Webster's
Home and Office
Handbook

From the Editors of **Webster's New World**™

Webster's
Home and Office
Handbook

SMITHMARK

REFERENCE

First published in the United States under the title *Webster's New World*^{TM} *Office Professional's Handbook*. Copyright © 1981, 1989, 1996 by Simon & Schuster, Inc. This edition published by arrangement with Macmillan Publishing, a division of Simon & Schuster, Inc. Webster's New World and colophons are trademarks of Simon & Schuster, Inc.

This edition published in 1999 by
SMITHMARK Publishers
a division of U.S. Media Holdings, Inc.
115 West 18th Street
New York, NY 10011

SMITHMARK books are available for bulk purchase for sales promotion and premium use. For details write or call the manager of special sales, SMITHMARK Publishers, 115 West 18th Street, New York, NY 10011; (212) 519-1300.

ISBN: 0-7651-1069-5

Printed in the United States of America

10 9 8 7 6 5 4 3 2 1

Library of Congress Catalog Card Number: 98-61771

Contributors

Susan C. Bauer, Associate Professor, Office Management, *State University Agricultural and Technical College,* Farmingdale, New York

Jeanette L. Bely, Ph.D., F.I.B.A., Professor of Education, *Bernard M. Baruch College of the City University of New York*

Murray Bromberg, Director, Supercenter, Council of Supervisors and Administrators, *The New York Board of Education,* and the *City University of New York*

Linda A. Bruce, President, *New York City chapter of Professional Secretaries International,* New York; Office Manager/Executive Secretary, American Academy, Rome, New York

Lois M. Burns, Ed.D., Assistant Professor, Department of Secretarial Science, *New York City Technical College,* Brooklyn, New York

William W. Cook, J.D., Director of Development, *Husson College,* Bangor, Maine

Rose A. Doherty, M.A., Instructor, Business Communications Department, *Katharine Gibbs School,* Boston, Massachusetts

Julie Eichenberger, M.Ed., former Instructor, *Long Island Business Institute,* Commack, New York

Joyce Gold, Adjunct Professor of English, *Fairleigh Dickinson University,* Rutherford, New Jersey; former Instructor, Business Communications Department, *Katharine Gibbs Secretarial School,* New York City

Charlotte B. Holmquest, M.Ed., Business Teacher, *Seabrook Intermediate School,* Seabrook, Texas

Audrey Katz, Legal Secretary

v

Milton Katz, Adjunct Assistant Professor, English Department, *State University Agricultural and Technical College,* Farmingdale, New York

Ruth Kimball Kent, M.A., Associate Editor (retired), Dictionary Division, *Simon & Schuster*

Doreen La Blanc, Assistant Professor, *Bronx Community College of the City University of New York,* Bronx, New York

Sheryl Lindsell-Roberts, President, *Sheryl Lindsell-Roberts & Co.,* a full-service communications company, Marlborough, Massachusetts.

James C. Matthews, Ed.D., Associate Professor, Department of Secretarial Sciences, *New York City Technical College,* Brooklyn, New York

John I. McCollum, Ph.D., Professor (retired), Department of English, *University of Miami,* Coral Gables, Florida

Ardis R. Morton, President, *National Association of Educational Office Personnel;* Secretary, Office of Human Relations, *Fairfax County Schools,* Connecticut

Emojean G. Novotny, B.S., Director, Secretarial Science Division, *Dyke College,* Cleveland, Ohio

Barry Persky, Chair, Education Department, *Walden University,* Minneapolis, Minnesota; Adjunct Assistant Professor, *Brooklyn College,* Brooklyn, New York

Naomi Dornfeld Platt, Ed.D., Professor and Director of GED Support Centers, *Kingsborough Community College,* Brooklyn, New York

Warren T. Schimmel, President, *The Berkeley School of Westchester,* White Plains, New York

Abba Spero, Ph.D., Associate Professor, Accounting, *Cleveland State University*

Contents

The Secretary Today

1

What It Means to Be a Professional Secretary

by Lois M. Burns, Ed.D.

- *Entering and Succeeding in the Profession*

- *Professional Development*

- *The Tools of the Profession*

  Language
  Professional Reading
  Information Processing
  A Professional Manner

- *The Competent Secretary*

- *Secretarial Specialties*

  The Executive Secretary
  The Secretary in Advertising, Radio and
    Television, Journalism, and the Arts
  The Secretary in Government
  The Secretary in Travel

- *Special Employment Situations*

  The Temporary Secretary
  The Part-time Secretary

- *The Secretary's Day*

  Time- and Work-Saving Units

- *Inventory Control*

- *Storage*

- *The Future*

The secretary is a professional—not only because of the knowledge and preparation necessary for the job but also because being a professional implies competence, pride in one's work, and a dedication to excellence. The secretary—sometimes known as an administrative assistant, administrative secretary, private secretary, or several other titles—is a professional with each of these qualities. Moreover, the secretary is an important member of the management team, responsible not only for carrying out the executive's wishes but also for helping to maintain a well-organized and efficient office.

The word *secretary* comes from the Latin *secretarius,* meaning "confidential employee." The secretary of today is still an employee who is privy to confidential information. In that respect, the job has not changed. However, the tools of the trade have changed over the years.

Office automation and computers have revolutionized the type of work that the secretary does, and changes are continuing at a rapid pace. The changes that will take place in the future are impossible to predict, but the professional secretary must be able to learn and adapt to each new challenge.

ENTERING AND SUCCEEDING IN THE PROFESSION

The relative ease with which a person can enter the secretarial profession is a plus. A high school education; typing, shorthand, machine transcription, and filing skills; and knowledge of office procedures, computer equipment, and software packages will enable one to advance along a career path. A post-secondary education is an additional asset.

The secretary entering the work force is faced with a multitude of possible job situations. Although the conditions under which a secretary works are fairly standard, a choice can certainly be made about location, the size of the company, and the company's services or products. Each area of the economy needs the expertise of a secretary, and the professional secretary has only to choose the field most interesting to him or her and the one in which career goals can be furthered. Weekly pay and fringe benefits are as important as ever, but today's secretary is also concerned with the possibilities for professional growth within a company.

Secretaries are professionals with career goals. Most large organizations have a human resources department that is concerned with the professional growth and development of their employees. By providing training and educational opportunities for employees from date of hire until retirement, these organizations are able to enhance the effectiveness of their operations and to enrich the lives of their employees.

Specialized training is a matter of professional survival in a world where the methods of handling information are changing rapidly. The secretary will be increasingly involved with office automation and needs to be familiar with the concept and the technology. The responsibilities of the secretary are multifunctional: typing/keyboarding; transcribing; processing mail; telephoning; scheduling appointments; greeting visitors; composing and editing documents;

researching; coordinating meetings, conferences, and teleconferences; making travel arrangements; handling reprographics; managing inventory; and organizing time and work. Supervisor and management education and advanced technical and professional education are available to those who are interested in moving ahead in the organization. One of the great benefits of a well-developed education and training program is that people on the secretarial level can move into supervisory, administrative, and managerial positions if they have the desire and the ability to do so.

Secretaries are encouraged to develop career paths and life plans just as executives do. The secretary's projected work life is just as long as the executive's. These years will be more pleasant if the individual takes steps to examine what kind of job will be the most personally satisfying now and in the future. This kind of examination also benefits the organization because it keeps people from changing companies when a change in work responsibility would be more satisfying.

Many organizations also encourage secretaries to avail themselves of outside educational opportunities through financial support or tuition reimbursement. Frequently these outside courses must be job related or related to a degree that the company agrees would benefit the employee and employer. Sometimes, however, these courses are promoted for the personal enrichment of the employee. All of these personnel-development efforts increase the secretary's satisfaction with the job and the employer.

PROFESSIONAL DEVELOPMENT

Participation in professional organizations is one way a secretary can grow professionally. Organizations offer the opportunity to network with other professionals and promote personal development by providing information, contacts, and support. Several professional organizations sponsor annual conventions, local conferences, seminars, and courses to enhance secretarial performance.

The following organizations provide many opportunities for service, educational, and professional growth: Professional Secretaries International (PSI), the Association of Information Systems Professionals (AISP), the American Association for Medical Assistants (AAMA), the American Association for Medical Transcription (AAMT), and the National Association of Legal Secretaries (International). Several of these organizations sponsor certification programs.

Professional Secretaries International (PSI) fosters an awareness of professional pride and the maintenance of high standards by promulgating the following definition:

> *A secretary shall be defined as an executive assistant who possesses a mastery of office skills, demonstrates the ability to assume responsibility without direct supervision, exercises initiative and judgment, and makes decisions within the scope of assigned authority.*

The importance of an organization like PSI cannot be overemphasized. All professional people take pride in their affiliation with organizations that attest to the importance of their field. Lawyers have bar associations; doctors have the American Medical Association; teachers have national educational organizations. In each of these groups the purpose is to set standards for the profession and to honor those who meet the standards. PSI awards the title of Certified Professional Secretary (CPS) to those who have passed a comprehensive two-day, six-part examination. The title of CPS brings respect from peers and superiors.

The examination that the aspiring secretary must take calls upon knowledge that has been gained through education and work experience. Office administration and communication, office technology, accounting, economics and management, business law, and behavioral science in business are the areas covered by the test. Membership in PSI and participation in the local chapter's activities will bring a sense of the importance of a secretary's job to the functioning of society and will introduce the secretary to others who have similar professional goals.

Additional information may be obtained from Professional Secretaries International, 10502 NW Ambassador Dr., Box 20404, Kansas City, MO 64195 (816-891-6600).

THE TOOLS OF THE PROFESSION

Keyboarding, shorthand, transcription, filing, office procedures, and knowledge of word processing systems and equipment are the skills for which the secretary was hired. However, the ability to use the language and a commitment to professionalism will earn respect and promotions.

Language

The raw material to which the secretary applies these skills is the English language. A command of and a respect for the English language, both in writing and in speaking, are essential. A good dictionary, a thesaurus, and a grammar book must be kept handy. In the automated office, equipment may have a built-in spell checker or a software program with a dictionary or grammar component. Work still has to be proofread, however, because programs cannot distinguish between homonyms, nor can they determine if the transcript omitted a word. Letters and all forms of communication represent the company, the employer, and the professional secretary. The recipient must never get the impression that any one of the three is less than first rate. Most executives have a good speaking command of the language. This asset is often one of the reasons why an individual reaches a top management position. However, it is the secretary's responsibility to check details of grammar, spelling, and punctuation. An employer with an excellent command of English presents a double challenge to the secretary. All communications must be absolutely perfect in composition, tone, and clarity.

The secretary may occasionally be the final check on grammar. An executive may have been hired for an area of technical expertise, not language ability. In this case the secretary will be responsible for editing all of the written communications from the office. The executive and the secretary in this situation must realize their mutual dependence and work to turn out superior written material. Correcting a dangling participle or making the verb and subject agree will demonstrate to the executive that the secretary is a professional with extremely valuable skills.

Professional Reading

Trade journals are published for each area of the economy and for each profession. By reading these publications, the secretary will demonstrate professional concern and learn new ideas and new vocabulary. The competent secretary does not have to read these magazines from cover to cover but will develop a system for skimming to stay abreast of developments, using the table of contents as a guide

Reading magazines such as *The Secretary, Fortune, Business Week, Forbes, Today's Office,* and *Office Administration and Automation* is part of the commitment to professional excellence.

Information Processing

Computers have revolutionized the way secretaries work and process information. More and more offices have acquired the most sophisticated technological equipment, and the secretary needs only the ability and the desire to grow and change with each new development or modification.

Such systems provide an automated information center that upgrades the quality of hard copy materials while improving office efficiency by increasing the speed with which the material is produced. Today's businesses must deal with more written information than ever before, and they must transmit that information quickly and accurately. Material for bulk mailing and form letters can be keyboarded in a much shorter time by the equipment. Having an executive decide to insert three paragraphs on page 60 of a 200-page document no longer means that the entire document must be re-keyboarded. The material to be inserted is keyboarded into the computer, and the finished document is produced, often in seconds. Complete documents of hundreds of pages can be sent from one office to another in minutes, rather than days. And, by using satellite communication, a subsidiary company's entire monthly report can be transmitted to the home office half a continent away in 30 seconds.

New vocabulary and procedures must be learned. The competent secretary will not only learn how to respond to the instructions of the system but will also make every effort to understand how the system works and how best to make use of the various options offered.

The future is unlimited for the secretary who takes advantage of all training opportunities and remains open and flexible to the changes that will certainly develop in the industry.

A Professional Manner

The secretary should view clothing as a uniform that fits the image of the office and thus advances the secretary's career goals along with the purpose of the office. If there is no declared dress code, clues about formality should be taken from the other employees in the office. If the men always wear conservative business suits and the women are always dressed in conservatively tailored clothing, striking a blow for individuality in dress will do nothing for one's personal goals. If the office is very informal, the secretary who wishes to be noticed and moved ahead will wear clothing that is just a shade more formal and more professional. The goal is not to alienate other workers but to make oneself stand out as the secretary who takes work seriously. When the executive office has an opening, the secretary who has demonstrated the most personal polish, in addition to superb skills, is the one who will be chosen.

A proper office manner should be cultivated by the secretary, and this manner should be based on the fact that the executive and the secretary are expected to work as a team. The secretary should follow the lead of the executive in office style. Whether working for an individual, a pair of executives, or a whole department, the secretary's duty is to help fulfill the executive job responsibilities. Therefore, assignments that appear in the job description (if there is one) are done conscientiously, and those chores that do not appear but that need to be done in order to free the executive from routine tasks will be done by the professional secretary without grumbling.

Much has been written about people moving ahead in careers because of the mentor/protégé system whereby a seasoned hand in the business takes on the education of someone younger who has promise. Although the superior may be grooming someone for a place on the management level, the secretary can also be a protégé who moves upward in salary and responsibility with the boss or with the boss's blessing.

As part of the team, the professional secretary protects the employer. He or she does not contribute information to office gossip but does report any rumor that may be helpful to the superior, first qualifying the information as gossip. Also, the professional does not spend company time on personal phone calls, in clock watching, or in being late.

THE COMPETENT SECRETARY

The secretary plans not only a career path but also short- and long-range work for the company. Short-range planning enables the secretary to do each day those things that must be done. For example, a routine is established whereby the secretary's and the employer's desks are ready for work at the beginning of each day. Standard procedures for handling mail, for advising the executive of telephone calls, and for handling dictation and transcription are set up, but this schedule does not lead to inflexibility. The competent secretary is capable of taking any kind of interruption in stride. When the emergency or interruption has been dealt with, the work routine is resumed at the point of interruption. Long-range planning makes it possible for the secretary to concentrate on low-priority projects at a slow time of the year and also makes it possible for the executive to call on secretarial aid at times when the work flow is heavy.

Effective Use of Time

The secretary's time is a valuable and perishable commodity. All duties are performed as quickly as possible so that the unexpected may be dealt with. A sense of the relative urgency of activities is developed with experience, so that it is possible to distinguish the important from the trivial. A long-distance caller does not distract the secretary from the necessity to transcribe an urgent letter. The unexpected visitor is started on his or her way courteously and firmly, rather than being allowed to waste company time.

Business calls are evaluated for length, and they are not continued beyond the time that is absolutely essential for courtesy and the exchange of information. The secretary should plan ahead. If one is making a call, a clear statement of purpose should open, followed by details, questions, or whatever the call must accomplish. The call should be completed by thanking the person on the other end, stating the action you or your boss expect to be taken, or getting a firm commitment for future action or the time of a return call. Remember that this is a business call and avoid those verbal ticks like "you know" and slang that would be appropriate in a personal call.

Responsibility and Follow-Up

By carefully following through on any tasks assigned, the secretary demonstrates a sense of responsibility every day. When the employer is out, the secretary displays professionalism by making sure that the office is covered at all times. Take, for example, a situation in which the executive and the secretary are the only ones who know all aspects of a given situation. When the boss is away, something that vitally affects that matter happens. The competent secretary is present and immediately gets in touch with the employer so that the appropriate course of action can be decided and so that the secretary can set the wheels in motion.

Relationship with Executive

The personal relationship between the executive and the secretary will vary according to the people involved and the formality of the company. The secretary should always remember that the relationship is a business arrangement and that the structure of any organization makes the executive more important than the secretary. Without the executive to set the overall objective and to plan for action to attain that objective, the secretary's job would not exist. Nevertheless, the indispensable contribution of the secretary to the execution of the executive's work should be a source of professional pride.

The executive may ask the secretary to explain a matter, but the secretary does not have the right to call upon the executive to justify decisions. When a good working relationship exists, both the secretary and the executive realize that they are there to make that office run at peak efficiency.

No job is without its dull routines as well as its stimulating aspect. No employer is without faults. There may be times when you consider your employer unreasonable. You may be asked to do chores that you consider demeaning or outside your province or job description. Decide how intrusive these jobs are, and discuss the matter with your employer. Perhaps the duties can be added to your job description. Otherwise, see if you can arrange for the writing of a job description if there is none.

Appropriate Behavior

Personal life must be separated from professional life. It is very possible to work well with people one does not like at all; likewise, it is possible to work professionally with people who are personal friends. Personal problems should not be brought into the office. However, worries about sickness at home, financial problems, and domestic difficulties do affect the quality of work, and the professional will do everything possible to keep the level of professional performance high. The fact that a doctor has personal troubles is not an acceptable excuse for a faulty diagnosis of a patient. One expects the doctor to perform well, and the executive has the right to expect the secretary to remain competent despite difficulties. People, however, are not machines and are not expected to behave as such. When overwhelming problems are present, the supervisor should be told before one's work is held up for censure.

Professional behavior as part of a team determines the relationships with the rest of the organization. In dealing with other members of the group, the secretary should make it clear that those others are viewed as the experts in their jobs. The professional secretary is courteous to everyone regardless of the individual's position on the company ladder.

Alertness to Mistakes

The secretary must be very honest in all relationships within the company. Everyone makes mistakes. The good secretary will do everything possible to avoid them and will accept responsibility when one has been made. The need to make use of other people's expertise must be recognized, and the secretary should help others in the office in an effort to foster a spirit of helpfulness to ensure that good work is turned out. For example, even if a secretary's typing is excellent, proofreading of important documents should be done by two people. The secretary should therefore try to make arrangements to proofread material with a co-worker.

Alertness to the mistakes of others so that the mistakes may be corrected is characteristic of the competent secretary. Especially if work is done under pressure, people have a tendency not to check a figure, proofread a page, or make certain that a statement conforms to policy. The secretary must check and double-check to avoid errors that are embarrassing or might affect important decisions.

Level of Authority

Differentiating between the executive's requests and the secretary's requests is necessary. In the first instance, the secretary has a lot of authority; in the second instance, there is much less. If the executive needs the report by 4 P.M., the department responsible will recognize that the effort and expense are inconsequential compared to the importance of meeting the deadline. However, the secretary must not push co-workers unless the pressure is justified. Everyone has a schedule to which he or she must adhere. Remember to respect the importance and the schedules of other people's work. Never claim authority for yourself when you are passing on the executive's wishes. "Professor Brown would like all class schedules completed by Friday" will get a better response than "I would like all class schedules completed by Friday." Even with suggestions the same rule is followed. A suggested course is far more likely to be implemented if put forward as the boss's idea, particularly if it involves difficulty.

Accurate Record Keeping

The secretary's filing system gets the same careful attention given to other duties. The employer must have an accurate record of what has happened in the past in order to take future action. For highly confidential matters or the employer's personal correspondence, a system consistent with filing rules but responsive to the needs of the office should be set up. If the company has a central files department, the secretary works closely with the assigned file clerk, whose expertise should be recognized.

Filing requires intelligence, knowledge of the subject matter, and an organized method of recording. The secretary should work with the file clerk. All material should be carefully marked to indicate whether there has been any previous correspondence on the subject. If the previous reference could not be easily identified by the file clerk, a notation indicating the subject with which it should be filed is a courtesy that will save time, prevent confusion, and contribute to a helpful attitude in the office, which will be to everyone's benefit. If a subject is especially important or unusually complicated, an exchange of ideas may enable the file clerk to set up the file intelligently. A sense of history on the part of the secretary and the file clerk will enable them to build up a file coherently, so that a person reading it will be able to determine the sequence of events and the actions taken. When the secretary recognizes the complexity of the file clerk's job, the employer will get the file or information sought, not an excuse.

Today, many firms have computer equipment, and documents are stored on disks and automatically filed in the system.

SECRETARIAL SPECIALTIES

A competent secretary may work in one particular type of office and become familiar with the equipment, vocabulary, procedures, and duties specific to that type of office. In some cases, specific training is required. A few secretarial specialties are discussed here and a more detailed discussion of some of the more common ones is provided in Chapters 2–6 in the major section titled "The Specialized Secretary."

The Executive Secretary

The executive secretary or the administrative assistant is more than just a secretary or an assistant to an executive. In some companies and organizations, the terms seem to be interchangeable; in other companies, one is placed above the other on the organizational ladder. Whether one uses the term executive secretary or administrative assistant, in terms of responsibility, knowledge of the company's business, judgment, and experience, this person is an executive. The executive secretary (the term we shall use in this discussion) may indeed employ a secretary or a whole staff. Making decisions that affect an important segment of the company's operations and, in some cases, taking charge of business while the executive is absent brings the executive secretary financial and personal rewards. But these benefits are earned. At this highest level of secretarial authority, the responsibilities are such that the greatest possible effort to check procedures and avoid errors is essential. Planning, discretion, knowledge, accuracy, efficiency, and dependability are watchwords of the job. The executive secretary has top skills and keeps them updated. Technical skills and knowledge of the latest automated equipment are essential.

Confidence of the executive's staff is built slowly and carefully. These are the people who have the responsibility to carry out the objectives of the company or department. The executive secretary's duty is to screen demands on the executive's time.

Decisions must be made promptly; action must be taken swiftly. Anything that slows that action is detrimental to the overall operation of the company. When a member of the staff has to see the boss, it may be because that person faces some decision beyond the scope of his or her particular authority. It may seem a simple matter to give notice that the subordinate has to see the executive, but what if the secretary has six or seven calls from different staff members? Who sees the executive first, who next, and who not at all?

It is up to the secretary to win the confidence of each member of the staff so that each person will be absolutely honest as to the urgency of any particular request. Each has to know that if the employee says, "I must have it five minutes before noon," he or she will have it if it is humanly possible, and that if the employee says, "Tomorrow will be fine," he or she will see the executive tomorrow without any further reminders to the secretary. In such circumstances, maximum use is made of everyone's time. The secretary can work out an orderly plan with the executive to conserve time. The subordinate can attend to other projects without wasting time calling back or attempting to waylay the executive in the hall. In this cooperative atmosphere, everyone realizes that the short-term advantage would not be worth the risk of losing the secretary's confidence.

The secretary must always be aware of being a representative of the executive, and while the staff is subordinate to the executive, the staff is not subordinate to the secretary. As the subordinates' confidence grows, they will ask advice or opinions on how the boss would like something done. The secretary has a responsibility to give accurate advice and to state only opinions that truly represent the executive's feelings. If the secretary's personal opinion is given, the subordinate may be misled as to the executive's actual sentiments on the matter.

The executive must view operations as a whole and must be able to depend upon the secretary to reflect this accurately in dealings with subordinates. It is important that each staff member be recognized as an integral part of the team and as making a contribution to the company. Each employee wants the good opinion of the boss, and perhaps even without consciously recognizing it, the secretary's reaction to an employee may be interpreted as a reflection of the boss's opinion. The secretary must remember that a personality trait that is unattractive to the secretary may be exactly the trait that makes the subordinate effective in a particular function. The subordinate who insists upon "dotting every *i* and crossing every *t*" may be far more effective in controlling costs than the easygoing, affable staff member who has difficulty in keeping even a personal expense account within proper bounds. The boss may have a higher opinion of the former than of the latter, and a secretary's favoring of the affable over the precise subordinate might be doing an injustice to both individuals and to the executive. By dampening the enthusiasm of one and giving a false sense of confidence to the other, the executive is misrepresented and the company's objectives may be impeded.

The job of executive secretary or administrative assistant is challenging and rewarding and a lot of hard work. Intelligence, interest, dedication, plus experience and training are essential for success.

The Secretary in Advertising, Radio and Television, Journalism, and the Arts

The skills required for these jobs are the same as for a job in any business, but the amount of contact with interesting personalities, public figures, and the public is increased. When dealing with public personalities, the secretary must be able to maintain a professional manner. If the employer does not wish to talk to a local public figure or a network newsperson, the secretary must be firm and diplomatic. Jobs in these fields require the ability to deal with people whose job it is to manipulate responses.

The professional secretary will decide just what kind of job will give the most satisfaction and the kind of atmosphere that will be pleasant. Will the high-pressure atmosphere of an advertising agency or television station make you nervous or will it challenge you? The fact that you are contributing to the success of a gallery or a museum may be the kind of reward that means the most to you. The excitement of putting any kind of publication "to bed" may be just what you want. Remember to take extras, such as house seats for a play, into consideration when you are considering a career.

The Secretary in Government

The federal government is the largest employer in the United States and should not be overlooked by the professional secretary. In order to become eligible for most governmental positions, the secretary must take a written civil service examination. Promotions are usually made from within based on availability and the demonstrated skill and industry of the applicant. Government positions offer annual salary increments, job security, and retirement systems.

There are also employment opportunities for secretaries in foreign countries. The Department of State has Foreign Service offices in over 300 cities worldwide.

Other jobs are also available in the public sector. State, county, and municipal governments, plus the many quasi-governmental agencies, all have need of skilled secretaries.

The secretary who is interested in public service should contact the Office of Personnel Management in the region in which he or she wishes to obtain employment.

The Secretary in Travel

Excitement and adventure are the fruits of secretarial work in the travel industry. Airlines, resorts, and travel agencies often offer free or reduced rates in transportation, hotel accommodations, and tours to their employees.

However, one does not get all this just for the asking. The job requires hard work. One must have a sincere liking for and a desire to help people. You are helping them to spend the money for which they have often worked hard all year. Also, you must deal with harried offices that may have to get an executive to Europe as quickly as possible.

A secretary in the travel industry must know geography well, be able to read different companies' timetables, plan itineraries, and make reservations through a computer. In short, you must know how to do everything and anything that will contribute to the comfort and enjoyment of your company's customers. Above all, you must be accurate. The pleasure of a vacation or a business opportunity can be lost by a single error.

Each year the volume of business and pleasure travel exceeds the previous year's. A person with the right combination or interest in people and ability to deal with details will find a bright future as a secretary in the travel field.

SPECIAL EMPLOYMENT SITUATIONS

Most secretaries are employed on a full-time basis. However, there are other types of employment situations, among them temporary work and part-time work.

The Temporary Secretary

Temporary employment services throughout the country fulfill a need for both employers and employees. The secretary who works on a temporary basis fills in vacancies created by vacations, illness, sudden resignations, or other short-term openings during peak workload periods.

Secretaries take on temporary employment for a number of reasons. Some use temporary employment as an opportunity to explore different industries, organizations, and working conditions so as to determine a preference and a career path. For others, family obligations or other responsibilities make a permanent position inconvenient and a temporary situation ideal. A temporary position also permits a flexible schedule and a choice of job locations, and these considerations may be important to someone pursuing further education or an avocation.

Agencies that engage temporary employees prefer secretaries who have had experience so that they will be able to immediately assume the responsibilities of the job. Temporary secretaries must be flexible, confident, and adaptable.

The pay in temporary work is slightly lower in many cases than that of permanent workers who have the same job skills and responsibilities. Fringe benefits are becoming more available to temporary workers. Some agencies that place temporary secretaries in offices now offer group life and medical insurance, paid holidays, paid vacations, referral bonuses, seniority or longevity bonuses, profit sharing, scholarships, and training on computers and related office equipment.

The Part-time Secretary

Doctors, educational institutions, small businesses, and large corporations often need part-time secretaries. The individual or firm may require only a few hours of work each day or only a few days per week. In other situations, a few weeks or a few months of the year may be required. Some companies are now willing to divide a full-time job between two part-time secretaries; two secretaries, in other words, share one full-time job. This is known as "job sharing."

Part-time work enables the secretary to maintain skills while freeing the individual for other responsibilities or interests.

THE SECRETARY'S DAY

Job descriptions make the task of organizing the workday a bit easier, but if your job does not have a formal description of duties, *organization* is the word to keep in mind. Not only must the secretary's desk be organized but also the work that flows across the executive's desk must be ordered. Decisions about what is important must be made constantly, since most secretaries will have more work to do in one day than can be reasonably accomplished. The key to deciding what is most important is the principle that keeps the executive and the secretary working together as a team.

The interests of the superior must come first, and the good secretary will be sure to perform tasks that the executive wants completed quickly and thoroughly. Deadlines between the secretary and the executive in the office may be missed because of extraordinary circumstances, but if the boss misses a deadline with higher company executives because the secretary's work was not completed on time, do not expect to have an excuse accepted.

Prepare the afternoon before. The schedule for each day begins the afternoon before when the secretary goes through the tickler or follow-up folder to determine exactly what must be done the next day. The follow-up file should be set up in whatever way the secretary finds most convenient. If the office operates on a yearly schedule with certain meetings, promotions, and correspondence scheduled for the same time each year, the secretary may wish to have monthly files with notations about the amount of time it took to plan last year's fall sales meeting and the list of tasks to be performed in connection with that meeting. In an office that does not have this repetitive schedule, the secretary may use a desk calendar to keep track of letters to be answered, telephone calls that must be made, shipments expected, and so forth. The secretary should make a list of the items that must be taken care of the next day and a list of appointments for the executive, along with pertinent information and the materials that should be prepared. To conclude the day, the equipment should be turned off and covered and the desk cleared so that the maintenance staff will be able to work.

Prompt morning start. The office must be ready to function at whatever time it opens, and the secretary should be at work in the office, not returning from the washroom or talking in the next office. Certain jobs must be performed each day, and the secretary taking over an office would be wise to make a list of these in the order in which they should be done until the routine becomes second nature.

After opening the mail and putting the most important items on top, the secretary may be required to call certain items to the executive's attention. This practice, however, should be begun only when permission has been given. The executive may ask that some of the journals and newspapers the office receives be skimmed and that pertinent articles, notices of new products, promotions, and so forth be marked for special notice.

Mail must be moved quickly from the secretary's desk to the appropriate correspondent; rerouting is done immediately. If some of the letters can be answered by the secretary, the executive may return them with notations about content. This will then be completed as soon as possible.

Priority of duties. The previous afternoon the secretary should have made a list of tasks for the following day by using the techniques of time management. Tasks fall into three categories: those that must be done immediately, those that may be done, and those that may be put off. Just as the executive has a list of appointments, the secretary should have a list of tasks and some notation after each entry to indicate its relative importance. All necessary items can be given an A or 1; the tasks that should be done when there is time, a B or 2; and the tasks that can be left until a slack period, a C or 3. The trap of putting down jobs that are part of the daily routine or filling the list from the third category must be avoided. Putting down small jobs just for the satisfaction of crossing them out is a dangerous game to play. The executive will not want to hear that all of the filing is up-to-date and that the invitation for the annual office party has been sent to the printers if the report that was due in the president's office at 11 A.M. has not been typed.

Importance of the memo pad. The duties of a secretary are as varied as are jobs and employers. But in any situation it is safe to assume that the secretary is responsible for handling the mail, making calls and answering the telephone, taking and transcribing dictation, following up orders and work in progress, and organizing office work. More often than not, the secretary must keep track of the employer's appointments and maintain a filing system—all in addition to the specifics of the job.

How can one keep all of these duties in mind? It is impossible; everything must be written down on a memo pad. Every request, every assignment, every message is noted. Nothing is left to memory or chance. The secretary's work procedure depends upon the nature of the job and the size of the company. Some offices have established routines; some employers will specify the methods they prefer; sometimes a departing secretary will train an incoming one. The basic tools of organization are a memo pad, a calendar, an appointment book, and a telephone-address book or file.

The memo pad will function as an added memory bank. Notations are made from each phone call, each request for an answer, each new assignment. By writing the information down, the secretary is freed from the need to keep small pieces of information in a mental notebook. Also, by writing all information down, the secretary is able to resume work at the point of interruption.

Keeping an appointment book. The appointment book is one of the most important records in the office. There are various methods of recording and following up appointments, but essential to each is the appointment book. In automated offices, there is an electronic calendar.

In some offices the appointment book is kept on the executive's desk. The secretary must maintain an accurate duplicate book so that both members of the office know how each day is to be spent. In other offices the executive assigns the appointment book to the secretary, who makes all of the appointments. To examine the book, the executive will have to go to the secretary's desk and read it there or temporarily remove it.

Before making appointments, the secretary must be familiar with the office procedures. Such matters as availability of executives, availability of conference rooms for meetings, daily arrival and departure times, and average schedules and length of conferences affect the making of appointments.

The appointment should be entered under the day and the hour agreed upon by the person requesting it and the secretary. The entry includes the names of the persons concerned, some notation of the topic to be discussed, and any other pertinent information. The secretary uses these notes to produce needed documents for the executive to read before the meeting. If the material is complex, the secretary may give it to the executive days ahead of time when the work flow is slow. On the day of the appointment the secretary follows through to be sure that there is no misunderstanding and to be sure that the appropriate materials and notes are on the executive's desk. If the appointment is canceled, arrangements for a new appointment should be made immediately.

Developing familiarity with sources of information. The secretary who can find the names of those whom the employer must reach most frequently and the names, addresses, and phone numbers for services, emergencies, and sources of information is a valuable asset to the office and is rewarded as such. Many secretaries in education and research organizations will keep a separate file of reference books or sources with notations about the contents and the call letters if they are in the public or the company library. The secretary would do well to become familiar with the area's Yellow Pages and with the various sources of information listed in the section on reference materials in this volume (Chapter 25).

Time- and Work-Saving Units

Time is one of a businessperson's most precious commodities. The secretary who learns to organize work and plan time wisely will save minutes out of every hour, hours out of every week. This free time will be used by the professional to expand knowledge and expertise.

Here are a few time- and work-saving suggestions:

1. *Make efficient use of your desk.* Keep the surface clear of everything except your immediate work. Form the habit of using filing folders for anything of a temporary nature—work in progress, incoming or outgoing communications, work being held for additional information—and keep these folders in the file drawer of your desk where they are instantly accessible but not in the way.

2. *Plan your time; never waste it.* When work is slow, plan ahead. Do what can be done to relieve the workload at peak periods. Try to learn more about your company's operations. Consider what you can do to make your part of it run more smoothly. Become familiar with reference

materials; learn how to use the reference books your boss consults frequently. The next time you may be able to find that chart or graph that is badly needed. Bring the address book up-to-date. Get to know the filing system.

3. *Learn to schedule your time realistically.* It may take you an hour to type a stack of letters, provided that you are not interrupted; but you will be. The telephone will ring, your employer will call upon you to take care of something urgent, and people will stop at your desk to ask questions. That one hour may become two or three hours. If you learn to expect interruptions, you will not be flustered by them or lose time trying to pick up where you left off. Interruptions are part of your work and require a place in your schedule.

4. *Be part of the team.* When the workload is heavy, when your employers and other members of the staff are up against a deadline to get a job done, be willing to pitch in and help even if it is a little after closing time. Your ability to function as a professional will be remembered when you have a favor to ask and when you wish a promotion.

INVENTORY CONTROL

The secretary who has the obligation to look after office supplies should keep a running record of what supplies are on hand and the frequency with which each item needs to be reordered. Place on the calendar or tickler file a reminder at the beginning of each month to check all or some of the office supplies. A yearly inventory is time-consuming; an ongoing monthly account is generally better.

A card record should be kept for each item. This record should include name of supplier, name of salesperson, quantities usually purchased, sizes, colors, and other details. The cards may be filed alphabetically by supplier, item, or category. They may be used as inventory records, showing the quantities coming in, the quantities distributed, and the minimum quantity to be kept in stock. As the record approaches the minimum, the item should be added to an order list or immediately placed on order. The minimum order should be of a quantity large enough that the stock is never exhausted and yet does not result in an overload of the item, for paper, printer cartridges, and certain other supplies deteriorate with age.

The following list includes common office supplies the secretary will need on the inventory record.

Paper and Filing Products
    typing paper
    stationery (letterhead)
    envelopes

correction fluid (with thinner; white and color as needed)
scratch pads and paper
manila or plastic file folders (color coded as needed)
hanging file folders
file folder tabs and labels
memo pads
dictation notebooks
alphabetized dividers
telephone message pads
file baskets, trays, and stacks
3" × 5" cards
4" × 6" cards
transparent tape
bookmarks
card files
calendars
planning diaries
business envelopes
manila envelopes
padded envelopes
binders
looseleaf covers and fillers
mailing tape
telex paper (in rolls)
address labels
paper for calculating machines
postage stamps
Do not overlook purchasing recycled products.

Computer Supplies
printer ribbons
printer cartridges
diskettes
diskette trays

Duplicating and Dictating Supplies
cassette tapes
tape storage unit

tape demagnetizer
tape splicer
microfilm
microfiche film
microfiche index
copier toner

Desk Supplies

staplers, staples, staple removers
letter openers
pen and pencil holders
tape dispensers
rulers
fineline, broad-nib, or felt-tip pens
paper clips
rubber bands
writing and marking pencils
magnifying glasses
erasers
scissors
rubber stamps, including date stamp
pushpins
book holders
ink pads for rubber stamps
bookends

Miscellaneous

postal scales
globe
first aid kit
maps
fire extinguisher
easels
keys
planning boards
batteries

Desk Reference Sources
>   desk dictionary
>   international area code booklet, if needed
>   secretarial handbook
>   current office supply catalog
>   office address and/or telephone directory (booklet, sheet, or rotary file)
>   style manual
>   almanac
>   chart for current postal rates
>   ZIP Code directory
>   telephone directory
>   telex directory, if needed

STORAGE

Office supplies in storage should be arranged according to age, with the oldest stock in front for immediate use. Only one box of a single item should be opened at a time. Like items may be stacked one in front of the other on shelves. Unlike items should be kept separate to ensure that no stock is concealed from sight and forgotten. Shelves, boxes, and packages should be plainly marked to show contents and date of purchase. It is important to store supplies so that humidity and temperature are as close to ideal as possible.

THE FUTURE

The need for skilled secretaries will continue to grow. The secretary of today and the future may be entering the field from high school, vocational school, or college; may be returning to work after many years of child-rearing; or may be making a midlife career change. What all these secretaries have in common is their professionalism and their recognition of the importance of the work they do. The secretary of today and the future recognizes that a life's work deserves to be planned, and the professional secretary chooses a career path carefully. The professional secretary who will assume an important place in business and society will need to be able to respond to the concept and technology of information processing, possess decision-making ability and human relations skills, and be adaptable to learning new skills in a rapidly changing office environment. Secretaries can expect to take more responsibility as the more repetitious aspects of their jobs are automated.

The Specialized Secretary

The Medical Secretary

by Lois M. Burns, Ed.D.

- *Insurance Claims Processing and Accounting*
    Procedures

    Insurance Claims
    Patient Billing
    Collections

- *Medical Office Technology*

    Machine Dictation and Transcription
      Equipment
    Word Processing
    Use of Computers
    Computer Software for the Medical
      Secretary

- *Medical Mini-Glossary*

A career as a medical secretary offers a challenging and rewarding experience with opportunity for professional and intellectual growth. Because of the ever-increasing need and demand for good medical care, the career of a medical secretary will continue to be available and growing. And, since medical research is ongoing with new diagnostic and treatment methods being developed, the medical secretary will find there is always something new to learn. Good medical care is not possible without the trained medical secretary.

To be successful, the medical secretary must possess good secretarial and English skills, a knowledge of medical terminology, and personal attributes necessary for working with physicians and patients.

To appreciate the importance of the medical secretary, it is essential to know what medical secretaries are, what tasks they perform, what qualifications they must have, where they are employed, what professional certifications they may obtain, and what professional organizations they may join. This chapter touches on all of these topics and then discusses medical communications, medical records, insurance claims processing and accounting procedures, and medical office technology. A brief glossary, which lists prefixes and suffixes commonly used in medical terms, completes the chapter.

WHAT A MEDICAL SECRETARY IS

A medical secretary performs the administrative and secretarial functions required at a particular medical facility and sometimes also performs some clinical functions by assisting the doctor in the examination and treatment of patients. The medical secretary is a trained member of the medical health-care team.

Tasks

The trained and competent medical secretary manages the medical office smoothly and efficiently, thus saving the doctor time and work. Some tasks may be routine. However, there can be no routine in handling patients. Each patient is different, with specific needs.

The specific tasks performed by the medical secretary are varied in scope. In general, they can be grouped as administrative or secretarial duties and clinical duties.

Administrative/Secretarial Duties
- handling the telephone
- obtaining and recording messages from the answering service
- scheduling, canceling, and rescheduling patients' appointments
- greeting patients
- recording patients' visits
- quoting and collecting fees

- sending out bills
- preparing and processing insurance claim forms
- maintaining financial records
- ordering and maintaining office supplies and equipment
- typing and transcribing dictated and handwritten correspondence and case histories
- composing correspondence
- maintaining patients' records
- opening, sorting, and distributing mail
- handling petty cash
- making bank deposits
- taking patients' medical histories
- assisting patients in understanding the doctor's instructions regarding their prescribed health-care treatment
- filing and pulling patients' charts, reports, and records for their visits
- arranging for patients' hospital reservations

Clinical Duties

- taking patients' medical histories
- measuring patients' vital signs: temperature, pulse, respiration, blood pressure
- sterilizing instruments and equipment
- positioning and draping patients for examination
- collecting specimens from patients and either sending them to a laboratory or performing certain diagnostic tests for which one has been trained
- taking electrocardiograms
- assisting doctors with the patients' examinations or treatment
- keeping medical supply cabinets well stocked

Qualifications

The qualifications for a medical secretary depend on whether the specific position requires mainly secretarial/administrative tasks, clinical tasks, or both; on the specialty of the physician; and on the nature and size of the medical facility. A medical secretary/assistant in a small office may be called on for a wide range of duties, whereas one in a large facility with a large staff and greater specialization may be required to perform only a limited number of specific tasks (*e.g.,* transcribing medical records).

In all situations the medical secretary should have a desire to help people, strong interpersonal skills, and personal characteristics such as patience, poise, tact, consideration, dependability, punctuality, and flexibility. Also important are carefulness, accuracy, and attention to detail, as well as respect for confidentiality. A well-groomed appearance is also important, since the medical secretary must convey a professional image and create an impression that office procedures and medical attention are efficient.

The medical secretary must be proficient in English pronunciation, spelling, grammar, and punctuation. In addition, a basic understanding of anatomy, medical terminology, and the legal implications of the practice of medicine is essential. Such knowledge is invaluable in transcribing and typing medical correspondence, case histories, laboratory reports, medical abstracts, and manuscripts.

The secretary must also know how to maintain patient records, quote and collect fees, process insurance claims, maintain financial records, and inventory and order office and medical supplies. Familiarity with computers is a plus as more and more medical facilities are using them to assist in patient record keeping, patient billing, insurance claims processing, and appointment scheduling. Courteous and efficient use of the telephone is also essential, as is familiarity with filing methods and the use of common office equipment.

If the medical secretary is required to perform some clinical duties, there are additional qualifications, some of which depend on the physician's specialty. The medical secretary must know the name and purpose of the instruments used in the medical practice and their proper care and use. To prevent infection, appliances and instruments used in the examination and treatment of patients must be sterilized. The assistant must be familiar with the methods of sterilization, although many items are now disposable. In assisting with an examination or treatment, the assistant is expected to hand the instruments to the physician as needed, assembling them in order of their use and making sure that all are clean and in working order.

Positioning and draping the patient for examination are important clinical functions of the medical secretary. He or she must know the standard positions for specific types of examinations and treatments. The assistant should also know how to take pulse, respiration, and temperature readings and how to measure blood pressure.

If the secretary/assistant is to perform or assist in any routine laboratory procedures, special training is usually needed. The assistant may be trained to collect and label specimens, prepare slides, and perform specific tests on the specimens or arrange for their delivery to a special laboratory. Absolute accuracy, honesty, and reliability are essential.

Educational Requirements

The minimum educational requirement for a job as a medical secretary is a high school diploma; however, many positions require additional education. Vocational/technical institutes offer three- to six-month training programs, and many two-year colleges offer an associate's degree program that provides a broad foundation in both clinical and administrative skills. Courses cover medical terminology, medicolegal topics, medical office procedures, medical transcription, medical assisting procedures, keyboarding, business English, accounting, word processing, basic biological sciences, basic laboratory techniques, cardiopulmonary resuscitation (CPR), and human relations.

Places of Employment

The medical secretary may be employed in a doctor's office, a medical clinic, a hospital, a public health facility, a health maintenance organization (HMO), a nursing home, a research center, a laboratory, an insurance company, a pharmaceutical company, a government or private health service agency, a medical transcription service, a business that manufactures medical supplies and equipment, or the medical department of any large business.

Medical Ethics and the Law

Medicine is perhaps the oldest profession to have developed a code to govern its practitioners. These principles of right and wrong are referred to as *medical ethics*. Medical ethics concerns itself with a standard of conduct; *medical etiquette* deals with courtesy, manners, and customs. These two areas complement each other and are often formally set forth in social contracts and codes.

About 400 B.C. Hippocrates, the Greek physician known as the Father of Medicine, devised a brief statement of principles to govern the conduct of physicians toward their patients and the public. The *Oath of Hippocrates* has been taken by physicians for centuries and remains an inspiration to the physicians of today.

The American Medical Association (AMA) formulated its own principles of medical ethics, which were accepted by the medical profession in the United States. They have been revised and updated several times, but their moral intent has never been changed. These principles are not laws but standards. A physician who violates the ethical standards of an association may be censured or have his/her membership in the organization suspended.

While the code and standards and their interpretation are directed toward the physician, the medical secretary is considered an agent of the physician and plays an important role in applying these same standards of conduct.

Law as applied to the practice of medicine holds many responsibilities for both the doctor and the medical team. The law is different in the different states. The *Medical Practice Act* of each state regulates all activities in the health field. Its general principles prescribe who must be licensed to perform various procedures, the requirements for licensure, the duties imposed by licensure, and government regulations. Violation of a law followed by conviction may result in punishment by fine, imprisonment, or revocation of licensure.

Professional liability encompasses all civil liability that a physician can incur as a result of professional acts. However, the *Good Samaritan Acts* protect the physician from liability for civil damages that may occur as a result of emergency care.

Negligence as applied to the medical profession is called *malpractice.* Most patients never consider taking legal action against their physicians. The medical secretary, who must understand the legal implications of the practice of medicine, can play a role in preventing litigation by

- establishing good patient rapport
- keeping all information confidential
- avoiding the transmittal of criticisms of physicians to a patient
- avoiding discussion of a patient's condition, diagnosis, or treatment with him or her
- keeping complete and accurate records
- obtaining proper authorizations, releases, and consents
- using discretion in telephone and office conversations
- notifying the physician if he or she learns that the patient is under treatment by another physician for the same condition
- being available to assist the doctor

The medical secretary must always remember that the relationship between the doctor and the patient is legally considered a contract. All information furnished to a doctor by the patient—information the medical secretary may have access to or be aware of—is considered confidential and may not be divulged to any unauthorized person.

Professional Organizations and Certifications

The professional medical secretary/assistant enjoys an enviable professional status. He or she is eligible to join professional associations and can apply for certification in the medical field.

The American Association of Medical Assistants (AAMA) and the American Association for Medical Transcription (AAMT) provide the opportunity for members to attend local, state, regional, and national meetings and conventions. Members may participate in workshops, learn of educational opportunities in the field, visit exhibits, hear prominent speakers, obtain continuing education units (CEUs), and establish networks.

The AAMA publishes a bimonthly journal, *The Professional Medical Assistant.* The AAMT publishes the *Journal of the AAMT* four times a year and the *AAMT Newsletter* six times a year.

Both the AAMA and the AAMT offer certifying examinations, the successful completion of which leads to certification. Passing the AAMA tests leads to recognition as a Certified Medical Assistant, either Administrative (CMA-A) or Clinical (CMA-C) or both. Passing the AAMT test leads to recognition as a Certified Medical Transcriptionist (CMT).

For more information contact the American Association of Medical Assistants, 20 North Wacker, Suite 1575, Chicago, IL 60606 (312-889-1500) and the American Association for Medical Transcription, P.O. Box 6187, Modesto, CA 95355 (800-982-2182).

By joining a professional organization and participating in the activities it offers, the medical secretary will grow personally and professionally and will keep abreast of current trends. Participation in a recognized professional organization indicates to an employer that you are serious about your career and would be an asset to his or her practice. The rewards are limitless.

MEDICAL COMMUNICATIONS

A medical secretary's ability to communicate effectively, both orally and in writing, is essential. Communication with those concerned with health-care delivery may be in person, by telephone, or by letter.

Telephone

Most medical office telephone contacts involve health problems, and the medical secretary should respond compassionately and tactfully in dealing with the patients' problems. The medical secretary is expected to exercise good judgment, courtesy, and calmness when answering patient calls.

The telephone should be answered by the second ring at the latest. When answering a phone in a medical office, it is acceptable to greet the caller with the doctor's name. Most calls involve scheduling appointments, requests to speak with the doctor, or inquiries about laboratory test results or information about a medical condition, medication, or charges and bill payment. Callers often ask to speak with the doctor, although most simply want to schedule an appointment. The medical secretary must screen and handle calls to save the doctor's time for examining and treating patients.

The medical secretary must obtain complete information for each call. Most medical offices use prepared telephone message pads or spiral-bound telephone message books with carbons so copies of messages can be kept. The information noted should include

- date and time of call
- person called
- caller's name
- caller's phone number, including area code
- action to be taken (return call, wants to see you, will call again, returned your call, urgent)
- complete message
- name of the person who took the call

Answering Service

Most physicians use an answering service for after-office hours and weekend calls. Some services receive calls automatically if they are not answered by the medical secretary; other services require the medical secretary to inform them when to begin answering, where the doctor can be reached, and when to stop answering. Upon entering the office, the medical secretary checks with the service for messages.

Some medical offices use a recorded message to give patients the regular office hours and a number where the doctor can be reached in case of emergency.

Scheduling, Canceling, and Rescheduling Appointments

The medical office depends on efficient management of the scheduling of appointments for patients and visitors. Appointments scheduled too closely may result in patients waiting unnecessarily, while appointments scheduled too far apart result in the doctor's loss of valuable time.

Patient appointments vary in length depending on the reason for the appointment and the specialty of the doctor. The doctor usually establishes a formula for standard appointments—for example, 30 to 45 minutes for new patients, physical examinations, consultations, and treatments; 15 to 20 minutes for routine follow-ups or injections.

Each patient's full name, telephone number, and reason for the appointment should be recorded in the appointment book beside the time of the appointment. As each patient is seen by the doctor, a check mark should be placed in the appointment book next to the name. Ditto marks should be used to indicate length of appointments, and diagonal lines should be used to indicate when the doctor will not be available for appointments with a brief explanation given.

If there is a medical emergency, the injured or ill patient must see the physician immediately. Waiting patients should be informed of the emergency and assured that the delay will not be lengthy. If the delay will be lengthy, patients who have not arrived at the office should be called and their appointments rescheduled.

Canceled appointments should be noted by a line drawn through the patient's name in the appointment book. This appointment slot then becomes available for another patient. Patients should be discouraged from canceling appointments and, when they must be canceled, should be encouraged to reschedule them.

All appointments that must be canceled should be rescheduled for the first available opening. The appointment book should show a line drawn through the patient's name and a notation beside the name indicating that the appointment has been rescheduled.

Greeting Patients and Visitors

Patients and visitors should be greeted with a cheerful attitude and a friendly smile. The medical secretary's goal should be to make the patient and visitor feel at ease. The patient or visitor should be identified, the name located in the day's schedule, and he or she should be asked to be seated in the waiting room.

Correspondence

Medical secretaries frequently compose routine letters that the physician asks them to compose for his or her signature or letters that explain, clarify, or transmit instructions and information. Correspondence may involve letters of referral and reference; the scheduling, canceling, and rescheduling of appointments; summaries of attending physicians' statements for insurance companies; preparation of instructions for laboratory tests and examinations; billing and insurance inquiries; and the ordering of supplies, equipment, and subscriptions.

The letters must be courteous, concise, complete, accurately typewritten, properly formatted, and proofread. Just as the proper use of the telephone is vital to the medical office, so too is the correspondence leaving the medical office.

RECORDS IN A MEDICAL OFFICE

The records in a physician's office consist of medical records of the patient's health and business records of general correspondence, financial files, insurance information, and so forth.

What a Medical Record Is

A patient's record includes the medical history or chart, medical reports, and correspondence pertaining to each patient. A medical history begins with the patient's first contact with the doctor and continues with subsequent visits, noting the patient's progress and discharge.

A patient's history contains the following information:

- chief complaint and date, or reason for initial visit
- medical history
- personal history
- family history
- results of examination
- diagnosis
- prognosis
- treatment and medication prescribed

- progress reports
- discharge summary

The history is obtained by questioning the patient. (The medical secretary may obtain part of the history before the patient sees the doctor.) Examination results and diagnostic, prognostic, and treatment reports are completed by the doctor, and the medical secretary types them into the medical report either from the doctor's notes or from dictation.

Filing Records

Each medical office has its own filing system, type of records, and filing equipment. Patients' medical records may be arranged alphabetically or numerically. Files that relate to the other areas of the medical office—for example, insurance or financial matters—may be arranged by subject. These filing systems will be briefly discussed.

Patient Files

Offices using alphabetic filing file by the patient's last name, given name, and middle initial. Prefixes such as De, Di, La, Le, Mac, and Mc are considered as an inseparable part of the surname. If two names are identical, then the city or town is used as the indexing unit.

Offices using numeric filing must have a way of assigning each patient a number. Many offices use the social security number for numeric systems.

Business Files

Business files are usually arranged by subject and placed in alphabetical order. The file label identifies the contents of the file. For example, the label may be Financial Statements, Insurance, Licensing, Memberships, Office Equipment Contracts, Office Supplies, or Payroll Records.

Storing Records

The storage of medical records can be centralized or decentralized, depending on the size of the medical facility. Centralized filing systems house files from many departments in one place and are usually overseen by a medical records person trained in records management. Decentralized files are those kept in each department and organized according to its own system.

Medical records must be protected from theft, fire, and water damage. Therefore, they are usually sorted in metal file cabinets, either lateral or vertical. There are lateral files that have drawers that do not open outward, saving aisle space, and folders can be filed either front to back or sideways. Vertical files have drawers that open outward with file folders standing upright and folders filed front to back.

INSURANCE CLAIMS PROCESSING AND ACCOUNTING PROCEDURES

Most people have some form of health-care insurance with benefits varying widely from policy to policy. The patient is responsible for the payment of his or her account and must pay any difference between the charges of the physician or medical provider and the insurance coverage.

Insurance Claims

When a patient with health insurance coverage is treated at a medical facility, either the patient or the medical facility files a claim with the insurance carrier for payment. The carrier reviews the claim and, if the patient is covered, mails a check to the physician or to the patient. Physicians sometimes require payment at the time of their service. The patient then pays the physician at the time of service and files a claim for reimbursement by the insurance company.

Health insurance may be designed for a group of people insured under one policy, or it may be designed to meet the needs of an individual and the individual's dependents. The major health-care coverage plans are Blue Cross and Blue Shield, Health Maintenance Organizations (HMOs), Medicare, Medicaid, and CHAMPUS (Civilian Health and Medical Program of the Uniformed Services). Workers Compensation is an income-maintenance and health-care insurance program established by law in each state to cover work-related occupational diseases, injury, or death.

Some physicians prefer that the medical secretary complete insurance claim forms for patients to reduce the possibility of errors. Other physicians prefer that the patient complete the top of the form and the medical secretary complete the bottom.

Patient Billing

One of the medical secretary's responsibilities may be to maintain the financial records of the office. These accounting duties may include recording patient charges and receiving payments from patients and insurance companies. Patients' billing statements can be computer generated, individually typewritten on statement forms, or photocopied from the patient's ledgers.

In an office in which a majority of the patients pay their bills at the time of service, a statement may be prepared, with one or more copies given to the patient and one filed. The statement will show that the full charges have been paid or what balance is due. The patient may use copies of the statement to submit to his or her insurance company for possible reimbursement.

Accounts may also be billed on a monthly basis, with all bills processed at the same time each month. A cyclical billing system in which accounts are billed on a staggered basis during the month may also be used.

When a computer is used for patient billing, a superbill or patient charge slip is usually prepared. The superbill is a one-page preprinted form with a multicarbon packet. It lists the comprehensive services a patient might receive from a medical facility and the fees for each of these services. The services actually received and their fees are marked off. A superbill eliminates the need for patient ledger cards.

In the ledger card system, each patient has a card that lists chronologically the dates of the doctor's services, a description of each service, the charge for the service, the payment received, and the balance remaining.

Collections

The medical secretary may have to handle collections, since patients do not always pay their accounts on time. A comprehensive collection policy involving letters, telephone calls, or use of collection agencies may be necessary for the doctor to receive payment for services rendered to patients.

Although each facility has its own collection policy, the general practice is to bill the patient. If no response is received after the mailing of two monthly statements, a third bill is mailed containing a reminder that the bill is overdue and a request for an explanation. There may be a series of follow-up collection letters, each expressing more urgency in settling the account.

Another way to effect collections is for the secretary to telephone the patient to determine why the patient has not paid or answered the collection inquiries. This collection effort requires tact, understanding, confidence, experience, and listening skills. After the telephone call is completed, a note of the conversation should be recorded.

The doctor may also collect on bad accounts by suing the patient and going to court or by using the services of a collection agency. These options are often costly and time-consuming.

MEDICAL OFFICE TECHNOLOGY

Advances in technology continue to provide more ways to handle written communication in the medical office. Because medical facilities have expanded, there is an increase in the volume of paperwork. The increased paperwork and higher production costs have led many medical offices to improve efficiency through the use of sophisticated dictation, word processing, and computer equipment.

Machine Dictation and Transcription Equipment

The dictation and transcription of correspondence and medical reports can be a large part of a medical secretary's job. Because machine dictation is less time-consuming and often more convenient than in-person dictation, many doctors prefer machine dictation.

Transcription of dictation into typewritten hard copy requires that the secretary have excellent listening skills, be familiar with the transcription equipment, and have a solid background in medical terminology, grammar, punctuation, spelling, and the formats to be used for different types of medical reports.

Word Processing

Word processing is the automated production of documents and correspondence using modern electronic equipment. Electronic typewriters, dedicated word processors, and personal computers may be used. Keyboarding (typing) speeds can range from 150 to over 600 words per minute. Word processing also provides memory for storing, producing, retrieving, revising, and correcting the documents and correspondence. It greatly improves the efficiency of any office.

Use of Computers

The medical office is being revolutionized by the use of the computer. Initially the computer was used in hospitals for billing and administrative purposes. Today, computers and word processing systems are used in most medical facilities for a wide range of applications, including patients' records, patients' ledgers, daily logs, insurance form processing, research, electronic appointment scheduling, and the production of graphics.

Computer Software for the Medical Secretary

There are software programs to enhance the office efficiency of general practitioners and specialists. Functions of these programs include tracking charges to patients; preparing monthly statements; preparing bills for insurance companies; generating appointment schedules; customizing procedure and diagnosing codes; keeping detailed information on insurance companies, providers, referring physicians, labs, and hospitals; preparing general ledgers, aged accounts receivable, form letters, and patients recaps; and tracking inventory, price quotes, and sales tax.

MEDICAL MINI-GLOSSARY

It is impossible for the medical secretary to become familiar with all medical terms and abbreviations. A medical dictionary, such as *Webster's New World/Stedman's Medical Dictionary,* is a must at all medical secretaries' desks. However, familiarity with prefixes and suffixes commonly used in medical terms greatly helps in understanding the meaning of a word. (See Tables 2.1 and 2.2.) Knowledge of the abbreviations used in medicine is also very important.

TABLE 2.1 Prefixes Commonly Used in Medical Terms

A prefix is a word part found at the beginning of a word; it is never used alone. Awareness of what a prefix means often leads to understanding of the full word. For example, *postoperative* = *post* (after) operation, or after an operation.

Prefix	Meaning	Prefix	Meaning
a, an	no; not; without	*endo*	in; within
ab	away from	*epi*	above; upon; on
ad	toward	*eso*	inward
ana	up; apart; excessive	*eu*	good
		ex	out; away from
ante	before; forward	*poly*	many
anti	against	*post*	after; behind
auto	self	*pre*	before; in front of
bi	two		
brachy	short	*pro*	before
brady	slow	*re*	back
cata	down	*retro*	behind
con	together; with	*semi*	half
contra	against; opposite	*sub*	under; below
de	lack of; down	*supra*	above
dia	complete; through	*sym*	together; with
		syn	together; with
dys	bad; painful; difficult	*tachy*	fast
		tetra	four
ec	out; outside	*trans*	across
ecto	out; outside	*tri*	three
em	in	*ultra*	beyond; excess
en	in; within	*uni*	one

TABLE 2.2 Suffixes Commonly Used in Medical Terms

A suffix is a word part found at the end of a word. Knowledge of the meaning of a suffix can often help the secretary figure out the meaning of the entire word. For example, *tendonitis* = *tendon* + *itis* (inflammation), or an inflammation of a tendon.

Suffix	Meaning	Suffix	Meaning
ac	pertaining to	*or*	one who
agia	excessive pain	*osis*	abnormal
al	pertaining to		condition
algia	pain	*ous*	pertaining to
ar	pertaining to	*pathy*	disease
ary	pertaining to	*penia*	deficiency
cele	hernia	*pexy*	fixation; to put
crine	secrete; separate		in place
crit	separate	*phagia*	eating; swal-
cyesis	pregnancy		lowing
cyte	cell	*plasty*	surgical repair
dynia	pain	*pnea*	breathing
eal	pertaining to	*ptosis*	drooping;
ectomy	removal; excision		sagging; prolapse
emia	blood	*rrhage*	bursting forth of
er	one who		blood
fusion	to pour	*rrhea*	flow; discharge
grade	to go	*scope*	instrument for
gram	record		visual examin-
graph	instrument for		ation
	recording	*sis*	state of; condition
ia	condition	*spasm*	sudden contraction
iac	pertaining to		of muscles
ic	pertaining to	*stomy*	new opening
ism	process	*therapy*	treatment
ist	specialist	*thorax*	pleural cavity;
itis	inflammation		chest
logy	study of	*tic*	pertaining to
megaly	enlargement	*tome*	instrument to cut
meter	measure	*tomy*	process of cutting
oid	resembling	*ule*	little; small
ole	little, small	*uria*	urination; urine
oma	tumor, mass	*us*	thing
opsy	view of	*y*	condition; process

3

The Legal Secretary

by Milton Katz

Although the duties of the legal secretary are similar in most respects to those of other secretaries, there are several important differences deriving from the major concern of a law firm—the practice of law. As a result, the legal secretary must be well versed in the terminology, forms, and procedures of the legal profession. In addition, because of the precise standards set by the law, the legal secretary must be particularly careful to follow correct procedures in exact sequence.

REQUIREMENTS

In addition to those common to all secretaries, the competent legal secretary should possess the following characteristics:

- comprehensive background in legal matters
- keen interest in the law
- thoroughness and high standards
- ability to deal with pressure and to work under severe time limitations
- interest in people
- ability to deal with people who may be in a highly emotional state
- respect for confidentiality
- strong oral communication skills.

The position of legal secretary is demanding, but it is also rewarding. Because a legal secretary requires training and skills greater than those of the average secretary, pay and fringe benefits are generally superior. In addition, involvement in human drama and a variety of social and economic experiences makes for more interesting work. Although many legal matters deal with such normal actions as the purchase of a house, people in trouble or crisis often turn to the law for help. The legal secretary is a participant in this search for redress and so is offered valuable insight into society's legal framework.

TYPES OF POSITIONS

Many kinds of positions are available to the legal secretary. They include working in a single-attorney office, in a partnership, in a large law firm, in the in-house law department of a large corporation, and in the local, state, and federal court systems. In addition, legal practices vary from the general to specialties in real estate law, corporate law, criminal law, tax law, estate planning, marital law, and labor law.

DUTIES

The functions of the legal secretary may be divided into three major areas: dealing with people, managing the law office, and preparing legal instruments and court papers. Many of the duties of the legal secretary are identical to those of other types of secretaries.

Dealing with People

The legal secretary comes into regular contact either personally or by written or phone communication with lawyers, fellow employees, clients and potential clients, and court personnel. Certain principles should guide the secretary's behavior with each of these four types.

The Attorney

The secretary must never be afraid to ask the attorney questions when unsure of what should be done. All attorneys would prefer to answer questions than to be presented with a legal paper done incorrectly. Moreover, the more a secretary knows about the attorney's clients, cases, and work habits, the more effective she or he can be in helping the attorney deal with the burden of work.

The secretary should also understand that each attorney adopts an individual approach and that it is the secretary's obligation to conform to each attorney's way.

This is certainly true in the sensitive area of formality/informality. There is increasing familiarity today between attorney and secretary. However, the wise secretary understands that individual preferences differ and that some attorneys do not wish to be addressed by their first name. Moreover, in the presence of a client, *always* use Mr., Ms., or Mrs. when talking to or referring to the attorney, no matter how informal the office is customarily.

The secretary must also understand that attorneys often work under pressure and, being human, sometimes erupt. No matter how slight the provocation, the secretary should not take the criticism personally. When the pressure abates, the emotional atmosphere will return to normal.

Finally, the secretary must always respect the confidentiality of legal matters. Opinions, information, and anecdotes must never be carried beyond the confines of the office. It is always possible that, for example, a derogatory comment about a client could find its way back to that client and affect the attorney-client relationship, or that a piece of information could reach the opposing counsel and adversely affect the case of the secretary's employer.

Fellow Employees

Verbal "buttoning up" is desirable in the secretary's relationship with fellow employees—other secretaries, paralegals, law clerks, and receptionists. Too much chitchatting at the expense of work can lead to negative productivity and perhaps even negative office morale. And even here, within the office, confidentiality must be respected.

It is essential to know what the secretary's duties are and how they differ from those of other employees. Don't infringe on someone else's territory, even with the best of intentions. For example, you may have nothing to do for the moment and see your fellow secretary knee-deep in legal papers; you may think that by going through that secretary's mail, you may be saving her or him time and effort, but your co-worker may be looking forward to a change of pace from the typing and so not appreciate your efforts. By all means help out, but ask first.

Also, if you're relatively new to the office, you can save yourself a good deal of time and trouble by enlisting the help of a veteran. Don't hesitate to ask; most secretaries will be glad to assist.

Clients

Much of the secretary's success in dealing with clients will spring from an instinctive reaction to their characters and needs. There are a few principles that apply to interacting with all clients. Unless the client specifically requests otherwise, always refer to him or her by surname. Many people resent the easy familiarity of a quick first-name basis.

Be patient, courteous, and never sarcastic. Be friendly, but don't get overly involved with the client's problems. Most important, don't give legal advice! Leave that to the attorneys. Even if you think you know the answer, don't offer it. Be sympathetic, but emphasize that your legal knowledge is limited.

Clients may sometimes ask to see their files, or to remove some document pertaining to their case. A client has the right to see personal papers, such as the deed to his or her house. Aside from personal papers, however, politely resist such requests, saying you need permission from your employer. It is a good idea to find out in advance what your attorney's policy is in regard to clients' requests to examine their files.

Court Personnel

The secretary will also come into contact with court personnel, most often through phone contact with court clerks. These contacts are usually important, involving requests for information, such as the postponement date of a trial, whether some legal papers were received, or whether certain exhibits need to be attached to papers (*e.g.,* a copy of a lease in a landlord-tenant dispute).

Have available the name of the case and the case index number. And when receiving information from the court clerk, *write it down.* You may think you'll remember it, but you may be interrupted as soon as you hang up and then find that an important detail has slipped your mind.

Managing the Law Office

Write it down is a good rule to follow at all times. Other practices experienced legal secretaries have learned to apply relate to key areas of time management, office machines, dictation and legal shorthand, correspondence, filing, books and records, and miscellaneous functions such as taking charge of mail. Our emphasis here will be on legal procedures, but many procedures discussed elsewhere in this handbook will also be helpful.

Sometimes the legal secretary may experience a lull, but more often than not she or he will be working under the pressure of time. One technique to help diminish this pressure is to bring a body of work to the attorney as soon as it is completed, rather than wait until the end of the day. Since changes are sometimes necessary, getting the work in early can help avoid the press of correction near departing time.

Another time-saving technique is to attach a client's file to any correspondence from or related to the client that has just arrived in that day's mail. This enables the attorney to have necessary information at his or her disposal while dealing with the communication.

Other time-management techniques include filing material as soon as it is completed; keeping phone conversations to a minimum length, but doing so courteously ("Excuse me, there's a call on another line. I'll get back to you."); and not photocopying or fastening court papers the attorney has dictated until he or she approves, for changes are often made.

Law offices employ the same machines found in other types of offices: computers, word processors, copying machines, dictaphones, fax machines, postage meters, etc. Of these, one that has been most adaptable to the law office is the computer. It can be used to set up formats for wills, caption boxes, attorney's affirmations, etc. For example, the opening of an attorney's affirmation ("John Jones, being duly sworn, deposes and says") can be placed on a computer, thus avoiding retyping. Also, since all wills contain *boilerplate* (specific material used over and over again), a paragraph such as the one that follows can be set up on a word processing file and copied onto each new will, thus avoiding much unnecessary typing.

I, (NAME), residing at (ADDRESS, CITY), County of (COUNTY), State of (STATE), do hereby make, publish and declare this to be my Last Will and Testament, hereby revoking any and all Wills and Codicils by me at any time heretofore made.

One kind of office machine peculiar to the law office is the stenotype. Although it is most often used by court reporters, some secretaries who have been schooled in its use and have the machine will use it for taking office dictation.

Familiarity with legal phrases and their meanings will help make a more efficient legal secretary. (A brief glossary of often-used legal terms appears at the end of this chapter.) Use can be made of such books as *The Legal Secretary: Terminology and Transcription* by Dorothy Adams and Margaret Kurtz, published by McGraw-Hill, and *Speedwriting for the Legal Secretary* by Berniece Craft, et al., a paperback published by Bobbs Merrill.

It is important to emphasize absolute accuracy in the law office: *Always proofread carefully.* Also, when sending correspondence to a business rather than a home address, ask the attorney if the envelope should be marked PERSONAL & CONFIDENTIAL. Another good policy is to state the position of the addressee when addressing a letter (*e.g.,* Vice President, Marketing).

Computer Software for the Legal Secretary

LEXUS and NEXUS are databases that are available to lawyers to supplement legal research. And there are many software packages that help the legal secretary. There are programs that keep an automatic tickler file for clients, perform docket tracking, store client's telephone numbers, print out daily schedules and to-do lists, track billable time, prepare monthly statements, and store standardized legal forms.

Hints for Correspondence

There are a number of routines involving correspondence that can diminish the secretary's frustrations. These include:

1. When opening mail, immediately stamp the date received on the letter.
2. If a copy of a pleading (answer, bill of particulars, etc.) is received in the mail, save the envelope. Sometimes the date stamp becomes important.
3. Always make a copy of an original for the file. Use a color other than white for the copy; this helps to distinguish office correspondence from letters received from clients or other lawyers.
4. When mailing an original and a copy (either to the same or different recipients), stamp COPY on the copy.
5. When sending out correspondence requesting or requiring a follow-up, make a calendar entry for the follow-up due date.
6. Don't throw out any written matter given to you by the attorney, such as a handwritten version of a letter. Let the attorney do the discarding.

Hints for Filing

The following suggestions apply particularly to the law office.

1. In opening a file, attach correspondence to one side of the manila folder (*e.g.,* the left) and legal papers to the other side (*e.g.,* the right).

2. When naming a file in a court proceeding, always put the client's name first: JONES *vs.* BROWN when the client is the plaintiff, JONES *adv.* BROWN when the client is being sued (*adv.* = adversus, Latin for against).

3. Smaller law firms generally file alphabetically. Large firms most often use a numerical system, with each case receiving a number. When writing concerning a case, always use the file number. (Of course, numerical systems must employ a reference file to trace correspondence without the file number.)

4. For a very large file, as in the handling of an estate, use a red expandable envelope, and within the envelope insert separate manila folders for such areas as CORRESPONDENCE, SURROGATE COURT MATTERS, BANK STATEMENTS, and STOCKS & BONDS.

5. On the outside of the file, in addition to the client's name, place home address and phone and business address and phone. This eliminates the need to go through the file when it is necessary to reach the client.

Miscellaneous

The keeping of books and records in a law office generally follows customary practice elsewhere. When there are unusual expenses incurred for a client, such as securing a copy of records from the county clerk or sending mail by express service (at the request of the client), such expenditures should be listed on a disbursement sheet kept in the client's file.

Miscellaneous functions, too, follow customary practice. These include such matters as taking care of the mail, arranging for travel, and social amenities.

Preparing Legal Instruments

Along with correspondence, legal instruments and court papers (pleadings) generally consume most of the legal secretary's time. A *legal instrument* is a formal written document such as a deed, contract, affidavit, or will. A legal instrument is not usually related to a court action. A *court paper,* on the other hand, is a statement to the court presenting the claims of the plaintiff or the answer of the defendant.

Preparation of Legal Instruments:

1. Double-space (although long agreements may sometimes be single-spaced, as may citations and land descriptions).
2. CAPITALIZE names of parties involved.
3. When referring to money or numbers, always write out the number and then, in parentheses, put the number in figures, as: four thousand (4,000).
4. Enumerate paragraphs (optional with an affidavit).
5. Do not fill in the complete date until there is certainty as to when the instrument will be signed.
6. On a preprinted form (such as a deed), if the signature must be notarized, fill in the acknowledgment for the notary.
7. When sending a paper to a client for a signature, put initials or a check mark lightly in pencil to indicate where the client should sign. Do the same where a notary's signature is required.
8. Type the client's name under the signature line where he or she has to sign (execute).
9. Use sequential page numbers.
10. When photocopying an executed paper of several pages (*e.g.*, a will), don't remove staples from the original document, since this might suggest tampering.

Types of Legal Instruments

A *deed* is a legal instrument that, when delivered, transfers a present interest in property. Deed forms are generally preprinted and can be readily gotten from a title company.

A *contract* is a legal agreement between two or more people to do something. Some contracts, such as those pertaining to real estate, are available as preprinted forms, obtainable from title companies. Contracts that are not preprinted are usually dictated by the attorney.

An *affidavit* is a written statement made on oath before a notary public or other person authorized to administer oaths. Below is an example of the format for an affidavit. (The first line is typed about ten spaces below the place where it normally would go.)

STATE OF NEW YORK)
)
) SS.:
COUNTY OF KINGS   )

        JOHN JAMES, being duly sworn, deposes and says:

    1.
        (Body of affidavit goes here and should be double-spaced. When completed, come down four spaces to the signature line.)

_____
JOHN JAMES

Sworn to me before this
1st day of September, 19—

_____
    Notary Public

    A *will* is a legal statement of a person's wishes concerning the disposal of his or her property after death. Simple wills are often assemblages of "boilerplate," paragraphs whose format is unvaried from will to will but whose information is individualized to the wishes of the testator (male who has made out the will) or testatrix (female who has made out the will).

    The signature line of the testator or testatrix and the several witnesses must always be together on the same page—never separated. In addition, these signatures must never appear on an otherwise blank page; the page must contain some section of the body of the will.

Preparing Court Papers

Please note that all the examples shown are for New York State; other states may have slight variations. The various types of court papers can be summarized most easily through an understanding of the sequence of pretrial procedures.

    In civil cases, a court action is initiated by the plaintiff's service of a *summons* and *complaint.* A *summons* is an official order to appear in court, to respond as a defendant to a charge. A *complaint* is a formal charge or accusation. It contains the plaintiff's explanation of the reason for the suit. Allegations are enumerated. The complaint ends with a *wherefore* clause asking for a favorable judgment and costs and disbursements in connection with the legal action. Though the summons and complaint can be served separately, most often they are served together.

The defense attorney replies with an *answer,* responding to the plaintiff's charges. The answer sometimes contains a *counterclaim,* clauses that present countercharges against the plaintiff's charges. The answer is sometimes accompanied by a *demand for a bill of particulars,* a request of the plaintiff by the defendant for a detailed list of the amounts of money asked for. The plaintiff responds with a *bill of particulars.*

In order to get the case on the court calendar, a series of papers must be presented, such as a *notice of issue* or a *request for judicial information.* The defendant may present a *demurrer,* a plea for the dismissal of the suit on the grounds that even if the plaintiff's statements are true, they do not sustain the claim because they are insufficient or otherwise legally defective. Also, attorneys frequently make *motions,* requests of the court, such as a request for an order to show cause. During trial, or on appeal, attorneys may file a *brief,* usually at the request of the court. A brief is a concise statement of the main points of the case.

General Procedures to Follow in Preparing Court Papers:

1. Send the original to the court and one copy to each of the attorneys involved, and keep one copy for office files.
2. For most pleadings, follow the sample format shown below:

Sample Pleading Format

SUPREME COURT OF THE STATE OF NEW YORK
COUNTY OF KINGS
_____X

JOHN JONES,

                              Plaintiff,

          -against-   ANSWER
                                       Index No. 1234/95

JAMES DOE,

                              Defendant.

_____X

(*Note:* The above caption box is used for most pleadings. The body of the work, whether a complaint, answer, etc., will be double-spaced. All pleadings will end with a WHEREFORE clause.)

DATED: New York, NY
Jan. 1, 1995

BROWN & SMITH
Attorneys for Defendant
10 Broad Street
New York, NY 10001
(212) 555-1234

TO: DAVID JAMES
Attorney for the Plaintiff
2 State Street
Brooklyn, NY 12201

The following is an example of a WHEREFORE clause in an answer:

"WHEREFORE defendant demands judgment dismissing the complaint herein, together with the costs and disbursements of this action and for such other relief as to this court may seem just and proper."

3. Assemble and fasten prepared court papers into a legal back, a preprinted, heavier paper, sometimes in a color such as blue or yellow. The *caption box* on the outside of the legal back must be completed. Part of the inside includes a space for *verification,* a swearing to the truthfulness of the statements made in the pleading. Usually, the verification must be signed by the client and notarized.

4. When a copy is mailed to the opposing attorney, the secretary should complete and mail to the court, along with the original paper, an *affidavit of service.* This states that on a particular date a copy of the paper was mailed to the attorney. Give the attorney's name, state that he or she is attorney for the plaintiff (or defense), and provide the attorney's address. The secretary should sign her or his name on the signature line and have the affidavit notarized.

5. With the papers sent to the court, enclose a stamped self-addressed postcard, following the sample below:

X	JONES vs. BROWN	X	(name of action)
X	Index # 123/95	X	(case number)
X	ANSWER	X	(name of pleading)
X	received and filed	X	
X	(stamped & returned	X	
X	by court clerk)	X	
X		X	

6. When sending pleadings to the court, with copies that must be returned (for example, for a signature, or for a copy to be conformed), always enclose a stamped self-addressed envelope.

ADVANCING A LEGAL CAREER

If a legal secretary wants to advance a legal career, he or she might consider becoming a legal assistant, or *paralegal*. A paralegal is a highly trained legal professional who performs tasks under the direct supervision of an attorney. A paralegal can compile and correlate legal research, interview clients, and prepare and interpret legal documents. A paralegal can perform many of the same tasks that would be performed by an attorney with the exception of giving legal advice, setting legal fees, and presenting cases in court.

Paralegals have more responsibilities than legal secretaries and are paid higher salaries. According to the U.S. Department of Labor and Industry, the paralegal profession is one of the fastest growing professions in the country. Therefore, paralegal courses are springing up all over. Courses—which include ethics, legal research, real estate, business organizations, domestic relations, bankruptcy, torts, personal injury, wills and estates, and a host of other selections—can be taken through colleges and through home-study programs.

GLOSSARY OF LEGAL WORDS AND PHRASES

Latin words and phrases are italicized. Terms defined in the preceding text are not included.

alleged so declared, but without proof; presumed

appellant person making an appeal

appellee person against whom the appeal is brought; respondent

attestation certification by oath or signature; testimony

bona fide in or with good faith

certiorari writ issued by a higher court to a lower court requesting the record of a case for review

codicil addition to or modification of a will

contra against

deposition testimony of a witness, made under oath but not in open court, written down to be used when the case comes to trial

docket court calendar

duress unlawful restraint by which a person is forced to perform or refrain from doing an act

et alii (et al.) and others

execution completion or validation of a legal instrument, as by signing, sealing, and delivering

fee simple absolute ownership (of land) with unrestricted rights of disposition

felony a major crime, as murder, arson, or rape; results in greater punishment than for a misdemeanor, a minor crime

habeas corpus writ directed to a person having custody of another to produce that person in court

id est (i.e.) that is

injunction writ or order from a court prohibiting a person or group from carrying out a given action or ordering a given action to be done

in re in the matter of

intestate without having made a will

jurat statement or certification added to an affidavit, telling when, before whom, and (sometimes) where the affidavit was made

lien the right of a creditor against the property of a debtor for payment of a debt or duty

mandamus writ issued by a superior court commanding that a specified thing be done

mortgagee one who receives a mortgage (creditor)

mortgagor one who mortgages his or her property (debtor)

nolo contendere I will not contest it

non compos mentos not of sound mind

per annum by the year

perjury willful telling of a lie while under lawful oath to tell the truth

plaintiff person who brings a suit into a court of law

postmortem after death

power of attorney written statement legally authorizing a person to act for another

prima facie at first sight; on the face of it

pro for; in behalf of

quid pro quo one thing in return for another; something for something

retainer type of contract in which a lawyer is employed by a client to perform services when needed

scilicet (ss.) to wit; that is to say

stipulation clause in a contract or any agreement; agreement between opposing lawyers in a civil case

subornation crime of inducing another to commit perjury

subpoena written legal order directing a person to appear in court to testify, show records, etc.

supra above

tort wrongful act, injury, or damage (not involving a breach of contract) for which a civil action can be brought

venue county or locality in which a cause of a legal action occurs or a crime is committed; county or locality in which a jury is drawn and a case tried

versus (vs.; v.) against

writ formal legal document ordering or prohibiting some action, such as a writ of *habeas corpus*

4

The Technical Secretary

by James C. Matthews, Ed.D.

Technology has fostered growth in research in both the public and private sectors. The technical secretary works for scientists, mathematicians, researchers, and others in scientific and technical fields. In addition to basic knowledge of secretarial procedures and skills for information gathering, the technical secretary needs special skills. The secretarial work will involve the formatting and handling of a variety of technical documents, such as scientific reports and abstracts, as well as the deciphering and interpretation of information. The secretary must deal with technical terms and symbols, be able to type or key technical data accurately, proofread, and make decisions with reference to mathematical equations, language symbols, and other technical data.

THE ROLE OF THE TECHNICAL SECRETARY

The role of the technical secretary in the office is different from that of secretaries in many other categories. Many scientists and researchers work in government-sponsored institutes and projects in both the public and the private sector. In many cases the security of records and personnel is an important factor. The technical secretary working in such areas may be bonded and may have a position involving certain security risks. These factors in themselves make the technical secretary's position more sophisticated.

The technical secretary, in addition to having a knowledge of routine secretarial skills, may be required to be familiar with a variety of electronic equipment and be able to understand and follow sophisticated organizational patterns. In general, the higher the technical level of the work, the greater the number of tasks, functions, and duties the secretary may be responsible for. The overall nature and scope of the job make it technical.

Because many tasks involve documents, inventions, diagrams, and designs that are subject to copyright or patent, confidentiality is most important. The technical secretary must develop an awareness of what is confidential material and should be well prepared never to slip and make a mistake, divulging information. The ability to keep a secret and act on confidential matters ensures professional integrity and stance as a trusted secretary who exhibits expertise in technical as well as general matters.

TYPES OF OFFICES

Career fields for the technical secretary are varied—aerospace, engineering, environmental control, chemistry, life sciences, mathematics, synthetics, and physics, to name just a few. Each field has subsets, and some subdivisions develop into full-blown separate technologies. In addition, fields often change as new technologies emerge, interface, and integrate with others.

Technical secretaries may work in conventional offices, but most work in modern electronic offices.

The Electronic Office

In the broadest sense, automation is a system of production and processing that uses machines to process information. The key is improved equipment that permits the technical secretary to streamline procedures and have several alternatives to do work more efficiently.

The electronic office, also called the automated and/or computerized office, uses new technologies to improve the quality of work and increase productivity and produce documents of high quality—and at a much greater speed than is possible without automation.

In the electronic office, the technical secretary will use personal computers, electronic typewriters, intelligent copiers, and a number of other machines to prepare technical documents and create technical databases. The technical secretary needs this equipment and should not be intimidated by it.

A Typical Day

A typical day for a technical secretary in an electronic office might include arriving at the office ahead of the scheduled time, deactivating security systems for database files and vaults, and checking messages electronically transmitted on a computer network. Also, he or she might schedule appointments on a managerial workstation and then print a copy for the executives. Other tasks might include "booting up" the systems and keying into specific networks in which formulas and equations may be stored. The next order of business might be to gather supplies and scientific manuals needed for special typing jobs to be handled during the day. For example, if a secretary is typing a scientific abstract of four pages on which a 66-line calculation has to be reduced 50 percent for one of the pages, including a freehand drawing and insertion of mathematical symbols, he or she would need access to special equipment or media, such as graphics and/or desktop publishing software, stencils, templates, and so forth. Access to a copier for reduction of work and a variety of forms rulers may also be required.

The technical secretary might be working directly with an executive for two to three hours. An assistant or another office worker may be assigned to handle the desk operations during this period, or perhaps the electronic managerial workstation can answer all calls, etc.

During the course of the day, he or she might work with a number of different technologies, including telecommunications, photocomposition or phototypesetting, optical character recognition, optical (laser) discs, and image processing. Peripheral devices might include pointing devices and cursor manipulations, such as a mouse, track ball, light pen, cursor disc, electronic pad, and so forth. These technologies become integrated tools to produce a final-quality product.

This hypothetical day in the life of a technical secretary is offered as an example only. Other work periods may include research in specialized libraries in completing data needed for meeting a deadline. You must also develop an ability to work on a "crisis" basis. You must learn to cope and deal with stressful periods; you must always identify positive measures to combat physical and mental intimidation that would hinder success.

The Conventional Office

The conventional office and its basic operations still exist in business, small and large. Conventional office procedures include handling business reports, shorthand and machine dictation including transcription activities, handling telephone duties, processing and distributing mail, making travel arrangements, preparing for meetings, and so forth. A small number of secretaries use manual machines, mostly in small businesses that cannot afford the cost of automated equipment. However, a large number of offices, especially those in technical fields, have switched to automation and electronic equipment.

The Office of the Future

No doubt you have heard of the "paperless office." Integrated, electronic transmission of data allows information to appear on visual display terminals, screens, and cathode-ray tubes (CRTs). However, a paper product is still needed in a majority of situations. The impact of word processing and personal computers long ago reared the hope of a paperless office and a paperless society. However, the effect of technology has generated more paperwork than ever before. Even though the office of the future has been speculated on as one with no or minimal paper output and handling, efforts are still being made to make this a reality. And, even in the paperless office, security is still a problem because systems can be entered by access sources other than those having rights to the information filed in databases.

Change is inevitable, and as a technical secretary, you must prepare for change. How? By becoming aware of what, where, and how changes are taking place and how you and your job are being affected. The technical secretary must update his or her knowledge and skills and create a plan, meeting change head-on for career advancement.

PREPARING TECHNICAL REPORTS

A technical report involves visuals; electronically prepared graphics; mathematical, scientific, chemical engineering, and other notations, such as equations; and technical text. The text is somewhat different from the business text used in accounting, banking, investment, insurance, real estate, fashion, advertising, and so forth. Technical text refers to that which is specialized, abstract or theoretical, scientific, and formal, rather than practical. Technical text thus exemplifies an air or sense of technicity, *i.e.,* something meaningful or relevant only to a specialist.

Parts of a Technical Report

A technical report basically includes the following elements: letter or memorandum of transmittal, title page, abstract, table of contents, list of illustrations and tables (or figures), body, appendix, bibliography, index, and distribution list. Theoretically, these parts are similar to the elements of a business report. However, there are differences. Since these reports are technical and scientific in nature, the main element—the body—includes these subsections: introduction, discussion, conclusions, and recommendations.

Letter or memorandum of transmittal. This section includes authorization, a brief background, and the purpose and scope of the report. It may be placed in an envelope and attached to the outside of the report.

Title page. The title page should include, in addition to the title of the report, the name, address, and contract number (if any) of the writer's company. If there is a government or foundation number, it should be listed in a conspicuous place.

Abstract. The abstract culls and summarizes the entire report. It serves as an outline for the report. It should be thorough, highly detailed, and phrased to correlate with corresponding headings in the text. The abstract should be typed double-spaced on a separate sheet of paper.

Body. This is the largest part and main section of the technical report. It follows the general format of the business report. However, there are three distinct subsections that should be included:

1. the introduction, which follows the abstract's statement
2. the discussion, in which the research method is clearly explained step by step
3. conclusions and recommendations, which include results, a summary, and, if appropriate, implications and/or recommendations for further research or study.

If there is a report number, it should be centered at the top of each page. Allow space for insertions of freehand symbols; if you are working on a first draft, insert symbols and other similar items with a pencil.

Appendix. The sequence may be different depending on the scientific style guide used. Identify each appendix by letter, *i.e.,* Appendix A, Appendix B, etc., each on a separate page. All data that need to be included in the report but for some reason cannot be placed in the body should be placed in this section.

Bibliography. In general, this section should follow the same format as it does in business reports. However, carefully check format variations depending on the manual used. In some scientific reports, references may be arranged in order of appearance, cross-referenced by the page number.

Index. An index is used only for lengthy reports (over 200 pages). It should include an alphabetical listing of all topics, names, etc., appearing in the complete report.

Distribution list. This is a separate list that provides the names of persons and officers (departments, units, firms) receiving the report. It should be typed on a separate page. In some cases, these data may be placed on the letter or memorandum of transmittal.

Scientific Manuscripts

A scientific manuscript is a specific type of technical report usually submitted to a professional journal for consideration for publication. Some standard parts in a scholarly writing are: title, by-line and supplemental data (similar to contract data listed on the title page of the basic technical report), abstract, acknowledgments, references, and index. *A word of caution:* The technical secretary may be asked to verify or complete incomplete references. As a check-and-balance technique, always check every reference for accuracy both in the body and the reference list. For scholarly writing, journals specify a style for references and footnotes. Obtain a copy of the style *first—*before you begin to type/key the report, if possible.

In the acknowledgment section, credit may be given to others who may have assisted: institutions, foundations, and/or individuals in business and industry, including both the private and public, governmental, sectors.

FORMATTING TECHNICAL MATERIALS

The technical secretary is expected to deal with varied and detailed material. Depending on the responsibilities, your employer's needs, and the nature of the firm, try to establish a good rapport at the beginning. There are many sciences; each with its own vocabulary, principles, subject content, and so forth. *Don't hesitate: When in doubt, ask.* Remember, you may be able to save yourself a great deal of trouble if you simply ask *first.*

Formatting technical material is a learning experience in itself. Once mastered, technical material becomes much easier to deal with. The following sections introduce you to some of the basic considerations used in formatting. Most of the signs and symbols are available on the computer. Check the user's manual if you have any questions.

Mathematics

Mathematical expressions consist of abbreviations and several types of symbols and signs, including English, Greek, and Roman letters; signs of operation and relation; and superscripts, subscripts, and primes.

The following are examples of English word abbreviations:

sin (sine)   *exp (exponent)*

Greek and Roman letters are used to note kinds of quantities:

A (alpha)

Superscripts (a°), subscripts (h$_1$), and primes (f ') are often used, and the technical secretary must be careful to type or draw freehand every character exactly as the originator wants it. Errors are much more serious than in standard text. For example, an error like "personel computer" is easy to spot when proofreading straight draft copy, but dropping a superscript from an equation may go unnoticed, thus making the equation incorrect.

Numbers and computation signs must also be carefully keyed and proofread for accuracy. Here is an example of an error in a computation sign:

$3 - 5 = 8$ *(Correct: 3 + 5 = 8)*

Signs of operation $(+, -, \times, \div)$ indicate specific mathematical operations. These can be carried out in letter symbols such as *abc,* which means $a \times b \times c$. Here, the multiplication signs are understood.

Typing elements may or may not have the symbol for the root of a quantity. You may draw this: $\sqrt{\ }$. This symbol is called the radical symbol; $\sqrt{9}$ is read as "the square root of 9."

Signs of relation, in contrast to signs of operation, indicate relationships among terms in expressions:

$<$ *Less than* $>$ *Greater than*

Thus $x < y$ is read as "x is less than y."

Fences are symbols of inclusion; they serve as punctuation marks in mathematics. Fences include the following:

Parentheses (left and right)
Brackets [ ]
Braces { }

The conventional order is { [( )] }.

Some electronic typewriters, word processors, and computer keyboards have special elements for these and other symbols. Use of typed, hand-drawn, or rub-on symbols depends on what is available to you. Remember, however, that the finished product must be clear and consistent.

TABLE 4.1 Some Abbreviations Used in Mathematics

Word	Abbreviation
constant	const
sine	sin
cosine	cos
secant	sec
cosecant	csc
tangent	tan
cotangent	cot
logarithm	log

TABLE 4.2 Some Symbols Used in Mathematics

Symbol	Meaning
~	similar to
∞	infinity, indefinitely great
α	directly proportional to
Σ	sum of
iff	if and only if
≠	does not equal
∴	therefore, hence
→	yields
≡	identical with
⊥	perpendicular to
∂	the partial
∈	belongs to
∉	does not belong to
:	ratio (is to); divided by
∫	integral
π	product; pi

When an experimental design is discussed in research, these symbols are used:

R	random selection of subjects or treatments
X	variable to be manipulated
C	control variable
O	test
_____	a line between levels represents equated groups

Thus:

$$\frac{R\ X\ O_1}{R\ C\ O_2}$$

Chemistry

The technical secretary may have to type and prepare reports containing chemical symbols and notations.

Style for Names and Symbols of Elements

- The first time the name of an element appears in the text, capitalize the first letter.

  … plus two other elements: Oxygen and Nitrogen …

- The first letter of the symbol for an element is always capitalized, but the second letter is not.

  C (carbon)

  Cl (chlorine)

  Fe (iron)

- Leave no space between a chemical symbol and its index numbers.
- The index number that represents the atomic number of the element is typed as a subscript or as a superscript on the left side of the symbol.

  $_{50}$Sn or ^{50}Sn

- The index number that represents the ionic charge is typed as a superscript on the right side of the symbol.

  Fe^3 (iron with an ionic charge of +3)

- The index number representing the number of atoms of an element in a molecule of a compound is typed as a subscript on the right side of the element symbol.

  CO_2 (two atoms of oxygen [O] in the molecule carbon dioxide [CO_2])

Equations and Formulas

The typing of equations and formulas must be accurate and artistic. As mentioned earlier, technical symbols not appearing on your typewriter may be drawn by hand or with a template or typed with interchangeable keys or elements. For word processors and personal computer software programs, check the operator's manual. Software packages can be purchased with a wide variety of symbols for equations and formulas.

General Guidelines for Typing Equations and Formulas

1. The "base" or "center line" is the main line of the equation and should be aligned with the major symbol(s) used:

$$A = \frac{R+b}{E_r}$$

   Use the variable line lever, called the ratchet release.

2. Space once before and after major symbols:

$$A = 2$$

3. Do not space in parenthetical expressions:

   $[b-2]$ $\qquad$ $(b-3p)$

4. Do not space between a number and a following letter:

   $a^2 + 3ac$

5. Do not use periods with abbreviations. Leave a space before and after:

   $P = 10 \log$

6. Use a lower-case o for super- and subscripts unless a zero is specified:

   X_o

7. Use the apostrophe to indicate prime:

   p'

8. Use half-space adjustments for super- and subscripts having letters and numbers superior or posterior below or above the main line:

$$K = \frac{C^{c^q} D}{C_A^m}$$

9. When two or more equations of varying lengths are grouped together, the longest should be centered. Align equal signs:

   $p = p''$

   $V = p' + abc'$

   $b = b' + 2(a \times b') + 2$

10. An equation should not be divided within parentheses, braces, or brackets; within an expression, such as $(a + b)$; or at the end of a page.

11. Use punctuation (, ; .) only when a mark adds to the equation's meaning. Three or four spaces should be allowed between the end of the equation and the mark of punctuation:

   $x = (y + z) = (x + y) = z \quad ;$
   $(xy)z = x(yz) = xyz \quad .$

12. Ellipsis (three periods with spaces before and after each) indicates omitted symbols within:

   $a_1 + b_2 \ldots + c = -x$

DEVELOPING A TECHNICAL VOCABULARY

The technical secretary should become familiar with the technical terms, particularly the frequently used words, of the field in which he or she is working. This section lists prefixes and suffixes used in various fields. Often a knowledge of what the prefix or suffix means will help in figuring out the meaning of the word.

The lists given here are selective. Consult standard references in your specialized field and find out if local business schools, universities, and technical institutes have special courses or other instruments by which you can improve your vocabulary—and your value as a technical secretary.

TABLE 4.3 Prefixes Commonly Used in Technical Terms

Prefix	Meaning	Example
alco-	relating to alcohols	alcohol
alk-	relating to alkyls	alkylate, alkiodide
alka-	relating to alkanes	alkaloid
anti-	opposed to	antiacid, antienzyme
bi-	double; two; a compound containing two rings	bifurcation, bimetallic, bimodal, binary
cyclo-	relating to a circle	cyclobarbital, cyclometer
hydr-	relating to water; hydrogen	hydraulic, hydroelectric
iso-	equal; denoting an isomer of a compound	isobutyl, isonuclear, isoctane
macro-	large; excessively developed	macroanalysis, macrocyte, macrophysics
micro-	small	microfilm, microorganism, microwave
naphth-	related to naphthalene	naphtha, naphthalia, naphthene
nitr-	pertaining to nitrogen	nitrate, nitric, nitride
par-, para-	closely related to; beside	paraformaldehyde, parallel, paragenesis
radio-	relating to energy or radiation	radioactive, radioisotope, radiometer
syn-	at the same time; with	syneresis, synergist, synthesize, synthol
therm-	related to heat	thermal, thermodynamics, thermolysis, thermonuclear
turbo-	related to driving a turbine	turbofan, turbogeneration, turbojet, turboprop
ultra-	beyond the limits of; the other side	ultrabasic, ultrasonic, ultraviolet

TABLE 4.4 Suffixes Commonly Used in Technical Terms

Suffix	Meaning	Example
-al	related to; characterized by dehydrogenated alcohols	butanal, ethanal, hormonal, medicinal
-amide	derived from ammonia	capramide, carboxamide, oleamide
-ane	a saturated or completely hydrogenated carbon compound	butane, ethane, methane, propane
-ate	relating to a chemical compound derived from another element that may modify it	butyrate, fractionate, nitrate
-ene	denoting unsaturation; carbon compound with one double bond	benzene, ethene, kerosene, terpene
-mer	belonging to a specific or specified class	isomer, copolymer, elastomer
-ol	may represent a chemical compound containing hydroxyl (alcohols and phenols classified as hydrocarbons noted by the suffix -ol)	ethanol, glycerol, phenol, mannitol
-on	an elementary particle or antiparticle; a unit	electron, meson, photon, proton, neutron
-one	a ketone, frequently used as a solvent	acetone, lactone, pentanone
-scope	viewing with the eye in any way	microscope, telescope
-scopy	viewing; examination	cryoscopy, microscopy, spectroscopy
-yne	unsaturated straight-chain hydrocarbon; presence of one triple bond	alkyne, butyne, pentyne
-yl	a radical containing oxygen	acetyl, butyl, vinyl, ethyl

REFERENCES AND SOURCES OF INFORMATION

The technical secretary is frequently called on to research information. The research may involve completing bibliographic references and checking specific dates or other facts for the researcher/executive, or it may involve the secretary's own need to understand symbols and technical terms. A skill for searching, retrieving, and analyzing information, either in a traditional manner through encyclopedias, textbooks, and other references or through modern electronic databases and software, is a skill required for the secretary of the 1990s, especially the technical secretary.

Books and Other References

Science encyclopedias such as *Van Nostrand's Scientific Encyclopedia* and *McGraw-Hill's Encyclopedia of Science and Technology* can be valuable references, as can specialized dictionaries (e.g., *Webster's New World/Stedman's Concise Medical Dictionary*) and directories (e.g., *American Medical Directory*). Indexes, such as *Applied Science and Technology Index,* can direct you to specific articles on various subjects.

Other sources of technical information may be found in public and private libraries, the U.S. Government (The Superintendent of Documents, U.S. Government Printing Office, Washington, DC 20442), and independent government agencies (see *U.S. Government Manual*). Agencies include the National Aeronautics and Space Administration and the Civil Aeronautics Board, among others, and public and private organizations and foundations. For specialized libraries, consult *The Directory of Special Libraries and Information Centers,* published by Gale Research Co., Detroit, MI.

For information on the metric system, see *Standard for Metric Practice,* American Society for Testing and Materials. The International System of Units (SI), the metric system, is a standard system for expressing units of measurement throughout the world. The U.S. Customary (English) system (feet, pounds) is now officially defined in SI units. The book listed includes common SI-derived units, the metric system, and conversion charts and is a useful guide.

For scientific journal writing and formatting, consult *The Chicago Manual of Style,* 14th edition (The University of Chicago Press) and *Writing for Technical and Professional Journals* by John H. Mitchell (John Wiley & Sons, Inc.).

Style and symbols notes in mathematics, physics, etc. can be found in *American Institute of Physics Style Manual,* 3rd edition. This book includes common mathematical operations, signs of relation, identification of symbols, and hints on spelling and typesetting.

Symbols in the Greek and Latin alphabets—the alphabets sometimes used in technical writing—are found in most major dictionaries.

Software

The technical secretary in the electronic office may also consult electronic databases for information. Among those to consult are:

Research Institute, Inc., New York, NY
Dialog, Lockheed's Information System
Bibliographic Retrieval Services (BRS)
NewsNet
OAG North American & Worldwide Electronic Edition
Cuadra Associates, Inc.'s *Directory of Online Databases* and *DataPro Directory of Online Services*

## 5

The Membership Secretary

by Linda A. Bruce

■ *What a Membership Secretary Is*

■ *Qualifications*

■ *Tasks*

■ *Summary*

WHAT A MEMBERSHIP SECRETARY IS

The membership secretary is a critical link in any organization that deals with a membership base, since without a satisfied, supportive, and growing membership constituency the parent organization cannot continue to exist. The secretary who deals with the members, therefore, must do so in an efficient and pleasant manner, since he or she is most often the first person with whom members come in contact, whether in person, on the telephone, or in writing.

Organizations that most often employ a membership secretary are usually in the nonprofit or service sector and run the gamut from trade and professional associations to educational and arts institutions (including their alumni associations) and charities.

QUALIFICATIONS

There are no specific rules about educational qualifications for a membership secretary. However, a knowledge of personal computers is becoming increasingly desirable as the use of PCs filters down into the nonprofit world.

Strong "people" skills are essential, since the focus of any membership department is servicing the members or potential members of the organization. A parallel function that requires these same skills is the role of liaison between other staff members, elected officials, volunteers, and the public at large.

Equally important are excellent administrative and organizational capabilities, a command of communication skills (both written and oral), and the ability to handle effectively a great amount of detail.

Finally, shorthand is still in demand by some executives, particularly in situations where minutes of meetings are required.

TASKS

There are a number of special tasks that a membership secretary may be asked to perform, depending on the size of the organization. In small organizations, greater flexibility and versatility is required of all staff members, whereas in larger organizations, there are usually enough employees to allow greater specialization.

Telephone Use

Responses to telephone inquiries can take up as much as 50 percent of the working day. The nature of the calls varies greatly, covering such things as general information about the organization, categories of membership and costs involved, membership status questions, services and programs, statistical information, complaints and compliments, and new product and service needs and suggestions. Whether the secretary is the first to answer the telephone in an organization or answers a referral call, he or she must give an impression of friendliness and efficiency.

List Maintenance and Record Keeping

In order to respond intelligently to questions about membership status—*i.e.,* affiliation, disaffiliation, transfers, etc.—the membership secretary is often required to keep such records current. The dates of membership activity, as well as accurate information on the payment of fees or dues, are essential to the smooth fiscal functioning of any organization. Records of contributions, addresses and telephone numbers, names of employers, job titles, and other types of detailed information are also maintained, depending on their intended uses.

Record keeping is increasingly being converted from a manual to a computerized operation as more and more membership database software packages come onto the market. For example, individually addressed letters (as well as labels or envelopes) may be generated on the computer to remind members of an upcoming dues renewal date, with the appropriate membership classification and dues amount inserted in each letter. The computer can also sort these letters by zip code for mailing, alphabetically by last name, or by membership category, affiliation date, or any number of other specific information needs. Letters soliciting annual or special-cause contributions might need to be sorted by dollar ranges based on previous giving, in order to tailor the newest appeal letters; or, lists of names and telephone numbers by geographic areas might be needed to send or phone invitations to regional events.

As can be seen from the few examples given, accurate record keeping is a cornerstone for meaningful and therefore successful mail or telephone communications between an organization and its membership base.

Handling Conventions, Conferences, and Seminars

Many nonprofit organizations hold conventions, annual meetings, conferences, seminars, and committee meetings regularly throughout the year. The membership secretary's involvement in organizing this type of activity depends on the size of the group and varies greatly, as does the extent of computerization.

The secretary may be responsible for the inspection and contracting of meeting sites, registration, setting up of workshops, production of meeting materials and name badges, collection of fees, hotel reservations, and on-site assistance.

Preparing for and assisting at any conventions, conferences, or seminars involve considerable contact with the membership base and requires flexibility and the ability to handle with grace numerous last-minute changes in complex and detailed information. Organizational and administrative talents must be brought into play as well, or disaster is inevitable. These tasks can be very demanding, challenging, and rewarding (when things run smoothly). They can also afford the opportunity for travel, which appeals to many secretaries.

Numerous books are available that provide more detail on planning meetings, site inspections, and meeting setups. Professional organizations for meeting planners (recommended for all membership secretaries involved in planning large meetings) and meeting planners' trade magazines provide additional information.

Bulk Mailings

Responsibility for numerous mailings to members and nonmembers alike is another aspect of the membership secretary's job. Such mailings might consist of an announcement of new services, programs and conferences/seminars, fundraising efforts, newsletters, and magazine subscriptions, among other things. They can involve thousands of single or multiple enclosures.

The membership secretary is often called on not only to affix postage and get the mail to the post office but also (if possessing these skills) to assist with the writing, editing, artwork, and reproduction of the enclosures. If a computer is available for the creation of mailing labels, the job becomes easier than it would be if names and addresses needed to be typed or handwritten. The computer will also make the process of sorting data into categories (such as those mentioned previously in the "List Maintenance and Record Keeping" section of this chapter) far more efficient than a manual system.

For large mailing projects, it is often a better use of the secretary's time to hire and supervise temporary help for manual addressing and sorting and affixing of postage. Depending on the degree of mechanical/technical sophistication and budget constraints within an organization, a great deal of time can also be saved by using computerized postal scales and meters. Gone are the days of having to carry the meter to the post office to have additional postage entered. It is now possible to do everything by telephone and computer, once an account has been established with a postal meter company.

Alternatively, it is possible to "farm out" the entire job to an office service bureau or mailing house that will even take the mail to the post office for you. When an outside firm is used, it is essential that accurate lists or computer data be provided since there is usually no "in-house" control of what actually goes out in the mail.

Fundraising

Fundraising is often the lifeblood of a membership-based organization, and it is critical that the tasks involved be carried out with skill and effectiveness.

Fundraising is often cyclical in nature—often annual or semiannual. Some organizations may restrict themselves entirely to fundraising by mail, in which case the "Bulk Mailings" section of this chapter would apply. However, in many organizations fundraising involves a special event or program. The membership secretary's involvement again depends on the size of the organization and also on the specialized skills or positions of others on the staff and on the interest and initiative of the secretary.

In the "Jack/Jill-of-all-trades" type of secretarial spot, the membership secretary may be called on to exercise all sorts of talents—from conceptualizing the type of event to negotiating contracts for facilities, entertainment, catering, advertising, decorating, speakers, and security. Invitation lists and responses must be tracked, place cards printed and set out, receiving lines and registration organized, and initial and follow-up mailings or phone calls made. A series of checklists based on tasks to be performed, staff assignments, and completion dates is an indispensable tool to ensure that small details do not "fall between the cracks." Indeed, the checklist system should be used for any multitask areas.

Correspondence, Reports, and Minutes

The underpinnings of any organization's functioning involve the documentation of decisions and actions. This documentation can take many forms, including correspondence typed from shorthand or dictation equipment or rough manuscript. In addition, reports and business plans need to be prepared and minutes of meetings taken. (In some organizations the membership secretary may need to know shorthand to take minutes at meetings.) Depending on demonstrated writing skills and the amount of autonomy given the membership secretary, he or she may be required to do a fair amount of original writing—letters, brief press announcements, etc.

SUMMARY

The work of a membership secretary may be broad or narrow in scope, has the potential of being very challenging, and may draw on a wide range of skills learned over the years. Involvement in any of the tasks mentioned varies not only with the size of the organization but also with the secretary's experience, willingness to learn (not only on the job but also through specialized classes and seminars), and initiative.

The Educational Secretary

by Ardis R. Morton

The educational secretary is one who is employed by any educational system, institution, or organization related to education. Such an institution might be a public, private, or church-affiliated school, a school for blind or hearing-impaired children or adults, a school for physically or mentally handicapped students, a correctional school, or a vocational school. The secretarial/clerical personnel employed by institutions of higher learning (colleges, universities, seminaries, business schools, community colleges, medical schools, etc.) are also termed "educational secretaries." In addition, there are many organizations, such as the National Education Association, the American Association of School Administrators, and others, that employ educational secretaries.

The responsibilities of secretaries on any educational level are as diversified as the levels of education. With the varied responsibilities come different job descriptions and titles. The educational secretary may be known as an administrative assistant, manager, coordinator, executive assistant, or other title reflecting the particular position. Although the school secretaryship probably started out as a clerical job, the technological and information age, coupled with the realization that administrators, teachers, and educational secretaries are partners in education, has brought new emphasis and a great number of responsibilities to this specialized aspect of the secretarial profession.

REQUIREMENTS

The educational secretary is on the "front line" with students, teachers, administrators, co-workers, parents, and the local community and must feel comfortable with this type of position. Frequently called upon to be a confidant, peacemaker, nurse, disciplinarian, and public relations expert, the educational secretary must remain calm and professional at all times. When confronted with myriad requests from several administrators and the need to do several things, the secretary must be able to make priority judgments and complete each task efficiently.

The basic educational requirements for the position of educational secretary vary from job to job. However, the minimum requirement in most educational systems or institutions is a high school diploma in addition to knowledge of basic secretarial and office functions. Many institutions require additional formal education: a business college or other college degree or specific business courses.

As with all secretaries, the educational secretary should be able to take and transcribe dictation and type accurately and quickly. A good knowledge of business English, spelling, arithmetic, and basic record keeping is essential, as is the ability to learn established policies and practices and plan and organize work schedules. Familiarity with office machines such as photocopiers, calculators, and computers is necessary.

FACETS OF THE EDUCATIONAL SECRETARY'S JOB

The educational secretary's job is usually multifaceted regardless of the educational level. Secretaries act as a liaison between school members and others, must develop a trusting working relationship with school administrators, and must handle special functions, such as assisting teachers and/or media experts in preparing teaching materials, maintaining centralized management information, and arranging for substitute teachers.

Public Relations

The educational secretary is often the first contact a caller or visitor has with the educational system. He or she gives in a very few minutes an impression of the entire school system or administration. The picture can be a masterpiece of organization, cooperation, and efficiency, or it can be a rough sketch of discordance and ineffectiveness. The staff of the school may be outstanding, but if the first contact—the office professional—fails, the school gains a critic, not a friend. Since many school districts and institutions of higher learning depend on taxes and contributions, such poor public relations can result not only in loss of a friend but also in loss of needed funds.

Relationship with Administrators

The secretary's relationship with the executive—the school principal, dean, university president, or other in an executive position—is very important. To create an atmosphere that allows each member of the team to function at full potential, a viable working relationship must be developed. Three important factors in this relationship are consideration, confidence, and communication.

Administrators and secretaries must be considerate and understanding of the goals, strengths, and weaknesses of the other. The educational secretary also needs to know that the administrator has confidence in him or her and trusts his or her ability to keep confidences. Finally, communication is the key to all good working relationships. The administrator must communicate in such a manner that the secretary knows what he or she wants, what is expected, and where authority lies. Conversely, the administrator needs to know in what areas the secretary has expertise and then to allow his or her input into daily work.

Liaison

The importance of communication extends beyond the secretary/executive relationship: it is important throughout the entire school family (students and staff) and with the surrounding community. The educational secretary serves as a liaison between staff and administrators; between administrators and superiors; between staff, administrators, and the public; and between staff and students. Good human relations skills are essential whether the secretary is communicating the administrator's wishes to the staff and her co-workers or providing the administrator with input from the staff. Always on the front line, the educational secretary must develop and nurture tact.

Special Duties

Media service is a new area in which some educational secretaries work. They are involved in working with the librarian at the local school level, in the ordering of films and library materials at the central level, and in processing library and media materials. They might also be involved in preparing materials for teachers and using laminators, paper cutters, and machines that cut out letters for posters and bulletin boards. Many secretaries assist in the preparation of school newspapers and newsletters that are sent to both students and parents. Included in the realm of media can also be assisting with photography and the preparation of television and video presentations.

Many school systems now have centralized management information systems. Secretaries who work with computers input attendance information for both students and employees, payroll information, enrollment information, and student grades; order classroom and lunchroom supplies; and keep financial records.

One important facet of working in many school districts is the hiring of substitute teachers. In some very large school systems this may be done through a centralized program, where several persons spend evenings calling for substitutes for the schools that need them the following day. However, in many school districts it is the secretary who calls each day for the substitutes using a list of persons eligible and approved for substitute work by the administration.

DUTIES AT DIFFERENT EDUCATIONAL LEVELS

In addition to the human relations skills and special duties referred to earlier, the educational secretary has responsibilities that vary with the level and size of the educational facility in which he or she works.

In Small Elementary Schools

The secretary in the elementary school handles all office responsibilities, unless the school is a large one that has two or more secretaries or other office personnel to assist the secretary. The responsibilities of the elementary school secretary may include those of receptionist, record keeper, bookkeeper, stenographer, counselor to both students and staff, office manager, lunch period clerk, attendance clerk, data processing clerk, and many other varied positions. The elementary school secretary must be able to relate to young children, for much of the time will be spent in direct contact with the students. Since the secretary must also deal with the teachers, maintenance personnel, and other people in the school building, he or she must be able to relate well with co-workers and convey the messages of the principal or other administrator effectively.

At Larger Elementary Schools and at the Secondary Level

At larger elementary schools and in secondary schools where there are more personnel in each office, the responsibilities of the secretary are more defined and limited. There may be separate positions such as secretary to the principal, bookkeeper, attendance clerk, guidance secretary, data processor, and receptionist.

In Administrative Positions

Educational secretaries who work in administrative areas may hold positions such as executive secretary (e.g., to the superintendent of the school district), administrative secretary, or technical clerk. Duties vary greatly depending on the specific office in which the secretary is employed. Almost all educational offices have personnel departments in which secretaries work with administrators who hire school employees; human relations departments that handle discrimination cases and affirmative action plans; employee assistance directors, who counsel employees with work-related or personal problems; benefits and retirement directors; and specialists who develop school calendars. Other educational offices handle the development of instructional programs and special education programs, maintenance problems, security, food services and school lunch programs, budgets, computer services, and many other specialized programs peculiar to the individual school district. Staff and organizational planning, tuition reimbursement for courses taken by both educational and support staff, planning of workshops for employees, and adult education programs are also activities that many school districts now have as part of their service to employees.

At Higher Educational Levels

Secretaries who work in universities or colleges might be the secretary to the dean, an administrator or director, or the university librarian or may work in the registrar's office. In many instances, secretaries may work with more than one administrator and perhaps with several professors in a department. Many secretaries in universities and colleges, and sometimes members of their families, receive free tuition, use of athletic facilities and libraries, and discount tickets to sporting and cultural events.

PROFESSIONAL ORGANIZATIONS AND CERTIFICATION

Membership in a professional organization is important, providing a means for further education and communication. In the United States, the only national professional association for office personnel in educational institutions is the National Association of Educational Office Personnel (NAEOP).

(The association is also represented in several foreign countries.) The U.S. NAEOP office is located at 1841 South Eisenhower, Wichita, KS 67277 (316-942-4822).

The NAEOP is dedicated to providing its members with opportunities and stimuli for professional growth. It works for increased recognition of educational office personnel as partners in the education team. Its goals are:

1. to promote the advancement of education by improving the quality of service by educational office personnel to institutions of learning and the profession
2. to provide professional growth opportunities
3. to recognize educational office personnel as members of the education team
4. to elevate the standards of office personnel in education.

The NAEOP has a four-point program: Service, Information, Recognition, and Fellowship. The Association also has a Code of Ethics in which it affirms its belief that an education is the birthright of every person and pledges itself to the preservation of that right. The Code of Ethics includes a commitment to the position, to the profession, and to the community.

Certification

NAEOP has a certification program—the Professional Standards Program. Successful completion of approved programs qualifies a member for a certificate at an appropriate level. The distinction of a Certified Educational Office Employee is awarded to those who meet the established criteria. These certificates are increasingly being recognized by educational administrators in both placement and monetary terms.

Computers and Their Applications

Computers and Other Electronic Equipment

by Sheryl Lindsell-Roberts

- *Personal Computers*

  Parts of the PC
  Portable Computers

- *Computer-Related Equipment*

  Modem
  Plotter
  Scanner
  *Combination Copier, Scanner, and
      Printer*
  Local Area Network (LAN)

- *Other Electronic (or Electronic-Related)
      Equipment*

  Fax Machines
  Surge Protectors
  Electronic Typewriters
  Paper Shredders

- *Selection of Office Equipment*

  Needs Analysis
  Demonstration
  Cost
  Vendors

The office has changed more in the last decade than it has in all the decades following the invention of the typewriter and the telephone. The impact of the computer on business has been growing by leaps and bounds since its introduction to the office after World War II. Computers have evolved from large, costly mainframes, which were capable of processing millions of instructions per minute, to the smaller, general-purpose minicomputers, which were often selected to meet the needs of the small-to-medium-size business, to the fastest growing category of computers, microcomputers, known as personal computers (PCs). The PCs of today are capable of outperforming the older mainframe computers both in the number of functions and in speed.

PERSONAL COMPUTERS

PCs, originally known as microcomputers, were named for the microprocessor chips that function as the brain. Originally developed for personal and home use, PCs make up the fastest growing category of computers. They are widely used in businesses, schools, and homes.

Parts of the PC

The basic computer system consists of a monitor, central processing unit (CPU), disk drives, keyboard, printer, and mouse. All this equipment is known as the *hardware*, as opposed to the programs, which are the *software*.

Monitor

The monitor is a television-like viewscreen, that is also called the screen or cathode ray tube (CRT). Many monitors have tilt-and-swivel bases so the user can position them for comfortable viewing. The sharpness of the image depends on the resolution, which is the number of pixels (dots) that make up the monitor's image. More pixels on the screen mean a higher resolution and therefore, a sharper image. So, if resolution is expressed as 640 x 480, that means there are 640 pixels per line on the horizontal axis and 480 pixels per line on the vertical axis. Although monochrome monitors are still used, most buyers are purchasing color monitors. The choice of a monitor depends on how the PC will be used. Is it for calculations and spreadsheets? Graphics? Desktop publishing? Multiple uses?

Central Processing Unit (CPU)

The CPU is where the operation of the PC is actually performed. It is the computer's brain. Think of the CPU in terms of an "orchestra conductor" who directs the orchestra (computer) according to the directions of the composer (user).

Memory. The computer has two kinds of memory: read-only memory (ROM) and random-access memory (RAM).

ROM is the permanent memory that contains the information to make the computer run. Even when the computer is turned off, ROM is not affected.

RAM is the memory that is discussed when buying a computer. It is a temporary work space where the computer runs and stores the information on which the user is working. RAM is wiped out as soon as the computer is turned off. RAM capacity is measured in kilobytes (K or KB, thousands of bytes) and megabytes (MB, millions of bytes.) Early computers had RAM capacities of 64K, which quickly expanded to 640K. Computers today have RAM capacities of 1, 2, 4, 8+ MB, and the microchip is much smaller. Most computer systems let users add RAM by placing an additional RAM chip on the motherboard.

Disk Drives

Computers have several disk options and most use more than one: *diskettes* (also called floppy disks or floppies), *hard disk*, *CD-ROM*, *Bernoulli*, and *tapes*.

Diskettes. Diskettes come in two sizes: 5¼ inches and 3½ inches, the latter of which does not bend. Diskettes are inserted into slots called *disk drives*, which copy information and record new information. Both size diskettes are portable. Diskette capacity = sides + density. Double-sided (DS) diskettes can record information on the top and bottom, while single-sided (SS) can only record information on the top. The density of the diskette refers to the spacing of the magnetic storage units used in recording data. In general, a high-density drive can accommodate either a high- or low-density diskette, but a low-density drive can accommodate only a low-density diskette. Most computers today are sold with only high-density drives.

Hard disks. The early PCs used diskettes only. As the amount of information grew and the size of the programs grew, managing these diskettes became a tremendous job. A hard disk then became available and widely used. A hard disk stores data and programs and is built into the computer. Information can be transferred to and from diskettes for portability. A hard disk can store much more information than a diskette (typically 40 – 200 + MB) and can retrieve information much faster.

CD-ROM. This is the third type of drive that users are beginning to buy. A CD-ROM (compact disk, read-only memory) comes as an external unit that can be placed in the computer. It is a permanent, nonreadable compact disk that holds vast amounts of information (typically more than 600 MB or 300,000 pages). A CD-ROM drive reads information with a laser beam; therefore, it is a read-only drive.

Bernoulli. Bernoulli offers the convenience of removable media up to 100 times more than the normal diskette. Bernoulli is a disk that requires either an internal or external Bernoulli box.

Tapes. Cartridge tapes are often used to back up a high-capacity hard drive.

Keyboard

The letters on the keyboard are laid out as they are on a typewriter. In addition, the keyboard has *cursor control keys* (arrows pointing up, down, left and right), which are used to move the cursor around the screen; *function keys* (labeled F1 through F12), which act as shortcuts to performing certain operations; and a *numeric keypad*, which looks like a calculator for computational input.

Printers

Printers provide the printed output, known as hard copy. Printers vary in speed, print quality, and cost. There are three types of printers that are commonly used: *dot-matrix*, *inkjet*, and *laser*. The secretary may find all three in the office and, if connected, can switch back and forth between them for different purposes.

Dot-matrix. The dot-matrix is an impact printer that has a row of small pins, wires, and hammers that shoot up to make dots on the paper, creating text and graphics. These printers are often categorized as 9-, 18- or 24-pin, referring to the number of pins located in the printer's printhead. The higher the number, the better the resolution.

The secretary can select "letter-quality" for final copy or "near-letter-quality" for drafts. Although the dot-matrix printers claim "letter quality," the quality is not as sharp as that of an inkjet or laser printer. The dot-matrix printer uses pin-fed, continuous-form paper, which runs through a tractor mechanism. The paper attaches to the tractor with holes that are part of a perforated strip that can be pulled away. Continuous-form envelopes, labels, and forms are also available.

Inkjet. The inkjet printer is somewhere between the dot-matrix and the laser in terms of print quality and cost. It uses tiny jets to spray droplets of ink on the page, and the refinement in the ink compound has made this technology very attractive. To the untrained eye, there is little difference between the print quality of an inkjet printer and laser printer. Some inkjet printers are capable of printing in color. A major advantage of the inkjet printer is its portability. It is lightweight and can be taken on the road and used with a laptop or notebook computer.

Laser. The original laser printers were used with mainframes and cost several thousand dollars. Small desktop laser printers are now available and the costs have dropped dramatically. Laser printer technology is borrowed from copier technology, using a laser beam to form images on a light-sensitive drum. These images are transferred onto paper, one page at a time. Laser-printed copies are of the highest quality, with some approaching typeset quality. A laser printer is so quiet, one would hardly know it is working. A laser printer is capable of printing a large variety of fonts, and some have color capabilities. The speed, print quality, and ability to be shared with several computers make the laser printer an attractive choice. The boom of the desktop publishing can be attributed to the advent of the desktop laser printer.

The laser printer does have a few drawbacks, however. It cannot handle multiple forms and cannot accept anything larger than legal-size paper. The onetime problem of feeding envelopes and adhesive labels has been solved, as some manufacturers are producing envelopes that can be fed smoothly and labels that can withstand the heat of the laser.

Mouse

The mouse is a hand-held pointing device that takes the place of the cursor control keys and many function keys in performing routine computing tasks. When the cursor is moved, a small arrow- or bar-shaped pointer moves on the screen. The mouse can be used to select words, sentences, or paragraphs from the text that need to be manipulated. Some people find the mouse difficult to get used to because they dislike taking their hands from the keyboard. However, it is an indispensable tool for certain tasks and is easy to use once the user becomes accustomed to it.

Portable Computers

For the pound-conscious traveler, portable computers range from laptops, which offer desktop performance, to notebooks, to subnotebooks, and finally, to palmtops, which weigh a few ounces. Some models have built-in modems, and color and/or printing capabilities. They can key in trip reports, place orders, retrieve information and E-mail, and perform other tasks. Portable computers allow executives to communicate with their offices while traveling—almost like taking their offices on a trip. Of course, as the models become smaller, functionality and power decrease.

COMPUTER-RELATED EQUIPMENT

Modem

The modem, which stands for "modulator-demodulator," allows the computer to communicate with other computers. The modem translates digital signals into analog signals so they can be sent via telephone lines, and then translates the analog signals back to digital signals for the receiving computer. Computers that have modems can communicate as easily as humans can by telephone. Modems are available in speeds of 1200, 2400, and 9600 bits per second (bps). The higher speed modems transmit faster, thereby reducing the charges for connect time.

Plotter

A plotter is used to print graphics. There are many types of plotters that produce pages or transparencies and draw curved lines, three-dimensional figures, bar charts, graphs, etc., according to the instructions of the computer. Some plotters are capable of adding text labels to the charts produced.

Engineering applications can include blueprints and schematics; business applications can include sales projections and presentation graphics. There is little difference in quality between the low-end and high-end plotters. The main difference is the ease of use.

Scanner

A scanner is a device that can "read" text and graphics. A copy of the scanned image is stored on magnetic media as it simultaneously reproduces on a monitor. Text, photographs, drawings, and charts can be scanned and used in desktop publishing or electronic filing. Accuracy depends on the quality of the document being scanned, so the wise user will review the scanned image for the occasional error the scanner may have misread.

A scanner works by using an array of light-sensitive conversion devices—usually charged-coupled devices (CCD)—to scan paper images and convert the images into computer code. Light is reflected off paper documents and into CCD rays, which then detect the amount of gray shading (ranging from white to black) or color. Most scanners come bundled with Optical Character Recognition (OCR) capability that can convert images into computer-editable format. Scanners are available at affordable prices for every level of user. They can range from hand-held to sophisticated table models.

Combination Copier, Scanner, and Printer

There are copiers that can also function as scanners and printers for graphic arts, business presentations, and other computer graphics applications. When connected to a computer via the optional intelligent processing unit, these units can print images created on a host computer in full color. They can scan images and transfer them to the host computer for viewing and editing.

Local Area Network (LAN)

The concept of personal computing in the business environment has been dramatically altered. Not long ago, businesses saw a single individual running a computer, using it for word processing or spreadsheets. Today, that same individual might be using a PC connected to other PCs via a LAN.

What is a network? A network is a collection of closely grouped PCs wired together to share data, programs, and hardware. The reason for the growth of LAN environments is that most people do not work alone. They must work with other people to share information and resources. Therefore, LANs can be more efficient and less costly than a series of stand-alone PCs. A LAN— with the key word being *local*—allows users to share software and data files within a building, department, campus, or other limited geographic area. A Wide-Area Network (WAN) provides this same capability over long distances. A typical LAN might include high-speed laser printers, a bank of fast hard disks, and communications links to other LANs or mainframes. A well-designed LAN can offer a number of advantages:

- It eliminates an individual's having to run around around the office, delivering and retrieving data. With the right software, users can do that electronically.
- Several computers can be hooked up to the same printer, thereby decreasing the cost of many individual printers. This cost-saving advantage also applies to other hardware that is shared.
- Users can send E-mail messages to local and remote users.
- New software products are being developed that can streamline the work process for groups of people, not just individuals.
- Money is saved because companies can populate the desktop with adequate computers and spend the big dollars on central, shared computers that can handle complex, processor-intensive tasks.

OTHER ELECTRONIC (OR ELECTRONIC-RELATED) EQUIPMENT

Fax Machines

Just as the bicycle messenger has been replaced by the overnight courier, the overnight courier is being replaced by the fax machine. Fax transmission is a flexible, inexpensive, and simple method of sending information in the form of image replication (facsimile). There are two ways a fax transmission can be generated: (1) from a fax machine, or (2) from a computer, the details of which will be discussed in chapter 8 under "Computer-Generated Fax Transmissions."

Suppose a business has to notify customers immediately that an error was found or it has to notify the sales force that an important deadline has been changed. The time involved in telephoning or mailing a letter to each recipient would be prohibitive. That is where fax transmissions come in.

Many people use the fax machine by dialing the number into the telephone keypad and pressing the "start" button. Fax machines, however, have a variety of options that are often overlooked. Fax transmissions have become an integral part of the way companies do business, and the smart secretary should read the user's manual or contact the dealer to become familiar with the capabilities of the fax machine(s) at the office. The following are some of the capabilities that might be available:

- Confirmation that the message has been sent.
- A speed dialer that can store frequently called fax numbers. The secretary can check the phone bill to determine which customers are receiving the bulk of the faxes generated.
- Incoming messages that can be sent directly to memory rather than to the printer, so that the machine remains free for transmitting. The document can be printed when time is available.
- Documents that can be scanned into memory and transmitted when phone rates are lower.
- Documents being sent to several locations that can be scanned at once and broadcast to multiple recipients rather than feeding the document though the machine over and over again.
- Incoming messages that can be stored in "mailboxes" and be retrieved by the person with the proper access code. This makes the messages less public.
- Gray-scale controls that can adjust the resolution of graphics.
- Power protectors that can safeguard the machine from electrical surges or inconsistencies.
- External devices that can enable the machine to receive multiple calls simultaneously by storing the messages in memory and forwarding them to the recipient's printer.

The secretary should fax only those messages that require priority handling. Unless there is a sense of urgency, sending messages through the postal system is less costly.

In a further effort to curtail costs, the secretary should consider eliminating the full-page cover sheet of a fax and substitute it with a Post-it® Fax Note. According to 3M General Offices, U.S. companies today spend an estimated $10 billion per year sending unnecessary full-page fax cover sheets. These charges are realized at both ends of the transmission in telephone and paper charges. On the following page is an example of one type of Fax Note that can be affixed to the first page of a transmission.

A word of caution about broadcasting (*i.e.,* sending a fax transmission to a list of fax numbers): As of December 20, 1992, it is illegal to send unsolicited fax transmissions (electronic junk mail) that advertise or sell services or products. The prudent secretary should check in advance to ensure that all recipients on a broadcast list wish to be included.

Surge Protectors

To prevent interrupted transmissions and possible damage to expensive equipment caused by power surges, a surge protector can be installed. Power surges are especially troublesome during thunder and lightning storms and during the summer months when air conditioners overload the lines.

Post-it® Fax Note 7672

		No. of Pages	Today's Date	Time

To	From

Company	Company

Location	Location	Dept. Charge

Fax #	Telephone #	Fax #	Telephone #

Comments	Original Disposition: ☐ Destroy ☐ Return ☐ Call for pickup

—— Attach Document At Line ——

3M

Contact: Linda Grams
            612-737-2783
            Facsimile: 612-736-8261

Media Backgrounder

BLOW THE COVER:
STOP THE SPREAD OF BAD FAX COVER SHEETS

ST. PAUL, MINN., (October 13, 1993) — Whether you consider the facsimile machine your greatest curse or convenience, it's here to stay. In 1988, there were fewer than one million facsimile machines in the United States. Today, there are an estimated eight million. And by next year, there will be an estimated 10 million facsimile machines operating in the United States.

David Day, author of *Facsimile Facts and Figures*, an annual publication of the International Facsimile Association, comments, "Fax has become our instant mailman — 24 hour service, global coverage and recorded delivery."

Of the hundreds of millions of pages being faxed every day, tens of millions are being thrown away within seconds of receipt. We're referring to the fax cover sheet — that make-shift instruction page that tells the person receiving the fax how many pages were sent and who to pass them along to.

"Full-page cover sheets waste everyone's time and money," adds Day.

Wasteful, certainly — extra telephone charges and paper. But frequently also irritating and illegible. Has our reliance on this convenient new technology grown faster than its effective use? Hundreds of thousands of companies are squandering time, money — and their visual image in the marketplace — using ill-conceived, poorly designed, full-page cover faxes to accompany routine correspondence.

(more)

Courtesy of 3M General Offices

Electronic Typewriters (ETs)

The birth of the ET was sandwiched sometime between the older electric type-writer and the word processor. Although the market for ETs has decreased in recent years, there is still a viable niche for them. They are durable and easy to use, and there are still jobs ETs can do faster and better than a computer. For example, ETs are more practical than computers to generate printed paper forms that have not been computerized, and ETs can generate a check, enve-lope, or index card quickly and easily. ETs do not have separate monitors or printers, but they do have small electronic displays that will show a partial page. ETs have become more sophisticated in recent years and many have built-in spell checking, text editing capabilities, spreadsheet and mail merge capabilities, limited font selection, and some can be networked to computers and used as printers.

Paper Shredders

Swelling landfills across the country have dispelled the myth of the "paperless office." Paper shredders cannot make paper disappear, but they can make in-formation disappear. Payroll lists, customer records, telephone logs, meeting minutes, personnel evaluations and pay scales, product specifications, market analyses, customer lists, design changes, and canceled checks are just a few types of sensitive materials that should remain confidential. Industrial espio-nage is a major concern today, and many top research companies are not only shredding top secret information, but also keeping the shreds.

Shredders come in a wide range of styles, capabilities, prices, and shred-ding options. Flat paper can be shredded into long strips as wide as egg noodles or as fine as angel hair pasta. The selection ranges from desktop models to large free-standing units that can handle hundreds of thousands of sheets per hour. When selecting a shredder, the main things to consider are the volume the shredder must handle and the kinds of material it is expected to shred (checks, letter-size paper, or computer printouts).

SELECTION OF OFFICE EQUIPMENT

The selection of office equipment involves a great deal more than product demonstrations and price comparisons. An assessment of organizational plans and needs must be made. In a large organization, the secretary's involvement will likely be concerned with the type of work done, ease of use of equipment or software, special features required, and what is currently being done and what needs to be done that cannot be done at the present time. On the other hand, a small company may have the secretary directly participate in the pro-cess of equipment selection, since the secretary is probably the person most knowledgeable about what is needed.

Only a few of the major considerations will be discussed here, since an entire chapter could be written on this subject. The discussion will center on the purchase of a single PC and software, but the basic factors discussed apply to the purchase of any major office equipment.

Among the factors to be considered in the purchase and selection of office equipment are a careful analysis of needs, the possibility of demonstration and follow-up support, cost, and choice of vendor.

Needs Analysis

Before any PC—or any major office equipment—is purchased, an analysis of the office or company needs must be made. This analysis should include consideration of the expected applications of the new equipment, the users of the equipment and the ease of use, and the versatility and upgradeability of the equipment as well as the documentation, instruction, and support services available for it.

Applications

When considering the purchase of a PC software applications should be addressed first. What do you want the computer to do? Word processing? Spreadsheets? Database management? Graphics? Desktop publishing?

Once the general applications have been determined, specifics need to be examined. What features are required? Can applications be linked together so changes on one are reflected on the other? What types of graphics are required? What are the limitations on bar, pie, and line graphs? Can desktop publishing software import documents prepared in the word processing package used? Can imported text be edited in desktop publishing or only in word processing? Does it support multipage documents? Samples of actual or anticipated applications should be carefully analyzed to determine the features needed.

Users

Who will use the equipment? Do the users require a dedicated piece of equipment or can it be shared by a department? Was the equipment purchased to run a particular application? If the equipment is purchased primarily for word processing, each secretary might require one. In an accounting or financial area each user would probably require a personal unit.

Versatility and Upgradeability

A major concern when purchasing equipment and software is the continual advances in technology. While one should purchase based on the needs of the present and foreseeable future, one does not want to overbuy. The cost of technology keeps going down, and it may cost less to upgrade later. If software upgrades are being planned, will they be compatible with earlier releases? Will new applications packages require upgrading of operating system software? Are there sufficient expansion slots for communications, second printer, etc.?

Ease of Use

The advances in technology have made more on-screen help available to the users. Some types of equipment use icons or pictures to represent the task to be performed. The pointer is moved to the desired icon—for example, a file drawer to represent filing—by moving the mouse and clicking a button to execute the task. Other types of equipment allow choices to be made by touching the screen or by using a light pen or probe to make the selection. Integrated software contributes to ease of use because of the similarity of instructions from application to application.

Most equipment is modular so that it can be arranged to the user's comfort. The brightness and contrast levels can be controlled by the user, and antiglare attachments are available. A vast array of adjustable furniture is available for the physical comfort of those using the equipment.

Documentation and Support

Documentation and support are primary areas of concern, especially for a novice. Equipment should come with detailed set-up instructions. Software may have a tutorial diskette to acquaint new users with the package. The instruction manual should be well organized and clearly written for the users—not for programmers or technicians.

Templates that fit over the keyboard and list the functions performed by various keys or combinations are of great help to the user. There is also an extensive selection of "how to" books on computers, operating systems, and software packages.

Do the equipment manufacturer and software developer have a toll-free number to answer questions about the workings of hardware or software, at least for the initial one-to-three-month period? In general, the level of support provided will be greater for a large company buying in quantity. And, a computer store will be able to provide more guidance than a mail-order house.

Vendors who provide training generally train an agreed-upon number of employees to use the equipment. After initial training, there is a fee for each additional person trained. Some types of training usually need to be provided on large systems for newly hired, upgraded, and transferred personnel. An in-house training department might be appropriate for a large corporation. A smaller company might bring a trainer in-house and individual users may have to attend a seminar or course or purchase an audiovisual training package.

What will happen when there is a problem with the functioning of equipment? Is a maintenance contract available through the vendor? Is the repair provided by the vendor or is it contracted to third parties? If the equipment is purchased from a computer store, does it have to be brought in for repair? Is a substitute available while the equipment is being repaired? These are all questions that should be answered before a purchase is made.

Software vs. Hardware Considerations

Once the appropriate software has been selected to do the job, other considerations need to be addressed. How much on-line storage is needed? With the abundance of software available, what software should be on-line? How many disks does the package have? How lengthy are the documents, spreadsheets, databases, etc.? Answers to these questions will aid in determining the size of hard disk and processing speed required. The more software stored on the system, the less room for manipulation and processing of data.

Is security an issue? If using a hard disk, how will the information be protected? How many levels of security are available? Where will the backup copies be stored, and how often will they be updated? Will confidential documents be communicated electronically? In a single computer operation, the entire computer may be locked or confidential documents transferred to tape or disk and stored in a safe.

If expansion is planned, is a site license available for software selected? Can software be purchased in a version that will run on a network? Can equipment be upgraded easily?

These are only a few of the questions that should be asked before any computer system is purchased. Similar detailed questions should be considered before the selection of any other type of office equipment.

Demonstration

A vendor demonstration will highlight the good features of the equipment or software. There are a few points to remember, however. Since demonstrations are done by experienced personnel who know the product well, features that may be difficult to use look like they are very simple. Features that are important to you might not even be part of the demonstration. Make sure the product demonstration is done with the applications of the user in mind.

Again, let's use the purchase of a PC and software as an example. After the choice of software has been narrowed down to one or two that seem to fit the requirements of the office, actual applications using the software should be tried. Assemble several jobs that are representative of the applications needed and that contain any special features that might be required. These applications should be tried by a person who will use the software on the job and is familiar with the company needs.

If possible, the software should be demonstrated on the type of equipment it will be used on. The same software can run at speeds that differ according to the equipment. Printers should also be tried.

Cost

Equipment can vary in cost for a number of reasons. Mail-order houses, which have low overhead costs, generally offer lower prices than do computer stores, but the trade-off may be technical support. Equivalent equipment, or "clones," of well-known brands made by different manufacturers are also usually less expensive. And, finally, the price per unit is usually lower when items are purchased in quantity.

Vendors

After the choice of equipment and software is made, a decision must be made regarding the vendor from whom it may be purchased. The preceding paragraph on costs mentions a few factors to be considered in choosing a vendor. With regard to equipment in particular, if a substantial investment is being made, will the vendor still be in business to honor commitments next year? Next month? Has the vendor's product line kept up with technological advances? Does the vendor enjoy a good reputation in the area?

8

Computer Applications

by Sheryl Lindsell-Roberts

- *Word Processing and Desktop Publishing Software*

    Electronic Clip Art

- *Spreadsheet Software*

- *Integrated Packages*

- *Communications Software*

    E-Mail
    Computer-Generated Fax Transmissions
    Electronic Data Interchange (EDI)

- *On-Line Services*

    Bulletin Board Systems (BBSs)
    Hobbies and Entertainment
    Databases and Research
    News and Finance

- *Database Management*

- *CD-ROM*

- *Videoconferencing*

- *Other Applications*

  Project Planning
  Employee Handbooks
  Bookkeeping and Accounting
  Money Management
  Starting a Business
  Maps

Many people ask, "What is the best software?" There is no best software; there is only software that best meets the user's needs. Any secretary who is purchasing software should identify what is really needed and not buy indiscriminately. For example, although integrated software that does everything may have great appeal, the features of a full-functioning spreadsheet program are not needed to reconcile the checkbook. On the other hand, software must be purchased with future needs in mind.

WORD PROCESSING AND DESKTOP PUBLISHING SOFTWARE

In the early days of computers, there was a major distinction between people who were word processing experts, people who created graphics, and people who designed page layout. With the new software that is currently on the market, those lines are becoming blurred. Today, virtually anyone who can type, write clearly, and has an eye for design can produce documents that would previously have been a team effort. Although people are still using dedicated word processors and text editors, they are not buying them. Purchasers have migrated from dedicated systems to computers and from character-based word processors to desktop publishing packages that incorporate graphical user interfaces (GUIs).

Inasmuch as most of the software packages on the market have the basics—text editing, cut and paste, print preview, search and replace, file management, spell checker, thesaurus, electronic clipboard, font manipulation, etc.—the following are some of the special features a secretary should look for in word processing and/or desktop publishing (WP/DTP) software, if the combination is needed. (It is important to note that not all secretaries need DTP capabilities. If the secretary's job requires basic typing and document preparation, WP software may be adequate. Basic WP software is less costly and is easier to learn and use.)

Styles. Can the software apply multiple formats to words, phrases, headers, footers, paragraphs, and documents? For example, if the secretary is preparing a newsletter and needs assorted fonts, is there an option for creating a style sheet?

Columnization. Does the software set up a page for multiple columns that can automatically wrap?

Importing Graphics. Can graphics be created in another source—chart, paint, or draw program, clip art, or spreadsheet—and be imported? Once imported, is the image static or can it be adjusted for size and shape?

Boxes and Lines. Can boxes and horizontal and vertical lines be created without using a line draw feature? Can the inside of a box be shaded to emphasize the text?

Leading and Kerning. "Leading" adjusts the spacing between lines and paragraphs, and "kerning" adjusts the spacing between characters. Can leading and kerning be adjusted to make the page more readable?

Headers and Footers. A "header" is information repeated at the top of several or all of the pages, and a "footer" is information repeated at the bottom of several or all of the pages. Does the software handle headers and footers with the versatility of odd and even pages?

Large Document Handling. Can the software separate files for sections of a large document, keep track of their order, and paginate for internal numbering (1-1, 1-2…2-1, 2-2…)?

Index and Table of Contents Generation. Can the software generate an index and/or table of contents electronically? Does it do automatic updates when changes are made to the document?

WYSIWYG (What You See Is What You Get). Does the software display on the screen what the printed page will look like?

Electronic Clip Art

Electronic clip art—a variety of ready-made graphics that can be used to improve the appearance of presentations, reports, newsletters, etc.—can be electronically "cut and pasted" into documents. Electronic clip art is available for a wide variety of businesses and industries, educational institutions, and personal uses, and it can be imported into most WP/DTP software.

SPREADSHEET SOFTWARE

The development of the electronic spreadsheet was the fuel that sent PC sales skyrocketing in the early years. Spreadsheets are arranged in a grid, with (vertical) columns and (horizontal) rows. The intersection of a column and a row is called a cell. Cells may be assigned a number, a formula, or be identified in a special way. Text, mathematical formulas, and values are placed in the cells. The beauty of the spreadsheet is that if a value or formula is changed, everything affected by the change is automatically recalculated. The format may be saved so that new information need only be entered. A year-to-date report, for example, only requires calling up the last report and adding the current month's figures. The spreadsheet will recalculate the rest automatically.

Add-on packages have been developed to give additional functions to spreadsheet information. For example, a WP add-on linking a table to a spreadsheet will update the information in the document to reflect the changes made in the spreadsheet. Graphic add-ons allow the user to display the spreadsheet information using a variety of graphs. The benefit is that the user does not have to exit the spreadsheet to utilize the add-on. The following is an example of an electronic spreadsheet:

	A	B	C	D	E	F	G	H
1								
2			Global Quality Corporation					
3			Sales Forecast					
4								
5	Monthly Increase	0.075						
6	Initial Target	32,000						
7								
8	Sales	January	February	March	April	May	June	July
9	Target	32,000	34,400	34,400	34,400	34,400	34,400	34,400
10	Jones	31,796	32,943	34,463	36,560	29,413	31,645	37,021
11	Johnson	32,774	37,405	38,566	40,510	33,677	31,360	36,954
12	Kerman	37,722	35,172	34,016	38,524	33,595	28,151	32,628
13	Lindholm	33,616	38,735	37,440	37,716	37,002	27,578	31,724
14	Mannison	35,355	35,787	33,537	35,352	38,034	28,130	27,692
15								
16								

INTEGRATED PACKAGES

An integrated package is one with different programs that can work together. All the programs in the package use similar menus and commands, so the user can move from one application to another. For example, if the user were preparing a sales report, the graphics program could display the sales information chart, the word processing program could add the text, the spreadsheet program could add the year-to-date information, and the communications program could distribute the report electronically.

Many integrated packages allow information from several documents to be displayed simultaneously on the screen through a facility called *Windows*, a product of Microsoft. Integrated packages allow the user to keep working in an environment without having to stop and exit from one program and enter another.

COMMUNICATIONS SOFTWARE

Communications packages allow PCs to "talk" to each other. Such software requires a modem and connection to telephone lines. The communications software handles logging on and off the communications network, dialing, saving messages, and sending or receiving information from a central computer.

E-Mail

E-mail is one of the most popular communications services. E-mail has message sending and receiving capabilities. The service accepts messages and delivers them in real time. E-mail service handles incoming mail by holding it in the recipient's electronic mailbox or dialing it to the recipient's terminal for delivery. Some services are limited to intercompany communications, others span the globe. There are also services that allow the user to send Mailgram messages, Cablegrams, telexes, telegrams, express documents, and priority letters.

As American companies are gaining more access to national and international markets, and as the world is becoming more global, people are spending fewer hours at their desks and are less reachable by phone. Additionally, the world time zone differences make people in other countries unavailable during normal working hours in the United States. Although E-mail is not essential for efficiency in every company, it is an effective and profitable connectivity tool that gives people another way to communicate. Stand-alone computers with modems, in addition to those connected to a LAN, can transmit E-mail.

Computer-Generated Fax Transmissions

With a fax/modem and the accompanying software, a computer becomes an instant fax machine that can send files to distant fax machines. Or, without a fax/modem, another popular approach is to use the fax delivery option of an E-mail service. The latter requires sending plain-vanilla ASCII files, but it is a good option for those who send text-oriented transmissions.

Fax transmissions can be sent to a vast number of people and locations within minutes at less than the cost of a regular letter or telephone call, and each transmission can be individualized. The following is a series of events that shows the basic sequence of a computer-generated fax transmission:

- The logo or company letterhead is electronically scanned into the computer's memory.
- The system's software creates a cover page using the logo or letterhead. (Once this is done, the cover page can be generated repeatedly.)
- The text is created via the keyboard, scanning, or disk or transfer file.
- At the user's command, the hardware dials each fax number while it simultaneously broadcasts the message to the locations designated by the user.

If the secretary does not have the capability of sending fax transmissions from his/her computer, there are fax broadcasting service bureaus that provide this assistance. The cost will generally be based on a per-page or per-second rate. The disadvantage of per-second billing is that fax machines send and receive at different rates of speed, and the cost will not be known until the transmission has been completed. It may be more advantageous to pay a flat rate.

Electronic Data Interchange (EDI)

EDI—a worldwide movement—is the computer-to-computer exchange of business information. It is rapidly changing the way companies do business. Any company that sells goods and/or services can benefit from EDI. A company can send purchase orders, invoices, confirmations, shipping papers, inquiries, financial reports, etc., directly from its computer to the computer of the trading partner. The information is keyed in a standardized, structured format. The information needs to be keyed in only once and can be processed for all related transactions. The following are just some of the industries using EDI: manufacturing, government, health care, grocery, logistics, transportation, publishing, and retail.

The American National Standards Institute (ANSI) is the recognized coordinator for national and international standards information. For detailed information about EDI standards, contact the Publications Department, Data Interchange Standards Association, Inc., 1800 Diagonal Road, Suite 355, Alexandria, VA 22314-2852. Or call (703) 548-7005.

The following is an example of how a standard invoice will look in an EDI-generated format.

Standard Invoice   *EDI-Generated Invoice*

Standard Invoice

Smith Corporation
900 Easy Street
Big City, NJ 15155
(618) 555-6765

INVOICE
No. 1001

CHARGE TO: Acme Distributing Co. / P.O. Box 33327 / Anytown, NJ 44509

INVOICE DATE 7/13/90   SALES PERSON NTO

SHIP TO: The Corner Store / 601 First Street / Crossroads, MI 48106

YOUR ORDER NO. P989320   CUST. REF. NO. 66043   ORDER DATE 6/25/90   TERMS 2% 10 Days

QUAN.	UNIT	NO.	DESCRIPTION	UNIT PRICE	TOTAL PRICE
3	Cse	6900	Cellulose Sponges	12.75	38.25
12	Ea	P450	Plastic Pails	.475	5.70
4	Ea	1640Y	Yellow Dish Drainer	.94	3.76
1	Dz	1507	6" Plastic Flower Pots	3.40	3.40

Please direct correspondence to:
C.P. Jones
(618) 555-8230

PLEASE PAY THIS AMOUNT $51.11

DATE SHIPPED 7/13/89   SHIPPED VIA Consolidated Truck

ORIGINAL

EDI-Generated Invoice

```
ISA*00*000000000*01*PASSWORDME
*01*123456789bbbbb*987654321bbbbb*
890714*2210*U*00204*000000008*0*P*:NL

GS*IN*012345678*087654321*900509
*2210*000001*X*002040NL

ST*810*0001NL

BIG*900713*1001*900625*P989320NL
```

	DATE	7/13/95
ORDER DATE	8/25/90
INVOICE #	1001
CUSTOMER ORDER #	P989320

```
N1*BT*ACME DISTRIBUTING COMPANYNL
N3*P.O. BOX 33327NL
N4*ANYTOWN*NJ*44509NL
```

CHARGE TO: Acme Distributing Company / P.O. Box 33327 / Anytown, NJ 44509

```
N1*ST*THE CORNER STORENL
N3*601 FIRST STREETNL
N4*CROSSROADS*MI*48106NL
```

SHIP TO: The Corner Store / 601 First Street / Crossroads, MI 48106

```
N1*SE*SMITH CORPORATIONNL
N3*900 EASY STREETNL
N4*BIG CITY*NJ*15455NL
```

REMIT TO (Selling Party): Smith Corporation / 900 Easy Street / Big City, NJ 15455

```
PER*AD*C.D.JONES*TE*6185558230NL
```

CORRESPONDENCE TO: Accounting Dept. / C.D. Jones / (618) 555-8230

```
ITD*01*3*2**10NL
```

TERMS OF SALE: 2% 10 days from invoice date

QUANTITY	UNIT	SUPPLIER BRAND CODE	DESCRIPTION	UNIT PRICE
IT1**3*CA*12.75**VC*6900NL				
3	Cse	6900	Cellulose Sponges	12.75
IT1**12*EA*.475**VC*P450NL				
12	Ea	P450	Plastic Pails	.475
IT1**4*EA*.94**VC*1640YNL				
4	Ea	1640Y	Yellow Dish Drainer	.94
IT1**1*DZ*3.4**VC*1507NL				
1	Dz	1507	6" Plastic Flower Pots	3.40

```
TDS*5111NL
```
Invoice Total

```
CAD*M****CONSOLIDATED TRUCKNL
```
Via Consolidated Truck

```
CTT*4*20NL
```
(4 Line Items, Hash Total 20)

```
SE*21*00001NL

GE*1*000001NL

IEA*1*000000008NL
```

b = Space Character   * = Data Element Separator   NL = Segment Terminator

ON-LINE SERVICES

On-line services are commercial communications networks that let the subscriber tie into massive databases. No matter what kind of information the user needs—annual revenues or annual rainfalls—there is a database that can find it. The world of on-line services is immense and is expanding constantly. The on-line service user can track stocks, check horoscopes, get help for PC problems, play interactive games, place orders, make travel arrangements, and much more. Prodigy Interactive Personal Service, The Source, CompuServe Information Service, GEnie, ZiffNet, Dow Jones News/Retrieval with MCI Mail, and America Online are a few of the popular services. Internet, another known name, is not actually a service. It is an electronic network of millions of computers at thousands of sites around the world that can share files and pass information. The user can communicate with universities, corporations, government agencies, and other private users.

When selecting a service, consider the following: the cost of the service in terms of set-up charges, access charges (per search, per hour), and monthly charges; how easy it is to access and use; and the specific communications features it offers. The following are just a few of the on-line features that are available:

Bulletin Board Systems (BBSs)

With BBSs, the user can retrieve messages and reply to other people's messages, get the answers to technical questions, get driving and weather updates, get information on shareware (public-domain software), improve vendor responsiveness, etc. BBSs are often less costly than major services and generally offer a page system operator who can walk the user through a particular process.

Hobbies and Entertainment

Play on-line games, get movie reviews, be privy to hobbyist discussions, obtain travel information and make travel arrangements.

Databases and Research

Virtually every important trade journal and reference publication is offered. Access government, academic, and business information via on-line encyclopedias, magazines and textbooks, and newspapers.

News and Finance

Get up-to-the-minute news from newswire services the newspapers use. Stay informed on local and international weather forecasts, stock quotations, brokerage services, company information, Dun & Bradstreet's profiles, Standard & Poor's profiles, and treasury fund rates.

DATABASE MANAGEMENT (DBM)

DBM software is used to enter, organize, store, and retrieve data. These programs organize data in a manner similar to a filing cabinet. Data are first organized into files relating to a particular subject, such as customer lists, accounts receivable, employees, and inventory. Within the files are individual records. These records could be compared to the folders in the file cabinet. Specific information in each record is broken down and contained in fields. An employee might have fields such as last name, first name, date of birth, address, department, date of hire, and position.

DBM software directs the computer to search the files and assemble specific information from the records into a report form that can be used to make informed decisions. Knowing what type of information will be needed aids the structure of the database so that retrieval will be efficient.

CD-ROM

Through full-motion video clips, animations, synchronized and digital sound, CD-ROM brings the computer to life, offering the user tremendous research capabilities and entertainment. Incredible amounts of information can be stored on a single 4.72-inch compact disk. CD-ROM can perform extensive searches in a few minutes. There are no ongoing charges after the disk has been purchased, such as the charges incurred for on-line services. And the disk can be used over and over again. The user can purchase CD-ROM disks that offer interactive encyclopedias, telephone directories, historical reference works, news reviews, science references, music, and a host of general and specific topics.

VIDEOCONFERENCING

Still in its infancy, desktop videoconferencing is expected to be the hottest computer application of the next decade. Telecommunications, networking, and compression are a few pieces of the puzzle that will allow people to be in several places at once.

OTHER APPLICATIONS

The following applications barely begin to skim the surface, but this list will give the reader an idea of the array of software that is on the market.

Project Planning

An efficient secretary will be a good project planner. Get software that will help with calendaring, planning projects, reports, and the preparation of Gantt and PERT charts.

Employee Handbooks

The secretary can purchase software that will help write an employment handbook. Such software includes information on how to find good employees, employment application forms, interview questions, new employee orientation guide, performance evaluations, etc.

Bookkeeping and Accounting

There are programs available from entry-level bookkeeping to advanced accounting "what-if" scenarios, cash control, credit card tracking, job costing, general ledger, accounts receivable and payable, payroll, inventory control, invoicing, income tax preparation, and much more.

Money Management

There are programs that help take control of finances. Use these programs to set budgets, write checks, track investments and expenses, collect financial data, set and modify financial goals, judge whether investments are performing as they should, learn how loans are front-loaded with interest, calculate interest rates, and much more.

Starting a Business

For those entrepreneurs who want to start their own businesses, software can lead the user to sources for business loans, grants, venture capital, and government contracts.

Maps

Get instant route planning and maps of major national and international cities.

Office Correspondence

## 9

Dictation and Transcription

by Lois M. Burns, Ed.D.

- *Types of Dictation*

  In-Person Dictation
  Machine Dictation
  Telephone Dictation
  Diskettes

- *Transcription*

  *Transcribing and Preparing the Final
     Copies*

- *Rough Drafts*

  Proofreading and Editing

- *Envelopes and Mailing Instructions*

- *Signature and Follow-up*

For many years secretaries took dictation; typed letters, memos, and reports; answered the telephone; and maintained filing systems. Today, secretaries still do many of these same things, but electronic technology has made office work much easier. Offices now use electronic typewriters, word processors, computers, and various types of dictation equipment and telephone hookups. The technology for processing, storing, and communicating information is changing rapidly. Much less time is spent on routine tasks, such as correcting errors and retyping, and greater efficiency has been the result.

The basic secretarial skills of dictation, transcription, keyboarding, and communication are still very much in demand. Shorthand dictation is generally requested at 80 to 100 words a minute, and typing speeds range from 60 to 80 words a minute. However, today's secretary must be able to adapt to the ever-changing technology and to transfer skills to the new office equipment and job requirements. For example, approximately 60% of offices now use machine dictation and transcription on word processors.

This chapter discusses the types of dictation, transcription, rough drafts, and final mailing and follow-up procedures for both a conventional and an electronic office.

TYPES OF DICTATION

There are many types of dictation methods used in today's electronic office.

In-Person Dictation

In an office where in-person dictation is used, the secretary must be prepared to take the executive's dictation and transcribe it. Efficiency is improved if tools such as a spiral-bound notebook and pens are kept ready; a routine is established, and special indicators (highligher, paper clip, etc.) are used to draw attention to pressing matters or items that need urgent attention.

If the dictation is too rapid, the secretary should signal the dictator, reading back the last few words taken down. To avoid breaking the dictator's line of thought, the secretary should wait until the end of a sentence or paragraph before interrupting. The secretary should feel free to ask that unusual names or terms be spelled and then write them in longhand. This can be done at the end of the dictation.

If the dictation should be interrupted by a phone call or visitor, the secretary should use the time to read back the notes, insert punctuation, or write in longhand anything that may have been scribbled. If the interruption is extended, the secretary should quietly gather up the materials and return to his or her desk.

Machine Dictation

Dictation equipment has become very sophisticated in recent years, and because people talk about five times as fast as they can write, dictation equipment is still widely used. Think of busy managers for a moment. They often juggle a full slate of appointments. It is very expedient for a manager to dictate a draft, have it transcribed while attending a meeting, and have the transcript ready when the meeting is completed.

Many of the dictating units on the market offer voice activation, electronic indexing, and variable recording speeds for improved sound quality. Dictation equipment can range in size from microcassettes and minicassettes to standard audiocassette tapes. The smaller units can weigh as little as a few ounces and can be stored in a desk drawer, pocket, or attaché case. The equipment is also easy to learn and operate. It can be used at meetings, on sales calls, in a waiting room, in an airplance or car, or from home.

In addition to tape-based units, digital systems are available. Digital systems have the advantages of allowing the dictator to insert new material without deleting material that was already dictated and of connecting to microcomputers to increase speed and efficiency. There are even sophisticated voice-processing systems that combine dictation, voice messaging, and computerized phone-in bulletin boards.

Telephone Dictation

Executives who travel frequently call to dictate by phone. The notes—especially the names, dates, and figures—should be read back before the conversation ends.

Diskettes

More and more executives have learned to keyboard. They realize that in this age of computers, without the much-needed skill of keyboarding, they run the risk of being excluded from important business transactions. Many executives, therefore, find it easier and more convenient to compose written material on their computers and then turn the diskette over to their secretaries for transcription. This allows the executive the opportunity to reread the text before giving it to his or her secretary for transcription, eliminating the need for the secretary to redo work because a word or sentence was misunderstood. It would then be the secretary's responsibility to format the text and to proofread it carefully.

TRANSCRIPTION

Before transcribing anything, whether it be shorthand or machine dictation, the secretary should establish priorities for the work to be done. Items may be sorted into stacks to be:

1. handled at once (this may be a mailgram, a phone call, or a letter to be typed, signed, and mailed immediately)
2. transcribed before the day is over
3. transmitted to others for handling

4. handled by the secretary, but under no deadline
5. placed in the tickler file for follow-up
6. filed
7. discarded

After the sorting has been completed, the secretary should proceed according to the priorities set.

Becoming Familiar with Standard Formats

Many companies have a standard format for correspondence and intracorporate memos and a different style for letters to customers or clients. The secretary should be familiar with these formats and follow them when transcribing. If there is no company standard, the secretary should use the style preferred by the executive or a style that is generally accepted in an up-to-date style manual.

Checking Notes and Other References

If the secretary has taken in-person dictation, he or she should read through the notes, inserting punctuation where necessary, paragraphing where necessary (if not dictated), checking the calendar for possible conflicts in days and times of meetings or appointments, correcting errors in grammar and facts, restructuring poor sentences, and so forth. Many executives rely on their secretaries to make whatever changes are necessary. However, if the secretary notices that a change in fact is necessary, he or she should mention it to the executive. And, if the executive wants the material transcribed exactly as dictated, the secretary should do so.

A dictionary and a current secretarial handbook should be on every secretary's desk so that he or she may check the spelling of unfamiliar words and place names, rules of punctuation, the division of words at the end of a line, and so forth. (One feature of *Webster's New World*™ *College Dictionary, Third Edition,* is a unique system of end-of-line hyphenation.)

Transcribing and Preparing the Final Copies

With experience, the secretary can easily determine the length of a letter to be transcribed and the margins to be set on the typewriter. It is necessary to take into consideration the size of the shorthand notes or the length of the dictation on the machine as well as the type style (pica, elite, and/or proportional spacing) of the typewriter. It may occasionally be necessary to type a rough draft when material not dictated, such as a list of names or a statistical tabulation, is to be inserted.

In a traditional office, the transcriptionist sets the margins, tab stops, and line spacing, and proofreads and edits the documents at the typewriter. Minor mistakes may be corrected with correction tape or correction fluid. More substantial errors may require retyping one or more pages. Today's transcriptionist may occasionally use a carbon packet for copies; however, photocopies and hard-copy originals are more commonly used.

If the transcription process is interrupted, the secretary should put a small check mark in the shorthand notes to indicate the place to resume typing.

In the word processing or electronic office, margins, tabs, and line spacing can be adjusted or changed automatically. Editing tasks such as adding or deleting words, lines, or paragraphs can be accomplished without retyping whole pages. Equipment may have a built-in spell checker or a software program with a dictionary or grammar checking component. The work still should be proofread, however, because the equipment and programs cannot distinguish between homonyms, nor can they determine if the transcript omits a word. The final transcript will be a clean, neat, original document with no trace of revisions.

With modern electronic equipment, the secretary can merge various pieces of information into one document. If the same letter is being sent to several different people, type the letter and merge it with a file that contains a list of names, addresses, and salutations. The computer will then print the same letter with the appropriate inside addresses and salutations.

ROUGH DRAFTS

The executive may request that the secretary type a rough draft of a letter, report, speech, or legal document. This should be done on inexpensive paper. A rough draft of a letter may be single spaced and corrections made in the margins. Speeches and reports should be double or triple spaced, leaving room for editorial changes. Rough drafts are retained until the final draft is approved.

On occasion the secretary may deem it advisable to type a rough draft of a letter without being asked, if experience dictates the probability of a rewrite. It could be diplomatically explained that the rough draft was for the secretary's own guidance in layout or because the shorthand notes were not clear. This will give the executive an opportunity to review the material before the final transcription and to make any changes desired.

Offices equipped with electronic typewriters, word processors, or computers enable secretaries to draft all items, make corrections, or rearrange paragraphs and then push a button to produce a final copy with centered headings, justified margins, and different type styles within the document. These machines are excellent timesavers for secretaries who type manuscripts, technical materials, routine specialized documents, or correspondence for executives who habitually make many changes in their dictation.

Proofreading and Editing

The prudent secretary will always create "letter perfect" business communications. Computers are capable of checking spelling and grammar, but the human eye is still necessary. For example, a spell or grammar checker will not detect homonyms that are used incorrectly ("The products cost *two* much."). They will not detect tenses or words that are used incorrectly ("Mr. Smith telephoned often" instead of "Mr. Smith telephones often"). Even though the secretary can rely on the spell checker to detect most spelling errors and the grammar checker to detect many grammatical errors, the secretary should be sensitive to the following:

- the spelling of all names and initials
- the continuity of all sequentially numbered items, even if they are electronically generated
- all numbers (money, addresses, telephones, invoices, etc.)
- small words (if, in, it, is)

Last, but certainly not least, be certain the communications make sense and have a pleasing appearance.

Every secretary who prepares drafts should know how to use proofreader's marks. A listing of these can be found on page 624 in Chapter 27 of this book.

ENVELOPES AND MAILING INSTRUCTIONS

Envelopes for letters should be typed as soon as the letter is transcribed. A method preferred by many executives is to place the letter and the enclosures, if any, under the flap of the envelope with the addressed side of the envelope on top. This same procedure may be used with those copies that are to be sent to another party.

Because of the extended use of automated equipment the Postal Service has made available a leaflet entitled "Secretarial Addressing for Automation" (Notice 23-B), which may be obtained from customer-service representatives and postmasters. Some suggestions included are:

1. The address area should be in block form with all of the lines forming a uniform left margin. It should be four inches from the left edge of the envelope and on the fourteenth line down from the top edge of the envelope. No print should appear to the right or below it.
2. Mail addressed to occupants of multiunit buildings should include the number of the apartment, room, suite, or other unit. The unit number should appear immediately after the street address on the same line— never above, below, or in front of the street address.
3. Street addresses or box numbers should be placed on the line immediately above the city, state, and ZIP Code. When indicating a box number at a particular station, the box number should precede the station name. Correct spelling of street names is essential, since some machines match the names in the address to those like it on the machine's memory.
4. City, state, and ZIP Code should appear in that sequence on the bottom line of the address block. Two-letter state abbreviations and nine-digit

zip codes should be used. Automatic sorting equipment is instructed to look for this information in that position. Mail presorted by ZIP Codes bypasses many processing steps in the post office and can get to its destination quicker.

5. Type addresses in uppercase letters without punctuation:

> GENERAL XYZ CORP
>
> ATTENTION SALES DEPT
>
> 1000 MAIN ST
>
> PO BOX 23302 CENTRAL STATION
>
> DALLAS TX 75223-1234

It should be noted that this style of addressing envelopes is not mandatory, and the secretary should consult with the executive before adopting it.

Special mailing instructions should be typed in all capital letters five or six spaces below the area where the postage will be placed, or special labels may be used if available.

If a letter states or implies that materials are to be sent separately, the material should be prepared, placed in an envelope or mailing container, and a mailing label typed. If the mailing is to be taken care of by a different person or by another department, the secretary should make a note to check and determine that the mailing was actually done.

SIGNATURE AND FOLLOW-UP

After the dictation has been transcribed and proofread and the envelopes and enclosures have been prepared, the secretary should review his or her notebook to be sure that no items or special instructions have been overlooked.

The secretary should then note any pertinent dates or reminders on the calendar and place follow-up items in the tickler file. The executive's appointment calendar should also be posted, if this was not done during the in-person dictation period.

The completed correspondence should be put in a folder marked "For Your Signature" and placed on the executive's desk. Rush items should be taken in to the executive immediately. Others may be accumulated and presented to the executive later in the day, but be sure to allow sufficient time for the letters to be signed and mailed on schedule.

Some executives prefer to sign each piece of mail personally. Others authorize their secretaries to sign for them. If authorized to sign, the secretary should place his or her initials after the dictator's/originator's signature, unless otherwise instructed.

10

Business Letter Format

by Lois M. Burns, Ed.D.

- *Letter Styles*

    Block Style
    Modified Block Style
    Simplified Letter Style

- *Business Letter Punctuation*

- *Basic Parts of a Business Letter*

    Letterhead
    Dateline
    Inside Address
    Salutation
    Body of the Letter
    Complimentary Closing
    Typewritten Signature and Title
    Reference Initials

- *Other Elements in a Business Letter*

    Attention Line
    Subject Line

Reply Reference Notation
Enclosure Notation
Copy Notation
Blind Copies
Postscript
Mailing Notation

■ *Multiple-Page Letters*

■ *Envelopes*

■ *Spacing Used with Punctuation Marks*

■ *Rules for the Division of Words*

Letters leaving a business office are, in a very real sense, ambassadors of good will. The impression an individual letter creates may mean the difference between the gain or loss of a prospective customer, a client, or an influential friend for your company. This impression depends as much on the appearance of the letter as on its tone or contents.

This chapter discusses different letter styles, the basic parts of a business letter and other parts that may be included, and rules for spacing with punctuation marks and division of words.

LETTER STYLES

It has often been said that an ideal letter should resemble a picture in an appropriate frame, but this is not always practical today because of the many different letterhead styles. Letters must be arranged and typed according to the style of the letterhead as well as the letter style the company has chosen. Most organizations have a procedural manual for their employees giving the letter style and explaining how they want the various parts of the business letter typed.

In the following pages, only modern letter styles and their variations will be illustrated.

Block Style (Letter 1)

The block style letter, also called a *full block style* letter, is typed with all lines beginning at the left margin. Paragraphs are not indented. This type of letter is easy to type because there are no tabular stops. The more tab stops there are in a letter, the longer it takes to type, and the greater the chance of typist errors.

Modified Block Style (Letters 2, 3)

The modified block style letter places the dateline, the complimentary close, and the sender's name and title in the center of the page. Paragraphs may be indented, or they may begin at the left margin. (The recent trend is not to indent unless a very short letter is double-spaced.)

Simplified Letter Style (Letter 4)

The simplified letter style, also known as the *AMS* (Administrative Management Society) letter, is the most modern letter style. This style eliminates the salutation and the complimentary close. A subject line typed on the third line below the inside address in all capital letters replaces the salutation. All lines begin at the left margin. The sender's name and title are typed in all capital letters three lines below the body of the letter. This style of letter eliminates salutation problems (whether to use Miss, Ms., Mrs., Gentlemen, or Ladies and Gentlemen) and increases the productivity of the typist.

SUPER COMMUNICATIONS COMPANY

2504 Mill Road / Richmond, VA 23230-1609 / (804) 555-9857

Date	September 11, 19___	(operate return 4 times)
Inside address	MRI Media Research, Inc.	
Attention line	Attention Communications Division	
	25 Main Street	
	Buffalo, NY 14222-5147 (DS)	
Salutation	Gentlemen (DS)	
Body of letter	Enclosed find Survey Form MR43 that you have requested from us. We have studied the results of your letter survey and are considering using this style for business letters. Let us go over each element. (DS)	
	This letter is typed in "block style." All lines begin at the left margin. The salutation and complimentary close are used. (DS)	
	The style is flexible. Some executives prefer to use the conventional marks of punctuation. More often, the colon after the salutation and the comma after the complimentary close are omitted. This punctuation style is known as "open punctuation."	
	You will see that the company name is given before the signature of the writer of the letter. It is typed in all capital letters. The typed signature follows the space for the written signature. Below or following the typed signature is the title of the writer. (DS)	
Complimentary close	Sincerely yours (DS)	
Company name	SUPER COMMUNICATIONS COMPANY	(operate return 4 times)

Joan R. Starr

Writer's name	Ms. Joan R. Starr	
Title	Public Relations Director (DS)	
Typist's initials	ms (DS)	
Enclosure	Enclosure	
Copy notation	pc Thomas Smith	

Letter 1: Block style, open punctuation

FERRIS INTERNATIONAL CORPORATION

308 Fifth Avenue / New York, NY 10001-4596 / (212) 789-1234

Date   October 3, 19_____   (operate return 4 times)

Inside address   Mr. William Sommers
                       Vice President
                       United Books International
                       909 Fifth Avenue
                       New York, NY 10001-4596 (DS)

Salutation   Dear Mr. Sommers: (DS)

Subject line   SUBJECT: The Modified Block Style Letter (DS)
centered

Body of   This letter is typed in modified block style with
letter   indented paragraphs. Mixed punctuation is used in the
                       opening and closing lines. This punctuation style calls
                       for a colon after the salutation and a comma after the
                       complimentary close. (DS)

                            In contrast to the block style letter, the date, compli-
                       mentary close, typed signature line, and title line have been
                       moved to the center point. All other lines begin at the left
                       margin. These modifications of the block style letter give
                       this letter its name—modified block. (DS)

                            If a subject line is used, it may be centered over the
                       body of the letter a double space below the salutation, or it
                       may begin at the left margin. (DS)

Complimentary   Sincerely,   (operate return 4 times)
close

                                            David C. Cannava

Writer's name   David C. Cannava
Title   Director (DS)

Typist's initials   lb

Letter 2: Modified block style, indented paragraphs, mixed punctuation

FERRIS INTERNATIONAL CORPORATION

308 Fifth Avenue / New York, NY 10001-4596 / (212) 789-1234

Date   October 3, 19__   (operate return 4 times)

Inside address   Mr. William Sommers
Vice President
United Books International
909 Fifth Avenue
New York, NY 10001-4596 (DS)

Salutation   Dear Mr. Sommers: (DS)

Subject line centered   SUBJECT: The Modified Block Style Letter (DS)

Body of letter   This letter is typed in modified block style with blocked
paragraphs. Mixed puncuation is used in the opening and
closing lines. This punctuation style calls for a colon
after the salutation and a comma after the complimentary close. (DS)

In contrast to the block style letter, the date, complimentary
close, typed signature line, and title line have been moved to
the center point. All other lines begin at the left margin.
These modifications of the block style letter give this letter
its name—modified block. (DS)

If a subject line is used, it begins at the left margin or is
centered over the body of the letter a double space below the
salutation. (DS)

Complimentary close   Sincerely,   (operate return 4 times)

David C. Cannava

Writer's name   David C. Cannava
Title   Director (DS)

Typist's initials   lb

Letter 3: Modified block style, blocked paragraphs, mixed punctuation

Date	October 3, 19__
Inside address	Ms. Joan Donner One Main Street Cleveland, OH 44224-5429 (TS)
Subject line	SIMPLIFIED STYLE LETTER (TS)
Body of letter	This letter is typed in the simplified style that is recommended by the Administrative Management Society (AMS). It is typed in block form with all lines beginning at the left margin. Note that there is no salutation and no complimentary close. This feature saves the typist time not only in typing, but sometimes in trying to determine what title is proper for a salutation. (DS)
	A subject line is typed in ALL CAPS a triple space below the inside address; the first line of the body is typed a triple space below the subject line. Note the word "subject" is omitted. (DS)
	The writer's name and title are typed in ALL CAPS four lines below the last line of the body of the lettr. (DS)
	The reference initials of the typist are typed a double space below the writer's name.
	Joseph H. Feng
Writer's name **Title**	JOSEPH H. FENG ASSISTANT MANAGER (DS)
Typist's initials	rm

Letter 4: Simplified style

BUSINESS LETTER PUNCTUATION

There are two punctuation styles for business letters. In *mixed punctuation style,* a colon is placed after the salutation and a comma is placed after the complimentary close. In *open punctuation style,* no punctuation is used after the salutation or the complimentary close.

BASIC PARTS OF A BUSINESS LETTER

Letterhead

Most business letters are typed on printed letterhead. The format of the letterhead differs with each firm, but the contents of the letterhead are fairly standard: the company name, the street address, the name of the city and state, and the ZIP code. Other elements that may appear in the letterhead are the telephone number (with area code) of the firm and the names and titles of the corporate officers.

Dateline

The dateline begins on about the third line below the company letterhead or on line 14, whichever is more eye-appealing for letter placement. The dateline consists of the month, the day, and the year.

The month is always spelled in full. The date and the year are given as numerals, and the date is followed by a comma.

Preferred style	October 3, 1995
Military style	3 October 1995
Unacceptable styles	October 3rd, 1995
	Oct. 3, 1995

In the block style letter (Letter 1) and the simplified style letter (Letter 4), the date is typed at the left margin. In the modified block style (Letters 2 and 3), the date begins at the center.

Inside Address

A complete inside address is very important to ensure not only that the letter is directed to the correct person but also that accurate files may be established. The inside address may be typed anywhere from three to twelve lines below the date line, depending on the length of the letter (see placement chart on page 137). It is typed at the left margin for all letter styles.

The inside address should include the following elements: person's name, person's title, name of company or organization, street address, city name, state name, and ZIP Code. If a company or organization is being addressed, or a person at a company or organization, the inside address should be typed exactly as it appears in the addressee's letterhead.

If you are unable to determine a specific person's name, then you may use an *attention line* with a business title. In this way, the letter will be directed to the proper person. The attention line is the second line of the inside address.

If the address includes an apartment number or room number, type these elements on the same line as the street. State names should be abbreviated in the address according to the two-letter state abbreviations. The nine-digit ZIP Code is typed one or two spaces after the state abbreviation.

Mr. John Alexander, President	The ABZ Company
ABZ Company	Attention Sales Manager
1234 East Sixth Street, Room 1410	1234 East Sixth Street
Buffalo, NY 14222-5147	Buffalo, NY 14222-5147
Mr. John Alexander	Mr. John Alexander
National Sales Manager	666 Fifth Avenue, Apt. 4D
ABZ Company	Buffalo, NY 14222-5147
P.O. Box 1614	
Buffalo, NY 14222-5147	

General guidelines to follow when typing the inside address:

1. Type names as they appear in the letterhead; always check the spelling of all proper names by referring to your files.
2. The number (#) symbol is not necessary when typing the house number, room number, or post office box number. House numbers, with the exception of one, are typed in figures.

   One East Sixth Street　　　　　　2 East Sixth Street

3. When street names are numbers, write out names below ten and use figures for names above ten.
4. When figures are used in street addresses, it is not necessary to use endings such as *st, d, nd,* or *rd* after the numbered street name.

   1234 East 12 Street

5. Type the city name, state name, and ZIP Code on the same line.
6. Type the city name in full, followed by a comma, and then the two-letter state abbreviation.
7. Type the ZIP Code one or two spaces after the two-letter state abbreviation. There is no punctuation after the state abbreviation.

Salutation

The salutation is typed two lines below the last line of the inside address. The salutation is omitted in the simplified letter. In all other letter styles, the salutation is typed starting at the left margin and followed by a colon if mixed punctuation is used.

Capitalization of salutations. Capitalize the first word, the title, and any noun in the salutation:

Dear Mr. Jones
My dear Professor Clark
Dear Mrs. Morgan
Your Excellency

Abbreviations in salutations. Mr., Ms., Mrs., Messrs., and Dr. are abbreviated. Write out other titles such as Captain, Professor, Father, Reverend, etc.

Forms of salutations. For the forms of salutations to use in addressing church or government officials, judges, doctors, etc., see Chapter 20.

When an organization is composed of men and women, the salutation used is still Gentlemen if the correspondence is addressed to a company. Although this style is frowned upon by some groups, it is still used simply because a more acceptable salutation has not yet evolved. Alternative salutations that are becoming more popular include Ladies and Gentlemen and the company's name.

Table 10.1 provides guidelines for salutations when a letter is addressed to a firm or an individual.

TABLE 10.1 Guidelines for Salutations

Addressee	Salutation
Firm's name	Gentlemen
Firm's name and an attention line is used	Gentlemen
Married woman, a widow, or a divorced woman who uses the title Mrs.	Dear Mrs. Jones
Unmarried woman	Dear Miss Jones Dear Ms. Jones
Unknown whether woman is married or single	Dear Ms. Jones
Group (composed of men and women)	Ladies and Gentlemen
Married couple	Dear Mr. and Mrs. Jones
Man and a woman	Dear Mr. Jones and Mrs. Black Dear Sir and Madam

Body of the Letter

The part of the letter containing the message is known as the "body." It is typed a double space below the salutation or a double space below the subject line. The paragraphs should be blocked or indented depending upon the letter style that is used. The paragraphs are single-spaced. Occasionally short letters are typed in double space.

Whether the lines are single-spaced or double-spaced, use only double spacing between paragraphs.

The body of the simplified letter style is typed on the third line below the subject line.

Letter Placement Guide

Type of Letter	Words in Body	Line Width	Spaces Pica	Elite	Set Margins Pica	Elite
Short letters	Under 100 words	4"	40	48	22–62	27–75
Medium letters	100 to 200 words	5"	50	60	17–67	21–81
Long letters	200 to 300 words	6"	60	72	12–72	15–87

The date is placed on line 14 on plain paper. When printed letterheads are used, the date is placed on the third line under the letterhead. However. if the letterhead is short (5 to 9 lines deep), bring date to line 14 for better placement.

Type of Letter	Words in Body	Lines from Date to Inside Address
Short letters	0–50	12
	51–75	11
	76–100	10
Medium letters	101–125	9
	126–150	8
	151–175	7
	176–200	6
Long letters	201–225	5
	226–250	4
	251–300	3

At least a triple line space must be kept between date, or last line in return address, and the inside address.

Raise the inside address one line for each extra line of introductory or closing material:

1.   Five-line inside address
2.   Subject line
3.   Postscript
4.   Enclosure line
5.   Copy notation line (one line for each name)
     cc—carbon copy; pc—photocopy; c—copy

Tabulated matter in body of the letter. Tabulated matter in the body of a letter is indented at least five spaces from both the left- and right-hand margins.

Enumerated paragraphs. Enumerated paragraphs are also indented five spaces from both the right- and left-hand margins. These paragraphs begin with a number followed by a period. Two spaces after the period, begin typing the paragraph. Single-space each enumerated paragraph but double-space between the enumerated paragraphs. (If each enumerated paragraph contains only one line, you may single-space between paragraphs.)

1.   _____

2.   _____

Complimentary Closing

The complimentary closing is typed two lines below the last line of the body of the letter.

Capitalize only the first word in the complimentary closing. Follow the complimentary closing by a comma, unless open punctuation is used. If open punctuation is used, no punctuation is needed.

Placement of complimentary closing. The placement of the complimentary closing depends upon which letter style is used (see Letters 1–3).

Degrees of formality. As with the salutation, there are also degrees of formality recognized in complimentary closings.

1. Formal tone: Yours truly, Yours very truly, Very truly yours.
2. More formal tone: Respectfully yours, Yours respectfully, Very respectfully yours, Yours very respectfully.
3. Less formal and more personal tone: Sincerely, Cordially, Sincerely yours, Cordially yours, Yours sincerely.

Typewritten Signature and Title

When a company name appears as part of the signature, it is typed in all capitals a double space below the complimentary closing. The typewritten signature is then typed on the fourth line below the company name or the complimentary closing. The penned signature is placed in the intervening space. If a letter is unusually short, place the typed signature on the sixth or eighth line below the company name or complimentary closing. If the writer's handwriting is unusually large, the signature may be typed from five to eight lines below the company name or complimentary closing.

The writer's title may appear on the same line with the typed signature or on the line below the typed signature, whichever gives a better balance to the page.

Yours very truly,   Yours very truly,

Clarence Brown   *Clarence Brown*

Clarence Brown, Manager   Clarence Brown
                                     Manager

In the simplified letter style, beginning at the left margin, type the writer's name and title on the fifth line below the body of the letter in all capital letters, or the name on the fifth line and the title on the sixth line (see Letter 4).

Joseph H. Feng

JOSEPH H. FENG
ASSISTANT MANAGER

Division or department. Frequently a division or department is used in the closing lines of a letter; it is typed below the typed signature and title.

Very truly yours,

R. M. Brown

R. M. Brown, Supervisor
Plastics Division

More than one signature. When a letter requires two signatures, you may use either of the following forms:

Sincerely yours,

Jane R. Jones   *Milton Trout*

Ms. Jane R. Jones   Milton Trout
District Manager   General Manager

OR

Sincerely yours,

Jane R. Jones

Ms. Jane R. Jones
District Manager

Milton Trout

Milton Trout
General Manager

Signature for the employer. If, as a secretary, you are required to sign a letter for your employer, you may use either one of the following forms:

Sincerely yours,   Sincerely yours,

Myrna Lane   *Myrna Lane*

Secretary to Ms. Jones   Ms. Myrna Lane
                                    Secretary to Ms. Jones

Signing someone else's name. When signing someone else's name, it is not necessary to write "per" or "by." Simply sign the individual's name and then your initials. If your employer has a facsimile signature, use it.

When the individual signing a letter for another person is not the person's secretary, use either one of these forms:

Sincerely yours,   Sincerely yours,

Milton Trout (L.W.)   *Milton Trout (L.W.)*

For Milton Trout   Milton Trout
General Manager   General Manager

Academic, military, and professional titles. These titles should appear in the typewritten signatures as given below.

Yours truly,

Grace Johnson

Ms. Grace Johnson, C.P.S.

Yours truly,

James Simpson

James Simpson, M.D.

Yours truly,

Laura Wilson

Laura Wilson, Ph.D.
Professor of Humanities

Yours truly,

Leonard J. Richardson

Leonard J. Richardson
Colonel, USAF

The salutations in replies to each of these would be, respectively, Dear Ms. Johnson, Dear Dr. Simpson, Dear Professor Wilson, and Dear Colonel Richardson.

Courtesy titles. When a first name could be a man's or a woman's name, or initials are used, the courtesy title of Mr. should be used.

Sincerely,

Dale Harrington

Mr. Dale Harrington

Sincerely yours,

D. K. Harrington

Mr. D. K. Harrington

It is customary for a woman to include her courtesy title (Ms., Miss, Mrs.) in her signature. If she does not, she presents a problem to the person replying to her letter. Without a signature that lets respondents know what title the woman prefers, they have little choice other than to use Ms., even though they risk offending some women who object to this title.

Sincerely yours,

Francine Booth

Mrs. Francine Booth

Sincerely,

Francine Booth

Miss Francine Booth

Yours truly,

Francine Booth

Ms. Francine Booth

If the writer is a single woman and wants to be recognized as being single, she should use Miss. If a woman is married and does not feel that her married status is relevant, she may use Ms. or Miss.

If a married woman prefers to be addressed by her husband's given name, then she should use the format:

Yours very truly,

Mrs. Paul A. Booth

Mrs. Paul A. Booth

A divorced woman may use any courtesy title she wishes regardless of whether she has resumed her maiden name or retained her married surname.

Reference Initials

All typed business letters should contain identifying initials. Today, most firms prefer only the typist's reference initials. Occasionally there are two sets of initials: the first set representing the author of the written document and the second set, the typist. If both sets of initials are used, the first set is typed in capital letters and the second set in lower case with either a slash or a colon separating the sets.

Reference initials are typed at the left margin a double space below the typewritten signature and title. Illustrations are as follows:

JRJ:lm   JRJ (author of document) and lm (typist)

JRJ/lm   JRJ (author of document) and lm (typist)

lm   (typist's initials only)

Occasionally an executive will type his or her own business letter. When this is done, the executive may repeat his or her initials (RK:rk) to indicate that a typist was not involved.

OTHER ELEMENTS IN A BUSINESS LETTER

In addition to the standard parts in all business letters, other elements are sometimes included.

Attention Line

The writer may wish to direct the letter to a particular person or department within the firm. When the inside address is directed to a firm name and the writer wishes a certain person or specific department also to be aware of the contents of the letter, an attention line should be used.

The attention line is typed after the company name and before the company address in the inside address. The word *attention* must appear; however, no punctuation is necessary after it.

ACE Recruitment International
Attention Mr. Samuel Jones
8225 Dunwoody Place
Atlanta, GA 30339-7329

Subject Line

When a subject line is used, it should be typed a double space below the salutation. The subject line may be typed starting at the left margin, centered, or indented five spaces, depending on the style of the letter. The word *Subject* may precede the subject line. It may be typed in all caps, or it may be typed in initial caps. Today many businesses prefer to type the subject line in all caps, without the word *Subject* preceding it.

If the simplified letter style is used, the subject line should replace the salutation and be typed on the third line below the last line of the inside address. The subject line should be typed at the left margin in all capitals. The word *Subject* does not precede the subject line.

Reply Reference Notation

Place the notation as you would a subject line. The word *Reference* or *Re* followed by a colon and two spaces may be shown before the notation.

Enclosure Notation

Whenever an item is to be enclosed with a letter, this should be indicated on the letter by typing an enclosure notation two lines below the reference initials at the left margin. This tells the recipient to check the envelope or package for additional items.

When more than one item is enclosed, any one of the following forms may be used:

Enclosures 2
Enclosures (2)
Enc. 2

Important enclosures should be listed:

Enclosure: check

Enclosures:
    check
    contract

Enclosures:
1. check
2. contract

Copy Notation

A record of every written communication that leaves the office must be prepared and filed. Carbon copies or photocopies may be used.

When a carbon is prepared for the information of a person other than the addressee of the letter, the notation *cc* followed by the name of the person receiving the copy is typed at the left margin, a double space below the reference initials or enclosure notation. If more than one person is to receive a copy, the names should be listed either in order of importance in the company or in alphabetical order. Common examples follow.

ms   ms

Enclosure   cc   Raymond Smith

cc: Raymond Smith
        Albert Wayne

Some organizations keep a record of their correspondence by preparing a photocopy of outgoing communications. The following notations may be used:

pc: Rosemarie Sweeting   pc   Rosemarie Sweeting

Other organizations make no distinction as to the type of copy made and use the following notations:

c: Sandra Delgado   c   Sandra Delgado

Blind Copies

There are instances when it is necessary to send a copy of a letter to one or more persons without the knowledge of the addressee. This is known as a blind copy (*bc*). To make this special notation, remove the original letter and any other copies on which the *bc* should not appear. Then type the *bc* notation on each of the remaining copies at the bottom of the letter at the left margin. Make sure the firm's file copy shows all the *bc* notations. The letters *bcc* indicate blind carbon copy.

Postscript

A postscript is often used to emphasize a special point by setting it apart from the rest of the letter or to relay a personal message to the recipient of the letter.

A postscript should be typed as a single-spaced paragraph a double space below the last notation. The letters *PS* are not necessary. Indent the paragraph if the paragraphs of the letter are indented.

Mailing Notation

Any special mailing notation (AIRMAIL, SPECIAL DELIVERY, REGISTERED, CERTIFIED, EXPRESS MAIL) should be typed midway between the date and the inside address. It should appear in all capital letters at the left margin.

MULTIPLE-PAGE LETTERS

When a letter consists of more than one page, the second page and successive pages are typed on plain paper of the same size, color, and quality as the letterhead. If possible, leave at least two lines of a paragraph at the bottom of the page and carry at least two lines to the next page. Do not end a page with a divided word.

Each successive page requires a *heading*. The heading consists of the name of the addressee, the page number of the letter, and the date, typed on the seventh line from the top edge of the paper. Triple-space after the heading and continue typing the remainder of the letter. Use the same side margins as for the first page.

There are two formats for headings for the second and subsequent pages of multiple-page letters: block style and horizontal style. The block style heading is typed at the left margin:

Miss Jane R. Smith
Page 2
October 7, 19--

In the horizontal style, the name of the addressee is typed at the left margin, the page number is centered, and the dateline ends at the right margin:

Miss Jane R. Smith   2   October 7, 19--

ENVELOPES

There are several guidelines that should be observed when typing business envelopes because the post office optical character readers are programmed to scan a specific area of the envelope. The address must be completely within the read zone, blocked and single-spaced. Two-letter state abbreviations must be used. Nine-digit ZIP Codes should be used. Apartment and room numbers should follow the street address on the same line. The U.S. Postal Service prefers the use of all capital letters and no punctuation in envelope addresses.

COMMUNICATIONS ASSOCIATES

385 Pennsylvania Avenue, NW / Washington, DC 20001-1438 1-800-432-5739

Date	October 7, 19__ (DS)
Mailing notation	REGISTERED (DS)
Inside address **Attention line**	Data Information Corporation Attention Purchasing Director 1945 West Parnell Road Jackson, MS 49201-1638 (DS)
Salutation	Ladies and Gentlemen (DS)
Subject line **or reply reference**	SPECIAL FEATURES IN BUSINESS LETTERS (DS)
Body of **letter**	We are delighted to enclose a copy of our latest booklet, SPE-CIAL FEATURES IN BUSINESS LETTERS. This booklet high-lights many of the special features used in today's business letters. (DS)
	The special features presented in this letter are: mailing nota-tion, attention line, subject line, company name in closing, enclosure notation, copy notation, and postscript. (DS)
	Most letters will not include all these special features; how-ever, one should understand these features and knowhow and when to apply them. (DS)
Complimentary close	Sincerely (DS)
Company name	COMMUNICATIONS ASSOCIATES
	Louise Rouse
Writer's name **Title**	Ms. Louise Rouse Communications Specialist (DS)
Typist's initials	lb (DS)
Enclosure	Enclosure
Copy notation	pc Diane Varadi (DS)
Postscript	Additional free copies of the booklet are available.

Letter 5: Block style, open punctuation, special features

The two standard-sized envelopes are:

No. 6³/₄ Envelope measures 6¹/₂ × 3⁵/₈"
No. 10 Envelope measures 9¹/₂ × 4¹/₈"

On a small envelope (No. 6³/₄) the address should start on line 12 from the top edge of the envelope and two and a half inches from the left edge of the envelope. On a large envelope (No. 10) the address should start on line 14 from the top edge and four inches from the left edge.

Special notations to the addressee (CONFIDENTIAL, HOLD FOR ARRIVAL, PERSONAL) are typed in all capitals about three lines below the return address.

Special mailing notations (AIRMAIL, SPECIAL DELIVERY, REGISTERED, CERTIFIED) are typed below the stamp (about line nine) to end five to six spaces from the right edge of the envelope; these notations are typed in all capitals.

The return address should start on the second line down from the top edge of the envelope and three spaces in from the left edge of the envelope.

ADDRESSING NO. 6³/₄ ENVELOPE FOR OPTICAL CHARACTER READER (preferred by U.S. Postal Service)

```
L M SMITH
245 MAIN STREET
GLENDALE, NY  11385-7342


HOLD FOR ARRIVAL




              MS ROBERTA ROGERS
              987 KINGSTON DRIVE  APT 7
              DES MOINES, IA  50310-3636
```

ADDRESSING NO. 10 ENVELOPE FOR OPTICAL CHARACTER READER (preferred by U.S. Postal Service)

L M S MITH
245 MAIN STREET
GLENDALE, NY 11385-7342

REGISTERED

DATA INFORMATION CORPORATION
ATTENTION PURCHASING DIRECTOR
1945 WEST PARNELL ROAD
JACKSON, MS 49201-1638

TRADITIONAL METHOD FOR ADDRESSING NO. 6¾ ENVELOPE

```
Mr. L. M. Smith
245 Main Street
Glendale, NY  11385-7342


HOLD FOR ARRIVAL




                    Ms. Roberta Rogers
                    987 Kingston Drive  Apt. 7
                    Des Moines, IA  50310-3636
```

SPACING USED WITH PUNCTUATION MARKS

The following spacing guidelines refer only to typewriter usage; when keyboarding on a computer, use only one space after all punctuation.

Period. Space twice after a period at the end of a sentence, after a term used as a subhead at the beginning of a line, or after a number as used in enumeration of items. Space once after the period following an abbreviation or following an initial.

Comma. Space once after a comma.

Question mark. Space twice after a question mark at the end of a sentence, once after a question mark within a sentence.

Exclamation point. Space twice after an exclamation point at the end of a sentence, once after an exclamation point within a sentence.

Semicolon. Space once after a semicolon.

Colon. Space twice after a colon. Exception: leave no space after the colon used in expressions of time (as 7:25).

Quotation marks. No space is left between the quotation marks and the material they enclose. When typing a list or quoting lines of poetry, leave the first quotation mark to the left of all the items or lines, so that the first words line up at the left. At the end of such material, the closing quotation marks come after the period (or closing word if no period is used) on the last line.

TRADITIONAL METHOD FOR ADDRESSING NO. 10 ENVELOPE

REGISTERED

Data Information Corporation
Attention Purchasing Director
1945 West Parnell Road
Jackson, MS 49201-1638

Mr. L. M. Smith
245 Main Street
Glendale, NY 11385-7342

Double quotation marks. For a quotation within a quotation, single quotation marks are used. No space in typing is left between the single and double quotation marks.

Parentheses. If the material in parentheses falls within a sentence, leave one space before the opening parenthesis, two spaces when the material in parentheses follows a sentence, and no space after the opening parenthesis. The closing parenthesis requires no space before it, one space after it when the material in parentheses falls within a sentence, and two spaces when the material in parentheses constitutes a complete sentence and is followed by another sentence outside the parentheses.

Apostrophe. No space is left after an apostrophe within a word; one space is left after an apostrophe at the end of a word within a sentence.

Asterisk. The asterisk, used to refer a reader to a footnote, is typed immediately after a word or a punctuation mark with no space before it. In the footnote itself, one space is left after the asterisk.

Diagonal. No space precedes or follows the diagonal, sometimes called the *slash mark* or *virgule.*

Dash. No space is used before or after a dash made up of two hyphens (or the longer dash on a typewriter with this character on one of its keys). The dash should never be used at the beginning of a line.

RULES FOR THE DIVISION OF WORDS

1. Avoid excessive word division.

2. Do not divide a word that contains only one syllable.
   Examples: brought, freight, friend

3. Divide only between syllables.
   Examples: ac knowl edg ment, har mo nize, tab u la tor

4. Do not divide a word unless it has at least six letters. Examples: ask ing, fil ter, man tel

5. Do not divide one or two letters from the remainder of a word. Examples: a gainst, agen da

6. Do not divide a word immediately before a one-letter syllable. Examples: co ag u late, o bit u ar y, spec u late
   If the one-letter syllable is part of a common suffix, such as *able* or *ible,* carry the suffix over to the next line (reli-able, convert-ible, etc.).

7. If a consonant is doubled where syllables join, generally divide the word between the consonants.
   Examples: admis sion, confer ring, sug gestion

8. If a suffix has been added to a root word that ends in a doubled letter, ordinarily divide before the suffix.

This rule could be considered an exception to the one preceding. A word such as *telling* is made up of the root *tell* and the suffix *ing*. It would logically be divided after the second *l*. Here are several other words that would be governed by this rule:

cross ing, drill ing, fall ing, miss ing, ebb ing, stuff ing

9. Divide a hyphenated word only at the hyphen.

   Examples: self- explanatory, non- participatory

10. Do not end more than two consecutive lines with a hyphen. Also, try to avoid dividing the first line of a paragraph.

11. Avoid the division of names. Proper nouns should be divided only when absolutely necessary. It is generally better to leave a line slightly short than to break words such as *Prendergast* or *Massachusetts*. Divide proper noun groups so that they can be read with ease. The name Donald S. Crenshaw might be typed with Donald S. at the end of one line and Crenshaw at the start of the next.

12. DO NOT DIVIDE THE LAST WORD OF A PARAGRAPH OR THE LAST WORD ON A PAGE.

13. Do not divide the following units:
    June 23, 1995
    8 percent
    12 pounds
    8:22 A.M.

11

Special Report Format

by James C. Matthews, Ed.D.

- *Business Reports*

    Types of Business Reports
    Format and Preparation
    Other Preparatory Tasks
    Parts of a Business Report
    Final Tasks

- *Office Memorandums*

    Types of Memos
    Parts of a Memo
    Memo Paper
    Memo Format

- *Minutes of a Meeting*

    Types of Meetings
    Preliminary Duties
    Preparing the Minutes
    Format of Minutes
    Resolutions

- *News Releases*

- *Copy for Publication*

    Desktop Publishing

- *Technical Reports*

- *Legal Documents*

    Software for Legal Documents

- *Handling Numbers in Reports*

- *Visual Aids*

    Kinds of Visuals
    Preparation of Visuals
    Formatting of Visuals

In addition to letters, other types of reports frequently have to be prepared by secretaries. The preparation may include dictation; transcription; typing or word processing; preparation and inclusion of charts, tables, and other visual aids; and other tasks to ensure that the final report is accurate and attractive. This chapter discusses the secretary's role in the preparation of business reports, office memorandums, minutes of a meeting or conference, news releases, copy for publication, technical reports, and legal documents.

BUSINESS REPORTS

A business report is a lengthy in-depth communication, with facts and ideas, to workers in a company. Reports can appear in several forms, and there is no authoritative list of all types of reports. Reports may be catalogical, analytical, or compartmentalized. The procedures described in this chapter put the elements together to produce an effective, quality report. Some reports are typeset and include artwork (as an annual report to stockholders or to a board of directors). Others are typewritten or word processed with unjustified or justified margins. Since reports are more in-depth than letters and memorandums, more time and effort are required. If possible, all reports should be keyed using a text-editing package. Storage and retrieval allows for easier final editing.

Types of Business Reports

There are several types of business reports, including corporate reports, executive summaries, and abstracts. The secretary must know how to format each element.

Corporate Report

This category includes memorandum reports, letter reports, and megareports (very lengthy, complex reports containing hundreds of pages). A corporate report might introduce and analyze a specific problem, discuss it, and provide impetus for its resolution. The content may be technical or general. The secretary may have responsibility for the production of the entire report, including careful proofreading, checking for accuracy, duplication, binding, collating, and distribution.

Executive Summary

An executive summary is a brief description and summation of a report's contents. Significant data are summarized. A summary of this type is used for problem solving and covers the problem, how it should be solved, and what the benefits are. Usually detailed data are not given. The summary may be part of a longer report.

Abstract

An abstract, like an executive summary, is a brief description or overview of the contents of a report. There are two types of abstracts: informative and descriptive. An *informative abstract* is a summary, an internal discussion. A *descriptive abstract* lists the elements covered in a complete report without stating the supporting data; it is an external discussion or framework.

Format and Preparation

Careful formatting and preparation of a business report are musts. Whether you cut and paste, type straight, or use a word processing or software package, you must be consistent in form, type style and fonts, and so forth to produce a quality document. Before beginning preparation of the report, the secretary must give thought to the paper, type style, and format as well as the special features of the report and the care and use of the equipment to be used in preparing the report.

Paper

Reports should use a good quality of paper, usually $8\frac{1}{2}" \times 11"$ white paper with rag content. The higher the rag content of paper, the longer its life. A watermark imprinted on rag-content paper tells the brand of paper and the percentage of cotton fiber in it. The right side of the paper shows a readable watermark. Use either 16-, 20-, or 24-pound paper. Type on the face of the paper showing the readable watermark.

Multiple originals can be generated by computers, and many offices use photocopiers to produce quality copies.

Type Style

Pica type (pitch 10) or a 12-point font is preferred for reports because its larger size makes it easier to read than elite type (pitch 12). As for design, the conventional roman type is still the most widely acceptable. A variation such as the square-serif roman may be available. Then again, a sturdy, modern sans-serif design is clean, easy to read, and makes single-spaced or tightly packed data appear less crowded. Neither script nor italic type is suitable for reports. However, italic type may be used to highlight certain words in the text of a report. Certain text-editing packages and some electric typewriters have this capability. If italic type is not available, italicized words are typed underscored. The underscoring equals and should be interpreted as the word(s) being in italics. In all cases the style must be good letter quality. Some dot-matrix printers are letter or near-letter print quality.

Format

The format, or arrangement and layout of material, in a report can vary in indentations, footnoting or citations, page numbering, spacing, etc. The secretary may be required to follow a certain format or have a preference for a certain style, but the format must be consistent throughout the report. Because of the increased use of text-editing equipment in the automated office, several software formatting packages can be obtained to assist with technical, detailed formatting projects. However, some caution is to be taken. Familiarity with the operation of automated equipment and its interface with commercial software packages is necessary to do the job effectively.

Format ruler. The format ruler, sometimes called a *word processing ruler* or *forms ruler,* is a handy tool used for checking margins, spacing, and counting the number of lines of a document. On a display terminal, it can be used to check vertical and horizontal spacing, centering, and so forth. The format ruler is usually 12, 15, or 18 inches in length and contains a centering scale, pitch 10 and 12 scales, lines of text, metric calculations, and so forth.

The format ruler is particularly useful if, for example, you are asked to produce an exact copy of a letter (or other document) with identical measurements. To find out the pitch, you would use the ruler to verify the spacing by placing a given line on the pitch-10 or pitch-12 scale. Exact placement would indicate the type style in which the letter was originally keyed. If line 12 is to be transposed to line 20, the number of lines scale could easily guide you to the appropriate line without the necessity of manually counting. This is most appropriate for stored text in a database file. The cursor should also be used to locate line 20. The cursor movement (vertical and horizontal) is correlated with the line count. By placing the format rule on the screen, quick line adjustments can be made without working from a hard copy.

Other Preparatory Tasks

Choice of appropriate software. If you will be using a computer or sophisticated word processor and a text-editing or similar software package, check beforehand that the features in the software package meet the needs of your company or the particular types of business reports you will be creating. If, for example, you will frequently want to use underscoring or superscripts, be sure that the software package you will use has these features.

Thousands of pre-packaged applications programs are available for personal computers to help produce quality documents. A microcomputer can handle alphanumeric or graphic information for text editing, depending on the type of program run on it. Dozens of text-editing programs are available, including, but not limited to, Multimate, Multimate Advantage, Word Perfect, Word Star, and Microsoft Word. Auxiliary features include dictionaries, spelling verification and grammar and math checkers, storing, list processing (mailing, inventory), a glossary, selective and global searches, style guides *(APA, Chicago Manual of Style),* a thesaurus, graphics (pie, line, bar, and graph charts), forms format (résumé), and graphic and text combinations (desktop publishing or electronic publishing, film, and blueprints).

Best-selling types of business software are listed periodically in two service publications: *PC World* (Subscriber Services, P.O. Box 55029, Boulder, CO 80322-5029) and *Administrative Management* (The Automated Office,

Ltd., 1123 Broadway, New York, NY 10010). When using electronic equipment to produce a business report, you might use a combination and/or integration of these various applications. Of special interest to the secretary is *The Secretary,* the professional publication of Professional Secretaries International (PSI) (301 East Armour Boulevard, Kansas City, MO 64111-1299). This magazine highlights new technologies affecting the modern-day secretary and discusses change as well as implementation of effective production measures.

Developing familiarity with electronic editing and printing. Many word processors and text-editing software programs used with personal computers have an automatic wraparound feature by which a long word keyed in near the right margin is carried to the beginning of the next line, triggered by a space before and after. If the program does have this feature, the secretary should check the right margin to be sure that too much white space is not left. Depending on the appearance, the secretary might want to impose hyphens and divide words in order to achieve evenly worded lines and an evenly formatted right margin. For example, with automatic wraparound the word *acknowledgment,* if keyed near the right margin, would automatically be wrapped around to the following line unless the secretary decided for appropriate word division and keys in the hyphen so that it became "acknowledgment" on two lines. In these cases, it is important to remember to delete the hyphen because later insertions, deletions, or other changes to the middle of a line may move the word where the hyphen would be inappropriate.

Extra care must be taken when editing documents on a screen. Adjust the contrast, clarity, and color. Use the cursor (pointer) to proofread from line to line or paragraph to paragraph. Check the printout for accuracy, since at times the text appearing on the screen may not be replicated on the hard copy due to slippage or movement in the printwheel or other part of the printer. With automatic typewriters and word processors, data are recorded by magnetic cards, disks, memory, or computer storage; with personal computers, by floppy and hard disks. Errors are corrected by backspacing and rekeying the correct character over the error. Once the correction has been made, the file must be updated to eliminate the original error.

The secretary should also make sure that the printwheel is clean, the ribbon fresh, and the printer producing evenly dark copy. An impression adjustment may be necessary.

Parts of a Business Report

The business report may include, along with the main body, all or some of the following: letter or memorandum of transmittal, title page, preface, table of contents, list of tables and/or figures, bibliography, appendix, and index. The secretary needs to know how to handle each of these elements and how to put them together. Secretaries play an important role in getting a report accepted. A report is much more likely to be looked upon with favor when it is properly formatted, well arranged, and easy to read.

Letter or Memorandum of Transmittal

A letter of transmittal is used to introduce the reader to the report. The content of the letter should tell the reader what the topic of the report is, why it was written, how it was compiled, who worked on it, and what major findings or conclusions resulted from the research.

The letter of transmittal appears directly after the title page, and it may be typed in any acceptable business letter or memorandum format.

Title Page

The title page will usually contain the name or title of the report, the name and title of the person or organization for whom it was written, the name and title of the person or group who wrote it, and the date it was submitted. The title page may also include more information if necessary.

Type the main title in all capital letters approximately two inches from the top of the page. Type the date two inches from the bottom of the page. Space the other information equally between the top and bottom margins, typed in lowercase letters with the first letter of each main word capitalized. Center each line horizontally.

There are various formats for title pages. For an acceptable style, see the illustration on page 160.

Preface

The preface, also called the *foreword,* is optional. It allows the writer to give a personal message to the reader. The author may, for example, provide special information not necessarily appearing in the body of the report (methods used, points of emphasis, pragmatic considerations, reasons for treatment of content).

Table of Contents

The table of contents is one of the last things prepared. It should be typed after all pages of the report are completed and numbered. The table of contents lists in order the numbers and titles of the sections or chapters in the report and the pages on which they begin. It should not be confused with the index, which is arranged alphabetically and includes more items.

Type the heading, TABLE OF CONTENTS, in all capital letters centered two inches from the top edge of the paper. Type "Page" a triple space below the heading, pivoted from the right margin.

Begin typing the contents a double space below "Page" at the left margin. Use the same margins that you use in typing the body of the report.

Use all capital letters in typing those entries of the contents page that refer to the major sections of the report. Those sections of lesser importance should be indented under their main heading, listed in the same sequence as they appear in the report, and typed in capital and lowercase letters. Leaders

INTRODUCING INFORMATION PROCESSING INTO THE BUSINESS CURRICULUM
AT ST. ANN'S TECHNICAL COLLEGE

The Effect of Change
The State University of New York Program in Office Management
by
Technical Consultants, Inc.

August 16, 19__

Sample title page.

should be used to guide the reader's eye across the page from a content's entry to the page number.

See page 162 for a sample of a TABLE OF CONTENTS.

List of Tables or Figures

When a report contains several tables and/or figures, separate lists of these enclosures should be included after the table of contents. Type the lists in a format similar to that of the table of contents. Should a report contain both tables and figures, the list of tables precedes the list of figures. In the separate lists, number each title or figure, and give the full caption or title of each. Type each list on a separate page.

Body of the Report

Use a report or manuscript typing guide for setting up reports. These may be purchased or you may design your own.

Margins. Margins for reports and manuscripts are a minimum of one inch; however, many authors prefer one and one-fourth inches. When the report is to be bound on the left side, allow for the binding by making the left margin one and one-half inches wide. This makes the center point of the writing line three spaces to the right of the present center; if you are centering lines at 51, you will now center them at 54. You can accomplish the same result by merely moving the paper one-fourth inch to the left of the spot where you normally keep it.

The top margin on the first page should be at least two inches; on the other pages, it should be one inch. If the report is to be bound at the top, allow an additional half inch for this. Keep the bottom margins at least one inch deep; in some cases you may want to make them as much as one and one-half inches deep.

Spacing. Usually reports are double-spaced, and the first line of each paragraph is indented five spaces. The number of spaces paragraphs are indented may be eight or ten, but paragraph indentions are always used.

When quotations are of three lines or more, indent the quoted material five spaces from the left and right margins or indent it the same number of spaces from these margins as you indent the paragraphs. Indent the first line of the quotation to show a paragraph indention. Copy the indented quotation in single spacing and omit the quotation marks. The indention tells the reader that the material is quoted.

If listings are included in your report, single-space them. Center the items on the page. If the length of items varies, select the longest one to be centered and line up the others with it. If your listings contain widely separated columns, use leaders to assist the eye in reading the material. Make these leaders by alternating periods with spaces. Note whether the periods fall on the odd or even spaces in the first line, and then match the location of the periods accordingly in succeeding lines.

TABLE OF CONTENTS

Sample table of contents.

the College, considering the above circumstances, was most under-standable. It was and is a risky undertaking at this period of time when college enrollment is declining.

Population Under Investigation

The population under investigation for this study is the administration of the College, the Business and Economics Division, the Secretarial Admin-istration Department, the students enrolled in the secretarial program, the surrounding business community, and the certificated and classified staff of San Bernardino Valley College.

Definition of Terms

Mag Card II Typewriter. Paula Cecil states in her word processing textbook:

> In April 1973 IBM introduced the use of "memory" in word processing typewriters with its new Mag Card II. Previously, recording of typing had been made directly onto the magnetic tape. But on the Mag Card II the recording is made "in memory" from which it can be played back. If the operator wants to store the recording on a card, a button is depressed which records all information that was typed into memory.[4]

Memory Typewriter. In the same textbook Ms. Cecil describes the Memory Typewriter:

> In March 1974, another member of the IBM family was introduced: the Memory Typewriter. This unit has all the features of the Mag Card II except the use of cards, thereby eliminating long storage and merging applications. The Memory Typewriter has a 50-page memory storage and a 4000-character-per-page capacity for revising, which means a total memory capacity of 200,000 characters. This unit is sold mainly to small offices for production of regular correspondence, some stored letters or paragraphs, and short-turnaround revisions.[5]

---

[4]Paula B. Cecil. Word Processing in the Modern Office (Menlo Park, California: Cummings Publishing Co., 1976), pp. 85-86.

[5]Ibid., p, 87.

Sample of a page from the body of a report.

Allow at least two lines of a paragraph to appear at the bottom and top of each page, adjusting the bottom margin, if necessary, to accommodate the ending and beginning lines. Avoid single lines that carry over to end a paragraph at the top of a new page. Avoid dividing the last word on a page.

White space. When preparing each page of the business report, avoid leaving excessive space without type. This distracts the reader and takes away from the appearance, organization, and format of the page. If white space is necessary before and after an illustration, artwork, or visual, leave not more than two inches. This applies to tables and figures; if they are typed and follow the text, allow at least triple linear spacing before and after. If reductions are necessary because of width, length, or both, make them; however, these reductions should fit within the margins.

Tables, Figures, Illustrations

The placement of tables, figures, and illustrations in the body of the business report is very important and must be carefully done. Each visual (whether a table, figure, or other type of illustration) must have its own identification number (Table 1, Table 2, and so forth; Figure 1, Figure 2, and so forth). Tables may present quantitative or qualitative data. The data should be arranged so that the significance of different items is obvious at a glance. Allow ample spacing between rows and columns; here, white space helps lend order to the data being displayed. Turning a report sideways to read a table or study a figure is often an inconvenience to the reader. If possible, reduce the visual so that it conforms to the margins. Remember, reducing the width of a visual reduces the length by the same percentages; for example, reducing a visual's width by 77% simultaneously reduces its length by 77%. The same applies for enlargements.

Headings

The main heading is centered in all capital letters at the beginning of the report. No other heading should be typed in all capital letters. If the report has a subheading (secondary heading that explains or amplifies the main heading), separate it from the main heading with a double space, then triple-space before beginning the body of the report. The subheading should be centered and the main word or words capitalized.

First-order side headings are preceded by a triple space and followed by a double space. Side headings should be typed at the left margin, underlined with main words capitalized, and have no terminal period (or other terminal punctuation).

Second-order side headings or paragraph headings are preceded by a double space. They are indented to the paragraph point (usually only the first word is capitalized), underlined, and followed by a period. Begin typing the paragraph on the same line as the heading.

Footnotes

Footnotes usually fall at the bottom or end of the page where the reference is made. The secretary must plan the page so that there is sufficient space for the footnotes.

Footnotes have a number of purposes: they may confirm or add meaning to the author's statements; they may refer to other parts of the report that have a bearing on the topic discussed; they may make acknowledgments; or they sometimes make additional explanations of the content or terms used.

Footnotes are identified in the text by raised figures called *superscripts*. The superscript is typed one-half space above the line of writing immediately after the word or statement to which the footnote applies. To type this super-script, engage the automatic line spacer and roll the paper down about one-half of the line. Type the figure and put the line-spacer lever back in typing position. Touch the platen knob gently, and the paper will resume its former position. It is more convenient to use the automatic line-spacer lever (sometimes called "line finder" or "ratchet release lever") than to use the variable spacer on the platen knob, because the former will automatically bring the platen back to its original line of writing. Most modern electric typewriters and word processing equipment have a special superscript (and subscript) key so manual paper adjustment is not necessary.

Some software packages have a footnote feature that makes the spacing and arrangement of footnotes fast and easy. Use a format ruler to check calculations whether you are using a preprogrammed package, checking the screen, or working from rough draft copy.

Footnotes may be numbered in one of two ways: consecutively throughout the article or chapter, or consecutively on each page, beginning with the number 1 for each new page. Be uniform in numbering the references. In rough-draft work and thesis work, it simplifies the typing if footnotes are numbered consecutively on each page. Then if there is an addition, deletion, or correction, subsequent footnotes need not be renumbered.

When using footnotes, type the reference figure in the text following the passage to which the footnote refers. Type the footnote on the same page on which the reference figure following the passage appears. Type footnotes to end one inch from the bottom edge of the page. Use the page-end indicator on your typewriter or a guide sheet to determine where to begin the footnote in order to have this one-inch margin. Usually it is safe to allow three or four lines for each footnote.

After typing the last line of the text before the footnote, single-space and type a horizontal underscore line one and one-half to two inches long, starting at the left margin and extending the line toward the center. Type the footnote a double space below this line. Precede the footnote with the corresponding reference number raised about one-half space above the line. Start the footnote at the paragraph indention. The second line of the footnote should begin at the left margin. Footnote entries should be single-spaced with a double space between each footnote.

For a footnote that refers to published material, give the same information that is given in a bibliographical reference plus the page number of the cited material. The examples given below follow the *Chicago Manual of Style*.

Example of a footnote: book with two authors.

---

[3] Rosemary T. Fruehling and Constance K. Weaver, *Electronic Office Procedures* (New York: McGraw-Hill Book Company, 1987), p. 29.

Example of a footnote: magazine article.

---

[4] Stephen McMillen, "Secretarial Development: The Other Side of the Coin," *The Secretary* (June/July, 1987), p. 26.

If two or more footnotes are identical, you do not need to retype the details. Use one of the following abbreviations for Latin phrases:

Ibid., meaning "in the same place." Use *Ibid.* when referring to the word cited in the immediately preceding footnote, without an intervening footnote. This abbreviation may be used several times in succession.

Example:

---

[5] *Ibid.* (Use when the reference is identical to the one in the preceding footnote.)

[6] *Ibid.,* p. 35. (Use when the reference is identical to the one in the preceding footnote but on a different page.)

loc. cit., meaning "in the place cited." Use *loc cit.* with nonconsecutive footnotes that refer to the same material, the same work, and the same page or pages. Repeat the author's name before *loc cit.*

op. cit., meaning "in the work cited." Use *op cit.* with nonconsecutive footnotes that refer to the same work but different pages. Repeat the author's last name.

Example:

---

[8] Walshe, *loc. cit.*
[9] Baker, *op. cit., p. 77.*

Sometimes footnotes appear at the end of a report on a separate sheet headed "Works Cited."

Notes or Endnotes

These are writer's comments appearing at the bottom of a page or at the end of a report. They may be writer's identification notes, content footnotes, or copyright permission footnotes. If there is a single author's note on a page, an asterisk (*) may be used, not a number. The asterisk in the text with a note at the bottom of the page is called a *natural footnote*. You must leave a one-inch bottom margin. At times, especially in technical reports, notes and endnotes are lengthy. Remember, a one-inch bottom margin must be left below the notes.

Header/Footer

A *header* is a line or two at the top of each page in the report or at the top of the first page of the report that contains identifying information. Usually, the header contains the topic or subtopic in that particular section of the report. It may also identify a specific section of the report by number.

With a top margin of one inch (6 lines), start on line 7. It is acceptable to use line 2 or 3 for the header. The header should not be more than two lines long.

```
                              TypeRight Software 1.1
                              Chapter 1.3: Compatibility    Header
```

```
     The program design of major software is copyrighted. Moreover, some
programs are compatible with major manufacturers' equipment. However,
caution must be taken as to
```

A *footer,* located at the bottom of a page, is also identifying information. Generally, it contains the date of the report, page number, and other data. The footer may also note the coding or file number assigned in the database if text-editing equipment is being used.

Note that the types of identifying information included in headers and footers vary from one company to another. The examples given are typical; however, always follow company procedures.

```
Recommendation:        Specifications must be drafted by the end of the third
                       quarter. The feasibility study will cost $30,000.

September 1, 1988                          Coding 23     FOOTER
```

Bibliography

A bibliography includes the references used in the preparation of the report. Arrange it alphabetically by names of authors. When listing books, copy the information from the title page, rather than from the outside cover. When listing references from periodicals, take the title from the article itself.

Depending on the content of some reports and the company's policy, items in the bibliography may be numbered in order of their appearance in the report. Sometimes you may be asked to use abbreviated (shortened) forms of citations in your draft copy and complete forms in the final copy.

Each reference lists the surname of the author, followed by given name or initials; the title of the work; the publisher; the place of publication; and the date of publication. When using references from periodicals, one may include such identifying information as volume and page numbers. Observe these rules:

- Underscore the titles of books and magazines.
- Enclose the titles of magazine articles in quotation marks.
- Type the author's initials after the surname. If some references use a full name and others only initials, be consistent, particularly when the references come close together. Usually it is better to use the full name.
- If the author has written some books alone and collaborated with other authors on some materials, list first those books the author wrote alone.
- If the publication has more than three authors, list the publication under the name of the first mentioned author and then use the words "and others" or *et al.*
- If the publication is out of print, indicate this in parentheses following the reference.
- Volume numbers of periodicals are written with Arabic numerals.
- To make the author's name stand out, type the first line of the entry at the left margin and indent all other lines.
- If there are many sources of reference material, classify them according to books, periodicals, pamphlets, or other documents.
- When two or more books by the same author are listed in succession, instead of retyping the author's name each time, simply use a solid line of five underscores followed by a comma.

Example:

Popyk, Marilyn K., *Word Processing: Essential Concepts,* New York: McGraw-Hill Book Company, 1983.

_____, *Word Processing and Information Systems: A Practical Approach to Concepts,* New York: McGraw-Hill Book Company, 1986.

References. Only citations used or referred to in the report are listed in the bibliography. Some reports provide a listing of suggested or recommended readings. These are separate from the bibliography and should be noted as such. In other words, the suggested or recommended readings (books, magazines, films, etc.) are neither cited nor used in the preparation of the report; they are intended for further study or review only.

There are a number of style manuals that can be used in preparing a bibliography (or other part of a report). Whatever manual you choose, use it properly: consistency, clarity, and common sense must prevail.

List of Style Manuals*

General

The Chicago Manual of Style

Kate Turabian's *A Manual for Writers of Term Papers, Theses, and Dissertations*

The MLA Handbook

The U.S. Government Printing Office's *Style Manual*

Technical

The American Psychological Association's *Publication Manual*

The American Institute of Physics' *Style Manual*

Harvard Law Review's *A Uniform System of Citation*

---

* "Publication style" means the way references appear on printed pages of
a journal in final form. "Manuscript-submission style" means the way
references appear in the original manuscript as submitted by the writer
(author). Note that the two styles are very different. Many journals print
bibliographic references as footnotes; however, most such journals also
require that references appearing in the manuscript be in end-note form (a
separate page at the end of the report).

Sometimes these references appear with the heading "Works Referenced."

Appendix

Material supportive to the report should be placed in a supplementary section called an appendix. It should follow the bibliography. Examples of items placed in the appendix are copies of questionnaires, maps, lists, tables, sample forms and letters, and detailed summaries of data. Because of electronic (desktop) publishing, visuals, tables, graphics, and other inserts may be reduced and incorporated into the body of a report. This procedure saves the reader from turning back and forth to refer to cited items.

BIBLIOGRAPHY

Books

Fruehling, Rosemary T., and Weaver, Constance K. Electronic Office
  Procedures. New York: McGraw-Hill Book Co., 1987. 544 pp.

Keene, Michael L. Effective Professional Writing. Lexington, MA:
  D.C. Heath and Co., 1987. 450 pp.

Popyk, Marilyn K. Word Processing and Information Systems: A
  Practical Approach to Concepts. New York: McGraw-Hill Book
  Co., 1983. 336 pp.

Journals

Hart, M.B. "Status of OS in 29 Texas Companies (With Implications for OS
  Curricula)," Office Systems Research Journal. (1986).

McEntee, A. "Determining Core Competencies Necessary for Success in
  the Automated Office," Journal of the Business Education Association of New York. (1985).

Munter, M. "Using the Computer in Business Communication Courses,"
  The Journal of Business Communication. (1986).

Unpublished Work

Xavier, Chris. "Office Needs" (Assessment Criteria, Star Associations,
  1988), "Mimeographed."

Sample bibliography page.

The appendix may be preceded by an introductory page entitled APPEN-DIX, typed in all capital letters and centered both horizontally and vertically. This page may also include a list of the items included in the appendix. If this is used, both the title and the listing are centered vertically, or the title may be typed two inches from the top of the paper with the listing beginning a triple space below the title. When more than one item is appended, each item should be numbered or lettered and placed under a separate heading, such as Appendix A, Appendix B, etc.

Should the style manual you are using specify that appendices be lettered and you have more than 26 appendices, begin the 27th by doubling the letter as AA, BB, CC, and so forth. If an attachment has internal pagination, indicate the pagination by using an asterisk superior to the appendix letter followed by a note at the bottom. (See example below.)

If an appendix is rather lengthy and bulky, label it "Enclosure" and attach it after the last appendix. If there is only one appendix, no letter or number is necessary. The word Appendix is sufficient. Triple-space and begin the text of that single appendix.

```
                        Appendix C*


                    Manual of Operations






        _____
        * This manual has internal pagination.
```

Sample appendix page.

Index

An index is a listing of subjects, their subsets, and cross-referenced, correlated subjects citing key words in the body of the report.

It may be necessary to prepare an index as well as a table of contents for some reports. Be sure the index is typed in alphabetical order. Put the entries first on 3" × 5" cards and then arrange them alphabetically. Then type the index from the cards.

However, index cards are awkward to handle in bulk form. If you have access to a personal computer, word processor, or electronic typewriter, use an electronic filing procedure. Create a database and print a hard copy when needed. Electronic keying allows quick additions, deletions, and insertions. By creating a database, you eliminate misfiling and loss of cards. By the same measure, always keep a backup disk of all your keyed documents.

Final Tasks

After the draft of a report has been completed and corrected and all lists, tables, charts, and visuals inserted in their proper places, the secretary must prepare the report in its final form.

First, the pages must be numbered. Number the pages in the body of the report with Arabic numbers and those in the preliminary section (for example, the Table of Contents or List of Tables) with small Roman numerals.

If the report is unbound or bound at the left, the page number of the first page (if numbered) is centered one-half inch (3 lines) from the bottom of the page. Other pages of the report are numbered in the upper right corner on line four, with the number ending flush with the right margin. Begin the first line of typing on line seven; this will leave a one-inch top margin for the body of the report. Usually, if a manuscript is bound at the top, it is numbered at the bottom, centered on the third line from the bottom of the page.

In the preliminary section, count the title page as "i" but do not type the numeral. Number the remaining preliminary pages with small Roman numerals (ii, iii, iv, v, vi, etc.) centered on the third line from the bottom of the page.

Most text-editing software packages have a feature for automatic pagination and repagination. For originally keyed data, automatic paging is done. When new pages or text are inserted that will expand the contents of a page, the secretary need only program the feature and all of the pages will automatically be repaginated. However, always remember to update the file to show all corrections and adjustments. Some advanced software packages will even automatically repaginate footnotes, notes, and endnotes.

OFFICE MEMORANDUMS

An office memorandum, almost universally referred to as a *memo,* is basically a letter between company employees and is less formal than a traditional letter. It may be short or long, single or multipage. The secretary may compose memos as well as type them for executives.

Like all other office communications, memorandums transmit information and provide a record that information was transmitted. Office memorandums are used for several purposes: a) for messages that are complicated; b) to avoid making unnecessary telephone calls for business that may not be urgent; and c) when a record is needed. They not only avoid situations that may be misunderstood but also protect people by having a written record. Usually, office memorandums are brief and direct. However, there are exceptions depending upon the nature, purpose, and scope of the subject discussed and the writer's purpose and intent.

The plural form of memorandum may be either *memorandums* (add "s") or *memoranda* (add "a"; Latin form). However, when composing or writing, be consistent and use only one form for the plural. Also, when typing from an originator's draft copy, always check for consistency in spelling.

Types of Memos

Interoffice Memorandum

The interoffice memorandum is an in-house communication and is sent to a person in your own firm or department within one location; in other words, it is confined. Forms vary widely from company to company. However, all the principles of writing and business correspondence apply to memorandums as they do to letters.

Intraoffice Memorandum

The intraoffice memorandum is used within the same company between offices in different buildings or locations. For example, Company A may have two offices in New York City and one in Westchester County. Thus, the written communication is external; that is, it is not distributed in one location but must be transmitted elsewhere.

Parts of a Memo

All memorandums, whether printed or not, are composed of similar elements (parts). However, format may differ. These elements include to/from, date, subject, body, and end references (*i.e.,* reference initials, distribution of copies, etc.). There may be slight differences in heading and closing information or in the order of the elements, especially if the forms are printed.

To/From

The "To/From" section may be reversed. Some feel that using "to" first is more courteous to the reader. However, follow the company preferences. Personal titles (Mr., Mrs., Ms., Miss) should be omitted, but you may use professional titles such as Prof., Dr., etc.

Usually, there is a name and a title in both the "To" and "From" sections, such as:

TO: Horace Denize, Executive Director
FROM: Julia Brown, Chairperson, Board of Directors

There is no salutation, complimentary close, or signature. However, the person who is sending the memorandum may initial it between the name and title or at the end of the "From" line.

Date

Follow a standard format. Do not use shortcuts. Type the date as:

September 29, 19-- or 9/29/--

When using the numeric form, proofread carefully to be sure that numbers are not transposed.

Subject

The "Subject" lines provides a short description of what the memorandum is about. It focuses attention and may serve as a subject category for filing and retrieval. It should be brief and to the point. Delete unnecessary words.

Body

This section contains the main idea and purpose of the memorandum. If there are enumerations, use an acceptable format, as: 1), 2) or a), b), etc.

Some special keyboarding symbols may be used before the enumeration to capture the reader's attention. These include dashes (—) and bullets (•).

- *Call Mr. Gomez and make an appointment.*
- *Cancel the Simmons' contract (No. 23-A).*
- *Print out file #23.A-9 (4.1).*

This technique calls immediate attention to enumerations and enhances the appearance. Numbering and/or lettering the items or points also makes it easier for the reader to follow the sequential development of ideas and comments.

Reference Information

Several types of reference information may be located at the end of a memorandum. These include reference initials, copy notations, enclosures, filing

Interoffice Communication

TO: Horace Denize, Executive Director

FROM: Julia Brown, Chairperson, Board of Directors

DATE: October 15, 19--

SUBJECT: Organizational Meeting

A Board of Directors meeting has been scheduled for Wednesday, October 30, 19--, in Conference Room A, East Building.

The agenda will include:

- Approval of Minutes
- Report for the Chairperson
- Discussion of Goals
- New Business

Since this is the first meeting, your attendance is necessary. Please bring business report No. 23-A, located in the central database file.

JB/TS 8.8a

Distribution:

Jerome L. Abrams
Bennette Von Brun
Josephine D'Allo
Maye Santiago
Norman Zapper

Sample interoffice memo.

code, and word processing code. Reference initials may be typed in lower- or uppercase:

    je or JE or E (transcriber)
JM:JE or jm:je (dictator and transcriber)

    At times, the composer or originator of a document may be someone other than the executive or principal. If this is the case, use:
    MC:CH:MI (Executive, composer or originator, transcriber)

Word/Information Processing Codes

Many documents are electronically memorized and processed. For ease of retrieval in these cases, codes are necessary:

    MJ/e 8.8
    MJ/CH 8.8a

    A colon (:) may be substituted for the slash (/). The code 8.8 may represent month, day, disk number, or another meaning such as file No. 8.8. Since such codes are not standardized, the secretary or executive should create one. If using electronic equipment (personal computer, word processor), keep a hard copy of the index for easy referral.

Copies/Distribution

This is the final section of the memorandum and alphabetically lists the names of those who were sent copies. The list may be ordered by seniority or by rank. Follow the company policy and check with your superior. The omission of a name may be an oversight, or it may be deliberate.
    With electronic mail and other automated communications, copies may be sent electronically through a network to various terminals. If this procedure is used, the usual distribution lists should be keyed in a database. The receipt of a transmission can easily be acknowledged by return transmission; a reply can also be keyed. If electronic messages are stored, keep an index. These data can then serve as boilerplates and standard paragraphs that can be inserted into other future memorandums without rekeying.

Memo Paper

Memorandums are often typed on plain paper or on printed forms that contain standard parts. If plain paper is used for one or more pages, use quality paper. If the memorandum is short, use a half sheet. If a preprinted form is used, align typing evenly with the printed headings.

Memo Format

The format of a memo—margins, paragraphs, special features, tabulation stops—should be uniform. Use the format procedures adopted by your company, and collect samples for a reference file.

Margins

Margins may vary. However, for plain paper, leave one-inch side margins and a one-and-one-half-inch top margin. Begin on line 10 (9 lines = $1^1/2$"). Leave sufficient space at the bottom.

If you are using text-editing equipment, an appropriate form may be keyed in and retrieved, thus eliminating the need for rekeying format instructions. In other words, the format would be set—similar to a standardized preset formatting software package.

For printed forms, the left margin should begin evenly with the "to/from" element printed on the form.

Spacing

Whether using typed or preprinted forms, begin typing two or three spaces from the colon. Triple-space between the subject line and the beginning of the text. Single-space the content of each paragraph, but double-space between paragraphs.

Tabulations in Body

Tabulation represents the keying of columns of information. It is used to present complex information in isolated, but related, columns for easier reading, comprehension, and comparison. Detailed, technical materials should be arranged logically to allow for comprehension. If space allows when keying long or multipage memorandums, use ruled columns to enhance the tabulated data. Single-space the text of columns and have equal horizontal spacing before and after the tabulated material.

MINUTES OF A MEETING

The executive may ask the secretary to take minutes at a formal or informal meeting. *Minutes* is a term used to describe an official record of the proceedings of a meeting. Keeping minutes of meetings is always advisable. Although the minutes may not be disseminated, they should be filed in case they are needed at a later date.

Types of Meetings

There are basically two types of meetings: formal and informal. A *formal meeting* is a preplanned, structured meeting, such as an annual conference or convention and its workshops and symposia. Usually, there is a prepared agenda. An *informal meeting* may be short and announced only a short time before it is held; it is usually held on company premises. To inform staff members of a quickly scheduled meeting, the secretary may use electronic calendaring, if available, or the telephone. Always confirm by sending a follow-up note.

Another type of meeting—a *teleconference*—has been made possible by modern technology. In a teleconference, two or more persons in different geographic locations communicate electronically (audio, video, computer). It is effective for informal meetings and serves as an adjunct to more formal, structured meetings. By using audio, video, and/or computer equipment, including the *electronic blackboard,* meetings can be held simultaneously or on a delayed basis with several groups participating in various locations. Everything in a teleconference is taped.

The minutes of a teleconference can be completed from the recorded media. This allows the secretary time to devote to other duties. The minutes, when completed, can be distributed electronically.

Preliminary Duties

Preliminary duties before a formal meeting may include reserving the meeting room, sending pertinent materials, preparing mailing lists, making calendar notations, preparing an agenda (the order of business), and handling last-minute details, such as supply and equipment needs (*e.g.*, overhead projector or VDT). If you plan to take shorthand notes at the meeting, be sure you have sufficient notebooks, pencils, and other supplies. If you plan to record the meeting, check reel-to-reel or cassette recorders to ensure the equipment is operating and that you have sufficient supplies.

Some companies employ technical assistants to be available during electronic transmissions if needed. At a computer conference, the secretary may be asked to keyboard messages and retrieve stored data. These types of conferences should be planned in advance.

MEETING OF THE EXECUTIVE COMMITTEE

April 2, 19__

AGENDA

1.   Review and vote for Contract No. 23-a.1.

2.   Update report on Contract No. 24.

3.   Report on service project for the first quarter.

4.   Proposed budget for Xavius Project, a government grant.

5.   New business.

Sample agenda.

Preparing the Minutes

The most important phase of preparing minutes is the accurate recording and reporting of the actions taken. The record should report what was said. At times, it is difficult to report what is done. For informal meetings, the minutes are compact and simple; for formal meetings, the minutes are complex. If you find that grouping the minutes around a central theme is clearer, do so. On the other hand, the executive may prefer chronological order.

Corporate minutes (official minutes of a formal nature) must be prepared in the order of occurrence, showing details and the exact wording of motions, resolutions, and so forth. By law, corporations are required to keep minutes of stockholders' and directors' meetings. These minutes are legal records and should be protected from tampering.

When preparing corporate minutes, use watermarked paper, and place the finalized minutes in keylock binders. Any corrections resulting from a sub-sequent meeting should be written. Incorrect portions are ruled out in *ink* and initialed in the margin. The official secretary of the corporation has responsibility for the completeness and accuracy of corporate minutes, but the secretary may have to type and prepare them.

Format of Minutes

Follow these suggestions in preparing minutes:

1. Use plain white paper (watermarked for official corporate stockholders' and directors' meetings).
2. Center and capitalize the title. Example:

MEETING OF THE EXECUTIVE COMMITTEE

3. Double-space the text. Allow a one-and-one-half-inch left margin, a one-inch right margin, and a generous top margin. The left margin should allow for hole-punching or binding. Be consistent.
4. Indent five to ten spaces.
5. List the name of the presiding officer and the recorder. The recorder should sign.
6. Follow the agenda's subject headings as closely as possible.
7. List absences and indicate quorums.
8. Follow the company's policy on capitalization of words such as *committee, department,* etc.
9. Paginate at the bottom consecutively.
10. If a formal resolution, motion, or vote is passed, record it word for word. Persist in making sure the wording is exact.
11. Record the time of adjournment.

MEETING OF THE EXECUTIVE COMMITTEE

April 2, 19__

ATTENDANCE

The weekly meeting of the executive committee was held in the office of Cortez Diaz, first Vice President of Operations, at 10 A.M. on April 2, 19__. Mr. Diaz presided. Present were James Madison, Frederick McAllison, Yolanda Smith, Anne Marie Johnson, and Lewis Smith. Patricia Mendea was absent.

ITEMS COVERED

1. Contract No. 23-a.1 was approved in the amount of $125,000,000.

2. Yolanda Smith gave an update report on Contract No. 24. Further information is to be presented at the May 21 meeting.

3. Anne Marie Johnson reviewed the service budget for the first quarter. Recommendations were made. A feasibility study is to be conducted for implementation of an improved MIS.

4. Lewis Smith presented the proposed budget for the Xavius Project, a government grant. A draft copy of his recommendations will be distributed before the May 21 meeting. This item will be discussed and voted upon at the May 21 meeting.

ADJOURNMENT

The meeting was adjourned at 12 noon.

James Madison

James Madison, Recorder

Sample minutes of a weekly committee meeting.

12. Use businesslike language. Avoid descriptive adjectives, such as *outstanding*.
13. List and summarize the gist of what was said.
14. Transcribe minutes while they are still fresh in your mind.
15. Prepare a rough draft for approval before finalizing. To avoid rekeying, electronically key and store, if possible.

Resolutions

A resolution is a formal statement of a decision voted (an expressed opinion or will of those voting). After a resolution is drafted and finalized, it is the secretary's responsibility to have it signed, distributed, and incorporated into the minutes. Areas of concern may include but not be limited to expressions of recognized achievements, stated objectives, sympathy, and so forth. Each paragraph in a resolution begins with WHEREAS or RESOLVED in solid capital letters or underlined.

RESOLUTION
Adopted December 29, 19__

WHEREAS, JoAnne Logan has been a member of the consultant firm of Kelaher & Kelaher, Inc., for the past fifteen years and has contributed significantly to the professional prestige of this company; and

WHEREAS, Mrs. Logan is retiring; therefore, be it

RESOLVED, that the members of this company go on record as expressing their deep appreciation of Mrs. Logan's professional service throughout the years and that they wish her well in her retirement; and be it

RESOLVED FURTHER, that our Secretary send a copy of this resolution to the Chairperson of the Board of Directors.

Judy Martinez
_____
Judy Martinez, Secretary

Lillian Marti
_____
Lillian Marti, President

Sample resolution.

NEWS RELEASES

News releases are typed double-spaced on 8½" x 11" plain paper or on a special news-release form. Side margins should be generous, at least one and one-half inches or wider, to give the editor room for notations. Try to limit the release to one page.

The editor likes to see identifying information at the top of the sheet. This information should include the date and the name, address, and telephone number of the person to whom requests may be made for more information.

The article itself starts with an indented date line consisting of the name of the city and the date. The city name is typed in all capital letters; the date is typed in capital and lowercase letters and is followed by a dash. The name of the state is given only if the city is not well known or if there is likely to be a doubt as to the identity of the city.

If the news release runs to more than one page, end each page with a complete paragraph and put the word MORE at the bottom, centered or at the right side of the page. Continuation pages should be numbered and have a

N E W S   R E L E A S E   From Sandra Demous
Free Press
500 South Broadway
Los Angeles, California 90055
Telephone (213) 666-5555

Release July 30, 19--

CENTERED TITLE OF A NEWS RELEASE

LOS ANGELES, July 30—continue typing the news release with

double spacing in report form.

This is an example of the bottom of a page of a news release that is continued to the next page.

MORE

This is an example of the last page or end of a news release with one of the concluding symbols.

# # # # # #

brief caption typed flush with the left margin near the top of the page. Copy is often divided so that it can be given to different typesetters. MORE tells the typesetters that there are more pages. End the news release with a concluding centered symbol such as ####, -0-, -end-, or (END).

See the sample news release heading above.

COPY FOR PUBLICATION

Typing/Keying

When the copy is to be printed, keep the typewritten lines six inches long and use double spacing. Avoid dividing words at the ends of lines as much as possible. Type headings in the position they will occupy on the printed page and be consistent in style. Type on one side of the paper; make side margins at least one inch wide. Keep the pages equal in length. Do not staple pages together.

Proofreading

Proofread the material. It is a good idea to lay the material aside before giving it a final check. The second reading may reveal errors overlooked the first time. Two heads are better than one for proofreading. When working with an assistant, the typist should follow the original and the assistant the final copy. The secretary is really a stand-in reader. It is the secretary's job to find those errors so elementary that they escape the author's attention.

Another method for proofreading is to read aloud. When reading copy aloud if you have missed a word, it is quickly obvious to the ear. If you have keyed copy on a word processor, you may print a copy and have a second person proofread it.

Correcting Copy

Use proofreading marks in making corrections. Short corrections can be made by crossing out the incorrect word and writing the correction over it. If the correction is lengthy, type it on a separate sheet of paper, which should then be attached to the original. If a whole paragraph needs correction, you may find it convenient to type the correction on a separate sheet and staple, tape, or glue it over the original. Use rubber cement for gluing. (Rubber cement allows for easy removal without tearing, which becomes a problem when using tape.)

The best time to number the pages of the manuscript is after the whole job has been typed and all corrections have been made. Pages are numbered consecutively, and the page number usually appears in the upper right-hand corner of each page, indented one inch from the right edge, on line four from the top of the page.

Artwork

Identify all artwork either by number or by some other system of labeling, and keep a list. If you use numbers, make certain that the numbering agrees with the order in which the items will appear in the finished job. Type the identification line on a separate label and attach it to the back of the illustration.

Avoid writing on photographs with either pen or pencil, because the marks may break the finish on the photograph and show in the reproduction. If writing is absolutely necessary, use special nonreproducing pens and pencils, which may be obtained from an art shop or stationery store.

Depending on the quality and sensitivity of the artwork, you may have to place onionskin paper or thin art paper over it. This protects the artwork and prevents running of colors, lines, etc.

Layout

The printer will advise on the layout and will make a dummy if it is part of your agreement. A dummy is a set of blank sheets, cut and folded to the size and shape of the finished job. The dummy indicates the location of any artwork.

Estimating Length

Often it is necessary to tell the printer the approximate length of the material. Select three or four lines of the copy and count the number of words in these lines. From this count determine the average number of words per line. Now count the number of lines on the page and multiply this by the number of words in each line. Suppose in four lines you count 44 words. This means that you have an average of 11 words to each line. If there are 27 lines on your page, 27 times 11 gives you 297 words, or nearly 300 words to the page. A report, then, of ten full pages would be about 3,000 words.

Galley Proofs

The printer returns the original manuscript with two or more copies, or proofs, set in the typeface selected. Compare the printer's copy, word for word, with the original. Again, it is always better if two people work together. Careful checking saves time and money, because the printer charges an extra fee for changes.

Reading these proofs, the galley proofs, is the next major step. This reading gives you the opportunity not only to detect and call attention to errors made by the printer but also to make any last-minute alterations you may find desirable. However, if your revisions deviate much from the original, you pay a heavy penalty in time rates. Changes in the galley proof become very costly. Read material through for continuity in thought. Some of the things to watch for in checking are:

- spelling and punctuation errors
- inconsistencies in style, spelling, or paragraphing
- transposition of letters and lines
- errors in page numbers

- continuity from page to page and line to line (Does the last word on a page make sense with the top of the next page?)
- omissions

If your employer frequently publishes manuscripts, keep a record of each manuscript on a 3" × 5" card or some other memory device. Record such facts as the title, the date the manuscript was submitted to the printer, how many pages it contained, and the number of illustrations or visuals included. Create a file for each manuscript to keep track of detailed supportive data.

Desktop Publishing

Desktop publishing, also called *electronic publishing,* is a new technology. It refers to a personal computer-based system or dedicated word processor that runs page composition. It is possible to include graphics and multiple type styles and fonts similar to a typeset page. A laser printer is used for the highest quality.

Desktop publishing software is appropriate for newspapers, advertising materials, and columns of text with limited length and complexity. The visual image on the screen gives you an idea of what the printed page, including graphics and other visuals, will look like.

TECHNICAL REPORTS

The typing done for engineers, chemists, mathematicians, scientists, and other professionals is often referred to as "technical typing." The material often involves equation typing. In such work accuracy is extremely important, much more important than speed. Because you are typing symbols in patterns, spacing both horizontally and vertically becomes a consideration that may require some experimentation and technical knowledge. Use of a format or word processing ruler may help in determining such calculations as insertions of visuals, equations, charts, etc.

Equations generally include raised and lowered symbols. Those symbols written above the regular line of writing are called *superscripts;* those written below, *subscripts.* It is essential, therefore, that technical reports be typed in double spacing to allow room for writing these subscripts and superscripts. Most modern electric typewriters and word processing equipment have special superscript and subscript keys.

Typewriters can also have special keys with mathematical symbols and Greek letters. If you are operating a typewriter that utilizes an element, you may purchase a special element called the "universal symbol element." This element has the mathematical symbols and the letters of the Greek alphabet used frequently in equation typing.

For the larger symbols you will want a template. This is a small plastic rectangular guide that resembles the letter guides for stencil work, except that

Common Business Symbols

Symbol	Meaning	Examples
` or ´	accent	Buenos días, Genève
& (ampersand)	and	Meyers & Jones
*	asterisk	*Note (used as a footnote symbol)
@	at, each	@ $2.45
[ ]	brackets	[Diskette 45]
¢	cents	30¢
°	degrees	45°F
/	diagonal/slash	either/or; and/or; 1/2
$	dollars	$85.00
'	feet; minutes	7'
"	inches; seconds	7"
#	number	#1 (before a numeral)
%	percent	99.99%
#	pound	45# (after a numeral)
/S/	signed	In legal documents, used before copied signature: /S/

it provides outlines of symbols used in scientific reports. You trace the stencil symbol with a sharp-pointed pencil.

Always leave a space before and after the arithmetical operational symbols: =, +, −, ÷, and ×. However, if the symbol is used adjectivally, as -3, there should be no space between the minus sign and the 3.

Multiplication is expressed by using the "×" or a centered period $(4 \cdot 6)$ or by parentheses enclosing an expression to be multiplied. Often the multiplication sign is omitted and the letters are typed together, as ab. Thus, in the equation $7ad(s - y) = mx$, there is no space between d and the opening parenthesis, but there is a space before and after the equal sign and the minus sign.

Type fractions as follows: If the equation is short, the fraction may be part of the running text and is typed in the shilling style, which looks like this: 4/5. If you use mixed numbers, put a space between the whole number and the shilling fraction; for example, 43 5/6.

Equations are numbered consecutively throughout a report to make it easy to refer to any equation in the text. Each equation number is put in parentheses at the right margin. Set a tab stop for this location. Arrange the tab setting so that the closing parenthesis will be just inside of the right margin of your page. When making reference to these equation numbers, abbreviate equation to "Eq." Your reference will look like this: (Eq. 5).

Usually punctuation is not used with equations. If your author requests punctuation in equations, then observe these rules:

- Consider each equation as a clause of a complex sentence and follow it with either a comma or semicolon.
- If the equation concludes the sentence, a period follows it.
- If you have a series of equations, introduce them by a colon in the line preceding the equations.

Sometimes equations are too long for one line and must be placed on several lines. Break them before the equal sign when possible. Before any one of the operational signs ($+, -, \times, \div$) is another good place to divide an equation. You may also divide it between fractions or after brackets and parentheses. Do not put part of an equation on one page and the rest of it on the next page.

Some authors help their typists to read the symbols in an equation by writing all lowercase symbols and printing upper-case symbols. It may also be helpful to draft all the equations in the report before typing. Let the author check your arrangement of the equations. If the author has no objection, then you are ready to do the finished report and can proceed with confidence that the material is arranged in the very best form.

Hints for Typing Symbols

If the typewriter does not have special keys for the symbols you need to make, you may try to produce the symbols by using other keys showing similar symbols or a combination of keys. For example, to make the symbol for inches or seconds, type double quotation marks; to make the symbol for feet, type a single quotation mark or an apostrophe.

If a symbol cannot be made on the typewriter, use a black pen and insert the symbol by hand. Be sure that the ink matches the color of the printwheel or the typewriter ribbon. Practice writing the symbol several times on a separate sheet of paper before writing it on the original and final form.

LEGAL DOCUMENTS

Even though you may not be employed in a law office, at times you may find it necessary to type a legal document or, at least, to complete a printed legal form. Accuracy is essential, because a changed word or a correction may affect the validity of the paper. If you have any doubt about making a correction, consult your supervisor. When changes must be made in a document after it has been signed, all changes must be initialed by the signers. In some instances, erasures or corrections are not acceptable; the document with a correction would not be legally binding.

Many legal documents are typed on "legal cap" paper. This paper is stronger than regular stationery and is usually slightly larger, measuring $8\frac{1}{2}" \times 13"$

Legal Binder: folded and endorsed (left), and flat with document in place.

or $8^{1}/_{2}$" × 14". It has a double-ruled line $1^{1}/_{4}$ inches from the left edge of the paper and a single-ruled line one-half inch from the right edge. Not all legal documents are put on these ruled sheets. Many wills, for example, are written on plain sheets of paper.

To avoid crowding the information in the document, type it double-spaced and use generous side margins (at least two spaces within the rulings). If your paper has no rulings, use a 1-inch left margin and a $^{1}/_{2}$-inch right margin. Start the first line of each page two inches from the top edge and end each page within an inch of the bottom. Indent all paragraphs ten spaces, and use only one side of the paper. Never end a page with the first line of a paragraph or begin a page with the last line of a paragraph. At least two lines of the document must appear on the page that is to have the signature.

Spell out sums of money and repeat them in figures enclosed within parentheses. Dates may be either spelled out or written in figures—but not both ways.

The first page is usually not numbered, except on a will. Numbers of subsequent pages are centered between the margins, three blank lines from the bottom of the page. Type a hyphen before and another after the page number.

Use the underscore for signature lines. The signature lines for the principal signers start at the center of the page and extend toward the right margin. The signature lines for witnesses begin at the left margin and extend toward the center. Lines should be at least three spaces apart. Lightly pencil the respective initials at the beginnings of the signature lines to guide the signers. If you prefer, use the small "x" to mark the spot where the parties are to sign.

Type the introductory and closing phrases in all capitals. Put either a comma or a colon after the phrases, depending on how the phrase is used.

Some of these phrases are:

KNOW ALL MEN BY THESE PRESENTS, that . . .
IN WITNESS WHEREOF, the parties . . .
THIS AGREEMENT, made June . . .
WHEREIN IT IS MUTUALLY AGREED AS FOLLOWS: 1.
   At that . . .

File copies can be made on onionskin paper. If carbon copies are to be signed, make the copies on the same quality of paper that you use for the original.

Some legal documents have cover sheets or binders, called *legal backs*. These are endorsed with a brief description of the document. To prepare the binder, lay it on the desk and bring the bottom edge up to within one inch of the top; crease. Bring the creased end up to approximately one inch from the top and fold again. Open this fold and insert the binder in the typewriter. Do not type beyond the crease. After typing the endorsement, turn the top edge of the backing sheet down, crease it, and insert the document in the crease. Staple it in place. Fold the document to fit the creases in the binder.

Software for Legal Documents

Because of the universal format of legal documents, several standardized software packages are available for basic contracts, wills, court orders, deeds, codicils, affidavits, and powers of attorney. Preprinted legal forms for several common documents are also available from stationery stores that supply legal offices. These are called *legal forms* or *law blanks*.

Most law offices today are equipped with automated text-editing equipment. A significant portion of many legal documents consists of standard paragraphs that have been court-tested. These paragraphs can be keyed in once (or be part of a software package) and serve as *boilerplates* that can be retrieved automatically each time needed. Since typographical errors and corrections are critical places in a legal document and can disqualify a document for court purposes, these boiler plates are very helpful. They provide error-free typing. All the secretary has to do is fill in the variables.

Lawyers often generate documents that have been created before. When merged with new or edited text, the final document is unique when seen as a whole. Computer networks have been set up to serve law offices by providing indexes for legal material, including opinions, reviews, cases, and decisions.

In many cases, the linkage with the network is a community word processor, terminal, or personal computer.

For processing legal documents, useful word processing features include automatic page numbering; line numbering facility; specialized spell-check dictionaries; redlining and strikeout; document assembly; merging; automatic table of authorities and contents; automatic indexing; outlining; columnized documents; file-find commands; header/footer controls; and automatic math calculations.

There are also several useful primary text-editing techniques. In a technique known as *macros,* memorized keystroke sequences are used to automate groups of keystrokes for names, terms, and sequences used frequently. (For example, the memorized sequence TWIC may automatically automate all the keystrokes needed for the frequently used phrase "To Whom It May Concern.") In *merging* techniques, fill-ins are used as variables in standard documents; in *segment retrieval,* standard paragraphs or parts of paragraphs are used to create documents in leases and contracts. And, finally, any variety of these techniques may be used together in a *combination.*

HANDLING NUMBERS IN REPORTS

There is no uniform or simple style for typing numerals, and the rules established by a variety of style manuals can sometimes be perplexing.

The following list provides some generally accepted basic rules.

Use figures for	*Use words for*

Exact numbers above ten
   35 club members
	Exact numbers, ten and below
	   mail five boxes

Amounts of money
   $29.95; $46; 9 cents
	Round or approximate numbers
	   four hundred people

Percentages
   6 percent
	Beginning of sentences
	   Fourteen years

Dimensions, measurements, etc.
   15 feet; size 9;
   4 ½ acres
	Names of centuries and decades
	   the sixteenth century
	   the Roaring Twenties

Exact age
   11 years, 4 months, 2 days
	Approximate age
	   seventeen years old

Time with A.M. or P.M.
   4 P.M.
	Time with "o'clock"
	   four o'clock

Street names above ten
   14 West 24 Street
	Street names ten and below
	   Fifth Avenue

Word "number" followed by figure
   No. 4
	Numbered sessions of Congress
	   Seventy-eighth Congress

House or building numbers	Fractions standing alone

Use figures for	Use words for
47 Genesee Street	send one-half of the order
Dates	Two numbers coming together
July 4, 1995	six 4-inch bolts
5th of May	210 six-pound crates
Plurals of numbers	Mixed numbers
16's or 16s	six and three-fourths
Large even amounts	Smaller amounts in round numbers
15 million dollars	fourteen hundred copies

Some additional guidelines for handling numbers in reports:

- Spell numbers from one to ten. However, if a sentence contains a series of numbers over ten, use numbers.

    The team won 24 games in 1993, 21 games in 1994, and 10 games in 1995.

    The group consisted of two group leaders, one recorder, and three secretaries for each of the projects.

- If a number begins a sentence, use the word form.

    Ten thousand students were present at the conference.

- Except in legal documents, type amounts of money in figures.

- Use ciphers after the decimal point when fractional amounts appear in the same context.

    The book was $19.51 with tax, but the magazine was only $5.00.

    The magazine was only $5.

- Use a hyphen to represent the word *to*.

    1984-1996.

- When a sum of money is used as an adjective, spell it out and hyphenate.

    He bought a twenty-dollar pen.

- Use figures for federal, state, and interstate highways.

    U.S. Route 67 (or U.S. 67)

    New York State Throughway 37

    Interstate 68 (or I-68)

VISUAL AIDS

Visuals are any display materials in business reports or other reports that make them clearer and more attractive. Visuals may be inserted into the text, in which case they often have a great impact on the reader, or, if they are lengthy, they may be placed in the appendices of a report.

Figure 11-1. Examples of Visuals from a Template.

The secretary should develop knowhow about when and where to use visuals. In general, visuals are used to:

- enhance a page
- clarify text
- emphasize a specific point or purpose
- motivate and arouse interest
- illustrate a point in greater detail
- explain or simplify technical material

Kinds of Visuals

The type of visual to use depends on the intended purpose of the visual, the audience, the subject, the type of paper to be used, and the printing process to be used for reproduction.

Basically there are two types of visuals: pictorial and numerical or other data. Pictorials include photographs, figures, and illustrations. Numerical data include tables, charts, and graphs.

Preparation of Visuals

Visuals may be prepared in several ways with automated equipment or with simple cut-and-paste techniques. With the increased use of automated equipment, many firms have established a separate unit or department to handle the work involving the production of different types of visuals. Some other firms contract the preparation of visuals to a professional service outside the firm. In these situations, the secretary's main responsibility becomes formatting. However, in some businesses visual preparation is still the secretary's responsibility.

Secretaries who do not have access to a sophisticated word processor or personal computer may have to use the cut-and-paste method and produce a mechanical which is then copied on the appropriate paper and serves as an original to be reproduced. This technique allows for reduction or enlargement of the visual so that the final version conforms to the page size and format of the report.

For pictorial visuals, draw—or hire an artist to draw—the desired likenesses and images. Sometimes a standard template can be used to draw or copy the image (see Figure 11-1). Alternatively, cut out the image and paste it on paper, photocopy it, or trace and generate it on a computer. When inserting visuals into the text, be sure that all lines are properly balanced, that the visual is crisp and defined, that all photographs are sharply focused, and, if the visual is not an original, that proper credit is given.

Numerical or other data visuals are easier to produce. Use numerical visuals when you wish to make comparisons and contrasts more vivid and when you want to pinpoint a detail clearly. For graphs, be sure to:

- list the scale used and indicate where zero is
- use an acceptable range of precision
- check that the graph reads left to right and bottom to top

Formatting of Visuals

Once the visuals—whether pictorial or numerical—are prepared, it is usually the secretary's responsibility to format them in the report. Mainly, format preparation involves the reduction, enlargement, and placement of visuals in the text. Care must be taken at all times to ensure quality, error-free reproduction.

Loose Material

Most visuals must be attached to paper. Use rubber cement or liquid or stick glue that will not tear the paper if the visual has to be removed.

Make sure that extraneous lines from the edge of the attached material do not appear in the copy to be reproduced. Such lines may be covered with tape or white-out liquid.

Reduction/Enlargement

If a visual is too large (too wide, too long, or both), reduce it to fit within the page format designed. Special reprographics equipment is available for reductions in a variety of percentages: 77%, 74%, 66%, 50%, 25%, and smaller. Conversely, visuals may be cut and then enlarged to show specific points more clearly. A well-equipped photocopy shop or department can provide a variety of enlargement and reduction services.

Placement

Avoid inserting visuals in such a way that they can be read only by turning the report. Always try to make the visual conform to the normal page of a report. If this is not possible and the visual must be inserted sideways, be sure that the heading of the visual is placed at the binding or spine (left side) of the report.

Figure 11-2 shows a typical visual—a process flow chart. The circles were drawn using a template. Then the illustration was enlarged. After the enlargement, the numbers and letters were typed and the connecting lines drawn using a black pen and a ruler. The visual was then reduced by 64% so that it would fit within the margins of an $8^1/_2$" × 11" sheet of paper. The final reduction was cut and pasted and then recopied.

Figure 11-2. Example of a Reduced Visual.

12

Communications Techniques

by James C. Matthews, Ed.D.

■ *The Office Mail*

> *Update on the U.S. Postal System*
> *Incoming Mail*
> *Outgoing Mail*
> *Special Postal Services*
> *Other Postal Services*
> *Other Instructions about Mail*
> *Express*

■ *Electronic Mail Services*

> *Electronic Mail*
> *Facsimile (Fax)*
> *Mailgram®*
> *Priority Letter*
> *Telegram*
> *Cablegram*
> *Telex*

- *The Telephone*

  Telephone Techniques
  Telephone Dictation
  Telephone Reference Materials
  Assembling Data for Outgoing Calls
  Long-Distance Services
  Telephone Record Keeping
  Special Telephone Equipment and Services
  Billing Numbers
  Telephone Answering Services
  Telephone Answering Devices

Effective and efficient communication is an essential for any business and is required of all employees. Some basic methods of communication have remained largely unchanged; others have changed greatly with technological developments and increasing sophistication. The secretary must be familiar with all communications techniques and how and when to use them. This chapter briefly discusses the major communications techniques: mail, telegrams, cables, radio messages, and the telephone.

THE OFFICE MAIL

The processing and handling of mail constitutes the most important method of communication between a company and its contacts in the business world. The way in which mail is handled by the secretary affects every phase of a company and its external and internal procedures of information processing. A secretary who can effectively deal with office mail is indeed a valuable asset to an employer.

Update on the U.S. Postal System

For the distribution of mail outside of the office, the U.S. Postal Service is still the oldest, most widespread, and cheapest way. In April 1988, massive changes and updates in the postal system occurred, including an increase in the cost of postage. Many of the changes have affected procedures as well as the handling of mail in general. Guidelines are still being released. For a current ready reference for those changes write for a copy of:

> POSTAL BULLETIN (Special Bulletin)
> PB 21666 (check with your local Post Office for the current
> publication)

The address is:

> U.S. Postal Service
> Washington, DC 20260-1571

This special bulletin contains the new rates, fees, and classifications as well as some changes in regulations necessary to implement them; all relate to the domestic rates and fees for various classes, services, and mail classifications. The bulletin also includes *interim* international rates and fees. Future issues will include notices of the adoption of final international rates and fees. This and related postal bulletins will serve to guide you in the handling of office mail via the U.S. Postal Service.

Incoming Mail

A new secretary may find a well-established system of handling mail within an organization. Changes may need to be suggested tactfully. The size of the organization has a great bearing on the system that evolves. In a small office one person may sort and open all mail except that marked "Personal" or "Confidential." (Letters so marked are delivered unopened to the person to whom they are addressed.) A large organization usually has a mailing department, where both incoming and outgoing mail are handled according to a fixed system. In an office where the secretary is assigned the responsibility for opening the mail for the employer, a routine procedure will permit rapid handling of each day's mail.

Necessary Supplies

The secretary will need supplies to open the mail. The following items and others you will need on your desk or workstation should be placed there *before* the mail is processed. Arrange the items in a circular fashion or another configuration for convenient and easy access. The suggested items are:

- envelope opener
- stapler or clips
- date or time stamp
- routing slips
- transparent tape
- pencils/pens (at least two different colors)
- memo pad
- mail register or log, if needed
- staple remover

If electric equipment, such as a mail opener or time stamp, is available, use it. It will save two-thirds of the time as compared to manual equipment.

Opening the Mail

The mail should be opened as soon as it is delivered to the secretary's desk, and an orderly procedure should be followed to ensure that nothing is misplaced or lost, that time is not wasted, and that the executive receives the information needed.

Opening the envelopes. All envelopes should be opened before the contents are removed from any of them. To ensure that the contents will not be torn while the letter is being opened, tap the envelope firmly on the edge of the desk so that the contents will slip away from the top. Slit the upper edge of the envelope with a letter opener. If the contents of a letter are cut by the opener, use transparent tape to paste the parts together.

Checking the contents. After removing the contents of an envelope, check the letter for a return address. If there is none, staple the envelope containing the return address to the contents. (*Caution:* If the contents include a punched card, use a paper clip for fastening rather than a staple.) The envelope should also be retained if the signature on the letter is not easily distinguishable.

Another check should be made to determine that all enclosures stipulated in the letter are accounted for. If not, a notation should be made immediately on the face of the letter, indicating what is missing.

Even though annotating a letter is one of the procedures encouraged, some companies do not like correspondence marked up, especially legal or business firms that might have to submit a piece of correspondence as evidence in a court of law. Always follow company policy. Some companies prefer that the secretary place a buck slip (adhesive) with the notation on the face of the letter. In theory, it serves the same purpose.

Dating the mail. It is always wise to affix each day's date on incoming mail. The easiest procedure is to use a rubber stamp. Such a procedure is helpful if the letter has arrived too late to meet a deadline requested, has been in transit longer than it should have been, or is undated. In either of the last two cases, it is well to staple the envelope to the letter in addition to dating the letter. This will give evidence of the date of mailing as well as the date of receipt.

Envelopes. Generally the envelope may be destroyed after it has been ascertained that everything has been removed and that there are no problems concerned with the names, addresses, or dates. However, in certain situations, especially legal matters, envelopes sometimes serve as evidence of date and time received (from the precanceled postage stamp). In such situations, envelopes may be kept and clipped or stapled to the back of the letter.

Preparation of Mail for Employer

In order to save the employer's time, the efficient secretary should take the time to prepare the mail. This involves two basic steps.

1. Read each letter, underlining important points that will aid you and your employer in answering the letter. Underline only those things that are of significance, such as publications, dates, and names of people.

2. Make annotations on each letter. This involves writing notes in the margins. Generally, annotations fall into three categories, namely, a note indicating:

   a. Action required by the letter—date of appointment for correspondent, reservations for a trip the employer may have to make as a result of the correspondence, etc.

   b. Procedures to be followed. These may depend upon former correspondence with the same person or related correspondence, which will have to be sought in the files.

   c. The priority the letter should receive, symbolized by a code. In an agreement with the employer a given place on each letter should be established for this code. For example, a red number may be written in the upper left corner. Such a code might be:

      Code 1. Mail and reports with high priority and requiring a decision. These should be answered the same day they are received. (It is assumed that personal or confidential mail is delivered unopened to the addressee as soon as it arrives on the secretary's desk.)

Code 2. Mail for which additional information must be procured and for which answering may have to be deferred for a day or two while data are being collected. *All mail should be answered within 48 hours of receipt,* except under very unusual circumstances.

Code 3. Routine mail that the secretary may be able to handle. Many employers want to see all mail; it is wise to determine an employer's preference in this regard. After the relationship is well established, many secretaries have their employers' permission to reply to routine letters. In such instances it is usually good procedure to supply the employer with carbons of the letters sent and the original letter.

Code 4. Letters that require notations but no reply.

As the secretary reads and annotates the mail, it becomes a simple matter to encode and sort the mail as it is prepared for the employer. A fifth or even a sixth category may be added as needed. Usually important reports require a special category, while weekly, monthly, or semimonthly periodicals may require no encoding. Most employers prefer to examine the periodicals before they are made available to others in the office.

Preparing supplementary material. As the letters are being annotated, an efficient secretary will also make a list of files or pieces of correspondence and other information to be looked up before presenting the correspondence to the employer.

Some employers wish to see the mail as soon as it has been opened. In that case the secretary may bring the mail in as soon as it has been annotated. While the mail is being read, the secretary may take the compiled list and seek the necessary files, reports, and other information for acting upon the urgent mail. To keep all papers pertaining to each piece of correspondence together, use file folders or small clips.

Arranging the mail. After the sorting process has been completed, the secretary may arrange the mail either in one pile with the high-priority mail on top or in any other arrangement that has been agreed upon. Whenever the mail is placed on the desk of the employer, some provision should be made to prevent others from reading the top letter. Some secretaries simply place the top letter face down.

Absence of the employer. When the employer is away from the office, letters requiring immediate replies may be handled in either of two ways. First, if a decision must be made immediately, it may be necessary to give the mail to the person in charge during the employer's absence. Second, if the employer will be in the office within a day or two and the decision can wait, the secretary should write the sender immediately and explain when a reply may be expected and the reason for the delay.

The efficient secretary to whom the employer has entrusted routine correspondence will maintain a file of materials handled during an absence of the employer. The folder should be readily at hand upon the employer's return.

Outgoing Mail

If the secretary is responsible for the preparation of outgoing mail, as the case may well be in a firm too small to have a separate mailing and shipping department, time and expense can be saved by learning about the various postal and shipping services available and the general regulations and normal charges pertinent to these services. It is important to be alert to frequent changes.

An accurate scale for weighing postal matter is a worthwhile piece of office equipment. It saves time and eliminates guesswork.

Sources of Mail Information

To obtain correct information on postal procedures and rates, which are subject to change, consult the local postal authorities. From them, or from the Superintendent of Documents, Government Printing Office, Washington, DC 20402, may be obtained a number of useful pamphlets that are periodically brought up to date. These are some of them:

> *Mailers Guide*
> *Packaging Pointers*
> *Domestic Postage Rates, Fees, and Information*
> *How To Prepare Second- and Third-Class Mailings*
> *Mailing Permits*
> *International Postage Rates and Fees*

Some of the information in these pamphlets is taken from the *Postal Manual*, which contains complete data on postal regulations and procedures.

A monthly publication called *Memo to Mailers* is available to business mailers without charge. It tells of rate and classification changes, along with other news of postal matters. Address:

MEMO TO MAILERS
U.S. Postal Service
Post Office Box 999
Springfield, VA 22150-0999

Stamps, Stamped Envelopes, and Postal Cards

Postage stamps may be purchased in several forms—single stamps, sheets, books, and coils—and denominations for both regular mail and overseas airmail. For the coil form, inexpensive dispensers are available at the post office.

Stamped envelopes are also sold at the post office; these may be obtained in two standard sizes. Postal cards are available with the stamp printed on the address side; they come in single or double (reply) forms, with or without postage on the reply half.

Precanceled and meter stamps are two means of reducing the time and cost of mail handling. In order to use precanceled stamps (*i.e.*, stamps canceled before mailing), a special permit must be obtained from the post office. For regulations applying to precanceled stamps, consult the *Postal Manual* or the local postal authorities.

Postage may be paid by printing meter stamps with a postage meter. Postage meters hasten the purchase, control, and attachment of postage and therefore facilitate mailing. Postage-meter machines may be leased from authorized manufacturers. Again, the *Postal Manual* or the local postal authorities should be consulted for regulations governing the leasing, use, and licensing of postal meters and also their manufacture and distribution.

Zip Codes and Two-Letter State Abbreviations

The U.S. Postal Service uses a set of two-letter abbreviations, to be followed by the nine-digit ZIP Code, for all of the states and possessions of the United States.

The U.S. Postal Service relies heavily on ZIP Codes in the processing of mail. While some letters (at this writing) are still delivered even if the ZIP Code is not used, they may be delayed by lack of the number code. On the other hand, the Postal Service will not accept quantity mailings of letters, circulars, brochures, catalogs, etc., unless the pieces to be mailed are ZIP Coded and sorted by the code.

ZIP stands for Zoning Improvement Plan. The ZIP Code itself is a designation by numbers that expedites mail deliveries by cutting down on the steps required to move a letter from sender to addressee. The digits identify state, city, and post office, enabling most efficient use of air, highway, and rail transportation of the letter or parcel.

The *National ZIP Code and Post Office Directory* is available from the Information Service, U.S. Postal Service, Washington, DC 20260, or at any post office or branch. Having the latest ZIP Code directory is important, for over a thousand ZIP Codes change each year. The *National ZIP Code and Post Office Directory* is printed by the Government Printing Office and is exchangeable free of charge each year for the annually revised edition. ZIP Code manuals printed by private companies must be paid for anew each time an updated printing is desired.

Because of the many changes in ZIP Codes, even the latest printing of such a handbook may not provide the secretary with the one needed. In that case, local post offices generally have a separate department for this and a ZIP Code can easily be ascertained by telephone.

Your local telephone directory will usually show local ZIP Codes.

AK	Alaska	KY	Kentucky	OH	Ohio
AL	Alabama	LA	Louisiana	OK	Oklahoma
AR	Arkansas	MA	Massachusetts	OR	Oregon
AZ	Arizona	MD	Maryland	PA	Pennsylvania
CA	California	ME	Maine	PR	Puerto Rico
CO	Colorado	MI	Michigan	RI	Rhode Island
CT	Connecticut	MN	Minnesota	SC	South Carolina
DC	District of	MO	Missouri	SD	South Dakota
	Columbia	MS	Mississippi	TN	Tennessee
DE	Delaware	MT	Montana	TX	Texas
FL	Florida	NC	North Carolina	UT	Utah
GA	Georgia	ND	North Dakota	VA	Virginia
HI	Hawaii	NE	Nebraska	VI	Virgin Islands
IA	Iowa	NH	New Hampshire	VT	Vermont
ID	Idaho	NJ	New Jersey	WA	Washington
IL	Illinois	NM	New Mexico	WI	Wisconsin
IN	Indiana	NV	Nevada	WV	West Virginia
KS	Kansas	NY	New York	WY	Wyoming

Coding for Mail to Canada

Canada uses a different coding system (called National Postal Code) to speed mail deliveries. The following two-letter abbreviations are recommended for use with this code:

AB	Alberta	NT	Northwest Territories
BC	British Columbia	ON	Ontario
LB	Labrador	PE	Prince Edward Island
MB	Manitoba	PQ	Quebec
NB	New Brunswick	SK	Saskatchewan
NF	Newfoundland	YT	Yukon Territory
NS	Nova Scotia		

Business offices that send a large amount of mail to Canada can write to the following address for Postal Code information:

> Mail Collection & Delivery Branch
> Postal Coding Division
> Canada Post
> Ottawa, Ontario K1A 0B1
> Canada

Classes of Mail

There are six classes of domestic mail, and these will be discussed in detail. Postal regulations and rates change quite frequently.

Private, commercial "mail" services are now established, providing an alternative to the U.S. Postal System, which has had problems in effecting speedy delivery. Often such services operate only within a metropolitan area, but a few nationwide services also exist. All of these will be listed in the Yellow Pages, generally under "Delivery Services." There, too, will be found a listing of companies that will pick up mail and deliver it to the post office for speedier handling or will make pickups of mail directed to a box number at a post office.

First class: all handwritten or typewritten material and all material sealed against postal inspection

Priority mail: any mailable matter that requires the speediest transportation and expeditious handling, weighing up to 2 pounds

Second class: newspapers and periodicals

Third class: circulars, books, catalogs, and other printed matter, and merchandise not included in first or second class, weighing less than 16 ounces

Fourth class: all mailable matter not included in first, second, or third class, weighing one pound or more, but no more than 40 pounds, and not exceeding 84 inches in combined length and girth (in some circumstances, 70 pounds and 108 inches)

Express mail: guaranteed fast, reliable overnight delivery, on a money-back basis, of mail and packages

First-Class Mail

The rate for first-class mail is determined by weight (the ounce or fraction thereof), without regard to the distance the article is to travel.

Address. To ensure prompt delivery, observe these precautions regarding the address:

- Write or type the address clearly and legibly.
- Mail addressed for delivery through a city-delivery post office must include the street and street number, or post office box number, or general delivery, or rural or star route designation. Mail for patrons on a rural route may be addressed to street names and numbers, provided that this type of address has been approved by the post office. The rural route number or the words "Rural Delivery" should be used in such addresses. Most patrons on rural routes have been assigned box numbers and this number should be included with the address.
- Be sure that all mail bears the name and address of the sender, either in the upper left corner or on the back flap.
- Include the nine-digit ZIP Code.

Remember that mail pieces bearing more than one street address, or the name of more than one city or town in the return address or in the recipient's address, are not acceptable for mailing.

Some firms use both a post office box number and the street address. The U.S. Postal Service will deliver the item to the address immediately above the city-state-ZIP Code line. Therefore, if the company wants addressees to know its street address, yet prefers to have mail directed to its post office box, the box number will come next to last in its return address or letterhead. The secretary should be sure to address the envelope for return mail with the elements in the order shown. For the secretary's own company, such preferred order should be carefully specified when ordering letterheads, envelopes, or other company paper bearing an address.

	The BCX Company	The BCX Company
	200 Main Street	P.O. Box 800456
Mail will be delivered →	P.O. Box 800456 ⟶	200 Main Street
	Small Town, NJ 06780-1243	Small Town, NJ 06780-1243

USPS-enhanced box numbers. The USPS has developed a new program for expediting and ensuring the delivery of mail to post office box numbers. The new system requires an adjustment of a post office box number to ensure the uniqueness of the number and decrease the likelihood of confusion. Before the new program was instituted, a box number was not unique because the same number could exist in a number of other post offices in the same borough, county, or locale. Therefore, mail containing a correct box number but an incorrect ZIP Code or no ZIP Code at all was difficult—if not impossible—to deliver to the correct box.

In the new system a prefix has been added to all post office box numbers. All box numbers now have been expanded to six digits or more. The first two digits are the last two digits of the five-digit ZIP Code. The last four digits are the current box number; if the box number has fewer than four digits, at least one zero precedes the box number.

Old	*New*
XYZ Company	XYZ Company
Post Office Box 22	Post Office Box 180022
Brooklyn, NY 11218-0006	Brooklyn, NY 11218-0006

Bar-coded envelopes. Specially printed bar-coded envelopes or labels, for which the originator has paid the postage, may be distributed for business reply mail or forwarding mail that is to be returned to the originator.

The location of the bar code must be on the address side of the mailpiece and within a clear space called the "bar code read area." This area extends $5/8$ inch from the bottom and at least $4^1/2$ inches from the right edge of the mailpiece. Within the read area, the leftmost bar of the bar code must be located between $3^1/4$ and 4 inches from the right edge of the mailpiece. The bottom of the bars must be positioned $1/4$ inch (plus or minus $1/16$ inch) from

1/4 inch maximum thickness

11-1/2"

5"

3-1/2"

6-1/8"

Figure 12-1. Dimensional Standards Template for Letter-size Mail. The full-size template with measurements shown is to be used for first-class mail of one ounce or less or third-class mail of two ounces or less. When the piece to be mailed is aligned with the lower left-hand corner, the tip of the upper right-hand corner must touch the shaded area, to be mailed at regular postage.

the bottom edge of the mailpiece. The bar code must be completely contained within the solid rectangle as shown in Figure 12-2. There should be typewritten or handwritten items on either side of the mailpiece or at the bottom. Mailpiece refers to envelopes, cartons, labels, and adhesive items.

These bar codes are read by optical character recognition (OCR) readers. In other words, the bars are scanned. Characters are converted into signals and are recorded and/or interpreted as to meaning and destination of the mailpiece. The OCR scanner allows reduced input time, increased accuracy, and faster output. Special print shops and the post office branch offices provide envelopes at cost; however, the forms of imprint must conform to the requirement of the U.S. Postal Service.

Envelope size. All envelopes differing widely from the standard sizes should be marked "FIRST CLASS." A rubber stamp is often used for this purpose, although it is not essential. First-class mail that weighs one ounce or less and exceeds $6^{1}/8$ inches in height, $11^{1}/2$ inches in length, and $^{1}/4$ inch in thickness, and whose length is less than 1.3 times the height or more than 2.5 times the height, is considered nonstandard mail. The secretary should call the post office to determine the rate for an outsize piece of mail or should alert the company mail department that a nonstandard piece of mail is going out.

Figure 12-2. Bar-coded Envelope. The envelope typing format remains the same. Do not write or type in the left and right margins. Nothing should appear below the bar codes or bottom margin of the mailpiece.

Source: Special Postal Bulletin, U.S. Postal Service.

Mail must be at least .007 inch thick, that is, about the thickness of a postcard. Mail that is $1/4$ inch thick or less must measure at least $3^1/2$ inches in height, be at least 5 inches in length, and be rectangular in shape.

Postcards. Government-printed postal cards measure $3^1/2" \times 5^1/2"$, while commercial postcards are $4" \times 6"$ or slightly larger. In order to be mailed at the postcard rate, which is lower than the first-class letter rate, cards cannot be larger than $4^1/4" \times 6"$. A larger card must bear the first-class letter postage.

Double postal cards are two attached cards, one of which is to be detached by the receiver and returned through the mail as a reply. The reply portion does not have to bear postage when originally mailed. Double cards must have the address of the reply portion on the inside.

Business-reply mail. Specially printed business-reply cards, envelopes, cartons, and labels may be distributed so that they can be returned to the original mailer without prepayment of postage. A permit must be obtained from the local postmaster in order to distribute such mail. Postage is collected on each piece of business-reply mail at the time it is delivered to the original mailer. The rates are the regular postage rates, plus an additional fee. No special services may be included in these rates.

No limitation is made on the quantity of business-reply mail, but it cannot be sent to any foreign country except to U.S. military post offices overseas.

The forms of imprint and address for business-reply mail must conform to the requirements of the Postal Service. One standard format is shown in Figure 12-3.

Priority Mail

Mailable matter that weighs more than 12 ounces and is to be sent by the fastest means of transportation with the most expeditious handling may be sent by priority mail. Matter cannot exceed 70 pounds in weight or 100 inches in length and girth combined.

Special envelopes or stickers should be used to clearly identify the package or envelope as priority mail. To ensure proper handling, the identification "PRIORITY MAIL" should be clearly marked in large letters on all sides.

Second-Class Mail

The category of second-class mail includes newspapers and other periodical publications. The secretary may be concerned with the mailing of such matter if the company puts out a newsletter regularly. Special rates apply, according to the nature of the publication, the frequency of publication, and so on.

Publications issued by, and in the interest of, nonprofit organizations and associations, such as religious, educational, scientific, philanthropic, agricultural, labor, and fraternal groups, are categorized for mailing under a special-rate structure.

Because of the variation and specialization of postal regulations in this category, the secretary to whom the responsibility of handling this kind of

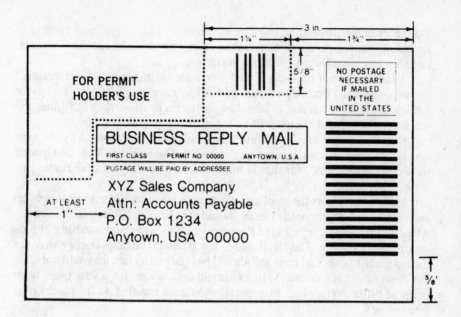

Figure 12-3. A standard format for the address side of a piece of business-reply mail.

mail is assigned should get specific information from the post office on the particulars applying to the publication with which the office is concerned. However, these few general observations on the wrapping or covering of second-class matter may be useful.

Preparation for mailing. Second-class mail must be prepared so that it can be easily examined. Even if envelopes, wrappers, or other covers are sealed, the use of second-class postage rates indicates that the sender consents to postal inspection of the contents.

Sealed or unsealed envelopes used as wrappers and sealed wrappers or covers must indicate, in the upper right corner, the "second-class" status, acknowledging the post office's right of examination. The upper left corner must have the name of the publication and the mailing address to which undeliverable copies or change-of-address notices are to be sent.

Special instructions must be followed for sorting the pieces before mailing. These are available through the local post office.

Third-Class Mail

All pieces in the third-class category—circulars, books, catalogs, and other printed matter, and merchandise weighing less than 16 ounces—must be legibly marked "THIRD CLASS" whether or not they are sealed. They may be mailed and charged by the single piece or in bulk. Bulk mail requires a permit and cannot contain more than 200 pieces or weigh more than 50 pounds. All the pieces in a bulk mailing must be identical in size, weight, and number of enclosures, although the printed textual matter need not be identical. Special rates are available for nonprofit organizations.

A single piece of third-class mail is considered nonstandard if it weighs 2 ounces or less and exceeds a height of $6^1/8$ inches, a length of $11^1/2$ inches, or a thickness of $1/4$ inch and is less than 1.3 times or more than 2.5 times the height. An additional charge will be made for such mail.

Preparation for mailing. Third-class mail must be prepared by the sender so that it can be easily examined. It need not be marked "May Be Opened for Postal Inspection," for this is implied in the sending of mail under this class.

Mailers must sort the mail and place each piece with the address side up and in the same position; the pieces should then be tied, lengthwise and crosswise, into packages, with twine strong enough to withstand handling in processing and shipping. The "Bulk Mail" labels should be large enough to cover the top piece of exposed mail and should be attached so that they will not slide out from under the twine. Mailers should follow special instructions from the post office. Wrapping, in general, should be handled as for parcel post (see below).

Writing permitted. Other than the address, the only writing permitted on the wrapper of third-class mail is in the form of instructions, such as "Printed Matter"; "Photograph—DO NOT BEND"; or "Do Not Open until Christmas."

Enclosures. With catalogs or booklets, one order form, a business-reply card or envelope, and one circular concerning the product being sent may be enclosed.

A letter may also be enclosed in the package if separate first-class postage is paid for the letter in addition to the third-class rate for the package and if the wrapper is marked "Letter Enclosed."

Fourth-Class Mail

Domestic parcel post makes up most of the fourth-class mail, but the classification also includes bound printed matter and the "special fourth-class rate" for books, 16-millimeter films (or films with less width), sound recordings, manuscripts, and a special library rate.

Fourth-class mail includes merchandise, mailable live animals, and all other matter not included in first, second, or third class.

Parcel post service is provided for packages weighing one pound or more. In the conterminous United States, packages mailed from larger post offices are limited to 35 pounds and 84 inches in length and girth combined. However, parcels mailed from smaller offices and any office in Hawaii or Alaska are accepted up to 70 pounds and 108 inches. Rates are determined by weight (fractions of a pound are computed as a full pound) and by distance or zone.

The zones are measured as follows:

- Local Zone (within delivery limits of local post office)
- Zone 1—Within the same sectional center area
- Zone 2—Up to 150 miles
- Zone 3—Up to 300 miles
- Zone 4—Up to 600 miles
- Zone 5—Up to 1,000 miles
- Zone 6—Up to 1,400 miles
- Zone 7—Up to 1,800 miles
- Zone 8—Beyond 1,800 miles

Note: These data represent pieces weighing up to 35 pounds.

Special fourth-class rates apply to books, library materials, educational materials, and some advertising matter. Educational materials include 16-millimeter films and 16-millimeter film catalogs (except films and catalogs mailed to commercial theaters); printed music; printed objective-test materials; sound recordings and magnetic tapes; manuscripts of books, periodical articles, and music; printed educational reference charts processed for preservation; and loose-leaf pages and their binders, consisting of medical information for distribution to doctors, hospitals, medical schools, and medical students. The outside of packages containing books or educational materials must be labeled "SPECIAL FOURTH-CLASS RATE: BOOK (or FILM, etc.)."

Wrapping and cushioning. Two or more packages may be mailed as a single parcel if they are about the same size or shape or if they are parts of one article. They must be securely wrapped or fastened together and must not, together, exceed the fourth-class weight and size limits.

Packages may be excluded from the mail unless they are wrapped in such a way as to ensure safe transport. A package sealed with masking tape or transparent adhesive tape is not acceptable for mailing. Special wrappers and envelopes in a variety of sizes are now available from the post office at cost. These wrappers and envelopes are manufactured to meet the packaging requirements of the U.S. Postal Service. The package to be mailed is simply inserted in an appropriate envelope or wrapper, and a label is prepared and affixed thereon.

Containers in which the goods are to be shipped should be strong enough to retain the contents and protect them from the weight of other parcels with which they will be transported. Corrugated cardboard may be used to protect contents. Cellulose materials, plastic bits, cotton, shredded paper, or tissue paper may be used for lighter items. Special wrappers and envelopes with cushioning interiors may be purchased from the post office at cost.

Nonfragile materials may be wrapped in heavy paper and sealed securely with tape. Thin paper bags are not acceptable. Articles that are self-contained may be mailed without outside packaging or wrapping. However, the post office is not responsible if the surface or finish of the article becomes marred or damaged. A cardboard carton in good condition may be wrapped and sealed with reinforced kraft paper tape or nylon filament tape. Avoid using twine if possible.

Addressing and mailing instructions. All parcel-post packages should be delivered to the post office and not deposited in mailboxes. The following rules should be followed in addressing and labeling the package.

1. The return address of the sender must be shown on the face of each package. If the addresses of the sender and the addressee are close together, label the return address "from" and the addressee's "to." It is always wise to include inside each package the name and address of the sender as well as of the addressee. Addresses should always be written with ink or an indelible marking pencil or typewritten on a label that is affixed to the package. Tied-on tags should be used only with packages too small to contain the complete address. Do not repeat the address on the back of the package.

2. Special inscriptions, such as "Merry Christmas," "Do Not Open until Christmas," or "Happy Birthday," may be written on the wrapper.

3. Packages containing fragile articles such as glassware, china, jewelry, and so forth, must be labeled "FRAGILE."

4. Products that may decay quickly, such as fresh meat or fresh produce, must be labeled "PERISHABLE."

5. The label "DO NOT BEND" may be used only when the contents are fully protected with fiberboard or corrugated cardboard.

Enclosures. Only certain types of handwritten and typewritten materials may be included in parcel-post packages. Invoices and customers' orders may be enclosed with the merchandise stipulated thereon. A letter may be enclosed, provided that the wrapper is marked "Letter Enclosed" or "First-class Enclosure" immediately below the place for postage. Separate first-class postage is charged for such an enclosure in addition to the fourth-class charge for the parcel.

Special handling. To ensure that a parcel-post package receives the fastest possible handling and transportation, the special-handling service may be used, for an additional fee. It does not include special-delivery service. Priority mail or express mail can be used for parcels going over long distances when faster delivery of the parcel is desired.

Express Mail

Express mail is a service provided by the postal system that guarantees overnight domestic delivery of mail. This service was implemented because of a continuing demand for speedier delivery of mail. Various private carriers also provide this service.

Under express mail, there are four offerings:

1. *Express Mail,* which allows for delivery the next day.
2. *Express Mail Custom Designed Service,* which provides for special shipments for customers who make regularly scheduled shipments on a routine basis.
3. *Express Mail Same Day Airport Service,* which provides service between major airports; for this service, the customer takes the mail to the airport.
4. *Express Mail International Service,* which provides service to different countries. A service agreement is required for this service. Check for countries providing this special international service.

Printed Matter

Books and catalogs of 24 or more bound pages (at least 22 of which are printed) and weighing less than 16 ounces apiece are considered third-class mail. Other material that may be mailed at the third-class rate includes circulars and other printed matter, such as proof sheets, corrected proof sheets with related manuscript copy, and bills or statements of account produced by any photographic or mechanical process.

All other matter wholly or partly in writing, except authorized additions to second-, third-, and fourth-class mail, should be sent as first-class mail.

Bulk Mailing

Items that are to be mailed at the special bulk-mailing rate should be enclosed in mail sacks or other suitable containers and separated accoding to ZIP Code area. The containers must be taken to the post office.

If the third-class rate is to be used, postage is computed by rates per pound on the entire mailing at one time. An annual bulk-mailing fee must be paid at or before the first mailing of each calendar year. In addition, a postage permit is required. Under this permit, which may be obtained from the post office for a fee, mail must be prepaid.

If an imprint is used instead of precanceled stamps or meter stamps, the permit imprint may be made by printing press, hand stamp, lithograph, mimeograph, multigraph, addressograph, or a similar device. It may not be typewritten or hand-drawn. The style must conform to the specifications set forth by the United States Postal Service. Each imprint must show the name of the post office and the permit number. The fourth-class bulk rate may be used if at least 300 separately addressed pieces are involved and if they are identical in weight.

Bulky mail, called *slugs,* usually is marked *Hand Stamp* in large red letters. This stamp alerts the handler not to place the bag in canceling machines, which may cause serious damage to the machine and to the contents of the mail piece because of its bulky nature.

Express Mail International Service Destinations

Argentina	Italy
Australia	Japan
Austria	Jordan
Bahamas	Korea, Republic of
Bahrain	Kuwait
Bangladesh	Luxembourg
Barbados	Macao
Belgium	Malaysia
Bermuda	Mali
Brazil	Mexico
Burkina Faso	Netherlands (Holland)
Canada	Netherlands Antilles
Cayman Islands	New Zealand
Chad	Niger
Chile	Nigeria
China, People's Republic of	Norway
Colombia	Oman
Côte d'Ivoire (Ivory Coast)	Pakistan
Cyprus	Panama
Denmark	Portugal
Djibouti	Qatar
Egypt	Saudi Arabia
Finland	Senegal
France	Singapore
Germany, Federal Republic of	South Africa, Republic of
Great Britain and Northern Ireland	Spain
Greece	Sweden
Guyana	Switzerland
Hong Kong	Taiwan
Hungary	Thailand
Iceland	Tunisia
India	Turkey
Indonesia	United Arab Emirates
Ireland	Uruguay
Israel	Venezuela

Airmail

Airmail is no longer specified as such within the 50 states of the United States, as all first-class mail with a destination more than a certain number of miles away is routinely transported by air. Airmail service is also available for some parcels and for overseas mail. The word "AIRMAIL" should appear on all sides of such a parcel. An adhesive label for this purpose is available without charge at the post office. The return address of the sender must be shown on the address side of each air parcel.

International Mail

International mail is mail sent between countries except to overseas military addresses: APO (Army Post Office) and FPO (Fleet Post Office). Certain articles of a dangerous or objectionable nature are generally prohibited in the international mail: poisons, narcotics, intoxicating liquors, most live animals, explosive or flammable articles, obscene or libelous matter, and so on. In addition to these, each country generally prohibits or restricts the importation of various other articles. Such information may be obtained at the post office, provided the country named has made its restrictions known to the post office.

A person or company that wishes to prepay a reply letter from another country may do so by sending the correspondent one or more international reply coupons, which may be purchased at U.S. post offices. To avoid delay and inconvenience, postage on all foreign mail should be prepaid according to weight.

Forwarding foreign mail. Mail arriving in this country from a foreign country may be forwarded to any destination within the United States without additional postage.

Mail may not be forwarded to another foreign country without rewrapping, procuring a customs declaration, and affixing new postage.

U.S. mail to be forwarded to a destination outside the country should always have any additional postage affixed before leaving the United States, because some countries charge double postage for mail arriving with postage due.

International postal union mail. International mail is divided into two general categories: International Postal Union mail and parcel post. Postal union mail includes two classes of matter:

1. LC mail (letters and cards): letters, letter packages, Aerogrammes (air letters), postcards, and postal cards.
2. AO mail (other articles): printed matter, samples, commercial papers, matter for the blind, and small packets.

The special postal services that apply to Postal Union mail are registration with a standard limited indemnity, insurance (though not to all countries), and special delivery in most countries. Consult the post office for details, including what marking the mail should bear.

For all Postal Union mail, the address on all articles must be legible and complete, showing the street name and house number or the post-office box number, the name of the post office, the province (if known), and the country (on the last line). If the item is addressed in a foreign language, the name of the post office, province, and country must also be shown in English. The sender's name and address should be shown in the upper left corner of the address side. All Postal Union articles except letters and letter packages are required to be left unsealed, even if registered.

Mailers must endorse the envelopes or wrappers of all Postal Union articles except letters and postcards to show the classification under which they are being mailed; for example, "Printed Matter," or "Printed Matter—Books." The words "Letter (Lettre)" should be written on the address side of letters or letter packages which, because of their size or manner of preparation, may be mistaken for mail of another classification.

In addition, airmail articles should be plainly endorsed "Par Avion" or have such a label affixed; articles intended for special delivery should be marked boldly as "Express" or "Special Delivery."

International parcel post. Parcel-post packages that exceed certain size limitations are not accepted for mailing to foreign countries. Consult the post office about these and other restrictions.

If the addressee has left a forwarding address, a package will be delivered and the addressee will be charged additional postage, depending upon the weight of the package and the distance forwarded. If there is no forwarding address, the package will be returned to the sender, and a charge will be made for the return postage.

Special Postal Services

Insurance. To assure the sender that payment may be obtained for loss of, rifling of, or damage to domestic mail insurance is available. The fee, which is charged in addition to the regular postage, is based on the assessed value of the parcel. By paying an additional charge, the sender is assured that an insured package will be delivered only to the addressee (see Figure 12-4).

Third-class and parcel-post mail may be insured up to $500. Insurance may be obtained for merchandise mailed at priority or first-class rates. The post office generally obtains a receipt of delivery from the addressee for all articles that are insured for more than $15. Insured mail may contain incidental first-class enclosures, so long as they are noted on the face of the package and paid for at the first-class rate. The mail must bear the complete names and addresses of sender and addressee. Articles not sufficiently well packed and wrapped to withstand normal handling are not acceptable for insurance.

Collect on delivery. A patron can mail an article that has not been paid for and have the price and the cost of the postage collected from the addressee when the article is delivered. Collect-on-delivery service may be used for merchandise sent by parcel-post, first-class, or third-class mail, and the article may be sent as registered mail. Collection is made for the cost of the merchandise and postage, plus the C.O.D. fee; the merchandise cost is returned to the sender by postal money order. The fees include insurance against loss or damage of the merchandise and are limited to a maximum valuation of $400; fees vary according to the amount to be collected.

Registered mail. Additional protection for valuable pieces; irreplaceable articles, regardless of value; and all items valued up to $25,000 may be obtained by using registered mail. This service gives the sender evidence of mailing and delivery and provides security; the mail is controlled throughout the postal system (see Figure 12-5).

The sender is required by law to tell the postal clerk or, if the sender is a company, to enter on the company mailing bill the full value of mail presented for registry. Table 12.1 provides a guide to the required declaration of values of various types of valuable mail.

Only first-class and priority mail may be registered. C.O.D. parcels may be registered, but they will be accepted only at the rate for first-class mail. The registry fees are in addition to postage and include insurance protection up to $25,000 for domestic mail only. In the registry of international mail, the indemnity varies according to the country of the addressee.

TABLE 12.1 Declaration of Value for Different Types of Mail

Kind of Mail	Value to Be Declared

Negotiable instruments
   Instruments payable to bearer and
      matured interest coupons
	Market value

Nonnegotiable instruments
   All registered bonds, warehouse
      receipts, checks, drafts, deeds, wills,
      abstracts, and similar documents
   Certificates of stock, including those
      endorsed in blank
	No value or replacement cost
	   if postal insurance
	   coverage is desired

Money	Full value
Jewelry, gems, precious metals	Market value or cost
Merchandise	Market value or cost

V-596 045 596

Receipt for Insured Mail
UNITED STATES POSTAL SERVICE *(Domestic or International)*

Sent To

Street & No.

PO, State, & ZIP Code

Postage	Airmail ☐	$
Insurance Coverage		Fee
Special Handling		
Domestic Only	Special Delivery	
	Restricted Delivery	
	Return Receipt (Except Canada)	
☐ Fragile ☐ Liquid	☐ Perishable	Total $
Postmark		Postmaster (by)

If Your Article is Lost or Damaged, See Instructions on the Reverse. SAVE THIS RECEIPT UNTIL ARTICLE IS ACCOUNTED FOR

PS Form 3813-P, September 1991

U S Insured Mail

V-596 045 596

NOTE: You must present the article, container, and packaging when filing a claim for damage.

Figure 12-4. Receipt form for insured mail—domestic and international.

Source: U.S. Postal Service

REGISTERED NO.   **POSTMARK**

To Be Completed By Post Office	Reg. Fee $	Special $ Delivery
	Handling $ Charge	Return $ Receipt
	Postage $	Restricted $ Delivery
	Received by	

Domestic Insurance
Is Limited To
$25,000; International
Indemnity Is Limited
(See Reverse)

Customer Must Declare
Full Value $

☐ With Postal Insurance
☐ Without Postal Insurance

FROM

TO

To Be Completed By Customer (Please Print)
All Entries Must Be In Ball Point or Typed

PS Form **3806**, **RECEIPT FOR REGISTERED MAIL** *(Customer Copy)*
April 1991   *(See Information on Reverse)*

SAVE THIS RECEIPT FOR REGISTERED MAIL CLAIMS & INQUIRIES

DECLARATION OF VALUE – Mailers are Required to declare the Full value at the time of mailing on all registered mail articles, whether insurance is desired or not.

WITH POSTAL INSURANCE – Domestic postal insurance against loss or damage may be purchased by paying the appropriate fee. Domestic insurance on registered mail is limited to the lessor of (1) the value of the article at the time of mailing if lost or totally damaged, or (2) the cost of repairs. Consult your postmaster for additional details of insurance limits and coverage for domestic and international registered mail. See sections 149 and 911, Domestic Mail Manual for limitations of coverage.

WITHOUT POSTAL INSURANCE – An article may also be sent by registered mail without postal insurance by paying the appropriate fee. No indemnity will be paid for articles mailed without postal insurance coverage.

TO FILE INSURANCE CLAIM – Claim must be filed within 1 year from the date of mailing. Present this receipt. Claims for complete or partial loss of contents, damage or alleged rifling must be filed immediately. The article, container, and packaging must be presented when filing a complete or partial loss of contents or damage claim. Submit evidence of value or repair costs to substantiate your claim. Inquiries on registered mail claims should not be filed for at least 3 months after the date the original claim was filed.

INTERNATIONAL REGISTERED MAIL – Indemnity coverage for International Registered Mail is limited to the maximum set by the Convention of the Universal Postal Union. Consult postmaster and the International Mail Manual for limitations of coverage and individual country prohibitions and restrictions.

PS Form **3806,** April 1991 (Reverse)

Figure 12-5. Receipt form for registered mail (front and reverse).

Source: U.S. Postal Service

Special delivery. Immediate delivery at the address of the recipient during prescribed hours and within certain distance limits may be assured by payment of a special-delivery fee. Payment of this fee does not ensure the safety of delivery or provide for payment of indemnity; therefore, money or other valuables sent special delivery should be registered also. Insured, certified, and C.O.D. mail may be sent special delivery.

Fees for special-delivery mail sent by regular first class are based on weight. For all other classes of mail, fixed special-delivery fees apply. Special-delivery fees must be paid in addition to regular postage.

Special handling. Special-handling service is available on third-and fourth-class mail only, including insured and C.O.D. mail. It provides preferential handling in transportation but does not provide special delivery. Special-handling parcels are delivered as regular parcel post is delivered. The special-handling fee, which is based upon weight, must be paid on all parcels that require special care, such as baby chicks and packaged bees.

Certified mail. Certified-mail service provides a receipt for the person mailing the item and a record of the delivery of the item from the post office from which it is delivered. No record is kept at the post office at which it is mailed. Certified mail is handled in the ordinary mails and is not covered by insurance. If the matter mailed has no intrinsic value, but the sender wishes to be sure that it has been sent to the correct point of receipt, this service is worthwhile (see Figure 12-6).

Any item on which first-class or priority postage has been paid will be accepted as certified mail. This matter may be sent special delivery if the required postage is also paid. An additional fee is involved if delivery is restricted (*i.e.*, delivery only to the person named in the address) or if a return receipt is requested.

Certificates of mailing. At a fee somewhat lower than that for certified mail, certificates of mailing furnish evidence of mailing only. No receipt is obtained upon delivery of mail to the addressee. The fee does not insure the article against loss or damage (see Figure 12-7).

Return receipt. For mail that is registered, certified, insured, or sent C.O.D. or by express mail, the sender may wish to have evidence that the mail was received. When such proof of delivery is desired, a return receipt should be requested at the time of mailing. It identifies the article by number, the signer, and the date of delivery. Evidence of the exact address of delivery may also be requested. Restricted delivery service may be requested if the sender wants the mail to be delivered only to the addressee or to a particular individual authorized in writing to receive the mail of the addressee. Each of these services requires an additional fee as well as the regular postage (see Figure 12-8).

Money orders. A practical and safe method of sending money through the mail is by postal money order. The fees vary according to the amount sent and also according to whether the order is domestic or international. There is usually no limitation on the number of orders that can be purchased at one time. Lost or stolen money orders can be replaced and copies of payments can be obtained for two years after date of payment.

Z 171 267 008

Receipt for Certified Mail

UNITED STATES
POSTAL SERVICE

No Insurance Coverage Provided
Do not use for International Mail
(See Reverse)

PS Form **3800**, March 1993

Sent to	
Street and No	
P.O. State and ZIP Code	
Postage	$
Certified Fee	
Special Delivery Fee	
Restricted Delivery Fee	
Return Receipt Showing to Whom & Date Delivered	
Return Receipt Showing to Whom, Date, and Addressee's Address	
TOTAL Postage & Fees	$
Postmark or Date	

Fold at line over top of envelope to the right of the return address

CERTIFIED

Z 171 267 008

MAIL

Figure 12-6. Receipt form for certified mail.

Source: U.S. Postal Service

Figure 12-7. Certificate of mailing.

Source: U.S. Postal Service

Thank You for using Return Receipt Service.

I also wish to receive the following services (for an extra fee):

1. ☐ Addressee's Address

2. ☐ Restricted Delivery

Consult postmaster for fee.

4a. Article Number

4b. Service Type
☐ Registered ☐ Insured
☐ Certified ☐ COD
☐ Express Mail ☐ Return Receipt for Merchandise

7. Date of Delivery

8. Addressee's Address (Only if requested and fee is paid)

DOMESTIC RETURN RECEIPT

SENDER:
- Complete items 1 and/or 2 for additional services.
- Complete items 3, and 4a & b.
- Print your name and address on the reverse of this form so that we can return this card to you.
- Attach this form to the front of the mailpiece, or on the back if space does not permit.
- Write "Return Receipt Requested" on the mailpiece below the article number.
- The Return Receipt will show to whom the article was delivered and the date delivered.

3. Article Addressed to:

5. Signature (Addressee)

6. Signature (Agent)

PS Form **3811**, December 1991   ☆U.S. GPO: 1993—352-714

Is your RETURN ADDRESS completed on the reverse side?

Figure 12-8. Domestic Return Receipt.

Source: U.S. Postal Service

Other Postal Services

The U.S. Postal Service also offers a variety of supplemental services to ensure that the mail reaches its destination. Among others, these include: Change of Address Requests for correspondents, publishers, and businesses (Figure 12-9); and a consumer service card for identifying specific mailing problems (Figure 12-10).

Other Instructions about Mail

Recall of mail. At times it is desirable to recall a piece of mail that has already been taken to a post office or dropped into a mailbox. In such instances the sender must go to the post office and complete a written application and present a similar envelope or wrapper to identify the piece of mail being recalled.

Change of address. Prior to moving, each individual or firm should procure from the post office and complete the official U.S. Postal Service change-of-address form. Change-of-address cards are available in quantity, so that all correspondents and publishers of periodicals regularly received may be notified of the new address and the date of its effect. If possible, it is wise to notify the publishers of periodicals six or eight weeks before the move takes place, so that magazines and newspapers are not sent to the old address.

Undeliverable mail. First-class mail that bears no return address cannot be returned to the sender in the event that it is undeliverable. Therefore, it is imperative that all mail have a return address typed or written on it.

Franked mail. The federal government uses "franked" mail—that is, mail sent free of postage. The franked envelope may be used only for surface mail; it may not be used for overseas airmail unless the airmail postage is affixed. There is a federal penalty for misuse of franked mail. A franked piece of mail must have a facsimile or real signature of the sender appearing in the place of the stamp. The words *Official Business* must appear on the address side.

The authorized use of franked mail is limited to certain categories: members and members-elect of Congress, resident commissioners, the Secretary of the Senate, the Sergeant at Arms of the Senate, and the Vice President of the United States.

Penalty mail. Mail pieces falling into this category are also official and free. Penalty mail is used for official government correspondence. The correspondence is enclosed in penalty envelopes or under penalty labels specificially marked *Official Business—Penalty for Private Use*. In some cases, the amount of the penalty may be printed.

Free mail. Mail pieces falling into this category are sent without postage by the general public, such as census mail and absentee ballot envelopes from members of the armed forces and military personnel of the United States.

Figure 12-9. Form for a change of address request.

Source: U.S. Postal Service

U.S. POSTAL SERVICE CONSUMER SERVICE CARD

| 1 PRINT FIRMLY | 2 REMOVE TOP COPY FOR CUSTOMER RECORD (do not separate remaining copies) | 3 FILL IN ADDRESS BLANK ON BACK OF LAST CARD | 4 MAIL (postage free) |

No. M 10 899 315

Name

Date (Mo., Day, Yr.)

Address (Apt./Suite No., No. and Street, City)

State   **ZIP Code**   **Customer Phone** (8 a.m.–5 p.m.)

Is This
☐ Information Request   ☐ Suggestion   ☐ Problem   ☐ Compliment

Did It Involve
If This Is A Problem With A Specific Mailing, Please Complete The Following:

Did It Involve	Was It	Was Mailing
Delay	Letter	First-Class
Nonreceipt	Package	Special Delivery
Damage	Newspaper/ Magazine	Certified
Misdelivery	Advertisement	Registered
Improperly Returned	Electronic Transmission	Insured
Change of Address		Express Mail
Vending Equipment		Other
Window Services		
Personnel		
Other		

This Section Is For USPS Use Only

Recording Employee Name

Date Customer Contacted   Customer Contacted By

USPS Action

Please Give Essential Facts (If this involves a change of address problem, please include previous address.)

THANK YOU. You will be contacted soon by your Post Office.

PS Form 4314-C, July 1991   CUSTOMER COPY - 1

Figure 12-10. Form for consumer service (card).

Source: U.S. Postal Service

Unmailable items. The following items may not be sent through the U.S. mails. In fact, penalties are imposed on the mailers of these items.

Meat and meat-food products without certificate of inspection

Plants and plant products not accompanied by required certificate; certain plants are prohibited from shipment into certain states by quarantine order (before attempting to mail plants, consult a postal authority)

Poisons, except those for scientific use and those sent to licensed dealers

Intoxicating liquors

Narcotics and other controlled substances as defined by federal regulations

Explosive, flammable, corrosive, or toxic substances

Live animals, except tiny ones that need no care, as bees, earthworms, or day-old chicks

Poisonous reptiles and insects and all kinds of snakes

Foul-smelling articles

Dangerous mechanical devices or machines

Sharp-pointed or sharp-edged tools insufficiently protected

Firearms capable of being concealed on the person (with exceptions)

Radioactive material, unless special permission is granted and special packaging and labeling requirements are met

Matter tending to incite arson, murder, assassination, insurrection, or treason

Indecent matter, written or other

Defamatory, dunning, or threatening matter on post cards or on the outside of any piece of mail

Endless-chain enterprises, or fraudulent matter

Mail opened by mistake. At times mail is delivered to the wrong address and opened by mistake. When this happens, the person who opens it should simply reseal the envelope with tape and write "Opened by Mistake." The mail should then be dropped into a mailbox or handed to the mail carrier.

Express

Most things that can be transported can be sent by express, but nothing irreplaceable should be sent by this means. Valuable papers, such as bonds, can be sent by express, provided that they can be replaced. Certain items are barred from express shipments, such as those containing acids or corrosives, antiques, artworks, coins, explosives, gems or jewelry, or uncrated household goods. Consult the nearest express agency office for other specific limitations.

Preparation for shipment. The following information must be given to the express company before a shipment can be made:

Consignee's name and local address
Value of shipment
Number of pieces of shipment and type of container
Weight
Description of articles shipped
Shipper's name and address
Information regarding payment

The address of the shipper and the consignee should both be written on the packing slip and also enclosed in the package.

Domestic Air Express

Air express is available for those cities having airports. The service is extended to the areas surrounding such cities, but an additional charge is made to "off-line" points outside the area served by the airport. The nearest express office should be queried as to the exact points to which delivery is made without additional charge.

Many airlines accept small packages and envelopes for airport-to-airport delivery; the item will be held for pickup at the luggage-return area or at the air express office.

Package Express by Bus

Bus lines offer package express within the United States and Canada. Consult them for information on rates, requirements, restrictions, and schedules.

Prohibited articles. The following are not accepted for shipment by bus:

Acids or corrosive substances
Alcoholic beverages and liquors
Animals, live, including birds and reptiles
Articles packed in wet ice or water
Batteries, electric-storage, wet
Dangerous articles, including ammunition, explosives, and flammable
    materials
Fluorescent signs
Gases in cylinders
Jewelry, when the declared value is more than $50
Materials having a disgreeable odor
Money
Neon signs or bent neon tubing
Wild game, killed
X-ray tubes

ELECTRONIC MAIL SERVICES

Electronic Mail

Electronic mail is the popular term for many of the new forms of communication that use computer and telecommunications technology. Commonly referred to as E-mail, it is the communication of text, data, voice, and image messages between a sender and a recipient using system links. The secretary should stay informed of new features as they become available because technology is constantly advancing.

There are several advantages to electronic mail. One is the high speed with which large amounts of data can be transmitted. Another is that data can be distributed to a specific location and stored in electronic form until they are needed by the recipient.

E-mail uses computers, modems, and telephone lines to transmit messages in a quick, reliable, and timely manner from one computer to another, turning your computer into an electronic mailbox. Messages can be sent to multiple destinations simultaneously and can be stored and retrieved at will. The transmittals do not require paper, time differences do not cause any difficulty, and systems operate 24 hours a day. Messages can be sent in-house, to other firms in the same city or across the country, or to foreign countries.

E-mail is rapidly becoming an indispensable tool in communications. Not only do companies use E-mail for in-house communication but also for many employees who work at home from computer workstations and terminals. With the use of public access networks, it is possible to link host computer facilities simply, through a local phone call from almost anywhere in the world.

E-mail is implemented with several different technologies, among them facsimile transmission, telex, communicating word processors, microcomputers and other computer-based networks, electronic document distribution systems, and voice technologies.

Facsimile (Fax)

Facsimile transmission is a rapidly advancing telecommunications technology. Facsimile, or fax, is becoming widely used nationally and internationally, because of its low cost and extreme ease of use. Fax machines are nowin many business offices and all secretaries should know how to use them effectively.

Facsimile is the transmission of a copy of a document by electronic means. A special copying machine, called a facsimile unit or copier, sends the images of a document over telephone lines to a similar copying machine in another location. The telephone line is the connection; without the telephone the system cannot work. The distance between two fax units is irrelevant. Information can be sent to another office in the same building or across the continent. Virtually any document—photographs, diagrams, statistical information, and handwritten or typewritten language messages—can be telecopied within a matter of minutes. The transmitted document looks exactly like the original.

Fax units can store and forward information. They also have delay features that permit automatic dialing of one of more stations so that unattended transmission to multiple locations is possible on a 24-hour basis. Also, fax transmissions can be sent directly from any computer that has a fax/modem.

Mailgram®

A Mailgram® is an electronic form of communication that is a joint venture between Western Union and the U.S. Postal Service. It has the advantage of a low-cost, high impact message. The messages are transmitted by the wire facilities of Western Union to any address in the United States, Puerto Rico, Guam, the U.S. Virgin Islands, or Canada for delivery the next business day. After the local Western Union office receives the message, it is sent electronically to the destination post office for delivery to the addressee. Western Union has installed in certain post offices equipment that receives messages on a continuous roll of paper. A post office employee tears off the message, inserts it in a window envelope, and distributes it for delivery in the next business day's mail. The cost of a Mailgram® depends on the number of words.

An International Mailgram® is a cost-effective overnight letter that can be sent to the United Kingdom, the Netherlands, Argentina, Denmark, and the Philippines. It is transmitted electronically to the destination country and delivered through the local postal system with the next day's mail.

Priority Letter

A priority letter is also a service of Western Union and is a low-cost alternative to a Mailgram®. It can be sent anywhere in the United States—just as a Mailgram®—and delivered within two days. The following characters are not permitted in a priority letter:

- =   equal sign
- >   greater than symbol
- <   less than symbol
- [left bracket
-]   right bracket

Telegram

A telegram does not have the popularity it once had because it has been replaced by newer forms of communication, such as E-mail and FAX. However, it is still a valid form of communications for sending messages anywhere in the continental United States. A telegram is transmitted through Western Union and the message will be telephoned to the recipient. If the sender wants a printed message to follow, that must be indicated. Many offices require that a typed copy be placed in their files. The typed telegram is

Figure 12-11. Western Union Mailgram® correctly filled out.

spaced to fit the printed lines on the form. The cost of a telegram may be charged to the sender's telephone number. The message should be brief because the number of words determines the cost.

Telegrams are accepted for immediate transmission for delivery within two hours by telephone and five hours by messenger, subject to the open hours of the delivery office and special holiday conditions.

Cablegram

A cablegram is an international telegram that can be sent to almost every country in the world in the language of the recipient. A cablegram is also sent via Western Union and is usually delivered within 24 hours. A cablegram is most often printed out and hand delivered, but in some areas of the world it may be mailed or telephoned to the recipient. The following characters are not permitted in a cablegram:

$ dollar sign
&   ampersand
#   pound sign
%   percent sign
/   slash
"   quotation marks
;   semicolon

Note: Mailgrams®, priority letters, telegrams, and cablegrams can be sent from a computer if the sender has a telex and/or E-mail service from a major

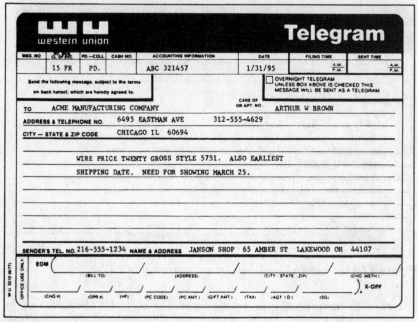

Figure 12-12. Western Union telegram form correctly filled out.

service provider. There are also local companies that provide these services. Many of these companies will be listed in the Yellow Pages.

Telex

Although telexes are very much part of the business environment, they are being replaced by E-mail and newer forms of electronic communications, especially for the transmission of domestic messages. Telexes offer the time-liness of a telephone call and the "paper copy" of a letter. Telex messages can be sent to domestic and international locations 24 hours a day, 7 days a week. International telex service requires a country code, which precedes the telex number. For a listing of telex numbers, consult a telex directory. For a listing of country codes, contact the local telex service company. (Some services offer on-line country codes.) To communicate with companies having telex equipment in their overseas offices, call the Telex Center of one of the international carriers, identify yourself, and give the area code for the country being called, plus the telex number of the receiver.

THE TELEPHONE

Despite the vast number of devices, methods, and alternatives for communicating information, the telephone remains the most popular means of communication. It allows for communication between two or more persons, and it is the key instrument in initiating telecommunications networks worldwide.

Since the telephone is such an important communication device, it is essential that the secretary use it to its maximum effectiveness and be familiar with its peripheral equipment.

Telephone Techniques

It is important for the secretary to keep up with the constantly expanding services available from the telephone company, as well as the many and varied pieces of equipment that can add to the efficient operation of the business office. The telephone is the most frequently used audio-communication medium in the business world. The dependence upon this instrument has grown so that currently over 900 million telephone calls are made daily.

The reputation and good will of the employer and the firm may depend upon the secretary's approach and skill in using the telephone. Although most people in our society begin to use the telephone in early childhood, perhaps the majority of them still need to be trained in proper telephone techniques. An impressive way to point out defects in techniques, and one that results in a rapid and desirable change, is to make a recording or tape of a telephone conversation. Such a recording emphasizes the faults in telephone techniques and vividly points out areas needing improvement. Many organizations, even though they are efficiently organized, lose customers, money, and good will simply because of employees' poor telephone habits.

Speaking Clearly and Pleasantly

People talking on a phone have no visual image on which to base impressions. The frame of reference is based entirely upon the voice coming over the wires. If these sounds are jarring or unpleasant, a busy executive may quickly lose patience and discontinue association with the firm in question. On the other hand, a pleasant and understanding voice coming over an inanimate instrument can accomplish wonders. The power of the spoken word can and does exert a great impact upon the listener.

The telephone is not a nuisance instrument designed to interrupt the secretary in the midst of some important or complicated task. It is, rather, a vital business communication facility that assists the employee in carrying out duties and responsibilities.

In order to enhance one's telephone personality, it is necessary to inject variety and flexibility into the voice, so as to convey mood and attitude in telephone conversations. These qualities can be obtained through pitch, inflection, and emphasis. The development of these qualities is individual. A high-pitched voice may convey an impression of childishness and immaturity or of impatience and irritability. On the other hand, a voice that is well modulated carries the impression of culture and polish. "Pitch" in speaking, like "pitch" in music, refers to the key in which one speaks. Everyone has a range of tone within which a pleasant speaking voice is possible, and it can be consciously controlled. Each person must be conscious of his or her own range and practice utilizing it effectively. An individual is said to speak in a "modulated" voice when the pitch is in the lower half of the possible range. This tonal range carries best and is easiest to hear over the telephone.

In cultivating an interesting telephone personality it is essential that the speaker enunciate clearly and distinctly. A garbled and indistinct speech pattern will annoy the listener who cannot understand what is being said. Do not be afraid to move the lips. One cannot form rounded vowel sounds or distinct consonants unless the lips accomplish their function. It is not necessary to exaggerate or to become stilted; clear enunciation and pronunciation should be made a part of the secretary's natural, daily speech pattern, because it is just as important in face-to-face conversations as in telephone conversations. The secretary's voice should reflect his or her personality and transmit alertness and pleasantness. It should be natural, distinct, and expressive, and neither too loud nor too soft. Avoid repetitious, mechanical words and phrases.

Answering Promptly

Answering a business telephone call is similar to welcoming a visitor. Therefore, it is essential that each call be greeted by a prompt, effective, and pleasing answer.

The telephone should be placed on the secretary's desk so that it is readily accessible. A pad and pencil or pen should be kept handy in order to jot down necessary information. These should not be used for doodling when speaking on the phone; this habit distracts the secretary from the business at hand and interferes with giving the caller undivided attention.

When the telephone rings, answer it promptly—at the first or second ring, if possible. Try not to put incoming calls immediately on "hold"; many callers find this practice infuriating. If it becomes increasingly necessary to do this, the employer should be alerted. It may be desirable to install another telephone line and to hire another person, if only for the busiest hours of the day, to help handle incoming calls.

If the secretary finds it necessary to leave the desk, arrangements should be made to have someone else answer the telephone and take the messages during that interval. The telephone should not be left unattended. An unanswered telephone becomes an instrument of failure—failure to the company because of the loss of customers and failure of the individuals responsible.

In many businesses, an answering unit is used. This machine will record a message after a "beep" usually preceded by a message.

Identifying Who Is Answering

For efficiency, the office should be identified immediately when the phone is answered. The secretary's name may also be given. It is correct to say, "Mr. Wright's office; Miss Dubrowski speaking," or the firm name may be used, as, "Smith and Grey; this is Mr. Lopez." When the telephone is answered in this fashion, the caller is assured that the proper office has been reached.

Avoid answering the business telephone by saying, "Hello." Using this form of greeting is much like saying, "Guess who this is," and is unbusinesslike. Business people have no time to play guessing games, and this form of address can become irritating.

In answering calls for others, identify yourself and the office of the person whose calls are being taken. For example, "Miss Jones's office; Mr. Liska speaking." Unless this is done, the caller will not know whether the right person has been reached at all. If the caller expects to hear the voice of Miss Jones's secretary, he or she may be taken aback when an unfamiliar voice comes over the wire. The fact that the correct office has been reached is made clear at once.

Identifying Who Is Calling

The wise secretary develops a keen ear and learns to recognize the voices of important or frequent callers. However, a word of caution. Do not become too sure of an infallible ear, for voices may sound different over the telephone. If the voice is known beyond a doubt, use the caller's name when speaking. If the voice has been identified correctly, the caller will be pleased to be recognized and addressed by name. Then speak *to the person* at the other end of the wire, not *at the telephone*. If the secretary was incorrect in identifying the voice before divulging any information, little harm was done, since the caller will make the correction. Apologize tactfully and take up the business at hand. However, when the name of the caller is not revealed and/or the nature of the business is not identified, the secretary's skill at diplomacy comes into play.

Many executives prefer their secretaries to screen incoming calls. This must be done with tact and discretion. In some cases the executive will speak with anyone who calls but would like to know beforehand who is calling and the nature of the business. It is the secretary's duty to obtain this information before transferring the call to the executive. Curtness and rudeness must be avoided in doing so. It is correct to say, for example, "May I tell Mr. Brown who is calling?" or "Mrs. Winslow is talking on another line. Would you care to wait, or may I have her call you? I believe her other call may take some time." or "Mr. Zobkiw is in conference. May I help you?" Be sincere and courteous in your explanation, but do not divulge information unnecessarily. Your goal is simply to find out tactfully who is calling.

Screening Calls

Although some executives answer the telephone themselves, many depend upon their secretaries to answer all incoming calls. The secretary must, therefore, be familiar with the executive's preferences. It is important to learn which calls the secretary is expected to handle, which are to be referred to the executive, and which should be transferred to someone else. Consequently, the secretary must classify telephone callers accurately and quickly. Every call is important. Enough information must be ascertained to classify the call. A caller cannot be allowed to get to the end of a long inquiry before being referred to the proper person. In order to forestall this, the secretary may make a discreet vocal sound that may cause the caller to pause slightly so that the secretary may say, "Mr. Chan in the shipping department should be able to help you with this. Please let me transfer your call to him."

Handling the Call

Generally the calls that can be handled by the secretary are as follows:

Requests for information. The secretary can handle this type of call if the information is not confidential and if there is no doubt concerning the facts. Sometimes it may be necessary to check with the employer before imparting information. If any complications arise, it is always wiser to turn the call over to the executive. In certain situations, the secretary may ask for a letter of request and, upon its receipt and approval, respond.

Requests for appointments. The secretary is sometimes authorized to make appointments for the employer. However, both the executive's and the secretary's diary should be checked before any appointments are made in order to avoid conflicts. If the employer is out of the office, the appointment should be verified immediately upon return. Commitments could easily have been made about which the executive had either forgotten to inform the secretary or the opportunity had not yet arisen to have had them entered in the desk calendars.

Receiving information. Often the secretary can conserve the employer's time by taking down telephone information. If the message is taken in shorthand, this must be transcribed as soon as possible and placed on the employer's desk.

Transferring calls. If the call cannot be handled by the secretary or the employer, it should be transferred to the office that can give the caller the information sought. This should be done only with the caller's permission. If transferral is refused, obtain the information and call back. If the caller agrees to a transfer, make sure that the right office is reached and give the person in that office sufficient information before hanging up so that the caller will not need to repeat it.

When taking calls from persons who wish to speak to the executive directly, the secretary must know how to handle the following situations tactfully, discreetly, and diplomatically.

1. The employer is in and free. The executive is informed of who is calling. On occasion, if the caller is well known to the employer and someone to whom the executive talks frequently, the secretary may signal the executive to pick up the telephone.
2. The employer is in but does not want to be disturbed. The caller is told that the executive is engaged at the moment and asks whether a message

may be taken. If the caller insists on speaking to the executive person-ally, ask if a callback may be made as soon as the employer is free.

3. The employer is in another office in the building. The secretary should ascertain whether the executive will be available for telephone calls when away from the office. Generally only the most urgent calls should be transferred under such circumstances.

Taking Messages

It is good practice to keep a written record of all incoming calls, particularly when the executive is away from the office. The secretary should indicate the time the call was received; the name, business affiliation, and telephone number of the caller; and the message. The note may be signed with the secretary's initials. If the message is from an out-of-town caller, the area code or the telephone operator's number should also be recorded. It is best when taking a message to read it back to the caller in order to avoid errors or misunderstandings. Messages should always be taken verbatim. Be patient and pleasant but persistent. Ask the caller to spell out both first and last names if necessary. If numbers are involved, repeat the sequence for verification.

When a call is taken, the "phone message" slip should be placed on the executive's desk immediately. The secretary will also anticipate the executive's needs by attaching to the slips any material (possibly annotated) that may be necessary for reference in order to conclude the transaction successfully—back correspondence, a bill, price lists, or whatever may assist the executive in handling the call intelligently.

To be able to handle the incoming calls more efficiently, the secretary should know where the executive will be when away from the office, whether urgent messages can be relayed, and the expected time of return to the office.

Also, in taking calls for other persons in the office, it is helpful if one can state when the person called will return or whether the call can be transferred somewhere else. It is best to offer whatever information is possible; otherwise the caller may get the impression of being put off with an excuse. Be courte-ous, and use discretion in explaining an absence from the office. It is less offensive to say, "Miss Jones is away from her desk just now. May I have her call you, or would you prefer to leave a message?" than to say bluntly, "She's out," or "This is her coffee break," or "I don't know where she is." The secre-tary must always use tact in dealing with callers, whether it be for one's own executive or for another secretary whose calls are being taken.

Taking Action

The secretary should promise the caller some definite action and see to it that the promise is kept. If the caller is told that the executive will call back, then this information must be conveyed to the employer so that the call can be made. A broken promise can result in a canceled order or a lost customer, and it may take many months to regain lost good will.

```
┌─────────────────────────────────────────────┐
│  To ____ Mr. Lopez _____             │
│                                    A.M. ☒    │
│  Date __10/21___ Time __10__       P.M. ☐    │
│                                              │
│        WHILE YOU WERE OUT                    │
│                                              │
│  M _s. Butler_____             │
│                                              │
│  of _Millenium, Inc._____             │
│                                              │
│  Phone __212 - 491 - 0001  x 24__            │
│  Area Code        Number        Extension    │
│  ┌──────────────┬──┬──────────────┬──┐       │
│  │ TELEPHONED   │ ✓│ PLEASE CALL  │ ✓│       │
│  ├──────────────┼──┼──────────────┼──┤       │
│  │ CALLED TO SEE YOU│ WILL CALL AGAIN│       │
│  ├──────────────┼──┼──────────────┼──┤       │
│  │ WANTS TO SEE YOU │              │  │       │
│  ├──────────────┤  │  URGENT      │  │       │
│  │ RETURNED YOUR CALL│            │  │       │
│  └──────────────┴──┴──────────────┴──┘       │
│                                              │
│  Message _The appointment is__               │
│  _at 2 p.m., 10/22._____               │
│  _____             │
│  _____             │
│  _____             │
│                        J.E.                  │
│                      Operator                │
└─────────────────────────────────────────────┘
```

Figure 12-13. Telephone message slip.

On some calls that the secretary can handle, more information may be needed than is within immediate reach. Therefore, it may become necessary to leave the telephone to look up the necessary information and to inform the caller of this fact and of the length of time it may take to obtain the material. Offer the caller a choice of waiting or of being called back. The caller should never be left waiting for an unreasonable amount of time. If a promise is made to call back with the needed information, this promise must be honored.

If the caller is waiting to speak to the executive, the secretary should reassure the caller periodically that the call will be connected as soon as the employer is free. Otherwise the caller will be uncertain as to whether the call is still connected, and a minute's silent delay will seem like a half-hour's wait. When the secretary is ready to transfer the call, thank the caller for waiting.

Completing the Incoming Call

At the completion of the call, indicate its end by summing up the details. Use the caller's name when saying a pleasant "Goodbye." It is courteous to wait for the caller to end the call. Permitting the caller to say "Goodbye" first also allows time for last-minute orders or special instructions. The receiver should be replaced gently in its cradle, for the pleasantest "Goodbye" can be spoiled by the jarring sound of a receiver dropped into position. Do not hang up until your caller has done so first.

Limiting Personal Calls

Because of the secretary's status and the prestige of that position, an example should be set for the office personnel by refraining from making and accepting personal calls during business hours except those that stay strictly within the rules set by the employer. The policy of the company or executive should be determined by the secretary at the very beginning of employment.

Telephone Dictation

The secretary might be called upon to take dictation over the telephone. For this reason a notebook and pen should be placed near the telephone and ready for use. The caller is always informed of the fact that the conversation will be taken by the secretary. The secretary picks up the receiver and indicates readiness to record the proceedings. In the case of telephone dictation the dictator cannot tell whether the secretary is getting all the information. Therefore it is necessary for the secretary to repeat the material phrase by phrase as it is taken down. This informs the dictator as to the rate of dictation, clarity of reception, and errors in grammar or facts. Corrections can then be made immediately instead of waiting until the end of the dictation. If the dictation is too fast, it is best to indicate this immediately. It is a good practice to read back the notes at the end of the dictation to ensure that the correct information was received and recorded. The notes should be transcribed as soon as possible, and a copy should be sent to the telephone dictator.

Telephone Reference Materials

The efficient secretary must be aware of the available sources of information that will be of help in placing a call expeditiously, skillfully, and economically. Directories and booklets published by the telephone company provide much information. A desk file for frequently used numbers should be maintained. A secretary with a computer terminal may create a database for telephone reference materials and retrieve information from it in a matter of seconds.

Telephone Directories

Telephone directories contain three general sections—the introductory pages, the alphabetical listing of subscribers (which may be divided into subsections), and the classified section, familiarly known as "the Yellow Pages." In many areas of the country, all three sections appear in one volume of the telephone directory. However, in metropolitan areas where the listings are voluminous, the classified section is a separate book.

The introductory section contains a lot of useful information. It gives instructions on what numbers to call in various types of emergencies, where to place service calls, how to ask for directory assistance, how to make mobile and marine calls, and the different types of calls that can be made. It lists area codes for faster calling and sample rates for long-distance and person-to-person calls. It explains how to make collect calls; how to call overseas; how to call the telephone company's business office and the operators who handle customer information; where to pay bills and transact business in person; and what modern telephone services are available to the customer. A map illustrates area code zones.

The subscriber section lists in alphabetical sequence the names, addresses, and telephone numbers of the telephone subscribers in a locality, borough, town, village, city, or county. Sometimes the kind of business or the occupation of a subscriber is also shown. In some large directories, business, professional, and organizational listings are given in a separate section from that for residences. Government offices may also be listed in still another section.

At the top outside corner of each page, guide names, or "telltales," indicate the first and last listings on the page for quick location of the page on which a particular name appears. If a name might be spelled in several ways, a cross-reference spelling directs the user to additional listings. The divisions, departments, or branch offices of an organization with separate telephone listings are usually indented under the firm name. Alternate call listings (telephone numbers to be called when no one answers the regular numbers) can be found in the telephone directory. These listings indicate Governmental agencies and state, county, and municipal offices are shown with major headings for the principal listing and indented entries for subordinate departments and divisions.

The local alphabetical and classified directories are usually distributed to all subscribers. Out-of-town directories may be purchased by calling the telephone business office.

Street-Address Directories

In some cities, street-address directories are available and may be rented from the telephone company. These directories list telephone numbers according to the alphabetical and numerical arrangements of streets in that city. They are of special value and usefulness to credit and collection agencies and for companies or organizations who desire to make up mailing lists.

Desk Telephone Files

For efficiency and expediency, a file of numbers and area codes should be compiled. This list consists of

1. business numbers the employer calls frequently and, possibly, taxi, railroad-terminal, and airline numbers

2. emergency numbers for ambulance service, fire department, police department, and so on
3. personal numbers of the employer's family
4. extension numbers in other offices
5. frequently called long-distance numbers, with notations indicating the difference in time zones

Unlisted numbers should be added to this list, with an identifying mark indicating the nature of such a number. Unlisted numbers are never revealed without specific instructions from the executive to do so. They were given to the employer for personal use, and this fact should be respected.

It is a good idea when compiling a telephone list to make it as informative as possible. The secretary should identify individual names by noting title and company affiliation in addition to the address and telephone number and area code. In entering the name, address, and telephone number of an organization, also indicate the name and title or department of the person or persons with whom the secretary or the employer talks most frequently.

The placement of the telephone list depends upon its size. If quite short, it may be taped neatly to the top or the slide panel of the desk; if long, it may be kept in a book or on a rotary file attached to or near the telephone.

Database Files

Because electronic communication is used in today's automated office, the secretary may have access to a terminal or workstation. To automate telephonic communications, create databases for telephone reference materials and desk telephone files. Then, you can easily retrieve complete citations for easy reference as well as make changes and additions within seconds. The advantage is not having to handle a book and check via a system to find the data needed. Simply key the data to initiate retrieval. Such databases help speed up directory assistance inquiries. Instead of paging through phone books, operators input a name, and a list of possibilities appears on the screen. Through scrolling, the desired number, if listed, is revealed.

Assembling Data for Outgoing Calls

In order to place outgoing calls quickly for the employer, the secretary should master all the telephone techniques that enable one to do this skillfully. Be absolutely certain of the telephone number before calling. Then assemble all the information that may be necessary to conduct the business transaction when the call is put through. It may be necessary to obtain materials from the files to refresh the executive's memory on previous business or other information that will be of help in making a successful call. All pertinent material should be placed on the executive's desk before the call is made.

It is also a good practice to be sure the executive will be free and available to take the call as soon as it goes through. Delay may not only lower the prestige of the company and the executive and cause annoyance but also prove costly to the firm making the call.

The question frequently arises as to which executive should answer first. Courtesy prescribes that the caller should be on the line, ready to talk, when the person called is put on the line by his or her own secretary, particularly if the person called outranks the caller. The secretary should put the executive on the line immediately, if possible. This can be done readily if the secretary identifies the employer when the call is answered. The secretary at the other end will then be able to transfer the call to the person called without delay or immediately inform the caller of how to reach that individual.

Long-Distance Services

In addition to business calls within the local community or surrounding areas, it frequently becomes necessary to place calls to more distant points.

Toll Calls

Long-distance calls are those made from one town or city to another town or city outside of a local calling area. A charge is made for such calls in addition to the charge for the regular telephone service. The amount of the charge depends upon the distance, the type of service requested, the time of day or night the call is made, and the time taken for the conversation.

There are two classes of long-distance calls—station-to-station and person-to-person.

Station-to-station calls. Any state in the United States can be reached by direct dialing today. The telephone directory carries a listing of cities and states and their area codes. In order to place a call to any of these localities, dial "1," the area code, and the local telephone number. If the city or town is not listed at the front of the telephone directory, refer to the area code directory.

A station-to-station call is made to a particular telephone number, and the caller speaks to anyone who answers the telephone. Therefore, if someone answers the ring, the individual making the call is charged for it, and the charges start as soon as the call is answered. However, this type of call is less costly, is more frequently made, and is usually faster than the person-to-person call.

Person-to-person calls. To place a person-to-person call, the secretary dials zero, the three-digit area code, and the telephone number; at this point the operator intercepts and the secretary gives the name of the individual being called. When the call is put through, the person called may not be present or available to take the call. Then a decision may have to be made as to whether someone else at that number can handle the transaction. A person-to-person call is made to a particular person only, and the caller is not charged for the call unless the person called is reached or the caller consents to speak to some other specifically identified individual. Charges start as soon as the caller consents to the call and begins speaking; therefore, the secretary should not start a conversation, but must make sure that the employer is ready to take the call immediately. A "1" is not needed in person-to-person calls because the operator intercepts.

Direct Distance Dialing.

Almost all calls in the United States and abroad may be put through by means of direct distance dialing. A "1" must precede the area code. A list of the area codes for direct dialing is found at the beginning of the telephone directory or in the expanded area code directory available from the telephone company. The direct dialing system works by dialing "1" and a three-digit area code, followed by the local telephone number. There are no two areas that have the same area code, nor are there two identical telephone numbers in an area. The numbers of adjacent geographical area codes are widely different numerically to help avoid confusion and error. It is a quick and accurate system. If a wrong number is reached, the secretary, before disconnecting, should find out the name of the city that was reached. He or she should then dial the operator, or in some cases the credit bureau, and promptly report that an incorrect destination was reached, so that the telephone bill will not reflect a charge for the wrong number. Also, if the transmission was poor or the call was cut off, the operator or the credit bureau should be called so that the appropriate adjustment may be made.

The phone directory also explains how to use direct dialing for credit card and collect calls and for overseas calls. A "1" must also precede the area code.

Time Differences

It is vital to check the differences in time when planning to place a long-distance call. One must be aware not only that this country is divided into time zones, but also that certain regions change to daylight saving time during the summer months and that differences in time exist in all countries. For example, the United States (excluding Alaska and Hawaii) is divided into four standard-time zones: Eastern, Central, Mountain, and Pacific. Each zone is one hour earlier than the zone immediately to the east of it: when it is 12 noon Eastern Standard Time, it is 11 A.M. in the Central zone, 10 A.M. in the Mountain zone, and 9 A.M. Pacific time. Greenwich Mean Time, which is the mean solar time of the meridian at Greenwich, England, is used as the basis for standard time throughout most of the world. For specific time information, consult the tables in Chapter 23.

Sequence Calls

The sequence-calls service is of value when a number of calls are to be made to out-of-town points. Much time is saved by furnishing the operator with a list, oral or written, of the calls to be made at the specified times. The secretary should supply the names of the individuals to be called, the cities and states where they are located, their telephone numbers, if known, and the hour at which the executive wishes to speak to each person on the list. However, it should be noted that this is an expensive procedure, as each call is charged at the "operator-assisted call" rate. If the secretary makes the calls by direct dialing, money is saved.

Collect Calls

Calls can be charged to the phone of the person who is being called. The individual called may either accept the call and be charged for it or refuse the call and not be charged. Collect call rates are higher than direct-dialed station-to-station rates. A subscriber can also charge to his or her own phone long-distance calls placed from other phones. The secretary should determine from whom collect charges will be honored. If in doubt, ask the operator to wait while the matter is checked with the executive.

Overseas Calls

The secretary can direct-dial many overseas points. Information on such calls can be obtained from the front pages of the directory, the International Dial brochures, or from the long-distance operator. For person-to-person overseas calls, the secretary must dial the long-distance operator and ask for an overseas operator. The name of the person to be called and the telephone number, if known, must be provided. The charges for this service are higher than those for domestic calls. There are reduced rates for evenings and for nights and weekends.

Calls to Ships, Planes, Trains, and Automobiles

Telephone calls to mobile conveyances by way of radiotelephone are similarly made by the operator. Such service is not available without the installation of special equipment by the telephone company in the car, plane, or ship, of course. Calls can then be placed directly from the office telephone to the destination desired.

Returning Long-Distance Calls

Frequently a long-distance call is received when the executive is not in the office to take it. In such a case, the long-distance operator will give the secretary the operator's number, the city calling, and the name and telephone number of the person calling. To return the call, the secretary must dial the operator, ask by number for the operator who placed the call, and identify the city from which the call originated. When the connection is made with the proper operator, the secretary should tell the employer the name and telephone number of the person who placed the call. Collect calls are excluded from this service.

Telephone Record Keeping

Many organizations require that a record be kept of all long-distance calls made, in order to verify the telephone bill, and have special printed forms for this purpose. The secretary may ask the telephone operator, when placing such calls, to provide the charges when the call is completed. However, the request for charges must be made in advance, not after the call is completed. If you log long-distance calls, record the following: date, time, length of conversation, and caller.

Special Telephone Equipment and Services

A good secretary should be familiar with the various types of telephone equipment and services available in order to meet the needs of the company and those of the executive. Huge strides have been made in the field of telephone research, and equipment and services are evolving at a rapid pace. The following are some of the customary features available from the telephone company or from the secondary services to your telephone subscription.

Multibutton phones are basic telephones that are typically used in small offices to place, answer, screen, and transfer calls. Electronic phones offer enhanced features such as touch-tone dialing, multiple-tone ringing, multiple-line pickup.

Automatic call distributor phones are used by companies that cater exclusively to call-in customers (hotels, airlines, mail-order firms, etc.). A taped message will inform the caller that he or she is queued and that the call will be answered by the next available operator.

Speakerphones allow for more than one person in a room to participate in a call.

Conference calls are available as an option from the telephone company. Those who are not subscribers can still make conference calls. Consult the long-distance carrier for details.

Call waiting will sound a short tone to let the user know there is someone else trying to call. The user can press down the switch hook, putting the original conversation on hold, and speak to the person waiting.

Call forwarding transfers calls to another number when the called party is not at the office or at home.

Three-way calling allows a third party to cut into an existing conversation.

Speed dialing enables the user to store those numbers that are dialed frequently and then to access the numbers with a simple code.

Voice mail plays a personalized message, generally with the name of the person or company being called, and the caller can then leave a message. Messages can often be retrieved from outside the office using a certain code.

Cellular or *mobile phones* are wireless units that are becoming increasingly popular. They are especially valuable to people who spend a lot of time in their cars, such as salespeople. When a caller dials a cellular phone number, he or she may get a recorded message that says the person is not within reach. This means the person may be between cells, and the caller should try again a few minutes later.

Beepers, also known as *pagers*, are small signaling devices that may be kept in a pocket, on a belt, in a purse, or in a briefcase. The user will be "beeped" when an incoming call has been placed (*ergo*, the name). The user can then go to the nearest telephone and receive the message. There are 800-number services that allow callers to reach the user at a toll-free number, and there are voice mail systems that will signal the user each time a caller leaves a recorded telephone message. It used to be that doctors wore beepers because of the life and death situations they deal with, but today many executives use beepers to deal with their own types of emergencies.

Billing Numbers

800 numbers can be provided toll-free for callers both nationally and internationally. The business that owns the 800 number pays for the calls. (*Note:* the telephone company is planning to introduce *888* as an additional toll-free number.)

900 numbers make use of prerecorded messages used by companies as a way of charging for customer services. The charges to callers are higher for 900 numbers than for regular phone calls.

WATS services (Wide Area Telecommunications Services) are business-wide volume reduced rates for outbound calls. WATS services can be restricted to a city, state, the entire United States, or particular countries.

Telephone Answering Services

Many offices maintain contact with customers or others in the business world through an answering service that takes calls at night and on weekends and holidays. For a small office that closes entirely for vacations, an answering service is valuable.

The answering service may transfer the messages taken by calling at the beginning of the next business day. However, it is more common for the secretary to call in periodically and take the messages that have been received. Trial and error may be necessary in finding a reliable answering service. If the service does not have enough lines or operators and callers are put on "hold" for unreasonable lengths of time, much good will can be lost. Then again, it is important to have a service that can be trusted to take messages accurately. The secretary planning to engage an answering service will do well to consult other secretaries and take their recommendations. Once the system is in operation, the secretary should check response time regularly by calling the number.

When it comes time to take the messages from an answering service, the secretary should have pen and paper on hand and be accurate in transcribing any messages given, and especially so if the answering device does not have playback equipment. A set of priorities may be set up in advance with the employer as to which messages call for immediate action and which may be delayed for a shorter or greater length of time.

A sophisticated service available through the telephone company has an apparatus by which the subscriber can dial a two-digit code and have incoming calls transferred to an answering service. This does not "tie up" the line, as the subscriber may still make outgoing calls. When the subscriber wishes to disengage the service, a second two-digit code will restore the incoming calls to the client's own telephone line. Telephone answering services also provide "wake-up" calls, courtesy calls, and reminder-of-appointment calls at an additional cost.

Telephone Answering Devices

A great variety of telephone answering devices, usually activating a cassette tape recorder, are available. The simplest of these give a recorded message, as for example a statement telling the caller when the person called will be available, telling hours when the business is open, or the like. An equally common type is the recorder in which the person called has prerecorded a message that invites the caller to leave a message. When a tone sounds, the caller can talk for varying lengths of time, depending upon the equipment.

Messages recorded by such a device should be transcribed by the secretary as early as possible at the start of a business day. If it is not possible to understand clearly any portion of a message, a notation should be placed on the transcript to alert the employer that the secretary was not sure of the message given.

A remote-control feature allows the user to call the device on any telephone from anyplace in the world and hear whatever messages have been recorded. One phone call plays all messages, and a special feature allows the user to replay any given message without waiting for the entire tape to rewind and replay.

Record Keeping

13

Data Management

by Charlotte B. Holmquest, M. Ed.
revised by Julie Eichenberger, M. Ed.

- *Traditional Filing Systems*

    Alphabetic Systems
    Combination Subject Systems
    Numeric Systems
    Phonetic Systems

- *Physical Setup of Files*

- *Preparation of Material for Filing*

- *Removing Files*

- *Card File*

- *Filing Equipment*

    File Cabinets
    Lateral or Open-Shelf Filing

- *Color Coding*

- *Indexing and Alphabetizing*

- *Records Retention Schedule*

- *Transferring Records*

- *Micrographics*

- *Filing Electronic Documents*

   Methods of Organizing Computer Documents
   Database
   Utilities
   Directories

An efficient filing system is one that reduces clutter, separates information into recognizable categories, and makes possible the rapid and accurate retrieval of documents. There are several standard methods, and each has its advantages and disadvantages. Nevertheless, it is not the system but the use of it that determines its effectiveness. Documents are filed so they can be found. This applies especially to information needed for making day-to-day management decisions. Given the system, the secretary should be able to pull a document from a file within five minutes of a request.

A large organization may employ a number of clerks who are responsible for maintaining company records kept in a central area. In a small office there may be only a few file cabinets. In either case, the secretary must be familiar with the systems commonly used, because every office depends on one or another of them.

In today's offices the processing of data in ever-increasing amounts has led to the proliferation of desktop computers. Many have the capability to tie in with mainframe computers. Even though traditional filing systems continue to be used, the secretary in the electronic office must be prepared to access computer-generated documents quickly and efficiently.

TRADITIONAL FILING SYSTEMS

The basic filing systems in use in the modern office are alphabetic, combination subject, numeric, and phonetic. Alphabetic filing encompasses filing papers by name, subject, or geographic location in alphabetical order. Combination subject systems utilize both numbers and words or numbers and letters arranged in alphabetical order. Such names as alphanumeric, subject-numeric, and duplex-numeric appear in this category. Nonalphabetic filing exercises the use of numbers for filing purposes; and such terms as numeric, decimal, terminal digit, triple digit, and middle digit are in this category. The phonetic filing system involves using letters and sounds in code number form.

Filing systems may be direct or indirect. In a *direct method of filing,* a person can locate a file immediately, without first having to refer to a cross-index file to find out where to look. In an *indirect filing system,* a person cannot immediately locate the file but must refer to a cross-index file to determine where to locate it. For example, if the basic filing system is a subject system and the secretary wishes to locate the file for a specific firm, he or she must either know the subject under which the firm is filed or refer to an alphabetical cross-index, looking up the firm name and finding out in which subject file the file is located.

Alphabetic Systems

Almost 90% of all filing that is done in the office is alphabetic. In this type of system the office correspondence and other papers are filed alphabetically according to name, geographic location, or subject.

Name

In a name file, all papers are filed alphabetically according to the last name of the person or the name of a company. It is a direct method of filing. It is very simple to expand a name file because any new name is filed alphabetically without disturbing the name before or after it.

Geographic Location

In the geographic system the papers are filed alphabetically according to the name of the state; then alphabetically according to the town or city within that state; then alphabetically according to the name of the correspondent within the town or city. Mail-order houses, public-utility companies, publishing houses, and organizations that serve a geographic district or have branch offices in different areas use this system of filing.

The geographic system of filing is an indirect system. It is not possible to locate the file for a specific firm without first referring to a cross-index that lists the names of the firms in alphabetical order and gives the location of each firm. In other words, if you do not know the location of the firm, you must refer to the cross index under the firm name and determine under what geographic location to find the file.

Subject

When a company deals with products, supplies, materials, advertising, and so forth, the subject system is used. It is an indirect system, because a cross-index file is used to save time in filing and finding material and in locating correspondence by firm name when the subject is in doubt. The folders in the subject file are arranged alphabetically by the name of the product. The material within the folders is arranged by date, with the latest date in the front of the folder.

Often a combination of subject file and name file is used. If there is not enough material to set up a separate subject file, the subject captions are set up in a name file.

Combination Subject Systems

Some companies that use the subject filing system have found it necessary to use major subject titles with separate subcategories relating to that major topic so that locating specific information is quicker. A major subject outline containing the most important titles is set up in alphabetical order. Next, subcategory subject titles within each area are placed beneath the major subject titles. Then, numbers are used in combination with the subjects in the outline to make up the *combination subject filing system.*

When a company uses the combination subject filing system, it is extremely important that an up-to-date list be kept of all subjects and their code letters and numbers. This list should be circulated to all persons and departments needing access to the files. Likewise, a *relative index* should be made, listing all possible subjects and where information might be located pertaining to that subject. This list, too, should be updated frequently and distributed to those using the files.

Types of Combination Subject Files

Some of the combination subject filing systems used are:

Subject-Numeric. This system uses the major subject title with numbers assigned to the subcategories underneath it. For example, the subject heading "Automobile Accessories" would be treated in this manner:

AUTOMOBILE ACCESSORIES

1	Automobile Accessories: Tires
1-1	Standard Black
1-2	Whitewall

Duplex-Numeric. This system makes use of both numbers and letters of the alphabet. A digit is selected for the subject; this is followed by a dash and another digit for a division of the subject, plus a letter for further subdivision. For example, the subject heading "Automobile Accessories" might be given the number 13; the division "Automobile Accessories: Tires" would be numbered 13-1; a further subdivision, "Automobile Accessories: Tires, Standard Black," would be numbered 13-1a; "Automobile Accessories: Tires, Whitewall" would be numbered 13-1b. The outline would look like this:

13	AUTOMOBILE ACCESSORIES
13-1	Automobile Accessories: Tires
13-1a	Standard Black
13-1b	Whitewall

Alpha-Numeric. This system uses letters of the alphabet for the major subject titles along with letters and numbers for subtopics:

A	ADMINISTRATION
A1	Long-Range Planning
A1-1	Guidelines and Schedules
A2	Competition
A2-1	Survey Reports
A3	Public Relations
G	GOVERNMENT RELATIONS
G1	Air Pollution Control
G1-1	Vehicle Emissions
G1-1-1	Health Hazards

Numeric Systems

Numeric filing systems are nonalphabetic. All records are filed solely by numbers.

When the numeric system is used, an *accession register* must be kept to make retrieving a particular file a quick process. The accession register is a book or card file that contains each file number beginning with the first number as well as the correspondent's name on that file. The correspondents' names should be alphabetized so that one can get the file quickly if a correspondent's file number has been forgotten.

Types of Numeric Filing Systems

There are several types of numeric filing systems, some used only in highly specialized businesses.

Straight numeric. This system has records filed according to strict numeric sequence. Folder number 1 is given to the first client or account; folder number 2 is given to the second, and so forth, in strict numeric order.

Terminal digit. In this system, numbers on a file are read from right to left. Usually, the last, or terminal, two digits are the drawer number, the next two digits are the folder number, and any other numbers indicate the sequence within the folders. For example, an insurance policy numbered 567,123 would be stored in drawer 23, folder 71, and the 56 would refer to its sequence in the folder.

Triple digit. This system is similar to the terminal-digit system, except that the numbers are read in three digit units instead of two. The terminal three digits of a number are called the *primary* numbers, and the remaining digits refer to the sequence of the papers in the folders bearing the primary numbers. For example, the insurance policy numbered 567,123 would be found in folder 123, and 567 would refer to its sequence in the folder.

Middle digit. The third and fourth digits from the right are separated from the last two digits on the right. For example, in the insurance policy number 567,123, the policy would be filed in folder 71, and 23 would refer to its sequence in the folder.

Decimal system. The decimal system is used only in highly specialized businesses. The system may be based on the Dewey decimal system, which is the system commonly used by public libraries, though many are switching to the Library of Congress Catalog card system.

Phonetic Systems

The phonetic filing system is a filing method based on the use of letters and sounds. Organizations that file records by individuals' surnames encounter the problem of filing names that sound alike but are spelled differently, such as Smith and Smyth or Schmidt and Schmitt. To eliminate this problem, the Remington Rand Office Systems Division of the Sperry Rand Corporation developed the Soundex Phonetic Filing System. Soundex is a combination of spelling, or sounds, and numbers. Basic sounds are represented by six fundamental letters, the consonants *B, C, D, L, M,* and *R,* which make up the entire Soundex alphabet. Each of these consonants is given a separate code number: B is 1, C is 2, D is 3, L is 4, M is 5, and R is 6. The remaining consonants in the alphabet have the same relative sounds as the six basic Soundex consonants and are grouped with the *basic* consonant. All vowels and the letters *W, H,* and *Y* have no number and are not coded. To use this system, look at the *first* letter of the *surname* and sort by *that letter* first. Then code the *remaining* letters in the surname by looking at the following chart.

Code	Key Letters and Equivalents
1	B F P V
2	C G J K Q S X Z
3	D T
4	L
5	M N
6	R

To file the surname "Snyder," the first letter, S, is recorded. The next letter to be coded is N, which is code 5. Y is disregarded, D is code 3, E is disregarded, and R is code 6. The surname "Snyder" is thus coded S536.

To file the surname "Day," code a D and three zeros to show that only vowels follow the first consonant, D. When no consonants or not enough consonants follow the first letter in the surname, use one, two, or three zeros to give the name a three-digit code. The code for "Day" is D000. The surname "Shaw" is S000, Levy is L100, and Kelly is K400.

PHYSICAL SETUP OF FILES

The file drawer contains primary guides that divide the file into alphabetic sections or numeric sections. These primary guides are placed at the beginning of each section. The tabs may be on the left-hand side or in the middle of the file drawer. Secondary guides are used to subdivide the section or to call attention to important names or numbers. Individual folders, arranged alphabetically, chronologically, or in numeric sequence, are placed directly behind the guides. Individual folders are used for correspondents who communicate frequently with the firm. When there are from five to eight pieces of correspondence from the same source, an individual folder is set up. The full name of the correspondent is on the tab. Tabs are usually alternated in position so that one does not come directly behind another. When material is arranged in an individual folder, the latest date is always in the front of the folder.

When material is placed in a miscellaneous folder, it should be arranged alphabetically with the latest date in front for each person or subject.

Miscellaneous folders follow the individual folders at the end of each major division. They are used for correspondence that does not warrant individual folders. The tab on the miscellaneous folder may be of a different size or be marked with a distinctive color so that it can easily located.

In preparing index tabs and labels for guides and folders, type the letter of the alphabet or the name. The first typing space below the fold of the file-drawer label should be used, and typing should start two spaces from the left of the label. Use initial capitals and indent the second and each succeeding line two spaces so that the first word on the top line will stand out. Use abbreviations if the name or subject is long. Use the largest type possible when typing file-drawer labels, or print these labels.

PREPARATION OF MATERIAL FOR FILING

Check all papers to see whether they are to be filed and have been released for filing. Sort the correspondence into personal, business, contracts, and the like. Remove all staples, paper clips, or other paper holders. Underline the name in colored pencil to indicate where the letter is to be filed. Indicate the guide number in the upper right-hand corner. Use a colored pencil to circle important words to help to locate a particular paper when it is needed. Make any cross-reference sheets that are required. A *cross-reference sheet* is made out when a letter or a record may be filed in one of two places. File the letter or record under the most important name and cross-refer the second name or subject. For example, a letter may be received from Jordan Marsh Company. It would be filed under Jordan (first unit) Marsh (second unit) Company (third unit), and a cross-reference made out for Marsh, Jordan Company. The cross-reference sheet would read:

> Marsh, Jordan Company
> SEE
> Jordan Marsh Company

Below is a simple step-by-step checklist to use when getting ready to file material:

1. *Inspection.* Read or scan the material. Put a check mark in the upper left-hand corner to signal that this material should be filed.
2. *Indexing.* Determine which name or subject to use for filing the material. This is vital, as poor indexing means poor "finding" and a loss of time.
3. *Coding.* Coding is the physical act of marking the name, subject, etc., under which the material is to be filed. Put the code in the upper right-hand corner. Make cross-reference sheets at this point.
4. *Sorting.* Sort the material in a rough, superficial manner—all As together, all Bs together, etc., in alphabetical order. Put all 10s together, all 20s

together, etc., for numeric filing. Then sort each stack according to "strict sorting," using the standard filing rules the firm uses.

5. *Filing.* Place correspondence in the folders, top to the left of the folder. Put material in the miscellaneous folder alphabetically, with the latest date on top. Place material in individual folders chronologically, latest date on top.

REMOVING FILES

When it is necessary to take material from the file, replace the record or correspondence with an "out" guide or card. On the "out" guide, record the date, the name of the record taken, who has it, and the date it is to be returned. The word *out* should be printed on the tab, and stock of a different color should be used so that the guide stands out. It is necessary to record the withdrawal of the material if it goes out of the office for a period of time or if the employer is going to use it away from the office. Confidential records should be used in the office and returned to the files immediately.

CARD FILE

A card file (usually with 3" × 5" cards) arranged alphabetically by name of person or subject is often imperative for finding needed manuscripts or correspondence. In many offices, two separate card files are maintained, one for subject and the second for the name of the writer of each piece of material. If there are a great many different sets of files in an office, each needs to be clearly identified to make the card file useful.

Each card should hold as much information as necessary for retrieval of needed material. It should contain subject, along with any pertinent subcategory; name of person and/or date (if pertinent); set of files in which the material is stored; and any notes that will aid the secretary or executive in learning exactly what will be found in the file being sought.

FILING EQUIPMENT

Files may be kept in standard four-drawer file cabinets or in open-shelf files.

File Cabinets

The standard office filing cabinet has four drawers that hold file folders enclosing material on the regulation $8^1/_2$" × 11" typing paper. A law office or company with many legal papers will need a wider cabinet to accommodate legal cap. The standard drawer will carry a load of from 60 to 70 pounds. For efficient filing, the file drawers should not be overcrowded. The secretary should take note at what intervals the files start to become overcrowded and take appropriate action.

The files should be arranged so that there is a minimum of walking required to and from the files. The file drawers may be labeled in either vertical (top to bottom) or horizontal (left to right) order. Space may be saved if the file cabinets are backed up against a wall. If there are many cabinets, it may be more efficient to arrange them in a cluster in the center of a room. Floor space is expensive; therefore, some consideration should be given to arranging cabinets economically. Adequate aisle space between cabinets must be allowed. At least 28 inches must be allowed for a file drawer when it is opened into the aisle. There should be gaps in long rows of cabinets to save time in getting from one row to another. This is particularly important for the file supervisor who has to make spot checks of the file drawers and to assist the file clerks.

Lateral or Open-Shelf Filing

For certain kinds of filing, the open-shelf method is more appropriate than the use of file drawers. This "lateral" or shelf filing may result in the saving of as much as 40 percent of the office floor space needed for files. The aisles between the shelves can be considerably narrower than those needed between cabinets with drawers, because the additional space for pulling out drawers is not needed. Also, files can be stacked higher than drawers—in many instances, to the ceiling.

Lateral filing is particularly useful for active files in which papers are inserted and withdrawn constantly and which are not to be retained for a long period of time. Proponents of lateral filing claim much time is saved by having the files immediately at hand and in sight.

COLOR CODING

Color coding can be a worthwhile expedient, permitting easier location of specific files or file sections. Before making a decision about color coding, the secretary should study the various methods available and determine which would be best for the particular type of material filed in the office for which the system is intended.

Color coding is usually employed to identify a filing series that has been categorized by the alphabetic system or any of the several numeric systems discussed earlier in this chapter. A specific color is assigned to each number or letter. One manufacturer of filing materials (Datafile) uses twelve colors twice, the second time with a white bar that sets it apart from the first. These 24 colors, with white for Y and gray for Z, serve for the 26 letters of the alphabet.

This represents one of the great variety of color coding systems that have been worked out. The pattern used depends on the complexity of the material to be filed. Datafile, using its twelve colors, also has folders with two color bands for identification of the first two letters of a word or name. By identifying two letters, the file is expanded from the 26 letters of the alphabet to about three or four hundred segments. The possible total is 26×26, or 676, but all combinations of letters do not occur at the beginning of words or names.

Color coding may be used with either open-shelf filing or with files in closed file cabinets.

With Open-Shelf Files

For some kinds of open-shelf filing, the plain manila folder and/or hanging file folders are used, with a much simpler color code. One company that keeps order files for exactly two years before discard uses a color-coded dot on the folders holding the records for alternate years. Thus the file at any particular time consists of folders marked in one color for one of the years represented, unmarked folders for another, and a second colored dot for the third. If, for example, the date is March 1995, the folders for April through December of 1993 (January through March having been discarded) have dots of one color, the folders for 1994 are plain, and the folders for January to date in 1995 have dots of a second color. Folders for 1996 will be plain, and the system will repeat.

In summary, color coding may be effected on shelf filing by folders of a solid color; by folders with color bands; by stick-on dots in an upper corner of a manila file folder; by tabs that protrude; or by tabs that slip on, clip on, or are pasted on the folders. The tabbed folders may be bought prepared or assembled by the secretary or file clerk.

In File Cabinets

Color coding of files within drawers can be equally effective. Durable plastic file folders may be purchased in a wide variety of colors, or a color tab may be affixed to manila folders or hanging dividers. One of the common ways to use these is to select a new color for each year within an alphabetic file.

INDEXING AND ALPHABETIZING

Indexing is the arrangement of the names on the folder tab or on cards. The folders and cards are arranged alphabetically for simplicity of filing and finding. The following indexing rules are standard rules for filing. The Association of Records Managers and Administrators, Inc. (ARMA) uses these guidelines with minor exceptions, which are noted toward the end of this section.

Individual names. Names of individuals are indexed by the last name (the surname) first, then the first name, and then the middle initial or middle name:

Name	Indexing Order
Alfred M. Amell	Amell, Alfred M.
Grace R. Gladd	Gladd, Grace R.
J. Thomas Williams	Williams, J. Thomas

Business names. The names of business establishments, institutions, and organizations are indexed as they are written, unless they embody the name of an individual. An exception to this rule is the names of schools. When the individual's name is part of a firm name, index by considering the last name (surname) first, then the first name and the middle initial or middle name, if any.

Name	Indexing Order
Atlantic Service Station	Atlantic Service Station
Earl A. Stone Book Publishers	Stone, Earl A. Book Publishers
General Department Store	General Department Store
James A. Carson Company	Carson, James A. Company
J. M. Morgan Sign Company	Morgan, J. M. Sign Company
Nathan Hale Junior High School	Nathan Hale Junior High School
Rose and Peter Beauty Supplies	Rose and Peter Beauty Supplies
Rose Peter Beauty Shoppe	Peter, Rose Beauty Shoppe
Rose's Beauty Salon	Rose's Beauty Salon
Stone and Book Publishing Company	Stone and Book Publishing Company
Stone Book Publishers	Stone Book Publishers
Thomas Milford Stiles Florist Shop	Stiles, Thomas Milford Florist Shop
Troy Sand and Gravel, Inc.	Troy Sand and Gravel, Inc.

Alphabetical order. Names are alphabetized by comparing each of their letters. If the first units are alike, compare the second units. If there is no second unit, the single name is filed first. The rule of "nothing before something" applies here. A surname followed by a first initial only goes before the same surname followed by a complete first name beginning with the same letter as the initial—again, "nothing before something."

	Indexing Order	
Name	*Unit 1*	*Unit 2*
Carson	Carson	
Carson Brothers	Carson	Brothers
J. Carson	Carson	J.
James Carson	Carson	James

Letters used as words. Consider any single letter as a word and not part of a cluster or part of an acronym.

	Indexing Order			
Name	*Unit 1*	*Unit 2*	*Unit 3*	*Unit 4*
N A P A Jobbers	N	A	P	A
N C R Accounting Company	N	C	R	Accounting
Pacific Car Company	Pacific	Car	Company	
R & B Auto Service	R	B	Auto	Service

Abbreviations. Abbreviations are indexed as though they are the words they represent written out in full; hence, "Mme." is indexed as "Madame."

	Indexing Order		
Name	*Unit 1*	*Unit 2*	*Unit 3*
Mme. Sophie's Boutique	Madame	Sophie's	Boutique
Mr. Pete's Grocery	Mister	Pete's	Grocery
St. Alexis Hospital	Saint	Alexis	Hospital

Article "the." When *the* is part of the name, it is disregarded in filing. If it is the initial word, it is placed at the end of the name in parentheses. If *the* occurs in the body of the name, it is placed in parentheses and disregarded.

Name	*Indexing Order*
The Cleveland Boat Company	Cleveland Boat Company (The)
Danny the Tailor	Danny (the) Tailor
Stanley of the Ritz	Stanley (of the) Ritz

Such words as *and, for, on, in, by,* and *of the* are disregarded in indexing and filing. However, they are placed in parentheses when writing names on folders and cards.

Hyphenated names. Hyphenated firm names are treated as separate names, because they represent separate individuals; when listed among other proper names, the second name is to be regarded as a given name for alphabetizing purposes.

Name	*Indexing Order*
Branch-Merrill Company	Branch Merrill Company
Richard T. Branch	Branch, Richard T.
Winifred I. Wilson	Wilson, Winifred I.
Wilson-Wyman, Inc.	Wilson Wyman, Inc.

Hyphenated individual names are treated as one name, because they represent one individual.

Name	Indexing Order
James A. Gladd-Monroe	GladdMonroe, James A.
Patricia Lloyd-Taylor	LloydTaylor, Patricia
Jane L. Marin-Jones	MarinJones, Jane L.

One- or two-word names. Names that may be spelled as one word or two words are usually considered as one word.

	Indexing Order		
Name	Unit 1	Unit 2	Unit 3
Raybrook Cleaners	Raybrook	Cleaners	
Ray Brook Paint Company	RayBrook	Paint	Company
South East Electric Shop	SouthEast	Electric	Shop
Southeast Supply Company	Southeast	Supply	Company
Good Will Cleaners	GoodWill	Cleaners	
Goodwill Industries	Goodwill	Industries	

Individual surnames with prefixes. Prefixes such as D', d', De, de, Del, Des, Di, Du, Fitz, l', La, Le, M', Mac, Mc, O', Van, Von, and so on, are indexed as written and treated as one word.

	Indexing Order		
Name	Unit 1	Unit 2	Unit 3
D'Aoust, James	D'Aoust	James	
Darling, John E.	Darling	John	E.
De Lancett, Morris	De Lancett	Morris	
DeLancey, Lincoln	DeLancey	Lincoln	
MacDonald, George H.	MacDonald	George	H.
McCasland, Raymond A.	McCasland	Raymond	A.
Van Cour, Elsie A.	Van Cour	Elsie	A.
Von Ottenfeld, Oscar M.	Von Ottenfeld	Oscar	M.

Words ending in "s." When a name ends s' or 's, the s is considered part of the name.

	Indexing Order		
Name	Unit 1	Unit 2	Unit 3
Bob's Sport Shop	Bob's	Sport	Shop
Boy Scout Camp	Boy	Scout	Camp
Boys' Clothing Store	Boys'	Clothing	Store
Williams' Dry Cleaning	Williams'	Dry	Cleaning
William's Service Station	William's	Service	Statio

Titles. A personal or professional title or degree is usually not considered in indexing and filing. When the name is written, the title is placed in parentheses at the end of the name.

Name	Indexed as
Dr. Richard P. Bellaire	Bellaire, Richard P. (Dr.)
Ms. Helen Hayles	Hayles, Helen (Ms.)
Grace M. Janson, D.D.	Janson, Grace M. (D.D.)

A religious or foreign title is considered as the first indexing unit when it is followed by a given name only.

Indexed and filed as

Brother Francis
Madame Eugenie
Prince Charles
Princess Anne
Sister Mary Megan

Married women's names. The name of a married woman is indexed according to the name by which she prefers to be known. Some women retain their maiden names after marriage and this preference should be respected. A married name could be a woman's given first name, her maiden surname, and her husband's surname, or it could be her given first and middle names (or initial for the middle name) and her husband's surname. The title "Mrs." is disregarded in filing, but it is placed in parentheses after the name. If signatures on correspondence from a married woman indicate that she prefers "Ms.," then that is the title placed in parentheses after her name. The name of the husband may be given in parentheses below the woman's legal name.

Name	Indexing Order
Mrs. John F. Matson (Mary Nelson)	Matson, Mary Nelson (Mrs.) (Mrs. John F. Matson)
Mrs. Lucien (Louise S.) Platt	Platt, Louise S. (Mrs.) (Mrs. Lucien Platt)
Mrs. Robert (Mary Lee) Young	Young, Mary Lee (Mrs.) (Mrs. Robert Young)

Names with numbers. When a name contains a number, it is considered as if the number was written as a single unit and is spelled as it is pronounced.

	Indexing Order		
Name	Unit 1	Unit 2	Unit 3
A 1 Garage	A	One	Garage
The 400 Club	Fourhundred	Club (The)	
7th Ave. Building	Seventh	Avenue	Building

Geographic names. An easy rule to follow in arranging geographic names is to treat them as they are written. Each element in a compound name of a geographic location is indexed as a separate unit.

	Indexing Order			
Name	*Unit 1*	*Unit 2*	*Unit 3*	*Unit 4*
Mount Holly, New Jersey	Mount	Holly	New	Jersey
New Bedford, Massachusetts	New	Bedford	Massachusetts	
Newburgh, New York	Newburgh	New	York	

When the first element of a geographic name is not of English origin, that element is considered part of the first unit.

	Indexing Order	
Name	*Unit 1*	*Unit 2*
Des Moines, Iowa	DesMoines	Iowa
Las Vegas Hotel	LasVegas	Hotel
Los Angeles, California	LosAngeles	California
San Francisco, California	SanFrancisco	California

Government offices and departments. The name of a federal government office is indexed as follows:

1. United States Government (whether or not it is written as part of the name)
2. Principal word or words in the name of the department
3. Principal word or words in the name of the bureau
4. Principal word or words in the name of the division

"Department of," "Bureau of," and "Division of" are disregarded but are usually placed in parentheses.

Name	*Indexing Order*
Bureau of the Census	United States Government
U.S. Department of Commerce	Commerce (Department of)
	Census (Bureau of the)
Office of Indian Affairs	United States Government
U.S. Department of the Interior	Interior (Department of)
	Indian Affairs (Office of)
U.S. Postal Service	United States Government
Bureau of Accounts	Postal Service
Division of Cost Ascertainment	Accounts (Bureau of)
	Cost Ascertainment (Division of)

Foreign government names. Names pertaining to foreign governments are indexed under names of countries and subdivided by title of the department and then by bureau, division, commission, or board.

Name	Indexing Order
Republic of India	India (Republic of)
Department of Energy	Energy Department

Other political divisions. Names pertaining to other political divisions are indexed under the name of the political division followed by its classification, such as *state, county,* or *city,* and then subdivided by the title of the department, bureau, division, commission, or board.

Name	Indexing Order
Bureau of Statistics	Maine, State (of)
State of Maine	Statistics (Bureau of)
Harris County	Harris, County (of)
Bureau of Personnel	Personnel (Bureau of)
Department of Safety	Anaheim, City (of)
City of Anaheim	Safety (Department of)

Banks. Banks are indexed under the names of the communities in which they are located, then by bank name. The state is the last indexing unit.

Name	Indexing Order
First National Bank Cleveland, Ohio	Cleveland: First National Bank, Ohio
Bank of New Jersey Newark	Newark: Bank of New Jersey, New Jersey
Wells Savings Bank Wells, Maine	Wells Savings Bank, Maine

If the name of the community is a part of the name of the bank, the name of the community is not repeated but is considered the first unit as it occurs.

Churches, schools, and other organizations. The names of churches, schools, and other organizations are indexed as follows. Cross-references may be used when necessary to file or find these names more efficiently.

Name	Indexing Order
American Legion	American Legion
University of California	California, University (of)
Lakewood Kiwanis Club	Kiwanis Club, Lakewood
First Lutheran Church	Lutheran Church, First
Martin Luther King High School	Martin Luther King High School
The Salvation Army	Salvation Army, The

Addresses. If two or more persons or firms have the same name but different addresses, alphabetize them according to city or town. In the event that the persons or firms also have the same city or town name, then alphabetize according to the state name. Should persons or firms having the same name be in the same community but have different addresses, alphabetize these names according to the name of the street. In the event that the same name has more than one address on the same street of that city or town, then index from the lowest to highest street number.

125 Main Street goes before 126 Main Street.

The Association of Records Managers and Administrators indexing and filing rules. The Association of Records Managers and Administrators, Inc., in its book of indexing rules, *Rules for Alphabetical Filing,* has established three classifications for indexing: individual names, business establishment names, and government/political designations. ARMA recommends separating index units with the diagonal (/). ARMA rules are essentially the same as the ones given above with the following differences:

1. The hyphenated company name is treated as one unit.

   Brown-Jacobs/Company/

2. Compound geographical names are treated as separate units.

   Las/Vegas/Construction/Company
   Del/Rio/Music/Store/

3. Company names that have compass points as part of the name are indexed as separate units.

Name	*Indexing Order*
North East Alignment	North/East/Alignment/
Southeastern Transfer	South/eastern/Transfer/

4. The *'s* is included as part of the indexing unit; that is, the apostrophe is disregarded.

Name	*Indexing Order*
Leon's Barbecue	Leon's/Barbecue/
Leons' Music Store	Leons'/Music/Store/

5. Company names that are numbers and written in figure form, such as *500 Club,* are arranged in strict numeric sequence and are *not* spelled out. They are filed at the *front* of the entire alphabetic file.

Name	*Indexing Order*
1 Hour Cleaners	1/Hour/Cleaners/
7th Street Auto Shop	7(th)/Street/Auto/Shop/

8 Ball Eatery	8/Ball/Eatery/
400 Executive Clothiers	400/Executive/Clothiers/
500 Club	500/Club/

RECORDS RETENTION SCHEDULE

The secretary should keep a copy of the company's records retention schedule and update it when revisions occur. This schedule is a listing of all types of records a firm has and how long these items are to be kept in the office or in the records center. The schedule lists which records must be microfilmed and how long they must be retained. Also, the schedule contains a timetable for disposing of records and a permanent records list.

The company's attorney and representatives of top management should set up the retention schedule following guidelines based on the many federal and state regulations that apply to the firm.

TRANSFERRING RECORDS

When records become inactive in the file, they should be transferred to storage files. Thus, the expensive filing equipment is used only for active material. The material that is removed from the active files and placed in the *inactive,* or *transfer,* files should be well arranged, so that no time is wasted in locating this material if it is needed. Many firms plan to transfer the material in the files annually. The entire file drawer is transferred to the inactive file. The secretary needs to make new guides and prepare new folders for the new files.

If the guides and folders are going to be kept in the office, the transferred material may be placed in inexpensive folders that have been labeled with the same captions as those in the active-file drawer.

All transfer files or boxes should be labeled to indicate their contents, dates, and so forth, so that they can easily be located when needed.

Many business papers, correspondence, and some records that will not be needed in the future may be destroyed to conserve space and save time in transferring files. Material should not be destroyed without consideration of the statute of limitations in the state and other laws that require business firms to retain certain types of records.

MICROGRAPHICS

Micrographics is the term used to designate reproduced information in minia-ture form on film. Storing information on microfilm has saved firms great amounts of money, space, and retrieval time. Records are photographed onto film in a microfilmer so that many small images in color or black and white will appear on a reel of 16-millimeter or 35-millimeter film. Records can be viewed in enlarged form on a reader.

Computer Output Microfilm (COM). COM is a method of microfilming in which data that are stored in a computer can be recorded directly onto microfilm. This process eliminates recording the data on paper printouts before microfilming can take place. COM speeds getting information to persons needing it on film rather than on paper.

Microfilm Storage

Microfilm may be stored in any of several ways.

Rolls. Roll film can be stored in cartons and cabinets. A plastic collar snapped over the film roll becomes a magazine that self-threads to readers.

Jackets. Jackets contain chambers that hold short lengths of film. A 4" × 6" jacket holds 70 images of letter-size documents.

Microfiche. Microfiche, often called simply "fiche," contains rows of documents on sheet film about 4" × 6". Full-color or black-and-white images can appear on microfiche (98 full-color or more than 300 black-and-white images).

Aperture cards. Aperture cards are tab-card-size cards that have chambers to hold one or more pieces of film and room on the card for identification.

Film folios. Film folios are a combination of aperture cards and jackets. They are cards the size of microfiche with chambers to hold film of microfiche size. The card also contains space for identification.

FILING ELECTRONIC DOCUMENTS

Because electronic documents (ED) can be manipulated in memory, storage and filing procedures differ greatly from standard filing practices.

Documents are stored on disks. A single floppy disk can hold many units of information, or *records*. Each record is composed of discrete areas called *fields*. For the purpose of filing, a field may be

> alphabetic, containing only letters and blanks
>
> numeric, containing only digits and certain characters, such as + or –
>
> alphanumeric, containing any characters

Within a field, numeric data are right justified; alphabetic and alphanumeric data are left justified. Examples of fields can be seen in Table 13.1.

File structure on a floppy disk is fairly simple. With a program such as DisplayWrite or Multimate, data control is increased by using the comment field, as illustrated in Table 13.2.

Methods of Organizing Computer Documents

There are three methods for organizing computer documents: sequential, direct, and indexed.

Sequential, or Serial, File

A sequential, or serial, file controls data on a medium such as magnetic tape. It is one-directional, and reading and writing are done while advancing the tape. Many files are intended to be used sequentially. Data to print onto a document are effectively handled as a serial file since printing itself is a serial process.

TABLE 13.1 Examples of Fields

Alphabetic	Numeric	Alphanumeric
ROGER	321	14 Oak St
CREDIT	9246	72,400
AMES CORP	100543	24 DOZ APPLES

TABLE 13.2 Display Directory

ID	Name	Ext	Date	Comment
a	TELEMEMO	TXT	04-01-95	Memo to H. Hadley
b	FILES	TXT	04-19-95	Personnel Change/IS Dept.
c	ANDREWS	TXT	04-24-95	Forsythe & Rhoades (Phillip)

Direct File

Any record stored on a direct file can be accessed immediately if its location or address is known. This is the method used by airline reservation agents. The flight number and date of flight are keyed in and the record is displayed on a terminal screen.

Indexed File

An indexed file offers the simplicity of sequential file processing and the capability for direct access. Using programs such as ISAM or VSAM, the indexes are searched for key values, which, in turn, provide the name of the record.

Database

A *database* is a set of logically related files organized for easy access and minimal overlap. In a database management system (DBMS), access usually is possible only through programming languages such as COBOL, FORTRAN, PL/I, or Pascal. With integrated software, a DBMS is capable of using files from outside sources. For example, data might be read into a word processing program. The secretary revises the text and then reads back into the DBMS for report generation.

A type of information network is called an online real-time information system, which provides two-way communication between individual terminals and a central processing unit (CPU). The database consists of large-volume, random-access files. The secretary in a sales office would use this system to good advantage. When an order is keyed in, the CPU responds with required data: cost, availability, quantity discount, shipping information, and so forth; creates an invoice, if the item is in stock; and updates inventory files. These programs are designed for specific applications; therefore, processing methods vary.

Utilities

Utilities are programs that manipulate files, disks, and subdocuments. Any electronic document can become an electronic subdocument (ESD), depending on how it is used. Pages, paragraphs, phrases, or text material common to many documents can be filed as an ESD and appended to future EDs. To create an ESD, request *block write* and give it a name, or request *phrase write* and give it a name. A phrase will be stored on the disk, but not in the text. Although a disk can be used hundreds of times, it is good practice to copy frequently used records onto a new disk to avoid the problems associated with worn or defective disks.

There are many occasions when the secretary will want to *sort* records and *merge* documents as part of file management. Most record processors will display a list of fields and an empty column for specifying the order of sort. Similarly, data from subfiles can be merged into a single document. Even though these features eliminate needless repetition, a quicker method is always welcome. Let us assume the secretary wants to compile a list of employees with dependents. Rather than scroll through records on the dependent field, it is less time-consuming to request all records *excluding* those with no dependents. Simply key in a dependent field value of 0, and that record will be excluded.

Directories

Directories provide information about existing documents. When the secretary reads a directory, it is presented either alphabetically by name, by creation date, by revision date, or in the order documents appear on the disk. Most record processors have a directory maintenance program, and most provide a single directory format.

Although some offices do keep records indefinitely, many documents are short-lived. A company report, for instance, may have several authors. After a first draft is assembled, the subdocuments can be disposed of. This procedure applies also to subsequent revisions. It is wise, however, to check with the author(s) before destroying any records. In any event, it is imperative that the secretary keep an up-to-date directory printout.

Subdirectories

The majority of computers in the modern office contain one floppy disk drive and one hard or fixed drive. Fixed drives cannot be removed and are capable of storing large amounts of data. Clearly, the greater the storage capability of a computer, the more precise the filing methods must be, not only to expedite retrieval but also to minimize the possibility of "losing" a file. There might be so many documents on a hard disk that to view all the file names and comments could, conceivably, take several hours. To avoid this, the secretary would set up *subdirectories* for greater control.

On most (if not all) computers, the "C" drive is the hard disk. Whenever subdirectories are established, all information is stored in C>. If, for example, you are the secretary to four people, and your program is DisplayWrite3, one of the subdirectories might read:

C   = "C" drive
cd   = a subdirectory
DW3   = first level of subdirectory: the program
TDE   = second level of subdirectory: TDE's files

The variations are endless: C>cd\DW3\1995\Budget\Variance. . . .

A word of caution, however. If too many subdirectories are set up, locating documents will become extremely difficult. A simple, broad-based system affords the two most desirable qualities of any filing system: easy access and rapid retrieval. It is always well to remember that documents are filed so they can be found.

14

Managing Funds, Bookkeeping, and Record Keeping

by Abba Spero, Ph. D.
revised by Linda A. Bruce

- *Managing Cash Transactions*

- *Handling the Bank Account*

    Making Bank Deposits
    Endorsing Checks
    Dishonored Checks
    Bank Statements
    Bank Reconciliation
    Bank Reconciliation Statements
    Investigating Outstanding Checks

- *Handling Cash Payments*

    Writing Checks
    Certified Checks
    Stopping Payment on a Check
    Petty-Cash Fund

■ *Bookkeeping*

    Business Records
    Tax Records

■ *Payroll*

A secretary will often be required to handle cash, either from the business operations or the employer's personal funds. This, in turn, may require the recording of these transactions. The figures recorded will be used in preparing income-tax returns and in determining the profitability of the firm's operations. It is important for the secretary to be able to handle various aspects of cash transactions and to be familiar with the basic procedures in record keeping. The purpose of this chapter is to provide information that will enable the secretary to carry out these duties proficiently.

Specifically, the chapter will deal with (1) managing all cash transactions, including receiving cash, writing checks, reconciling bank statements with records, and handling petty cash; (2) record keeping as it affects the determination of profits; and (3) record keeping for income-tax and payroll purposes.

MANAGING CASH TRANSACTIONS

Cash will come into the company from various sources, especially as fees collected for services or as the personal funds of the employer. Personal funds can be received for salaries, interest and dividends on investments, and rents from income-producing property. Usually this money will be in the form of checks; occasionally, cash itself is received.

It is important that all monies received be deposited into the appropriate bank account on the day they are received. This procedure is the best insurance against thefts and robberies. Checks should be examined to determine whether they are properly made out. Attention should be paid to the date; postdated checks cannot be deposited or cashed before the date written on the check. Checks that are not made out correctly should be set aside to be discussed with the employer. Whenever cash is received, the secretary should prepare a receipt in duplicate (blank forms are available at any stationery store), one copy to be given to the person making payment and the other to be retained as a record of the transaction.

If the secretary's duties include record keeping, entries should be made in the proper records. Arrangements for night deposits should be made if funds cannot be deposited before the bank closes.

HANDLING THE BANK ACCOUNT

Making Bank Deposits

When cash is to be deposited in a bank, a deposit slip is made out (see next page). Although banks do accept deposit slips improperly prepared, the competent secretary is careful to do the job correctly. The company bank-deposit slips are usually imprinted with the company name and the bank account number. If these are not available, then this information must be filled in on a blank slip. The account number is important since it is the number, rather than the name, that the bank uses for its records.

CHECKING DEPOSIT	00061-015-781	NATIONAL CITY BANK		
SUBJECT TO RULES AND REGULATIONS GOVERNING CHECKING ACCOUNTS		CLEVELAND, OHIO		

DATE *Aug. 14, 19-* ACCOUNT NO. 0 4 7 5 2 6 1

	CASH Coin Checks Single	22	50
		150	00
		43	75

CREDIT THE ACCOUNT OF *Dorothy Jones*

OFFICE WHERE ACCOUNT IS CARRIED *Broadway — 65th*

Be Sure Each Item is Properly Endorsed.

TOTAL	276	25

⑆041000124⑈

Currency is counted, and the total is entered on the slip. Coins, if in large quantities, should be rolled in wrappers provided by the bank. Each check included in the deposit is listed separately. Occasionally traveler's checks or money orders may be a part of the deposit. These are entered in the same manner as ordinary checks. After all checks have been listed, the amounts of all items on the slip are added and the total is placed in the space provided.

The bank will give a receipt for the deposit. The receipt should be retained until the bank statement is received and then used to check the statement and be sure that all deposits have been properly recorded.

Endorsing Checks

Checks are written orders by which the depositor, known as the *drawer,* directs the bank, referred to as the *drawee,* to pay money to the *payee* or to a third party designated by the payee. Checks are sometimes made payable to *bearer,* a practice generally frowned upon because they are negotiated by simple delivery and can be cashed by persons who wrongfully receive them. Checks need not be made payable to real persons. Business checks are frequently made out to "Petty Cash" or to "Payroll." A check is made payable to Payroll, for example, when money is needed to make up pay envelopes.

If a check is made out to a definite payee, this person must write on the back of the check directions for its disposition and sign his or her name. This is known as an *endorsement.* Endorsements are placed on the back of the check on the left-hand side. The endorser should sign exactly as the name is written on the face of the check. If the name is misspelled or differs in any manner from the way it appears on the bank records, the payee should sign twice, first as it is written on the face of the check and then correctly.

Forms of Endorsement

There are three principal forms of endorsement: blank, in full, and restrictive (see Figure 14-1).

Blank Endorsement
Payable to bearer
without further endorsement

Blank Endorsement
Name misspelled

Endorsement in Full
Payable as James Cavanaugh directs

Restrictive Endorsement
Further negotiation prohibited

Figure 14-1.

Blank endorsement. In a blank endorsement, the endorser's signature is simply written across the back of the check. The effect of a blank endorsement is to make the check payable to the bearer. If it is lost or stolen, it can be cashed by the holder without further endorsement. Although they are commonly used, blank endorsements are not recommended. They should be made only at the time a check is being cashed or deposited at the bank.

Endorsement in full. In an endorsement in full, the endorser transfers the check to a designated party by writing the words "Pay to the order of" followed by the name of the person to whom payment is to be made and then signs the check. A check so endorsed can be cashed or negotiated only after the person named in the endorsement has signed it. It is not good in the hands of a person who wrongfully possesses it.

Restrictive endorsement. In a restrictive endorsement, the endorser limits further negotiation of the check by writing above his or her signature definite instructions on what may be done with it. Thus, a check might be made payable to one person only or it might be endorsed "For deposit only." Except when checks are being deposited in the bank, restrictive endorsements are almost never used. Business checks are usually endorsed for deposit with a rubber stamp; no written signature is needed.

Dishonored Checks

A bank accepts checks for deposit subject to their final payment. If the drawer has directed the bank to refuse payment or if there are insufficient funds on deposit, the bank will return the check and charge it to the drawer's account. Such a check is known as a *dishonored check,* or an "NSF (insufficient funds) check." Informal arrangements for payment or redeposit of a dishonored check are usually made with the drawer. However, if the drawer is a stranger, it would be advisable for the holder of a dishonored check to take legal steps and file a formal notice of protest. In this way, the holder is assured of protecting full rights against the drawer.

Dishonored checks that have been returned by the bank should be deducted from the bank balance on the depositor's cash records and then be redeposited or filed for safekeeping until the drawer has made settlement. Any fees that may have been paid for the protest or collection can rightfully be collected from the drawer.

Bank Statements

At regular intervals, usually monthly, or sometimes upon request of the depositor, the bank renders a bank statement, showing what has taken place in the account since the last statement was prepared and the present balance according to the bank's records. The statement shows the balance carried forward from the previous statement, all deposits and all charges made to the account during the period, and the balance on the date the statement was rendered. Sent along with the statements are canceled checks, credit memos, and debit memos.

Today, many financial institutions provide checkbooks that make self-carbon copies of checks written. These copies remain in the check register and are used just as the traditional canceled and returned checks at the end of the statement period to balance the account.

Canceled checks are the depositor's checks that have been returned to the bank, charged against the account, and stamped "PAID." *Credit memos* are notices of amounts added to the account for such sums as interest allowed by the bank or proceeds of items left with the bank for collection—notes and bond coupons, for example. *Debit memos* are notices of deductions made from the account for service charges, interest on bank loans, and the like.

Bank Reconciliation

Seldom will the balance showing in the checkbook agree with the balance reported on the bank statement, even though no errors have been made in either place. Disagreement results from the following causes:

- Deposits that were made near or after the date of the statement have not yet been posted on the bank records. They do, however, appear in the checkbook.

- Credits that have been made to the account by the bank, as indicated on the credit memos, have not yet been entered in the checkbook.
- Checks issued by the depositor and deducted in the checkbook are still outstanding; that is, they have not yet been presented to the bank for payment and therefore do not appear on the bank statement.
- Charges that have been made against the account by the bank, as indicated on the debit memos, have not yet been entered in the checkbook.
- Errors have been made either in the checkbook or on the bank's records, or in both places.

As soon as possible after receiving a statement, the depositor should locate the reasons for differences between the bank statement and the checkbook and find the correct balance in the account. This is done on a bank reconciliation statement, prepared by the following steps:

1. Compare deposits entered in the checkbook with those recorded on the bank statement. Check discrepancies against deposit slips to determine which record is correct. Make a note of deposits that do not appear on the bank statement and credits made by the bank that have not been added in the checkbook.
2. Take checks returned by the bank or self-carbon copies in the checkbook and arrange them in numerical order. Compare them with their stubs or other notations in the checkbook, taking careful notice to see whether the amounts agree. Make a note of differences. Place a check mark or other symbol on stubs of the checks that have been returned. Prepare a list of the outstanding checks, noting the check numbers, the dates, and the names of the payees. Do not include certified checks on this list, since they have already been charged against the account. Make a note of any bank charges that have not been entered in the checkbook.
3. Arrange the information that has been assembled on a bank reconciliation statement. The form and preparation of this statement are explained and illustrated below.

If the checkbook and bank statement are both correct, the balances can be brought into agreement and the reconciliation is complete. If the accounts cannot be reconciled after adjustments have been made for omissions, there is probably an error in addition or subtraction in the checkbook. Check the check stubs, paying particular attention to the balances carried forward from one stub to another.

Bank Reconciliation Statements

Bank reconciliation statements are prepared in three ways:

1. Adjustments are made to the balance reported by the bank to bring it into agreement with the checkbook balance.

2. Adjustments are made in the checkbook balance to bring it into agreement with the balance according to the bank statement.
3. Adjustments are made to both balances to get the correct balance.

Since neither of the first two methods provides the correct balance, the third method is the preferred procedure and is the one explained here. The sources of the data are the bank statement and the checkbook or a cash ledger account if one was prepared.

Comparison of the deposits that were made during the month with those recorded on the bank statement reveals that the bank has not entered a deposit of $1,000 made on July 31; this amount is added to the balance reported by the bank. Comparison of the canceled checks returned by the bank with the checks drawn during the period shows that the following checks are still outstanding:

Check No.	Date	Payee	Amount
633	7/22	Bean & Co.	$2,180
634	7/28	Blue Cross	50
			$2,230

Reconciliation Statement (July 31)

Balance on bank statement	$7,328
Deposits made after date of statement	1,000
Add	$8,328

Checks Outstanding

Check No.	Date	Payee	Amount
633	7/22	Bean & Co.	$2,180
634	7/28	Blue Cross	50
			$2,230

Deduct checks outstanding	2,230
Corrected bank balance	6,098
Balance according to checkbook	6,100
Service charge not recorded	2
Corrected checkbook balance	$6,098

The total of the outstanding checks is deducted from the balance reported on the bank statement. Adding the unrecorded deposits and deducting the outstanding checks takes care of all omissions on the bank statement. The correct bank balance is determined to be $6,098.

The bank statement shows a service charge of $2.00 that has not been entered in the cash records; this amount is deducted from the checkbook balance. Now the corrected checkbook balance is also $6,098, and it has been proved that no errors have been made.

After the reconciliation has been completed, errors should be corrected and entries should be made in the depositor's cash records and checkbook for any omissions, such as the service charge discussed above, so that the records will reflect the correct balance. Adjustments in the checkbook can be made on the stub for the last check drawn. It is not necessary to correct all preceding balances. Any bank errors uncovered in the reconciliation should be reported to the bank immediately.

The bank reconciliation statement should be filed for future reference. It will prove useful when the next reconciliation is made. The canceled checks are receipts for payments that have been made. They should be kept on file as long as proof of payment might be necessary.

Investigating Outstanding Checks

Ordinarily checks should clear through the bank and be returned to the depositor (not the case with self-carbon checks) within a few weeks after issue. Checks that have been outstanding for unreasonably long periods of time should be investigated. Outstanding checks are not only annoying when bank accounts are being reconciled but also pose a question as to what may have happened to them. Perhaps the checks have been lost or mislaid by the payee. Communication with the payee is in order.

If the payee claims not to have received a check, a new one will have to be issued in its place. This should be done, however, only after a stop-payment notice has been filed on the old check. How to stop payment on a check is described later in this chapter.

HANDLING CASH PAYMENTS

The secretary who takes care of the company bills accepts responsibility for paying the correct amount at the right time. To ensure proper payment, the secretary should (1) check to make sure that bills submitted to the employer are correct and (2) take measures to ensure that bills are at hand for payment when they are due.

Before drawing checks for the employer's signature, the secretary should thoroughly check the accuracy of the statements received. Compare the charges listed on the statement with the sales slips that are attached or other supporting evidence and make sure that proper credits have been allowed for returns and for payments that have been made on the account. The mathematical accuracy of all calculations on the statement should be verified.

Prompt payment of all bills is desirable; on some bills, payment on or before a given date is essential. Particular attention must be paid to insurance premiums, because policies lapse if premiums are not paid before a certain date, and to those bills that are subject to some form of additional charge if payment is not made within a stated period. Also, bills that allow for cash discount if paid within a certain time should be earmarked for timely payment. For example, the expression "2/10; n/30" stands for a 2-percent discount if paid within ten days; if not taken, the total is due within thirty days. In terms of annual notes, this is the equivalent of almost a 35-percent interest charge if the discount is not taken. One method of ensuring payment at the right time is the use of a tickler file in which bills are filed by the dates on which they should be paid.

Occasionally payments must be made in a foreign currency. The easiest means of making remittances to foreign countries is a draft payable in the funds of the country to which payment is to be sent. Drafts can be purchased at any bank. Personal checks can be used in some instances; however, this poses the problem of exchange rates and presents the possibility of over- or underpayment. The exchange rates fluctuate.

Writing Checks

Care should be exercised in writing checks. It is good policy to fill in the check stub first, to prevent the possibility of drawing a check without recording it. The date, the check number, the name of the payee, and the reason for the payment should all be listed on the stub. The reason for payment should contain enough information to permit later entry in the cash records. The check is filled in with the number (if not preprinted), the date, the name of payee, the amount in both figures and words, and the signature. Checks should be written legibly. No blank spaces that might be used to alter the check should be left. The amount in figures is placed close to the dollar sign, and the amount in words is started close to the left-hand side. The amount in words should agree with the amount in figures. In case of disagreement, the bank may refuse to honor the check. If the check is honored, the amount written in words governs. If the amount of the check is less than one dollar, it is customary to cross out the word "Dollars" and write "Only . . . cents."

Titles such as "Dr." or "Rev." are not used; it is "Ben Kildare," not "Dr. Ben Kildare." "Mrs." is used only in connection with the husband's name; it is either "Mrs. Roy Roe" or "Ruth Roe." Checks issued to organizations should be made payable to the organization, not to some individual in the organization. Likewise, checks should be made payable to companies rather than to their agents. Checks for insurance premiums, for example, would be drawn in favor of the insurance company rather than the agent who handles the account.

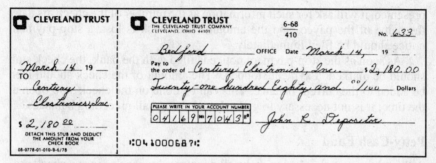

Figure 14-2.

It is not wise to sign blank checks. Should this be necessary when the employer will be absent from the office, the checkbook should be kept in a place where it will be safe from theft. Checks, like money, are a medium of exchange and should be guarded as carefully as money.

Erasures and alterations should never be made on checks. Banks are reluctant to accept checks if there is any suspicion that they have been tampered with. If mistakes are made in preparing a check, the word "VOID" should be written across the face of the check and on its stub. If the checks are prenumbered, spoiled checks should not be discarded; they should be kept with canceled checks so that there can be no question concerning the whereabouts of a missing check.

Certified Checks

Often checks for large amounts drawn by a person whose financial status is unknown to the payee must be certified by the bank before they are issued. To secure certification, the depositor takes a completed check to the bank. After the cashier has ascertained that the account has sufficient funds to cover it, the cashier stamps the check "CERTIFIED" and signs it. Immediately upon certification, the amount of the check is charged against the depositor's account. There can be no question concerning whether funds are available for payment when the check is presented. So far as the bank is concerned, it has already been paid. Thus in a bank reconciliation, a certified check is never outstanding, since it has been charged in advance.

Certified checks should never be destroyed. In the event that they are not sent to the payee, they should be redeposited in the bank.

Stopping Payment on a Check

The drawer of a check has the power to stop payment on it at any time prior to its presentation to the bank for payment. This is accomplished by filing a stop-payment notice at the bank on a form that the bank will provide. Oral notice is insufficient. So that the bank can identify the check when it is presented, it will ask for such information as the number of the check, its date, the name of the payee, and the amount. If a check is lost, a stop-payment notice should be filed immediately.

As soon as the stop-payment notice is filed with the bank, the check stub should be marked "Payment stopped." The amount of the check should then be added to the current balance. This can be done on the check stub open at the time; it is not necessary to go back and correct all preceding balances.

Petty-Cash Fund

Although it is good policy to make all payments by check, since a check provides a written record of the transaction and serves as a receipt, it is impractical to write checks for small amounts to cover items such as collect telegrams, postage due, carfare, supper money, and incidental purchases of office supplies. In some instances, too, cash is needed immediately. To meet these needs, it is customary to set up what is generally called a "petty-cash fund." Operation of the petty-cash fund is described in the following paragraphs.

Establishing the petty-cash fund. First, it is decided how much cash should be placed in the fund. This is determined by the expenditures that are anticipated. The amount should not be too high, yet it should not be so low that too-frequent reimbursements are required. When the amount has been set, a check is drawn payable to Petty Cash. The check is cashed and the funds are placed in a locked cash box or drawer, generally referred to as the petty-cash drawer. Responsibility for the fund should be placed in one person, and this person alone should have access to it.

Payments from the petty-cash fund. All payments from the petty-cash fund should be supported by documentary evidence in the form of a petty-cash voucher, showing the date of payment, the name of the payee, the reason for payment, and the amount paid out (see Figure 14-3). The petty-cash voucher is initialed by the person making payment and signed by the person who has received the cash. Printed forms for this purpose can be purchased at any stationery store.

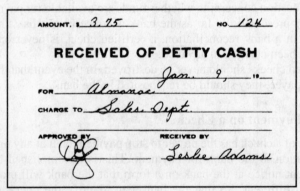

Figure 14-3.

Paid vouchers are placed in the petty-cash drawer or in a special envelope kept for this purpose. In addition, some firms maintain a petty-cash record. This is simply a form on which paid vouchers can be summarized. Columns are provided for the voucher number, date, name of payee, explanation of payment, and a summary of the expenditures made. Seldom is there a real need for such a record; the petty-cash vouchers themselves usually provide an adequate record. However, in a company with a system of bookkeeping that accounts for every expenditure, regardless of how small, the inclusion of petty-cash payments in the accounting books as part of the daily record may be the best procedure.

Replenishing the petty-cash fund. Whenever the cash in the petty-cash fund gets low, the fund is replenished. A check is written payable to Petty Cash for the amount that has been spent from the fund. The check is cashed and the proceeds are placed in the petty-cash drawer. After replenishment, the cash in the fund should amount to the fund originally established. If replenishment of the fund is taking place too often, consideration should be given to increasing the size of the fund.

BOOKKEEPING

There is a need to properly record the income and expense transactions of any business operation. There are two major purposes for this record keeping. One objective is to determine the profitability of the business. By being able to calculate the profit or loss of the operation and then to be able to analyze in detail the individual items of income and expense, the company is in a position to act with greater knowledge in its decisions. The second objective is to gather the necessary information required by the governmental tax agencies such as the Internal Revenue Service. These tax reports not only require a calculation of net income (income less total expense) but also detailed substantiation of individual amounts.

The preparation of these financial statements is usually the responsibility of the accountant. Much of the initial work, however, may be done by the bookkeeper. A secretary may be called upon to handle these bookkeeping duties. At this point, a brief description of the duties will be given. It should be understood that some of these tasks can be handled with little or no experience, while others require complete training as an accountant.

Business Records

Careful records of all payments, expenses, and other transactions must be kept to determine the profitability (or losses) of a business. Some of the tasks involved in keeping complete business records follow.

- Recording business transactions originally in journals. Most companies use what is referred to as a *double entry* system that has a "debit" and "credit" entry for each item.

- Posting the journal to the ledger. There will be a general ledger and there may be subsidiary ledgers for specific accounts, such as accounts receivable and accounts payable.
- Calculating a trial balance of all accounts in the ledger to determine if the accounts are in balance in terms of debits and credits.
- Adjusting journal entries to bring all accounts up to date. For example, any bills owed at the end of the year are recorded even though they will not be paid until the next year.
- Preparing the financial statements, primarily the Balance Sheet and the Income Statement. This usually involves the use of a worksheet.

The first two items and possibly the third are considered work normally done by the bookkeeper. The last two items are more often the job of the accountant. How a secretary fits into this process will depend upon the practice of the individual company.

Tax Records

Aside from the bookkeeping described above, there is a need to keep adequate tax records. Every business must pay a tax on its profits. A corporation pays its own income tax; income from a partnership or an individually owned business is added to the personal tax return of the individual owner. In each case there must be proof of the amounts recorded in the tax returns for income and expense. Save all receipts.

A sales invoice, a bill, a receipt for cash payment—all of these can be useful in providing the necessary documentation. A filing system that allows the accountant to find the necessary papers easily should be maintained.

A filing system can be set up on the basis of (1) date, with bills and invoices filed according to month; (2) type of expense—for example, office supplies or utilities; or (3) type of document—for example, invoice, cash receipt, or bill. Combinations of these systems are often used. The main point is that the system be based on a commonsense approach that other people can follow. The secretary is in a central position to see to it that the filing is correctly handled.

Travel and Entertainment Expenses

There are specific expense items for which the IRS requires a detailed record. An example of this type of expense and the additional record keeping involved is the travel and entertainment deduction (T & E). Adequate records would include:

- the amount of the expenditure
- the dates of departure and return for each trip and the number of days spent on business

- the business purpose of the expenditure
- the place of travel or entertainment
- the business relationship to the taxpayer of the person(s) being entertained

Documentary evidence in the form of credit card stubs and receipts of paid bills is required for (1) all expenditures for lodging while traveling away from home, and (2) any expenditure over the amount specified by the Internal Revenue Service. It is good practice to record all expenditures in an account book or diary and to attach receipts, paid bills, and other substantiating documents to the back of the page on which the expenditure is recorded. Employers will expect secretaries to handle this type of detailed record keeping. Usually the employer will turn over the raw information to the secretary and expect the secretary to put it together in a formal record (see Figure 14-4).

Automobile Expense Record

The taxpayer who uses a personal automobile in connection with business or employment is entitled to deduct automobile expenses (in whole if the auto is used exclusively for business, or in part if it is used for both business and pleasure) on the income-tax return. Expenses include not only all the operating costs but also a reasonable allowance for depreciation. To ensure receiving full benefit from allowable deductions, the taxpayer would be wise to keep careful account of expenses and mileage on an automobile-expense record. A simple form for this purpose, set up to accumulate expenses on an annual basis, is shown in Figure 14-5.

The secretary can keep the record by using information supplied by the employer or, better yet, by making entries from bills routinely filed. The calculation for depreciation can best be made by the accountant responsible for preparing the tax return.

If records are not kept on automobile expenses, an optional tax-deduction method is allowed by the IRS. A standard mileage rate for business use each year instead of a record of the actual operating and fixed expenses and separate deduction for depreciation may be used by an individual. Interest payments on loans and state and local taxes (other than the gasoline tax) attributable to the business use of the car are deductible in addition to the standard mileage rate.

Always check current IRS booklets for detailed information and for rules on necessary record keeping.

Employer's Personal Tax Records

There are a number of different nonbusiness expenses that are deductible on the individual's personal income-tax return. As with business expenses, it is important that there exist adequate evidence of the payment of these expenses.

TRAVEL EXPENSE REPORT

Name	Harriet Blasko		Sales No		Dept No. 510-076		Date 8/16		Approvals *PBM*		
Business Purpose	Annual Convention of Purchasing Agents			Debit Acct				Credit Acct.		Amt	

Day	Date	Mil./Dr.	Location	Hotel	Meals	Ent'm't	Tel/Tel	Air	Transportation Gas/Oil	Other	Park/Tolls	Other	TOTALS
Sun.													
Mon.													
Tue.													
Wed.													
Thu.	8/12		Kansas City	28.50	21.75	45.00	2.30	82.73	10.30		50.00		240.58
Fri.	8/13		"	--	19.80				10.50				30.30
Sat.													
			TOTALS										270.88

ITEMIZED ENTERTAINMENT RECORD

Date	Location	Business Purpose	Persons Ent'ed/Business Relationship	Amount
8/12	Jet Night Club	Inquiry on discounts for processing equipment	Elvin Hayes & Adele Vasquez, Acme Products	45.00

Miles @ 10¢	
TOTAL	270.88
Less Airline Charges	82.73
Less Other Charges	
TOTAL	188.15
Cash Advance	
Due Me	188.15
Returned Herewith	

DETAIL OF OTHER EXPENDITURES

Date	Item	Total
8/12	cab: airport - hotel	10.30
8/13	" hotel - airport	10.50
8/12	Convention Registration fee	50.00

INSTRUCTIONS

1. Receipts for lodging, the customer copy of airline tickets, receipts for supplies and each item over $25 should be attached to the report.
2. Meal charges may be included in the report if the employee is away from home "overnight."
3. Include tips for meals and taxis in meal and transportation charges. Tipping for other services should be listed under "Other" expenses and itemized in the space provided.
4. Under "Other" expenditures include items such as luggage tips, supplies, postage, valet, and laundry.
5. Charges for transportation should be identified, such as bus, taxi, train, or rental car. Rental car receipts should be attached to the report.
6. If the space provided for entertainment is inadequate, use a separate memorandum for the overflow.
7. Expense reports are to be submitted weekly and should be sent to the office no later than the Friday following the week in which the expenditures occur.

Signed *Harriet Blasko*	Send Check To	Harriet Blasko, Purchasing Dept.

Figure 14-4.

The secretary may be called upon by the employer to keep an additional set of records for these personal expenses. The expense deductions include: (1) contributions to charities, colleges, etc., (2) medical and dental expenses, (3) interest on mortgages, loans, etc., and (4) taxes. The most important proof is the canceled check indicating payment. In most situations this is usually sufficient. However, occasionally more evidence is required. Thus a file of the bills would be helpful in substantiating a tax deduction. The employer should turn over personal bank statements with the canceled checks, or at

RECORD OF AUTOMOBILE UPKEEP FOR THE   Month of *January*   1994

DATE	MILEAGE	GASOLINE		OIL AND GREASE	STORAGE and PARKING	AUTO REPAIRS	CLEANING AND WASHING	ACCESS-ORIES	MISCEL-LANEOUS
		No. Gals.	Amount						
1									
2	22,346	10	11 40						
3					2 00				
4							3 75		
5					2 75				
6				16 00		18 00			54 30
7		14	15 96						
29					3 15				
30		12	13 72						
31	24,180								
TOTAL	1,834			16 00	10 70	18 00	7 50		54 30

Figure 14-5.

least the ones to be recorded, along with the bills received. The degree that the employer wants the secretary involved in personal financial matters will obviously affect the amount of record keeping that will be necessary.

PAYROLL

The secretary may be called in to handle the payroll of the company. This will involve (1) calculating the net amount to be paid out and (2) keeping payroll records required for computing the various kinds of payroll taxes and for the government reports. The following section describes these procedures in some detail.

The federal government requires that the employer withhold from each employee's salary a sufficient amount that will at year's end add up to the amount of income tax due. The employee when first hired must fill out a form indicating the number of exemptions claimed. The number of exemptions is then used in calculating, according to IRS guidelines, how much tax should be withheld for each salary level.

There also may be state and city income taxes that will require additional withholdings from the employee's payroll check. While the general procedures are basically the same, it is important that the secretary follow the specific requirements of each governmental agency.

Beside the various income taxes, the Federal Insurance Contributions Act (FICA) requires employees to pay a percentage of their salary as their contribution to the Social Security program. (There is a matching contribution that is paid by the employer.) The rate is fixed at a certain percentage of the annual salary up to a given amount. After this figure is reached, no more FICA tax is to be paid. Each year FICA tables are prepared for the various salary levels.

The following example uses the figure 7.65% FICA tax to be withheld from the annual salary:

> Employee A, married with two children, may claim four exemptions. If A's weekly salary were $300, the payroll check would be calculated as follows:

Gross Pay		$300.00
Less: Federal Income Tax Withheld	$33.30	
FICA Tax Withheld (7.65% × $300)	22.95	
Total Withheld		−56.25
Net Pay—Amount of Check		243.75

The illustration could have been more complex if state and city income taxes were included. Beside the taxes that are withheld, the company sometimes withholds medical insurance, union dues, contributions to charity or retirement programs, and other agreed-upon items.

The monies withheld from the employee's paycheck have to be remitted periodically to the respective agencies. Thus, for example, the federal income tax withheld, plus the FICA tax withheld, and the employer's matching FICA tax contribution must be sent to the Internal Revenue Service (or a bank authorized to act as the depositor). How often this is to be done depends upon the dollar amount:

> Less than $500 a month—Every three months
>
> More than $500 but less than $3000 a month—Every month
>
> More than $3000 a month—Every two weeks

At the end of each three-month period, a payroll tax return form is required to be filed with the IRS. This requirement normally is not the responsibility of the secretary. However, keeping the detailed payroll records may be one of the duties. This will require a record of each pay period showing the dates, hours, and earnings of each employee and a record of each employee's earnings showing date of employment and discharge, social security number, rate or method of pay, and summary of wages and all deductions by quarter and calendar year.

There are additional reports required at the end of each year. These include the *Employer's Annual Federal Unemployment Tax Return* (Form 940) and a *Wage and Tax Statement* (Form W-2) for each employee. On the state and local governmental level, quarterly and annual income and unemployment tax returns may be required depending on state and local regulations.

It is important to point out that the ability to manage all of these tax and payroll reports is normally *not* the responsibility of the secretary. Usually the company has an accountant who handles these items. However, the accountant may delegate much of the work to the bookkeeper or the secretary and act only as a supervisor. Therefore, it is helpful to be familiar with payroll procedures and tax reports in case these areas become your responsibility.

Special Functions

15

Special Secretarial Functions

by Jeanette L. Bely, Ph.D., F.I.B.A.
revised by Barry Persky

■ *Organizing Meetings and Conferences*

Preparation Phase
During the Meeting
After the Meeting

MAKING TRAVEL ARRANGEMENTS

Many firms today have extended and expanded their interests and scope into the international picture. This broadening of the horizons makes it more likely that the executive will travel to maintain contacts with the firm's branches and customers, to attend meetings and conventions, to lecture, or just to relax. With the need for increased travel, the means of transportation have become more convenient and many-faceted. To ensure a smooth and enjoyable trip for the employer, the secretary should be familiar with the various means of transportation that are available. It is the secretary's responsibility to make sure that the executive gets to the destination on time and in comfort and that the supplies and documents necessary for a successful trip are at the disposal of the traveler.

Before the secretary can make any arrangements for the trip, certain facts need to be compiled. The planner must know departure date and time, cities to be visited, length of time to be spent in each locality, the purpose of each visit, the time and day the traveler must arrive in each city to keep scheduled appointments, preferences as to means of travel, and how many people will be traveling. Supplied with this information, the secretary can take the next step in making travel arrangements—the compiling of an itinerary—and then proceed to complete all other tasks necessary.

Compiling an Itinerary

As bits and pieces of information are gathered, it is a good practice to draw up a tentative itinerary or a worksheet on which notations of alternate flights, alternate train schedules, costs, and so forth can be presented for the executive's approval and selection. Such a worksheet might contain the following information: dates, destination, airport, railroad station, departure time, time of arrival, hotel accommodations, appointments (where and with whom), and reference materials.

The secretary should start the preliminary planning of the itinerary from the dates and times provided by the executive. Then a listing of whatever travel methods the employer prefers that are available at the times indicated should be added to the worksheet. If the means of transportation are left open, complete information on all airlines and railroads serving the city of destination, with arrival and departure times and the costs of each, should be obtained. Information about car rental agencies at the various destinations may be included. It is wise to indicate all possible choices available and permit the executive to make the decision as to which means of travel is preferred. The worksheet should be revised periodically with the approval of the executive until the decisions are complete and the itinerary is ready to be finalized.

In planning an itinerary, the secretary must bear in mind that the traveler must eat regularly while traveling, must rest, must have enough time to get from a terminal to the place of an appointment, and so forth. Therefore, the following information should be included in the schedule:

- eating locations (plane, train, hotel, restaurant, etc.)
- allowance of time to go from the point of arrival to the appointment at the designated hour and without pressure
- applicable time zones, noted in indicated time on the itinerary (EST, EDST, etc.)
- all confirmations for hotel accommodations, attached to the itinerary
- all confirmations for transportation, airline tickets, etc., attached to the itinerary

Multiple copies of the final draft should be prepared: one for the office files, one or two for the executive, one for the traveler's family, and, if customary, copies for key people in the organization.

Data and Supplies for the Trip

If the executive's trip is entirely for business or is part business and part pleasure, the secretary's duties in making travel arrangements do not stop with the completion of the itinerary. The secretary should prepare an appointments schedule; pertinent files, including past correspondence and memory refresher notes; stationery and other supplies that might be needed; an expense record book; and any other supplies the traveler may need to be prepared for the calls, be able to communicate with the home office, and keep necessary records.

Appointments Calendar

The secretary should prepare an appointments calendar listing all the calls to be made while traveling. Such a schedule is usually made only for the executive and secretary, and it is not distributed to anyone else. It can be either combined with the itinerary or prepared as a separate schedule, depending on the executive's preference.

The appointments schedule should include the following:

- name of the city and state in which the call is to be made
- date and time of the appointment
- name and address of the firm to which the executive is going
- name of the individual with whom the appointment is made
- telephone number of the firm or individual (if known)
- remarks or special reminders about each visit
- reference to the file number of the data the traveler is taking along for each call

Pertinent Files

The secretary should prepare a file for each company to be visited. Then, the executive will not need to rely on memory alone for information regarding the company and past associations. A memory refresher file may, indeed, help make the call productive.

A separate folder should be prepared for each call, and each folder should bear a reference number that is keyed to the schedule of appointments. The folders should be arranged in the order in which the calls will be made.

Each folder should contain:

- copies of past correspondence with the firm or individual
- letters or memos concerning the problem to be discussed
- a list of the persons to see and their positions in the company
- a list of the officers and executives of the organization
- a list of the persons with whom the executive has had contact in the past, other than those with whom appointments are scheduled, and the circumstances of these contacts
- other bits of information, regardless of how insignificant they may seem

Stationery and Other Supplies

In addition to the files of correspondence and other data that the executive will take along, it is wise to provide the traveler with some stationery and supplies for communication with the office and with others while traveling. For this purpose the secretary should draw up a checklist of those supplies to be taken, assemble all the materials, and pack them in the briefcase. Supplies that the executive might require include company stationery, plain paper, envelopes of various sizes, memo paper or pads, a legal pad, an address book, legal-size folders, letter-size folders, business cards, dictation equipment (portable recorder), cassette tapes for recorder, mailing folders or boxes for dictation tapes, office account checks, expense forms, other office forms, pens and pencils, erasers, clips, scissors, rubber bands, transparent tape, paste, calendar, pins, a bottle opener, a ruler, a timetable, and postage stamps. The materials that the executive selects from the checklist should be assembled by the secretary, checked by the executive, and made ready for packing at least a day before departure.

Expense Record Book

The expense record forms or expense book should be packed on top, so that expenses can be recorded as the executive goes along. This is a very important detail, because the expense record is needed for income-tax and

Charles Murray Itinerary February 19, 19__

Tuesday, February 19 (New York to Raleigh)

10:00 a.m.	Leave West Side Airline Terminal, New York, by limousine or van for Newark airport.
11:10 a.m.	Leave Newark airport on Eastern Airlines Flight #275 (lunch). (Ticket attached)
1:19 p.m.	Arrive Raleigh. Van to Hotel Hilton. (Reservation attached)
2:00 p.m.	Robert Lee, Office Manager at Raleigh branch, will pick you up at the Hilton. Conference scheduled at branch office. (File #1 in briefcase)

Wednesday, February 20 (Raleigh)

9:00 a.m.	Robert Lee will pick you up at the hotel for inspection of Raleigh plant. (File #2 in briefcase contains facts and statistics on plant operation)
8:00 p.m.	Company dinner at Hotel Hilton. (Speech in File #3 in briefcase)

Thursday, February 21 (Raleigh to Winston-Salem via Greensboro)

9:30 a.m.	Robert Lee will pick you up at the hotel and drive you to the airport.
9:56 a.m.	Leave Raleigh on Delta Airlines Flight #101. (Ticket attached)
10:18 a.m.	Arrive Greensboro airport. Limousine or van to Winston-Salem Hotel in Winston-Salem. (Reservation attached) Lunch at hotel.
3:00 p.m.	Appointment with John Spaaks, Office Manager at Winston-Salem branch, and Al Smith, Sales Director. Hotel Winston-Salem, Green Room. (File #4 in briefcase)
7:00 p.m.	Dinner at Bill Lawson's home. (Telephone 722-1234)

Friday, February 22 (Winston-Salem)

9:00 a.m.	Golf with Bill Lawson.
1:00 p.m.	Conference with staff at Winston-Salem offices. (File #5 in briefcase)
8:00 p.m.	Company dinner at Winston-Salem Hotel. (Speech in File #6 in briefcase)

Saturday, February 23 (Winston-Salem to Greenville via Asheville)

9:02 a.m.   Leave Winston-Salem on Southern Airlines Flight #501. (Ticket attached)

10:10 a.m. Arrive Asheville. Limousine or van to Greenville Hotel in Greenville. (Reservation attached) Lunch at hotel.

2:00 p.m.   Conference with Greenville branch office manager Jim Turrell at Greenville Hotel, Mezzanine Lounge. (File #7 in briefcase)

7:00 p.m.   Company dinner at hotel. (Speech in File #8 in briefcase)

Sunday, February 24 (Greenville to Columbia)

3:00 p.m.   Leave Greenville/Spartanburg airport on Southern Airlines commuter flight #38. (Ticket attached)

4:00 p.m.   Arrive Columbia. George Lewis, Office Manager, will meet you at airport. Magnolia Hotel. (Reservation attached)

Monday, February 25 (Columbia)

9:00 a.m.   Conference at Columbia offices. George Lewis will pick you up at the hotel. (File #9 in briefcase contains statistics and progress reports from this branch)

7:00 p.m.   Dinner meeting of Columbia staff at Magnolia Hotel. (Speech in File #10 in briefcase)

Tuesday, February 26 (Columbia to New York)

10:00 a.m. George Lewis will pick you up to take you to the airport.

11:07 a.m. Leave Columbia on Eastern Airlines Flight #666 (lunch). (Ticket attached)

2:33 p.m.   Arrive Newark airport. Limousine to New York offices.

accounting purposes. Generally the following information is needed if the executive is to be reimbursed in part or whole for the trip or to be able to deduct business-incurred travel expense from income tax: date of trip; description of how expense was incurred; types of expense (transportation, entertainment, breakfast, lunch, dinner, and so forth); and amount reimbursed by the company. In some instances receipts must be obtained for travel expenses. Therefore, a secretary should be familiar with the company and income-tax requirements in this area and should attach a reminder to the expense forms or expense book for the traveling executive to obtain these receipts as the occasions arise.

Arrangements for Domestic Trips

Large organizations generally have departments that make all the arrangements pertinent to a trip. If the company has such a department, the executive's secretary submits to this department the data that have been obtained from the executive about the trip, and then the department takes over. It works out the itinerary with the traveler's approval, makes all the reservations for transportation and accommodations, and obtains the confirmations. This information is sent to the executive's office well in advance of the departure date.

Where there is no department in an organization, the secretary may either call on the services of a reliable travel agency or take care of the arrangements personally.

An easy way to obtain reservations for domestic and foreign travel is through the services of a reliable travel agency. Many executives rely on these services to plan their trips and to make their reservations. This method saves the secretary considerable time. Furthermore, travel agencies can usually obtain better and faster services than an individual who lacks their contacts and their specialized experience and knowledge.

If the secretary or the executive does not know the name of a good travel agency, he or she can contact The American Society of Travel Agents, Inc., at 1101 King Street, Alexandria, VA 22314. However, not all of the good travel agents belong to this society. Others may be listed in the classified telephone directory.

The secretary must provide the travel agent with the executive's name, business and home telephone numbers, credit card number (if pertinent), detailed information on dates and times of arrival and departure desired for each city to be visited, and the type of transportation preferred. Although the agent will report periodically the progress made, it is the secretary's responsibility to keep in touch with the agent in order to see to it that tickets and reservations arrive at the office in plenty of time to check the dates, times, destinations, and so forth before they are turned over to the traveler.

Agencies do not charge for making airline or hotel reservations, since they receive a commission from the hotel or airline with which the reservation is placed. There is sometimes a charge, however, for rail reservations unless they are part of a prearranged package tour. Refunds for any unused tickets are obtained by the agency and should be reflected as deductions from the charges made on bills. The agency should be instructed that all bills are to be sent to the attention of the executive or the secretary, so that they can be checked before being forwarded to the accounting department.

If the secretary has access to on-line services, one of the services might be the Official Airline Guide Electronic Edition (OAGEE). The following are just some of the on-line services OAGEE offers: the latest flight information; ticketing; credit card arrangements; seating preferences; meal selection; hotel and motel reservations, including banquet and conference facilities and restaurant information; weather conditions and travel tips throughout the world.

Making Reservations for Transportation

Plane travel. The types of plane service available are first class, business class, and coach. All types of accommodations are often available on the same plane. The main differences are the size and comfort of the seats and the type of meals. First-class passengers enjoy wider seats and more legroom. They are served restaurant-like meal on china and complimentary alcoholic beverages. Business-class passengers sit in slightly smaller seats, and there are no middle seats. The meals are similar to those in first class. The coach section of the plane may be larger with smaller seats set closer together. The meals are less elaborate and alcoholic beverages must be purchased separately.

It has become the policy of many companies to request traveling personnel to use business class service on plane travel. The executive who prefers to travel first class must personally pay the difference. The secretary should check company policy on this and then determine the executive's preference each time a trip is to be made. The executive may be willing to pay the difference if a very long flight is involved. If a first-class flight is to be made, the difference in cost must be entered in the correct place in the expense sheet.

Shuttle plane service may offer only a single class, especially when the flight is made in a smaller plane.

The secretary whose executive travels extensively should add an airline guidebook to the desk reference library for information on airlines servicing each city in the nation. The *Official Airlines Guide* may be obtained by writing to Official Airlines Guide, 2000 Clearwater Drive, Oak Brook, IL 60521 (1-800-323-3537). Each city in the United States and its possessions and each city in Canada that is serviced by an airline is listed in this book; the book indicates the airlines that service each city and gives information on car-rental and taxi service in each city.

Airline schedules may be kept on hand and the executive and the secretary may check the schedule before calling for reservations. The schedules need to be updated regularly, because flights may have been added or canceled or have changes of time. All the major airlines have 800 numbers.

To make a plane reservation, the secretary should call the reservation desk of the airline chosen by the executive and give the executive's name, the name and address of the firm, the credit card number, the executive's home telephone number, the desired flight number, the city of departure and the city of destination, and the time that the flight is scheduled to leave. If the flight is already filled or a considerable change in time has been posted, the secretary should ask for alternative suggestions. If none of the suggestions is acceptable to the executive, ask to be placed on the standby list and then try to make reservations on some other airline. As soon as a reservation is available and a definite confirmation is received, the secretary should immediately cancel all the other pending alternative arrangements. This will ensure the good will of persons the secretary may want to deal with in the future.

In placing airline reservations, the secretary should get the name of the airline clerk who makes the original reservations. If flight plans are extremely involved, with layovers in different cities and changes of time zones, the secretary may avoid repeating the information if the same clerk is available when checking or changing plans.

Payment for airline tickets is generally made by credit card or standard billing. The secretary should be absolutely certain that there is time for an airline ticket to arrive in the mail prior to a flight. If there is some doubt, the executive should pick up the ticket at the airport before boarding the plane. If the ticket comes in advance, the various parts must be checked carefully against the information on the itinerary as to the correctness of flight numbers, the time of departure, the departure airport, and the city of destination. If any discrepancies are noted, the secretary must immediately notify the reservation clerk.

Train travel. The choice of available train accommodations may depend upon the length of the trip and the price of the accommodations. The least expensive way of traveling is by coach. For long trips, the traveler may prefer a Pullman accommodation. For the most part, Pullman accommodations offered are roomettes and bedrooms. A roomette is a private room, usually for one person, with a bed folding into the wall, a sofa seat for daytime use, and toilet facilities in the same room. A bedroom is a private room with lower and upper berths, the lower berth serving as a sofa for daytime use, and toilet facilities in the same room. Bedrooms are more expensive than roomettes.

The secretary should be aware that not all trains provide all the above accommodations. Railroad connections to many destinations are increasingly limited. For more rail information, contact *The National Railway Publication* at 424 W. 33 Street, New York, NY 10001.

Automobile travel. Sometimes a trip may be more easily and conveniently made by car, or the executive may rent a car to reach the desired destination after disembarking from plane or train. In that case, and if the executive is a member of the American Automobile Association (AAA), help can be obtained from its travel department in planning the route that should be followed on the trip. The AAA will prepare a *Triptik,* which is a detailed, up-to-the-minute strip map of the entire trip, listing recommended hotels and AAA service stations along the route. This association also assists members in obtaining hotel and resort accommodations.

If the executive is not a member of the AAA, the secretary's task is more complicated. Road maps and city maps may be obtained from the Tourist Bureaus in the various states and cities, but they must be sent for well in advance. Nowadays there is sometimes a fee involved, and the secretary will have to write a second letter after the amount of this is made known.

Most drivers have a preferred method of mapping out the route for a trip. If the secretary is asked to determine the best driving route to a destination, the executive's preferred method of recording this should be determined. Some drivers mark out a route directly on the map with a transparent felt-tipped pen. Others write out an itinerary to be followed.

If a car is to be rented, arrangements should be made as far in advance as possible. Rates vary according to the size of car to be rented, so the executive's preference should be determined before the reservations are made. If the car is to be left at a different city or airport from the one where it is rented, the secretary will need to make sure that the car-rental agency has a branch at the second location.

Bus travel. With the improvements in equipment and services offered by bus lines, the economy-minded traveler may choose to use this means of travel for all or intervening portions of a trip. Bus lines have passenger service agents who will assist in planning either long or short trips. Timetables should be obtained and the route laid out well before reservations are placed for a bus trip.

Refunds for Unused Tickets

On occasion the executive may need to change travel plans en route. In such a case the traveler is entitled to a refund on the unused portion of the ticket. The transportation line should be informed at once when the need for cancellation becomes apparent.

The secretary may send an unused flight ticket with a covering letter to the Refund Accounting Department of the airline involved. In the letter the secretary should mention the date of the flight that the executive was to have taken, the city of departure, the city of destination, the ticket number, the flight number, the credit card number, and the cost of the ticket. Refunds for train travel may be handled in a similar fashion.

Making Motel or Hotel Reservations

Reservations for motel or hotel accommodations should be made as soon as possible. Delay can cause the executive to arrive in a strange city without any place to stay. Therefore, the secretary must be certain that reservations for all motel or hotel accommodations have been made and confirmed before the executive leaves on a trip.

If the motel or hotel at which the executive plans to stay is part of a chain, the easiest and quickest way for the secretary to make reservations is to call the chain's toll-free number for the central location through which all reservations for motels or hotels in the chain are handled.

In making reservations for overnight accommodations, the following sources contain information:

- *Hotel and Motel Red Book,* published annually by the American Hotel and Motel Association Directory Corporation, 1201 New York Avenue NW, Washington, DC 20036. This book lists the hotels and motels by city and state; indicates the number of rooms, rates, and plans under which they operate (American, with meals; European, without meals); lists recreational facilities; gives telephone and toll-free telephone numbers for each hotel; and indicates whether the hotel or motel belongs to a chain. A special section lists number and types of meeting rooms of various seating capacities, along with facilities available in these rooms for PA systems, lecterns, showing of films, etc.

- Chamber of Commerce or Tourist Information Bureau in city of destination.

- Folders from the American Automobile Association, which list motels, hotels, and inns for automobile travelers.

In making reservations for overnight accommodations, the following information must be supplied to the person taking reservations: the name and address of the traveler, the type of accommodations desired, the date of arrival, the approximate time of day of arrival, and the probable departure date. The secretary should be sure to obtain the checkout time, since this varies from one place to another, and to request a confirmation of the reservation by mail. These confirmations should be attached to the traveler's itinerary. Unless a request for accommodations has been confirmed, there is no assurance that a room will be held for the traveler. Some motels and hotels confirm reservations only if a deposit is made in advance.

Generally if a reservation is not picked up by 6 P.M., the room is not held. Therefore, if the traveler will arrive later than 6 P.M., it would be wise to either make a deposit or put the room charges on a credit card to ensure that the room will be held. If such a deposit is not made and the traveler is held up along the way, he or she should call the motel or hotel if possible and ask that the reservation be held.

If the executive changes plans about itinerary or hotel after the reservation is made, the secretary should contact the motel or hotel to cancel the reservation.

Arrangements for Foreign Travel

Preparations for foreign travel should be made far in advance of the departure date. There are many more details to be considered than in domestic travel arrangements, and many phases of such an undertaking involve much time. Before any arrangements for travel accommodations are started, the traveler should know

- the names of the persons to be seen in what countries and for how long
- the U.S. government requirements regarding travel to foreign countries
- the requirements of the government of the country or countries to be visited
- any conditions that are imposed on business travelers but not on tourists, and
- something about the countries to be visited

Using a travel agency. It is advisable that the arrangements for foreign travel be made by a reliable travel agency, unless the organization has a traffic department and foreign branches in the countries to be visited. Under any circumstances, the executive's secretary must know where to obtain information in preparation for the executive's trip abroad and the data that will be needed for such a trip. The travel agency chosen should be one that will work out a personal itinerary for the traveling executive, rather than an agency that specializes in package tours. A reliable agency will take care of all of the details pertaining to the trip and will perform the following services for its clientele:

- Prepare a tentative itinerary, which the executive can approve or change.
- Handle all the arrangements for traveling, for hotels, and perhaps for sightseeing for the entire trip.
- Provide information as to exactly which documents will be needed (passport, visas, health and police certificates, etc.) and how to obtain them.
- Obtain all the documents that they can (certain documents the executive must obtain personally).
- Help to obtain a letter of credit or traveler's checks.
- Arrange to have a rental car waiting for the executive at the destination point, if desired.
- Handle both personal and baggage insurance, if desired.
- If the executive is uncertain about accommodations and is unable to make arrangements before leaving, supply the name of a desirable hotel in the country of destination, as well as a letter of introduction to the manager of the hotel

Preliminary preparations. For help in arranging a foreign business trip, the secretary can contact the Bureau of International Commerce in the Department of Commerce. This government department maintains a staff of specialists on individual countries and can contact foreign-trade experts who are stationed at each of the Department's field offices. This bureau will supply information on economic developments, regulations and trade statistics on any country, distribution methods, foreign costs and their effect on sales prices, types of distributors, and names of key commercial officers to contact both in the United States and in the countries to be visited. It will also set up the executive's overseas appointments and will notify all U.S. Foreign Service posts, such as the embassies, consulates, and consuls general, that the executive is coming to those countries and alert them as to the purpose of the visit. The bureau will request that these posts provide any assistance that is needed. Furthermore, the Washington Bureau of International Commerce maintains a trade complaint service, with which a traveler can communicate if any dispute with a foreign country should arise; this bureau safeguards and protects the industrial property rights to patents, trademarks, and copyrights abroad.

A very important secretarial duty in making preparations for the executive's trip abroad is writing letters to pave the way for a good reception in the countries to be visited. The secretary should write to the companies to be visited to make and confirm appointments, giving the time of arrival, the length of time the executive expects to stay, the address where reservations have been made, and any other pertinent information that will make it possible to aid the executive in the country of destination. The secretary should not overlook checking the holiday dates of the countries to be visited, so that an appointment will not be planned for a day when the offices will be closed. It should be borne in mind that many countries celebrate holidays that differ from those in the United States.

Passports. All U.S. citizens traveling abroad are required to carry a passport. Anyone requiring a passport can apply for one at a passport agent's office or through a clerk of a Federal court, state court, or court of record; a judge or clerk of a probate court; or a designated postal clerk. Passport agencies are located in Boston, Chicago, Honolulu, Houston, Los Angeles, Miami, New Orleans, New York, Philadelphia, San Francisco, Seattle, Stamford (Connecticut), and Washington, D.C. For passport information contact Passport Services, Bureau of Consular Affairs, 1425 K Street NW, Washington, D.C. 20524, or call 202-647-0518.

The traveler should allow several weeks for a passport application to be processed if it is being handled by mail. One can be obtained in person the same day. The applicant is required to show proof of citizenship (birth certificate with embossed seal, certificate of naturalization, baptismal certificate, or voter registration certificate). Two full-face, front-view passport photos must be presented. Many photo shops offer this service. Once a passport has been issued, it is valid for ten years.

Visas. Some countries require that visitors obtain permission to enter the country through a document referred to as a "visa." Therefore the secretary should call the consulates of the countries that the executive intends to visit and find out whether a visa is necessary. If it is, a passport must be presented by the traveler at the consulate and a visa form filled out. Since the length of time it takes to process a visa varies with the country to be visited, this must be done well in advance of the set departure date. The secretary should also find out from the consulate what the fee for the visa will be, since a charge for this document is generally made.

Customs regulations. In order to avoid difficulties upon the traveler's return to this country, the secretary should obtain information about the customs regulations for travelers abroad and present it to the executive. Such information can be procured from pamphlets issued by the U.S. Treasury Department, Bureau of Commerce, Washington, D.C., and from the travel agent who is arranging the trip.

The secretary should remind the executive that if a watch, a camera, or any other item of foreign manufacture that was purchased in the United States is being taken abroad, it will be necessary to carry proof of purchase such as a sales slip for each of the items. Such possessions should also be registered with the U.S. Customs officials before the executive leaves, in order to eliminate possible customs problems upon reentry.

During the trip, the executive will expect to be kept posted on events occurring at the home office. Therefore, it is important to determine which items are to be referred to other people in the organization and which are to be forwarded to the traveler. Some employers request that the secretary keep a log of daily events and send it on to them at specific times. If the secretary keeps abreast of the traveler's itinerary and uses fax transmissions, the traveler can be kept informed about events in the home office. The secretary should keep a duplicate copy of all correspondence that is forwarded and number each packet sent, so that any loss can be detected.

If it is necessary to send a package to the executive in some foreign country, the secretary should first check with the post office about mailing regulations, restrictions, and requirements.

For urgent messages that need immediate attention, the secretary can rely on E-mail, telephone, telegram, or cablegram services.

The Traveling Secretary

At times it is necessary for the executive to take along a secretary on a business trip. Although today the executive has several means to facilitate business needs, such as portable recorders, public stenographers, etc., an employer may prefer to take the secretary on the trip because much of the work to be done would take a great deal of explaining to one unfamiliar with it.

A secretary who travels with an employer should be prepared for and try to foresee all contingencies that may arise during the trip. The secretary should determine which supplies should be taken along and which will be easily available at the destination.

If the executive will want material typed, arrangements for a computer must be made. A laptop or notebook may be taken along if one is available. If not, the secretary may write ahead to the hotel or motel and arrange for a rental. Then again, it may be possible for the traveling secretary to type up reports or speeches as needed in a branch office of the company. If arrangements for this courtesy can be made in advance, the way may be paved for a harmonious sharing of space and office equipment during the trip.

SOCIAL AMENITIES

Visiting Cards

Executives must use both business and personal cards. A secretary encloses an executive's business card when sending a gift to a business associate. However, if the individual becomes a personal friend—that is, someone whom the executive sees outside of business hours—the executive's personal card should be used. The secretary should also enclose the executive's personal card in greetings and presents that are sent to personal friends and to relatives.

Visiting cards that are collected from clients or other visitors should be stored in a reference file for easy access when they are needed.

Donations

An executive usually receives many requests for donations annually, and many individuals respond to these pleas. It is not the secretary's responsibility to screen such requests before submitting them to the employer. Every request for a donation must be submitted for the executive's attention and decision. However, it is the secretary's responsibility to keep a record, and (if possible) a receipt, for all donations made by the executive to educational, religious, and philanthropic organizations. These records are very important for income-tax purposes and for the donor's own information.

When a request for a donation or contribution comes into the office, it will aid the executive if the secretary notes on each request the amount given to that organization in the preceding year and the total amount of contributions made during the current year. If a pledge was made that is payable in installments, the due dates of the payments should be entered on the secretary's calendar or in the card tickler and brought to the executive's attention as they occur. At the end of the year a list should be compiled of all the organizations to which the executive has contributed, with the amounts of the donations given to each organization clearly shown.

Invitations

Invitations extended by the executive to two types of functions are of particular concern to the secretary. These functions are formal dinners that are given personally and official entertainments given by the executive in an official capacity. Invitations for either of these functions are usually formal in style. This means that they should be written in the third person. They may be engraved, partly engraved, or handwritten.

An executive who entertains frequently may wish to have a quantity of partially engraved invitations made up. When the time comes to put them to use, the name of the guest, the kind of gathering, and the time and date can be filled in by hand. A partially engraved invitation generally follows this form:

Mr. and Mrs. Harold Jones
request the pleasure of
(name written in)
company at
on
at   o'clock
35 Woodlawn Avenue

Answers to Invitations

Etiquette requires that an invitation be answered promptly in the same form in which it was issued; that is, if the invitation was issued in the third person, it should be answered in the third person. Formal answers are used in reply to formal invitations.

The full name of the person answering the invitation should appear. If the invitation is sent in more than one name, all the names mentioned should be shown in the reply. The date and the hour that the function is to take place should be specified in an acceptance, but only the date need be mentioned in a regret. The year of the date is omitted. When referring to the invitation in a reply, it is courteous to refer to it as a "very kind invitation."

Answers to invitations to social business functions, such as luncheons, dinners, or receptions, should be on business letterhead paper. If it is necessary to explain the reason for declining the invitation, a letter of explanation should follow the formal note of regret. Generally no reason need be given.

The secretary should keep a record of invitations received by the executive. The events should also be marked on the calendar or in the tickler file so that the employer can be reminded of them in advance. Also, if the employer should take the invitation home, the secretary will have a record of the host, time, place, and date of the affair, so that the invitation can be answered correctly when the decision on attendance is made.

If the invitation originates with the executive, the secretary should type a list of the guests to whom the invitations were sent. As the acceptances and regrets come in, a notation should be made next to the name of each guest, and the letters should be attached to the list. It is helpful to make a daily summary of the total number of acceptances, regrets, and nonresponses to the invitations sent out. This summary should be placed on the executive's desk at the end of each day.

When dinner or luncheon invitations have specified a definite return date for reply and no reply has been received from some of the guests on the list, it is perfectly permissible for the secretary to telephone the invited guests three or four days before the event. This is done in order to determine the number of guests who will be present.

Theater Tickets

A secretary is sometimes called upon to obtain theater tickets for the executive and guests. The executive may name several shows in order of preference. The usual procedure in buying tickets is to call the box office and charge tickets to the executive's credit card account. Or, the secretary may go in person to a Ticketron location if there is one nearby.

It is often difficult to obtain tickets by either of these methods for hit shows unless they are bought far in advance. However, advance notice is not always possible. The secretary may establish an account in the executive's name with a reliable theater-ticket agency in order to have a better chance of obtaining tickets on short notice.

When the tickets arrive at the office, the secretary should enclose them in an envelope on which have been noted the date and day of the week of the performance, the curtain time, the name and address of the theater, and the name of the show.

If the tickets must be sent through the mail for any reason, the secretary should enclose with them a letter of transmittal in which reference has been made to the name of the show, the name and address of the theater, the date of the performance, and the seat numbers. Thus, if the tickets are lost, and particularly if the executive has planned to attend several different shows, the copy of the letter contains all the information necessary for follow-up. The letter also provides all the pertinent information to the individual receiving the tickets and acts as a reminder of the date.

Gift and Card Lists

A secretary may also have the responsibility of reminding the executive of an approaching occasion such as a birthday, anniversary, or graduation. He or she may also be expected to send holiday remembrances. For this purpose, a record of these events and lists of the persons to whom the executive sends cards and presents must be kept. Separate lists should be maintained for friends, relatives, and business acquaintances to whom holiday greetings are sent by the executive, those to whom cards are sent by the executive jointly with husband or wife, those who receive company cards, those to whom holiday gifts are given, and those who receive gifts at other times of the year.

These lists and records should be kept up to date, with names added or deleted and addresses checked periodically. It will aid the executive in the selection of gifts if the secretary keeps a cumulative record of the gifts previously given the individual, their cost, and the occasions for which they were given. Since the secretary in many cases is asked to select and purchase the cards and gifts and to address and mail them, these lists should be submitted to the employer well in advance of the occasion, so that sufficient time will be allowed for shopping, preparation, and mailing.

Holiday gifts or greeting cards should be thought of at least six or eight weeks in advance, particularly if the gift is to be sent abroad. If greeting cards are to have the executive's name imprinted, they need to be ordered early.

At Time of Death

At the time of a death, a friend or acquaintance of the deceased usually expresses sympathy by sending a token remembrance to the bereaved family. The form of this expression of sympathy depends upon the religious affiliation, if any, of the deceased. These expressions may take any one or a combination of several of the following forms:

Flowers. It is customary to send flowers to the bereaved family, except one of the Jewish faith. From close friends or relatives, prepared dishes for meals that will save the family from food preparation is considered a proper and accepted expression of sympathy to the Jewish family in mourning.

Flowers may take the form of a floral piece—a spray, wreath, or basket. It is also appropriate to send a floral piece to memorial services when the deceased is cremated or buried immediately. A card should always accompany the floral piece. If a visiting card is used for this purpose, the engraved name should be crossed out in ink and a few words of sympathy added. The floral piece is usually ordered by the secretary from the florist by telephone, and the florist supplies an appropriate card on which the name of the person sending the flowers is written, along with any message the sender desires. When ordering the floral piece, the secretary must be prepared to tell the florist the name of the deceased, where the flowers are to be sent, the time and date of the services, and the kind and size of floral piece desired.

Letters of sympathy. Letters expressing sympathy to the bereaved family may be sent to people of any faith and may be sent in addition to flowers, fruit, or any of the other expressions noted here. The secretary should inquire about the customs in the business and social community of the executive.

Mass cards. Mass cards indicate that arrangements have been made to have a Mass or Masses said in memory of the deceased and for the repose of the soul. It is appropriate to send such cards to a Roman Catholic family. They may be sent by either a Roman Catholic or a non-Catholic. The cards may be obtained from a priest, church office, or sometimes a funeral parlor. It is customary to make an offering when such cards are obtained. Although a Roman Catholic could ask a priest to say Mass for a non-Catholic, Mass cards are not usually sent to a non-Catholic family.

Charitable contributions. Some families specify that, instead of flowers, they would prefer friends and business associates to send contributions to charities or organizations in which the deceased was interested. If this is done, the organization that receives these donations in the name of the deceased usually notifies the bereaved family that such contributions were received. The donor may also write to the family to inform them that a donation is being sent to the charitable or educational institution in the name of the deceased.

Death of a member of the executive's family. When a member of the executive's family dies, the secretary may be asked to keep a record of those who send expressions of sympathy and what was sent. A description of the floral piece that was received should be written on the back of each accompanying card. In addition, a separate alphabetic file of all Mass cards and letters should be kept. From these data, separate lists can be made of those who sent flowers alone, of those who sent both Mass cards and flowers, of those who wrote and also sent flowers or Mass cards, and of those who sent contributions to institutions, and appropriate acknowledgments sent.

Two opinions exist concerning the type of acknowledgment that is appropriate at this time. According to one, the cards acknowledging expressions of sympathy should be formal and engraved. According to the other, it is perfectly proper to have the acknowledgments handwritten. Acknowledgments may be written out in longhand if only a few need to be sent, but if the deceased was a prominent person and hundreds of remembrances were received, engraved cards should be sent only to those who are unknown to the bereaved, not to acquaintances. The type of remembrance sent—flowers, Mass cards, or contributions—should be mentioned in the acknowledgment.

The secretary should also keep a list of the names and addresses of those who performed outstanding services, such as doctors, nurses, a priest, minister, or rabbi, editorial writers, and the like, so that letters of appreciation can be sent to them for their kindness and understanding. Also, thank-you letters should be sent to those who sent memorial contributions to organizations.

All the lists should be submitted to the executive, who will select those to whom letters will be dictated, those to whom acknowledgments will be written in longhand, and those for whom the secretary is to draft and type acknowledgments.

Death of the executive. The details that the secretary takes care of in the event of the executive's death depend upon the wishes of the family. The secretary can offer assistance in a number of ways:

• Help to compile material for newspaper obituaries. This would include dates and history of the executive's career and the names of organizations to which the executive belonged and offices held in each. The secretary can write or help to write the obituary or call the newspapers and give the information to the writer responsible for this.

The funeral director supplies the funeral notice to the newspapers; the secretary can supply information for this.

- Notify branch offices, foreign offices, or affiliates of the company of the death of the executive.

- Notify the executive's lawyer and the secretaries of organizations to which the executive belonged.

- Notify the insurance company or companies, the Social Security Administration, and any other institution or agency from which a monetary death benefit may derive.

- Arrange for the personal effects of the executive to be removed from the office and taken home or disposed of as the family requests.

- Keep a file of clippings from the newspapers bearing items about the deceased.

TALKING TO VISITORS

When visitors arrive they should find a courteous, professional secretary who is pleasant and attentive. The secretary should take the visitor's name, company, and reason for the visit and notify the executive that the person is waiting. It may help the executive if the secretary escorts the visitor to the office or conference room and announces or introduces the person to the executive. If the visitor is required to wait and wishes to talk, the secretary should engage in light conversation and avoid details about office matters.

Some executives suggest that visitors be offered coffee or tea while they wait. The secretary should ask if the visitor wishes refreshments and either serve it or direct the visitor to the area in the office where coffee and tea can be obtained.

Visitors without appointments should be told politely that the executive has a very busy schedule and cannot see people without an appointment. Then, the person's name, company, and phone number should be taken and arrangements for a future appointment made.

TALKING TO REPORTERS

If the executive is a government official or in the public eye, the secretary may find it necessary to deal with reporters and others from the media. Be courteous and professional; however, do not volunteer information. If the executive has a prepared statement, have it ready and distribute it without comment. If the executive asks the secretary to make a verbal statement, prepare the statement beforehand, type it, and read it as written. After the statement is read, it may be necessary to make a dismissal statement such as "This is the information that has been prepared for you. There is no further statement at this time. Thank you for your cooperation." If reporters persist, security may need to be called.

ORGANIZING MEETINGS AND CONFERENCES

The secretary may be called upon to assist with meetings and conferences—the preparation phase, tasks during the meeting, and the completion of tasks after the meeting.

Preparation Phase

During the preparation phase the secretary may be responsible for notifying the staff, directors, and persons outside the office headquarters, sometimes in other cities or countries, of the planned meeting or conference. Invitations may be mailed or telephoned. The secretary should make a list of those to be notified, check that all are informed, and check responses so that a final list of those who will be able to attend is prepared. If invitations are mailed, a reply card and a self-addressed envelope are enclosed.

The secretary may also work with the executive in preparing the agenda and materials for the participants; arranging for special services, sites, and speakers; arranging the physical site (the size of the room, the positioning of tables and chairs, etc.); and taking care of other miscellaneous details (providing water for the participants, locating coat racks, etc.)

The following page shows a typical agenda for a monthly staff meeting.

During the preparation phase special services such as multimedia equipment, tours of plants or offices, printing of agendas, mailing press coverage, security, and duplicating and organizing information folders will be attended to by the secretary. The secretary should also make sure that microphones, slide projectors, overhead projectors, video machines, and the like are available and functioning.

During the Meeting

During the meeting or conference, the secretary should be sure that everything ordered has arrived in working order and should organize material such as folders, pencils, and pads for the speakers and those who attend. The secretary may also arrange for greeting those who speak and attend, directing participants and speakers to conference rooms, and making introductions.

In addition, the secretary may be required to take the minutes, list participants, handle correspondence and telephone messages, deal with last-minute problems or changes, distribute press releases, arrange for luncheons, and summarize presentations.

After the Meeting

After the meeting or conference the secretary may be asked to prepare the minutes for distribution, collect extra agendas and materials, and list persons who will receive copies of the minutes, "thank-you" letters, and conference-related information.

Agenda for Monthly Staff Meeting
January 15, 19__

SCHEDULE	EVENT	PLACE
9:30 A.M.	Call to Order Old Business Read Minutes of Last Meeting Committee Reports	Suite 1215

10 A.M.	New Business
	
	1. Peter Doyle—
	   Demonstration of New
	   Computer System for
	   Accounting
	2. Helen Brown—
	   Dealing with Executive
	   Stress: New Techniques
		Suite 1221

Noon	President's Report	Suite 1221
1-2 P.M.	Lunch	Suite 1232

Daily Agenda for a Conference
Monday, February 15

9 A.M.-Noon	Phillip White, Susan MacKay Our New Line of Sofware	Harrison Room
Noon-1 P.M.	Informal Discussion	Harrison Room
1-2:30 P.M.	Lunch Mary Alice Bender New Market Opportunities	Sky Terrace

Tuesday, February 16

9-11 A.M.	James Williams, Dawn Petersen Hardware—Old and New	Columbia Room
11:35 A.M.-1 P.M.	Plenary Margaret Snow and Anita Cuttitta Management Systems for Small Companies	Wintergreen Room
1:15-2:30 P.M.	Lunch Karen Trainer Business Run by Women	Sky Room

Meeting/conference minutes should be prepared according to a specific format. The secretary will need copies of the agenda, notices of the meeting, lists of those who attended and spoke, and the file on current papers related to the meeting/conference.

Annual meetings and conferences require knowledge of the last meeting, the schedule, people involved, travel arrangements, contacts such as caterers, hotels, sites, and speakers. This job is easier if the office maintains a tickler file. One need only locate the conference folder from the last meeting or conference to begin the cycle of preparation.

Time Management

by Murray Bromberg

In an attempt to improve employee performance, many large corporations routinely administer needs assessment questionnaires to staff members. In so doing, they seek to find out employee weaknesses and needs and determine in which areas training should be focused.

Research into the responses has shown that the entire range of office personnel, including secretaries, middle-management people, and top executives, often pinpoint similar concerns, such as how to handle stress, reduce paperwork, gain greater familiarity with state-of-the-art equipment, improve human relations, read faster, and comprehend better. However, almost without exception, the single topic that appears most often on most respondents' surveys is *time management*.

Some secretaries are able to deal with a tremendous workload within the normal working day without appearing frazzled or harassed. They rarely need to stay late to catch up on correspondence, get out a critical mailing, meet a deadline, or photocopy the agenda for the next day's important conference. As the popular saying goes, it's not that they work harder, but that they work smarter.

Admittedly, such performers are in the minority. Most secretaries in a busy environment complain that there just is not enough time during the normal workday to do everything required. When the pressure becomes intense ("I need that contract typed in a half hour," "Fish out everything we have on those mortgage applications before lunch," etc.), some secretaries almost panic and yearn for more time. But what they need are time-management skills.

The good news about time management is that it is a skill that almost anyone can master. Application of the suggestions given in this chapter will restore a secretary's confidence, probably bring about renewed job satisfaction, and possibly even help the secretary advance in his or her career.

The remainder of this chapter discusses ten proven methods of time management for secretaries.

ONE: ANALYZING THE WAY YOU USE TIME NOW

Before you start to draw up meaningful rules for streamlining your performance and managing your time, you should diagnose the problem. In short, try to determine how you spend your time now and decide whether or not you are using it to its best advantage. After you have analyzed how you spend your time now, you can determine how you can make better use of it in the future.

Just as a research-oriented employer might bring in a time-study expert to watch employees in action, you, the secretary, should keep a log of your daily expenditure of time. Over a period of two weeks, record your activities every half hour. Then study the log and focus on the recurring items that cause you to use your time inefficiently. Is it numerous trips to the mail room (and possible socializing en route)? Is it repeated jaunts to the executive's office for clarification of dictation, instructions, or other matters?

With the patterns apparent, you will be in a better position to draw up a trim schedule that will enable you to function in an orderly environment.

After analyzing your movements, you may find that personally attending to every phase of every job that comes across your desk is a poor way to budget your time. Is it really necessary for you to collate multiple copies, to staple a newsletter, or to run envelopes through a postage meter? Are clerical assistants available for such tasks?

When executives enroll in time-management seminars, they spend many hours learning how to delegate responsibility. Assuming that there is help available in the office, the secretary should also learn how to delegate. If you instruct and train personnel properly, you will very likely be able to assign them routine tasks, thus freeing yourself for those tasks that you and only you were hired to do.

TWO: LIVING WITH A SCHEDULE

The next step is the organization of a daily schedule. It may be more interesting to ad lib, and of course it is necessary to vary routines once in a while, but secretaries who do careful planning are on the road to becoming successful time managers. Let's look at one secretary's schedule:

9:00 to 9:15 A.M.	– Play back telephone messages
9:15 to 9:40	– Go through the morning's mail
9:40 to 10:40	– Complete yesterday's correspondence
10:40 to 11:30	– Make business calls; set up appointments; respond to inquiries
11:30 to 12:00	– Clip relevant articles from daily newspapers
12:00 to 1:00 P.M.	– Lunch
1:00 to 2:00	– Take dictation
2:00 to 3:00	– Type the letters
3:00 to 4:00	– Take minutes at office meeting and transcribe them
4:00 to 5:00	– Filing, mailing

Of course, the typical secretary is not a robot. There are coffee breaks, minor crises, photocopying, trips to the mailroom, etc. However, those secretaries who are guided by a schedule—somewhat rigid, somewhat flexible—will often find that they have those extra minutes each day to accomplish the tasks they need to complete.

An important hint: one sure way to negate the advantages to be gained from a daily schedule is to be intransigent and to tolerate no deviations from the schedule. In short, the secretary should be guided by the planned schedule but not shackled by it. Special needs will require modifying the schedule, but after that, the secretary can go back to its general outline.

THREE: WORKING WITH A "TO DO" LIST

Going hand in hand with the daily schedule is the "to do" list, a compilation of outstanding matters that require the secretary's attention. A typical "to do" list might include:

- Type letters to new sales reps
- Call service company for copying machine
- Order office supplies
- Revise file card tabs
- Prepare labels for mailing to prospective customers
- Place help wanted ad for office receptionist
- Have Mr. Berman's new business cards picked up at the printers
- Call DHL for pickup of letter to our Bangkok office
- Confirm Mr. Berman's reservation with Delta Airlines
- Order new name stamp for Mr. Berman

The "to do" list should be drawn up at the start of the week, reviewed daily, and updated as progress is made.

Some secretaries combine the "to do" list with a control sheet. Next to each important or multistep item, they record steps taken toward its completion. In that way, they have a progress report as well as a visible reminder.

It is reasonable to assume that there will usually be about ten or more items on the "to do" list. The list is likely to have some tasks that will take five minutes to accomplish (*e.g.*, a phone call) and some that are multistep and challenging (*e.g.*, reviewing the minutes of all unit meetings for the previous year and preparing an executive summary). In addition, some tasks require immediate attention; others are long-range in nature.

Start by grouping the tasks on the list: those that are routine and can be accomplished promptly in one column and other, more complex and time-consuming tasks in another column. The tasks in each column can then be prioritized so that the more important ones and/or the ones to which the executive gives greater weight are at the top. It is good practice to divide the larger tasks into smaller parts and do one part at a time.

FOUR: HESITATING TO TAKE ON OTHERS' RESPONSIBILITIES

A secretary naturally wants to please not only the executive but also co-workers. This can sometimes lead to problems if, for example, the secretary takes on responsibilities that are not his or hers and in so doing becomes overburdened with work that other staff members should be doing. Let's examine some practical examples.

Your fellow secretary, Miss Adams, makes personal calls throughout the day. As a result, she doesn't have enough time to complete an important assignment from the vice president for whom she works. She asks for your assistance. While you are willing to help a colleague, when you repeatedly undertake such activities your own work suffers. The time-management strides that you have been making are seriously threatened. How do you get Miss Adams to stop taking advantage of your good nature? You might say, "Gloria, you have to respect the fact that my time is as important as yours. I'll pitch in whenever I have nothing pressing to do, but if you are a real friend, you won't ask me to bail you out regularly." (Notice, you are not lecturing her about her telephone activity, since that would chill your relationship permanently, but you are leading her to feel the guilt and to change her ways—if that is at all possible.)

Another example: The account executive for whom you work, Mr. Baker, asks you to shop for him, return purchases for credit, pick up theater tickets, etc. He tells you to take a two-hour lunch, leave the office an hour early, or punch in an hour late as compensation for taking care of his personal errands. One possible way to handle this is to say, "Mr. Baker, I love the job, and I think I'm making a genuine contribution toward our unit's effectiveness. If you want me to help you out on the special missions, I'm pleased to be of service, too, but I'm concerned about completing my basic daily tasks. Of course, the final decision is yours."

FIVE: HANDLING THE MAIL EFFICIENTLY

Some secretaries receive a daily bag of mail for all the staff and sort it before delivering it to the correct desks. The personal or executive secretary, however, usually opens the executive's mail and some secretaries, usually experienced ones in whom the executive has a great deal of confidence, have complete jurisdiction over the mail. They know which letters require immediate attention from their employers, which should be forwarded to other office personnel for action, which are considered to be the kind of junk mail that the executive does not wish to see, and which should be routinely filed.

Tackling the mail in a large office can be an onerous, time-consuming job that may wreak havoc with a well-planned schedule. Obviously, there is nothing to be gained by reading every word of every document. The secretary who is managing time efficiently determines the importance of each letter swiftly and steers it in the right direction.

Just as the executive's time-management skills can be improved by handling each piece of mail once (and only once), so can the secretary's. If the mail is to be placed in the executive's in-basket, do so. If it goes to his or her associate, send it there promptly without keeping it on your desk, where it might be subjected to multiple handling. If it is a solicitation from an organization that your executive has told you to ignore, put it directly into the trash basket.

SIX: LEARNING TO USE THE PHONE EFFICIENTLY

The telephone can upset the most carefully thought out schedule, but there are some general guidelines to follow in using it. Skillful secretaries make sure that their telephone conversations are brief, concise, and businesslike—albeit friendly. Some executives simply want to know the name of the caller, but others prefer that the secretary elicit the purpose of the call. Whatever the protocol in your particular office, be sure to follow it expeditiously. (Refer to Chapter 12 for additional advice on telephone communications.) Here are a few sample lines experienced secretaries use:

"Good morning, M & S Furniture. May I help you?"

"For Miss Carter? Whom shall I say is calling?"

"Does Miss Carter know what the call is about?"

"Miss Carter is out of the office. May I take a message?"

As you can see, there are no wasted words in these brief exchanges, but they are polite.

If the secretary needs to make several outside calls, it is advisable to set aside a specific time of the day, group the calls, and place them. This saves interruptions during other daily tasks.

Needless to say, personal phone calls, incoming and outgoing, should be kept to a minimum. In a survey done at a large insurance company employing more than 50 secretaries, a time study expert found that 40% of secretarial telephone activity involved personal calls.

SEVEN: AVOIDING COSTLY INTERRUPTIONS

Concentrating on business without being distracted by a host of interruptions can spell success for a secretary's time-management program. When a steady stream of people swirl around a secretary's desk and engage him or her in conversation, all good resolutions and time-management plans are worthless. Some time-management consultants advise clients about the placement of office furniture to lessen interruptions. A person who can be seen from the hallway is often the one people interrupt. Consider moving your desk, if your particular office situation will permit it. A secretary's behavior does not have to be austere just to demonstrate concern for proper time management. As in all things, moderation is called for. When there is no pressure to complete a task, a little sociability is in order, but when pressing business is being conducted, social exchanges must take a back seat.

EIGHT: KEEPING YOUR DESK NEAT AND CLEAN

A secretary should have a clean and orderly desk for the obvious reason that it makes a good impression on staff and visitors. It's impossible to maintain one's self-esteem when seated behind a sloppy desk with mounds of paper, coffee cups, leftover food, etc. However, the more important reason for keeping a neat desk, especially for the purposes of this chapter, is that it is very difficult to locate material on a messy desk. Time spent searching for misplaced notes, files, or messages is time lost. Get into the habit of using clearly marked file folders for the temporary storage of materials—until you are ready to file them in the central system.

NINE: BEING SURE THE FILING SYSTEM IS A HELP, NOT A HINDRANCE

Consider whether your filing system is an aid or a detriment. If it takes many minutes to locate a needed document, and questions such as "Is it filed under 'Correspondence' or 'Conference Notes'?" come up, you should consider setting up a new filing system.

Filing is discussed in detail in Chapter 13. In the context of time management, the best advice is simply to draw up a list of every category now being used in the filing system and review it with a supervisor or an experienced co-worker. Eliminate what is no longer relevant; consolidate where you find redundancies; revise categories for greater clarity, etc. The small time investment in reviewing the filing system will pay huge dividends in time saved later.

TEN: SOME FINAL DON'TS

There are a few additional hints that are helpful for secretaries trying to manage their time efficiently. First, don't allow yourself to be sidetracked. You should have goals for every job you engage in, and not until these objectives are met should you be ready to move on to a new project. (Of course, when a legitimate "crisis" arises, all current matters must be delayed to accommodate the emergency.)

Second, don't take on more work than you can handle. Be realistic about your workload, and do not take on extra assignments if you do not realistically have the time. It will only dilute your effectiveness in all areas.

Third, don't say "yes" to every request. If another secretary stops by and asks "May I see you for a few minutes?" it is not essential that you drop whatever you are doing. You may politely say that you are busy and cannot interrupt what you are doing but that you will see him or her later, perhaps at lunch.

A FINAL WORD

Following the ten suggestions given in this chapter will help a secretary stretch his or her working day and improve overall performance. In closing, it should be noted that another aspect of office efficiency is the way a secretary manages the time of the executive for whom he or she works. Maintaining an executive's calendar intelligently, confirming or canceling meetings or appointments, and using tickler files to ensure compliance with deadlines and other commitments are critical time-management assets discussed elsewhere in this book. Suffice it to say that if you are the type of secretary who is eager to enhance your time-management skills, you will also be the team player who enables the executive to make every minute count. Secretaries with such attitudes possess the hallmarks of the respected professional.

Business English

17

Sample Business Letters and Memos

by Lois M. Burns, Ed. D.

- *Business Letters*

  Basic Principles
  Samples

- *Interoffice Memorandums*

  Use and Format
  Samples

One essential skill that a secretary must possess is the ability to compose letters and memorandums. Being asked to write letters for your employer indicates confidence in your ability, and it gives you the opportunity to show your creativity.

There are certain basic principles you must adhere to when you write a letter or a memorandum. This chapter presents guidelines and discusses procedures for preparing several kinds of written communications that a secretary may be asked to compose. Included are sample letters that show how to use the principles and procedures for specific kinds of letters and sample memos that illustrate typical interoffice communication.

BUSINESS LETTERS

The most important principle to remember in writing a business letter is to plan—before you begin to write. Then, follow a logical sequence in writing the letter. The following guidelines and sample letters should be helpful.

Basic Principles

General Guidelines for Organizing a Business Letter

1. Establish what type of letter you are writing (the purpose of the letter). Is it a request for information, an order, or an acknowledgment? } First paragraph

2. State items that need action, answer questions, and give information. In other words, give the details of the letter. } Middle paragraphs

3. Summarize briefly. End with a friendly greeting, if appropriate. } Last paragraph

Other Guidelines in Writing an Effective Business Letter

1. Reflect the employer's style of writing in presenting the message.
2. Write with clarity.
3. Write concisely.
4. Write the message in a personal tone.
5. Write with a positive approach.
6. Write with diplomacy and tact.
7. Endeavor to create good will and interest.

Guidelines for Answering a Letter

1. Read the letter to be answered carefully.
2. Jot down points of inquiry or other important points.
3. Place these items in priority order.
4. Decide the answers to all questions.
5. Verify all data.
6. Organize the letter and begin to write.

Guidelines for Initiating a Letter

1. Establish the purpose of the letter.
2. Collect all necessary material—information, enclosures, etc.
3. Organize material.
4. Compose the letter in a style suitable for the intended purpose.

Sample Acknowledgment Letter

1. Answer immediately.
2. State what you are acknowledging.
3. Give information requested.
4. If appropriate, end with a "thank you" or an expression of interest.

December 3, 19__

Mr. Joseph Peters
124 Main Street
New York, NY 11201-6734

Dear Mr. Peters:

Your letter regarding the figures in our current window display has been received. The dolls that aroused your curiosity were made in Yugoslavia. They are not antique, but were made and purchased within the past year.

Thank you for your kind words about this display. Our decorators spent many hours planning and setting up the scene, and it is nice to know it is appreciated and enjoyed.

Sincerely,

Jane Jones

Ms. Jane Jones
Senior Decorator

ss

Sample Adjustment Letter

1. Describe original action or purchase.
2. State complaint.
3. Request adjustment.

May 23, 19__

Mr. Richard White
Sales Manager
Richard Office Equipment Corporation
888 Mill Road
Abilene, TX 79601-5739

Dear Mr. White:

On February 14 of this year, your company shipped a paper shredder to our office. It is the Prestige brand labeled Model 433. It was installed by your local agency, Richard Electric Company.

At our request, Richard Electric Company service representatives came to try to adjust this piece of equipment twice in February and four times in March. It is inoperative most of the time, and at this time it is again not working. It seems fairly clear by now that we have a defective machine. Richard Electric Company says we must deal directly with you regarding this matter.

Please have a representative contact us for arrangements to replace this paper shredder.

Sharon Flemmings

Miss Sharon Flemmings
Office Manager

rm

Sample Appointment Letter

1. Be specific as to time, place, and date of appointment.
2. State purpose of appointment.
3. Specify any special information, file, etc., necessary for the appointment.
4. Ask for confirmation.

July 26, 19___

Mr. John Lettier
Auditing Department
Muskins and Sells, Inc.
876 Indiana Avenue
Washington, DC 20001-1438

Dear Mr. Lettier:

Mr. Thomas will be returning from his vacation next week and will be able to meet with you to discuss the audit report in the Board Room, Thursday, August 9, at 10 A.M.

Please bring File No. 306 with you to the meeting, as there are a few questions to be answered.

We would appreciate your confirming this appointment by Monday, August 6.

Sincerely

Mrs. Catherine Thompson
Administrative Assistant

ia

Sample Cancelation of Appointment Letter

1. Be specific about time and date of appointment being cancelled.
2. Give reason for cancelation, if appropriate.
3. Request rescheduled appointment.

OLYMPIA GREENE, M.D.
22 CENTRAL AVENUE
GLENDALE, NY 11385-7342
(718) 381-2345

October 13, 19_

Dr. Matthew Bavetta
123 Myrtle Avenue
Glendale, NY 11385-7342

Dear Dr. Bavetta:

Dr. Greene would like to cancel her appointment for Saturday, October 18, at 10:30 A.M. She will be out of town attending a seminar on that day.

Please reschedule Dr. Greene's appointment for the same time on Saturday, October 25.

If this is inconvenient, please telephone our office.

Sincerely,

Marilyn Landry

Ms. Marilyn Landry
Medical Secretary

Sample Appreciation Letter

1. State ceremony or occasion for which thanks is being expressed or enjoyment is being acknowledged.
2. State briefly subsidiary reasons, if any, for writing letter.
3. If appropriate, express wishes for future success.

October 3, 19__

Miss Margaret Bauer
21 Applegate Drive
Hamden, CT 06514-3456

Dear Margaret:

    The speech that you gave at the in-house workshop last week was stimulating as well as informative. The people I spoke with after your presentation also responded favorably.

    It has been ten years since we were in college, and it was good to see you again. It certainly brought back many memories for me.

    I look forward to your presentation next weekend and know that it will be as successful as the last one.

                     Sincerely yours,

                     Judith Karp

                     Ms. Judith Karp
                     Office Administrator

es

Sample Collection Letter

1. State the problem—that is, the amount due, dates of letters or orders, and mention of specific merchandise where necessary. This should usually be done in the first paragraph, unless the first paragraph is an attention-arousing device.
2. Present the argument for payment (two paragraphs).
3. Motivate action in the closing paragraph.

July 24, 19__

Mr. Walter Whitcomb
Administrator
XYZ Company
123 Main Street
Philadelphia, PA 30001-3456

Dear Mr. Whitcomb:

In our letters of June 17, July 2, and July 16, we tried unsuccessfully to obtain payment of your past-due account of $184.02 or to gain some explanation from you.

We are sorry that you have made no reply because we want to help our customers whenever possible. We filled your order promptly and in a manner that must have been satisfactory to you since you have made no reply to our offer of adjustment.

As you know, our credit terms call for payment within 30 days. You have not complied with these terms or given us the facts by which we might arrive at a solution.

Won't you use the enclosed envelope to send us your check or an explanation of why your payment is so long overdue.

Yours truly,

Jane Adams

Ms. Jane Adams
Credit Manager

ms

Enclosure

Sample Request for Payment Letter

1. State the problem.
2. Express concern about lack of payment.
3. Request a response.

OLYMPIA GREENE, M.D.
22 CENTRAL AVENUE
GLENDALE, NY 11385-7342
(718) 381-2345

October 13, 19__

Mr. Stanley Bailey
97-81 111 Street
Richmond Hill, NY 11418-2901

Dear Mr. Bailey:

After reviewing our accounts, I find that your account is three months
overdue.

Enclosed is a copy of the statement.

Dr. Greene is a little concerned that the bill has not been paid.
Perhaps you would like to discuss it with her.

Please telephone Dr. Greene at your earliest convenience.

Sincerely,

Marilyn Landry

Ms. Marilyn Landry
Medical Secretary

Enclosure

Sample Covering Letter

1. Inform recipient of what is being sent and whether it is enclosed or sent separately.
2. Tell when item was (or will be) sent.
3. Tell by what class of mail or method of shipment.
4. Give further information (if appropriate).

December 4, 19__

Professor John Hunter
Communications Department
Woods Collegiate School
22 Fifth Avenue
New York, NY 10001-1017

Dear Professor Hunter:

Your request to rent an 8-mm film, "Telephone Techniques," has been received. The film was sent this afternoon via Special Delivery.

We have other films on this subject and can furnish a list upon request.

Sincerely,
DUART FILMS, INC.

Joseph De Martino

Joseph DeMartino
Film Supervisor

bd

Sample Letter Acknowledging Applications for Credit

1. Welcome new customer.
2. Explain firm's policy.
3. Request that credit references be sent or that a credit form be filled out.
4. Provide an incentive to action.
5. Close with a sales statement about service, quality of merchandise, or your future mutual relationship.

SUPERIOR BUSINESS FORMS, INC.
222 Main Street
Hamden, CT 06514-5678
(203) 479-1234

December 3, 19__

Mr. James Weldon
Office Manager
New Business Systems, Inc.
333 Park Avenue
New York, NY 10001-3456

Dear Mr. Weldon:

We certainly appreciate the opportunity you have given us in your first order to do business with your firm. Your expression of confidence in us is most gratifying, and we will do everything in our power to live up to it.

Since you probably need this merchandise as soon as possible, we are shipping your order by express tomorrow. So that we can handle your future needs without delay, we would appreciate your sending us your financial statement. Or, if you prefer, just fill out and return the enclosed credit form.

This credit information will, of course, be kept absolutely confidential. We are looking forward to having you as a regular customer. May we have your credit information soon?

Cordially yours,

Harvey Froman

Harvey Froman
Purchasing Manager

lb
Enclosure

Sample Follow-Up or Reminder Letter

1. Make reference to previous letter or request.
2. State what is needed and why.
3. Emphasize deadline.

June 24, 19__

Professor Arlene Smith
Advertising Department
Institute of Technology
300 Jay Street
Brooklyn, NY 11201-2983

Dear Professor Smith:

At the June Directors' Meeting, the chairpersons were asked to submit their department budgets to the Vice President within two weeks.

Three weeks have elapsed and your budget is needed in order that we may be able to submit the overall budget report to the President. Our deadline is next week.

Office Services will be able to assist you in typing the report.

Sincerely,

Wanda Spear

Ms. Wanda Spear
Secretary to Vice President

ws

pc: Division Dean

Sample Notice of Meeting Letter

1. Specify day, date, time, place, and purpose of meeting.
2. Specify if it is a special meeting.
3. State agenda of meeting.
4. Inquire about additional items to be placed on agenda.
5. Request reply.

October 3, 19__

Mr. Clark Cason
Vice President
XYZ Company
228 Clark Street
Brooklyn, NY 11201-2983

Dear Mr. Cason:

An Advisory Committee meeting will be held in the Board Room, Thursday, October 19, at noon. This is a special meeting, called because of the upcoming change in the price of our product.

An agenda for the meeting is enclosed. If you have any additional items to be placed on the agenda, please send them to Mr. Price by October 13.

Please notify me by Monday, October 16, of whether or not you will attend the meeting.

Sincerely,

Herbert Price

Herbert Price
Vice President

lmb

Enclosure

Sample Letter of Regret or Rejection

1. State circumstances.
2. Give background information telling why decision was made.
3. End with expression of good will, showing appreciation or interest.

July 1, 19__

Ms. Mary Popkins, Secretary
Delta Pi Epsilon
2 Stuyvesant Oval
New York, NY 10001-1234

Dear Ms. Popkins:

Our President, Mrs. Beatrice R. Stokes, has received your letter asking
her to speak to your membership on "The Office of the Future," Saturday,
August 4.

Unfortunately, Mrs. Stokes will be on a business trip at that time. Thus, it
will not be possible for her to accept your kind invitation.

If your organization has a need for a speaker at some other time, Mrs.
Stokes hopes you will remember her then.

Sincerely,

Judith McGee

Miss Judith McGee
Secretary to President

jm

Sample Reservation Letter

1. State who wants the reservation and the number of people in the party.
2. State number of rooms and type of accommodations (single, double, suite, deluxe suite) desired.
3. State planned length of stay and approximate rate desired.
4. State arrival time and departure time. If arriving late, ask about guaranteed arrival and deposit requirements.
5. Request confirmation.

February 2, 19__

Glenpointe Hotel
Attention Reservations Manager
Route 80 West
Teaneck, NJ 07728-0897

Dear Sir:

Please reserve a medium-priced living room and bedroom suite for Mr. and Mrs. Albert Clark, who will arrive late Monday evening, April 6. They will leave Thursday afternoon, April 9, on a 3 P.M. flight and will require transportation to the airport.

Please confirm the room reservation for late arrival and advise me of your deposit requirements.

Mr. Clark, Vice President of the ABZ Corporation, will be attending the NSW workshop that will be held in your hotel.

Sincerely,

Janice Theodore

Ms. Janice Theodore
Secretary to Vice President

jt

Sample Deferral Letter

1. Answer immediately.
2. State matter under discussion.
3. Explain why answers must be deferred.
4. Tell when answer may be expected.

October 3, 19__

Ms. Nancy Adams, Marketing Manager
Adams Associates, Inc.
234 Maple Avenue
Maplewood, NJ 07748-9876

Dear Ms. Adams:

Your letter to Ms. Jones asking her approval of your new sales
brochures has been received.

Ms. Jones is attending our annual international conference in
Denver.

I am sure she will give your letter her immediate attention when
she returns. You should hear from her within the next three
weeks.

Sincerely,

Renee Johnson

Ms. Renee Johnson
Executive Secretary

rj

Sample Letter of Inquiry or Request

1. Give background to explain why letter is being written.
2. Ask question or make request.
3. Tell when information or material is needed.
4. Close with expression of appreciation or good will.

December 15, 19__

Mr. Alfred Reed
Marketing Manager
Consumers Corporation
189 Tacoma Street
Seattle, WA 98765-4321

Dear Mr. Reed:

Our company is planning its annual sales meeting, to be held in Seattle. Over 200 salespersons will attend.

We would appreciate having copies of your booklet "The Way to a Consumer's Heart" to pass out to those attending our conference.

Could you please have them sent directly to the Seattle Hotel, addressed to me, by January 15?

Your cooperation would be greatly appreciated.

Sincerely yours,

Thomas J. Jones

Thomas J. Jones
Consumer Affairs Specialist

jv

Sample Order Letter

1. Tell where order is to be sent.
2. List items wanted, giving all pertinent numbers, description of the products, price, and any other necessary information such as color and size.
3. Tell how payment is to be made (check is enclosed, bill is to be sent to a specified address, the order is to be put on a regular account, etc.).
4. Tell when order should be sent.

BUSINESS SYSTEMS, INC.
8 Jay Street
Brooklyn, NY 11201-2983
(718) 843-4567

October 3, 19__

Manhattan Stationers, Inc.
Attention Order Department
5 Lafayette Street
New York, NY 10001-2345

Gentlemen:

Please send the following items to the above address:

Quantity	Catalog No.	Item	Unit Price	Total
200	N238	No. 2 pencils Eberhard (blue)	.15	$30.00
25	N357	wooden rulers (blue)	.84	21.60
				$51.60
			sales tax	4.13
				$55.73

Our check for $55.73 is enclosed. We would appreciate having these items sent at once.

Yours truly,

Joan Bennett

Ms. Joan Bennett

Final Check after Writing the Letter

After you have planned and written the letter, ask yourself these questions:

1. Is my message clear?
2. Will the recipient interpret my message as I intended?
3. Have I presented facts clearly and correctly?
4. Have I kept the message concise?
5. Have I been diplomatic?
6. Have I used personal, positive, and natural tones throughout?
7. Have I created good will regardless of the situation?

INTEROFFICE MEMORANDUMS

Use and Format

The written communications passing between offices, departments, or branches of an organization are usually transmitted in a form known as an "interoffice memorandum." This form has the advantage of dispensing with the salutation, the complimentary close, and the signature of the dictator or originator.

The headings most frequently found on all interoffice memorandums are TO, FROM, DATE, and SUBJECT. In most firms, this heading, together with the firm name and, perhaps, address, are printed. Signed initials are frequently placed on the memo to show that it has been read and approved. The initials of the typist appear on the memorandum, just as in a letter. Enclosures and attachments should be indicated.

Some organizations have memorandum forms prepared in carbon packs. Other organizations prepare an original and use the copier for multiple copies. Several names may be typed after TO or they may be listed at the bottom of the memorandum. In this way, the recipients know which persons will be receiving the same message.

Interoffice correspondence should include most of the essential characteristics of a good letter. The tone should be considerate and courteous. The message should be clear, concise, and complete. (See also Chapter 11.)

Electronic Mail

E-mail should be considered a serious business document. As with all other interoffice correspondence, it should have a polite, respectful tone and a succinct message. For more information on electronic mail, see Chapter 12.

ABZ CORPORATION
INTEROFFICE MEMORANDUM

TO: Lori Nichols, Accounting Department
FROM: Arthur J. Brown, Administrator
DATE: October 3, 19__
SUBJECT: Salary Increases

We are sending memos to all our employees informing them of their salary increases effective next month.

Since the recommendations for salary increases start at your level, you should be prepared to answer any questions that members of your department may have. In those cases where my office decided on a salary increase other than that you recommended, I will be happy to discuss the increase with you and with the person who is to receive it.

The attached list of salary increases represents our best effort to be fair and remain within our budget.

ms

Attachment

OFFICE COMMUNICATIONS SYSTEMS, INC.

INTEROFFICE MEMORANDUM

TO: John Doyle
FROM: William Jones
DATE: October 23, 19__
SUBJECT: Employees' Sick Days

Your memo about the increase in the number of days of sick leave that our employees are taking has been given my attention.

A study of our sales reports and conversations with many of our employees revealed the cause of the problem.

For many years it was our policy to close down our operations completely for the month of June. All of our employees took their vacations at the same time, and most of our workers were very happy with this arrangement. Our decision to keep the plant in operation 12 months of the year was supposed to increase production. It has not worked.

Perhaps if we returned to the previous vacation time policy, our workers would be much happier and the number of days of sick leave would decrease to its previous level.

lb

COMMUNICATIONS ASSOCIATES

22 North Broad Street/Philadelphia, PA 19185-4752

INTEROFFICE COMMUNICATION

TO: All Information Processors

FROM: Catherine Quintana

DATE: December 2, 19__

SUBJECT: Interoffice Correspondence

Correspondence within a company is frequently formatted on interoffice forms, either half or full sheets, depending on the length of the message. The following points describe the features of a memorandum prepared on a printed form:

1. Space twice after the colon in the first line of the printed heading and set the left margin. The heading items will begin at this point. The body of the memo may begin at the same point, or it may be aligned with the letter "S" in the word SUBJECT. Set the right margin stop an equal distance from the right edge.

2. Omit full addresses, the salutation, the complimentary close, and the signature.

3. Omit personal titles from the memo heading. They are included on the interoffice envelope, however.

4. Triple-space between the last item in the heading and the body of the message. Single-space the paragraphs, but double-space between them. Double-space above and below a table or a numbered list when one is included in the message. Space twice after the number in an enumerated list; align the whole paragraph under the first line.

5. Include reference initials, enclosure or attachment notations, and copy notations.

6. Be sure the originator initials the memo opposite his or her name to show that it has been read and approved.

Special colored envelopes usually are used for memorandums. Type the addressee's name, title or name of department, and room number for the address.

ms

pc Naomi Greenfield

Grammar and Usage

by John I. McCollum, Ph.D.

Brackets
Colon
Comma
Dash
Ellipsis
Exclamation Point
Hyphen
Italics
Parentheses
Period
Question Mark
Quotation Marks
Semicolon
Solidus (Slash or Virgule)

■ *Capitalization*

■ *Use of Numbers*

■ *Spelling Rules*

■ *Usage*

Contrary to the view held by a majority of people, grammar and rhetoric are not devices conjured by fiendish teachers to bewilder defenseless students. They are useful studies, the mastery of which is the mark of a sophisticated person. In general, it may be said that their value is both functional and esthetic. There is efficiency in a precisely worded statement, just as there may be pleasure in a well-turned phrase.

Of the various theories relative to the development of language, the social view seems most reasonable. The theory that languages have arisen, developed, and modified as a result of social necessity or convenience is the one from which most of the advice contained in the following pages springs. That is to say, the statements as to practice reflect usage widely adopted by informed writers and speakers. "Good" English is, in general, a somewhat debatable issue. What may at one time or in one place be good English may vary significantly from what is so considered at another time or in another place. The assumptions here are based on practices that may currently be considered acceptable by those who use the language clearly, efficiently, effectively, and artistically.

This section of the book contains basically useful advice for the development of an acceptable writing and speaking style. No attempt has been made to give a complete survey of the intricacies of grammar and rhetoric, and there is little or no theorizing. In many ways the material here is in the nature of a reminder of what should be brought to one's writing.

In matters of debate, and there are many, the practice is to adopt the more conservative position. To those who would argue that some of the best writers ignore, overlook, or transcend "mere rules," we offer the counterargument that in so doing such writers offer significant stylistic or artistic compensation and that they are generally capable of such compensation only after a long apprenticeship in which they acquired the tools with which to shape their greater achievement.

It may be argued, as well, that many decisions concerning propriety and style are essentially matters of taste. Indeed, such may be the case; one may, therefore, adopt a single rule: What is clearest, most precise, most useful, and most pleasing should prevail. One must learn to perceive and avoid vague, slovenly, ineffectual, and inaccurate language.

The purpose of this section is to record useful statements of practice in the hope of leading secretaries easily and quickly through what is often considered a tangle of rule and rhetoric. What we generally call grammar is simply a description of the way words function and relate to one another in a sentence. This is to say that instead of prescribing a set of rules handed down by grammarians, rhetoricians, and linguists, we merely describe the way people have used their language in the past and thereby suggest possibilities for success through similar practice.

Effective communication is not easy, but we can reduce the difficulty somewhat by developing as great a familiarity with language as possible. The more we understand about how our sentences can be put together, how we can by punctuation marks pull together or separate a variety of ideas, how we can substitute one word for another to gain a more precise meaning or a more pleasing manner of expression, the easier and more successful our communication will be.

PARTS OF SPEECH

Sentences are composed by combining a series of words, each of which functions in a specific way within the particular context. That is to say, the word itself is called a *noun* or a *verb* or an *adjective* or an *adverb* because it functions as such in a sentence, not because it is arbitrarily a particular part of speech. In identifying parts of speech, always think of the *function* of the word (or word group) in a specific sentence. For example, the word *light* may function as a noun, a verb, or an adjective.

> The *light* shines in the night. (Noun)
> *Light* the fire. (Verb)
> She struck him a *light* blow. (Adjective)

Functions of Words

Obviously, it is necessary to identify a word (or word group) not as a particular part of speech but as a *functioning* part of the sentence. In this sense words may be divided according to four general functions:

1. To name or identify—a word or word group (noun, pronoun, gerund, infinitive, noun phrase, or noun clause—all substantives) that names a person, place, thing, condition, quality, or action.
2. To assert—a word or word group (verb) that indicates action, state of being, or occurrence.
3. To modify—a word, phrase, or clause (adjective, adverb, or participle) that describes, limits, restricts, or qualifies the meaning of another word or word group.
4. To connect—a word (preposition) that may join a substantive to another word in the sentence; a word (conjunction) that may join words, phrases, or clauses.

Nouns

A noun is a word that names a person, place, thing, action, idea, quality, group, etc.

Classification

All nouns belong to one of two main classifications:

a. *Proper nouns* name specific persons, groups, organizations, places, things, or ideas.

> *John Smith, Hamlet, Pittsburgh, White House*

b. *Common nouns* name members of a group of persons, places, things, ideas, or conditions.

> *book, health, house, man, children, city, liberty*

Common nouns are variously classified according to what they name: *collective, concrete, abstract, mass.*

Agreement

a. For consistency, every verb must agree in number with its subject.

FAULTY:	In each room *is* ten *typists.*
IMPROVED:	In each room *are* ten *typists.*
FAULTY:	The *quality* of a company's products often *determine* the reputation of the company.
IMPROVED:	The *quality* of a company's products often *determines* the reputation of the company.

b. Nouns or pronouns placed between the subject and the verb do not affect the number of the subject.

> The *sound* of the violins *seems* very faint.

c. The number of the subject is not changed by the use of parenthetical expressions that begin with such terms as *as well as, no less than, including, together with,* etc.

> *Dr. Smith,* together with his wife and two sons, *is* to arrive on the evening flight.

d. Usually subjects joined by *and* take a plural verb.

> A *dictionary* and a *typewriter are* two tools of a secretary.
>
> *Mother, Father,* and *I were* at home when he called.

When the words joined by *and* refer to the same person or thing, the verb is singular:

> Your family *physician* and *friend* is the man to see.

e. When *each* or *every* precedes a singular subject, the verb is singular. When *each* follows the subject and the subject is plural, the verb is plural.

> *Each* member of the class *has* been urged to vote.
>
> *Every* person *is* to vote if he possibly can.
>
> They *each want* to go.

f. Singular subjects joined by *or, nor, either . . . or,* and *neither . . . nor* generally take a singular verb.

> *Neither* a doctor *nor* a nurse *was* available.
>
> *Either* the teacher *or* the principal *attends* the conference.

When one part of the subject is singular and one is plural, the verb usually agrees with the one closer to it.

> Neither Bill nor his *parents are* at home.
>
> He did not know where his pencil or his *books were.*
>
> Either the eggs or the *milk has* to be used.
>
> Either the milk or the *eggs have* to be used.

When the two parts of the subject are pronouns in different persons, usage is generally according to the following: If the sense is singular, the verb is singular and agrees with the closer pronoun.

> Either you or *I am* able to attend the conference.

If the sense is plural, the verb is plural.

> Neither you nor I *are* able to attend the conference.

g. Special care must be taken with sentences beginning with *there is* or *there are. There* is an expletive, not a substantive, and therefore cannot serve as a subject.

> There *are* to be at least ten *floats* in the parade. (*Floats,* not the expletive *there,* is the subject.)
>
> There *is* no *point* in questioning him further.

h. A collective noun (*class, committee, jury*) may be either singular or plural, depending upon the meaning of the noun in the particular context: If the items or people are considered as a group, the noun takes a singular verb; if they are considered as separate individuals in a group, the noun takes a plural verb. (Remember, too, that a collective noun can also be used in the plural form when more than one group is meant: *classes, committees, juries.* For some collective nouns the plural form is the same as the singular: *offspring.*)

The *jury was* in session for two days. (A group)

The *jury come* from several areas of the city. (Separate individuals)

A collective noun should not be used in both the singular and plural numbers within the same sentence.

> FAULTY: Since the school *board hires* the teachers, *they may* also *dismiss* them. (*Board* is singular with *hires,* then inconsistently plural with *they.*)
>
> IMPROVED: Since the school *board hires* the teachers, *it may* also *dismiss* them.

i. Some nouns that are plural in form but singular in meaning take singular verbs. *Esthetics, civics, economics, linguistics, mathematics, mumps, news,* and *semantics,* for example, are regularly singular. Verb agreement with words like *measles, physics,* and *politics* depends upon the specific use of the word.

> Your *politics* are going to get you into trouble with the company. (Your political opinions are going to. . . .)
>
> *Politics has* always interested him. ([The subject of] politics has always interested him.)

Checking your dictionary will help you with similar words you are not sure of.

j. The title of a single published work or work of art takes a singular verb.

> *Canterbury Tales* was written by Chaucer.

k. A word used as a word, even when it is plural in form, takes a singular verb.

> *They is* a pronoun.
>
> *Scissors comes* before *scissortail* in the dictionary.

Case

Differentiations between the nominative and objective cases of nouns are not observed in the English language. A few special rules, however, are generally applied to nouns in the possessive case.

a. The possessive case of nouns denoting inanimate objects is usually formed with an *of* phrase. (See also *Apostrophe* in the section on punctuation later in this chapter.)

> FAULTY: The room's ceiling
>
> IMPROVED: The ceiling *of* the room

Exceptions to this practice are found in certain familiar expressions that are idiomatically correct.

a year's labor	his heart's content
a moment's notice	for heaven's sake
a stone's throw	a mile's end

b. A noun preceding a gerund is usually in the possessive case.

FAULTY: I don't understand William being gone so long.

IMPROVED: I don't understand William's being gone so long. (It is not *William* that is not understood; it is *being gone,* which is adjectivally identified by the word *William's.*)

Distinction should be made between gerunds and participles. (See *Verbals,* under *Verbs,* in this chapter.)

Everett doesn't like *Mary's working.* (Everett disapproves of the fact that Mary works. *Working* is a gerund here.)

Everett doesn't like *Mary working.* (Everett doesn't like Mary when she is at work. *Working* is a participle here.)

Nouns Used as Adjectives

Although many nouns are used as adjectives effectively, especially when no suitable adjectives can be found, such forms should be avoided if they are awkward or ambiguous.

a. Nouns used acceptably as adjectives:

opera tickets   *automobile* race

b. Nouns used awkwardly or ambiguously as adjectives:

FAULTY: Many people now become seriously involved in a race argument. (Race is ambiguous; does the writer mean *racing* or *racial* issues?)

IMPROVED: Many people now become seriously involved in arguments about *racial issues.*

Many people now become seriously involved in arguments about *horse racing.*

Pronouns

A *pronoun* is a word that may be substituted for a noun. It performs all the functions of a noun but is not as specific. Because a pronoun is a substitute and depends on other words for its meaning, it must refer expressly or by clear implication to a noun or another pronoun previously mentioned (called the *antecedent*).

Classification

Pronouns are usually classified descriptively.

a. *Personal pronouns* designate the person speaking, the person spoken to, or the person or thing spoken of.

Declension of Personal Pronouns

Person	Case	Singular	Plural
1st person	nominative	I	we
	objective	me	us
	possessive	my, mine	our, ours
2nd person	nominative	you	you
	objective	you	you
	possessive	your, yours	your, yours
3rd person	nominative	he, she, it	they
	objective	him, her, it	them
	possessive	his, her, hers, its	their, theirs

(Note that the possessive forms *ours, yours, hers, its,* and *theirs* are each written without the apostrophe.)

b. *Demonstrative pronouns* point out or identify specific objects (*this, that, these, those, such*). The choice of pronoun depends on the relative proximity of the speaker to the object.

this house, these houses (Near)

that house, those houses (Farther away)

c. *Relative pronouns* connect a subordinate clause to the main clause. *Who, whom, whose* (and the compounds *whoever, whomever, whosoever,* and *whomsoever*) refer to persons; *which* and *whichever* refer to things or objects and to living creatures (but not to persons except groups of people regarded impersonally or categories of persons regarded as such); *that* and *what* may refer to either persons or objects.

Homer, *who* is the first among the epic writers, has been called the father of heroic literature.

The writer of *whom* I speak is Sylvia Warner.

Is he the man *whose* hat is on my desk?

Whoever is first receives the award.

Grace will admit *whomever* she sees first.

This is the book of *which* I spoke.

The television set, *which* was repaired only last week, is broken again.

You may have *whichever* book you want.

He is a man *that* we all admire.

Is this the face *that* launched a thousand ships?

She is *what* I call a genius.

This is about *what* I would expect of him.

d. *Interrogative pronouns* are used to introduce a question. The pronouns *who, whose, which,* and *what* (and the compounds *whoever* and *whatever*) can become *interrogative.*

Who shall cast the first stone?

Whose gloves are these?

Which is yours?

What do you want?

Whoever told you that lie?

Whatever does she mean?

e. *Indefinite pronouns* are ones whose antecedents are not explicit or precise persons, places, or things. Some of the most frequently used indefinite pronouns are listed below.

all	each one	neither	other
another	either	nobody	some
any	everybody	none	somebody
anyone	everyone	no one	someone
anything	everything	nothing	something
both	few	one	such
each	much		

f. *Reflexive pronouns* direct or reflect the action back to the subject. In form they represent a compound of one of the personal pronouns and *self* or *selves.*

He taught *himself* to read.

She taught *herself* to sing.

g. *Intensive pronouns* appear in an appositive position and serve to emphasize or intensify a substantive. The forms are the same as the reflexive forms above.

The students *themselves* made the decision.

h. *Reciprocal pronouns* indicate an interchange or mutual action. *Each other* and *one another* are the only two such pronouns in English.

The two girls very seldom saw *each other.*

As they passed, all the soldiers nodded to *one another.*

Case

The case of a pronoun is determined not by its antecedent but by the construction that it is a part of.

    a.   *Personal pronouns* have different forms for different cases. (See the table *Declension of Personal Pronouns,* above.)

        (1)   The subject of the verb is in the nominative case.

            He and *I* are going.

            Dave and *she* are going.

        (2)   The complements of all forms of the verb *to be* (except the infinitive) are in the nominative case.

            This is *she* speaking.

            The speaker was neither *he* nor *she.*

            It is *they* whom you seek.

            It is *we* who must remain to spread your message.

        (3)   The subject and the complement of the infinitive are in the objective case if the subject is also the object of a verb or preposition.

            He invited *them* and *us* to go to the party.

            We believed *him* to be wrong.

            He asked *you* and *me* to be ready at noon.

            The judges declared the winner to be *her.*

        (4)   The object of a preposition is in the objective case.

            Let's keep this secret *between you* and *me.*

            I bought birthday presents *for him* and *her.*

            Come to lunch *with Judy* and *me.*

            I typed the letters *for Mr. Miller* and *him.*

Note: In (1) through (4) above, when a pronoun follows *and,* it sometimes becomes a problem to choose the correct case (*I* or *me, he* or *him, she* or *her, we* or *us, they* or *them*). Very often the correct form can be determined if the sentence is tried out with the *pronoun in question used by itself.* Some of the sentences above would be tried out as follows:

    Come to lunch *with* [Judy and] *me.*

    I typed the letters *for* [Mr. Miller and] *him.*

    He invited *them* [and us] to go to the party.

    He invited [them and] *us* to go to the party.

    He asked [you and] *me* to be ready at noon.

(5) The proper case for a pronoun used in an elliptical clause introduced by *than* or *as* can be determined by the meaning of the complete form of the clause.

> He is more understanding than *I* [am understanding]. (*I* is the subject of the verb in the clause *I am understanding.*)
>
> I can write as well as *he* [can write]. (*He* is the subject of the verb in the clause *he can write.*)
>
> She speaks to Helen more often than [she speaks to] *me.* (*Me* is the object of the preposition *to.*)
>
> She speaks to Helen more often than *I* [speak to Helen]. (*I* is the subject of the verb *speak* in the clause *I speak to* Helen.)

(6) With gerunds the possessive case is most often used, although the choice of case sometimes depends on the emphasis intended.

> *Your* reading aloud disturbs me.
>
> Have you ever thought about *his* leaving the company? (The *leaving* is emphasized here.)
>
> Have you ever thought about *him* leaving the company? (The person named [*him*] is emphasized here.)

(See *Verbals,* under *Verbs.*)

(7) The possessive case of *it* has no apostrophe.

> The bird built *its* nest in the tree.

b. The case of a *relative pronoun* is determined by the construction of the clause in which it appears. Difficulties frequently arise in the use of *who* and *whom.* In formal English *who* and *whoever* serve as subjects of a verb; *whom* and *whomever* serve as objects.

Nominative Case	Objective Case	Possessive Case
who	whom	whose
whoever	whomever	whosever
that	that	of that
which	which	of which, whose
what	what	of what

> Jean, *who* lives next door, was married last week. (Subject of the verb *lives*)
>
> Ann, *whom* I have known all my life, was there. (Object of the verb *have known*)
>
> John, to *whom* we looked for help, was not at home. (Object of the preposition *to*)

He spoke to *whoever* answered the telephone. (Subject of the verb *answered* in a noun clause that serves as the object of the preposition *to*)

Whose is often used as the possessive of *which,* in place of *of which,* to avoid an awkward or formal-sounding construction.

I'd like to have a desk the drawers *of which* don't stick.

I'd like to have a desk *whose* drawers don't stick.

c. Some *indefinite pronouns* can be made possessive in form through the addition of an apostrophe and an *s.*

another's glove   anyone's house   everybody's responsibility

d. A *pronoun* used *in apposition* with a noun or another pronoun is in the same case as the noun or other pronoun.

We—James and *I*—will never betray your confidence. (*I,* in apposition with *we,* the subject, is in the nominative case.)

He asked three men—Bob, Joe, and *me*—to be ready. (*Me,* in apposition with *men,* the subject of the infinitive *to be,* is in the objective case.)

The men—Bob, Joe, and *I*—met him at the river. (*I,* in apposition with *men,* the subject, is in the nominative case.)

Note: The correct form may be determined easily be dropping the noun with which the pronoun is in apposition and allowing the pronoun to function alone; *e.g., I* met him at the river.

Reference

A pronoun should refer clearly to its antecedent if the meaning is to be precise. Each pronoun should refer to a definite person, place, or thing in order to avoid the following difficulties:

a. Remote antecedent. The pronoun should be placed as close as possible to its antecedent.

FAULTY: He wore a flower in his lapel, *which* he had received from an admirer. (What had he received from an admirer, his lapel or a flower?)

IMPROVED: In his lapel he wore a flower, *which* he had received from an admirer.

b. Ambiguous reference. There should be no question as to the specific antecedent for each pronoun; if the antecedent involves the possibility of choice, it is ambiguous and thus the reference is faulty.

FAULTY:	Last Tuesday James told Mr. Adams that *he* must find the money or face bankruptcy. (Who is to find the money or face bankruptcy?)
IMPROVED:	Last Tuesday James told Mr. Adams to find the money or face bankruptcy.
or:	
IMPROVED:	Last Tuesday James told Mr. Adams, "You must find the money or face bankruptcy."
or:	
IMPROVED:	Last Tuesday James told Mr. Adams, "I must find the money or face bankruptcy."

c. Broad or weak reference. A pronoun should refer to a definite word, not to an entire clause, idea, action, modifier, or understood or unexpressed word.

FAULTY:	Bill was the star of the game, *which* led to his promotion to the first string.
IMPROVED:	Bill's starring in the game led to his promotion to the first string.
FAULTY:	Helen is learning to play the piano. *It* is a subject I know nothing about.
IMPROVED:	Helen is learning to play the piano. I know nothing about piano music.

d. Indefinite reference with second- and third-person pronouns. Consistency of reference must be applied, or the passive voice may be used.

FAULTY:	If you hope to pass, you must study; however, *anybody* can get help if *you* ask for it.
IMPROVED:	If you hope to pass, you must study; however, *you* can get help if *you* ask for it.
or:	
IMPROVED:	If one hopes to pass, he must study; however, *anyone* can get help if *he* asks for it.
FAULTY:	*They* have no income-tax law in the state of Florida.
IMPROVED:	Florida has no state income-tax law.

Agreement

Although pronouns are effective instruments by which we can secure variety, emphasis, and economy, they may merely confuse if consistent grammatical patterns are not maintained.

a. The pronoun should agree with its antecedent in number, person, and gender.

If a new *secretary* wants to succeed, *he* or *she* must work hard. (Singular antecedent requires a singular pronoun.)

She is one of those people *who hate* early morning appointments. (*Who* refers to *people*; it is therefore plural and thus takes the plural form of the verb *hate*.)

b. The indefinite pronouns (*each, one, someone, somebody, any, anyone, everyone, everybody, none, nobody, either, neither*) are usually considered singular.

If *anyone* wishes to speak, *he* may do so now.

Neither of the men would answer when *he* was questioned.

Everyone present cast *his* vote.

Everybody must turn in *his* expense account by Thursday.

Verbs

A verb is a word that makes a statement about a subject. Its function is to convey a positive assertion, to make a statement of condition or probability, to give a command, to ask a question, or to make an exclamation.

Classification

a. A *transitive verb* is one that requires a direct object to complete its meaning (as the word *transitive* suggests, the action passes from one thing to another).

I *carried* the *book*.

Donne *wrote* intriguing *poetry*.

Alice *closed* the *book* with a sigh of relief.

b. An *intransitive verb* simply states something about the subject; there is no direct object to receive the action.

The sun *rose* at six o'clock.

The old dog *lay* sleeping in the sun.

James *sat* for two hours waiting for the train.

c. A *linking verb,* or *copula,* is an intransitive verb that makes no complete statement itself but links the subject with a subjective complement (predicate noun or predicate adjective). *To be* is the most common linking verb; other principal ones are *taste, smell, become, feel, seem,* and *appear.*

The coffee *tastes* good.

I *am* the victor.

His account *seems* improbable.

She *felt* bad.

d. Many verbs serve an *auxiliary,* or *helping,* function; that is, they are used with another verb to form a verb phrase. They help indicate tense, mood, and voice. (See *Properties,* below.) Among the more common auxiliaries are *be, have, do, may, can, shall,* and *will.*

> I *am* going.
>
> She *has been* ill.
>
> I *do* want to go.

Properties

Verbs regularly show the following qualities, or properties: *person, number, mood, voice,* and *tense.*

a. Verbs (except *to be*) change in form to denote *person* and *number* only in the third person singular of the present tense.

To stop	Singular	Plural
1st person:	I stop	we stop
2nd person:	you stop	you stop
3rd person:	he, she, it stops	they stop

To be	Singular	Plural
1st person:	I am	we are
2nd person:	you are	you are
3rd person:	he, she, it is	they are

b. *Mood* (or *mode*) is the property of a verb that denotes the state of mind in which the action is conceived:

(1) The *indicative* mood makes a statement or asks a question.

> He *closed* the door.
>
> Who *is* the hero of the play?

(2) The *imperative* mood expresses a command or makes a request.

> *Take* time to compose a letter.
>
> *Listen* well; *respect* wisdom.
>
> *Stop!*
>
> Please *come* as early as you can.

(3) The *subjunctive* mood expresses a condition contrary to fact, a doubt, a regret or a wish, a concession, or a supposition.

> If I *were* you, I would study more regularly.
>
> I wish I *were* in command here.
>
> I move that the treasurer *be* instructed to pay our debts.
>
> Suppose she *were* too late to be considered.
>
> He acts as though he *were* the only person present.
>
> If this *be* treason, make the most of it.

In English, the subjunctive mood has largely been displaced by the indicative. The subjunctive occurs most frequently in the third person singular of the present tense (*I desire that he go at once,* instead of the indicative form, *I desire that he goes at once)* and in the verb *to be,* as indicated below:

Present Indicative		Present Subjunctive	
I am	we are	if I be	if we be
you are	you are	if you be	if you be
he is	they are	if he be	if they be

c. *Voice* is the property of the verb that indicates whether the subject of a sentence or of a clause is *acting* or *being acted upon.* When the subject performs the action, the verb is said to be in the *active voice.* When the subject is acted upon, it is said to be in the *passive voice;* the subject is literally passive and is a receiver rather than an actor. The passive is formed by the use of some form of the verb *to be* as an auxiliary to the past participle of another verb.

> The ball *struck* the player. (Active)
>
> The player *was struck* by the ball. (Passive)
>
> Mary *started* a rumor about two of her co-workers. (Active)
>
> A rumor *was started* about two of Mary's co-workers. (Passive)

Although the passive voice is sometimes weak, it has certain uses that are worth consideration by the careful writer.

(1) The passive voice may be used when the subject is not known or is not to be revealed.

> A bomb *was found* in the railway station.
>
> The invoice *was mailed* under separate cover.

(2) It may be used to emphasize the *action* rather than the *actor.*

> Good health *is sought* by everyone.
>
> This lesson *will be learned* before we leave.

(3) It may be used to achieve variety in sentence structure.

Inexperienced writers often use the passive in an attempt to create an impression of authority and learning, but excessive use of the passive often results in vague and wordy constructions. When possible, use the active voice.

d. The word *tense* comes from the Latin word *tempus* (time) and refers to the forms of verbs denoting the time and the distinct nature of the action or existence (continuing or completed). In English six tenses are commonly used: present, past, future, present perfect, past perfect, and future perfect.

Principal Parts

The *principal parts* of a verb are the *present stem,* which is the same as the infinitive (*jump*), the *past tense (jumped),* and the *past participle (jumped).* The past tense and past participle of most verbs in English are formed by adding -*ed* to the present stem; these verbs are called "regular" verbs. The principal parts of many other verbs in English are formed in an "irregular" manner—some through a vowel change (*sing, sang, sung*), others in some other "irregular" manner (*catch, caught, caught*). The principal parts are important because the six tenses are built from the three principal parts. From the present stem are formed the present and future tenses; from the past participle are formed the present perfect, past perfect, and future perfect tenses.

The word list in Chapter 19 includes the principal parts of all irregularly formed verbs. You may also consult this list to learn when the final consonant is doubled to form the past tense, past participle, and present participle of a verb (*hop, hopped, hopping*) and to learn when a final *e* is dropped before the -*ed* is added to form the past tense and past participle or before the -*ing* is added to form the present participle (*hope, hoped, hoping*).

Verbals

Because *participles, gerunds,* and *infinitives* are derived from verbs, they are called *verbals.* They are like verbs in that they have different tenses, may have subjects and objects, and may be modified by adverbs; but they cannot make a statement and therefore cannot be used in the place of verbs.

a. A *participle* may be used as an adjective.

> A *working* man is generally busy. (Present participle used as an adjective to modify the noun *man*)
>
> *Polished* silver always looks elegant. (Past participle used as an adjective to modify the noun *silver*)
>
> *Having completed* his work, he retired for the night. (Perfect participle used as an adjective to modify the pronoun *he*)

b. A *gerund* ends in *–ing* and functions as a noun.

> Your *working* is greatly appreciated. (Gerund used as the subject of the sentence)
>
> He objected to my *speaking* without permission. (Gerund used as the object of the preposition *to*)

A noun or pronoun preceding a gerund is usually in the possessive case.

> Most companies disapprove of an *employee's* being late.

However, a plural noun preceding a gerund is often not in the possessive case.

> Most companies disapprove of *employees* being late.

When the noun preceding the gerund denotes an inanimate object or an abstract idea, the noun is usually not in the possessive case.

> They blamed the plane crash on the *engine* falling in midair.

c. An *infinitive* is usually preceded by *to* and functions as a noun, an adjective, or an adverb.

> *To succeed* was my greatest ambition. (Infinitive used as a noun, subject to the verb *was*)
>
> The person *to choose* is the one now in office. (Infinitive used as an adjective to modify the noun *person*)
>
> We came to *help*. (Infinitive used as an adverb to modify the verb *came*)

Conjugation

Following is the conjugation of the verb *to see* in its various forms (principal parts: *see, saw, seen*).

Indicative Mood

Present Tense

1st person
ACTIVE: I see   we see
PASSIVE: I am seen   we are seen

2nd person
ACTIVE: you see   you see
PASSIVE: you are seen   you are seen

3rd person
ACTIVE: he, she, it sees   they see
PASSIVE: he, she, it is seen   they are seen

Past Tense

1st person
ACTIVE: I saw · we saw
PASSIVE: I was seen · we were seen

2nd person
ACTIVE: you saw · you saw
PASSIVE: you were seen · you were seen

3rd person
ACTIVE: he saw · they saw
PASSIVE: he was seen · they were seen

Future Tense

1st person
ACTIVE: I shall see · we shall see
PASSIVE: I shall be seen · we shall be seen

2nd person
ACTIVE: you will see · you will see
PASSIVE: you will be seen · you will be seen

3rd person
ACTIVE: he will see · they will see
PASSIVE: he will be seen · they will be seen

Present Perfect Tense

1st person
ACTIVE: I have seen · we have seen
PASSIVE: I have been seen · we have been seen

2nd person
ACTIVE: you have seen · you have seen
PASSIVE: you have been seen · you have been seen

3rd person
ACTIVE: he has seen · they have seen
PASSIVE: he has been seen · they have been seen

Past Perfect Tense

1st person
ACTIVE: I had seen   we had seen
PASSIVE: I had been seen   we had been seen

2nd person
ACTIVE: you had seen   you had seen
PASSIVE: you had been seen   you had been seen

3rd person
ACTIVE: he had seen   they had seen
PASSIVE: he had been seen   they had been seen

Future Perfect Tense

1st person
ACTIVE: I shall have seen   we shall have seen
PASSIVE: I shall have been seen   we shall have been seen

2nd person
ACTIVE: you will have seen   you will have seen
PASSIVE: you will have been seen   you will have been seen

3rd person
ACTIVE: he will have seen   they will have seen
PASSIVE: he will have been seen   they will have been seen

Subjunctive Mood

Active Voice   *Passive Voice*

Present Tense

SINGULAR: if I, you see (if he sees)   if I, you, he be seen
PLURAL: if we, you, they see   if we, you, they be seen

Past Tense

SINGULAR: if I, you, he saw   if I, you, he were seen
PLURAL: if we, you, they saw   if we, you, they were seen

Active Voice	*Passive Voice*

Present Perfect Tense	
SINGULAR: if I, you have seen (if he has seen) PLURAL: if we, you, they have seen	if I, you have been seen (if he has been seen) if we, you, they have been seen

Past Perfect Tense	
(Same as the Indicative Mood)	

Imperative Mood

Present Tense	
see	be seen

Infinitives

Present Tense	
to see	to be seen

Present Perfect Tense	
to have seen	to have been seen

Participles

Present Tense	
seeing	being seen

Past Tense	
seen	been seen

Present Perfect Tense	
having seen	having been seen

Gerunds

Present Tense	
seeing	being seen

Present Perfect Tense	
having seen	having been seen

In addition to the six simple tenses in English, there are two other forms that are frequently recognized:

a. *Progressive* verb forms show action in progress.

> I *am seeing.*
>
> I *was seeing.*
>
> I *am being seen.*

b. *Emphatic* verb forms employ *do* or *does* as an auxiliary. (These forms are used also for questions and negations.)

> I *do see;* he *does see.*
>
> *Does* he *see* it? *Did* he *see* it?
>
> He *does* not *see* it; he *did* not *see* it.

Sequence of Tenses

Tense reveals not only the time of the action (present, past, and future) but also the continuity of related action. Shifts in tense must conform to the logical order or sequence of action. In most instances a knowledge of the denotation of time in the six tenses and the application of common sense will aid in developing consistent practices.

a. The tense of a verb in a subordinate element should *agree* logically with the thought suggested by the governing verb in the main clause. Note that statements regarded as universally or permanently true are expressed in the present.

> FAULTY: This book *is written* for an audience that *felt* that political favors *are* to be dispensed without particular regard for merit or justice.
>
> IMPROVED: This book *was written* for an audience that *feels* that political favors *are* to be dispensed without particular regard for merit or justice.

b. A major difficulty arises from the use of verbals.

   (1) The *present infinitive* is used to express action of the same time as, or future to, that of the governing verb.

       She wants *to read* each new book.

       He wanted *to improve* his efficiency.

   (2) The *perfect infinitive* is used to express action previous to that of the governing verb.

       I *should* like to *have seen* his face when you told him.

       I consider it a privilege *to have worked* with him in the recent political campaign.

   (3) The *present participle* is used to express action simultaneous with that of the governing verb.

       Looking up from her book, she was startled to see her supervisor enter the room.

   (4) The *perfect participle* is used to express action prior to that of the governing verb.

       Having found his place, he sat down hurriedly.

Shall and Will, Should and Would

Although in informal usage the differences between *shall* and *will* and *should* and *would* are hardly discernible, careful writers still recognize the distinctions. In more conservative practice the use of *should* and *would* follows the same patterns as those established for *shall* and *will.*

  a. In expressing expectation and in the simple future, *shall* is used in the first person and *will* in the second and third persons.

I shall	we shall
you will	you will
he, she, it will	they will

       I *shall* be in the office next Monday at 10 o'clock.

       They said that they *would* be on time.

       I *should* think that they *would* be more careful.

  b. *Will* is used in the first person and *shall* in the second and third persons to express determination, command, or promise.

       I *will* have my way in this matter.

       I *would* do it if I could.

       They *shall* not pass.

c. *Should* may be used in all persons to express obligation or condition.

> I *should* follow your advice, but I'm too lazy.
> If he *should* leave now, all work would stop.

d. *Would* may be used in all persons to express determination, habitual action, or a wish.

> Only on one condition *would* we be willing to consider such a proposal.
> I *would* read for an hour or two each night before going to sleep.
> If he *would* leave now, all work would stop.

Adjectives and Adverbs

Modifiers are words or groups of words that describe or qualify other words. To *modify* means to describe, limit, or in any other way make the meaning more precise or exact. The two kinds of modifiers are *adjectives* and *adverbs*.

Adjectives

An *adjective* is a word that *modifies a noun or pronoun.*

blue bird	*the* chair
easy assignment	*his* grade
crushed flower	*several* people
a book	*seventh* day
an apple	*former* employer

Some adjectives form the comparative degree by adding *–er* and the superlative by adding *–est;* others form the comparative degree by the use of *more* (*less*) and *most* (*least*) for the superlative degrees. Still others have an irregular comparison.

Positive	Comparative	Superlative
cool	cooler	coolest
tired	more tired	most tired
bad	worse	worst
good	better	best

The comparative degree should be used to indicate the relationship between two persons or things.

> I am the *taller* of the two children in our family.
> This book is *better* than that one.
> I am *more optimistic* than he.

The superlative degree should be used when three or more persons or things are compared.

This is the *warmest* day of the year.

I am the *tallest* of the three boys.

This is the *most pleasant* experience I can recall.

Adverbs

An *adverb* is a word that *modifies an adjective, a verb, or another adverb.* Frequently, adverbs can be distinguished from adjectives only by the context in which they appear.

Children like books. (No modifier)

Young children *usually* like *story* books. (*Young* and *story* are adjectives; *usually* is an adverb.)

Very *young* children *almost always* like *highly illustrated* books, books *that can be read quickly.* (*Young, illustrated,* and the clause *that can be read quickly* are adjectives; *very, almost, always, highly,* and *quickly* are adverbs.)

In the comparison of adverbs, some shorter adverbs form the comparative degree by adding *-er* (*fast, faster*) and the superlative by adding *-est* (*fastest*), but most adverbs form the comparative degree by using *more (less)* and the superlative by adding *most (least).* Others are irregularly formed.

Positive	Comparative	Superlative
calmly	more calmly	most calmly
badly	worse	worst
well	better	best

Adverbs have certain distinguishing characteristics:

a. They are frequently distinguished from corresponding adjectives by ending in *-ly.* Although many adverbs end in *-ly,* this ending is not a certain device for recognizing this part of speech; some adverbs do not and some adjectives *(early, cowardly)* do end in *-ly.* Several common words that do not end in *-ly* may be either adjectives or adverbs depending on their function in a given context: *fast, little, near, late, well.*

b. Some adverbs are distinguished from corresponding nouns by *-wise* or *-ways* used as a suffix: *sideways, lengthwise.*

c. Some adverbs are distinguished from the same word used as a preposition in that they have no noun as an object.

The sun came *up.* (Adverb)

Henry came *up* the hill. (Preposition)

   d. Adverbs, like adjectives, may be preceded by words that intensify their meaning.

> The *very hastily* written paper was much better than the author had expected.
>
> He walked *right by* without speaking.

Prepositions

Simple Prepositions

A *simple preposition* shows the relationship of a noun or a pronoun (the object of the preposition) to some other word: stayed *at* school, lived *in* the house, the neighborhood *across* the way. The following list contains the words most commonly used as prepositions:

about	beside	in	since
above	besides	inside	through
across	between	into	throughout
after	beyond	like	till
against	but	near	to
along	by	of	toward
amid	concerning	off	until
among	despite	on	under
around	down	onto	underneath
at	during	outside	up
before	except	over	upon
behind	excepting	per	with
below	for	regarding	within
beneath	from	save	without

   A preposition is usually followed by its object, which may be a noun, a pronoun, a noun phrase, or a noun clause. Occasionally, however, the object may appear earlier in the sentence:

> Which church are you going *to*?
>
> The company I am employed *by* is a reliable one.
>
> This is the sort of foolishness that we will not put up *with*.
>
> We will not put up *with* this sort of foolishness.

Although some writers object to the use of a preposition at the end of a sentence, others accept such usage unless the final preposition is weakening. The practice should always depend upon its effectiveness.

Compound Prepositions

A *compound preposition* serves the same purpose as a single one.

as for	for fear of	in view of
as to	for the sake of	on account of
aside from	in accordance with	owing to
because of	in addition to	pertaining to
by means of	in behalf of	regardless of
by way of	in case of	with reference to
contrary to	in favor of	with regard to
due to	in regard to	with respect to
exclusive of	in spite of	with the exception of

Conjunctions

Conjunctions are used to connect words or groups of words in sentences; they are identified generally according to their function as *coordinating* or *subordinating* elements. If the words or word groups are of equal value in the sentence, the conjunction is said to be *coordinating;* if the words or word groups are unequal, the conjunction is said to be *subordinating*.

Coordinating Conjunctions

Coordinating conjunctions link words, phrases, clauses, or sentences of equal rank—elements that are not grammatically dependent on one another.

a. *Pure,* or *simple,* conjunctions join two or more words, phrases, clauses, or sentences of equal rank—that is, having similar importance in the grammatical unit. The simple conjunctions are *and, but, for, or,* and *nor* (some writers include *yet* and *so*).

b. *Correlative* conjunctions are words used in pairs to emphasize the relationship between two ideas. The most commonly used correlatives are *either . . . or, both . . . and, neither . . . nor, and not only . . . but also.*

Subordinating Conjunctions

Subordinating conjunctions relate a noun clause or an adverbial clause to its independent clause. (The adjective clause is usually related by a relative pronoun.) Some common subordinating conjunctions are *because, if, since, as, while, although, unless, before,* and *so that.*

Although English grammar is not difficult, many students never
master it.

Peter cannot hope to buy a car *unless* he begins to save money.

Conjunctive Adverbs

Conjunctive adverbs are words or phrases that ordinarily are used parentheti-
cally but also are often used to relate two independent clauses or two words,
phrases, or sentences; the more common are *however, thus, in fact, for
example, still,* and *then.*

I worked for three hours on the bookkeeping; *then* I began to review the
correspondence.

English grammar is not difficult; *however,* many students never master it.

Interjections

An *interjection* is an exclamatory or parenthetical word that has little relation
to the remainder of the sentence. Frequently it is a sentence in itself:

Ouch!

Oh, why didn't you come earlier?

Alas, youth too soon is gone.

Commonly used interjections include the following:

ah	boo	hurrah	pshaw
aha	bravo	hush	so
ahoy	encore	indeed	tut
alas	gosh	lo	what
amen	hello	O	whoa
ay	hey	off	whoopee
bah	ho	oh	why
behold	huh	ouch	woe

Interjections should be used sparingly in serious writing because they are
for the most part colloquial and conversational. When overused, they give the
effect of a strained, melodramatic, or immature style.

CLAUSES AND PHRASES

The sentence, which is in itself a group or cluster of words in a meaningful pattern, is often made up of a number of subordinate groups or clusters of words that form *clauses* and *phrases* and that function as individual parts of speech. A *clause* is a closely related group of words containing a subject and a verb. There are two general types of clauses:

Independent Clauses

An *independent* (principal or main) *clause* expresses a complete thought and may stand alone as a sentence. The underscored sections represent the independent clause.

Today's newspaper is on my desk.

The theater section, which begins on page 30, reviews the new play.

Dependent Clauses

A *dependent* (subordinate) *clause* cannot stand alone as a sentence, although it contains a subject and a verb. Such a clause depends for its meaning upon the principal clause of the sentence in which it occurs; it functions as a noun or a modifier, and it is usually introduced by a subordinating conjunction, an adverb, or a relative pronoun. Dependent clauses are used as adverbs (adverbial clause), as adjectives (adjective clause), or as nouns (noun clause) and are identified according to their function.

   a. An *adverbial clause* modifies a verb, an adjective, or an adverb.

   When the humidity is high, we suffer from the heat. (The adverbial clause modifies the verb *suffer.*)

   We are sorry *that he is ill.* (The adverbial clause modifies the adjective *sorry.*)

   She does her work more quickly *than I do.* (The adverbial clause modifies the adverbs *more quickly.*)

   b. An *adjective clause* modifies a noun or a pronoun.

   We saw a replica of the capsule *that John Glenn used in his orbital flight.* (The adjective clause modifies the noun *capsule.*)

   The employee *who applies himself* will succeed. (The adjective clause modifies the noun *employee.*)

   The woman *who applies herself* will succeed. (The adjective clause modifies the noun *woman.*)

   Give the book to anyone *who may want to use it.* (The adjective clause modifies the pronoun *anyone.*)

c. A *noun clause* serves as a subject, a complement, or an object.

> *What we need most* is more money. (The noun clause is the subject of the verb *is.*)

> That is *what he had in mind.* (The noun clause is a predicate nominative following the linking verb *is.*)

> Macbeth stated *that he was governed only by his vaulting ambition.* (The noun clause is the direct object of the verb *stated.*)

> Give *whoever needs one* a book. (The noun clause is the indirect object of the verb *give.*)

> I will speak to *whoever answers the telephone.* (The noun clause is the object of the preposition *to.*)

Phrases

A *phrase* is a group of related words having no subject and predicate. It is used as a noun or as a modifier (adjective or adverb) and is connected to the rest of the sentence by a preposition, a participle, a gerund, or an infinitive.

> Her ambition was *to learn another language.* (The infinitive phrase is used as a noun, serving as a predicate nominative.)

> Milton hoped *to write the great English epic.* (The infinitive phrase is used as a noun, serving as the direct object of the verb.)

> *To succeed* was my greatest ambition. (The infinitive phrase is used as a noun, serving as the subject of the sentence.)

> Her energies were directed to *writing a notable epic.* (The gerund phrase is used as a noun, serving as the object of the preposition *to.*)

> *Fishing with his friends* was his favorite pastime. (The gerund phrase is used as a noun, serving as the subject of the sentence.)

> He considered *peddling old clothes* undignified. (The gerund phrase is used as a noun, serving as the object of the verb.)

> The Greeks sailed *to Troy.* (The prepositional phrase is used as an adverb.)

> We went *to visit our brother at camp.* (The infinitive phrase is used as an adverb.)

> The cover *of the book* was blue. (The prepositional phrase is used as an adjective.)

> Her ambition *to climb the mountain* was never fulfilled. (The infinitive phrase is used as an adjective.)

> The mysterious stranger, *wearing a black coat,* disappeared into the night. (The participial phrase is used as an adjective.)

The *absolute phrase* is somewhat unlike other kinds of phrases in that it usually consists of a noun followed and modified by a participle or participial phrase. Because it cannot stand alone as a sentence, it is a phrase; but it modifies no single word in the sentence, although it is closely related in thought to the rest of the sentence or to some part of it. The phrase is *absolute* in that it has no grammatical relationship to the main clause.

> *The dishes having been done,* she curled up in the chair for a nap.

> *The king having died,* the prince assumed the throne.

An *appositive phrase* is a group of words naming again a substantive previously mentioned.

> Washington, *our first president,* was an astute politician.

> Chicago, *an inland city,* has grown in importance as an ocean port since the opening of the St. Lawrence Seaway.

SENTENCES

Communication in English begins with the sentence. Depending on the circumstances, a sentence may be a fully developed statement or it may contain implied elements. In many instances, our spoken language can be reduced to writing; however, the written statement does not have accompanying aids like gesture and vocal intonation, nor does it permit immediate questioning or requests for repetition when it is unclear. A good sentence, and thus effective communication, requires clarity, unity, and propriety. In order to achieve these qualities, writing generally follows a set of rules and conventions.

With the proper inflection a single word could be considered a sentence— or at least a sentence by implication.

> Oh? (Is that so?)
> Oh! (That hurts!)
> Come! (You come here!)
> [Who is that?] John. (That is John.)

As questions, exclamations, commands, and responses, such units may function satisfactorily as sentences. In general, however, it is convenient to define a sentence as *a group of words conveying a single complete thought.* If the group of words contains more than one statement, such statements should be so closely related that they convey a single impression.

Parts of a Sentence

The typical English sentence contains a *subject* and a *predicate.* As previously suggested, either the subject or the predicate may be expressed or implied. In order to work meaningfully with such matters, one must understand the structure of the sentence; one must recognize the function of words as they stand in a particular relationship with one another. The following comments are basic to that understanding.

a. The *subject (S)* is the person, thing, or idea about which an assertion is made. The *predicate (P)* (in its most expanded form composed of a verb, its modifiers, and its object and modifiers) makes an assertion (of action, state of being, or condition) about the subject.

I read a book.
S   P

The old man spoke softly.
S   P

b. Both the subject and the predicate may be simple or compound.

John and Mary read and sing well.
S (compound)   P (compound)

John stated his opinion and sat down.
S (simple)   P (compound)

John and Mary are present.
S (compound)   P (simple)

John's briefcase and hat were found beside the wreck.
S (compound)   P (simple)

Note: A simple device by which the subject may be located is to ask *who* or *what* of the verb. Observe the sentences above:

Who read and sing well? *John and Mary* are thus identified as the subject.

Who stated his opinion and sat down? *John.*

Who are present? *John and Mary.*

What were found beside the wreck? *John's briefcase and hat.*

c. Although a sentence needs only a subject and a verb to fulfill the requirement of the definition, many sentences contain other elements to complete their meanings. Among these are two general classifications: *objects* and *complements.*

(1) The *direct object (DO)* is a word or group of words that receives the action of a transitive verb.

DO
Joan typed the *letter.*

DO
I have read *War and Peace.*

(2) The *indirect object (IO)* identifies the person or thing receiving the action suggested by the verb and direct object. The indirect object usually precedes the direct object; the preposition *to* or *for* is implied.

IO   DO

He gave *her* a *box* of candy.

IO   DO

She told *him* a bedtime *story.*

IO   DO

Bring *me* the *report.* (Subject *you* understood)

(3) The *object of a preposition (OP)* is the substantive that follows a preposition *(P)* and completes its meaning. The complete prepositional phrase functions either as an adjective or as an adverb.

P   OP

She wore a dress *with* lace *trim.*

P   OP

Your money is *in* the *bank.*

P   OP

He spoke *to* the *manager.*

P   OP

The boat was built *by* three old *men.*

(4) A *subjective complement (SC)* (also called a *predicate nominative* when a noun or pronoun, and a *predicate adjective* when an adjective) is a noun, pronoun, or adjective following a linking verb and completing the assertion made about the subject or modifying the subject. (For more about linking verbs, see *Verbs* earlier in this chapter.)

SC (or predicate nominative)

Tom is the *hero* of the play.

SC (or predicate nominative)

This is *he* speaking.

SC (or predicate adjective)

This coffee smells *good.*

(5) The *objective complement (OC)* is a noun, pronoun, or adjective following the direct object and completing the assertion made about the object.

OC

The president appointed him *chairman.*

OC

He washed his face *clean.*

Types of Sentences

Sentences may be classified according to their purpose or according to their structure.

Purpose

According to their purpose, sentences are classified as declarative, imperative, interrogative, or exclamatory.

> I enjoy my work. (A declaration or a statement)
> Learn to write well. (An imperative request or command)
> Have you read the *Odyssey*? (An interrogation or question)
> Look out! (An exclamation)

Structure

Sentences may also be classified according to their *structure,* that is, according to the kind and number of clauses of which they are composed.

a. A *simple sentence* contains one independent clause.
> I work in an office.

b. A *compound sentence* contains two or more independent clauses.
> She works in the city, but John works on the farm.
> I like the theater; Bill, however, prefers the movies.

c. A *complex sentence* contains one independent and at least one dependent clause.
> Although she has traveled a great deal, she still finds charm in new places.

d. A *compound-complex sentence* contains two or more independent clauses and one or more dependent clauses.
> My black dress, which I wore to the party last week, is at the cleaner's, and my blue dress is not suitable for the occasion.

Sentence Fragments

Usually, every sentence should be grammatically complete. Sometimes, however, a group of words stands alone as a sentence but is not grammatically complete and therefore not really a sentence in the strictest meaning. Such a group of words is called a *sentence fragment.*

a. Although many skilled writers use fragments purposely to achieve particular effects, the inexperienced writer should be certain that he or she is able to write complete sentences when appropriate and that fragments are used knowingly and purposefully. The following sentences, while grammatically incomplete, are not considered real fragments, for the reader understands the writer's intent and the communication is complete.

QUESTIONS AND ANSWERS: Why are you going? Because I want to. Do you want to speak with me? No.

EXCLAMATIONS: Too bad!   So sorry!

The sentence fragments that should be avoided are those that have no specific meaning for the reader and do not communicate the intent of the author.

Increasingly large numbers of young people are seeking admission to colleges and universities, which are already overcrowded with students who have difficulty completing their work. Business and professions are demanding men and women with college degrees. *Because of a widespread idea that everyone should have a college education.*

The fragment is not clearly related to the sentences preceding it. Are large numbers of young people seeking admission to colleges and universities because of the widespread idea that everyone should have a college education, or do businesses and professions demand men and women with college degrees for that reason? The ambiguity cannot be resolved without grammatically associating the fragment with one of the complete sentences.

b. Many fragments occur because the writer is careless in making dependent elements a part of the sentence to which they belong; correction can usually be made by *modifying the punctuation.*

FAULTY: He asked me to forgive him. *Although I don't know why.*

IMPROVED: He asked me to forgive him, although I don't know why.

FAULTY: I was unable to gain admittance to the supply room. *The door having been locked five minutes before my arrival.*

IMPROVED: I was unable to gain admittance to the supply room, the door having been locked five minutes before my arrival.

c. A sentence fragment is not to be confused with *elliptical construction* (also called *ellipsis*), an acceptable construction in which a word or more is omitted but whose meaning can be supplied from the rest of the sentence.

He is as tall as she [is tall].

Characteristics of an Effective Sentence

Effective sentences must be more than grammatically correct; they must be unified, coherent, and skillfully arranged through the coordination and subordination of ideas and structure. Poor sentences frequently result from a failure to organize ideas in such a way as to indicate clearly their relationship and relative importance to one another.

Coordination

The basic principle of coordination is parallelism, a means of achieving unity, emphasis, and coherence. Ideas of equal importance and elements with similar functions in a sentence should be made structurally parallel; that is, coordinate elements in a compound structure are most effectively stated when given similar word patterns. In such compound constructions, nouns will be parallel with nouns, verbs with verbs, phrases with phrases, dependent clauses with dependent clauses, independent clauses with independent clauses.

(1) Coordinating conjunctions (*and, but, for, or, nor*) are definite indicators of parallel structure; they should warn the writer to be careful in constructing the sentence and alert the reader to look for ideas or elements of equal importance in the statement.

> FAULTY: I like *to read, to listen* to good music, and *watching* television. (The conjunction *and* joins improperly in this sentence two infinitive phrases—*to read, to listen*—and a gerund—*watching*.)
>
> IMPROVED: I like *to read, to listen* to good music, and *to watch* television.
>
> *or:*
>
> IMPROVED: I like *reading, listening* to good music, and *watching* television.
>
> FAULTY: The duties of the president are *presiding* at meetings, *appointment* of committees, and *to call* special meetings.
>
> IMPROVED: The duties of the president are *to preside* at meetings, *to appoint* committees, and *to call* special meetings.

(2) Comparisons should be stated in parallel structures.

> FAULTY: A ditchdigger is a less rewarding occupation than teaching. (A ditchdigger is not an occupation; teaching is.)
>
> IMPROVED: Ditchdigging is a less rewarding occupation than teaching.
>
> FAULTY: He protested that his job was more rewarding than a common laborer.
>
> IMPROVED: He protested that his job was more rewarding than a common laborer's [job].
>
> *or:*
>
> IMPROVED: He protested that his job was more rewarding than that of a common laborer.

(3) A frequent error in parallelism occurs in the improper use of correlative conjunctions (conjunctions occurring in pairs): *either . . . or, neither . . . nor, not only . . . but also, both . . . and.* Elements compared or contrasted through the use of such conjunctions are best stated in parallel form: The second conjunction should be followed by a construction parallel to that following the first; if a prepositional phrase follows one conjunction, a prepositional phrase should follow the other conjunction.

> FAULTY: She is not only *a tennis player* but *plays softball* as well.
>
> IMPROVED: She is not only *a tennis player* but also *a softball player.*
>
> FAULTY: He either was *a successful industrialist* or *an accomplished liar.*
>
> IMPROVED: He was either *a successful industrialist* or *an accomplished liar.*
>
> FAULTY: I talked both *to the student* and *his parents.*
>
> IMPROVED: I talked to both *the student* and *his parents.*

Subordination

The mature writer recognizes that not all details and thoughts are of equal importance. He or she learns to give certain details a primary or secondary position in the sentence in order to communicate accurately to the reader; in other words, the writer learns to apply the principle of *subordination.* The relationships of the writer's ideas are thus revealed with greater exactness. The main clause will convey the major idea, and the modifiers (words, phrases, dependent clauses) will convey additional and clarifying information. Effective subordination is a means of achieving not only clarity but also variety and coherence.

(1) Short, choppy sentences (often a mark of immature writing) may be eliminated.

> FAULTY: He is a man. He is fifty years old. He works hard. He wants to give his family a good home.
>
> IMPROVED: He is a fifty-year-old man who works hard to give his family a good home.

(2) Rambling sentences composed of short clauses joined by *ands* and *buts* may be improved.

> FAULTY: The alarm rings and she sits up in bed and she rubs her eyes.
>
> IMPROVED: When the alarm rings, she sits up in bed and rubs her eyes.

(3) Important ideas may be expressed emphatically in main clauses, and less important ideas through subsidiary constructions (modifying words; prepositional, infinitive, participial, and gerund phrases; appositives; dependent clauses).

> FAULTY: I came to the office and found that I was behind in my work.
>
> IMPROVED: When I came to the office, I found that I was behind in my work.

(4) Faulty subordination frequently results when conjunctions fail to express clearly the relationship between ideas. (*Like* is not a subordinating conjunction and is not used to join two clauses: *as* is ordinarily used to show time, not causal, relationships.)

> FAULTY: I don't know *as* I want to go.
>
> IMPROVED: I don't believe I want to go.
>
> *or:*
>
> IMPROVED: I don't want to go.
>
> FAULTY: It looked *like* he would win the match.
>
> IMPROVED: It looked *as if* he would win the match.
>
> FAULTY: I liked the play *while* I didn't care for the movie.
>
> IMPROVED: *Although* I liked the play, I didn't care for the movie.
>
> FAULTY: I read in the paper *where* he had been elected.
>
> IMPROVED: I read in the paper *that* he had been elected.

(5) *Because, where,* and *when* are subordinating elements and should not be used as the subject or the complement of a verb.

> FAULTY: The reason he won is *because* he is fifty pounds heavier than his opponent.
>
> IMPROVED: He won *because* he is fifty pounds heavier than his opponent.
>
> FAULTY: Trusting him is *where* I made my mistake.
>
> IMPROVED: My mistake was trusting him.
>
> *or:*
>
> IMPROVED: Trusting him was my mistake.
>
> FAULTY: A quatrain is *when* you have a verse of four lines.
>
> IMPROVED: A quatrain is a verse of four lines.

Consistent Construction

The careful writer avoids unnecessary or illogical shifts within the structure of an individual sentence or of closely related sentences. Although such a shift may not obscure the meaning, it may result in awkwardness, incongruity, and general loss of effectiveness and emphasis. In order to present ideas clearly and appropriately, the writer must be as consistent as possible in the use of voice, tense, mood, person, number, and style.

FAULTY:	When Meg returned to her home, a new car was found waiting for her. (Illogical shift from active to passive)
IMPROVED:	When Meg returned to her home, she found a new car waiting for her.
FAULTY:	When he hears that his friend is there, he hurried home. (Inconsistence in sequence of tenses)
IMPROVED:	When he heard that his friend was there, he hurried home.
FAULTY:	Everyone should be careful of their grammar. (Inconsistency of number)
IMPROVED:	Everyone should be careful of his grammar.
FAULTY:	If a man is to succeed, you must work hard. (Illogical shift in person)
IMPROVED:	If a man is to succeed, he must work hard.
FAULTY:	First prepare your notes carefully; then the report may be written. (Unnecessary shift in voice)
IMPROVED:	You should first prepare your notes carefully and then write your report.
FAULTY:	She asked me would I help her with her expense account. (Inappropriate shift from indirect to direct discourse)
IMPROVED:	She asked me to help her with her expense account.
FAULTY:	Although the party has made significant contributions to the community, the big wheels grab all the glory. (Inappropriate shift from formal to colloquial diction)
IMPROVED:	Although the party has made significant contributions to the comunity, the leaders do not recognize the contributions of others.

Correct Use of Modifiers

Modifiers, for clarity, must refer to specific words and should be placed as close as possible to the words they modify. A modifier is *misplaced* if it seems to modify a word that it logically should not or cannot; it is considered *dangling* if it has nothing to modify.

(1) Misplaced modifiers may be corrected by revising the sentence to place the modifier in such a position that its object of modification may be clearly discerned.

FAULTY:	After driving blindly for hours, a local resident helped us find our way back to the main road.
IMPROVED:	A local resident helped us find our way back to the main road after we had driven blindly for hours.
FAULTY:	I only need a few more minutes.
IMPROVED:	I need only a few more minutes.

(2) Dangling modifiers may be corrected by supplying the word that the phrase logically describes or by revising the dangling construction to make a complete clause.

FAULTY: Having taken our seats, the players began the game. (Dangling participial phrase)

IMPROVED: After we had taken our seats, the players began the game.

FAULTY: To appreciate good music, vigorous study must be undertaken. (Dangling infinitive phrase)

IMPROVED: To appreciate good music, one must study vigorously.

PUNCTUATION

Formal writing generally employs close punctuation because the sentences are often long and tend to contain more involved construction than informal writing. Punctuation serves two purposes: to make the structure of the sentence readily apparent and to establish minor relationships within the sentence. The marks of punctuation with conventional applications are listed in alphabetical order below.

Ampersand &

The ampersand (&) is a symbol meaning "and." In general, it should not be used in formal writing. There are, however, a few situations in which its use is correct:

a. when it is part of the official name of a company

Johnson & Johnson

Little, Brown & Co.

b. in reports in which author-date references are given in parentheses (not in the body of the text)

(Smith & Robbins 1987)

Smith and Robbins (1987)

c. in tables, directories, advertising copy, and some informal writing to save space.

Apostrophe ’

The apostrophe is used to indicate possession, contraction, and plurality of certain words and symbols.

a. To show possession in singular nouns and indefinite pronouns, add an apostrophe and *s.*

Tom's book   anybody's guess

b. To show possession in plural nouns ending in *s,* add only an apostrophe.

the students' grades   the soldiers' allegiance

c. To show possession in plural and collective nouns that end in a letter other than *s,* add an apostrophe and *s.*

the people's choice   the children's wishes

d. To show possession with names of inanimate objects, it is more common to use an "of" phrase, but the apostrophe with *s* is also used. Sound, meaning, rhythm in the sentence, and the emphasis desired determine the choice.

the brightness of the sun   the sun's brightness
the lesson of today   the power of the state
the state's power   today's lesson

e. To indicate measurement (of time, amount, degree, etc.), add an apostrophe (and with the singular an *s*).

one day's work   a week's time
two weeks' notice   three dollars' worth

f. To show joint possession, add an apostrophe and *s* only to the last element.

Tom and Robert's office (Both share one office.)

Note: Individual or alternative possession may be indicated by adding an apostrophe and *s* to each element.

Tom's and Robert's offices (Each has a separate office.)
Hitler's or Mussolini's dictatorship

g. To form the possessive of compounds, add an apostrophe and *s* to the last element of the unit only.

my brother-in-law's request   anyone else's belief

h. To indicate omission of letters in contractions, insert an apostrophe at the point of elision.

Can't, isn't, won't, haven't

Note: It's is a contraction of *it is; its* is the possessive pronoun.

i. To indicate the omission of the first figures from dates, insert an apostrophe at the point of elision.

Class of '09   Spirit of '76

j. To form the plural of a word used as a word, without regard to its meaning, add an apostrophe and *s*.

There are too many *but's* in this sentence.

k. To indicate the plural of symbols and letters, add an apostrophe and *s*.

10's, two 5's, H's, &'s

Note: The possessive forms of personal and relative pronouns do not require the apostrophe: *his, hers, its, ours, theirs, whose.* The possessive forms of indefinite pronouns do require an apostrophe: *one's* book, *anyone's* opinion, *somebody's* mistake.

Brackets   [ ]

---

a. Brackets are commonly used to enclose comments, insertions, corrections, etc., made by a person other than the author of the quoted material.

"He [Abraham Lincoln] became known as a great humanitarian."

b. Brackets are used to enclose material within parentheses to avoid the confusion of double parentheses.

The Voyages of the English Nation to America, before the Year 1600, from Hakluyt's Collection of Voyages (1598–1600 [III, 121–128]). Edited by Edmund Goldsmid.

Colon   :

---

a. The colon is a formal mark indicating introduction or anticipation. It ordinarily is used to precede a series or a statement that has already been introduced by a completed statement.

There is only one course of action: We must work more conscientiously.

The library has ordered the following books: *Don Quixote, The Pilgrim's Progress,* and *Alice in Wonderland.*

There are several schools and colleges in the university system: arts and sciences, business administration, education, music, and engineering.

b. The colon may be used to introduce an extended quotation.

> In a long speech President Roosevelt said: "We have nothing to fear but. . . ."

c. The colon is conventionally used after a formal salutation in a letter.

> Dear Sir:
> Dear Mr. Adams:

d. The colon is used to separate chapter and verse numbers in biblical citations and volume and page numbers in references containing Arabic numerals.

> John 3:16   I Corinthians 13:1–12   PMLA 72:19–25

e. The colon is regularly used between numerals designating hours and minutes.

> 12:15 A.M.

Comma   ,

The comma is the most frequently used mark of punctuation; its misuse often produces confusion and misunderstanding.

a. A comma is used to separate two independent clauses joined in a compound sentence by a coordinating conjunction (*and, but, for, or, nor*).
He spoke clearly, but his father did not hear him.

Note: In less formal writing the comma is frequently omitted between short clauses joined by *and;* it is rarely omitted before *or* or *but*.

b. The comma is used to set off nonrestrictive modifiers. (A nonrestrictive modifier is one that is not essential to the meaning of the sentence but that supplies incidental information about a word already identified. A restrictive modifier restricts, limits, or defines; it cannot be left out without changing the meaning of the sentence.)

> NONRESTRICTIVE MODIFIER: Grace's father, *who is a grocer,* ran for the city council. (The clause *who is a grocer* can be eliminated without robbing the sentence of meaning.)
>
> RESTRICTIVE MODIFIER: An employee *who is always late* may be fired. (The clause *who is always late* is necessary to the meaning of the sentence.)

c. The comma is used to separate elements (words, phrases, clauses) in a series of three or more.

> The vegetables included corn, beans, tomatoes, and asparagus.
>
> Tell me what you wore, where you went, and what you did.

Note: Commas should not be used before the first or after the last element in the series unless needed for other reasons.

d. The comma is used to set off terms of direct address.

> Professor Jones, please be seated.

e. The comma is used after a long introductory phrase or clause. Such "signal" words as *when, although, as, if, while, since,* and *because* usually indicate that a comma will occur before the main clause.

> After setting up our tent and getting the camp in order, we took a swim.
>
> Although I am no scholar, I enjoy historical research.

f. The comma is used both before and after a dependent clause that appears in the body of a sentence.

> His car, although he bought it only last year, looked ready for the junk heap.

g. The comma is used to separate elements of a date, an address, or other statistical details.

> Monday, September 1, 1952, was an important day.
>
> The address is 1172 Louis Plaza, Arlington, Kentucky.
>
> The quotation occurs on page 16, line 6, of the manual.

h. The comma is used to set off direct quotations.

> He said, "I am prepared."

i. The comma is used between coordinate adjectives (usually coordination can be tested by substituting *and* for the comma).

> COORDINATE: He sat in a poorly made, old-fashioned chair.
> NOT COORDINATE: He was a member of the large freshman class.

j. Commas should not be used to separate the subject from the verb or the verb from the complement.

> FAULTY: Careful study, may produce good grades.
> IMPROVED: Careful study may produce good grades.

k. One of the most common errors in punctuation is the *comma splice,* the separation of two independent clauses by only a comma. Fused or run-together sentences result when two or more independent clauses are included in a single sentence without punctuation to separate them. Independent clauses should be separated by a comma and a coordinating conjunction or by a semicolon.

> FAULTY: It was raining, he could not walk to work.
> IMPROVED: It was raining, and he could not walk to work.
> *or:*
> IMPROVED: It was raining; he could not walk to work.

 (1) Frequently a comma splice can be best corrected by effective subordination.

> FAULTY: It was raining, he could not walk to work.
> IMPROVED: Because it was raining, he could not walk to work. (The first clause is now a subordinate clause.)
> *or:*
> IMPROVED: Because of the rain he could not walk to work. (The first clause is now a prepositional phrase.)
> *or:*
> IMPROVED: The rain kept him from walking to work. (The two clauses are combined to form one simple sentence.)

 (2) If the two independent clauses are not closely related in meaning, each may be made into a sentence.

> FAULTY: Swimming is good exercise, I like to swim in the summer.
> IMPROVED: Swimming is good exercise. I like to swim in the summer.

l. Conjunctive adverbs (such as *moreover, therefore, thus, hence, then,* and *still*) should not be used to connect independent clauses unless a semicolon or a coordinating conjunction is also used.

> FAULTY: The two boys meet each morning, then they spend the day together.
> IMPROVED: The two boys meet each morning; then they spend the day together.
> *or:*
> IMPROVED: The two boys meet each morning, and then they spend the day together.

m. When a conjunctive adverb of more than one syllable (*however, moreover, consequently, therefore,* etc.) is used to connect two independent clauses, a semicolon comes before the adverb and a comma after it.

The flood destroyed many houses; however, the church remained undamaged.

n. The comma is used to set off conjunctive adverbs or short transitional phrases.

> We do not, moreover, need your advice.

o. The comma is often used before the conjunction *for* to avoid faulty interpretation.

> We hurried, for the plane was about to leave.

p. The comma is used after the complimentary closing of a letter.

> Very truly yours,   Sincerely,

q. The comma is used after the salutation of a personal letter.

> Dear Sandra,

Dash   —

Dashes are frequently overused by inexperienced writers; they are more emphatic than commas and less emphatic than parentheses.

a. The dash is used to emphasize or to indicate hesitation or a sharp break or change in thought.

> I must tell you—now what was I going to tell you?
> He ought to be satisfied—if he is ever to be satisfied.

b. The dash is used to set off parenthetical material when commas might be confusing or inadequately emphatic.

> Three books—a dictionary, a grammar book, and a novel—lay on the desk.

c. The dash is used before a statement or word that summarizes what has been said.

> The mayor, the aldermen, the lesser officials, and the citizenry—all were gathered in front of the city hall.
> Kindness, understanding, and honor—these are needed virtues.

Ellipsis   . . .

The ellipsis (. . .) is used to indicate the omission of a part of quoted material or of words needed to complete a sentence. Three dots are used to indicate the omission; if the ellipsis occurs at the end of a sentence, a period is added.

The war, which had been in progress for ten years, was ended by mutual agreement.

The war . . . was ended by mutual agreement.

The war . . . was ended. . . .

Exclamation Point   !

The exclamation point is used to indicate an emphatic utterance.

> For heaven's sake!   Ready, set, go!

Hyphen   -

Whenever possible, avoid breaking words from one line to the next. When hyphenation is necessary, (a) the hyphen should be placed at the end of a line, never at the beginning, and (b) only words of two or more syllables should be divided, with the division occurring only between syllables. The word list in Chapter 19 shows these syllable breaks.

a. The hyphen is used to divide at syllable breaks a word that must be carried over from one line to another. Words should be so divided that a single letter does not stand alone (*fault-y, a-bove*). Hyphenated words should be divided at the hyphen.

b. The hyphen is used to join compound numbers from twenty-one through ninety-nine.

c. The hyphen is used to join words that function as a single adjective before a substantive.

> a broken-down nag   up-to-date methods

d. The hyphen is often used to join such prefixes as *self-, ex-,* and, when it is followed by a capital letter, *anti-*.

> self-help   ex-governor   anti-American

e. The hyphen is used in compounds containing forms like *-elect* and *-in-law*.

> President-elect Jones   sister-in-law

f. The hyphen may be employed to eliminate confusion in the meaning of words to which prefixes are added.

> re-creation (in contrast to *recreation*)
> re-form (in contrast to *reform*)

g. The hyphen is now frequently used to join a single capital letter to a noun.

> H-bomb,   I-beam,   U-boat

h. The hyphen is used to join a verb modifier except when the adverb ends in *-ly* or following such common adverbs as *very* and *most*.

> a fast-paced horse
> a widely known author

Be careful to recognize that some words ending in *-ly* are adjectives (*cowardly, friendly*) and that there may be times when the adjective and another word should be joined with a hyphen to form a modifier of a noun.

> a friendly-acting animal
> a cowardly-looking bullfighter

i. Although many modifiers are hyphenated when they come before the word they modify, they usually are not hyphenated when they are in the predicate position.

> He is a well-known scientist. The scientist is well known.

Sometimes, however, the meaning of the modifier is such that the hyphen should be retained even in the predicate position.

> That man is big-hearted.
> His appearance was awe-inspiring.

j. Usage is divided on hyphenating noun phrases used as modifiers (*income tax* laws, *income-tax* laws; *life insurance* policies, *life-insurance* policies). Usually a hyphen is not needed when the significance of the compound modifier is so well established that no ambiguity can result (*public health* program).

k. Sometimes two words mean one thing hyphenated and quite another without the hyphen. Contrast the difference in meaning between:

> a light green coat   and   a light-green coat

Be careful not to use hyphens in constructions like *a long telephone conversation,* where each word modifies the noun separately.

> a new company policy
> a large cardboard box

The hyphen should be used in two-word modifiers like the following:

> a four-year term
> a first-class cabin

Italics *italic*

Italics are indicated in manuscript and typescript by underlining.

a. Italics are used to identify the titles of books, magazines, newspapers, and the names of ships and aircraft.

> I have recently read Hemingway's novel *The Sun Also Rises*.
> The *Queen Mary* was one of the world's finest ships.

b. Italics may be used to indicate emphasis.

> I am *always* on time.

c. Italics are used to identify foreign words or phrases.

> He is *persona non grata* in this country.
> She lacks *joie de vivre*.

d. Italics (but frequently quotation marks) are used to identify words used as words (that is, without reference to their meanings).

> The word *go* will be the signal.

e. Italics are used for Latin expressions used in bibliographical references.

> *op. cit.*
> *ibid.*

f. italics are used for legal citations.

> *Smith v. Jones*

g. Italics are used for the scientific (Latin) name of an organism.

> *Homo sapiens* (human)
> *Pelecanus occidentalis* (brown pelican)
> *Paeonia officinalis* (common peony)

h. Italics are used for algebraic symbols.

> $a + b + c$

Parentheses   ( )

Parentheses are used to set off explanatory or supplementary material (definitions, additional information, illustration) not essential to the meaning of the sentence or to enclose numbers or letters in enumeration.

> Many of our Presidents (Washington, Lincoln, Wilson, and Roosevelt, for example) rose above mere party politics.
>
> (1), (a)

Period   .

The period is used to indicate the end of a sentence and to mark abbreviations.

> The sky is blue.
>
> Mr.   Mrs.

Question Mark   ?

a. The question mark is used to mark the end of a question.

> Do you really care?

b. A question mark is used to show doubt, uncertainty, or approximation.

> Sir Thomas Wyatt, the English poet, lived from 1503? to 1542.

c. Question marks are used in a series of questions.

> Several questions remained to be answered: How many were going? How many cars would be needed? What time would we return?

d. The question mark is not needed at the end of a courteous request that is phrased as a question.

> Will you please return the completed form as soon as possible.

e. A question mark is not used after an indirect question.

> He asked whether he would be allowed to go.

f. When quotation marks and a question mark are used together, the question mark is placed *before* the closing quotation marks if the quoted material is a question and *after* the closing quotation marks if the whole sentence is a question. (If both are questions, only one question mark is used, *before* the closing quotation marks.)

> He said, "Are you here?"
> Did he say, "I am here"?
> Did he say, "Are you here?"

(See also *Quotation Marks.*)

Quotation Marks   " "

Quotation marks serve to indicate spoken dialogue and to acknowledge specifically reproduced material.

a. Quotation marks are used to enclose direct quotations.

> The supervisor said, "Come to my desk, young man."

Note: Single quotation marks (' ') are used to enclose a quotation within a quotation.

> The student asked, "Who popularized the statement 'This is the best of all possible worlds'?"

b. Quotation marks should be used to enclose titles of short poems, stories, and articles that are usually printed as a part of a larger work.

> She read "Ode on a Grecian Urn" from an anthology.

c. Quotation marks may be used to enclose a word used as a word (rather than for its meaning). (See also item *d* under *Italics.*)

> The word "school" brings back pleasant memories.
> Do not overuse the word "and" in formal writing.

Note: When other marks of punctuation are used with quotation marks, the following practices should be observed:

(1) A question mark or an exclamation point is placed inside the final quotation mark if it is a part of the quotation, outside if it is a part of the sentence that includes the quoted material.

(2) Periods and commas are always placed inside the closing quotation marks.

(3) Semicolons and colons are always placed outside the closing quotation marks.

Semicolon   ;

a. A semicolon is used to separate two independent clauses not joined by a coordinating conjunction.

> He annoyed me; I regretted having invited him.

b. A semicolon is used to separate two independent clauses that are joined by a coordinating conjunction when either or both of the clauses contain one or more commas.

> The office manager, a woman I admired, was pleased with the results of the survey; but she was not happy to lose two of her best workers.

c. A semicolon is used to separate two independent clauses joined by a conjunctive adverb.

> We placed our order with your sales representative two weeks ago; however, we have not yet received delivery.

d. A semicolon is used to separate two independent clauses when the second is introduced by such expressions as *namely, for example, that is,* and *in fact.*

> She is a poor example of what we expect; that is, she just doesn't meet our requirements for a person in such a position.

e. The semicolon may be used to separate items in a series containing internal punctuation.

> Our tour carried us to all parts of the country—from Seattle, Washington, to Miami, Florida; from El Paso, Texas, to Bangor, Maine.

> Among our greatest Presidents we include George Washington, the father of our country; Abraham Lincoln, the great emancipator; and Theodore Roosevelt, the hero of San Juan.

Solidus (Slash or Virgule)   /

The solidus, or slash, should be used only in specific situations:

a. to represent the word *per*

> 9 ft/sec

b. to indicate periods of time or seasons that exend over two successive calendar years

> fiscal year 1987/88
> winter 1986/87

c. to indicate alternatives, as in *and/or*

> my son and/or daughter

d. to mark the end of a line of poetry when more than one line is run into the text

> She quoted William Blake's lines, "To see a world in a grain of sand/ And a heaven in a wild flower."

CAPITALIZATION

The use of the capital letter generally is standardized, but some situations call for personal judgment based on the writer's taste and the level of writing in question. The following conventions are generally employed in formal writing.

1. Capitalize the first word of a sentence and of each line of poetry.
2. Capitalize the first word of a direct quotation. No capitalization is required at the resumption of a quotation interrupted by such expressions as *he said* and *he responded.*

> He said, "This is your last opportunity to change your mind."
> "This is your last chance," he said, "and I advise you to take it."

3. Capitalize proper nouns and adjectives derived from such nouns.

   a. Capitalize the names of specific persons and places, as well as their nicknames and titles.

   > Winston Churchill, Professor Smith, Major Adams, Grandma Moses, Boston, Bostonians

   b. Some words that were originally proper names but are no longer identified with those names are not capitalized. (Check the dictionary when in doubt.)

   > manila paper   india ink

   c. Titles used with a name, as on the envelope or inside address of a letter, are capitalized; but they are not capitalized when used alone.

   > John Jones, Director of Training
   > ABC Company
   > John Jones, the director of training of the ABC Company

   d. Capitalize racial, religious, and political designations.

   > Indian, Baptist, Republican

e. Capitalize names of languages.

French, English, Latin, Aramaic

f. Capitalize days of the week, the months, and the holidays.

Monday, July, Christmas, Labor Day, Easter

g. Capitalize names of organizations and membership designations.

Phi Beta Kappa, Boy Scouts, Rotary Club, Rotarians, Socialists

h. Capitalize references to a divine being.

Lord, Jehovah, Christ, Savior, Holy Ghost, God

i. Capitalize names of historical events and documents.

Renaissance, Monroe Doctrine, French Revolution, Magna Carta

j. Capitalize names of specific institutions, ships, airplanes, academic courses, geographical features, and regions.

First National Bank of Miami, *Queen Mary*, *Columbine*, History 101 (as distinguished from my history class), World War II (as distinguished from a world war), the South (as distinguished from turn south on Main Street)

k. Words denoting a definite geographical region or locality are proper names and therefore should be capitalized. However, compass points or words designating mere direction or position are not proper names and therefore should not be capitalized.

the Far East

Traveling south, we arrived . . .

4. Capitalize the first word and all important subsequent words (nouns, pronouns, adjectives, adverbs, verbs) in the titles of books, articles, musical compositions, motion pictures, and works of art.

The Sun Also Rises   *A Place in the Sun*

5. Capitalize names of family relationship when used with the person's name or in place of the name, but not otherwise.

I bought Mother a box of candy.

I bought my mother a box of candy.

6. Capitalize the pronoun *I* and the interjection *O* (but not *oh*, except at the beginning of a sentence).

7. Capitalize the word *the* in the title of a company or organization only when it is actually part of the name.

> The Ohio Electric Company
> the Girl Scouts of America

8. Once an organization or group has been referred to by name in full in a letter or other piece of writing, a shortened version of the name, using one of the words in the name, should be capitalized.

> Acme Life Insurance Company .... the Company
> Federal Communications Commission .... the Commission
> Federal Bureau of Investigation .... the Bureau

(In expressions such as *our company policy, company* is not capitalized.)

9. Names of the seasons are ordinarily not capitalized.

10. Government organizations are capitalized when they are referred to by specific name.

> House of Representatives   Peace Corps
> Senate   Internal Revenue Service

11. Capitalize the material that follows a colon if it is in the form of a complete sentence. Do not capitalize it when it is not a sentence (unless the first word following the colon is capitalized for some other reason).

> We had two alternatives: We could either go to the movies or stay home and watch television.
> We had two alternatives: to go to the movies or to stay home and watch television.
> We had two alternatives: Aileen's plan or Marilyn's plan.

USE OF NUMBERS

Numbers often present a problem in formal writing. Should they be written out, or should numerals be used? The handling of numbers in reports is covered in Chapter 11, "Special Report Format," but some general guidelines are repeated here.

Use numerals (figures) for

- exact numbers above ten, except when the number begins a sentence
- ages (5 years old)
- exact amounts of money ($15.67)

- percentages (35%)
- measurements and dimensions (6 feet 4 inches)
- time of day when A.M. or P.M. is used (4 A.M.)
- plurals of numbers (6's)
- street names above ten (98 West 32 Street)
- dates (July 4, 1776)
- enumeration (1. dictation; 2. transcription; 3. proofreading)
- large even amounts (24 billion dollars)
- house or building numbers (19 Liliac Drive)
- federal, state, and interstate highways (U.S. 67)

Use words for

- numbers at the beginning of a sentence (Twenty-four boys were on the team.)
- numbers preceding figures (eleven 17-pound turkeys)
- exact numbers below ten (five boys and three girls)
- approximate numbers (about six hundred cars in the lot)
- approximate age (about fourteen or fifteen years old)
- sessions of Congress (Eighty-seventh Congress)
- centuries and decades (the twentieth century; the eighties)
- sums of money used as adjectives (fifty-dollar wallet)
- ordinals (the third person to enter; Third Avenue).

SPELLING RULES

Spelling rules represent generalizations that are applicable to large numbers of words; however, it should be noted that exceptions often occur. Proper understanding of prefixes, suffixes, syllabification, pronunciation, and definition will eliminate many spelling errors. Chapter 19 of this book is a guide to the correct spelling and syllabification of the 33,000 most frequently used words in English.

1. When the sound is long *e* (as in *believe*), *i* is placed before *e* except after *c*.

   achieve, chief, relief, yield, piece, receive, deceive, conceive, ceiling

   EXCEPTIONS: neither, either, seize, weird, leisure

   When the *ie* combination is pronounced as separate syllables, the rule does not apply.

   society, science

When the *ie* combination follows a *c* to produce the *sh* sound, *i* is placed before *e*.

deficient, efficient, conscience, ancient

2. The final *e* preceded by a consonant is dropped before a suffix beginning with a vowel and retained before a suffix beginning with a consonant.

hope—hoping	pure—purely
desire—desirable	use—useful
allure—alluring	state—statement

After *c* or *g*, the *e* is retained before a suffix beginning with *a, o,* or *u* to preserve the soft *c* or *g*.

peaceable, courageous, changeable, serviceable

3. Monosyllables and words accented on the last syllable ending in a single consonant preceded by a single vowel *double* the consonant before a suffix beginning with a vowel.

prefer—preferred	hop—hopped
occur—occurrence	forbid—forbidden
red—redder	control—controlled

When the accent shifts to another syllable with the addition of the suffix, the stress in the new word determines the application of the rule.

confer—conference	refer—reference
prefer—preference	

4. Words ending in *y* usually change the *y* to *i* before all suffixes except *-ing*.

lonely—loneliness   try—tried   lady—ladies

The *y* is usually retained if preceded by a vowel.

valleys plays

EXCEPTIONS: lay—laid   pay—paid   say—said

5. In the formation of plurals, most nouns add *s* or *es*. Some ending in *z* double this letter.

a. Nouns ending in *s, z, x, sh,* or *ch* add *es*.

church—churches	box—boxes
quiz—quizzes	loss—losses

    b. Nouns ending in *y* preceded by a consonant or by *qu* change the *y* to *i* and add *es.*

fly—flies	lily—lilies
sky—skies	soliloquy—soliloquies

    c. Compound nouns usually form the plural by adding *s* or *es* to the principal word.

attorneys-at-law	brothers-in-law
consuls-general	master sergeants
commanders in chief	

    d. When the noun ends in *fe,* the *fe* is usually changed to *ve* and *s* is added.

knife—knives	wife—wives

    e. Nouns ending in *o* usually add s to form the plural.

radio—radios	cameo—cameos

    EXCEPTIONS: echo—echoes   hero—heroes

6. When diacritical marks are a part of the foreign spelling, such marks are retained when the words are used in English sentences (fiancé, auto-da-fé, chargé d'affaires), but many words completely Anglicized no longer require diacritical marks.

    cafe, canape, fete, habitue, naive, depot, denouement

7. Only one word ends in *sede (supersede);* three words end in *ceed (exceed, proceed, succeed);* all other words with this final sound end in *cede (precede, secede).*

USAGE

This section contains a list of words and phrases that are often used incorrectly or for some other reason cause a writer or speaker difficulty. In addition, the word list in Chapter 19 has many cross-references to help you decide which is the appropriate word to use when confusion might arise (for example, *adapt, adept, adopt*).

A, AN: *a* is used before words beginning with consonants or with initial vowels that have consonant sounds (*a* book, *a* one-way street, *a* historian, *a* uniform); *an* is used before words beginning with vowels or with a silent *h* (*an* apple, *an* hour). Before an abbreviation that consists of letters sounded separately, use the article that agrees with the *pronunciation* of the first letter of the abbreviation (an SOS, an FM radio, a UN committee).

ACCEPT, EXCEPT: *accept* means *to receive something offered; except,* as a verb, means *to exclude;* as a preposition, *except* means *with the exclusion of.*

ACCIDENTLY: used incorrectly for *accidentally;* the *-ly* suffix should be added to the adjective and not to the noun.

ACQUIRE: often pretentious for *get.*

AFFECT, EFFECT: *affect* is a verb meaning, in one sense, *to pretend* or *to assume* and, in another sense, *to influence* or *to move; effect,* as a verb, means *to bring about;* as a noun, *effect* means *result* or *consequence.*

AGGRAVATE: in formal English, *to make worse or more severe;* in colloquial English, *to annoy or irritate.*

ALL RIGHT, ALRIGHT: *all right* means *satisfactory, correct,* or *yes; alright* is a misspelling.

ALOT: used incorrectly for *a lot.*

ALREADY, ALL READY: frequently confused: *Already* means *before* or *before this time; all ready* means *completely ready.*

ALTOGETHER, ALL TOGETHER: frequently confused: *Altogether* means *completely, on the whole; all together* means *in a group.*

A.M., P.M., a.m., p.m.: should not be used as synonyms for *morning* and *afternoon;* the abbreviations should be used only with the figures designating the time.

AND ETC.: redundant: *Etc.* is an abbreviation of the Latin *et* (and) *cetera* (others); *and etc.* would mean *and and so forth.*

AND WHICH: correct only when the clause that follows it is coordinate with a previous clause introduced by *which.*

ANECDOTE, ANTIDOTE: an *anecdote* is a short, entertaining account of some event; an *antidote* is a remedy for poison.

ANGRY: *at* a thing and *with* a person.

ANYPLACE, EVERY PLACE, NO PLACE, SOMEPLACE: colloquialisms for *anywhere, everywhere, nowhere, somewhere.*

ANYWAY: sometimes misspelled as *anyways.*

ANYWHERES: a misspelling of *anywhere.*

AS: sometimes used as a weak synonym for *since* or *because;* used incorrectly as a conjunction in place of *for, that,* or *whether* in sentences like these: "I didn't buy the hat, *as* [use *for*] red is not my color." "I don't know *as* [use *that* or *whether*] I can go." See also LIKE.

AT: redundant in such sentences as "Where are we at?"

AWFUL, AWFULLY: overworked intensives for *very.*

AWHILE: an adverb improperly used as the object of the preposition *for;* the acceptable form is *for a while.* Use *awhile* without the preposition *for:* He has been gone *awhile.*

BAD, BADLY: linking verbs *appear, be, seem, sound, taste, smell, feel, look,* and *become* are followed by an adjective; hence *bad* is the proper form in such sentences as "This coffee tastes *bad.*" Remember, however, that a linking verb can also be used as a transitive verb, and the modifier may be an adverb, as in "He sounded the bell *loudly.*"

BADLY: colloquial for *very much, greatly.*

BECAUSE: a conjunction should not be used as a subject, object, or complement; thus, the construction beginning "The reason is because ... " is incorrect.

BEFORE: redundant in such usage as *"Before, I used to* get sick if I saw blood."

BEING THAT, BEING AS HOW: misused for *as, since, because.*

BESIDE, BESIDES: only *beside* can be used as a preposition ("That is *beside* the point"), but both *beside* and *besides* can be used as an adverb (*"Besides,* there is no place to go." *"Beside,* there is no place to go").

BIANNUAL, BIENNIAL: *biannual* means *twice* (at any two times) *every year* (as distinguished from *semiannual,* which means *once regularly every six months*); *biennial* means *once every two years.*

CONTINUAL, CONTINUOUS: *continual* means *happening again and again; continuous* means *going on without interruption.*

CUTE: overused as a vague term of approval.

DEFINITELY: overused as an intensive modifier.

DEPRECIATE IN VALUE: redundant: *depreciate* means *lessen in value.*

DIFFERENT THAN: improperly used for *different from* except when the object is a clause: "This room is *different from* that one." "This room is *different than* I expected."

DUE TO: controversy among authorities exists about the use of *due to.* Some insist that *due to* should be used only as an adjective ("The leak was *due to* a break in the line"), never as a preposition (*"Due to* a break in the line, there was a leak"). They recommend that *owing to, because of,* or *as a result of* be substituted for *due to* in the second example.

EACH AND EVERY: needless repetition; use one word or the other.

EFFECT: see AFFECT.

ENTHUSE: colloquially used as a verb; not acceptable in formal writing as a substitute for *be enthusiastic about.*

EQUALLY AS: redundant; use *equally* ("Both men were *equally* guilty").

EXCEPT: improperly used for *unless.* See also ACCEPT.

EXCEPT FOR THE FACT THAT: wordy for *except that.*

FARTHER, FURTHER: now infrequently distinguished; in formal usage *farther* indicates distance and *further* indicates degree or extent.

FEWER, LESS: *fewer* refers to number; *less* refers to quantity or degree.

FIRST OFF: use instead *in the first place.*

FLAUNT, FLOUT: *flaunt* means *to display defiantly or impudently* ("The little girl *flaunted* her new dress in front of her friends"); *flout* means *to show scorn or contempt for* ("The employee who continually reports late to work *flouts* discipline").

GOES ON TO SAY: wordy for *adds, continues.*

HARDLY: do not use a negative before *hardly* when you mean *with effort or difficulty* ("I can *hardly* read his handwriting"; not "I *can't hardly* . . .").

HAVE: see OF.

IDEA: often vague for *belief, scheme, theory, conjecture,* or *plan.*

INCREDIBLE, INCREDULOUS: *incredible,* said of a situation, means *unbelievable* ("That he went swimming in the ocean in freezing weather is *incredible*"); *incredulous,* said of a person, means *unbelieving* ("I was *incredulous* that he would do such a thing").

INDULGE: often used improperly for *take part.*

INFER, IMPLY: often confused: *Infer* means *to draw a conclusion from facts or premises; imply* means *to hint or suggest.*

IN MY ESTIMATION, IN MY OPINION: often unnecessary or pretentious for *I think, I believe.*

IN REGARDS TO: a confusion of the British idiom *as regards* with the American idiom *in regard to.*

INSIDE OF: colloquial for *within* when used in a time sense ("I will see you *within* an hour").

IS WHEN, IS WHERE: frequently used erroneously in definitions; the verb *to be* requires a noun or an adjective as a complement.

IT BEING, THERE BEING: awkward for introducing a clause that should be introduced by *since* ("There being little time left, we hurried to the airport" should be changed to "Since there was little time left, . . . ").

ITS, IT'S: *its* is the possessive form of the pronoun *it; it's* is a contraction of *it is.*

KIND OF: colloquial for *somewhat.*

LAY, LIE: often confused: *Lay* is a transitive verb meaning *to put* or *to place something* ("*Lay* the book on the table"); its principal parts are *lay, laid, laid.*

Lay is also the past tense of the intransitive verb *lie,* meaning *to recline, to assume a position,* or *to remain in a position* ("I will *lie* here until morning"); the principal parts of the verb *lie* are *lie, lay, lain.*

LEARN: not to be confused with or used as a synonym for *teach.*

LEAVE, LET: *leave* should not be used as a synonym for *permit* or *let;* use *let me alone* to mean *do not bother me.*

LIABLE, LIKELY: *liable* means *subject to the possibility of,* but in a disagreeable way ("He is *liable* to be caught if he continues stealing"); *likely* means, simply, *subject to the possibility of* ("If the Pirates continue to win games, they are *likely* to win the pennant this year").

LIKE: should not be used as a substitute for *as* or *as if; like* is a preposition and governs a noun or pronoun ("He looks *like* me"); *as* and *as if* introduce clauses ("He looks *as if* he wants to speak to me").

-LOOKING: often a redundant suffix to an adjective.

LOT, LOT OF: vague, colloquial terms suggesting *many* or *much.*

MANNER: often unnecessarily used in phrases such as "in a clumsy manner"; a single adverb or a *with* phrase would suffice.

MARVELOUS: overused as a vague word of approval.

MINUS: colloquial for *lacking* or *without.*

MR., MRS.: in American usage the abbreviations are followed by a period and are now rarely written out except ironically.

MYSELF: often improperly used as a substitute for *I* or *me.*

NEVER-THE-LESS: should be written as one solid word (*nevertheless*).

NOT TOO: colloquial for *not very.*

NOWHERES: incorrect for *nowhere.*

OF: *could of, may of, might of, must of, should of,* and *would of* are often used incorrectly for *could have, may have, might have, must have, should have,* and *would have.*

OFF OF, OFF FROM: a doubling of prepositions that should be reduced to *off* (She stepped *off* the escalator). However, verb-adverb combinations ending with *off* may be followed by *of* or *from* ("The helicopter *took off from* the roof").

ONE AND THE SAME: needless repetition.

ONLY: should be placed in the sentence according to the meaning intended: contrast the following meanings: "*Only* men work in these rooms." "Men *only* work in these rooms." "Men work in *only* these rooms."

OUTSIDE OF: *of* is usually superfluous; *outside of* should not be used as a substitute for *aside from, except,* or *besides.*

PERSONS, PEOPLE: *persons* is used when the separateness of the individuals in a group is stressed ("Five *persons* applied for the job"); *people* is used when a large, indefinite, and anonymous mass is meant ("Jackson was a man of the *people*").

PLAN ON: the idiom is *plan to.*

PLENTY: should not be used adverbially as a substitute for *very,* as in *plenty good* or *plenty tired.*

PLUS: colloquial for *in addition to, having something added.*

PRACTICAL, PRACTICABLE: *practical* stresses effectiveness as tested by actual experience; *practicable* stresses capability of being put into effect ("Before the era of electronics, television did not seem *practicable;* today, however, it is only one of the *practical* applications of the science").

PRETTY: colloquial for *rather, somewhat,* or *very.* (Faulty: "He is a *pretty* good clerk." Improved: "He is a *rather* good clerk." "He is a *very* good clerk.")

PRINCIPAL, PRINCIPLE: often confused: *Principal* may be used as a modifier meaning *first in importance,* or as a noun naming a person or a thing of chief importance; *principle* is always a noun meaning *fundamental truth* or *motivating force.*

REASON WHY: *why* is redundant. See also BECAUSE.

SEEING THAT, SEEING AS HOW: an appropriate subordinating conjunction (*since, because,* etc.) should be substituted for these phrases.

SO: colloquial as a conjunction meaning *with the result that* between independent clauses. Colloquial as an intensive ("He's *so* handsome"); substitute *very.*

SOME TIME, SOMETIME, SOMETIMES: *some time* is used when a vague lapse of time is stressed (It has been *some time* since the objects were first sighted); *sometime,* used as an adverb, means at some unspecified time, usually in the future ("He will come back *sometime*"), and, used as an adjective, it means *having been formerly* or *occasional* ("the *sometime* president of the company"); *sometimes* means *on various occasions, usually unspecified* ("*Sometimes* I wish I were still working there").

-STYLE, -TYPE: redundant suffixes to adjectives.

SURE: an adjective used colloquially as an adverb, as in "He was *sure* thorough."

THEIR, THERE, THEY'RE: frequently confused in spelling: *Their* is the possessive form of *they; there* is an adverb meaning *in that place; they're* is a contraction of *they are.*

TOO: overused as a substitute for *very.*

TRY AND: colloquial for *try to.*

WHILE: frequently overused as a substitute for *although, but,* and *whereas.*

YOU: often improperly used indefinitely, in the sense of *a person, anyone, someone,* or *one.*

19

33,000-Word Spelling and Syllabification List

■ *Basic Hints*

> *Word Division*
> *Accent Marks*
> *Parts of Speech*
> *Inflected Forms*
> *Use of Identifying Definitions*
> *More than One Accepted Spelling*
> *Prefixes*

■ *Word Finder Table*

■ *33,000-Word Spelling and Syllabification List*

This chapter provides a quick, accurate, up-to-date guide to the correct spelling and syllabification of more than 33,000 words, based on the widely accepted *Webster's New World Dictionary®* *of the American Language, Second College Edition.* A special feature is the *Word Finder Table,* which will help you locate a word even though all you know about the word is how to pronounce it.

Many of the entries will settle questions as to whether a certain term is written as one word or with a hyphen or as two words. Answers to specific questions such as the following can be found easily: Do I want the word *anecdote* or *antidote?* When is *hanged* preferred as the past tense and past participle of *hang?* Is the word I want spelled *moot* or *mute?* When is *ringed* used correctly as a verb?

An almost infinite number of words can be formed through the addition of certain prefixes or suffixes to base words. Many of these derived words have been entered. Those that present any question of spelling have been included. For example:

a·gree´a·ble   di·ag´o·nal   di·dac´tic   gar´lic

a·gree´a·bly   di·ag´o·nal·ly   di·dac´ti·cal·ly   gar´lick·y

Obsolete, rare, and archaic forms have been omitted. Many technical terms, especially those in general use, and many colloquial words in common use have been included.

This list has been designed to be a complete and timesaving aid. A few general rules and an explanation of the symbols used in the list are given first. And, don't forget to use the Word Finder Table if you have trouble locating a word in the list.

BASIC HINTS

Each of the words in the alphabetical list in this chapter is referred to here as an *entry* or *entry word.* Symbols are used with the entry words to indicate word divisions, accents, parts of speech, and other useful information.

Word Division

All the entry words have been divided into syllables. Each syllable break is indicated by a centered dot, an accent mark, or, in certain cases, a hyphen. Wherever a hyphen is used in an entry word, that hyphen is part of the spelling of the word.

A word can be divided from one line to the next between any of its syllables except in the following cases:

- *a.* Never separate from the rest of the word a first or last syllable of only one letter or, if you can avoid it, two letters.
- *b.* Never divide a hyphenated word at any point other than the hyphen.

Accent Marks

Accent marks are included to help you find words more quickly. In some cases the accent mark will distinguish one word from another word spelled almost the same way.

> lo´cal / lo·cale´   kar´at / ka·ra´te

Two kinds of accent marks are used. The accent mark in heavy type shows that the syllable preceding it receives the main stress, or accent. The lighter one, wherever used, indicates that the preceding syllable receives less stress than the main one but somewhat more than an unmarked syllable.

> ag´gra·vate´ / dem´on·stra´tion / su´per·vise´

Parts of Speech

Part-of-speech labels (*n.* = noun, *v.* = verb, *adj.* = adjective, *adv.* = adverb) are included here only in special cases. Sometimes this label will give you information about current usage. In all cases the main purpose is to help you be sure you have the word you are looking for. Two of these special cases are explained here.

a. Sometimes a word is accented and syllabified in one way as one part of speech and differently as another. These changes in accent and syllabification are indicated, and the word is identified with the appropriate part-of-speech label; for example: re·cord´ *v.* / rec´ord *n.*

b. Sometimes two words are related in meaning and close in spelling and pronunciation. A part-of-speech label is all that is needed to identify each word:

> ad·vice´ *n.*   proph´e·cy *n.*
>
> ad·vise´ *v.*   ·cies
>
> ·vised´   ·vis´ing   proph´e·sy´ *v.*
>
> ·sied´   ·sy´ing

Inflected Forms

Inflected forms include the plurals of nouns, the parts of the verb, and the comparative and superlative forms of the adjective and adverb. All irregular inflected forms have been entered as part of the entry for the base word. To save space, these forms have been shortened in most cases to show only those syllables that are different from the base word:

> please   li´a·bil´i·ty   pic´nic
>
> pleased   pleas´ing   ·ties   ·nicked   ·nick·ing

fly		eas´y			date	
flies		·i·er	·i·est		dat´ed	dat´ing
flew	flown	fly´ing				

For verbs, when two forms are given, the first is the past tense and past participle and the second is the present participle. When three forms are given, the first is the past tense, the second is the past participle, and the third is the present participle. Noun, adjective, and adverb forms are easy to identify.

Again to save space, inflected forms of some compound words and derived words have been omitted. These forms can easily be found with the entry for the base word:

po·lice´man	pre·pack´age	un´der·score´

Occasionally certain inflected forms are used for certain meanings. These are identified. For example:

staff	ring
staffs *or* staves	rang rung ring´ing
(*sticks; music*)	(*sound ...*)
staffs	ring
(*people*)	ringed ring´ing
	(*circle ...*)

This system of entering inflected forms as part of the entry for the base word accomplishes at least three things:

(1) It helps you distinguish between words that might be confused if entered separately:

hop	hope
hopped hop´ping	hoped hop´ing

(2) It saves the time and trouble of searching for a word you might think is spelled one way but is, in fact, spelled differently:

swim

    swam   swum   swim´ming

(3) It establishes, without further identification under a separate entry, the specific inflected form that you are looking for (see *fly,* above).

One last point: when an entry contains verb forms, this does not necessarily mean that the word is used only as a verb. On the contrary, many of the entries represent the spelling for more than one part of speech. If, for example, a word used as an adjective is already entered as a verb form, and the spelling and syllabification are exactly the same, this word is not entered again separately. You may accept the verb form as the correct spelling for the adjective (see *please,* above). If, too, a noun has the same spelling as a verb, no special notation is given (see *picnic,* above). Where confusion might exist, some kind of identification is given.

Use of Identifying Definitions

It is no doubt clear that this list is not meant to replace the dictionary. It is also clear that in attempting to learn the correct spelling for a specific word, you may run into the difficulty of confusing another word with it. Many instances of such confusion are present in the English language. To help you find the exact word you are seeking, this list contains many cross-references. Each cross-reference supplies you with a very short *identifying definition* and refers you to another word that may be the one you want.

Confusion may result for any of several reasons. Two of the most common are:

(1) similar (but not exactly the same) pronunciation:

mou´ton´   mut´ton

   (*fur;* see mutton)   (*food;* see mouton)

(2) exactly the same pronunciation but, usually, a different spelling (such words are called *homonyms*):

la´ma   leak

   (*monk;* see llama)   (*escape;* see leek)

lla´ma   leek

   (*animal:* see lama)   (*vegetable:* see leak)

Often the words involved are very close alphabetically. In such cases only the identifying terms are given, as in:

less´en   les´son

   (*make less*)   (*instruction*)

less´er   les´sor

   (*smaller*)   (*one who leases*)

An important thing to note here is that these *identifying definitions* are meant only as an aid to your locating or identifying the word you want. They are not meant to replace or by any means cover the entire dictionary definition.

More than One Accepted Spelling

Many words in the English language have more than one accepted spelling in use today. Because of space limitations, only the variant spellings of the more common words have been included. To help you identify them as variants of the same word, they have, in most cases, been entered together, as part of the same entry. Usually, the first spelling given is the one more frequently used. Sometimes, if they are far apart alphabetically, they are entered as separate entries. Whichever variant spelling you decide on, it is advisable to be consistent and use that same spelling throughout any one piece of writing.

Prefixes

Many derived words have been entered. Since all such words cannot possibly be included, the information given below about certain prefixes will be helpful.

The prefix . . . is usually added to the base word . . .

self	with a hyphen.
out	without a hyphen.
over	without a hyphen.
anti	without a hyphen *except* when the prefix is followed by a capital letter.
pre	
pro	
semi	
un	
non	without a hyphen *except* when the prefix is followed by a capital letter or a word that has a hyphen in it.
re	without a hyphen *except* to distinguish between a word in which the prefix means *again* or *anew* and a word having a special meaning (*re-lay* and *relay*).

WORD FINDER TABLE

Have you ever tried to look up a word in order to find its spelling when you don't have any idea how to find it—simply because you can't spell it? This *Word Finder Table,* which gives the most common spellings for sounds, will help you end this vicious circle.

Think of the word in terms of its pronounced syllables. *Be sure you are pronouncing the word correctly.*

If the sound is like the	*try also the spelling . . .*	*as in the words . . .*
a in fat	ai, au	pl*ai*d, dr*au*ght
a in lane	ai, au, ay, ea, ei, eigh, et, ey	r*ai*n, g*au*ge, r*ay*, br*ea*k, r*ei*n, w*eigh*, sach*et*, th*ey*
a in care	ai, ay, e, ea ei	*ai*r, pr*ay*er, th*e*re, w*ea*r, th*ei*r
a in father	au, e, ea	g*au*nt, s*e*rgeant, h*ea*rth
a in ago	e, i, o, u, *and combinations, as* ou	*a*gent, san*i*ty, c*o*mply, foc*u*s, vici*ou*s
b in big	bb	ru*bb*er
ch in chin	tch, ti, tu	ca*tch*, ques*ti*on, na*tu*re
d in do	dd, ed	pu*dd*le, call*ed*
e in get	a, ae, ai, ay, ea, ei, eo, ie, u	*a*ny, *ae*sthete, s*ai*d, s*ay*s, br*ea*d, h*ei*fer, l*eo*pard, fr*ie*nd, b*u*ry
e in equal	ae, ay, ea, ee, ei, eo, ey, i, ie, oe	alumn*ae*, qu*ay*, l*ea*n, fr*ee*, dec*ei*t, p*eo*ple, k*ey*, mach*i*ne, ch*ie*f, ph*oe*nix
e in here	ea, ee, ei, ie	*ea*r, ch*ee*r, w*ei*rd, b*ie*r
er in over	ar, ir, or, our, re, ur, ure, yr	li*ar*, elix*ir*, auth*or*, glam*our*, ac*re*, aug*ur*, meas*ure*, zephy*r*
f in fine	ff, gh, lf, ph	cli*ff*, lau*gh*, ca*lf*, *ph*rase
g in go	gg, gh, gu, gue	e*gg*, *gh*oul, *gu*ard, prolo*gue*
h in hat	wh	*wh*o
i in it	a, e, ee, ia, ie, o, u, ui, y	us*a*ge, *E*nglish, b*ee*n, carr*ia*ge, s*ie*ve, w*o*men, b*u*sy, b*ui*lt, hymn
i in kite	ai, ay, ei, ey, ie, igh, uy, y, ye	*ai*sle, *ay*e, sl*ei*ght, *ey*e, t*ie*, n*igh*, b*uy*, fl*y*, r*ye*
j in jam	d, dg, di, dj, g, gg	gra*d*uate, ju*dg*e, sol*di*er, a*dj*ective, ma*g*ic, exa*gg*erate
k in keep	c, cc, ch, ck, cqu, cu, lk, q, qu, que	*c*an, a*cc*ount, *ch*orus, ta*ck*, la*cqu*er, bis*cu*it, wa*lk*, *q*uick, li*qu*or, baro*que*
l in let	ll, sl	ca*ll*, i*sl*e
m in me	chm, gm, lm, mb, mm, mn	dra*chm*, paradi*gm*, ca*lm*, li*mb*, dru*mm*er, hy*mn*
n in no	gn, kn, mm, nn, pn	*gn*u, *kn*eel, *mn*emonic, di*nn*er, *pn*eumatic
ng in ring	n, ngue	pi*n*k, to*ngue*
o in go	au, eau, eo, ew, oa, oe, oh, oo, ou, ough, ow	m*au*ve, b*eau*, y*eo*man, s*ew*, b*oa*t, t*oe*, *oh*, br*oo*ch, s*ou*l, d*ough*, r*ow*
o in long	a, ah, au, aw, oa, ough	*a*ll, Ut*ah*, fr*au*d, th*aw*, br*oa*d, *ough*t
oo in tool	eu, ew, o, oe, ou, ough, u, ue, ui	man*eu*ver, dr*ew*, m*o*ve, sh*oe*, gr*ou*p, thr*ough*, r*u*le, bl*ue*, fr*ui*t

If the sound is like the	*try also the spelling . . .*	*as in the words . . .*
oo in look	o, ou, u	w*o*lf, w*ou*ld, p*u*ll
oi in oil	oy	t*oy*
ou in out	ough, ow	b*ough*, cr*ow*d
p in put	pp	cli*pp*er
r in red	rh, rr, wr	*rh*yme, be*rr*y, *wr*ong
s in sew	c, ce, ps, sc, sch, ss	*c*ent, ri*c*e, *p*sychology, *sc*ene, *sch*ism, mi*ss*
sh in ship	ce, ch, ci, s, sch, sci, se, si, ss, ssi, ti	o*ce*an, ma*ch*ine, fa*ci*al, *s*ure, *sch*wa, con*sci*ence, nau*se*ous, ten*si*on, i*ss*ue. fi*ssi*on, na*ti*on
t in top	ed, ght, pt, th, tt	walk*ed*, bou*ght*, *pt*omaine, *th*yme, be*tt*er
u in cuff	o, oe, oo, ou	s*o*n, d*oe*s, fl*oo*d, d*ou*ble
u in use	eau, eu, eue, ew, ieu, iew, ue, ui, you, yu	b*eau*ty, f*eu*d, qu*eue*, f*ew*, ad*ieu*, v*iew*, c*ue*, s*ui*t, *you*th, *yu*le
ur in fur	ear, er, eur, ir, or, our, yr	l*ear*n, g*er*m, haut*eur*, b*ir*d, w*or*d, sc*our*ge, m*yr*tle
v in vat	f, lv, ph	o*f*, sa*lv*e, Ste*ph*en
w in will	o, u, wh	ch*o*ir, q*u*aint, *wh*eat
y in you	i, j	on*i*on, hallelu*j*ah
z in zero	s, sc, ss, x, zz	bu*s*y, di*sc*ern, *sc*issors, *x*ylophone, bu*zz*er
z in azure	ge, s, si, zi	gara*ge*, lei*s*ure, fu*si*on, gla*zi*er

Sometimes, certain letter combinations (rather than single sounds) cause problems when you are trying to find a word. Here are some common ones:

If you've tried . . .	*then try . . .*	*If you've tried . . .*	*then try . . .*	*If you've tried . . .*	*then try . . .*
pre	per, pro, pri, pra, pru	cks, gz us	x ous	fiz ture	phys teur
per	pre, pir, pur, par, por	tion	sion, cion, cean, cian	tious air	seous, cious are
is	us, ace, ice	le	tle, el, al	ance	ence
ere	eir, ear, ier	kw	qu	ant	ent
wi	whi	cer	cre	able	ible
we	whe	ei	ie	sin	syn, cin,
zi	xy	si	psy, ci		cyn

33,000-WORD LIST

A

aard'vark'
aard'wolf'
·wolves'
ab'a·cus'
·cus·es or ·ci'
ab'a·lo'ne
a·ban'don
a·base'
·based' ·bas'ing
a·bash'
a·bat'a·ble
a·bate'
·bat'ed ·bat'ing
ab'a·tis
ab'at·toir'
ab'ax'i·al
ab'ba·cy
·cies
ab'bé
ab'bess
ab'bey
ab'bot
ab·bre'vi·ate'
·at'ed ·at'ing
ab·bre'vi·a'tion
ab·bre'vi·a'tor
ab'di·cate'
·cat'ed ·cat'ing
ab'di·ca'tion
ab'di·ca·tor
ab'do·men
ab·dom'i·nal
ab·duct'
ab·duc'tion
ab·duc'tor
ab·er'rant
ab'er·ra'tion
a·bet'
·bet'ted ·bet'ting
a·bey'ance
ab·hor'
·horred' ·hor'ring
ab·hor'rence
ab·hor'rent
a·bide'
·bode' or ·bid'ed
·bid'ing
a·bil'i·ty
·ties
ab'ject
ab·jec'tion
ab'ju·ra'tion
ab·jure'
·jured' ·jur'ing
ab'la·tive
a·blaze'
a'ble
·bler ·blest
a'ble-bod'ied
ab·lu'tion
ab'ne·gate'
·gat'ed ·gat'ing
ab'ne·ga'tion

ab·nor'mal
ab'nor·mal'i·ty
·ties
ab·nor'mi·ty
·ties
a·board'
a·bode'
a·bol'ish
ab'o·li'tion
A'-bomb
a·bom'i·na·ble
a·bom'i·nate'
·nat'ed ·nat'ing
a·bom'i·na'tion
a·bom'i·na'tor
ab'o·rig'i·nal
ab'o·rig'i·ne
·nes
a·bort'
a·bor'ti·cide
a·bor'ti·fa'cient
a·bor'tion
a·bor'tive
a·bound'
a·bout'-face'
-faced' -fac'ing
a·bove'bóard'
ab'ra·ca·dab'ra
ab·rade'
·rad'ed ·rad'ing
ab·ra'sion
ab·ra'sive
ab·re·act'
ab're·ac'tion
a·breast'
a·bridge'
·bridged'
·bridg'ing
a·bridg'ment
or ·bridge'ment
a·broad'
ab'ro·gate'
·gat'ed ·gat'ing
ab'ro·ga'tion
ab'ro·ga'tor
a·brupt'
ab'scess
ab'scessed
ab·scis'sa
·sas or ·sae
ab·scond'
ab'sence
ab'sent adj.
ab·sent' v.
ab'sen·tee'ism
ab'sent-mind'ed
ab'sinthe or ·sinth
ab'so·lute'
ab'so·lu'tion
ab'so·lut'ism
ab·solve'
·solved' ·solv'ing
ab·solv'ent
ab·sorb'
·sorbed' ·sorb'ing
ab·sorb'a·ble
ab·sorb'en·cy
ab·sorb'ent

ab·sorp'tion
ab·stain'
ab·ste'mi·ous
ab·sten'tion
ab'sti·nence
ab'sti·nent
ab·stract'
ab·strac'tion
ab·struse'
ab·surd'
ab·surd'i·ty
·ties
a·bun'dance
a·bun'dant
a·buse'
·bused' ·bus'ing
a·bus'er
a·bu'sive
a·but'
·but'ted ·but'ting
a·but'ment
a·but'ter
a·bys'mal
a·bys'mal·ly
a·byss'
a·ca'cia
ac'a·de'mi·a
ac'a·dem'ic
ac'a·dem'i·cal
ac'a·dem'i·cal·ly
a·cad'e·mi'cian
ac'a·dem'i·cism
a·cad'e·my
ac'a·jou'
a·can'thus
·thus·es or ·thi
a'cap·pel'la
A'ca·pul'co
ac·cede'
·ced'ed ·ced'ing
(agree; see
exceed)
ac·cel'er·an'do
ac·cel'er·ant
ac·cel'er·ate'
·at'ed ·at'ing
ac·cel'er·a'tion
ac·cel'er·a'tor
ac·cel'er·om'e·ter
ac'cent
ac·cen'tu·al
ac·cen'tu·al·ly
ac·cen'tu·ate'
·at'ed ·at'ing
ac·cen'tu·a'tion
ac·cept'
(receive; see
except)
ac·cept'a·bil'i·ty
ac·cept'a·ble
ac·cept'a·bly
ac·cept'ance
ac'cep·ta'tion
ac·cept'ed
(approved; see
excepted)
ac·cep'tor

ac'cess
(approach; see
excess)
ac·ces'si·bil'i·ty
ac·ces'si·ble
ac·ces'sion
ac·ces'so·ry
or ·sa·ry
·ries
ac'ci·dent
ac'ci·den'tal
ac'ci·den'tal·ly
ac·claim'
ac'cla·ma'tion
ac'cli·mate'
·mat'ed ·mat'ing
ac·cli'ma·tize'
·tized' ·tiz'ing
ac·cliv'i·ty
ac·cli'vous
ac'co·lade'
ac·com'mo·date'
·dat'ed ·dat'ing
ac·com'mo·da'·
tion
ac·com'pa·ni·
ment
ac·com'pa·nist
ac·com'pa·ny
·nied ·ny·ing
ac·com'plice
ac·com'plish
ac·com'plished
ac·cord'
ac·cord'ance
ac·cord'ant·ly
ac·cord'ing
ac·cor'di·on
ac·cost'
ac·count'
ac·count'a·bil'·
i·ty
ac·count'a·ble
ac·count'a·bly
ac·count'ant
ac·count'ing
ac·cou'ter
ac·cou'ter·ments
ac·cred'it
ac·cred'it·a'tion
ac·cre'tion
ac·cru'al
ac·crue'
·crued' ·cru'ing
ac·cul'tu·rate'
·rat'ed ·rat'ing
ac·cul'tu·ra'tion
ac·cu'mu·la·ble
ac·cu'mu·late'
·lat'ed ·lat'ing
ac·cu'mu·la'tion
ac·cu'mu·la'tive
ac·cu'mu·la'tor
ac'cu·ra·cy
ac'cu·rate
ac'cu·rate·ly
ac·curs'ed or
ac·curst'

ac·cus'al
ac'cu·sa'tion
ac·cu'sa·tive
ac·cu'sa·to'ry
ac·cuse'
·cused' ·cus'ing
ac·cus'tom
ac·cus'tomed
a·cer'bi·ty
·ties
ac'e·tate'
ac'e·tone'
a·cet'y·lene'
ache
ached ach'ing
a·chiev'a·ble
a·chieve'
·chieved'
·chiev'ing
a·chieve'ment
ach'ro·mat'ic
a·chro'ma·tism
a·chro'ma·tize'
·tized' ·tiz'ing
A'chro·my'cin
ach'y
ach'i·er ach'i·est
ac'id-fast'
ac'id-form'ing
a·cid'ic
a·cid'i·fi'er
a·cid'i·fy'
·fied' ·fy'ing
a·cid'i·ty
ac'i·do'sis
a·cid'u·late'
·lat'ed ·lat'ing
a·cid'u·lous
ac·knowl'edge
·edged ·edg·ing
ac·knowl'edge·
ment or
·edge·ment
ac'me
ac'ne
ac'o·lyte'
ac'o·nite'
a'corn
a·cous'tic or
·ti·cal
a·cous'ti·cal·ly
ac·quaint'
ac·quaint'ance
ac'qui·esce'
·esced' ·esc'ing
ac'qui·es'cence
ac'qui·es'cent
ac·quir'a·ble
ac·quire'
·quired' ·quir'ing
ac·quire'ment
ac'qui·si'tion
ac·quis'i·tive
ac·quit'
·quit'ted
·quit'ting

ac·quit'tal
a'cre
a'cre·age
ac'rid
a·crid'i·ty
ac'ri·mo'ni·ous
ac'ri·mo'ny
ac'ro·bat'
ac'ro·bat'ic
ac'ro·bat'i·cal·ly
ac'ro·nym
ac'ro·pho'bi·a
a·crop'o·lis
a·cross'
a·cros'tic
a·cryl'ic
act'a·ble
act'a·bil'i·ty
act'ing
ac·tin'i·um
ac'ti·nom'e·ter
ac'ti·no·my'cin
ac'tion
ac'ti·vate'
·vat'ed ·vat'ing
ac'ti·va'tion
ac'ti·va'tor
ac'tive
ac'tiv·ism
ac'tiv·ist
ac·tiv'i·ty
·ties
ac'tiv·ize'
·ized' ·iz'ing
ac'tor
ac'tress
ac'tu·al
ac'tu·al'i·ty
·ties
ac'tu·al·ize'
·ized' ·iz'ing
ac'tu·al·ly
ac'tu·ar'i·al
ac'tu·ar'y
·ies
ac'tu·ate'
·at'ed ·at'ing
ac'tu·a'tion
ac'tu·a'tor
a·cu'i·ty
·ties
a·cu'men
ac'u·punc'ture
a·cute'
a·cute'ly
ad'age
a·da'gio
·gios
ad'a·mant
a·dapt'
(fit; see adept,
adopt)
a·dapt'a·bil'i·ty
a·dapt'a·ble
ad'ap·ta'tion or
a·dap'tion
a·dapt'er or
a·dap'tor

a·dap'tive
add'a·ble *or* ·i·ble
ad·den'dum
·da
ad'der
(*snake*)
add'er
(*one who adds*)
ad'dict
ad·dic'tion
ad·dic'tive
ad·di'tion
(*an adding;* see edition)
ad·di'tion·al
ad·di'tion·al·ly
ad'di·tive
ad'dle
·dled ·dling
ad'dle·brained'
ad'dress'
ad'dress·ee'
ad·duce'
·duced' ·duc'ing
ad·duc'i·ble
ad·duc'tion
ade'e·noi'dal
ad'e·noids'
ad·ept'
(*skilled;* see adapt, adopt)
ad'e·qua·cy
ad'e·quate
ad'e·quate·ly
ad·here'
·hered' ·her'ing
ad·her'ence
ad·her'ent
ad·he'sion
ad·he'sive
ad' hoc'
ad' hom'i·nem'
a·dieu'
ad in'fi·ni'tum
ad in'ter·im
ad'i·pose'
ad·ja'cen·cy
ad·ja'cent
ad'jec·tive
ad·join'
(*be next to*)
ad·journ'
(*suspend*)
ad·judge'
·judged'
·judg'ing
ad·ju'di·cate'
·cat'ed ·cat'ing
ad·ju'di·ca'tion
ad·ju'di·ca'tor
ad'junct
ad'ju·ra'tion
ad·jure'
·jured' ·jur'ing
ad·just'
ad·just'a·ble
ad·just'er *or*

·jus'tor
ad·just'ment
ad'ju·tant
ad'-lib'
-libbed' -lib'bing
ad'man'
·men'
ad·min'is·ter
ad·min'is·tra·ble
ad·min'is·trate'
·trat'ed ·trat'ing
ad·min'is·tra'tion
ad·min'is·tra·tive
ad·min'is·tra'tor
ad'mi·ra·ble
ad'mi·ra·bly
ad'mi·ral
ad'mi·ral·ty
·ties
ad'mi·ra'tion
ad·mire'
·mired' ·mir'ing
ad·mir'er
ad·mis'si·bil'i·ty
ad·mis'si·ble
ad·mis'si·bly
ad·mis'sion
ad·mit'
·mit'ted ·mit'ting
ad·mit'tance
ad·mit'ted·ly
ad·mix'
ad·mix'ture
ad·mon'ish
ad·mo·ni'tion
ad·mon'i·to'ry
ad' nau'se·am
a·do'
a·do'be
ad'o·les'cence
ad'o·les'cent
a·dopt'
(*choose;* see adapt, adept)
a·dop'tion
a·dop'tive
a·dor'a·ble
ad'o·ra'tion
a·dore'
·dored' ·dor'ing
a·dorn'
a·dorn'ment
a·dre'nal
ad·re'nal·in
a·drift'
a·droit'
ad·sorb'
ad·sor'bent
ad·sorp'tion
ad'u·late'
·lat'ed ·lat'ing
ad'u·la'tion
a·dul'ter·ant
a·dul'ter·ate'
·at'ed ·at'ing
a·dul'ter·a'tion
a·dul'ter·er
a·dul'ter·ess *n.*

a·dul'ter·ous *adj.*
a·dul'ter·y
a·dult'hood
ad·um'brate
·brat·ed ·brat·ing
ad' va·lo'rem
ad·vance'
·vanced'
·vanc'ing
ad·vance'ment
ad·van'tage
ad'van·ta'geous
ad·ven·ti'tious
ad·ven'ture
·tured ·tur·ing
ad·ven'tur·er
ad·ven'ture·some
ad·ven'tur·ous
ad'verb
ad·ver'bi·al
ad'ver·sar'y
·ies
ad'verse'
(*opposed;* see averse)
ad·verse'ly
ad·ver'si·ty
·ties
ad·vert'
ad·vert'ent
ad'ver·tise' *or* ·tize'
·tised' *or* ·tized'
·tis'ing *or* ·tiz'ing
ad'ver·tise'ment *or* ·tize'ment
ad·vice' *n.*
ad·vis'a·bil'i·ty
ad·vis'a·ble
ad·vis'a·bly
ad·vise' *v.*
·vised' ·vis'ing
ad·vis'ed·ly
ad·vise'ment
ad·vis'er *or* ·vi'sor
ad·vi'so·ry
ad'vo·ca·cy
ad'vo·cate'
·cat'ed ·cat'ing
Ae·ge'an
ae'gis
ae'on
aer'ate'
·at'ed ·at'ing
aer·a'tion
aer'a·tor
aer'i·al
aer'i·al·ist
aer'ie *or* ·y
aer'o·bal·lis'tics
aer'o·bat'ics
aer'obe
aer'o·dy·nam'i·cal·ly
aer'o·dy·nam'ics
aer'o·me·chan'·ics

aer'o·med'i·cine
aer'o·nau'ti·cal
aer'o·nau'tics
aero'o·neu·ro'sis
aer'o·sol'
aer'o·space
aer'o·stat'ics
Ae'sop
aes'thete'
aes·thet'ic
aes·thet'i·cal·ly
aes·thet'i·cism
af'fa·bil'i·ty
af'fa·ble
af'fa·bly
af·fair'
af·fect'
(*to influence;* see effect)
af'fec·ta'tion
af·fect'ed
af·fec'tion
af·fec'tion·ate
af·fec'tive
(*of feelings;* see effective)
af·fi'ance
·anced ·anc·ing
af·fi·da'vit
af·fil'i·ate'
·at'ed ·at'ing
af·fil'i·a'tion
af·fin'i·ty
af·firm'
af·fir·ma'tion
af·firm'a·tive
af·firm'a·tive·ly
af·fix'
·fixed' *or* ·fixt'
·fix'ing
af·flict'
af·flic'tion
af'flu·ence
af'flu·ent
(*rich;* see effluent)
af·ford'
af·fray'
af·front'
af'ghan
a·fi'cio·na'do
a·field'
a·fire'
a·flame'
a·float'
a·fore'men'tioned
a·fore'said'
a·fore'thought'
a·fore'time'
a·foul'
a·fraid'
A'-frame'
a·fresh'
Af'ri·can
af'ter
af'ter·birth'
af'ter·burn'er
af'ter·damp'

af'ter·ef·fect'
af'ter·glow'
af'ter·im'age
af'ter·life'
af'ter·math'
af'ter·noon'
af'ter·shock'
af'ter·taste'
af'ter·thought'
af'ter·ward'
a·gain'
a·gainst'
a·gape'
ag'ate
ag'ate·ware'
age
aged, ag'ing *or* age'ing
age'less
age'long'
a'gen·cy
·cies
a·gen'da
a'gent
age'-old'
ag·glom'er·ate'
·at'ed ·at'ing
ag·glom'er·a'tion
ag·glu'ti·nant
ag·glu'ti·nate'
·nat'ed ·nat'ing
ag·glu'ti·na'tion
ag·gran'dize'
·dized' ·diz'ing
ag·gran'dize·ment
ag'gra·vate'
·vat'ed ·vat'ing
ag'gra·va'tion
ag'gre·gate'
·gat'ed ·gat'ing
ag'gre·ga'tion
ag·gres'sion
ag·gres'sive
ag·gres'sor
ag·grieve'
·grieved'
·griev'ing
a·ghast'
ag'ile
ag'ile·ly
a·gil'i·ty
ag'i·tate'
·tat'ed ·tat'ing
ag'i·ta'tion
ag'i·ta'tor
ag'it·prop'
a·gleam'
ag'let
a·glow'
ag·nos'tic
ag·nos'ti·cal·ly
ag·nos'ti·cism
a·gog'
ag'o·nize'
·nized' ·niz'ing
ag'o·ny
·nies

ag'o·ra·pho'bi·a
a·grar'i·an
a·gree'
·greed' ·gree'ing
a·gree'a·bil'i·ty
a·gree'a·ble
a·gree'a·bly
ag'ri·busi'ness
ag'ri·cul'tur·al
ag'ri·cul'ture
ag'ri·cul'tur·ist
or ·tur·al·ist
a·gron'o·my
a·ground'
a'gue
a'gu·ish
a·head'
aid
(*help*)
aide
(*assistant*)
aide'-de-camp' *or* aid'-de-camp'
aides'- *or* aids'-
ail
(*be ill;* see ale)
ai'le·ron'
ail'ing
ail'ment
aim'less
air
(*gases;* see heir)
air base
air'borne'
air brake
air'bra'sive
air'brush'
air coach
air'-con·di'tion
air'-con·di'tioned
air conditioner
air conditioning
air'-cool'
air'-cooled'
air'craft'
air'drome'
air'drop'
·dropped'
·drop'ping
air'-dry'
-dried' -dry'ing
air express
air'field'
air'foil'
air force
air'frame'
air gun
air hole
air'i·ly
air'i·ness
air'ing
air lane
air'lift'
air'line'
air'lin'er
air lock
air'mail'

air'man
·men
air'-mind'ed
air'mo'bile
air'plane'
air'port'
air pressure
air'proof'
air pump
air raid
air'scape'
·at'ed ·at'ing
air'ship'
air'sick'
air'space'
air'speed'
air'-sprayed'
air'stream'
air'strip'
air'tight'
air'waves'
air'wor'thy
air'y
   air'i·er air'i·est
aisle
   (passage; see isle)
a·kim'bo
Al'a·bam'a
al'a·bas'ter
a' la carte'
a·lac'ri·ty
à' la king'
a' la mode'
   or à' la mode'
a·larm'ing
a·larm'ist
A·las'ka
al'ba·core'
al'ba·tross'
al·be'it
al'bi·nism
al·bi'no
·nos
al'bum
al·bu'men
   (egg white)
al·bu'min
   (class of proteins)
Al'bu·quer'que
al'che·mist
al'che·my
al'co·hol'
al'co·hol'ic
al'co·hol'i·cal·ly
al'co·hol'ism
al'cove
al'der·man
·men
ale
   (a drink; see ail)
a'le·a·to'ry
ale'house'
a·lert'ly
A·leu'tian
ale'wife'
·wives'
al·fal'fa
al·fres'co
al'gae

al'gae·cide'
al'ge·bra
al'ge·bra'ic
al'ge·bra'i·cal·ly
al'i·as
al'i·bi'
·bis'
·bied' ·bi'ing
al'ien
al'ien·ate'
·at'ed ·at'ing
al'ien·a'tion
a·light'
·light'ed or ·lit'
·light'ing
a·lign' or a·line'
·ligned' or ·lined'
·lign'ing or
·lin'ing
a·lign'ment
or a·line'ment
a·like'
al'i·men'ta·ry
(nourishing; see
elementary)
al'i·mo'ny
al'i·quant
al'i·quot
a·live'
al'ka·li'
·lies' or ·lis'
al'ka·line
al'ka·lize'
·lized' ·liz'ing
al'ka·loid'
al'kyd
all'-A·mer'i·can
all'-a·round'
al·lay'
·layed' ·lay'ing
all'-clear'
al'le·ga'tion
al·lege'
·leged' ·leg'ing
al·leg'ed·ly
Al'le·ghe'ny
al·le'giance
al'le·gor'i-cal
al'le·go·rize'
·rized' ·riz'ing
al'le·go'ry
·ries
al'le·gret'to
al·le'gro
al·le·lu'ia
al'ler·gen
al'ler·gen'ic
al·ler'gic
al'ler·gist
al'ler·gy
·gies
al·le'vi·ate'
·at'ed ·at'ing
al·le'vi·a'tion
al'ley
·leys
(narrow lane;
see ally)

al'ley·way'
al·li'ance
al·lied'
al'li·ga'tor
all'-im·por'tant
all'-in·clu'sive
al·lit'er·ate'
·at'ed ·at'ing
al·lit'er·a'tion
al'lo·cate'
·cat'ed ·cat'ing
al'lo·ca'tion
al·lot'
·lot'ted ·lot'ting
al·lot'ment
al·lot'tee'
all'-out'
all'o'ver
al·low'
al·low'a·ble
al·low'ance
al·lowed'
(permitted; see
aloud)
al'loy
all'-pur'pose
all right
all'spice'
all'-star'
all'-time'
al·lude'
·lud'ed ·lud'ing
(refer to; see
elude)
al·lure'
·lured' ·lur'ing
al·lu'sion
(mention; see
elusion, illusion)
al·lu'sive
(mentioning; see
elusive, illusive)
al·lu'vi·al
al·lu'vi·um
·vi·ums or ·vi·a
al·ly' v. al'ly n.
·lied' ·ly'ing
·lies
(join; partner;
see alley)
al'ma ma'ter
al'ma·nac'
al·might'y
al'mond
al'mon·er
al'most
alms
a·loft'
a·lo'ha
a·long'shore'
a·long'side'
a·loof'
a·loud'
(loudly; see
allowed)
al·pac'a
al'pen·stock'
al'pha·bet'

al'pha·bet'i·cal
al'pha·bet'i·cal·ly
al'pha·bet·ize'
·ized' ·iz'ing
al·read'y
al'so-ran'
al'tar
(table for
worship)
al'ter
(to change)
al'ter·a'tion
al'ter·cate'
·cat'ed ·cat'ing
al'ter·ca'tion
al'ter·nate'
·nat'ed ·nat'ing
al'ter·na'tion
al·ter'na·tive
al'ter·na'tor
al·though'
al·tim'e·ter
al'ti·tude'
al'to
·tos
al'to·geth'er
al'tru·ism
al'tru·is'tic
a·lu'mi·num
a·lum'na n.fem.
·nae
a·lum'nus
n.masc.
·ni
al'ways
a·mal'ga·mate'
·mat'ed ·mat'ing
a·mal'ga·ma'tion
a·man'u·en'sis
·ses
am'a·ryl'lis
am'a·teur'
am'a·to'ry
a·maze'
·mazed'
·maz'ing
a·maze'ment
Am'a·zon'
am·bas'sa·dor
am·bas'sa·do'ri·al
am'ber
am'ber·gris'
am'bi·ance
am·bi·dex·ter'i·ty
am'bi·dex'trous
am'bi·ent
am·bi·gu'i·ty
am·big'u·ous
am·bi'tion
am·bi'tious
am·biv'a·lence
am'ble
·bled ·bling
am·bro'sia
am'bu·lance
am'bu·late'
·lat'ed ·lat'ing
am'bu·la·to'ry

am'bus·cade'
·cad'ed ·cad'ing
am'bush
a·me'ba
·bas or ·bae
a·me'li·o·rate'
·rat'ed ·rat'ing
a·me'lio·ra'tion
a·me'lio·ra'tive
a·me'na·bil'i·ty
a·me'na·ble
a·mend'
(revise; see
emend)
a·mend'ment
a·men'i·ty
·ties
A·mer'i·can
A·mer'i·ca'na
A·mer'i·can·ism
A·mer'i·can·i·
za'tion
A·mer'i·can·ize'
·ized' ·iz'ing
Am'er·ind'
am'e·thyst
a'mi·a·bil'i·ty
a'mi·a·ble
a'mi·a·bly
am'i·ca·bil'i·ty
am'i·ca·ble
am'i·ca·bly
a·mid'
a·mid'ships
a·midst'
a·mi'no
Am'ish
a·miss'
am'i·ty
·ties
am'me'ter
am·mo'nia
am·mu·ni'tion
am·ne'sia
am·ne'si·ac' or
am·ne'sic
am'nes·ty
·ties, ·tied ·ty·ing
a·moe'ba
·bas or ·bae
a·mok'
a·mong'
a·mongst'
a·mon'til·la'do
a·mor'al
a'mor·al'i·ty
am'o·rous
a·mor'phous
am'or·ti·za'tion
am'or·tize'
·tized' ·tiz'ing
a·mount'
a·mour'
am'per·age
am'pere
am'per·sand'
am·phet'a·mine'
am·phib'i·an

am·phib'i·ous
am'phi·the'a·ter
am'pho·ra
·rae or ·ras
am'ple
am'pli·fi·ca'tion
am'pli·fi'er
am'pli·fy'
·fied' ·fy'ing
am'pli·tude'
am'ply
am'pul
am·pul'la
·las or ·lae
am'pu·tate'
·tat'ed ·tat'ing
am'pu·ta'tion
am'pu·tee'
a·muck'
am'u·let
a·muse'
·mused'
·mus'ing
a·muse'ment
a·nach'ro·nism
a·nach'ro·nis'tic
an'a·con'da
a·nae'mi·a
a·nae'mic
an'aes·the'sia
an'aes·thet'ic
an·aes'the·tize'
·tized' ·tiz'ing
an'a·gram'
a'nal
an'al·ge'si·a
an'al·ge'sic
an'a·log' computer
a·nal'o·gize'
·gized' ·giz'ing
a·nal'o·gous
a·nal'o·gy
·gies
a·nal'y·sis
·ses'
an'a·lyst
(one who
analyzes; see
annalist)
an'a·lyt'i·cal
or an'a·lyt'ic
an'a·lyt'i·cal·ly
an'a·lyze'
·lyzed' ·lyz'ing
an'a·pest'
an·ar'chic
or an·ar'chi·cal
an'ar·chism
an'ar·chist
an'ar·chis'tic
an'ar·chy
·chies
an'as·tig·mat'ic
a·nas'tro·phe
a·nath'e·ma
·mas
a·nath'e·ma·tize'
·tized' ·tiz'ing

an'a·tom'i·cal
or an'a·tom'ic
an'a·tom'i·cal·ly
a·nat'o·mist
·nat'o·mize'
·mized' ·miz'ing
a·nat'o·my
·mies
an'ces'tor
an'ces'tral
an'ces'tress
an'ces'try
·tries
an'chor
an'chor·age
an'cho·rite'
an'cho'vy
·vies
an'cient
an'cil·lar'y
n·dan'te
and'i'ron
nd/or
n'dro·gen
n'ec·dot'al
n'ec·dote'
(story; see
antidote)
·ne'mi·a
·ne'mic
·nem'o·graph'
n'e·mom'e·ter
·nem'o·ne'
n'er·oid'
n'es·the'sia
n'es·the'si-
ol'o·gy
n'es·thet'ic
n·es'the·tist
n·es'the·tize'
·tized' ·tiz'ing
n'gel
(spirit; see angle)
n'gel·fish'
n·gel'ic
or an·gel'i·cal
n·gel'i·cal·ly
n'ge·lus
n'ger
n·gi'na
n'gle
·gled ·gling
(corner; scheme;
see angel)
n'gler
n'gle·worm'
an'gli·can
an'gli·cism
an'gli·cize'
·cized' ·ciz'ing
n'gling
n'glo-A·mer'i-
can
n'glo·ma'ni·a
n'glo·phile'
n'glo-Sax'on
n·go'ra
n'gos·tu'ra

an'gri·ly
an'gry
·gri·er ·gri·est
an'guish
an'gu·lar
an'gu·lar'i·ty
·ties
an'gu·la'tion
an·hy'drous
an'ile
a·nil'i·ty
an'i·mad·ver'
sion
an'i·mal
an'i·mal'cule
an'i·mal·ism
an'i·mal·is'tic
an'i·mal·ize'
·ized' ·iz'ing
an'i·mate'
·mat'ed ·mat'ing
an'i·ma'tor
or ·mat'er
an'i·ma'tion
an'i·mism
an'i·mos'i·ty
·ties
an'i·mus
an'i'on
an'ise
an'i·seed'
an'i·sette'
ankh
an'kle
an'kle·bone'
an'klet
an'nal·ist
(a writer of
annals; see
analyst)
an'nals
An·nap'o·lis
an·neal'
an'ne·lid
an·nex' v.
an'nex n.
an'nex·a'tion
an·ni'hi·late'
·lat'ed ·lat'ing
an·ni'hi·la'tion
an·ni'hi·la'tor
an'ni·ver'sa·ry
·ries
an'no·tate'
·tat'ed ·tat'ing
an'no·ta'tion
an·nounce'
·nounced'
·nounc'ing
an·nounce'ment
an·nounc'er
an·noy'
an·noy'ance
an'nu·al
an'nu·al·ly
an·nu'i·tant
an·nu'i·ty
·ties

an·nul'
·nulled'
·nul'ling
an'nu·lar
an·nul'ment
an'nu·lus
·li' or ·lus·es
an·nun'ci·ate'
·at'ed ·at'ing
(announce; see
enunciate)
an·nun'ci·a'tor
an'ode
an'o·dize'
·dized' ·diz'ing
an'o·dyne'
a·noint'
a·nom'a·lous
a·nom'a·ly
·lies
an'o·mie
a·non'ym'i·ty
a·non'y·mous
a·noph'e·les'
an·oth'er
an'swer
ant·ac'id
an·tag'o·nism
an·tag'o·nis'tic
an·tag'o·nize'
·nized' ·niz'ing
ant·al'ka·li'
·lies' or ·lis'
ant·arc'tic
Ant·arc'ti·ca
an'te
·ted or ·teed
·te·ing
an'te- prefix
(before; see
anti-)
ant'eat'er
an'te·bel'lum
an'te·cede'
·ced'ed ·ced'ing
an'te·ced'ence
an'te·ced'ent
an'te·cham'ber
an'te·date'
an'te·di·lu'vi·an
an'te·lope'
an'te me·ri'di·em
an·ten'na
·nae or ·nas
an'te·pe'nult
an·te'ri·or
an'te·room'
an'them
an'ther
an·thol'o·gist
an·thol'o·gy
·gies
an'thra·cite'
an'thrax
·thra·ces'
an'thro·poid'
an'thro·pol'o·gist
an'thro·pol'o·gy

an'thro·po·mor'-
phic
an'ti- prefix
(against; see
ante-)
an'ti·air'craft
an'ti·bac·te'ri·al
an'ti·bi·ot'ic
an'ti·bod'y
·ies
an'tic
·ticked ·tick·ing
an·tic'i·pant
an·tic'i·pate'
·pat'ed ·pat'ing
an·tic'i·pa'tion
an·tic'i·pa·to'ry
an'ti·cli·mac'tic
an'ti·cli'max
an'ti·de·pres'sant
an'ti·dote'
(remedy; see
anecdote)
an'ti·freeze'
an'ti·gen
an'ti·he'ro
an'ti·his'ta·mine'
an'ti·knock'
an'ti·la'bor
An·til'les
an'ti·ma·cas'sar
an'ti·mat'ter
an'ti·mo'ny
an'ti·nov'el
an'ti·par'ti·cle
an'ti·pas'to
an'ti·pa·thet'ic
an·tip'a·thy
·thies
an'ti·per'son·nel'
an'ti·phon
an·tiph'o·nal
an·tip'o·dal
an'ti·pode'
an·tip'o·des'
an'ti·quar'i·an
an·tiq'ua·ry
·ies
an'ti·quate'
·quat'ed
·quat'ing
an·tique'
·tiqued'
·tiqu'ing
an·tiq'ui·ty
·ties
an'ti-Sem'ite
an'ti-Se·mit'ic
an'ti-Sem'i·tism
an'ti·sep'sis
an'ti·sep'tic
an'ti·so'cial
an·tith'e·sis
·ses'
an'ti·thet'i·cal
an'ti·thet'i-
cal·ly
an'ti·tox'in

an'ti·trust'
ant'ler
an'to·nym'
an'trum
·trums or ·tra
a'nus
·nus·es or ·ni
an'vil
anx·i'e·ty
·ties
anx'ious
an'y·bod'y
an'y·how'
an'y·one'
an'y·thing'
an'y·way'
an'y·where'
A'-OK' or
A'-O·kay'
a·or'ta
·tas or ·tae
a·pace'
a·part'heid
a·part'ment
ap'a·thet'ic
ap'a·thet'i-
cal·ly
ap'a·thy
·thies
ap'er·ture
a'pex
a'pex·es or
ap'i·ces
a·pha'si·a
aph'o·rism
aph'ro·dis'i·ac'
a'pi·ar'y
·ies
a·piece'
a·plomb'
a·poc'a·lypse'
a·poc'a·lyp'tic
a·poc'ry·phal
ap'o·gee'
a·pol'o·get'ic
a·pol'o·gize'
·gized' ·giz'ing
ap'o·logue'
a·pol'o·gy
·gies
ap'o·plec'tic
ap'o·plex'y
a·pos'ta·sy
a·pos'tate
a'·pos·te'ri·o'ri
a·pos'tle
ap'os·tol'ic
a·pos'tro·phe
ap'os·troph'ic
a·pos'tro·phize'
·phized'
·phiz'ing
a·poth'e·car'y
·ies

ap'o·thegm'
(short saying)
ap'o·them'
(math. term)
a·poth'e·o'sis
·ses
Ap'pa·la'chi·an
ap·pall' or ·pal'
·palled' ·pal'ling
ap'pa·loo'sa
ap'pa·ra'tus
·tus or ·tus·es
ap·par'el
·eled or ·elled
·el·ing or ·el·ling
ap·par'ent
ap'pa·ri'tion
ap·peal'
ap·pear'ance
ap·peas'a·ble
ap·pease'
·peased'
·peas'ing
ap·pease'ment
ap·peas'er
ap·pel'lant
ap·pel'late
ap'pel·la'tion
ap·pend'
ap·pend'age
ap·pend'ant or
·ent
ap·pen·dec'to·my
·mies
ap·pen'di·ci'tis
ap·pen'dix
·dix·es or
·di·ces'
ap'per·cep'tion
ap·per·tain'
ap'pe·tite'
ap'pe·tiz'er
ap'pe·tiz'ing
ap·plaud'
ap·plause'
ap'ple·jack'
ap'ple·sauce'
ap·pli'ance
ap'pli·ca·bil'i·ty
ap'pli·ca·ble
ap'pli·cant
ap'pli·ca'tion
ap'pli·ca'tor
ap·plied'
ap'pli·qué'
·quéd' ·qué'ing
ap·ply'
·plied' ·ply'ing
ap·pog'gia·tu'ra
ap·point'
ap·point'ee'
ap·poin'tive
ap·point'ment
ap·por'tion
ap'po·site
ap'po·si'tion
ap·prais'a·ble
ap·prais'al

ap·praise'
·praised'
·prais'ing
(estimate; see
apprise)
ap·prais'er
ap·pre'ci·a·ble
ap·pre'ci·ate'
·at'ed ·at'ing
ap·pre'ci·a'tion
ap·pre'ci·a·tive
ap'pre·hend'
ap'pre·hen'sion
ap'pre·hen'sive
ap·pren'tice
·ticed ·tic·ing
ap·prise' or
·prize'
·prised' or
·prized'
·pris'ing or
·priz'ing
(inform; see
appraise)
ap·proach'
ap·proach'·
a·ble
ap'pro·ba'tion
ap·pro'pri·ate'
·at'ed ·at'ing
ap·pro'pri·ate·ly
ap·pro'pri·a'tion
ap·prov'a·ble
ap·prov'al
ap·prove'
·proved'
·prov'ing
ap·prox'i·mate'
·mat'ed ·mat'ing
ap·prox'i·mate·ly
ap·prox'i·ma'·
tion
ap·pur'te·nance
a'pri·cot'
A'pril
a'pri·o'ri
ap'ro·pos'
ap'ti·tude'
apt'ly
aq'ua·cade'
aq'ua·lung'
aq'ua·ma·rine'
aq'ua·naut'
aq'ua·plane'
a·quar'i·um
·i·ums or ·i·a
a·quat'ic
aq'ua·tint'
aq'ue·duct'
a'que·ous
aq'ui·line'
ar'a·besque'
A·ra'bi·an
Ar'a·bic
ar'a·ble
a·rach'nid
ar'bi·ter
ar'bi·tra·ble

ar·bit'ra·ment
ar'bi·trar'i·ly
ar'bi·trar'i·ness
ar'bi·trar'y
ar'bi·trate'
·trat'ed ·trat'ing
ar'bi·tra'tion
ar'bi·tra'tor
ar'bor
ar·bo're·al
ar'bo·re'tum
·tums or ·ta
ar'bor·vi'tae
arc
arced or arcked
arc'ing or arck'ing
(curve; see ark)
ar·cade'
ar'chae·o·log'i·cal
ar'chae·ol'o·gy
ar·cha'ic
arch'an'gel
arch'bish'op
arch'dea'con
arch'di'o·cese
arch'duch'y
·ies
arch'duke'
arched
arch'en'e·my
·mies
ar'che·o·log'i·cal
ar'che·ol'o·gy
arch'er·y
ar'che·type'
arch'fiend'
ar'chi·pel'a·go'
·goes or ·gos'
ar'chi·tect'
ar'chi·tec·ton'ics
ar'chi·tec'tur·al
ar'chi·tec'tur·
al·ly
ar'chi·tec'ture
ar'chi·trave'
ar'chives
arch'priest'
arch'way'
arc'tic
ar'dent
ar'dor
ar'du·ous
ar'e·a·way'
a·re'na
aren't
Ar'gen·ti'na
ar'gon
ar'got
ar'gu·a·ble
ar'gu·a·bly
ar'gue
·gued ·gu·ing
ar'gu·ment
ar'gu·men·
ta'tion
ar'gu·men'ta·
tive
a'ri·a

a·rid'i·ty
ar'id·ness
a·rise'
·rose' ·ris'en
·ris'ing
ar'is·toc'ra·cy
·cies
a·ris'to·crat'
a·ris'to·crat'ic
a·ris'to·crat'i·
cal·ly
Ar'is·to·te'li·an
Ar'is·tot'le
a·rith'me·tic' n.
ar'ith·met'ic adj.
ar'ith·met'i·cal
ar'ith·met'i·
cal·ly
ar'ith·me·ti'cian
Ar'i·zo'na
ark
(enclosure;
see arc)
Ar'kan·sas'
ar·ma'da
ar'ma·dil'lo
·los
ar'ma·ment
ar'ma·ture
arm'chair'
armed
arm'ful
·fuls
arm'hole'
ar'mi·stice
arm'let
ar'mor
ar'mored
ar'mor·plat'ed
ar'mor·y
·ies
arm'pit'
arm'rest'
ar'my
·mies
ar'ni·ca
a·ro'ma
ar'o·mat'ic
ar'o·mat'i·cal·ly
a·round'
a·rous'al
a·rouse'
·roused'
·rous'ing
ar·peg'gio
·gios
ar·raign'
ar·range'
·ranged'
·rang'ing
ar·range'ment
ar·rang'er
ar'rant
ar·ray'
ar·ray'al
ar·rear'age
ar·rears'
ar·rest'

ar·riv'al
ar·rive'
·rived' ·riv'ing
ar'ro·gance
ar'ro·gant
ar'ro·gate'
·gat'ed ·gat'ing
ar'ro·ga'tion
ar'row·head'
ar'row·root'
ar·roy'o
·os
ar'se·nal
ar'se·nic
ar'son
ar'son·ist
ar'te·fact'
ar·te'ri·al
ar·te'ri·o·scle·
ro'sis
ar·te'ri·o·scle·
rot'ic
ar'ter·y
·ies
ar·te'sian
art'ful
art'ful·ly
ar·thrit'ic
ar·thri'tis
Ar·thu'ri·an
ar'ti·choke'
ar'ti·cle
ar·tic'u·late'
·lat'ed ·lat'ing
ar·tic'u·late·ly
ar·tic'u·la'tion
ar'ti·fact'
ar'ti·fice
ar·tif'i·cer
ar·ti·fi'cial
ar·ti·fi'cial·ly
ar'ti·fi'ci·al'i·ty
·ties
ar·til'ler·y
art'i·ness
ar'ti·san
art'ist
ar·tiste'
ar·tis'tic
ar·tis'ti·cal·ly
art'ist·ry
art'less
art'mo·bile'
art'sy-craft'sy
art'y
·i·er ·i·est
Ar'y·an
as·bes'tos
as·cend'
as·cend'a·ble
as·cend'an·cy
as·cend'ant
as·cen'sion
as·cent'
(a rising; see
assent)
as'cer·tain'
as·cet'ic

as·cet'i·cal·ly
as·cet'i·cism
a·scor'bic
as'cot
as·crib'a·ble
as·cribe'
·cribed'
·crib'ing
as·crip'tion
a·sep'tic
a·sep'ti·cal·ly
a·sex'u·al
a·shamed'
ash'can'
ash'en
ash'es
a·shore'
ash'y
·i·er ·i·est
A'sia
A'si·at'ic
as'i·nine'
as'i·nin'i·ty
·ties
a·skance'
a·skew'
a·sleep'
a·so'cial
as·par'a·gus
as'pect
as'pen
as·per'i·ty
as·perse'
·persed' ·pers'ing
as·per'sion
as'phalt
as·phyx'i·a
as·phyx'i·ant
as·phyx'i·ate'
·at'ed ·at'ing
as·phyx'i·a'tion
as·phyx'i·a'tor
as'pic
as'pir·ant
as'pi·rate'
·rat'ed ·rat'ing
as'pi·ra'tion
as'pi·ra'tor
as·pire'
·pired' ·pir'ing
as'pi·rin
as·sail'
as·sail'ant
as·sas'sin
as·sas'si·nate'
·nat'ed ·nat'ing
as·sas'si·na'tion
as·sault'
as·say'
(analyze; see
essay)
as·sem'blage
as·sem'ble
·bled ·bling
as·sem'bly
·blies
as·sem'bly·man
·men

as·sent'
(consent; see ascent)
as·sert'
as·ser'tion
as·ser'tive
as·sess'
as·ses'sor
as'set
as·sev'er·ate'
·at'ed ·at'ing
as·sev'er·a'tion
as·si·du'i·ty
as·sid'u·ous
as·sign'
as·sign'a·ble
as'sig·na'tion
as·sign'ee'
as·sign'ment
as·sim'i·la·ble
as·sim'i·late'
·lat'ed ·lat'ing
as·sim'i·la'tion
as·sim'i·la'tive
as·sim'i·la'tor
as·sist'
as·sist'ance
as·sist'ant
as·size'
as·so'ci·ate'
·at'ed ·at'ing
as·so'ci·a'tion
as·so'ci·a'tive
as'so·nance
as'so·nant
as·sort'
as·sort'ed
as·sort'ment
as·suage'
·suaged'
·suag'ing
as·sua'sive
as·sum'a·ble
as·sume'
·sumed'
·sum'ing
as·sump'tion
as·sur'ance
as·sure'
·sured' ·sur'ing
as·sur'ed·ly
As·syr'i·a
as'ter·isk'
as'ter·oid'
asth'ma
asth·mat'ic
asth·mat'i·cal·ly
as'tig·mat'ic
as'tig·mat'i·cal·ly
a·stig'ma·tism
as·ton'ish
as·tound'
a·strad'dle
as'tra·khan
or ·chan
as'tral
a·stride'
as·trin'gen·cy
as·trin'gent

as'tro·dome'
as'tro·labe'
as·trol'o·ger
as'tro·log'i·cal
as·trol'o·gy
as'tro·naut'
as'tro·nau'ti·cal
as'tro·nau'tics
as·tron'o·mer
as'tro·nom'i·cal
  or ·nom'ic
as'tro·nom'i·cal·ly
as·tron'o·my
as'tro·phys'i·cal
as'tro·phys'i·cist
as'tro·phys'ics
as·tute'
a·sun'der
a·sy'lum
a·sym·met'ri·cal
  or ·met'ric
a·sym'me·try
as'ymp·tote'
at'a·vism
at'a·vis'tic
at'el·ier'
a'the·ism
a'the·ist
a'the·is'tic
ath'lete'
ath·let'ic
ath·let'i·cal·ly
at-home'
a·thwart'
a·tin'gle
At·lan'tic
at'las
at'mos·phere'
at'mos·pher'ic
at'mos·pher'i·
  cal·ly
at'oll
at'om
a·tom'ic
a·tom'ics
at'om·ize'
  ·ized' ·iz'ing
at'om·iz'er
a·ton'al
a'to·nal'i·ty
a·tone'
  ·toned' ·ton'ing
a·tone'ment
a'tri·um
  ·tri·a or ·tri·ums
a·tro'cious
a·troc'i·ty
  ·ties
at'ro·phy
  ·phied ·phy·ing
at·tach'
at'ta·ché'
at·tach'ment
at·tack'
at·tain'
at·tain'a·ble
at·tain'der
at·tain'ment

at·taint'
at'tar
at·tempt'
at·tend'
at·tend'ance
at·tend'ant
at·ten'tion
at·ten'tive
at·ten'u·ate'
  ·at'ed ·at'ing
at·ten'u·a'tion
at·ten'u·a'tor
at·tes·ta'tion
at'tic
at·tire'
  ·tired' ·tir'ing
at'ti·tude'
at'ti·tu'di·nal
at·tor'ney
  ·neys
at·tract'
at·trac'tion
at·trac'tive
at·trib'ut·a·ble
at'tri·bute' n.
at·trib'ute v.
  ·ut·ed ·ut·ing
at'tri·bu'tion
at·trib'u·tive
au'thor
au·thor'i·tar'i·an
au·thor'i·ta'tive
au·thor'i·ty
  ·ties
au·thor·i·za'tion
au'thor·ize'
  ·ized' ·iz'ing
au'to
  ·tos
  ·toed ·to·ing
au'to·bi'o·
  graph'ic or
  graph'i·cal
au'to·bi·og'ra·
  phy
  ·phies
au·toc'ra·cy
  ·cies
au'to·crat'
au·to·crat'ic
au·to·crat'i·
  cal·ly
au'to·graph'
au'to·mat'
au'to·mate'
  ·mat'ed ·mat'ing
au·to·mat'ic
au·to·mat'i·cal·ly
au·to·ma'tion
au·tom'a·tism
au·tom'a·ton'
  ·tons' or ·ta
au'to·mo·bile'
au'to·mo'tive
au·to·nom'ic
au·ton'o·mous
au·ton'o·my
  ·mies

au na·tu·rel'
au'ra
  ·ras or ·rae
au'ral
  (of the ear; see
  oral)
au're·ole'
Au're·o·my'cin
au' re·voir'
au'ri·cle
  (earlike part;
  see oracle)
au·ric'u·lar
au·ro'ra bo're·
  a'lis
aus'cul·ta'tion
aus'pi·ces'
aus·pi'cious
aus·tere'
aus·tere'ly
aus·ter'i·ty
  ·ties
Aus·tral'ia
au·then'tic
au·then'ti·cal·ly
au·then'ti·cate'
  ·cat'ed ·cat'ing
au·then·ti·ca'tion
au'then·tic'i·ty
au'thor
au·thor'i·tar'i·an
au·thor'i·ta'tive
au·thor'i·ty
  ·ties
au'thor·i·za'tion
au'thor·ize'
  ·ized' ·iz'ing
au'to
  ·tos
  ·toed ·to·ing

au'top·sy
  ·sies
au'to·sug·ges'·
  tion
au'tumn
au·tum'nal
aux·il'ia·ry
  ·ries
a·vail'a·bil'i·ty
a·vail'a·ble
a·vail'a·bly
av'a·lanche'
  ·lanched'
  ·lanch'ing
a·vant'-garde'
a·vant'-gard'ism
a·vant'-gard'ist
av'a·rice
av'a·ri'cious
a·venge'
  venged'
  ·veng'ing
a·veng'er
av'e·nue'
a·ver'
  ·verred'
  ·ver'ring
av'er·age
  ·aged ·ag·ing
a·verse'
  (unwilling; see
  adverse)
a·ver'sion
a·vert'
a'vi·ar'y
  ·ies
a'vi·a'tion
a'vi·a'tor
a'vi·a'trix
av'id·ly
av'o·ca'do
  ·dos
av'o·ca'tion
a·void'a·ble
a·void'a·bly
a·void'ance
av'oir·du·pois'
a·vow'al
a·vowed'
a·vun'cu·lar
a·wait'
a·wake'
  woke' or
  ·waked',
  ·waked',
  ·wak'ing
a·wak'en
a·wak'en·ing
a·ward'
a·ware'
a·weigh'
awe'some
awe'-struck'
aw'ful
aw'ful·ly
aw'ful·ness
a·while'
awk'ward

awn'ing
a·wry'
ax or axe
ax'es
axed ax'ing
ax'i·om
ax'i·o·mat'ic
ax'i·o·mat'i·
  cal·ly
ax'is
ax'es
ax'le
Ax'min·ster
a·zal'ea
az'i·muth
Az'tec
az'ure

B

bab'bitt
bab'ble
  ·bled ·bling
ba·boon'
ba·bush'ka
ba'by
  ·bies
  ·bied ·by·ing
ba'by-sit'
  -sat' -sit'ting
baby sitter
bac'ca·lau're·ate
bac'ca·rat'
bac'cha·nal
bac'cha·na'li·an
bac'chant
  ·chants or
  bac·chan'tes
bac·chan'te
bach'e·lor
ba·cil'lus
  ·li
back'ache'
back'bite'
  ·bit', ·bit'ten or
  ·bit', ·bit'ing
back'bend'
back'board'
back'bone'
back'break'ing
back'court'
back'date'
  ·dat'ed ·dat'ing
back'door'
back'drop'
back'field'
back'fire'
  ·fired' ·fir'ing
back'gam'mon
back'ground'
back'hand'
back'lash'
back'list'
back'log'
  ·logged'
  ·log'ging

back'rest'
back'side'
back'slide'
  ·slid', ·slid' or
  ·slid'den, ·slid'ing
back'space'
  ·spaced'
  ·spac'ing
back'spin'
back'stage'
back'stairs'
back'stop'
back'stretch'
back'stroke'
  ·stroked'
  ·strok'ing
back'track'
back'up' or
back'-up'
back'ward
back'wash'
back'wa'ter
back'woods'man
  ·men
ba'con
bac·te'ri·a
  (sing. bac·te'ri·um)
bac·te'ri·cide'
bac·te'ri·o·log'i·
  cal·ly
bac·te'ri·ol'o·gist
bac·te'ri·ol'o·gy
bad
  worse worst
badge
  badged badg'ing
badg'er
bad'i·nage'
  ·naged' ·nag'ing
bad'lands'
bad'min·ton
bad'-tem'pered
baf'fle
  ·fled ·fling
bag
  bagged bag'ging
bag'a·telle'
ba'gel
bag'ful'
  ·fuls'
bag'gage
bag'gy
  ·gi·er ·gi·est
bag'pipe'
ba·guette' or
  ·guet'
Ba·hai'
Ba·ha'mas
bail
  (money; see
  bale)
bai'liff
bai'li·wick
bails'man
  ·men
bait'ed
  (lured; see
  bated)

bake
  baked bak'ing
bak'er
bak'er·y
  ·ies
bal'a·lai'ka
bal'ance
  ·anced ·anc·ing
bal'ance·a·ble
bal·brig'gan
bal'co·ny
  ·nies
bal'der·dash'
bald'faced'
bald'head'ed
bald'ness
bale
  baled bal'ing
  (*bundle;* see
  bail)
bale'ful
balk'y
  ·i·er ·i·est
ball
  (*round object;*
  see bawl)
bal'lad
bal'lad·eer'
bal'last
ball bearing
bal'le·ri'na
bal'let
bal·lis'tic
bal·loon'ist
bal'lot
ball'park'
ball'play'er
ball'room'
balm'y
  ·i·er ·i·est
ba·lo'ney
bal'sa
bal'sam
Bal'tic
Bal'ti·more'
bal'us·ter
bal'us·trade'
bam·bi'no
  ·nos or ·ni
bam·boo'
bam·boo'zle
  ·zled ·zling
ban
  banned ban'ning
ba'nal
ba·nal'i·ty
  ·ties
ba·nan'a
band'age
  ·aged ·ag·ing
band'-aid' or
  band'aid'
ban·dan'na
band'box'
ban·deau'
  ·deaux'
ban'de·role'
ban'dit

band'mas'ter
ban'do·leer'
  or ·lier'
band saw
bands'man
  ·men
band'stand'
band'wag'on
ban'dy
  ·died ·dy·ing
ban'dy·leg'ged
bane'ful
ban'gle
bang'-up'
ban'ish
ban'is·ter
  or ban'nis·ter
ban'jo
  ·jos or ·joes
ban'jo·ist
bank'book'
bank note
bank'roll'
bank'rupt
bank'rupt·cy
  ·cies
ban'ner
banns or bans
  (*marriage notice*)
ban'quet
ban'tam
ban'tam·weight'
ban'ter
ban'zai'
bap'tism
bap·tis'mal
bap'tis·ter·y
  or ·tis·try
  ·ies or ·tries
bap'tize
  ·tized ·tiz·ing
bar
  barred bar'ring
bar·bar'i·an
bar·bar'ic
bar'ba·rism
bar·bar'i·ty
  ·ties
bar'ba·rous
bar'be·cue'
  ·cued' ·cu'ing
barbed wire
bar'bel
  (*hairlike growth*)
bar'bell'
  (*bar with weights*)
bar'ber
bar'ber·shop'
bar'bi·tal'
bar·bi'tu·rate
bar'bule
bare
  bared bar'ing
  (*uncover;* see
  bear)
bare'back'
bare'faced'
bare'fac'ed·ly

bare'foot'
bare'foot'ed
bare'hand'ed
bare'head'ed
bare'leg'ged
bare'ly
bar'gain
barge
  barged barg'ing
bar'i·tone'
bar'keep'er
bark'en·tine'
bark'er
bar'ley·corn'
bar'maid'
bar'man
  ·men
bar mitz'vah or
  bar miz'vah
bar'na·cle
bar'na·cled
barn'storm'
barn'yard'
bar'o·graph'
ba·rom'e·ter
bar'o·met'ric
bar'on
  (*nobleman;* see
  barren)
bar'on·ess
bar'on·et
ba·ro'ni·al
ba·roque'
ba·rouche'
bar'racks
bar'ra·cu'da
bar·rage'
  ·raged' ·rag'ing
barred
bar'rel
  ·reled or ·relled
  ·rel·ing or
  ·rel·ling
bar'ren
  (*empty;* see
  baron)
bar·ette'
  (*hair clasp;*
  see beret)
bar'ri·cade'
  ·cad'ed ·cad'ing
bar'ri·er
bar'ring
bar'ris·ter
bar'room'
bar'row
bar'tend'er
bar'ter
Bart'lett pear
bas'al
bas'al·ly
ba·salt'
bas'cule
base
  bas'es
based bas'ing
  (*foundation; vile;*
  see bass)

base'ball'
base'board'
base'born'
base'burn'er
base hit
base'less
base line
base'ly
base'man
  ·men
base'ment
base'ness
bas'es
  (*pl. of* base)
ba'ses
  (*pl. of* basis)
bash'ful
bash'ful·ly
bash'ful·ness
bas'ic
bas'i·cal·ly
bas'il
ba·sil'i·ca
ba'sin
ba'sis
  ·ses
bas'ket
bas'ket·ball'
bas'ket·work'
bas'-re·lief'
bass
  (*singer;* see base)
bass
  (*fish*)
bass clef
bass drum
bas'set
bass horn
bas'si·net'
bas·soon'
bass viol
bass'wood'
bas'tard
baste
bast'ed bast'ing
bas·tille'
bas'tion
bat
  bat'ted bat'ting
batch
bate
  bat'ed bat'ing
ba·teau'
  ·teaux'
bat'ed
  (*held in;* see
  baited)
bathe
  bathed bath'ing
bath'er
bath'house'
bath'i·nette'
ba'thos
bath'robe'
bath'room'
bath'tub'
bath'y·sphere'
ba·tik'

ba·tiste'
bat mitz'vah or
  bat miz'vah
ba·ton'
bat·tal'ion
bat'ten
bat'ter
bat'ter·y
  ·ies
bat'ting
bat'tle
  ·tled ·tling
bat'tle-ax' or -axe'
bat'tle·dore'
bat'tle·field'
bat'tle·ground'
bat'tle·ment
battle royal
battles royal
bat'tle-scarred'
bat'tle·ship'
bau'ble
baux'ite
bawd'y
  ·i·er ·i·est
bawl
  (*shout;* see ball)
bay'o·net'
  ·net'ed or ·net'ted
  ·net'ing or ·net'ting
bay'ou
ba·zaar'
  (*market;* see
  bizarre)
ba·zoo'ka
be
  was or were,
  been be'ing
beach
  (*shore;* see
  beech)
beach'comb'er
beach'head'
bea'con
bead'ing
bead'work
bead'y
  ·i·er ·i·est
bea'gle
beak'er
bean'bag'
bean'stalk'
bear
  (*animal;* see
  bare)
bear
  bore, borne or
  born,
  bear'ing
  (*carry;* see bare)
bear'a·ble
bear'a·bly
beard'ed
bear'ish
bear'skin'
beast'li·ness
beast'ly
  ·li·er ·li·est

beat
  beat beat'en
  beat'ing
be·a·tif'ic
be·at'i·fi·ca'tion
be·at'i·fy'
  ·fied' ·fy'ing
be·at'i·tude'
beat'nik
beau
beaus or beaux
  (*sweetheart;* see
  bow)
beau'te·ous
beau·ti'cian
beau'ti·fi·ca'tion
beau'ti·fi'er
beau'ti·ful
beau'ti·ful·ly
beau'ti·fy'
  ·fied' ·fy'ing
beau'ty
  ·ties
bea'ver
bea'ver·board'
be·calm'
be·cause'
beck'on
be·come'
  ·came' ·come'
  ·com'ing
bed
  bed'ded
  bed'ding
bed'bug'
bed'cham'ber
bed'clothes'
bed'cov'er
be·dev'il
  ·iled or ·illed
  ·il·ing or ·il·ling
bed'fast'
bed'fel'low
bed'lam
Bed'ou·in
bed'pan'
bed'post'
be·drag'gle
  ·gled ·gling
bed'rid'den
bed'rock'
bed'roll'
bed'room'
bed'side'
bed'sore'
bed'spread'
bed'spring'
bed'stead'
bed'time'
beech
  (*tree;* see beach)
beech'nut'
beef
  beeves or beefs
beef'eat'er
beef'steak'
beef'y
  ·i·er ·i·est

bee'hive'
bee'keep'er
bee'line'
beer
  (*drink;* see bier)
beer'i·ness
beer'y
 ·i·er ·i·est
bees'wax'
Bee'tho·ven
bee'tle
bee'tle-browed'
be·fall'
 ·fell' ·fall'en
·fall'ing
be·fit'
 ·fit'ted ·fit'ting
be·fog'
 ·fogged'
·fog'ging
be·fore'hand'
be·friend'
be·fud'dle
·dled ·dling
beg
begged beg'ging
be·get'
 ·got', ·got'ten or
 ·got', ·get'ting
beg'gar
be·gin'
 ·gan' ·gun'
 ·gin'ning
 (*start;* see beguine)
be·gin'ner
be·gird'
 ·girt' or ·gird'ed,
 ·girt', ·gird'ing
be·gone'
be·go'nia
be·grime'
 ·grimed'
·grim'ing
be·grudge'
 ·grudged'
·grudg'ing
be·guile'
 ·guiled' ·guil'ing
be·guine'
 (*dance;* see begin)
be·half'
be·have'
 ·haved' ·hav'ing
be·hav'ior
be·head'
be·he'moth
be·hest'
be·hind'hand'
be·hold'
 ·held' ·hold'ing
be·hold'en
be·hoove'
 ·hooved'
·hoov'ing
beige
be·jew'el
 ·eled or ·elled
 ·el·ing or ·el·ling

be·la'bor
be·lat'ed
be·lay'
 ·layed' ·lay'ing
belch
be·lea'guer
bel'fry
 ·fries
be·lie'
 ·lied' ·ly'ing
be·lief'
be·liev'a·bil'i·ty
be·liev'a·ble
be·liev'a·bly
be·lieve'
 ·lieved' ·liev'ing
be·liev'er
be·lit'tle
 ·tled ·tling
be·lit'tler
bel'la·don'na
bell'boy'
 (*errand boy*)
bell buoy
 (*signal bell*)
belle
 (*pretty girl*)
belles-let'tres
bell'-bot'tom
bel'li·cose'
bel'li·cos'i·ty
bel·lig'er·ence
bel·lig'er·en·cy
bel·lig'er·ent
bell'-like'
bell'man
 ·men
bel'low
bell'weth'er
bel'ly
 ·lies
 ·lied ·ly·ing
bel'ly·band'
be·long'
be·lov'ed
be·low'
belt'ing
be·mire'
 ·mired' ·mir'ing
be·moan'
be·smirch'
bend
 bent bend'ing
be·neath'
ben'e·dict'
Ben'e·dic'tine
ben'e·dic'tion
ben'e·fac'tion
ben'e·fac'tor
ben'e·fac'tress
ben'e·fice
be·nef'i·cence
be·nef'i·cent
ben'e·fi'cial
ben'e·fi'ci·ar'y
 ·ar'ies
ben'e·fit
 ·fit·ed ·fit·ing
be·nev'o·lence

be·nev'o·lent
ben'ga·line'
be·night'ed
be·nign'
be·nig'nan·cy
be·nig'nant
be·nig'ni·ty
ben'i·son
be·numb'
ben'zene
 (*in chemistry*)
ben'zine
 (*cleaning fluid*)
be·queath'
 ·queathed'
·queath'ing
be·queath'al
be·quest'
be·rate'
 ·rat'ed ·rat'ing
be·reave'
 ·reaved' or ·reft'
·reav'ing
be·reave'ment
be·ret'
 (*flat cap;* see barrette)
ber'i·ber'i
Berke'ley
Ber·mu'da
ber'ry
 ·ries
 ·ried ·ry·ing
 (*fruit;* see bury)
ber·serk'
berth
 (*bed;* see birth)
ber'yl
be·ryl'li·um
be·seech'
 ·sought' or
 ·seeched'
·seech'ing
be·set'
·set' ·set'ting
be·side'
be·sides'
be·siege'
 ·sieged' ·sieg'ing
be·smirch'
be·sot'
 ·sot'ted ·sot'ting
Bes'se·mer
bes'tial
bes'ti·al'i·ty
 ·ties
be·stow'
best seller
bet
 bet or bet'ted
bet'ting
be'ta·tron'
be·tray'al
be·troth'
be·troth'al
be·trothed'
bet'ter
 (*compar. of* good)

bet'tor or ·ter
 (*one who bets*)
between'
be·twixt'
bev'a·tron'
bev'el
 ·eled or ·elled
 ·el·ing or ·el·ling
bev'er·age
bev'y
 ·ies
be·wail'
be·ware'
 ·wared' ·war'ing
be·wil'dered
be·witch'
be·yond'
bez'el
bi·an'nu·al
bi·an'nu·al·ly
bi'as
 ·ased or ·assed
 ·as·ing or ·as·sing
Bi'ble
Bib'li·cal
Bib'li·cal·ly
bib'li·og'ra·phy
 ·phies
bib'li·o·phile'
bib'u·lous
bi·cam'er·al
bi·car'bon·ate
bi·cen·te'nar·y
 ·ies
bi'cen·ten'ni·al
bi'ceps
 ·ceps or ·ceps·es
bick'er
bi·cus'pid
bi'cy·cle
 ·cled ·cling
bi'cy·clist
bid
 bade or bid,
 bid'den or bid,
 bid'ding
bid'da·ble
bi·det'
bi·en'ni·al
bi·en'ni·al·ly
bier
 (*coffin stand;* see beer)
bi'fo'cals
bi'fur·cate'
 ·cat'ed ·cat'ing
big
 big'ger big'gest
big'a·mist
big'a·mous
big'a·my
 ·mies
big'gish
big'heart'ed
big'horn'
big·no'ni·a
big'ot
big'ot·ed

big'ot·ry
 ·ries
bi'jou
 ·joux
bi·ki'ni
bi·la'bi·al
bi·lat'er·al
bilge
bi·lin'gual
bil'ious
bill'board'
bil'let
bil'let-doux'
 bil'lets-doux'
bill'fold'
bill'head'
bil'liards
bill'ing
bil'lings·gate'
bil'lion
bil'lion·aire'
bill of fare
bill of lad'ing
bill of sale
bil'low
bil'low·i·ness
bil'low·y
 ·i·er ·i·est
bil'ly
 ·lies
bi·man'u·al
bi·man'u·al·ly
bi'me·tal'lic
bi·met'al·lism
bi·month'ly
bin
 binned bin'ning
bi'na·ry
bind
 bound bind'ing
bind'er
bind'er·y
 ·ies
binge
bin'go
bin'na·cle
bin·oc'u·lars
bi·no'mi·al
bi·no'mi·al·ly
bi'o·as'tro-
 nau'tics
bi'o·chem'ist
bi'o·chem'is·try
bi'o·cide'
bi'o·e·col'o·gy
bi·og'ra·pher
bi'o·graph'i·cal
bi'o·graph'i·cal·ly
bi·og'ra·phy
 ·phies
bi'o·log'i·cal
bi'o·log'i·cal·ly
bi·ol'o·gy
bi·on'ics
bi'o·phys'ics
bi'op'sy
 ·sies
bi'o·sat'el·lite'

bi·par'ti·san
bi·par'tite
bi'pro·pel'lant
bi·quar'ter·ly
bi·ra'cial
bird'bath'
bird'call'
bird'ie
bird'lime'
bird'man'
 ·men'
bird'seed'
bird's'-eye'
bi·ret'ta
birth
 (*being born;* see berth)
birth'day'
birth'mark'
birth'place'
birth'rate'
birth'right'
birth'stone'
bis'cuit
bi·sect'
bi·sec'tion
bi·sec'tor
bi·sex'u·al
bi·sex'u·al·ly
bish'op
bish'op·ric
bis'muth
bi'son
bisque
bis'tro
bitch
bite
 bit, bit'ten or
 bit, bit'ing
bit'ter
bit'tern
bit'ter·sweet'
bi·tu'men
bi·tu'mi·nous
bi·va'lent
bi'valve'
biv'ou·ac'
 ·acked' ·ack'ing
bi·week'ly
 ·lies
bi·year'ly
bi·zarre'
 (*odd;* see bazaar)
bi·zarre'ly
black'-a·moor'
black'-and-blue'
black'ball'
black'ber'ry
 ·ries
black'bird'
black'board'
black'en
black'face'
black'guard
black'head'
black'heart'ed
black'jack'
black'list'

black'mail'
black'out'
black'smith'
black'top'
· topped'
· top'ping
blad'der
blam'a · ble *or*
blame'a · ble
blame
blamed blam'ing
blame'wor'thy
blanc · mange'
blan'dish
blan'ket
blare
blared blar'ing
blar'ney
bla · sé'
blas · pheme'
· phemed'
· phem'ing
blas'phe · mous
blas'phe · my
· mies
blast'off' *or*
blast'-off'
bla'tan · cy
· cies
bla'tant
blaze
blazed blaz'ing
blaz'er
bla'zon
bleach'ers
bleak'ly
blear'i · ness
blear'y
· i · er · i · est
blear'y-eyed'
bleed
bled bleed'ing
blem'ish
blend
blend'ed *or* blent
blend'ing
blend'er
bless
blessed *or* blest
bless'ing
bless'ed · ness
blight
blind'fold'
blintz
bliss'ful
bliss'ful · ly
blis'ter
blithe
blithe'some
blitz'krieg'
bliz'zard
bloat'ed
bloc
(*group*)
block
(*solid piece*)
block · ade'
· ad'ed · ad'ing

block'bust'ing
block'head'
block'house'
blond *or* blonde
blood bank
blood count
blood'cur'dling
blood'hound'
blood'i · ness
blood'i · ly
blood'less
blood'let'ting
blood'mo · bile'
blood pressure
blood'shed'
blood'shot'
blood'stained'
blood'stream'
blood test
blood'thirst'y
blood vessel
blood'y
· i · er · i · est
· ied · y · ing
Bloody Mary
blos'som
blot
blot'ted blot'ting
blotch'y
· i · er · i · est
blot'ter
blouse
bloused
blous'ing
blous'on
blow
blew blown
blow'ing
blow'gun'
blow'hole'
blow'out'
blow'pipe'
blow'torch'
blow'up'
blow'y
· i · er · i · est
blowz'y
· i · er · i · est
blub'ber
blu'cher
bludg'eon
blue
blued, blu'ing *or*
blue'ing
blue'ber'ry
· ries
blue'bird'
blue'-blood'ed
blue book
blue'-chip'
blue'-col'lar
blue'fish'
blue'grass'
blue jay
blue law
blue'-pen'cil
· ciled *or* · cilled
· cil · ing *or* · cil · ling

blue'print'
blue'stock'ing
bluff'er
blu'ing *or*
blue'ing
blu'ish *or*
blue'ish
blun'der
blun'der · buss'
blunt'ly
blur
blurred blur'ring
blur'ri · ness
blur'ry
· ri · er · ri · est
blus'ter
blus'ter · y
bo'a
boar
(*hog;* see bore)
board'er
board foot
board feet
board'ing · house'
boarding school
board'walk'
boast'ful
boast'ful · ly
boat'house'
boat'ing
boat'load'
boat'man
· men
boat'swain
bob'bin
bob'ble
· bled · bling
bob'o · link'
bob'sled'
· sled'ded
· sled'ding
bob'white'
bode
bod'ed bod'ing
bod'ice
bod'ied
bod'i · ly
bod'kin
bod'y
· ies
bod'y · guard'
bo'gey
· geys
· geyed · gey · ing
(*golf term*)
bog'gy
· gi · er · gi · est
(*like a bog*)
bo'gus
bo'gy
· gies
(*spirit*)
boil'ing
bois'ter · ous
bold'face'
bold'faced'
bo · le'ro
· ros

boll
(*pod;* see bowl)
boll weevil
boll'worm'
bo · lo'gna
bol'ster
bom · bard'
bom'bar · dier'
bom'bast
bom · bas'tic
bom · bas'ti · cal · ly
bomb'proof'
bomb'shell'
bomb'sight'
(*spoils;* see
bootee)
bo'na fi'de
bo · nan'za
bon'bon'
bond'age
bonds'man
· men
bone'-dry'
bon'fire'
bon'go
· gos
bon'i · ness
bon' mot'
bons' mots'
bon'net
bon'ny
· ni · er · ni · est
bon · sai'
bo'nus
bon' vi · vant'
bons' vi · vants'
bon' voy · age'
bon'y
· i · er · i · est
boo'by
· bies
boo'hoo'
· hoos'
· hooed' · hoo'ing
book'bind'er
book'case'
book club
book'end'
book'ish
book'keep'er
book'keep'ing
book'let
book'mak'er
book'mark'
book'mo · bile'
book'plate'
book'rack'
book'sell'er
book'shelf'
· shelves'
book'stack'
book'stall'
book'stand'
book'store'
book'worm'
boom'er · ang'
boom'let
boon'docks'
boon'dog'gle
· gled · gling

boor'ish
boost'er
boot'black'
boot'ee
(*baby's shoe;* see
booty)
boot'leg'
· legged'
· leg'ging
boot'leg'ger
boot'strap'
boo'ty
· ties
(*spoils;* see
bootee)
bo'rax
bor'der
bor'der · line'
bore
(*dull person;*
see boar)
bore
bored bor'ing
bore'dom
born
(*brought into
life*)
borne
(*participle of
bear*)
bor'ough
(*town;* see burro,
burrow)
bor'row
borsch *or* borsht
bos'om
boss'i · ness
boss'y
· i · er · i · est
bo · tan'i · cal
bot'a · nist
bot'a · ny
botch
both'er · some
bot'tle
· tled · tling
bot'tle · neck'
bot'tle · nose'
bot'tom
bot'u · lism
bou · clé' *or*
bou · cle'
bou'doir
bouf · fant'
bough
(*tree branch;*
see bow)
bought
bouil'la · baisse'
bouil'lon
(*broth;* see
bullion)
boul'der
boul'e · vard'
bounce
bounced
bounc'ing
bounc'er

bound'a · ry
· ries
bound'en
bound'less
boun'te · ous
boun'ti · ful
boun'ti · ful · ly
boun'ty
· ties
bou · quet'
bour'bon
bour · geois'
bour'geoi · sie'
bourse
bou · tique'
bou'ton · niere'
bo'vine
bow
(*curve;* see beau)
bow
(*of a ship;* see
bough)
bowd'ler · ize'
· ized' · iz'ing
bow'el
bow'er
Bow'er · y
bow'ie knife
bow'knot'
bowl
(*dish;* see boll)
bow'leg'ged
bow'line
bowl'ing
bow'sprit'
bow'string'
bow tie
box'car'
box'er
box office
box'wood'
boy
(*child;* see buoy)
boy'cott
boy'friend'
boy'hood'
boy'ish
boy'sen · ber'ry
· ries
brace
braced brac'ing
brace'let
brack'et
brack'ish
brad'awl'
brag
bragged
brag'ging
brag · ga · do'ci · o'
brag'gart
Brah'ma
Brah'man · ism
braid
Braille
brain'child'
brain'i · ness
brain'pow'er
brain'storm'

brain'wash'
brain wave
brain'y
· i · er · i · est
braise
  braised brais'ing
  (*cook;* see braze)
brake
  braked brak'ing
  (*stop;* see break)
brake'man
  · men
bram'ble
branch'ing
bran'dish
brand'-new'
bran'dy
  · dies
  · died · dy · ing
bras'sard
brass'ie *n.*
bras · siere'
brass'i · ness
brass'ware'
brass'-wind' *adj.*
brass winds
brass'y *adj.*
  · i · er · i · est
braun'schwei'ger
bra · va'do
brave
  braved brav'ing
brave'ly
brav'er · y
bra'vo
  · vos
brawl
brawn'y
  · i · er · i · est
braze
  brazed braz'ing
  (*solder;* see
  braise)
bra'zen
bra'zen · ness
bra'zen · faced'
bra'zier
Bra · zil'
bra · zil'wood'
breach
  (*a gap;* see
  breech)
bread'bas'ket
bread'board'
bread'box'
breadth
  (*width;* see
  breath)
breadth'ways'
bread'win'ner
break
  broke bro'ken
  break'ing
  (*smash;* see
  brake)
break'a · ble
break'age
break'down'

break'fast
break'front'
break'neck'
break'out'
break'through'
break'up'
break'wa'ter
breast'bone'
breast'-feed'
  -fed' -feed'ing
breast stroke
breast'work'
breath
  (*air;* see breadth)
breath'a · lyz'er
breathe
breathed
breath'ing
breath'er
breath'less
breath'tak'ing
breech
  (*rear;* see
  breach)
breech'cloth'
breech'es
breech'-load'ing
breed
  bred breed'ing
breez'i · ly
breez'i · ness
breeze'way'
breez'y
  · i · er · i · est
breth'ren
bre'vi · ar'y
  · ies
brev'i · ty
brew'er · y
  · ies
brib'a · ble
bribe
  bribed brib'ing
brib'er · y
  · ies
bric'-a-brac'
brick'bat'
brick'lay'ing
brick'work'
brick'yard'
brid'al
  (*wedding;* see
  bridle)
bride'groom'
brides'maid'
bridge
  bridged
  bridg'ing
bridge'a · ble
bridge'head'
bridge'work'
bri'dle
  (*harness;* see
  bridal)
brief'case'
bri'er *or* bri'ar
bri · gade'
brig'a · dier'

brig'and
brig'an · tine'
bright'en
bril'liance
bril'liant
bril'lian · tine'
brim
brimmed
brim'ming
brim'ful'
brim'stone'
brin'dled
brine
  brined brin'ing
bring
  brought
  bring'ing
brin'i · ness
brink'man · ship'
brin'y
  · i · er · i · est
bri · oche'
bri · quette'
  or · quet'
bris'ket
brisk'ly
bris'tle
  · tled · tling
bris'tli · ness
bris'tly
  · tli · er · tli · est
Bris'tol board
Brit'ain
  (*place*)
Brit'i · cism
Brit'on
  (*person*)
brit'tle
brit'tle · ly *or*
  brit'tly
broach
  (*open;* see
  brooch)
broad'ax' *or* · axe'
broad'cast'
  · cast' *or* · cast'ed
  · cast'ing
broad'cloth'
broad'leaf'
broad'-leaved'
broad'loom'
broad'-mind'ed
broad'side'
broad'sword'
bro · cade'
  · cad'ed · cad'ing
broc'co · li
bro · chette'
bro · chure'
bro'gan
brogue
broil'er
bro'ken-down'
bro'ken · heart'ed
bro'ker
bro'ker · age
bro'mide
bro · mid'ic

bro'mine
bro'mo selt'zer
bron'chi · al
bron · chi'tis
bron'chus
  · chi
bron'co
  · cos
bron'to · sau'rus
bronze
  bronzed
  bronz'ing
brooch
  (*pin;* see broach)
brood'i · ness
broom'stick'
broth'el
broth'er-in-law'
  broth'ers-in-law'
brougham
brought
brou'ha · ha'
brow'beat'
  · beat' · beat'en
  · beat'ing
brown'ie
brown'out'
brown'stone'
browse
  browsed
  brows'ing
bruise
  bruised bruis'ing
bruis'er
bru · net' *or*
  bru · nette'
brush'wood'
brush'work'
brusque
brusque'ly
brusque'ness
Brus'sels sprouts
bru'tal
bru · tal'i · ty
  · ties
bru'tal · ize'
  · ized' · iz'ing
brut'ish
bub'ble
  · bled · bling
bub'bler
bub'ble-top'
bub'bly
bu · bon'ic
buc'ca · neer'
buck'board'
buck'et · ful'
  · fuls'
bucket seat
buck'le
  · led · ling
buck'-pass'er
buck'ram
buck'saw'
buck'shot'
buck'skin'
buck'tooth'
  · teeth'

buck'toothed'
buck'wheat'
bu · col'ic
bud
  bud'ded bud'ding
Bud'dha
Bud'dhism
budge
  budged budg'ing
budg'et
budg'et · ar'y
buf'fa · lo'
  · loes' *or* · los'
buff'er
buf'fet
buf · foon'er · y
bug'bear'
bug'gy
  · gies
  · gi · er · gi · est
bu'gle
  · gled · gling
build
  built build'ing
build'up' *or*
  build'-up'
built'-in'
built'-up'
bul'bar
bul'bous
bulge
  bulged bulg'ing
bulg'i · ness
bulk'i · ness
bulk'y
  · i · er · i · est
bull'dog'
bull'doze'
  · dozed' · doz'ing
bull'doz'er
bul'let
bul'le · tin
bul'let · proof'
bull'fight'er
bull'frog'
bull'head'ed
bull'horn'
bul'lion
  (*gold;* see
  bouillon)
bull'ish
bull'ock
bull'pen'
bull's'-eye'
bull'whip'
bul'ly
  · lies
  · lied · ly · ing
bul'rush'
bul'wark
bum'ble · bee'
bum'bling
bump'er
bump'kin
bump'tious
bump'y
  · i · er · i · est
bun'combe

bun'dle
  · dled · dling
bun'ga · low'
bung'hole'
bun'gle
  · gled · gling
bun'ion
bunk'er
bun'ting
Bun'sen burner
buoy
  (*marker;* see boy)
buoy'an · cy
buoy'ant
bur'ble
  · bled · bling
bur'den · some
bu'reau
  · reaus *or* · reaux
bu · reau'cra · cy
  · cies
bu'reau · crat'
bu'reau · crat'ic
bu'reau · crat'i · cal · ly
bu · rette' *or* · ret'
bur'geon
bur'glar
bur'gla · rize'
  · rized' · riz'ing
bur'gla · ry
  · ries
Bur'gun · dy
bur'i · al
bur'lap
bur · lesque'
  · lesqued'
  · lesqu'ing
bur'ley
  (*tobacco*)
bur'li · ness
bur'ly
  · li · er · li · est
  (*muscular*)
burn
  burned *or* burnt
burn'ing
burn'a · ble
bur'nish
bur · noose'
burn'out'
bur'ro
  · ros
  (*donkey;* see
  burrow, borough)
bur'row
  (*hole;* see burro,
  borough)
bur'sa
  · sae *or* · sas
bur'sar
bur · si'tis
burst
  burst burst'ing
bur'y
  · ied · y · ing
  (*cover;* see
  berry)

bus
bus'es or bus'ses
bused or bussed
bus'ing or bus'sing
(motor coach; see buss)
bus'boy'
bus'by
·bies
bush'el·bas'ket
bush'ing
bush'man
·men
bush'rang·er
bush'whack'er
bush'y
·i·er·i·est
bus'i·ly
busi'ness
busi'ness·like'
busi'ness·man'
·men'
busi'ness·wom'an
·wom·en
bus'kin
bus'man
·men
buss
(kiss; see bus)
bus'tle
·tled·tling
bus'y
·i·er·i·est
·ied·y·ing
bus'y·bod'y
·ies
bus'y·ness
butch'er·y
but'ler
butte
but'ter·fat'
but'ter·fin'gers
but'ter·fly'
·flies'
but'ter·milk'
but'ter·nut'
but'ter·scotch'
but'ter·y
but'tocks
but'ton-down'
but'ton·hole'
·holed·hol'ing
but'tress
bux'om
buy
bought buy'ing
buz'zard
buz'zer
by'gone'
by'law'
by'line'
by'pass'
by'path'
by'play'
by'prod'uct or
by'-prod·uct
by'road'
by'stand'er

by'way'
by'word'

C

ca·bal'
·balled'·bal'ling
cab'a·lism
ca'bal·le'ro
·ros
ca·ba'na
cab'a·ret'
cab'bage
cab'driv'er
cab'in
cab'i·net
cab'i·net·mak'er
cab'i·net·work'
ca'ble
·bled·bling
ca'ble·gram'
ca·boose'
cab'ri·o·let'
cab'stand'
ca·ca'o
cac'ci·a·to're
cache
cached cach'ing
ca·chet'
cach'in·nate'
·nat'ed·nat'ing
cach'in·na'tion
cack'le
·led·ling
ca·cog'ra·phy
ca·coph'o·nous
ca·coph'o·ny
cac'tus
·tus·es or·ti
ca·dav'er
ca·dav'er·ous
cad'die or·dy
·dies
·died·dy·ing
(in golf)
cad'dish
cad'dy
·dies
(tea box)
ca'dence
ca·den'za
ca·det'
cad'mi·um
ca'dre
ca·du'ce·us
·ce·i
Cae·sar'e·an
cae·su'ra
·ras or·rae
ca·fé' or ca·fe'
caf'e·te'ri·a
caf'fe·ine or·in
cage
caged cag'ing
ca'gey or ca'gy
·gi·er·gi·est

ca'gi·ly
ca'gi·ness
cais'son
cai'tiff
ca·jole'
·joled'·jol'ing
ca·jole'ment
ca·jol'er·y
cake
caked cak'ing
cal'a·bash'
ca·lam'i·tous
ca·lam'i·ty
·ties
cal·car'e·ous
cal'ci·fi·ca'tion
cal'ci·fy'
·fied'·fy'ing
cal'ci·mine'
·mined'·min'ing
cal'ci·um
cal'cu·la·ble
cal'cu·late'
·lat'ed·lat'ing
cal'cu·la'tion
cal'cu·la'tor
cal'cu·lus
·li or·lus·es
cal'dron
cal'en·dar
(table of dates)
cal'en·der
(roller; see colander)
cal'ends
ca·les'cent
calf
calves
calf'skin'
cal'i·ber or·bre
cal'i·brate'
·brat'ed·brat'ing
cal'i·bra'tion
cal'i·co'
·coes' or·cos'
Cal'i·for'ni·a
cal'i·pers
ca'liph
cal'is·then'ics
calk
call'board'
cal·lig'ra·phy
cal'lous adj.
cal'low
call'-up'
cal'lus n.
·lus·es
calm'ly
ca·lor'ic
cal'o·rie or·ry
·ries
cal'o·rim'e·ter
cal'u·met'
ca·lum'ni·ate'
·at'ed·at'ing
ca·lum'ni·ous
cal'um·ny
·nies

Cal'va·ry
(Biblical place; see cavalry)
calve
calved calv'ing
Cal'vin·ism
ca·lyp'so
ca'lyx
ca'lyx·es or ca'ly·ces'
ca·ma·ra'de·rie
cam'ber
cam'bric
Cam'bridge
cam'el
ca·mel'li·a
Cam'em·bert'
cam'e·o'
·os'
cam'er·a
cam'er·a·man'
·men'
cam'er·a-shy'
cam'i·sole'
cam'o·mile'
cam'ou·flage'
·flaged'·flag'ing
cam·paign'
cam·pa·ni'le
·les or·li
camp'er
camp'fire'
camp'ground'
cam'phor
cam'phor·ate'
·at'ed·at'ing
camp'o·ree'
camp'site'
camp'stool'
cam'pus
cam'shaft'
can
canned can'ning
Ca'naan
Can'a·da
Ca·na'di·an
ca·naille'
ca·nal'
ca·nal'boat'
ca·nal'ize'
·ized·iz'ing
ca'na·pé'
(food; see canopy)
ca·nard'
ca·nar'y
·ies
ca·nas'ta
can'can'
can'cel
·celed or·celled
·cel·ing or·cel·ling
can'cel·la'tion
can'cer
can'cer·ous
can'de·la'bra
·bras

can'de·la'brum
·bra or·brums
can·des'cence
can·des'cent
can'did
(frank; see candied)
can'di·da·cy
·cies
can'di·date'
can'died
(sugared; see candid)
can'dle·light'
candle power
can'dle·stick'
can'dle·wick'
can'dor
can'dy
·dies
·died·dy·ing
can'dy-striped'
cane
caned can'ing
ca'nine
can'is·ter
can'ker
can'na·bis
can'ner·y
·ies
can'ni·bal
can'ni·bal·ize'
·ized'·iz'ing
can'ni·ly
can'ni·ness
can'non
(gun; see canon, canyon)
can'non·ade'
·ad'ed·ad'ing
can'not
can'ny
·ni·er·ni·est
ca·noe'
·noed'·noe'ing
can'on
(law; see cannon, canyon)
ca·non'i·cal
can'on·ize'
·ized'·iz'ing
can'o·py
·pies
(hood; see canapé)
can·ta'bi·le'
can'ta·loupe' or·loup'
can·tan'ker·ous
can·ta'ta
can·teen'
can'ter
(gallop; see cantor)
can'ti·cle
can'ti·le'ver
can'to
·tos

can'ton
can·ton'ment
can'tor
(singer; see canter)
can'vas
(cloth)
can'vass
(to solicit)
can'yon or ca'ñon
(valley; see cannon, canon)
caou·tchouc'
cap
capped cap'ping
ca·pa·bil'i·ty
·ties
ca'pa·ble
ca'pa·bly
ca·pa'cious
ca·pac'i·tance
ca·pac'i·tor
ca·pac'i·ty
·ties
ca'per
cap'ful'
·fuls'
cap'il·lar'y
·ies
cap'i·tal
(city; chief; see capitol)
cap'i·tal·ism
cap'i·tal·is'tic
cap'i·tal·is'ti·cal·ly
cap'i·tal·i·za'tion
cap'i·tal·ize'
·ized'·iz'ing
cap'i·tal·ly
cap'i·ta'tion
cap'i·tol
(building; see capital)
ca·pit'u·late'
·lat'ed·lat'ing
ca·pit'u·la'tion
ca'pon
ca·price'
ca·pri'cious
cap'ri·ole'
·oled'·ol'ing
cap'size
·sized·siz·ing
cap'stan
cap'stone'
cap'su·lar
cap'sule
·suled·sul·ing
cap'sul·ize'
·ized'·iz'ing
cap'tain
cap'tain·cy
·cies
cap'tion
cap'tious
cap'ti·vate'
·vat'ed·vat'ing

cap'tive
cap·tiv'i·ty
·ties
cap'tor
cap'ture
·tured ·tur·ing
car'a·cul
ca·rafe'
car'a·mel
car'a·mel·ize'
·ized' ·iz'ing
car'a·pace'
car'at
(weight; see
caret, carrot)
car'a·van'
car'a·van'sa·ry
·ries
car'a·way'
car'bide
car'bine
car'bo·hy'drate
car·bol'ic
car'bon
car'bo·na'ceous
car'bon·ate'
·at'ed ·at'ing
car'bon·a'tion
car'bon-date'
-dat'ed -dat'ing
car'bon·if'er·ous
car'bon·ize'
·ized' ·iz'ing
car'bo·run'dum
car'bun·cle
car'bu·re'tion
car'bu·re'tor
car'cass
car·cin'o·gen
car·ci·no'ma
car'da·mom
card'board'
card'-car'ry·ing
car'di·ac'
car'di·gan
car'di·nal
car'di·o·gram'
car'di·o·graph'
card'sharp'
care
cared car'ing
ca·reen'
ca·reer'
care'free'
care'ful
care'ful·ly
care'less
ca·ress'
ca·res'sive·ly
car'et
(insert mark; see
carat, carrot)
care'tak'er
care'worn'
car'fare'
car'go
·goes or ·gos
car'hop'

Car'ib·be'an
car'i·bou'
car'i·ca·ture
·tured ·tur·ing
car'i·ca·tur·ist
car'ies
(decay; see
carries)
car'il·lon'
car'load'
car'man
·men
car'mine
car'nage
car'nal
car'nal·ly
car·na'tion
car·nel'ian
car'ni·val
car'ni·vore'
car·niv'o·rous
car'ol
oled or olled
·ol·ing or ·ol·ling
car'ol·er or ·ol·ler
Car'o·li'nas
Car'o·lin'i·an
car'om
car'o·tene' or ·tin
ca·rot'id
ca·rous'al
ca·rouse'
·roused'
·rous'ing
car'ou·sel'
car'pen·ter
car'pen·try
car'pet
car'pet·bag'ger
car'pet·ing
carp'ing
car'port'
car'riage
car'ri·er
car'ries
(form of carry;
see caries)
car'ri·on
car'rot
(vegetable; see
carat, caret)
car'rou·sel'
car'ry
·ried ·ry·ing
car'ry·all'
car'ry·out'
car'ry-o'ver
car'sick'
cart'age
carte' blanche'
cartes' blanches'
car·tel'
car'ti·lage
car'ti·lag'i·nous
car'to·gram'
car·tog'ra·phy
car'ton
car·toon'

car·toon'ist
car'tridge
carve
carved carv'ing
car'wash'
car'y·at'id
·ids or -i·des'
ca·sa'ba
or cas·sa'ba
cas'bah
cas·cade'
·cad'ed ·cad'ing
cas·car'a
case
cased cas'ing
case'book'
case'hard'ened
ca'se·in
case'load'
case'mate'
case'ment
case'work'er
cash'-and-car'ry
cash'book'
cash'ew
cash·ier'
cash'mere
cas'ing
ca·si'no
·nos
(gambling room)
cas'ket
cas·sa'va
cas'se·role'
cas·sette'
cas·si'no
(card game)
cas'sock
cas'so·war'y
·war'ies
cast
cast cast'ing
cas'ta·nets'
cast'a·way'
caste
(social class)
cas'tel·lat'ed
cast'er
cas'ti·gate'
·gat'ed ·gat'ing
cast'-i'ron
cas'tle
cast'off'
cas'tor
cas'trate
·trat·ed ·trat·ing
cas·tra'tion
cas'u·al
cas'u·al·ly
cas'u·al·ty
·ties
cas'u·ist
cas'u·is'tic
cas'u·ist·ry
cat'a·clysm
cat'a·comb'
cat'a·falque'
cat'a·lep'sy

cat'a·lep'tic
cat'a·lo'
·loes' or ·los'
cat'a·log' or
·logue'
·loged' or
·logued'
·log'ing or
·logu'ing
cat'a·log'er or
·logu'er
ca·tal'y·sis
·ses'
cat'a·lyst
cat'a·ma·ran'
cat'a·pult'
cat'a·ract'
ca·tarrh'
ca·tarrh'al
ca·tas'tro·phe
cat'a·stroph'ic
cat'a·stroph'i·
cal·ly
cat'a·to'ni·a
cat'call'
catch
caught catch'ing
catch'all'
catch'er
catch'ing
catch'pen'ny
·nies
catch'up
catch'word'
catch'y
·i·er ·i·est
cat'e·chism
cat'e·chize'
·chized' ·chiz'ing
cat'e·chu'men
cat'e·gor'i·cal
cat'e·go·rize'
·rized' ·riz'ing
cat'e·go'ry
·ries
ca'ter
cat'er-cor'nered
ca'ter·er
cat'er·pil'lar
cat'er·waul'
cat'gut'
ca·thar'sis
ca·thar'tic
ca·the'dral
cath'e·ter
cath'e·ter·ize'
·ized' ·iz'ing
cath'ode
cath'o·lic
Ca·thol'i·cism
cath'o·lic'i·ty
ca·thol'i·cize'
·cized' ·ciz'ing
cat'i'on
cat'nap'
napped'
nap'ping
cat'nip

cat'-o'-nine'-tails'
cat's'-eye'
Cats'kill'
cat's'-paw'
cat'sup
cat'tail'
cat'ti·ly
cat'ti·ness
cat'tle
cat'tle·man
·men
cat'ty
·ti·er ·ti·est
cat'ty-cor'nered
cat'walk'
Cau·ca'sian
Cau'ca·soid'
cau'cus
cau'dal
cau'date
caul'dron
cau'li·flow'er
caulk
caus'a·ble
caus'al
caus'al·ly
cau·sal'i·ty
·ties
cau·sa'tion
caus'a·tive
cause
caused caus'ing
cau'se·rie'
cause'way'
caus'tic
cau'ter·i·za'tion
cau'ter·ize'
·ized' ·iz'ing
cau'ter·y
·ies
cau'tion
cau'tion·ar'y
cau'tious
cav'al·cade'
cav'a·lier'
cav'al·ry
·ries
(troops; see
Calvary)
cav'al·ry·man
·men
cave
caved cav'ing
ca've·at' emp'tor
cave'-in'
cav'ern
cav'ern·ous
cav'i·ar'
cav'il
·iled or ·illed
·il·ing or ·il·ling
cav'i·ty
·ties
ca·vort'
cay·enne'
cease
ceased ceas'ing
cease'-fire'

cease'less
ce'dar
cede
ced'ed ced'ing
ce·dil'la
ceil'ing
ceil·om'e·ter
cel'e·brant
cel'e·brate'
·brat'ed ·brat'ing
cel'e·bra'tion
cel'e·bra'tor
ce·leb'ri·ty
·ties
ce·ler'i·ty
cel'er·y
ce·les'ta
ce·les'tial
cel'i·ba·cy
cel'i·bate
cel'lar
cel'lar·et'
cel'lar·way'
cel'list
or 'cel'list
cell'-like'
cel'lo
or 'cel'lo
·los or ·li
cel'lo·phane'
cel'lu·lar
cel'lu·loid'
cel'lu·lose'
Cel'o·tex'
Cel'si·us
ce·ment'
cem'e·ter'y
·ies
cen'o·bite'
Ce'no·zo'ic
cen'ser
(incense box)
cen'sor
(prohibiter)
cen'sored
cen·so'ri·al
cen·so'ri·ous
cen'sor·ship'
cen'sur·a·ble
cen'sure
·sured ·sur·ing
(blame)
cen'sus
cen'taur
cen·ta'vo
cen'te·nar'i·an
cen'te·nar'y
cen·ten'ni·al
cen·ten'ni·al·ly
cen'ter
cen'ter·board'
cen'tered
cen'ter·piece'
cen·tes'i·mal
cen·tes'i·mal·ly
cen'ti·grade'
cen'ti·gram'
cen'ti·li'ter

cen'time
cen'ti·me'ter
cen'ti·pede'
cen'tral
cen'tral·i·za'tion
cen'tral·ize'
· ized' · iz'ing
cen·trif'u·gal
cen'tri·fuge'
cen·trip'e·tal
cen'trist
cen'tu·ple
cen·tu'ri·on
cen'tu·ry
· ries
ce·phal'ic
ce·ram'ic
ce·ram'ist or
ce·ram'i·cist
ce're·al
(grain; see serial)
cer'e·bel'lum
· lums or · la
cer'e·bral
cer·e'bral·ly
cer'e·brate'
· brat'ed · brat'ing
cer'e·bro·spi'nal
cer'e·brum
· brums or · bra
cer'e·ment
cer'e·mo'ni·al
cer'e·mo'ni·al·ly
cer'e·mo'ni·ous
cer'e·mo'ny
· nies
ce·rise'
cer'tain
cer'tain·ly
cer'tain·ty
· ties
cer'ti·fi'a·ble
cer'ti·fi'a·bly
cer·tif'i·cate
cer'ti·fi·ca'tion
cer'ti·fy'
· fied' · fy'ing
cer'ti·o·ra'ri
cer'ti·tude'
ce·ru'le·an
ce·ru'men
cer'vi·cal
cer'vix
vi·ces' or · vix·es
ces·sa'tion
ces'sion
(a giving up; see
session)
cess'pool'
chafe
chafed chaf'ing
(rub)
chaff
(husks of grain)
chaf'finch
cha·grin'
· grined'
· grin'ing

chain'man
· men
chain'-re·act'
chain'-smoke'
chair'lift'
chair'man
· men
chair'wom·an
· wom·en
chaise longue
chaise or chaises
longues
chaise lounge
chaise lounges
chal·ced'o·ny
cha·let'
chal'ice
chalk'board'
chalk'i·ness
chalk'y
· i·er · i·est
chal'lenge
lenged · leng·ing
chal'leng·er
chal'lis
cham'ber
cham'ber·lain
cham'ber·maid'
cham'bray
cha·me'le·on
cham'fer
cham'ois
· ois
· oised · ois·ing
cham'o·mile'
cham·pagne'
(wine)
cham·paign'
(open field)
cham'pi·on
chance
chanced
chanc'ing
chan'cel
chan'cel·ler·y
· ies
chan'cel·lor
chance'-med'ley
chan'cer·y
· ies
chan'cre
chan'croid
chanc'y
· i·er · i·est
chan'de·lier'
chan·delle'
chan'dler·y
· ies
Cha·nel'
change
changed
chang'ing
change'a·bil'i·ty
change'a·ble
change'a·bly
change'ful
change'ful·ly
change'less

change'ling
change'o'ver
change'-up'
chan'nel
· neled or · nelled
· nel·ing or
· nel·ling
chan'nel·ize'
· ized' · iz'ing
chan·teuse'
chan'tey or · ty
· teys or · ties
Cha'nu·kah
cha'os
cha·ot'ic
cha·ot'i·cal·ly
chap
chapped
chap'ping
chap·ar·ral'
cha·peau'
· peaus' or
· peaux'
chap'el
chap'er·on'
or · one'
· oned' · on'ing
chap'fall'en
chap'lain
chap'let
chap'ter
char
charred
char'ring
char'ac·ter
char'ac·ter·is'tic
char'ac·ter·is'ti·
cal·ly
char'ac·ter·i·
za'tion
char'ac·ter·ize'
· ized' · iz'ing
cha·rade'
char'coal'
chare
chared char'ing
charge
charged
charg'ing
charge'a·ble
charge plate or
charge'-a-plate'
charg'er
char'i·ly
char'i·ness
char'i·ot
char'i·ot·eer'
cha·ris'ma
char'is·mat'ic
char'i·ta·ble
char'i·ty
· ties
cha·riv'a·ri'
char'la·tan
charm'ing
char'nel
char'ry
· ri·er · ri·est

char'ter
char·treuse'
char'wom·an
char'y
· i·er · i·est
chase
chased chas'ing
chasm
chas·sé'
· séd' · sé'ing
chas'sis
· sis
chas·ten
chas·tise'
· tised' · tis'ing
chas·tise'ment
chas'ti·ty
chas'u·ble
chat
chat'ted
chat'ting
châ·teau'
· teaux' or · teaus'
chat'e·laine'
cha·toy'ant
chat'tel
chat'ty
· ti·er · ti·est
Chau'cer
chauf'fer
(stove)
chauf'feur
(driver)
chau·tau'qua
chau'vin·ism
chau'vin·ist
chau'vin·is'tic
chau'vin·is'ti·
cal·ly
cheap
(low in cost;
see cheep)
cheap'en
cheat'er
check'book'
check'er·board'
check'ered
check'list' or
check list
check'mate'
· mat'ed · mat'ing
check'off'
check'out' or
check'-out'
check'point'
check'rein'
check'room'
check'up'
Ched'dar
cheek'bone'
cheek'i·ly
cheek'i·ness
cheek'y
· i·er · i·est
cheep
(sound; see cheap)
cheer'ful

cheer'ful·ly
cheer'i·ly
cheer'i·ness
cheer'lead'er
cheer'less
cheer'y
· i·er · i·est
cheese'burg'er
cheese'cake'
cheese'cloth'
chees'i·ness
chees'y
· i·er · i·est
chee'tah
chem'i·cal
che·mise'
chem'ist
chem'is·try
· tries
chem'ur·gy
che·nille'
cher'ish
Cher'o·kee'
che·root'
cher'ry
· ries
cher'ub
· ubs or · u·bim
che·ru'bic
che·ru'bi·cal·ly
cher'vil
chess'board'
chess'man'
ches'ter·field'
chest'nut
chev'i·ot
chev'ron
chew'y
· i·er · i·est
Chi·an'ti
chi·a'ro·scu'ro
· ros
chic
chic'quer
chic'quest
chi·can'er·y
chi'chi or chi'-chi
chick'en-heart'ed
chicken pox
chic'le
chic'o·ry
chide
chid'ed or chid,
chid'ed or chid
or chid'den,
chid'ing
chief'ly
chief'tain
chif·fon'
chif·fo·nier'
chig'ger
chi'gnon
chig'oe
· oes
Chi·hua'hua
chil'blain'
child
chil'dren

child'bear'ing
child'bed'
child'birth'
child'hood'
child'ish
child'like'
chil'i
· ies
chill'i·ness
chill'y
· i·er · i·est
chime
chimed chim'ing
chi·me'ra
chi·mer'i·cal
chim'ney
· neys
chim'pan·zee'
chin
chinned
chin'ning
chi'na·ware'
chin·chil'la
Chi·nese'
chi'no
chin'qua·pin
chintz
chip
chipped
chip'ping
chip'munk'
chi·rog'ra·phy
chi·rop'o·dist
chi·rop'o·dy
chi'ro·prac'tic
chi'ro·prac'tor
chir'rup
chis'el
· eled or · elled
· el·ing or · el·ling
chis'el·er or
chis'el·ler
chi'-square'
chit'chat'
chit'ter·lings
chiv'al·rous
chiv'al·ry
chlor'dane
chlo'ric
chlo'ride
chlo'ri·nate'
· nat'ed · nat'ing
chlo'ri·na'tion
chlo'rine
chlo'ro·form'
chlo'ro·phyll'
or · phyl'
chlo'rous
chlor·tet'ra·cy'·
cline
chock'a·block'
chock'-full'
choc'o·late
choice
choic'er choic'est
choir
(singers; see
quire)

choke
  choked chok'ing
chok'er
chol'er·a
chol'er·ic
cho·les'ter·ol'
choose
  chose cho'sen
choos'ing
chop
  chopped
  chop'ping
chop'house'
chop'pi·ness
chop'py
  ·pi·er ·pi·est
chop'sticks'
chop su'ey
cho'ral
  (of a chorus)
cho·rale' or ·ral'
  (hymn tune)
chord
  (music; see cord)
chore
cho·re'a
chor'e·og'ra·pher
chor'e·o·graph'ic
chor'e·o·graph'·
  i·cal·ly
chor'e·og'ra·phy
chor'is·ter
chor'tle
  ·tled ·tling
cho'rus
cho'sen
chow'der
chow mein
chrism
chris'ten
Chris'ten·dom
Chris'tian
Chris'ti·an'i·ty
Chris'tian·ize'
  ·ized' ·iz'ing
chris'tie or ·ty
Christ'like'
Christ'mas
Christ'mas·tide'
chro·mat'ic
chro'ma·tin
chrome
chro'mic
chro'mi·um
chro'mo·some'
chron'ic
chron'i·cle
  ·cled ·cling
chron'o·log'i·cal
chro·nol'o·gy
chro·nom'e·ter
chro·nom'e·try
chrys'a·lis
chrys·an'the·
  mum
chrys'o·lite'
chrys'o·prase'
chub'bi·ness

chub'by
  ·bi·er ·bi·est
chuck'-full'
chuck'hole'
chuck'le
  ·led ·ling
chug
  chugged chug'ging
chuk'ka boot
chuk'ker or ·kar
chum'mi·ness
chum'my
  ·mi·er ·mi·est
chunk'i·ness
chunk'y
  ·i·er ·i·est
church'go'er
church'man
church'wom'an
church'yard'
churl'ish
churn
chute
chut'ney
chyle
chyme
ci·bo'ri·um
  ·ri·a
ci·ca'da
  ·das or ·dae
cic'a·trix
  ci·cat'ri·ces
cic'e·ly
Cic'er·o'
ci'der
ci·gar'
cig'a·rette'
  or ·ret'
cig'a·ril'lo
  ·los
cil'i·a
  (sing. cil'i·um)
cil'i·ar'y
cin·cho'na
Cin'cin·nat'i
cinc'ture
  ·tured ·tur·ing
cin'der
cin'e·ma
cin'e·mat'o·
  graph'
cin'e·rar'i·um
  ·rar'i·a
cin'er·a'tor
cin'na·bar'
cin'na·mon
cinque'foil'
ci'pher
cir'ca
cir'cle
  ·cled ·cling
cir'clet
cir'cuit
cir·cu'i·tous
cir'cuit·ry
cir'cu·lar
cir'cu·lar·i·
  za'tion

cir'cu·lar·ize'
  ·ized' ·iz'ing
cir'cu·late'
  ·lat'ed ·lat'ing
cir'cu·la'tion
cir'cu·la·to'ry
cir'cum·cise'
  ·cised' ·cis'ing
cir'cum·ci'sion
cir·cum'fer·ence
cir'cum·flex'
cir'cum·lo·
  cu'tion
cir'cum·nav'i·
  gate'
  ·gat'ed ·gat'ing
cir'cum·po'lar
cir'cum·scribe'
  ·scribed' ·scrib'ing
cir'cum·
  scrip'tion
cir'cum·spect'
cir'cum·spec'tion
cir'cum·stance'
cir'cum·stan'tial
cir'cum·stan'ti·
  ate'
  ·at'ed ·at'ing
cir'cum·vent'
cir'cum·ven'tion
cir'cus
cir·rho'sis
cir'ro·cu'mu·lus
cir'ro·stra'tus
cir'rus
  ·ri
cis·al'pine
cis·at·lan'tic
cis'tern
cit'a·del
ci·ta'tion
cite
  cit'ed cit'ing
  (mention; see
  sight)
cit'i·fied'
cit'i·zen
cit'i·zen·ry
cit'i·zen·ship'
cit'rate
cit'ric
cit'ron
cit'ron·el'la
cit'rous adj.
cit'rus n.
cit'y
  ·ies
cit'y·scape'
cit'y·state'
civ'et
civ'ic
civ'il
ci·vil'ian
ci·vil'i·ty
  ·ties
civ'i·li·za'tion
civ'i·lize'
  ·lized' ·liz'ing

civ'il·ly
civ'vies
claim'ant
clair·voy'ance
clair·voy'ant
clam
  clammed
clam'ming
clam'bake'
clam'ber
clam'mi·ness
clam'my
  ·mi·er ·mi·est
clam'or
clam'or·ous
clan·des'tine
clan·des'tine·ly
clan'gor
clan'gor·ous
clan'nish
clans'man
clap
  clapped
  clap'ping
clap'board
clap'per
clap'trap'
claque
clar'et
clar'i·fi·ca'tion
clar'i·fi'er
clar'i·fy'
  ·fied ·fy'ing
clar'i·net'
clar'i·net'ist or
  clar'i·net'tist
clar'i·on
clar'i·ty
clas'sic
clas'si·cal
clas'si·cal·ly
clas'si·cism
clas'si·cist
clas'si·fi'a·ble
clas'si·fi·ca'tion
clas'si·fi'er
clas'si·fy'
  ·fied' ·fy'ing
class'mate'
class'room'
clat'ter
clause
claus'tro·
  pho'bi·a
clav'i·chord'
clav'i·cle
cla·vier'
clay'ey
clay'i·er
clay'i·est
clean'a·ble
clean'-cut'
clean'er
clean'hand'ed
clean'li·ly
clean'li·ness
clean'ly
  ·li·er ·li·est

clean'ness
cleanse
  cleansed
  cleans'ing
cleans'er
clean'shav'en
clean'up'
clear'ance
clear'-cut'
clear'eyed'
clear'head'ed
clear'ing·house'
clear'sight'ed
cleats
cleav'age
cleave
  cleaved or cleft
  or clove, cleaved
  or cleft or
  clo'ven,
  cleav'ing
  (to split)
cleave
  cleaved cleav'ing
  (to cling)
cleav'er
clem'en·cy
clem'ent
clere'sto'ry
  ·ries
cler'gy
  ·gies
cler'gy·man
  ·men
cler'ic
cler'i·cal
cler'i·cal·ly
cler'i·cal·ism
clev'er
clew
cli·ché'
click
cli'ent
cli'en·tele'
cliff'-dwell'ing
cliff'hang'er or
  cliff'-hang'er
cli·mac'ter·ic
cli·mac'tic
  (of a climax)
cli·mac'ti·cal·ly
cli'mate
cli·mat'ic
  (of climate)
cli·mat'i·cal·ly
cli'ma·tol'o·gy
cli'max
climb'er
clinch'er
cling
  clung cling'ing
clin'ic
clin'i·cal
cli·ni'cian
clink'er
cli·nom'e·ter
clip
  clipped clip'ping

clip'board'
clip'per
clique
cli'to·ris
clo·a'ca
  ·cae
cloak'room'
clob'ber
cloche
clock'wise'
clock'work'
clod'dish
clod'hop'per
clog
  clogged
clog'ging
cloi'son·né'
clois'ter
close
  closed clos'ing
close
  clos'er clos'est
closed'-end'
close'fist'ed
close'fit'ting
close'grained'
close'-hauled'
close'ly
close'mouthed'
clos'et
close'-up'
clo'sure
clot
  clot'ted clot'ting
cloth n.
clothe v.
  clothed or clad
cloth'ing
clothes'line'
clothes'pin'
clothes'press'
cloth'ier
cloth'ing
clo'ture
cloud'burst'
cloud'i·ness
cloud'y
  ·i·er ·i·est
clo'ver·leaf'
  ·leafs'
cloy'ing·ly
clown'ish
club
  clubbed
  club'bing
club'foot'
club'house'
clue
  clued clu'ing
clum'si·ly
clum'si·ness
clum'sy
  ·si·er ·si·est
clus'ter
clut'ter
coach'man
co·ad'ju·tor
co·ag'u·la·ble

co·ag'u·lant
co·ag'u·late'
· lat'ed · lat'ing
co·ag·u·la'tion
co·ag'u·la'tor
co'a·lesce'
· lesced' · lesc'ing
co'a·les'cence
co'a·les'cent
co'a·li'tion
coarse
(common; see
course)
coarse'grained'
coars'en
coarse'ness
coast'al
coast'er
coast guard
coast'land'
coast'line'
coat'ing
coat'tail'
co·au'thor
co·ax'i·al
coax'ing·ly
co'balt
cob'ble
· bled · bling
cob'bler
cob'ble·stone'
co'bel·lig'er·ent
co'bra
cob'web'
co·caine'
or ·cain'
coc'cus
coc'ci
coc'cyx
coc·cy'ges
cock'a·lo'rum
cock'boat'
cock'crow'
cock'er·el
cock'eyed'
cock'i·ly
cock'i·ness
cock'ney
· neys
cock'pit'
cock'roach'
cocks'comb'
cock'sure'
cock'tail'
co'coa
co'co·nut'
or co'coa·nut'
co·coon'
cod'dle
· dled · dling
code
cod'ed cod'ing
co'de·fend'ant
co'deine'
co'dex
· di·ces'
cod'fish'
codg'er

cod'i·cil
cod·i·fi·ca'tion
cod'i·fy'
· fied' · fy'ing
co'ed·u·ca'tion
co'ef·fi'cient
co·erce'
· erced' · erc'ing
co·er'cion
co·er'cive
co·e'val
co'ex·ist'ence
cof'fee·house'
cof'fee·pot'
cof'fer
cof'fer·dam'
cof'fin
co'gen·cy
co'gent
cog'i·tate'
· tat'ed · tat'ing
cog·i·ta'tion
co'gnac
cog'nate
cog·ni'tion
cog'ni·tive
cog'ni·zance
cog'ni·zant
cog·no'men
· no'mens or
· nom'i·na
cog'wheel'
co·hab'it
co·hab'i·ta'tion
co'heir'
co·here'
· hered' · her'ing
co·her'ence
co·her'ent
co·he'sion
co·he'sive·ness
co'hort
coif·fure'
coign
(position; see
coin, quoin)
coin
(metal money;
see coign, quoin)
coin'age
co'in·cide'
· cid'ed · cid'ing
co·in'ci·dence
co·in'ci·dent
co·in'ci·den'tal
co·in'ci·den'tal·ly
co·i'tion
co'i·tus
col'an·der
(draining pan;
see calender)
cold'blood'ed
cold'heart'ed
co'le·op'ter·ous
cole'slaw'
col'ic
col'ick·y
col'i·se'um

co·li'tis
col·lab'o·rate'
· rat'ed · rat'ing
col·lab'o·ra'tion
col·lab'o·ra'tor
col·lage'
col·lapse'
· lapsed' · laps'ing
col·laps'i·bil'i·ty
col·laps'i·ble
col'lar
col'lar·bone'
col·late'
· lat'ed · lat'ing
col·lat'er·al
col·lat'er·al·ly
col·la'tion
col·la'tor
col'league
col·lect'a·ble
or ·i·ble
col·lec'tion
col·lec'tive·ly
col·lec'tiv·ism
col·lec'tiv·is'tic
col·lec·tiv'i·ty
col·lec'tiv·ize'
· ized' · iz'ing
col·lec'tor
col'leen
col'lege
col·le'gi·al'i·ty
col·le'gi·an
col·le'giate
col·lide'
· lid'ed · lid'ing
col'lie
col'li·gate'
· gat'ed · gat'ing
col'li·mate'
· mat'ed · mat'ing
co·lin'e·ar
col·li'sion
col'lo·ca'tion
col·lo'di·on
col'loid
col·loi'dal
col·lo'qui·al
col·lo'qui·al·ism
col·lo'qui·um
· qui·a
col'lo·quy
· quies
col'lo·type'
col·lude'
· lud'ed · lud'ing
col·lu'sion
col·lu'sive
co·lo'cate'
· cat'ed · cat'ing
co'lo·ca'tion
co·logne'
co'lon
colo'nel
(officer; see
kernel)
co·lo'ni·al
col'o·nist

col'o·ni·za'tion
col'o·nize'
· nized' · niz'ing
col'on·nade'
col'o·ny
· nies
col'o·phon'
col'or
Col'o·rad'o
col'o·rant
col'or·a'tion
col'o·ra·tu'ra
col'or·bear'er
col'or·blind'
col'or·cast'
· cast' or cast'ed
· cast'ing
col'ored
col'or·fast'
col'or·ful
col'or·less
co·los'sal
Col'os·se'um
co·los'sus
· los'si or
· los'sus·es
colt'ish
Co·lum'bi·a
col'umn
co·lum'nar
col'um·nist
co'ma
(stupor; see
comma)
com'a·tose'
com·bat'
· bat'ed or
· bat'ted
· bat'ing or
· bat'ting
com'bat·ant
com·bat'ive
comb'er
com·bin'a·ble
com·bi·na'tion
com·bine'
· bined' · bin'ing
comb'ings
com·bus'ti·
bil'i·ty
com·bus'ti·ble
com·bus'ti·bly
com·bus'tion
com·bus'tor
come
came come
com'ing
come'back'
co·me'di·an
co·me'dic
co·me'di·enne'
come'down'
com'e·dy
· dies
come'li·ness
come'ly
· li·er · li·est
co·mes'ti·ble

com'et
come'up'pance
com'fit
com'fort
com'fort·a·ble
com'fort·a·bly
com'fort·er
com'ic
com'i·cal
com'i·cal·ly
com'i·ty
· ties
com'ma
(punctuation
mark; see coma)
com·mand'
com·man·dant'
com·man·deer'
com·mand'er
com·mand'ment
com·man'do
· dos or · does
com·mem'o·rate'
· rat'ed · rat'ing
com·mem'o·
ra'tion
com·mem'o·
ra'tive
com·mence'
· menced'
· menc'ing
com·mence'
ment
com·mend'
com·mend'a·ble
com·mend'a·bly
com·men·da'tion
com·mend'a·
to'ry
com·men'su·
ra·ble
com·men'su·
ra·bly
com·men'su·rate
com'ment
com'men·tar'y
· ies
com'men·tate'
· tat'ed · tat'ing
com'men·ta'tor
com'merce
com·mer'cial
com·mer'cial·ism
com·mer'cial·i·
za'tion
com·mer'cial·ize'
· ized' · iz'ing
com·min'gle
· gled · gling
com·mis'er·ate'
· at'ed ·at'ing
com·mis'er·
a'tion
com'mis·sar'
com·mis·sar'i·at
com'mis·sar'y
· ies
com·mis'sion

com·mis'sion·er
com·mit'
· mit'ted · mit'ting
com·mit'ment
com·mit'ta·ble
com·mit'tal
com·mit'tee
com·mit'tee·man
com·mode'
com·mo'di·ous
com·mod'i·ty
· ties
com'mo·dore'
com'mon·al·ty
· ties
com'mon·er
com'mon·ness
com'mon·place'
com'mon·weal'
com'mon·wealth'
com·mo'tion
com'mu·nal
com'mu·nal·ly
com'mu·nal·ism
com·mune' v.
· muned'
· mun'ing
com'mune n.
com·mu'ni·ca·ble
com·mu'ni·cant
com·mu'ni·cate'
· cat'ed · cat'ing
com·mu'ni·
ca'tion
com·mu'ni·
ca'tive
com·mu'ni·ca'tor
com·mun'ion
com·mu'ni·qué'
com'mu·nism
com'mu·nist
com'mu·nis'tic
com·mu·nis'ti·
cal·ly
com·mu'ni·ty
· ties
com'mu·nize'
· nized' · niz'ing
com·mut'a·ble
com'mu·tate'
· tat'ed · tat'ing
com·mu·ta'tion
com'mu·ta'tive
com·mu·ta'tor
com·mute'
· mut'ed
· mut'ing
com·mut'er
com·pact'
com·pan'ion
com·pan'ion·
a·ble
com·pa·ny
· nies
com·pa·ra·ble
com·pa·ra·bly
com·par'a·tive
com·par'a·tive·ly

com·pare'
·pared' ·par'ing
com·par'i·son
com·part'ment
com·part'men'·
tal·ize'
·ized' -iz'ing
com'pass
com·pas'sion
com·pas'sion·ate
com·pat'i·bil'i·ty
com·pat'i·ble
com·pat'i·bly
com·pa'tri·ot
com'peer
com·pel'
·pelled' ·pel'ling
com·pen'di·ous
com·pen'di·um
·ums or ·a
com·pen'sa·ble
com'pen·sate'
·sat'ed ·sat'ing
com'pen·sa'tion
com'pen·sa'tive
com·pen'sa·tor
com·pen'sa·to'ry
com·pete'
·pet'ed ·pet'ing
com'pe·tence
com'pe·ten·cy
com'pe·tent
com·pe·ti'tion
com·pet'i·tive
com·pet'i·tor
com·pi·la'tion
com·pile'
·piled' ·pil'ing
com·pil'er
com·pla'cence
com·pla'cen·cy
com·pla'cent
(smug; see
complaisant)
com·plain'
com·plain'ant
com·plaint'
com·plai'sance
com·plai'sant
(obliging; see
complacent)
com'ple·ment
(completing part;
see compliment)
com'ple·
men'ta·ry
com·plete'
·plet'ed ·plet'ing
com·ple'tion
com·plex'
com·plex'ion
com·plex'i·ty
·ties
com·pli'ance
com·pli'ant
com'pli·cate'
·cat'ed ·cat'ing
com'pli·ca'tion

com·plic'i·ty
com·pli'er
com'pli·ment
(praise; see
complement)
com'pli·men'·
ta·ry
com'pli·men·
tar'i·ly
com·ply'
·plied' ·ply'ing
com·po'nent
com·port'ment
com·pose'
·posed' ·pos'ing
com·pos'er
com·pos'ite
com'po·si'tion
com·pos'i·tor
com'pos men'tis
com'post
com·po'sure
com·pote'
com·pound' v.
com'pound n.
com·pre·hend'
com'pre·hen'si·
ble
com'pre·hen'sion
com'pre·hen'sive
com·press'
com·pressed'
com·pres'si·ble
com·pres'sion
com·pres'sor
com·prise'
·prised' ·pris'ing
com'pro·mise'
·mised' ·mis'ing
comp·tom'e·ter
comp·trol'ler
com·pul'sion
com·pul'sive
com·pul'so·ri·ly
com·pul'so·ri·ness
com·pul'so·ry
com·punc'tion
com·punc'tious
com·put'a·bil'i·ty
com·put'a·ble
com'pu·ta'tion
com·pute'
·put'ed ·put'ing
com·put'er
com·put'er·ize'
·ized' ·iz'ing
com·put'er·i·
za'tion
com'rade
con·cat·e·na'tion
con·cave'
con·cav'i·ty
·ties
con·ca'vo-con·
cave'
con·ca'vo-con·
vex'
con·ceal'

con·cede'
·ced'ed ·ced'ing
con·ceit'
con·ceit'ed
con·ceiv'a·
bil'i·ty
con·ceiv'a·ble
con·ceiv'a·bly
con·ceive'
·ceived' ·ceiv'ing
con'cen·trate'
·trat'ed ·trat'ing
con'cen·tra'tion
con·cen'tric
con·cen'tri·cal·ly
con'cept
con·cep'tion
con·cep'tu·al
con·cep'tu·al·ize'
·ized' ·iz'ing
con·cep'tu·al·i·
za'tion
con·cep'tu·al·ly
con·cern'
con·cerned'
con·cern'ing
con'cert
con·cert'ed
con·cer·ti'na
con'cert·mas'ter
con·cer'to
·tos or ·ti
con·ces'sion
con·ces'sion·aire'
conch
conchs or
conch'es
con·chol'o·gy
con·ci'erge'
con·cil'i·ar
con·cil'i·ate'
·at'ed ·at'ing
con·cil'i·a·to'ry
con·cise'
con·cise'ly
con·cise'ness
con'clave
con·clude'
·clud'ed
·clud'ing
con·clu'sion
con·clu'sive
con·coct'
con·coc'tion
con·com'i·tance
con·com'i·tant
con'cord
con·cord'ance
con·cor'dat
con'course
con·crete'
con·cre'tion
con·cu'bine'
con·cu'pis·cence
con·cu'pis·cent
con·cur'
·curred'
·cur'ring

con·cur'rence
con·cur'rent
con·cus'sion
con·demn'
con·dem'na·ble
con·dem·na'tion
con·dem'na·to'ry
con·demn'er
con·den'sa·ble
or ·si·ble
con·den·sa'tion
con·dense'
·densed'
·dens'ing
con·dens'er
con·de·scend'
con·de·scend'ing
con·de·scen'sion
con·dign'
con·di·ment
con·di'tion
con·di'tion·al
con·di'tion·al·ly
con·do'la·to'ry
con·dole'
·doled' ·dol'ing
con·do'lence
con'dom
con·do·min'i·um
·i·ums or ·i·a
con·do·na'tion
con·done'
·doned' ·don'ing
con'dor
con·duce'
·duced' ·duc'ing
con·du'cive
con'duct'
con·duct'ance
con·duct'i·ble
con·duc'tion
con·duc·tiv'i·ty
con·duc'tor
con'duit
co'ney
·neys or ·nies
con·fab'u·late'
·lat'ed ·lat'ing
con·fec'tion
con·fec'tion·ar'y
adj.
con·fec'tion·er
con·fec'tion·er'y
n.
·ies
con·fed'er·a·cy
·cies
con·fed'er·ate'
·at'ed ·at'ing
con·fed·er·a'tion
con·fer'
·ferred' ·fer'ring
con'fer·ee'
con'fer·ence
con·fer·en'tial
con·fer'ment
con·fer'ral
con·fess'

con·fes'sed·ly
con·fes'sion
con·fes'sion·al
con·fes'sor
con·fet'ti
con·fi·dant' n.
con·fide'
·fid'ed ·fid'ing
con'fi·dence
con'fi·dent adj.
con'fi·den'tial
con'fi·den'tial·ly
con·fig·u·ra'tion
con·fin'a·ble or
con·fine'a·ble
con·fine'
·fined' ·fin'ing
con·fine'ment
con·firm'
con·fir·mand'
con'fir·ma'tion
con·firm'a·to'ry
con·firmed'
con'fis·cate'
·cat'ed ·cat'ing
con'fis·ca'tion
con·fla·gra'tion
con·flict'
con·flic'tion
con'flu·ence
con·form'
con·form'a·ble
con·form'a·bly
con·form'ance
con'for·ma'tion
con·form'ist
con·form'i·ty
con·found'ed
con·front'
con'fron·ta'tion
Con·fu'cius
con·fuse'
·fused' ·fus'ing
con·fu'sion
con'fu·ta'tion
con·fute'
·futed' ·fut'ing
con·geal'
con·gen'ial
con·gen'ial·ly
con·ge'ni·al'i·ty
con·gen'i·tal
con·gen'i·tal·ly
con·gest'
con·ges'tion
con·glom'er·ate'
·at'ed ·at'ing
con·glom·er·a'tion
con·grat'u·late'
·lat'ed ·lat'ing
con·grat'u·
la'tion
con·grat'u·
la·to'ry
con'gre·gant
con'gre·gate'
·gat'ed ·gat'ing
con·gre·ga'tion

con·gres'sion·al
con'gress·man
con'gru·ence
con'gru·ent
con·gru'i·ty
con'gru·ous
con'ic
con'i·cal
con'i·cal·ly
co·nif'er·ous
con·jec'tur·al
con·jec'ture
·tured ·tur·ing
con·join'
con·joint'ly
con'ju·gal
con'ju·gal·ly
con'ju·gate'
·gat'ed ·gat'ing
con·ju·ga'tion
con·junc'tion
con·junc'tive
con·junc·ti·vi'tis
con·junc'ture
con'jure
·jured ·jur·ing
con'jur·er or ·or
con·nect'
Con·nect'i·cut
con·nec'tion
con·nec'tive
con·nec'tor
or ·nect'er
conn'ing tower
con·niv'ance
con·nive'
·nived' ·niv'ing
con'nois·seur'
con·no·ta'tion
con·no·ta'tive
con·note'
·not'ed ·not'ing
con·nu'bi·al
con'quer
con'quer·or
con'quest
con·quis'ta·dor
·dors or ·dores
con'science
con·sci·en'tious
con'scious
con·script'
con'se·crate'
·crat'ed ·crat'ing
con'se·cra'tion
con·sec'u·tive
con·sen'sus
con·sent'
con'se·quence'
con'se·quen'tial
con'se·quent'ly
con·ser'van·cy
con·ser·va'tion
con·ser'va·tism
con·ser'va·tive
con·ser'va·to'ry
·ries

con·serve'
·served'
·serv'ing
con·sid'er
con·sid'er·a·ble
con·sid'er·a·bly
con·sid'er·ate
con·sid·er·a'tion
con·sid'ered
con·sign'
con·sign'a·ble
con·sign·ee'
con·sign'ment
con·sign'or
 or ·er
con·sist'
con·sis'ten·cy
·cies
con·sis'tent
con·sis'to·ry
·ries
con·sol'a·ble
con·so·la'tion
con·sol'a·to·ry
con·sole'
·soled' ·sol'ing
con'sole
con·sol'i·date'
·dat'ed ·dat'ing
con·sol·i·da'tion
con·sol'i·da'tor
con'som·mé'
con'so·nance
con'so·nant
con'so·nan'tal
con'sort
con·sor'ti·um
·ti·a
con·spec'tus
con·spic'u·ous
·cies
con·spir'a·cy
·cies
con·spir'a·tor
con·spire'
·spired' ·spir'ing
con'sta·ble
con·stab'u·lar'y
·ies
con'stan·cy
con'stant
con'stel·la'tion
con'ster·na'tion
con'sti·pate'
·pat'ed ·pat'ing
con'sti·pa'tion
con·stit'u·en·cy
·cies
con·stit'u·ent
con'sti·tute'
·tut'ed ·tut'ing
con'sti·tu'tion
con'sti·tu'tion·al
con'sti·tu'tion·
al'i·ty
con'sti·tu'tion·
al·ly
con·strain'
con·straint'

con·strict'
con·stric'tion
con·stric'tor
con·stru'a·ble
con·struct'
con·struc'tion
con·struc'tive
con·struc'tor or
con·struct'er
con·strue'
·strued' ·stru'ing
con'sul
con'sul·ar
con'sul·ate
con·sult'
con·sult'ant
con·sul·ta'tion
con·sul'ta·tive
con·sum'a·ble
con·sume'
·sumed'
·sum'ing
con·sum'er
con'sum·mate'
·mat'ed ·mat'ing
con·sum'mate·ly
con'sum·ma'tion
con·sum·ma'tor
con·sump'tion
con·sump'tive
con'tact
con·ta'gion
con·ta'gious
con·tain'er
con·tain'er·ize'
·ized' ·iz'ing
con·tain'ment
con·tam'i·nant
con·tam'i·nate'
·nat'ed ·nat'ing
con·tam'i·na'tion
con·tam'i·na'tor
con·temn'
con'tem·plate'
·plat'ed
·plat'ing
con'tem·pla'tion
con'tem·pla'tive
con'tem·pla'tor
con·tem'po·
ra'ne·ous
con·tem'po·rar'y
con·tempt'
con·tempt'i·bil'·
i·ty
con·tempt'i·ble
con·tempt'i·bly
con·temp'tu·ous
con·tend'
con·tent'
con'tent
con·tent'ed·ly
con·ten'tion
con·ten'tious
con·tent'ment
con·test'
con·test'a·ble
con·test'ant

con'text
con·tex'tu·al
con'ti·gu'i·ty
con·tig'u·ous
con'ti·nence
con'ti·nent
con'ti·nen'tal
con·tin'gen·cy
·cies
con·tin'gent
con·tin'u·a·ble
con·tin'u·al
con·tin'u·ance
con·tin'u·a'tion
con·tin'ue
·ued ·u·ing
con·tin'u'i·ty
·ties
con·tin'u·ous
con·tin'u·um
·u·a or ·u·ums
con·tort'
con·tor'tion
con'tour
con'tra·band'
con'tra·bass'
con'tra·cep'tion
con'tra·cep'tive
con'tract
con·tract'i·bil'i·ty
con·tract'i·ble
con·trac'tile
con·trac'tion
con'trac·tor
con·trac'tu·al
con·trac'tu·al·ly
con'tra·dict'
con'tra·dic'tion
con'tra·dic'to·ry
con'tra·dis·
tinc'tion
con'trail'
con·tral'to
·tos or ·ti
con'tra·pun'tal
con'trar·i·ly
con'trar·i·ness
con'trar·i·wise'
con'trar·y
con·trast'
con'tra·vene'
·vened' ·ven'ing
con'tra·ven'tion
con·trib'ute
·ut·ed ·ut·ing
con'tri·bu'tion
con·trib'u·tor
con·trib'u·to'ry
con·trite'
con·tri'tion
con·triv'a·ble
con·triv'ance
con·trive'
·trived' ·triv'ing
con·trol'
·trolled'
·trol'ling
con·trol'la·bil'i·ty

con·trol'la·ble
con·trol'ler
con'tro·ver'sial
con'tro·ver'sy
·sies
con'tro·vert'
con'tro·vert'i·ble
con'tu·ma'cious
con'tu·ma·cy
con'tu·me'li·ous
con'tu·me·ly
con·tuse'
·tused' ·tus'ing
con·tu'sion
co·nun'drum
con'ur·ba'tion
con'va·lesce'
·lesced' ·lesc'ing
con'va·les'cence
con'va·les'cent
con·vec'tion
con·vec'tive
con·vec'tor
con·vene'
·vened' ·ven'ing
con·ven'ience
con·ven'ient
con·vent'
con·ven'ti·cle
con·ven'tion
con·ven'tion·al
con·ven'tion·
al'i·ty
con·ven'tion·
al·ize'
·ized' ·iz'ing
con·ven'tion·eer'
con·verge'
·verged'
·verg'ing
con·ver'gence
con·vers'a·ble
con·ver'sant
con'ver·sa'tion
con'ver·sa'tion·al
con·verse'
·versed' ·vers'ing
con'verse
con·ver'sion
con·vert'
con·vert'er
 or ·ver'tor
con·vert'i·ble
con·vex'
con·vex'i·ty
con·vex'o-con·
cave'
con·vex'o-con·
vex'
con·vey'
con·vey'ance
con·vey'or or ·er
con·vict'
con·vic'tion
con·vince'
·vinced'
·vinc'ing

con·vin'ci·ble
con·viv'i·al
con·viv'i·al'i·ty
con·vo·ca'tion
con·voke'
·voked' ·vok'ing
con'vo·lut'ed
con·vo·lu'tion
con'voy
con·vulse'
·vulsed'
·vuls'ing
con·vul'sion
con·vul'sive
cook'book'
cook'out'
cook'ie or ·y
·ies
cool'ant
cool'head'ed
coo'lie
(Oriental laborer;
see coolly,
coulee)
cool'ly
(in a cool manner;
see coolie,
coulee)
co'-op
co·op'er·ate'
 or co-op'·
·at'ed ·at'ing
co·op'er·a'tion
 or co-op'·
co·op'er·a·tive
 or co-op'·
co-opt'
co·or'di·nate'
 or co-or'·
·nat'ed ·nat'ing
co·or'di·na'tor
 or co-or'·
co·part'ner
cope
coped cop'ing
co'pra
cop'u·late'
·lat'ed ·lat'ing
cop'u·la'tion
cop'y
·ies
·ied ·y·ing
cop'y·cat'
cop'y·hold'er
cop'y·read'er
cop'y·right'
cop'y·writ'er
co·quet'
quet'ted
·quet'ting
co'quet·ry
co·quette'

co·quet'tish
co·quille'
cor'al
cor'bel
cord
(string; see
chord)
cord'age
cor'date
cor'dial
cor·di·al'i·ty
·ties
cor'dil·le'ra
cord'ite
cor'don
cor'do·van
cor'du·roy'
cord'wood'
core
cored cor'ing
co're·spond'ent
(in law; see
correspondent)
Cor'fam
co'ri·an'der
Co·rin'thi·an
cork'screw'
cor'mo·rant
corn borer
corn bread
corn'cob'
cor'ne·a
cor'nered
cor'ner·stone'
cor'ner·wise'
cor·net'
cor·net'ist
 or ·net'tist
corn'field'
corn'flow'er
corn'husk'ing
cor'nice
corn'meal'
corn'stalk'
corn'starch'
cor'nu·co'pi·a
corn'y
·i·er ·i·est
co·rol'la
cor'ol·lar'y
·ies
co·ro'na
·nas or ·nae
cor'o·nar'y
cor'o·na'tion
cor'o·ner
cor'o·net'
cor'po·ral
cor'po·rate
cor'po·ra'tion
cor'po·ra·tive
cor·po're·al
corps
corps
(group of people)
corpse
(dead body)
corps'man

cor'pu·lence
cor'pu·lent
cor'pus
  cor'po·ra
cor'pus·cle
cor·ral'
  ·ralled' ·ral'ling
cor·rect'
cor·rect'a·ble
cor·rec'tion
cor·rec'tive
cor·rec'tor
cor're·late'
  ·lat'ed ·lat'ing
cor're·la'tion
cor·rel'a·tive
cor're·spond'
cor're·
  spond'ence
cor're·
  spond'ent
  (*writer;* see
  corespondent)
cor'ri·dor
cor'ri·gi·ble
cor'ri·gi·bly
cor·rob'o·rate'
  ·rat'ed ·rat'ing
cor·rob'o·ra'tion
cor·rob'o·ra'tive
cor·rob'o·ra'tor
cor·rode'
  ·rod'ed ·rod'ing
cor·rod'i·ble
cor·ro'sion
cor·ro'sive
cor'ru·gate'
  ·gat'ed ·gat'ing
cor'ru·ga'tion
cor·rupt'
cor·rupt'i·bil'i·ty
cor·rupt'i·ble
cor·rupt'i·bly
cor·rup'tion
cor·rup'tive
cor·sage'
cor'sair
corse'let
cor'set
cor'se·tiere'
cor·tege' or ·tège'
cor'tex
  ·ti·ces'
cor'ti·cal
cor'ti·cal·ly
cor'ti·sone'
cor'run'dum
cor'us·cate'
  ·cat'ed ·cat'ing
cor·vette'
co·se'cant
co'sign'
co'sign'er
co·sig'na·to'ry
  ·ries
co'sine
cos·met'ic
cos'me·ti'cian

cos·me·tol'o·gy
cos'mic
cos'mi·cal·ly
cos·mog'o·ny
cos·mog'ra·phy
cos'mo·line'
cos·mol'o·gy
cos'mo·naut'
cos·mop'o·lis
cos'mo·pol'i·tan
cos'mop'o·lite'
cos'mos
cos'mo·tron'
co'spon·sor
cost
  cost cost'ing
cost'li·ness
cost'ly
  ·li·er ·li·est
cost'-plus'
cos'tume
  ·tumed ·tum·ing
cos·tum'er
co·tan'gent
co'te·rie
co·til'lion
cot'tage
cot'ton
cou'gar
cough
cou'lee
  (*gulch;* see
  coolie, coolly)
cou·lomb'
coun'cil
  (*legislature;* see
  counsel)
coun'cil·man
coun'ci·lor
  or ·cil·lor
  (*council member;*
  see counselor)
coun'sel
  ·seled or ·selled
  ·sel·ing or
  ·sel·ling
  (*advice; advise;*
  see council)
coun'se·lor
  or ·sel·lor
  (*adviser;* see
  councilor)
count'down'
coun'te·nance
count'er
  (*one that counts*)
coun'ter
  (*opposite*)
coun'ter·act'
coun'ter·action
coun'ter·at·tack'
coun'ter·bal'·
  ance
coun'ter·claim'
coun'ter·clock'
  wise
coun'ter·feit
coun'ter·foil'

coun'ter·ir'ri·
  tant
coun'ter·man'
coun'ter·mand'
coun'ter·march'
coun'ter·meas'·
  ure
coun'ter·move'
coun'ter·of·fen'·
  sive
coun'ter·pane'
coun'ter·part'
coun'ter·plot'
coun'ter·point'
coun'ter·poise'
coun'ter·sign'
coun'ter·sink'
  ·sunk' ·sink'ing
coun'ter·spy'
coun'ter·weight'
count'ess
count'less
coun'tri·fied'
coun'try
  ·tries
coun'try·man
coun'try·side'
coun'ty
  ·ties
coup de grâce'
coup d'é·tat'
coupe
cou'ple
  ·pled ·pling
cou'pler
cou'plet
cou'pon
cour'age
cou·ra'geous
cou'ri·er
course
  coursed
  cours'ing
  (*way; run;* see
  coarse)
cour'te·ous
cour'te·san
cour'te·sy
  ·sies
  (*polite act;*
  see curtsy)
court'house'
cour'ti·er
court'li·ness
court'ly
  ·li·er ·li·est
court'-mar'tial
courts'-mar'tial
  ·tialed or
  ·tialled
  ·tial·ing or
  ·tial·ling
court'room'
court'yard'
cous'in
cou·ture'
cou·tu·rier'
cou·tu·rière'

cov'e·nant
Cov'en·try
cov'er·age
cov'er·alls'
cov'ered
cov'er·ing
cov'er·let
cov'ert
cov'er-up'
cov'et·ous
cov'ey
cow'ard
cow'ard·ice
cow'ard·li·ness
cow'ard·ly
cow'boy'
cow'catch'er
cow'er
cow'herd'
cow'hide'
  ·hid'ed ·hid'ing
cowled
cow'lick
cowl'ing
co'-work'er
cow'pox'
cow'rie or ·ry
  ·ries
cow'shed'
cox'comb'
cox'swain
coy'ly
coy·o'te
co'zi·ly
co'zi·ness
co'zy
  ·zies
  ·zi·er ·zi·est
crab
  crabbed crab'bing
crab'bed
crab'bi·ness
crab'by
  ·bi·er ·bi·est
crack'brained'
crack'down'
cracked
crack'er
crack'ing
crack'le
  ·led ·ling
crack'lings
crack'up'
cra'dle
  ·dled ·dling
cra'dle·song'
craft'i·ly
craft'i·ness
crafts'man
craft'y
  ·i·er ·i·est
crag'gi·ness
crag'gy
  ·gi·er ·gi·est
cram
  crammed
  cram'ming
  cramped

cram'pon
cran'ber'ry
  ·ries
crane
  craned cran'ing
cra'ni·al
cra'ni·ol'o·gy
cra'ni·um
  ·ni·ums or ·ni·a
crank'case'
crank'i·ness
crank'shaft'
crank'y
  ·i·er ·i·est
cran'ny
  ·nies
crap'u·lence
crash'-land'
crass'ly
crass'ness
cra'ter
cra·vat'
crave
  craved crav'ing
cra'ven
crawl'er
cray'fish'
cray'on
craze
  crazed craz'ing
cra'zi·ly
cra'zi·ness
cra'zy
  ·zi·er ·zi·est
creak
  (*squeak;* see
  creek)
creak'i·ness
creak'y
  ·i·er ·i·est
cream'er·y
  ·ies
cream'i·ness
cream'y
  ·i·er ·i·est
crease
  creased
  creas'ing
cre·ate'
  ·at'ed ·at'ing
cre·a'tion
cre·a'tive
cre'a·tiv'i·ty
cre·a'tor
crea'ture
cre'dence
cre·den'tial
cre·den'za
cred'i·bil'i·ty
cred'i·ble
cred'i·bly
cred'it·a·bil'i·ty
cred'it·a·ble
cred'it·a·bly
cred'i·tor
cre'do
  ·dos
cre·du'li·ty

cred'u·lous
creek
  (*stream;* see
  creak)
creep
  crept creep'ing
creep'i·ness
creep'y
  ·i·er ·i·est
cre'mate
  ·mat·ed ·mat·ing
cre·ma'tion
cre'ma·to'ry
  ·ries
cre'o·sote'
  ·dos
cres'cent
crest'fall'en
cre'tin
cre'tonne
cre·vasse'
crev'ice
crew'el·work'
crib'bage
crick'et
cri'er
crim'i·nal
crim'i·nol'o·gy
crim'son
cringe
  cringed
  cring'ing
crin'kle
  ·kled ·kling
crin'o·line
crip'ple
  ·pled ·pling
crip'pler
cri'sis
  ·ses
crisp'er
crisp'i·ness
crisp'y
  ·i·er ·i·est
criss'cross'
cri·ter'i·on
  ·i·a or ·i·ons
crit'ic
crit'i·cal
crit'i·cal·ly
crit'i·cism
crit'i·cize'
  ·cized' ·ciz'ing
cri·tique'
croak
cro·chet'
  ·cheted'
  ·chet'ing
crock'er·y
croc'o·dile'
cro'cus
crois·sant'
crom'lech
cro'ny
  ·nies
crook'ed·ness

croon'er
crop
  cropped
  crop'ping
crop'-dust'ing
cro·quet'
  ·queted'
  ·quet'ing
  (game)
cro·quette'
  (food)
cro'sier
cross'bar'
cross'beam'
cross'bow'
cross'breed'
  ·bred' ·breed'ing
cross'-check'
cross'-coun'try
cross'cur'rent
cross'cut'
cross-ex·am'i·
  na'tion
cross-ex·am'ine
cross'-eyed'
cross'-fer'ti·lize'
cross'-grained'
cross'hatch'
cross'-in'dex
cross'ing
cross'-leg'ged
cross'o·ver
cross'piece'
cross'-pur'pose
cross'-re·fer'
cross'-ref'er·ence
cross'road'
cross'ruff'
cross section
cross'-stitch'
cross'tie'
cross'-town'
cross'walk'
cross'wise'
cross'word'
crotch'et·i·ness
crotch'et·y
crou'pi·er'
crou'ton
crow'bar'
crowd'ed
crow's'-foot'
  -feet'
crow's'-nest'
cru'cial
cru'cial·ly
cru'ci·ble
cru'ci·fix'
cru'ci·fix'ion
cru'ci·form'
cru'ci·fy'
  ·fied' ·fy'ing
crude'ly
cru'di·ty
  ·ties
cru'el·ly
cru'el·ty
  ·ties

cru'et
cruise
  cruised cruis'ing
cruis'er
crul'ler
crum'ble
  ·bled ·bling
crum'bly
  ·bli·er ·bli·est
crum'by
  ·bi·er ·bi·est
crum'pet
crum'ple
  ·pled ·pling
crunch'i·ness
crunch'y
  ·i·er ·i·est
crup'per
cru·sade'
crush'a·ble
crus·ta'cean
crust'ed
crust'i·ness
crust'y
  ·i·er ·i·est
crux
  crux'es or cru'ces
cry
  cries
  cried cry'ing
cry'o·gen'ics
crypt
cryp'tic
cryp'ti·cal·ly
cryp'to·gram'
cryp'to·gram'mic
cryp'to·graph'ic
cryp'to·graph'i·
  cal·ly
cryp·tog'ra·phy
crys'tal
crys'tal·line
crys'tal·liz'a·ble
crys'tal·li·za'tion
crys'tal·lize'
  ·lized ·liz'ing
crys'tal·log'ra·phy
cub'by·hole'
cube
  cubed cub'ing
cu'bic
cu'bi·cal
  (cube-shaped)
cu'bi·cal·ly
cu'bi·cle
  (compartment)
cu'bit
cuck'old
cuck'oo'
cu'cum·ber
cud'dle
  ·dled ·dling
cud'dly
  ·dli·er ·dli·est
cudg'el
  ·eled or ·elled
  ·el·ing or
  ·el·ling

cue
  cued cu'ing
  or cue'ing
  (signal; see
  queue)
cui·rass'
cui·sine'
cul'-de-sac'
cu'li·nar'y
cull
cul'mi·nate'
  ·nat'ed ·nat'ing
cul'mi·na'tion
cu·lottes'
cul'pa·bil'i·ty
cul'pa·ble
cul'pa·bly
cul'prit
cult'ist
cul'ti·va·ble
cul'ti·vate'
  ·vat'ed ·vat'ing
cul'ti·va'tion
cul'ti·va'tor
cul'tur·al
cul'ture
  ·tured ·tur·ing
cul'vert
cum'ber·some
cum'mer·bund'
cu'mu·late'
  ·lat'ed ·lat'ing
cu'mu·la'tive
cu'mu·lous adj.
cu'mu·lus n.
  ·li
cu·ne'i·form'
cun'ning·ly
cup'board
cup'ful'
  ·fuls'
cu·pid'i·ty
cu'po·la
cur'a·ble
cu'ra·çao'
cu'rate
cur'a·tive
cu·ra'tor
curb'stone'
cur'dle
  ·dled ·dling
cure
  cured cur'ing
cure'-all'
cur'few
cu'rie
cu'ri·o'
  ·os'
cu·ri·os'i·ty
  ·ties
cu'ri·ous
curl'i·cue'
curl'i·ness
curl'y
  ·i·er ·i·est
cur·mudg'eon
cur'rant
  (fruit)

cur'ren·cy
  ·cies
cur'rent
  (a flowing)
cur·ric'u·lar
cur·ric'u·lum
  ·u·la or ·u·lums
cur'ry
  ·ried ·ry·ing
cur'ry·comb'
curse
  cursed or curst
  curs'ing
cur'so·ri·ly
cur'so·ri·ness
cur'so·ry
cur·tail'
cur'tain
curt'ness
curt'sy
  ·sies
  ·sied ·sy·ing
  (knee bend;
  see courtesy)
cur'va·ture
curve
  curved curv'ing
cur'vi·lin'e·ar
curv'y
  ·i·er ·i·est
cush'ion
cus'pid
cus'pi·dor'
cus'tard
cus·to'di·al
cus·to'di·an
cus'to·dy
cus'tom
cus'tom·ar'i·ly
cus'tom·ar'y
cus'tom-built'
cus'tom·er
cus'tom·house'
cus'tom-made'
cut
  cut cut'ting
cu·ta'ne·ous
cut'a·way'
cut'back'
cut'i·cle
cut'lass or ·las
cut'ler·y
cut'let
cut'off'
cut'out'
cut'-rate'
cut'ter
cut'throat'
cy'a·nide'
cy'ber·cul'ture
cy'ber·na'tion
cy'ber·net'ics
cy'cla·mate'
cy'cle
cy'cled cy'cling
cy'clic
cy'cli·cal

cy'clist
cy'cli·zine'
cy'clom'e·ter
cy'clone
cy'clo·pe'di·a
cy'clo·ra'ma
cy'clo·tron'
cyg'net
cyl'in·der
cy·lin'dri·cal
cym'bal
  (brass plate;
  see symbol)
cyn'ic
cyn'i·cal
cyn'i·cal·ly
cyn'i·cism
cy'no·sure'
cy'press
cyst'ic
cyst'oid
cy·tol'o·gy
cy'to·plasm
czar
Czech'o·slo·
  va'ki·a

D

dab'ble
  ·bled ·bling
dachs'hund
Da'cron
dac'tyl
dad'dy
  ·dies
da'do
  ·does
daf'fo·dil'
dag'ger
da·guerre'o·type'
dahl'ia
dai'ly
  ·lies
dain'ti·ly
dain'ti·ness
dain'ty
  ·ties
  ·ti·er ·ti·est
dai'qui·ri
dair'y
  ·ies
dair'y·maid'
dair'y·man
da'is
dai'sy
  ·sies
dal'li·ance
dal'ly
  ·lied ·ly·ing
Dal·ma'tian
dam
  dammed
  dam'ming
  (barrier; see
  damn)

dam'age
  ·aged ·ag·ing
dam'age·a·ble
dam'a·scene'
dam'ask
damn
  damned
  damn'ing
  (condemn; see
  dam)
dam'na·ble
dam'na·bly
dam·na'tion
dam'na·to'ry
damp'-dry'
  -dried' -dry'ing
damp'en
damp'er
dam'sel
dance
  danced danc'ing
danc'er
dan'de·li'on
dan'dle
  ·dled ·dling
dan'druff
dan'ger
dan'ger·ous
dan'gle
  ·gled ·gling
Dan'ish
dan·seuse'
dap'ple
  ·pled ·pling
dare
  dared dar'ing
dare'dev'il
Dar·jee'ling
dark'en
dark'room'
dar'ling
Dar·win'i·an
dash'board'
das'tard·li·ness
das'tard·ly
da'ta
  (sing. da'tum)
date
  dat'ed dat'ing
daugh'ter
daugh'ter-in-law'
  daugh'ters-
  in-law'
daunt'less
dav'en·port'
dav'it
daw'dle
  ·dled ·dling
day'bed'
day'book'
day'break'
day'dream'
day letter
day'light'
day'long'
day room
day'time'
day'-to-day'

day'work'
daze
dazed daz'ing
daz'zle
·zled ·zling
D'-day'
dea'con
dea'con·ess
de·ac'ti·vate'
dead'en
dead'-end'
dead'head'
dead'line'
dead'li·ness
dead'lock'
dead'ly
·li·er ·li·est
dead'wood'
deaf'en·ing·ly
deaf'-mute'
deal
dealt deal'ing
deal'er·ship'
dean'er·y
·ies
dear'ly
dearth
death'bed'
death'blow'
death'less
death'ly
death'trap'
death'watch'
de·ba'cle
de·bar'
barred' bar'ring
de·bark'
de'bar·ka'tion
de·base'
based' bas'ing
de·bat'a·ble
de·bate'
bat'ed bat'ing
de·bauch'
deb·au'chee'
de·bauch'er·y
·ies
de·ben'ture
de·bil'i·tate'
tat'ed tat'ing
de·bil'i·ta'tion
de·bil'i·ty
·ties
deb'it
deb'o·nair'
or ·naire'
deb'o·nair'ly
de·brief'
de·bris'
debt'or
de·bunk'
de·but'
deb'u·tante'
dec'ade
dec'a·dence
dec'a·dent
dec'a·gon'
dec'a·gram'

dec'a·he'dron
·drons or ·dra
de·cal'ci·fy'
fied' ·fy'ing
de·cal'co·ma'ni·a
dec'a·li'ter
Dec'a·logue'
or ·log'
dec'a·me'ter
de·camp'
de·cant'
de·cant'er
de·cap'i·tate'
tat'ed ·tat'ing
de·cap'i·ta'tion
de·cath'lon
de·cay'
de·cease'
ceased'
·ceas'ing
de·ce'dent
de·ceit'ful
de·ceiv'a·ble
de·ceive'
ceived'
·ceiv'ing
de·cel'er·ate'
at'ed ·at'ing
de·cel'er·a'tion
de·cel'er·a'tor
de·cel'er·on'
De·cem'ber
de'cen·cy
·cies
de·cen'ni·al
de'cent
(proper; see
descent, dissent)
de·cen'tral·i·
za'tion
de·cen'tral·ize'
·ized' ·iz'ing
de·cep'tion
de·cep'tive·ly
dec'i·bel
de·cide'
·cid'ed ·cid'ing
de·cid'ed·ly
de·cid'u·ous
dec'i·mal
dec'i·mal·ize'
·ized' ·iz'ing
dec'i·mal·ly
dec'i·mate'
·mat'ed ·mat'ing
de·ci'pher
de·ci'sion
de·ci'sive
deck'le
de·claim'
dec'la·ma'tion
de·clam'a·to'ry
de·clar'a·ble
dec'la·ra'tion
de·clar'a·tive
de·clare'
·clared'
·clar'ing

de·clas'si·fy'
·fied' ·fy'ing
de·clen'sion
dec'li·na'tion
de·cline'
·clined' ·clin'ing
de·cliv'i·ty
·ties
de·code'
de·cod'er
dé·col'le·tage'
dé·col'le·té'
de'com·pos'a·ble
de'com·pose'
de'com·po·si'tion
de'com·pres'sion
de'con·gest'ant
de'con·tam'i·nate'
de·con'trol'
·trolled'
·trol'ling
de·cree'
·creed' ·cree'ing
de·crep'it
de·crep'i·tude'
de'cre·scen'do
de·cres'cent
de·cri'al
de·cry'
·cried' ·cry'ing
de·crypt'
de·cum'bent
ded'i·cate'
·cat'ed ·cat'ing
ded'i·ca'tion
ded'i·ca·to'ry
de·duce'
·duced' ·duc'ing
de·duc'i·ble
de·duct'
de·duct'i·ble
de·duc'tion
de·duc'tive
de·em'pha·sis
de·em'pha·size'
deep'-chest'ed
deep'-dyed'
deep'freeze'
·froze' or
·freezed'
·fro'zen or
·freezed'
·freez'ing
deep'-fry'
·fried' -fry'ing

deep'-laid'
deep'-root'ed
deep'-seat'ed
deep'-set'
deer'skin'
de·es'ca·late'
de·es'ca·la'tion
de·face'
de·fac'to
de·fal'cate
def'a·ma'tion
de·fam'a·to'ry
de·fame'
·famed'
·fam'ing
de·fault'
de·fea'sance
de·feat'
de·feat'ist
def'e·cate'
·cat'ed ·cat'ing
def'e·ca'tion
de·fect'
de·fec'tion
de·fec'tive
de·fec'tor
de·fend'
de·fend'ant
de·fense'
de·fen'si·ble
de·fen'sive
de·fer'
·ferred' ·fer'ring
def'er·ence
def'er·en'tial
de·fer'ment
de·fi'ance
de·fi'ant
de·fi'cien·cy
·cies
de·fi'cient
def'i·cit
de·fi'er
de·file'
·filed' ·fil'ing
de·fin'a·ble
de·fine'
·fined' ·fin'ing
def'i·nite
def'i·ni'tion
de·fin'i·tive
de·flate'
·flat'ed ·flat'ing
de·fla'tion
de·fla'tion·ar'y
de·fla'tor
de·flect'
de·flec'tion
de·flec'tor
de·flow'er
de·fo'li·ate'
·at'ed ·at'ing
de'for·ma'tion
de·formed'
de·form'i·ty
·ties
de·fraud'

de·fray'
de·fray'al
de·frost'
de·funct'
de·fuse'
de·fy'
·fied' ·fy'ing
dé'ga·gé'
de·gen'er·a·cy
de·gen'er·ate'
·at'ed ·at'ing
de·gen'er·a'tion
de·gen'er·a·tive
de·grad'a·ble
deg'ra·da'tion
de·grade'
·grad'ed
·grad'ing
de·gree'
de'hu·mid'i·fy'
de·hy'drate
·drat·ed ·drat·ing
de'hy·dra'tion
de·hy'dra·tor
de·ic'er
de'i·fi·ca'tion
de'i·fy'
·fied' ·fy'ing
deign
de'ism
de'i·ty
·ties
de·ject'ed
de·jec'tion
Del'a·ware'
de·lay'
de·lec'ta·ble
del'e·gate'
·gat'ed ·gat'ing
del'e·ga'tion
de·lete'
·let'ed ·let'ing
del'e·te'ri·ous
de·le'tion
delft'ware'
de·lib'er·ate
de·lib'er·ate·ly
de·lib'er·a'tion
del'i·ca·cy
·cies
del'i·cate
del'i·cate·ly
del'i·ca·tes'sen
de·li'cious
de·light'ful
de·light'ful·ly
de·lin'e·ate'
·at'ed ·at'ing
de·lin'e·a'tion
de·lin'e·a'tor
de·lin'quen·cy
de·lin'quent
de·lir'i·ous
de·lir'i·um
de·liv'er·a·ble
de·liv'er·ance
de·liv'er·y
·ies

de·lude'
·lud'ed ·lud'ing
del'uge
·uged ·ug·ing
de·lu'sion
de·lu'sive
de·luxe'
delve
delved delv'ing
de·mag'net·ize'
dem'a·gog'ic
dem'a·gog'i·cal·ly
dem'a·gogue'
or ·gog'
dem'a·gog'y
de·mand'ing
de·mar'cate
·cat·ed ·cat·ing
de'mar·ca'tion
de·mean'or
de·men'tia
de·mer'it
de·mesne'
dem'i·john'
de·mil'i·ta·rize'
de·mise'
dem'i·tasse'
de·mo'bi·lize'
de·moc'ra·cy
·cies
dem'o·crat'ic
dem'o·crat'i·cal·ly
de·moc'ra·ti·
za'tion
de·moc'ra·tize'
·tized' ·tiz'ing
de·mog'ra·phy
de·mol'ish
dem'o·li'tion
de'mon
de·mon'e·tize'
·tized' ·tiz'ing
de·mo'ni·ac'
de·mon'ic
de·mon'i·cal·ly
de·mon'stra·ble
dem'on·strate'
·strat'ed
·strat'ing
dem'on·stra'tion
de·mon'stra·tive
de·mon·stra'tor
de·mor'al·ize'
de·mote'
·mot'ed ·mot'ing
de·mo'tion
de·mount'
de·mul'cent
de·mur'
·murred'
·mur'ring
(to object)
de·mure'
(coy)
de·mur'rage
de·mur'rer
de·na'tion·al·ize'
de·nat'u·ral·ize'

de·na'ture
 ·tured ·tur·ing
de·ni'a·ble
de·ni'al
de·nier'
de·ni'er
den'im
den'i·zen
de·nom'i·nate'
 ·nat'ed ·nat'ing
de·nom'i·na'tion
de·nom'i·na'tor
de·no·ta'tion
de·note'
 ·not'ed ·not'ing
de·noue'ment
de·nounce'
 ·nounced'
 ·nounc'ing
dense
 dens'er dens'est
dense'ly
den'si·ty
 ·ties
den'tal
den'tal·ly
den'ti·frice'
den'tin
den'tist
den'tist·ry
den'ture
de·nude'
 ·nud'ed ·nud'ing
de·nun·ci·a'tion
de·ny'
 ·nied' ·ny'ing
de·o'dor·ant
de·o'dor·ize'
 ·ized' ·iz'ing
de·o'dor·iz'er
de·part'ed
de·part'ment
de·part'men'tal
de·part'men'tal·
 ize'
 ·ized' ·iz'ing
de·par'ture
de·pend'a·bil'i·ty
de·pend'a·ble
de·pend'a·bly
de·pend'ence
de·pend'en·cy
 ·cies
de·pend'ent
de·per'son·al·ize'
de·pict'
de·pic'tion
de·pil'a·to·ry
 ·ries
de·plane'
de·plete'
 ·plet'ed ·plet'ing
de·ple'tion
de·plor'a·ble
de·plore'
 ·plored'
 ·plor'ing
de·ploy'

de·pon'ent
de·pop'u·late'
de·port'a·ble
de·por·ta'tion
de·port'ment
de·pose'
de·pos'it
de·pos'i·tar'y
 ·ies
dep'o·si'tion
de·pos'i·tor
de·pos'i·to'ry
 ·ries
de'pot
dep'ra·va'tion
 (a corrupting;
 see deprivation)
de·prave'
 ·praved'
 ·prav'ing
de·prav'i·ty
 ·ties
dep're·cate'
 ·cat'ed ·crat'ing
dep're·ca'tion
dep're·ca·to'ry
de·pre'ci·a·ble
de·pre'ci·ate'
 ·at'ed ·at'ing
de·pre'ci·a'tion
dep're·da'tion
de·pres'sant
de·pressed'
de·press'ing
de·pres'sion
de·pres'sive·ly
dep'ri·va'tion
 (a taking away;
 see depravation)
de·prive'
 ·prived' ·priv'ing
depth
dep'u·ta'tion
dep'u·tize'
 ·tized' ·tiz'ing
dep'u·ty
 ·ties
de·rail'
de·range'
 ·ranged'
 ·rang'ing
der'e·lict'
der·e·lic'tion
de·ride'
 ·rid'ed ·rid'ing
de ri·gueur'
de·ri'sion
de·ri'sive
de·riv'a·ble
der'i·va'tion
de·riv'a·tive
de·rive'
 ·rived' ·riv'ing
des'o·late'
der'ma·tol'o·gist
de·rog'a·to'ri·ly
de·rog'a·to'ry
der'rick

der·ri·ère'
der'ring·do'
der'rin·ger
de·sal'i·na'tion
de·salt'
des'cant
de·scend'
de·scend'ant
de·scend'i·ble
de·scent'
 (going down; see
 decent, dissent)
de·scrib'a·ble
de·scribe'
 ·scribed'
 ·scrib'ing
de·scrip'tion
de·scrip'tive
de·scry'
 ·scried'
 ·scry'ing
des'e·crate'
 ·crat'ed ·crat'ing
des·e·cra'tion
de·seg're·gate'
 ·gat'ed ·gat'ing
de·seg're·ga'tion
de·sen'si·tize'
de·sen'si·tiz'er
de·sert'
 (abandon; see
 dessert)
des'ert
 (dry area)
de·ser'tion
de·serts'
 (reward, etc.)
de·serve'
 ·served'
 ·serv'ing
de·serv'ed·ly
des'ic·cant
des'ic·cate'
 ·cat'ed ·cat'ing
des'ic·ca'tion
de·sign'
de·sig'nate'
 ·nat'ed ·nat'ing
des'ig·na'tion
des'ig·na'tor
de·signed'
de·sign'er
de·sir'a·bil'i·ty
de·sir'a·ble
de·sir'a·bly
de·sire'
 ·sired' ·sir'ing
de·sir'ous
de·sist'
des'o·late'
 ·lat'ed ·lat'ing
des'o·la'tion
de·spair'
des'per·a'do
 ·does or ·dos
des'per·ate
 (hopeless; see
 disparate)

des'per·a'tion
des'pi·ca·ble
de·spise'
 ·spised'
 ·spis'ing
de·spite'
de·spoil'
de·spo'li·a'tion
de·spond'en·cy
de·spond'ent
des'pot
des·pot'ic
des·pot'i·cal·ly
des'pot·ism
des·sert'
 (food; see desert)
des·sert'spoon'
des'ti·na'tion
des'tine
 ·tined ·tin·ing
des'tin·y
 ·ies
des'ti·tute'
des'ti·tu'tion
de·stroy'er
de·struct'
de·struct'i·bil'i·ty
de·struct'i·ble
de·struc'tion
de·struc'tive
de·struc'tor
des'ue·tude'
des'ul·to'ry
de·tach'
de·tach'a·ble
de·tach'ment
de·tail'
de·tain'
de·tect'
de·tect'a·ble
 or ·i·ble
de·tec'tion
de·tec'tive
de·tec'tor
dé·tente'
de·ten'tion
de·ter'
 ·terred'
 ·ter'ring
de·ter'gent
de·te'ri·o·rate'
 ·rat'ed ·rat'ing
de·te'ri·o·ra'tion
de·ter'ment
de·ter'mi·na·ble
de·ter'mi·na·bly
de·ter'mi·nant
de·ter'mi·nate
de·ter'mi·na'tion
de·ter'mine
 ·mined ·min·ing
de·ter'min·ism
de·ter'rence
de·ter'rent
de·test'
de·test'a·ble
de·test'a·bly
de·tes·ta'tion

de·throne'
 ·throned'
 ·thron'ing
det'o·nate'
 ·nat'ed ·nat'ing
det'o·na'tion
det'o·na'tor
de'tour
de·tract'
de·trac'tor
det'ri·ment
det'ri·men'tal
de·tri'tus
deuce
de·val'u·a'tion
de·val'ue
dev'as·tate'
 ·tat'ed ·tat'ing
dev'as·ta'tion
de·vel'op·ment
de·vel'op·men'tal
de'vi·ant
de'vi·ate'
 ·at'ed ·at'ing
de'vi·a'tion
de·vice'
dev'il·ish
dev'il·ment
dev'il·try
 ·tries
de'vi·ous
de·vis'a·ble
 (that can be devised;
 see divisible)
de·vise'
 ·vised' ·vis'ing
de·vi'tal·ize'
de·void'
de·volve'
 ·volved'
 ·volv'ing
de·vote'
 ·vot'ed ·vot'ing
dev'o·tee'
de·vo'tion
de·vour'
de·vout'
dew'drop'
dew'lap'
dew'y
 ·i·er ·i·est
dex·ter'i·ty
dex'ter·ous
 or dex'trous
dex'trose
di'a·be'tes
di'a·bet'ic
di'a·bol'ic
di'a·bol'i·cal
di'a·bol'i·cal·ly
di'a·crit'i·cal
di'a·dem'
di'ag·nos'a·ble
di'ag·nose'
 ·nosed' ·nos'ing
di'ag·no'sis
 ·no'ses
di'ag·nos'tic

di'ag·nos'ti·cal·ly
di'ag·nos·ti'cian
di·ag'o·nal
di·ag'o·nal·ly
di'a·gram'
 ·gramed' or
 ·grammed'
 ·gram'ing or
 ·gram'ming
di'a·gram·mat'ic
di'al
 ·aled or ·alled
 ·al·ing or ·al·ling
di'a·lect'
di'a·lec'tal
di'a·lec'tic
di'a·lec·ti'cian
di·al'o·gist
di'a·logue' or
 ·log'
di·am'e·ter
di'a·met'ri·cal
di'a·met'ri·cal·ly
di'a·mond
di'a·pa'son
di'a·per
di·aph'a·nous
di'a·phragm'
di'a·rist
di·ar·rhe'a
 or ·rhoe'a
di'a·ry
 ·ries
di'a·stase'
di'a·ther'my
di'a·ton'ic
di'a·tribe'
dib'ble
 ·bled ·bling
dice
 diced dic'ing
 (sing. die or dice)
di·chot'o·mize'
 ·mized' ·miz'ing
di·chot'o·my
dick'er
dick'ey
 ·eys
Dic'ta·phone'
dic'tate
 ·tat·ed ·tat·ing
dic·ta'tion
dic'ta·tor
dic'ta·to'ri·al
dic'tion·ar'y
 ·ies
Dic'to·graph'
dic'tum
 ·tums or ·ta
di·dac'tic
di·dac'ti·cal·ly
die
 dice
 (cube)
die
 dies
 died die'ing
 (mold; stamp)

die
  died dy'ing
  (*stop living;*
  see dye)
die'-hard' *or*
die'hard'
diel'drin
di·e·lec'tric
di·er'e·sis
 ·ses'
die'sel
die'sink·er
di'e·sis
 ·ses'
di'e·tar'y
di'e·tet'ic
di'e·tet'i·cal·ly
di'e·ti'tian
 or ·cian
dif'fer·ence
dif'fer·ent
dif'fer·en'tial
dif'fer·en'ti·ate'
 ·at'ed ·at'ing
dif'fer·en'ti·a'tion
dif'fi·cult
dif'fi·cul'ty
 ·ties
dif'fi·dence
dif'fi·dent
dif·fract'
dif·frac'tion
dif·fuse'
 ·fused' ·fus'ing
dif·fus'i·ble
dif·fu'sion
dif·fu'sive
dig
 dug dig'ging
dig'a·my
di'gest
di·gest'i·ble
di·ges'tive
dig'ger
dig'it
dig'it·al
dig'i·tal'is
dig'i·ti·grade'
dig'ni·fy
 ·fied' ·fy'ing
dig'ni·tar'y
 ·ies
dig'ni·ty
 ·ties
di·gress'
di·gres'sion
di·lan'tin
di·lap'i·date'
 ·dat'ed ·dat'ing
di·lat'a·ble
di·late'
 ·lat'ed ·lat'ing
di·la'tion
dil'a·to'ry
di·lem'ma
dil'et·tante'
 ·tantes' *or* ·tan'ti
dil'et·tant'ish

dil'i·gence
dil'i·gent
dil'ly·dal'ly
 ·lied ·ly·ing
dil'u·ent
di·lute'
 ·lut'ed ·lut'ing
di·lu'tion
di·lu'vi·al
dim
dim'mer
dim'mest
dimmed
dim'ming
di·men'sion
di·min'ish
di·min'u·en'do
dim'i·nu'tion
di·min'u·tive
dim'i·ty
dim'out'
dim'ple
 ·pled ·pling
din
dinned din'ning
dine
 dined din'ing
din'er
 (*person eating;*
 see dinner)
din·ette'
din'ghy
 ·ghies
 (*boat*)
din'gi·ness
din'gy
 ·gi·er ·gi·est
 (*not bright*)
din'ner
 (*meal;* see diner)
din'ner·ware'
di'no·saur'
di·oc'e·san
di'o·cese
di'o·ra'ma
di·ox'ide
dip
 dipped dip'ping
diph·the'ri·a
diph'thong
di·plo'ma
di·plo'ma·cy
 ·cies
dip'lo·mat'
 (*government
 representative*)
dip'lo·mate'
 (*doctor*)
dip'lo·mat'i·cal·ly
dip'so·ma'ni·a
di·rect'
di·rec'tion
di·rec'tive
di·rec'tor
di·rec'tor·ate
di·rec'to'ri·al
di·rec'to·ry
 ·ries

dire'ful
dirge
dir'i·gi·ble
dirn'dl
dirt'i·ness
dirt'y
 ·i·er ·i·est
dis'a·bil'i·ty
 ·ties
dis·a'ble
 ·bled ·bling
dis'a·buse'
 ·bused' ·bus'ing
dis'ad·van'tage
dis·ad'van·ta'·
 geous
dis·af·fect'ed
dis'a·gree'
dis'a·gree'a·ble
dis'a·gree'a·bly
dis'a·gree'ment
dis·al·low'
dis'ap·pear'ance
dis'ap·point'ment
dis'ap·pro·ba'tion
dis'ap·prov'al
dis'ap·prove'
dis·ar'ma·ment
dis·arm'ing
dis'ar·range'
dis'ar·ray'
dis·as·sem'ble
dis·as·so'ci·ate'
dis·as'ter
dis·as'trous
dis·a·vow'
dis'a·vow'al
dis·band'
dis·bar'
dis·be·lief'
dis·be·lieve'
dis·be·liev'er
dis·burse'
 ·bursed'
 ·burs'ing
dis·burse'ment
disc
dis·card'
dis·cern'
dis·cern'i·ble
dis·cern'ing
dis·cern'ment
dis·charge'
dis·ci'ple
dis'ci·plin·a·ble
dis'ci·pli·nar'i·an
dis'ci·pli·nar'y
dis'ci·pline
 ·plined ·plin·ing
disc jockey
dis·claim'
dis·claim'er
dis·close'
dis·clo'sure
dis·cog'ra·phy
dis'coid
dis·col'or
dis·col'or·a'tion

dis·com'fit
dis·com'fi·ture
dis·com'fort
dis·com·pose'
dis·com·po'sure
dis·con·cert'
dis·con·nect'
dis·con'so·late
dis·con·tent'
dis·con·tin'u·ance
dis·con·tin'ue
dis·con·tin'u·i·ty
dis·con·tin'u·ous
dis'co·phile'
dis'cord
dis·cord'ant
dis'co·thèque
dis'count
dis·cour'age
 ·aged ·ag·ing
dis·cour'age·ment
dis'course
dis·cour'te·ous
dis·cour'te·sy
dis·cov'er
dis·cov'er·er
dis·cov'er·y
 ·ies
dis·cred'it
dis·creet'
 (*prudent;* see
 discrete)
dis·crep'an·cy
 ·cies
dis·crete'
 (*separate;* see
 discreet)
dis·cre'tion
dis·cre'tion·ar'y
dis·crim'i·nate'
 ·nat'ed ·nat'ing
dis·crim'i·na'tion
dis·crim'i·na·
 to'ry
dis·cur'sive
dis'cus
 ·cus·es *or* dis'ci
dis·cuss'
dis·cus'sion
dis·dain'ful
dis·ease'
 ·eased' ·eas'ing
dis·em·bark'
dis·em·bod'y
dis·em·bow'el
 ·eled *or* ·elled
 ·el·ing *or*
 ·el·ling
dis·en·chant'
dis·en·cum'ber
dis·en·gage'
dis·en·tan'gle
dis·es·tab'lish
dis·fa'vor
dis·fig'ure
dis·fig'ure·ment
dis·fran'chise
 ·chised ·chis·ing

dis·gorge'
dis·grace'
 ·graced'
 ·grac'ing
dis·grace'ful
dis·grun'tle
 ·tled ·tling
dis·guise'
 ·guised'
 ·guis'ing
dis·gust'
dis'ha·bille'
dis·har'mo·ny
dish'cloth'
dis·heart'en
di·shev'el
 ·eled *or* ·elled
 ·el·ing *or*
 ·el·ling
dis·hon'est
dis·hon'es·ty
dis·hon'or
dis·hon'or·a·ble
dish'pan'
dish towel
dish'wash'er
dish'wa'ter
dis·il·lu'sioned
dis·in·cli·na'tion
dis·in·cline'
dis·in·fect'
dis·in·fect'ant
dis·in·gen'u·ous
dis·in·her'it
dis·in'te·grate'
 ·grat'ed
 ·grat'ing
dis·in'te·gra'tion
dis·in'ter'
dis·in'ter·est·ed
dis·join'
dis·joint'
dis·junc'tion
disk
dis·like'
dis'lo·cate'
dis'lo·ca'tion
dis·lodge'
dis·loy'al
dis·loy'al·ty
dis'mal
dis'mal·ly
dis·man'tle
dis·may'
dis·mem'ber
dis·miss'
dis·miss'al
dis·mount'
dis·o·be'di·ence
dis·o·be'di·ent
dis·o·bey'
dis·or'der
dis·or'der·ly
dis·or'gan·i·za'·
 tion
dis·or'gan·ize'
dis·o'ri·ent'
dis·own'

dis·par'age
 ·aged ·ag·ing
dis'pa·rate
 (*not alike;* see
 desperate)
dis·par'i·ty
dis·pas'sion·ate
dis·patch'
dis·patch'er
dis·pel'
 ·pelled' ·pel'ling
dis·pen'sa·bil'i·ty
dis·pen'sa·ble
dis·pen'sa·ry
 ·ries
dis'pen·sa'tion
dis·pense'
 ·pensed'
 ·pens'ing
dis·pen'ser
dis·per'sal
dis·perse'
 ·persed' ·pers'ing
dis·pers'i·ble
dis·per'sion
dis·pir'it·ed
dis·place'
dis·place'ment
dis·play'
dis·please'
dis·pleas'ure
dis·port'
dis·pos'a·ble
dis·pos'al
dis·pose'
 ·posed' ·pos'ing
dis'po·si'tion
dis'pos·sess'
dis·proof'
dis'pro·por'tion
dis'pro·por'tion·
 ate
dis·prove'
dis·pu'ta·ble
dis·pu'tant
dis'pu·ta'tion
dis'pu·ta'tious
dis·pute'
 ·put'ed ·put'ing
dis·qual'i·fi·ca'·
 tion
dis·qual'i·fy'
dis·qui'et
dis·qui'e·tude
dis'qui·si'tion
dis're·gard'
dis're·pair'
dis·rep'u·ta·ble
dis·rep'u·ta·bly
dis're·pute'
dis're·spect'ful
dis·robe'
dis·rupt'
dis·rup'tion
dis·rup'tive
dis·sat'is·fac'tion
dis·sat'is·fy'
 ·fied' ·fy'ing

dis·sect'
dis·sec'tion
dis·sec'tor
dis·sem'blance
dis·sem'ble
·bled ·bling
dis·sem'i·nate'
·nat'ed ·nat'ing
dis·sem'i·na'tion
dis·sen'sion
dis·sent'
(*disagree*; see
decent, descent)
dis·sen'tient
dis·sen'tious
dis·ser·ta'tion
dis·serv'ice
dis·sev'er
dis'si·dence
dis'si·dent
dis·sim'i·lar
dis·sim'i·lar'i·ty
dis·sim'i·la'tion
dis·sim'u·late'
dis'si·pate'
·pat'ed ·pat'ing
dis'si·pa'tion
dis·so'ci·ate'
·at'ed ·at'ing
dis·so'ci·a'tion
dis·sol'u·ble
dis'so·lute'
dis·so·lu'tion
dis·solv'a·ble
dis·solve'
·solved'
·solv'ing
dis·sol'vent
dis'so·nance
dis'so·nant
dis·suade'
·suad'ed
·suad'ing
dis·sua'sion
dis·sym'me·try
dis'taff
dis'tance
dis'tant
dis·taste'ful
dis·tem'per
dis·tend'
dis·ten'si·ble
dis·ten'tion *or*
dis·ten'sion
dis'tich
dis·till' *or* ·til'
·tilled' ·till'ing
dis'til·late
dis'til·la'tion
dis·till'er
dis·till'er·y
·ies
dis·tinct'
dis·tinc'tion
dis·tinc'tive
dis·tin·gué'
dis·tin'guish
dis·tin'guish·a·ble

dis·tin'guish·a·bly
dis·tort'
dis·tor'tion
dis·tract'
dis·tract'i·ble
dis·trac'tion
dis·trait'
dis·traught'
dis·tress'
dis·trib'ut·a·ble
dis·trib'ute
·ut·ed ·ut·ing
dis'tri·bu'tion
dis·trib'u·tive
dis·trib'u·tor
dis'trict
dis·trust'ful
dis·turb'
dis·turb'ance
dis·un'ion
dis'u·nite'
dis·u'ni·ty
dis·use'
ditch
dith'er
dit'to
·tos
·toed ·to·ing
dit'ty
·ties
di'u·ret'ic
di·ur'nal
di'va
di·van'
dive
dived *or* dove
dived div'ing
di·verge'
·verged'
·verg'ing
di·ver'gence
di·ver'gent
di'vers
(*sundry*)
di·verse'
(*different*)
di·ver'si·fi·ca'·
tion
di·ver'si·form'
di·ver'si·fy'
·fied' ·fy'ing
di·ver'sion
di·ver'sion·ar'y
di·ver'si·ty
di·vert'
di·ver'tisse·ment
di·vest'
di·vest'i·ture
di·vid'a·ble
di·vide'
·vid'ed ·vid'ing
div'i·dend'
div'i·na'tion
di·vine'
·vined' ·vin'ing
di·vin'i·ty
·ties
di·vis'i·bil'i·ty

di·vis'i·ble
(*that can be divided*;
see devisable)
di·vi'sion
di·vi'sor
di·vorce'
·vorced' ·vorc'ing
di·vor'cé' *masc.*
di·vor'cée' *or*
·cee' *fem.*
div'ot
di·vulge'
·vulged'
·vulg'ing
di·vul'gence
diz'zi·ly
diz'zi·ness
diz'zy
·zi·er ·zi·est
·zied ·zy·ing
do'a·ble
dob'bin
do'cent
doc'ile
doc'ile·ly
do·cil'i·ty
dock'age
dock'et
dock'yard'
doc'tor
doc'tor·al
doc'tor·ate
doc'tri·naire'
doc'tri·nal
doc'trine
doc'u·ment
doc'u·men'tal
doc'u·men'ta·ry
·ries
doc'u·men·ta'tion
dod'der·ing
dodge
dodged
dodg'ing
dodg'y
·i·er ·i·est
do'er
does
doe'skin'
does'n't
dog'catch'er
dog'ear'
dog'ged·ly
dog'ger·el
dog'gy *or* ·gie
·gies
(*dog*)
do'gie *or* ·gy
·gies
(*calf*)
dog'ma
·mas *or* ·ma·ta
dog·mat'ic
dog·mat'i·cal·ly
dog'ma·tism
dog'ma·tize'
·tized' ·tiz'ing
dog'nap'

di·vis'i·ble
do'-good'er
dog'trot'
dog'watch'
dog'wood'
doi'ly
·lies
do'-it-your·self'
dol'ce
dol'drums
dole
doled dol'ing
dole'ful
dol'lar
dol'lop
dol'man
·mans
(*robe*)
dol'men
(*tomb*)
do'lor·ous
dol'phin
dolt'ish
do·main'
do·mes'tic
do·mes'ti·cate'
·cat'ed ·cat'ing
do'mes·tic'i·ty
·ties
dom'i·cile'
dom'i·nance
dom'i·nant
dom'i·nate'
·nat'ed ·nat'ing
dom'i·na'tion
dom'i·neer'ing
do·min'i·cal
do·min'ion
dom'i·no'
·noes' *or* ·nos'
don
donned don'ning
do'nate
·nat·ed ·nat·ing
do·na'tion
do·nee'
Don' Ju'an
don'key
·keys
don'ny·brook'
do'nor
do'-noth'ing
Don' Qui·xo'te
don't
doo'dle
·dled ·dling
doo'hick'ey
dooms'day'
door'bell'
do'-or-die'
door'jamb'
door'keep'er
door'knob'
door'man'
door'mat'
door'nail'
door'plate'
door'sill'
door'step'

door'stop'
door'-to-door'
door'way'
dope
doped dop'ing
dor'man·cy
dor'mant
dor'mer
dor'mi·to'ry
·ries
dor'mouse'
·mice'
dor'sal
do'ry
·ries
dos'-à-dos'
dos'age
dos'si·er'
dot
dot'ted dot'ting
dot'age
dot'ard
dote
dot'ed dot'ing
dou'ble
·bled ·bling
dou'ble-bar'reled
dou'ble-breast'ed
dou'ble-check'
dou'ble-cross'
dou'ble-date'
dou'ble-deal'ing
dou'ble-deck'er
dou'ble-edged'
dou'ble-
en·ten'dre
dou'ble-faced'
dou'ble-head'er
dou'ble-joint'ed
dou'ble-knit'
dou'ble-park'
dou'ble-quick'
dou'ble-space'
dou'blet
dou'ble-tongued'
dou'bly
doubt
doubt'ful
doubt'ful·ly
doubt'less
douche
douched
douch'ing
dough
dough'i·ness
dough'nut'
dough'y
·i·er ·i·est
doup'pi·o'ni *or*
dou'pi·o'ni
douse
doused dous'ing
dove'cote'
dove'tail'
dow'a·ger
dow'di·ness
dow'dy
·di·er ·di·est

dow'el
dow'er
down'beat'
down'cast'
down'fall'
down'grade'
down'heart'ed
down'hill'
down'i·ness
down'pour'
down'range'
down'right'
down'spout'
down'stage'
down'stairs'
down'state'
down'stream'
down'swing'
down'time'
down'-to-earth'
down'town'
down'trod'den
down'turn'
down'ward
down'wash'
down'wind'
down'y
·i·er ·i·est
dow'ry
·ries
dox·ol'o·gy
doze
dozed doz'ing
doz'en
drab
drab'ber
drab'best
draft·ee'
draft'i·ness
drafts'man
draft'y
·i·er ·i·est
drag
dragged
drag'ging
drag'gle
·gled ·gling
drag'gy
·gi·er ·gi·est
drag'net'
drag'o·man
·mans *or* ·men
drag'on
drag'on·fly'
·flies'
dra·goon'
drain'age
drain'pipe'
dra'ma
dra·mat'ic
dra·mat'i·cal·ly
dram'a·tist
dram'a·ti·za'tion
dram'a·tize'
·tized' ·tiz'ing
dram'a·tur'gy
drape
draped drap'ing

dra'per·y
·ies
dras'tic
dras'ti·cal·ly
draughts'man
·men
draw
drew drawn
draw'ing
draw'back'
draw'bridge'
draw·ee'
draw'er
draw'knife'
·knives'
drawl
drawn'work'
draw'string'
dray'age
dray'man
dread'ful
dread'ful·ly
dread'nought'
dream'i·ly
dream'i·ness
dream'y
·i·er ·i·est
drear'i·ly
drear'i·ness
drear'y
·i·er ·i·est
dredge
dredged
dredg'ing
drenched
dress
dressed or drest
dress'ing
dress'er
dress'i·ly
dress'i·ness
dress'ing-down'
dress'mak·er
dress'y
·i·er ·i·est
drib'ble
·bled ·bling
drib'let
dri'er or dry'er
drift'wood'
drill'mas·ter
drill press
drink
drank drunk
drink'ing
drink'a·ble
drip
dripped or dript
drip'ping
drip'-dry'
drive
drove driv'en
driv'ing
drive'-in'
driv'el
·eled or ·elled
·el·ing or
·el·ling

driv'er
drive'way'
driz'zle
·zled ·zling
driz'zly
droll'er·y
·ies
droll'ly
drom'e·dar'y
·ies
drone
droned dron'ing
droop'i·ly
droop'i·ness
droop'y
·i·er ·i·est
drop
dropped
drop'ping
drop'cloth'
drop'-forge'
·forged'
·forg'ing
drop'let
drop'out'
drop'per
dross
drought
or drouth
dro'ver
drown
drowse
drowsed
drows'ing
drow'si·ly
drow'si·ness
drow'sy
·si·er ·si·est
drub
drubbed
drub'bing
drudge
drudged
drudg'ing
drudg'er·y
drug
drugged
drug'ging
drug'gist
drug'store'
drum
drummed
drum'ming
drum'beat'
drum'head'
drum'mer
drum'stick'
drunk'ard
drunk'en·ness
drunk·o'me·ter
drupe'let
dry
dri'er dri'est
dried dry'ing
dry'as·dust'
dry'-clean'
dry cleaner
dry cleaning

dry'er
dry'-eyed'
dry ice
dry'ly or dri'ly
dry'ness
du'al
(of two; see duel)
du'al·ism
du'al·is'tic
du'al·ly
du'al-pur'pose
dub
dubbed dub'bing
du·bi'e·ty
du·bi·ous
du'bi·ous
du'cal
duc'at
duch'ess
duch'y
·ies
duck'ling
duck'pins'
duc'tile
duct'less
dudg'eon
due bill
du'el
·eled or ·elled
·el·ing or
·el·ling
(fight; see dual)
du·et'
duf'fel or ·fle
dug'out'
dul'cet
dul'ci·mer
dull'ard
dull'ness
dul'ly
(in a dull manner)
du'ly
(as due)
dumb'bell'
dumb'found' or
dum'found'
dumb'ly
dumb'wait·er
dum'dum'
dum'my
·mies
dump'i·ness
dump'ling
dump'y
·i·er ·i·est
dun
dunned
dun'ning
dun'der·head'
dun·ga·ree'
dun'geon
dung'hill'
dun'nage
du'o
du'os or du'i
du·o·dec'i·mal
du'o·de'nal
du'o·logue'
du·op'o·ly

du'o·tone'
du'o·type'
dupe
duped dup'ing
du'ple
du'plex
du'pli·cate'
·cat'ed ·cat'ing
du'pli·ca'tion
du'pli·ca'tor
du·plic'i·ty
·ties
du·ra·bil'i·ty
du'ra·ble
du'ra·bly
dur'ance
du·ra'tion
du·ress'
dur'ing
du'rum
dusk'i·ness
dusk'y
·i·er ·i·est
dust'i·ness
dust'pan'
dust'y
·i·er ·i·est
du'te·ous
du'ti·a·ble
du'ti·ful
du'ti·ful·ly
du'ty
·ties
du'ty-free'
dwarf
dwarfs or
dwarves
dwell
dwelt or dwelled
dwell'ing
dwin'dle
·dled ·dling
dy'ad
dyb'buk
dye
dyed dye'ing
(color; see die)
dyed'-in-the-wool'
dy'er
dye'stuff'
dy·nam'ic
dy·nam'i·cal·ly
dy'na·mism
dy'na·mite'
·mit'ed ·mit'ing
dy'na·mo'
·mos'
dy'na·mom'e·ter
dy'na·mo'tor
dy'nas·ty
·ties
dyne
dy·nel'
dys'en·ter'y
dys·func'tion
dys·pep'si·a
dys·pep'tic
dys'tro·phy

E

ea'ger
ea'gle
ea'gle-eyed'
ear'ache'
ear'drum'
ear'ly
·li·er ·li·est
ear'mark'
ear'muffs'
ear'nest
earn'ings
ear'phone'
ear'plug'
ear'ring'
ear'shot'
earth'en·ware'
earth'i·ness
earth'ly
earth'quake'
earth'shak'ing
earth'ward
earth'y
·i·er ·i·est
ear'wax'
ease
eased eas'ing
ea'sel
ease'ment
eas'i·ly
eas'i·ness
east'er·ly
east'ern
east'ward
eas'y
·i·er ·i·est
eas'y·go'ing
eat
ate eat'en
eat'ing
eat'a·ble
eaves'drop'
ebb tide
eb'on·y
e·bul'lient
e'bul·li'tion
ec·cen'tric
ec·cen'tri·cal·ly
ec'cen·tric'i·ty
·ties
ec·cle'si·as'ti·cal
ech'e·lon'
ech'o
·oes
e·cho'ic
é·clair'
é·clat'
ec·lec'tic
ec·lec'ti·cism
e·clipse'
·clipsed'
·clips'ing
e·clip'tic
ec'o·log'i·cal

ec'o·log'i·cal·ly
e·col'o·gist
e·col'o·gy
e'co·nom'ic
e'co·nom'i·cal
e'co·nom'i·cal·ly
e·con'o·mist
e·con'o·mize'
·mized' ·miz'ing
e·con'o·my
·mies
e'co·sys'tem
e'co·tone'
ec'ru
ec'sta·sy
·sies
ec·stat'ic
ec·stat'i·cal·ly
ec'u·men'i·cal
ec'ze·ma
ed'dy
·dies
e'del·weiss'
e·de'ma
·mas or ·ma·ta
edge
edged edg'ing
edge'ways'
edge'wise'
edg'i·ly
edg'i·ness
edg'y
·i·er ·i·est
ed'i·bil'i·ty
ed'i·ble
e'dict
ed'i·fi·ca'tion
ed'i·fice
ed'i·fy'
·fied' ·fy'ing
e·di'tion
(form of book;
see addition)
ed'i·tor
ed'i·to'ri·al
ed'i·to'ri·al·ize'
·ized' ·iz'ing
ed'i·to'ri·al·ly
ed·u·ca·bil'i·ty
ed'u·ca·ble
ed'u·cate'
·cat'ed ·cat'ing
ed'u·ca'tion
ed'u·ca'tive
ed'u·ca'tor
e·duce'
·duced' ·duc'ing
e·duc'i·ble
ee'rie or ·ry
·ri·er ·ri·est
ee'ri·ly
ee'ri·ness
ef·face'
·faced' ·fac'ing
ef·face'a·ble
ef·fect'
(result; see
affect)

ef·fec'tive
(having effect;
see affective)
ef·fec'tu·al
ef·fec'tu·ate'
·at'ed ·at'ing
ef·fem'i·na·cy
ef·fem'i·nate
ef'fer·ent
ef'fer·vesce'
·vesced'
·vesc'ing
ef'fer·ves'cence
ef'fer·ves'cent
ef·fete'
ef·fi·ca'cious
ef'fi·ca·cy
ef·fi'cien·cy
ef·fi'cient
ef'fi·gy
·gies
ef·flo·resce'
·resced'
·resc'ing
ef·flo·res'cence
ef'flu·ence
ef'flu·ent
(flowing; see
affluent)
ef·flu'vi·um
·vi·a or ·vi·ums
ef'fort
ef·fron'ter·y
·ies
ef·ful'gence
ef·fu'sion
ef·fu'sive
e·gal'i·tar'i·an
egg'nog'
egg'shell'
e'go
e'go·cen'tric
e'go·cen'tri·cal·ly
e'go·ism
e'go·ist
e'go·ma'ni·a
e'go·tism
e'go·tist
e'go·tis'tic
e'go·tis'ti·cal·ly
e·gre'gious
e'gress
e'gret
ei'der·down'
ei·det'ic
eight'een'
eighth
eight'i·eth
eight'y
·ies
ei'ther
ei'ther-or'
e·jac'u·late'
·lat'ed ·lat'ing
e·jac'u·la'tion
e·jac'u·la'tor
e·ject'
e·jec'tion

e·jec'tor
eke
eked ek'ing
e·kis'tics
e·kis'ti·cal
e·lab'o·rate'
·rat'ed ·rat'ing
e·lab'o·rate·ly
e·lab·o·ra'tion
e·lapse'
·lapsed'
·laps'ing
e·las'tic
e·las'tic'i·ty
e·las'ti·cize'
·cized' ·ciz'ing
e·late'
·lat'ed ·lat'ing
e·la'tion
el'bow·room'
eld'er·ly
eld'est
e·lec'tion
e·lec'tion·eer'
e·lec'tive
e·lec'tor
e·lec'tor·al
e·lec'tor·ate
e·lec'tric
e·lec'tri·cal
e·lec'tri·cal·ly
e·lec·tri'cian
e·lec·tric'i·ty
e·lec·tri·fi·ca'tion
e·lec'tri·fy'
·fied' ·fy·ing
e·lec'tro·cute'
·cut'ed ·cut'ing
e·lec'tro·cu'tion
e·lec'trode
e·lec·trol'y·sis
e·lec'tro·lyte'
e·lec'tro·lyt'ic
e·lec'tro·lyze'
·lyzed' ·lyz'ing
e·lec'tro·mag'net
e·lec'trom'e·ter
e·lec'tro·mo'tive
e·lec'tron
e·lec·tron'ic
e·lec·tron'i·cal·ly
e·lec'tro·plate'
e·lec'tro·scope'
e·lec'tro·stat'ics
e·lec'tro·ther'a·py
e·lec'tro·type'
e·lec'tro·typ'y
el·ee·mos'y·nar'y
el'e·gance
el'e·gant
el'e·gi'ac
el'e·gize'
·gized' ·giz'ing
el'e·gy
·gies
el'e·ment
el'e·men'tal
el'e·men'ta·ri·ness

el'e·men'ta·ry
(basic; see
alimentary)
el'e·phant
el'e·phan·ti'a·sis
el'e·phan'tine
El'eu·sin'i·an
el'e·vate'
·vat'ed ·vat'ing
el'e·va'tion
el'e·va'tor
e·lev'enth
elf
elves
elf'in
e·lic'it
(draw forth;
see illicit)
e·lide'
·lid'ed ·lid'ing
el'i·gi·bil'i·ty
el'i·gi·ble
el'i·gi·bly
e·lim'i·nate'
·nat'ed ·nat'ing
e·lim'i·na'tion
e·li'sion
e·lite' or é·lite'
e·lix'ir
E·liz'a·be'than
el·lipse'
el·lip'sis
·ses
el·lip'ti·cal
el·lip'ti·cal·ly
el'o·cu'tion
e·lon'gate
·gat·ed ·gat·ing
e·lon·ga'tion
e·lope'
·loped' ·lop'ing
e·lope'ment
el'o·quence
el'o·quent
else'where'
e·lu'ci·date'
·dat'ed ·dat'ing
e·lu'ci·da'tion
e·lude'
·lud'ed ·lud'ing
(escape; see
allude)
e·lu'sion
(an escape; see
allusion, illusion)
e·lu'sive
(hard to grasp;
see allusive,
illusive)
e·ma'ci·ate'
·at'ed ·at'ing
e·ma'ci·a'tion
em'a·nate'
·nat'ed ·nat'ing
em'a·na'tion
e·man'ci·pate'
·pat'ed ·pat'ing
e·man'ci·pa'tion

e·man'ci·pa'tor
e·mas'cu·late'
·lat'ed ·lat'ing
e·mas'cu·la'tion
e·mas'cu·la'tor
em·balm'
em·bank'ment
em·bar'go
·goes
·goed ·go·ing
em·bark'
em·bar·ka'tion
em·bar'rass
em·bar'rass·ment
em'bas·sy
·sies
em·bat'tle
·tled ·tling
em·bed'
em·bel'lish
em'ber
em·bez'zle
·zled ·zling
em·bez'zler
em·bla'zon
em'blem
em'blem·at'ic
em·bod'i·ment
em·bod'y
·ied ·y·ing
em·bold'en
em'bo·lism
em'bo·lus
·li
em·boss'
em'bou·chure'
em·brace'
·braced'
·brac'ing
em·brace'a·ble
em·bra'sure
em·broi'der
em·broi'der·y
·ies
em·broil'
em'bry·o'
·os'
em'bry·ol'o·gy
em'bry·on'ic
em'cee'
·ceed' ·cee'ing
e·mend'
(to correct;
see amend)
e'men·da'tion
em'er·ald
e·merge'
·merged'
·merg'ing
(appear; see
immerge)
e·mer'gence
e·mer'gen·cy
·cies
e·mer'i·tus
em'er·y
e·met'ic
em'i·grant

em'i·grate'
·grat'ed
·grat'ing
em'i·gra'tion
em'i·nence
em'i·nent
(prominent; see
imminent)
em'is·sar'y
·ies
e·mis'sion
e·mit'
·mit'ted
·mit'ting
e·mol'li·ent
e·mol'u·ment
e·mo'tion·al
e·mo'tion·al·ize'
·ized' ·iz'ing
em·path'ic
em'pa·thize'
·thized' ·thiz'ing
em'pa·thy
em'pen·nage'
em'per·or
em'pha·sis
·ses'
em'pha·size'
·sized' ·siz'ing
em·phat'ic
em'phy·se'ma
em'pire
em·pir'i·cal
em·pir'i·cism
em·place'ment
em·ploy'
em·ploy'a·ble
em·ploy'ee
em·ploy'er
em·ploy'ment
em·po'ri·um
·ri·ums or ·ri·a
em·pow'er
em'press
emp'ti·ly
emp'ti·ness
emp'ty
·ti·er ·ti·est
·ties
·tied ·ty·ing
emp'ty-hand'ed
emp'ty-head'ed
em'u·late'
·lat'ed ·lat'ing
em'u·la'tion
em'u·lous
e·mul'si·fi·ca'tion
e·mul'si·fi'er
e·mul'si·fy'
·fied' ·fy'ing
e·mul'sion
en·a'ble
·bled ·bling
en·act'ment
en·am'el
·eled or ·elled
·el·ing or
·el·ling

en·am'el·ware'
en·am'ored
en·camp'ment
en·case'
·cased' ·cas'ing
en·caus'tic
en·ceph·a·li'tis
en·chant'ment
en'chi·la'da
en·cir'cle
en'clave
en·close'
·closed'
·clos'ing
en·clo'sure
en·code'
en·co'mi·ast'
en·co'mi·um
·ums or ·a
en·com'pass
en'core
en·coun'ter
en·cour'age
·aged ·ag'ing
en·cour'age·ment
en·croach'
en·cum'ber
en·cum'brance
en·cyc'li·cal
en·cy·clo·pe'di·a
or ·pae'di·a
en·dan'ger
en·dear'
en·dear'ment
en·deav'or
en·dem'ic
end'ing
en'dive
end'less
end'most'
en'do·crine'
en·dog'a·my
en'do·me'tri·um
en·dorse'
·dorsed'
·dors'ing
en·dor·see'
en·dorse'ment
en·dors'er
en·dow'
en·dow'ment
end'pa'per
en·dur'a·ble
en·dur'a·bly
en·dur'ance
en·dure'
·dured' ·dur'ing
end'ways'
en'e·ma
en'e·my
·mies
en'er·get'ic
en'er·get'i·cal·ly
en'er·gize'
·gized' ·giz'ing
en'er·giz'er
en'er·gy
·gies

en'er·vate'
·vat'ed ·vat'ing
en·fee'ble
·bled ·bling
en'fi·lade'
·lad'ed ·lad'ing
en·fold'
en·force'
·forced'
·forc'ing
en·force'a·ble
en·fran'chise
en·gage'
·gaged' ·gag'ing
en·gage'ment
en·gen'der
en'gine
en·gi·neer'
Eng'lish
en·gorge'
·gorged' ·gorg'ing
en·grave'
·graved'
·grav'ing
en·grav'er
en·gross'
en·gulf'
en·hance'
·hanced'
·hanc'ing
e·nig'ma
e·nig·mat'ic
e·nig·mat'i·cal·ly
en·join'
en·joy'a·ble
en·joy'a·bly
en·joy'ment
en·kin'dle
·dled ·dling
en·lace'
en·large'
·larged'
·larg'ing
en·large'ment
en·larg'er
en·light'en
en·light'en·ment
en·list'
en·list'ment
en·liv'en
en masse'
en·mesh'
en'mi·ty
·ties
en·no'ble
·bled ·bling
en·nui'
e·nor'mi·ty
·ties
e·nor'mous
e·nough'
en·plane'
en·rage'
en·rap'ture
·tured ·tur·ing
en·rich'
en·roll' or ·rol'
·rolled' ·roll'ing

en·roll'ee'
en·roll'ment or
en·rol'ment
en·route'
en·sconce'
·sconced'
·sconc'ing
en·sem'ble
en·shrine'
·shrined'
·shrin'ing
en'sign
en·slave'
en·snare'
en·snarl'
en·sue'
·sued' ·su'ing
en·sure'
en·tail'
en·tan'gle
en·tente'
en'ter·prise'
en'ter·pris'ing
en'ter·tain'
en·thrall' or
en·thral'
·thralled'
·thrall'ing
en·throne'
en·thuse'
·thused'
·thus'ing
en·thu'si·asm
en·thu'si·as'tic
en·thu'si·as'ti·
cal·ly
en·tice'
·ticed' ·tic'ing
en·tice'ment
en·tire'
en·tire'ly
en·tire'ty
·ties
en·ti'tle
·tled ·tling
en'ti·ty
·ties
en·tomb'
en'to·mol'o·gy
(insect study; see
etymology)
en'tou·rage'
en·tr'acte'
en'trails
en·train'
en'trance
en·trance'
·tranced'
·tranc'ing
en'trant
en·trap'
en·treat'
en·treat'y
·ies
en·tree' or ·trée
en·trench'ment
en'tre·pre·neur'
en·trust'

en'try
·tries
en·twine'
e·nu'mer·ate'
·at'ed ·at'ing
e·nu'mer·a'tion
e·nu'mer·a'tor
e·nun'ci·ate'
·at'ed ·at'ing
(pronounce; see
annunciate)
e·nun'ci·a'tion
e·nun'ci·a'tor
en·vel'op v.
en've·lope' n.
en·ven'om
en'vi·a·ble
en'vi·a·bly
en'vi·ous
en·vi'ron·ment
en·vi'ron·men'tal
en·vi'rons
en·vis'age
·aged ·ag·ing
en·vi'sion
en'voy
en'vy
·vies
·vied ·vy·ing
en'zyme
e'o·lith'ic
e'on
ep'au·let' or
·lette'
e·pergne'
e·phem'er·al
ep'ic
(poem; see
epoch)
ep'i·cen'ter
ep'i·cure'
ep'i·cu·re'an
ep'i·dem'ic
ep'i·der'mis
ep'i·glot'tis
ep'i·gram'
ep'i·gram·mat'ic
ep'i·gram·mat'i·
cal·ly
ep'i·graph'
ep'i·graph'ic
ep'i·graph'i·cal·ly
ep'i·lep'sy
ep'i·lep'tic
ep'i·logue' or
·log'
E·piph'a·ny
e·pis'co·pal
E·pis'co·pa'li·an
ep'i·sode'
ep'i·sod'ic
ep'i·sod'i·cal·ly
e·pis'tle
e·pis'to·lar'y
ep'i·taph'
ep'i·the'li·al
ep'i·the'li·um
·li·ums or ·li·a

ep'i·thet'
e·pit'o·me
e·pit'o·mize'
·mized' ·miz'ing
ep'och
(period; see epic)
ep'och·al
ep'o·nym'
ep·ox'y
ep'si·lon'
eq'ua·bil'i·ty
eq'ua·ble
eq'ua·bly
e'qual
·qualed or
·qualled
·qual·ing or
·qual·ling
e·qual'i·tar'i·an
e·qual'i·ty
e'qual·i·za'tion
e'qual·ize'
·ized' ·iz'ing
e'qual·ly
e'qua·nim'i·ty
e·quate'
·quat'ed
·quat'ing
e·qua'tion
e·qua'tor
e·qua·to'ri·al
eq'uer·ry
·ries
e·ques'tri·an
e·ques'tri·enne'
e'qui·an'gu·lar
e'qui·dis'tant
e'qui·lat'er·al
e·quil'i·brant
e·quil'i·brate'
·brat'ed ·brat'ing
e'qui·lib'ri·um
·ri·ums or ·ri·a
e'quine
e'qui·noc'tial
e'qui·nox'
e·quip'
·quipped'
·quip'ping
eq'ui·page
e·quip'ment
e'qui·poise'
e'qui·pol'lent
eq'ui·ta·ble
eq'ui·ta·bly
eq'ui·ty
·ties
e·quiv'a·lence
e·quiv'a·lent
e·quiv'o·cal
e·quiv'o·cal·ly
e·quiv'o·cate'
·cat'ed ·cat'ing
e·quiv'o·ca'tion
e·quiv'o·ca'tor
e'ra
e·rad'i·ca·ble

e·rad'i·cate'
·cat'ed ·cat'ing
e·rad'i·ca'tion
e·rad'i·ca'tor
e·ras'a·ble
e·rase'
·rased' ·ras'ing
e·ras'er
e·ra'sure
e·rect'
e·rec'tile
e·rec'tion
e·rec'tor
erg
er'go
er·gos'ter·ol'
er'got
er'mine
e·rode'
·rod'ed ·rod'ing
e·rog'e·nous
e·ro'sion
e·ro'sive
e·rot'ic
e·rot'i·ca
e·rot'i·cal·ly
e·rot'i·cism
er'o·tism
e·ro'to·gen'ic
err
er'ran·cy
·cies
er'rand
er'rant
er·ra'ta
(sing. er·ra'tum)
er·rat'ic
er·rat'i·cal·ly
er·ro'ne·ous
er'ror
er'satz
erst'while'
e·ruct'
e·ruc'tate
·tat·ed ·tat·ing
e·ruc'ta'tion
er'u·dite'
er'u·di'tion
e·rupt'
e·rupt'i·ble
e·rup'tion
e·rup'tive
e·ryth'ro·my'cin
es'ca·drille'
es'ca·lade'
·lad'ed ·lad'ing
es'ca·late'
·lat'ed ·lat'ing
es·ca·la'tion
es'ca·la'tor
es·cal'lop or ·op
es'ca·pade'
es·cape'
·caped' ·cap'ing
es·cap·ee'
es·cape'ment
es·cap'ism
es·cap'ist

es'ca·role'
es·carp'ment
es'cha·rot'ic
es'cha·tol'o·gy
es·cheat'
es·chew'
es·chew'al
es'cort
es'cri·toire'
es'crow
es'cu·lent
es·cutch'eon
Es'ki·mo'
·mos' or ·mo'
e·soph'a·gus
·a·gi'
es'o·ter'ic
es'o·ter'i·cal·ly
es'pa·drille'
es·pal'ier
es·pe'cial
es·pe'cial·ly
Es'pe·ran'to
es'pi·o·nage'
es'pla·nade'
es·pous'al
es·pouse'
·poused' ·pous'ing
es·pres'so
·sos
es·prit' de corps'
es·py'
·pied' ·py'ing
es·quire'
es·say'
(try; see assay)
es'say·ist
es'sence
es·sen'tial
es·sen'ti·al'i·ty
es·sen'tial·ly
es·tab'lish
es·tab'lish·ment
es·tate'
es·teem'
es'thete
es·thet'ic
es·thet'i·cal·ly
es·thet'i·cism
es'ti·ma·ble
es'ti·mate'
·mat'ed ·mat'ing
es'ti·ma'tion
es'ti·ma'tor
es'ti·val
es'ti·vate'
·vat'ed ·vat'ing
es·trange'
·tranged'
·trang'ing
es·trange'ment
es'tro·gen
es'trous adj.
es'trus n.
es'tu·ar'i·al
es'tu·ar'y
·ies
et cet'er·a

et·cet'er·as
etch'ing
e·ter'nal
e·ter'nal·ly
e·ter'ni·ty
 ·ties
e'ther
e·the're·al
e·the're·al·ize'
 ·ized' ·iz'ing
e'ther·ize'
 ·ized' ·iz'ing
eth'i·cal
eth'i·cal·ly
eth'ics
eth'nic
eth'ni·cal·ly
eth'no·cen'tri·
 cal·ly
eth'no·cen'trism
eth·nog'ra·phy
eth'no·log'i·cal
eth·nol'o·gy
e'thos
eth'yl
e'ti·ol'o·gy
et'i·quette
é'tude
et'y·mo·log'i·cal
et'y·mol'o·gy
 ·gies
 (word study; see
 entomology)
et'y·mon'
eu·ca·lyp'tus
 ·tus·es or ·ti
Eu'cha·rist
eu'chre
eu·gen'i·cal·ly
eu·gen'ics
eu'lo·gize'
 ·gized' ·giz'ing
eu'lo·gy
 ·gies
eu'nuch
eu'phe·mism
eu'phe·mis'tic
eu'phe·mis'ti·
 cal·ly
eu'phe·mize'
 ·mized' ·miz'ing
eu·phon'ic
eu·pho'ni·ous
eu·pho'ni·um
eu'pho·ny
 ·nies
eu·pho'ri·a
eu·phor'ic
eu'phu·ism
eu'phu·is'tic
Eur·a'sian
Eur'a·tom'
eu·re'ka
Eu'ro·crat'
Eu'ro·dol'lars
Eu'ro·pe'an
eu·ryth'mics
eu·ryth'my

Eu·sta'chi·an
eu'tha·na'si·a
e·vac'u·ate'
 ·at'ed ·at'ing
e·vac'u·a'tion
e·vac'u·ee'
e·vade'
 ·vad'ed ·vad'ing
e·val'u·ate'
 ·at'ed ·at'ing
e·val'u·a'tion
ev'a·nesce'
 ·nesced' ·nesc'ing
ev'a·nes'cence
ev'a·nes'cent
e'van·gel'i·cal
e'van·gel'i·cal·ly
e·van'gel·ism
e·van'gel·ist
e·van'gel·is'tic
e·van'gel·ize'
 ·ized' ·iz'ing
e·vap'o·rate'
 ·rat'ed ·rat'ing
e·vap'o·ra'tion
e·va'sion
e·va'sive
e'ven·hand'ed
eve'ning
e'ven·ness
e·vent'
e'ven-tem'pered
e·vent'ful
e·ven'tu·al
e·ven'tu·al'i·ty
 ·ties
e·ven'tu·al·ly
e·ven'tu·ate'
 ·at'ed ·at'ing
ev'er·glade'
ev'er·green'
ev'er·last'ing
ev'er·more'
e·vert'
ev'er·y·bod'y
ev'er·y·day'
ev'er·y·one'
ev'er·y·thing'
ev'er·y·where'
e·vict'
e·vic'tion
ev'i·dence
 ·denced ·denc·ing
ev'i·dent
ev'i·den'tial
e'vil·do'er
e'vil·ly
e'vil-mind'ed
e·vince'
 ·vinced'
 ·vinc'ing
e·vis'cer·ate'
 ·at'ed ·at'ing
e·vis'cer·a'tion
ev'o·ca'tion
e·voke'
 ·voked' ·vok'ing

ev'o·lu'tion
ev'o·lu'tion·ar'y
ev'o·lu'tion·ist
e·volve'
 ·volved' ·volv'ing
ewe
 (sheep; see yew)
ew'er
ex·ac'er·bate'
 ·bat'ed ·bat'ing
ex·ac'er·ba'tion
ex·act'
ex·act'ing
ex·ac'tion
ex·ac'ti·tude'
ex·act'ly
ex·ag'ger·ate'
 ·at'ed ·at'ing
ex·ag'ger·a'tion
ex·ag'ger·a'tor
ex·alt'
ex'al·ta'tion
ex·am'i·na'tion
ex·am'ine
 ·ined ·in·ing
ex·am'in·er
ex·am'ple
ex·as'per·ate'
 ·at'ed ·at'ing
ex·as'per·a'tion
ex'·ca·the'dra
ex'ca·vate'
 ·vat'ed ·vat'ing
ex'ca·va'tion
ex'ca·va'tor
ex·ceed'
 (surpass; see
 accede)
ex·ceed'ing·ly
ex·cel'
 ·celled' ·cel'ling
ex'cel·lence
ex'cel·len·cy
 ·cies
ex'cel·lent
ex·cel'si·or'
ex·cept'
 (omit; see accept)
ex·cept'ed
 (left out; see
 accepted)
ex·cep'tion
ex·cep'tion·a·ble
ex·cep'tion·al
ex·cep'tion·al·ly
ex·cerpt'
ex·cess'
 (surplus; see
 access)
ex·ces'sive
ex·ces'sive·ly
ex·change'
 ·changed'
 ·chang'ing
ex·change'·
 a·bil'i·ty
ex·change'a·ble
ex·cheq'uer

ex·cis'a·ble
ex'cise
ex·cise'
 ·cised' ·cis'ing
ex·ci'sion
ex·cit'a·bil'i·ty
ex·cit'a·ble
ex·cit'a·bly
ex·ci·ta'tion
ex·cite'
 ·cit'ed ·cit'ing
ex·cite'ment
ex·claim'
ex'cla·ma'tion
ex·clam'a·to'ry
ex'clave
ex·clud'a·ble
ex·clude'
 ·clud'ed
 ·clud'ing
ex·clu'sion
ex·clu'sive
ex'clu·siv'i·ty
ex'com·mu'ni·
 cate'
 ·cat'ed ·cat'ing
ex·co'ri·ate'
 ·at'ed ·at'ing
ex·co'ri·a'tion
ex'cre·ment
ex·cres'cence
ex·crete'
 ·cret'ed
 ·cret'ing
ex·cre'tion
ex'cre·to'ry
ex·cru'ci·ate'
 ·at'ed ·at'ing
ex'cul·pate'
 ·pat'ed ·pat'ing
ex'cul·pa'tion
ex·cur'sion
ex·cus'a·ble
ex·cus'a·bly
ex·cuse'
 ·cused' ·cus'ing
ex'e·cra·ble
ex'e·crate'
 ·crat'ed
 ·crat'ing
ex'e·cra'tion
ex'e·cute'
 ·cut'ed ·cut'ing
ex·e·cu'tion
ex'e·cu'tion·er
ex·ec'u·tive
ex·ec'u·tor
ex'ec·u'tor
ex'e·ge'sis
ex·em'plar
ex·em'pla·ri·ly
ex·em'pla·ri·ness
ex·em'pla·ry
ex·em'pli·fi·
 ca'tion
ex·em'pli·fy'
 ·fied' ·fy'ing
ex·empt'
ex·emp'tion

ex'er·cis'a·ble
ex'er·cise'
 ·cised' ·cis'ing
 (use; see exorcise)
ex·ert'
ex·er'tion
ex'e·unt
ex·ha·la'tion
ex·hale'
 ·haled' ·hal'ing
ex·haust'
ex·haust'i·ble
ex·haus'tion
ex·haus'tive
ex·hib'it
ex'hi·bi'tion
ex'hi·bi'tion·ism
ex·hib'i·tor
ex·hil'a·rant
ex·hil'a·rate'
 ·rat'ed ·rat'ing
ex·hil'a·ra'tion
ex·hort'
ex'hor·ta'tion
ex·hu·ma'tion
ex·hume'
 ·humed'
 ·hum'ing
ex'i·gen·cy
 ·cies
ex'i·gent
ex'ile
ex·ist'
ex·ist'ence
ex·ist'ent
ex·is·ten'tial
ex·is·ten'tial·ism
ex'it
ex'o·dus
ex' of·fi'ci·o'
ex·og'a·my
ex·on'er·ate'
 ·at'ed ·at'ing
ex·on'er·a'tion
ex'o·ra·ble
ex·or'bi·tance
ex·or'bi·tant
ex'or·cise' or
 ·cize'
 ·cised' or ·cized'
 ·cis'ing or ·ciz'ing
 (expel; see
 exercise)
ex'or·cism
ex'o·ter'ic
ex·ot'ic
ex·ot'i·ca
ex·ot'i·cal·ly
ex·pand'
ex·panse'
ex·pan'si·ble
ex·pan'sion
ex·pan'sive
ex·pa'ti·ate'
 ·at'ed ·at'ing
ex·pa'ti·a'tion
ex·pa'tri·ate'
 ·at'ed ·at'ing

ex·pa'tri·a'tion
ex·pect'
ex·pect'an·cy
ex·pect'ant
ex'pec·ta'tion
ex·pec'to·rant
ex·pec'to·rate'
 ·rat'ed ·rat'ing
ex·pec'to·ra'tion
ex·pe'di·ence
ex·pe'di·en·cy
 ·cies
ex·pe'di·ent
ex'pe·dite'
 ·dit'ed ·dit'ing
ex'pe·dit'er
ex·pe·di'tion
ex·pe·di'tion·ar'y
ex·pe·di'tious
ex·pel'
 ·pelled' ·pel'ling
ex·pel'la·ble
ex'pel·lee'
ex·pend'
ex·pend'a·bil'i·ty
ex·pend'a·ble
ex·pend'i·ture
ex·pense'
ex·pen'sive
ex·pen'sive·ly
ex·pe'ri·ence
 ·enced ·enc·ing
ex·pe'ri·en'tial
ex·per'i·ment
ex·per'i·men'tal
ex·per'i·men·
 ta'tion
ex'pert
ex·pert'·ise'
ex'pi·a·ble
ex'pi·ate'
 ·at'ed ·at'ing
ex'pi·a'tion
ex'pi·a'tor
ex·pi·ra'to·ry
ex·pire'
 ·pired' ·pir'ing
ex·pla·na'tion
ex·plan'a·to'ry
ex'ple·tive
ex'pli·ca·ble
ex'pli·cate'
 ·cat'ed ·cat'ing
ex·pli·ca'tion
ex·plic'it
ex·plod'a·ble
ex·plode'
 ·plod'ed
 ·plod'ing
ex'ploit
ex'ploi·ta'tion
ex·plo·ra'tion
ex·plor'a·to'ry
ex·plore'
 ·plored'
 ·plor'ing

ex·plor'er
ex·plo'sion
ex·plo'sive
ex·po'nent
ex'po·nen'tial
ex·port'
ex'por·ta'tion
ex·pose'
 posed' pos'ing
ex'po·sé'
ex'po·si'tion
ex·pos'i·tor
ex·pos'i·to'ry
ex post fac'to
ex·pos'tu·late'
 ·lat'ed ·lat'ing
ex·pos'tu·la'tion
ex·pos'tu·la'tor
ex·po'sure
ex·pound'
ex·press'
ex·press'age
ex·press'i·ble
ex·pres'sion
ex·pres'sion·ism
ex·pres'sion·
 is'tic
ex·pres'sive
ex·press'man
ex·press'way
ex·pro'pri·ate'
 ·at'ed ·at'ing
ex·pro'pri·a'tion
ex·pul'sion
ex·punge'
 ·punged'
 ·pung'ing
ex'pur·gate'
 ·gat'ed ·gat'ing
ex'pur·ga'tion
ex'qui·site
ex'tant
 (*existing;* see
 extent)
ex·tem'po·ra'ne·
 ous
ex·tem'po·re
ex·tem'po·rize'
 ·rized' ·riz'ing
ex·tend'
ex·ten'si·ble
ex·ten'sion
ex·ten'sive
ex·tent'
 (*scope;* see extant)
ex·ten'u·ate'
 ·at'ed ·at'ing
ex·ten'u·a'tion
ex·te'ri·or
ex·ter'mi·nate'
 ·nat'ed ·nat'ing
ex·ter'mi·na'tion
ex·ter'mi·na'tor
ex·ter'nal
ex·ter'nal·ize'
 ·ized' ·iz'ing
ex·tinct'
ex·tinc'tion

ex·tin'guish
ex'tir·pate'
 ·pat'ed ·pat'ing
ex'tir·pa'tion
ex·tol' *or* ·toll'
 ·tolled' ·tol'ling
ex·tort'
ex·tor'tion
ex·tor'tion·ate
ex·tor'tion·er
ex·tor'tion·ist
ex'tra
ex·tract'
ex·tract'a·ble
 or ·i·ble
ex·trac'tion
ex·trac'tor
ex'tra·cur·ric'u·
 lar
ex'tra·dit'a·ble
ex'tra·dite'
 ·dit'ed ·dit'ing
ex'tra·di'tion
ex'tra·le'gal
ex'tra·mar'i·tal
ex'tra·mu'ral
ex·tra'ne·ous
ex·traor'di·
 nar'i·ly
ex·traor'di·
 nar'y
ex·trap'o·late'
 ·lat'ed ·lat'ing
ex'tra·sen'so·ry
ex'tra·ter'ri·
 to'ri·al
ex·trav'a·gance
ex·trav'a·gant
ex·trav'a·gan'za
ex'tra·ve·hic'u·lar
ex·treme'
ex·treme'ly
ex·trem'ism
ex·trem'ist
ex·trem'i·ty
 ·ties
ex'tri·cate'
 ·cat'ed ·cat'ing
ex'tri·ca'tion
ex·trin'sic
ex·trin'si·cal·ly
ex'tro·ver'sion
ex'tro·vert'
ex·trude'
 ·trud'ed
 ·trud'ing
ex·tru'sion
ex·u'ber·ance
ex·u'ber·ant
ex'u·da'tion
ex·ude'
 ·ud'ed ·ud'ing
ex·ult'
ex·ult'ant
ex'ul·ta'tion
ex'urb'
ex·ur'ban·ite'
ex·ur'bi·a

eye
 eyed eye'ing
 or ey'ing
eye'ball'
eye'brow'
eye'-catch'er
eye'cup'
eye'ful'
eye'glass'
eye'hole'
eye'lash'
eye'let
 (*hole;* see islet)
eye'lid'
eye liner
eye'-o'pen·er
eye'piece'
eye shadow
eye'shot'
eye'sight'
eye'sore'
eye'strain'
eye'tooth'
eye'wash'
eye'wink'
eye'wit'ness

F

fa'ble
 ·bled ·bling
fab'ric
fab'ri·cate'
 ·cat'ed ·cat'ing
fab'ri·ca'tion
fab'ri·ca'tor
Fab'ri·koid'
fab'u·lous
fa·çade' *or* ·cade'
face
 faced fac'ing
face'plate'
face'-sav'ing
fac'et
fa·ce'tious
fa'cial
fac'ile
fa·cil'i·tate'
 ·tat'ed ·tat'ing
fa·cil'i·ta'tion
fa·cil'i·ty
 ·ties
fac·sim'i·le
 ·led ·le·ing
fac'tion
fac'tious
fac·ti'tious
 (*artificial;* see
 fictitious)
fac'tor
fac·to'ri·al
fac'to·ry
 ·ries
fac·to'tum
fac'tu·al
fac'tu·al·ly

fac'ul·ty
 ·ties
fad'dish
fad'dism
fade
 fad'ed fad'ing
fade'-in'
fade'-out'
fag
 fagged
 fag'ging
fag'ot·ing
Fahr'en·heit'
fail'-safe'
fail'ure
faint
 (*weak;* see feint)
faint'heart'ed
fair'ground'
fair'-haired'
fair'ly
fair'-mind'ed
fair'-spo'ken
fair'-trade'
fair'way'
fair'-weath'er
fair'y
 ·ies
fair'y·land'
faith'ful
faith'ful·ly
faith'less
fake
 faked fak'ing
fak'er
 (*fraud*)
fa·kir'
 (*Moslem beggar*)
fal'cate
fal'con
fal'con·ry
fall
 fell fall'en
fall'ing
fal·la'cious
fal'la·cy
 ·cies
fal'li·bil'i·ty
fal'li·ble
fal'li·bly
fall'ing-out'
fall'off'
fall'out'
fal'low
false
 fals'er fals'est
false'heart'ed
false'hood'
fal·set'to
fal'si·fi·ca'tion
fal'si·fi'er
fal'si·fy'
 ·fied' ·fy'ing
fal'si·ty
 ·ties
fal'ter
fa·mil'ial
fa·mil'iar

fa·mil'i·ar'i·ty
 ·ties
fa·mil'iar·i·
 za'tion
fa·mil'iar·ize'
 ·ized' ·iz'ing
fam'i·ly
 ·lies
fam'ine
fam'ish
fa'mous
fan
 fanned fan'ning
fa·nat'ic
fa·nat'i·cal·ly
fa·nat'i·cism
fan'ci·ful
fan'cy
 ·cies
 ·ci·er ·ci·est
 ·cied ·cy·ing
fan'cy-free'
fan'cy-work'
fan'fare'
fan'light'
fan'tail'
fan·ta'si·a
fan·ta·size'
 ·sized' ·siz'ing
fan·tas'tic
fan·tas'ti·cal·ly
fan'ta·sy
 ·sies
 ·sied ·sy·ing
far
 far'ther
 far'thest
far'ad
far'a·day'
far'a·way'
farce
 farced farc'ing
far'ci·cal
far'ci·cal·ly
fare
 fared far'ing
fare'well'
far'fetched'
far'-flung'
fa·ri'na
far'i·na'ceous
farm'hand'
farm'house'
farm'stead'
farm'yard'
far'o
far'-off'
far'-out'
far'-reach'ing
far'row
far'see'ing
far'sight'ed
far'ther
far'thing
fas'ces
fas'ci·cle
fas'ci·nate'
 ·nat'ed ·nat'ing

fas'ci·na'tion
fas'ci·na'tor
fas'cism
fas'cist
fash'ion
fash'ion·a·ble
fash'ion·a·bly
fast'back'
fas'ten
fas'ten·er
fas'ten·ing
fas·tid'i·ous
fat
 fat'ter fat'test
 fat'ted fat'ting
fa'tal
fa'tal·ism
fa'tal·ist
fa'tal·is'tic
fa·tal·is'ti·cal·ly
fa·tal'i·ty
 ·ties
fa'tal·ly
fate'ful
fa'ther·hood'
fa'ther-in-law'
 fa'thers-
 in-law'
fa'ther·land'
fa'ther·less
fa'ther·li·ness
fa'ther·ly
fath'om
fath'om·a·ble
fath'om·less
fat'i·ga·ble
fa·tigue'
 ·tigued'
 ·tigu'ing
fat'-sol'u·ble
fat'ten
fat'ti·ness
fat'ty
 ·ti·er ·ti·est
fa·tu'i·ty
 ·ties
fat'u·ous
fat'-wit'ted
fau'cet
fault'find'ing
fault'i·ness
fault'less
fault'y
 ·i·er ·i·est
faun
 (*deity;* see fawn)
fau'na
 ·nas *or* ·nae
faux' pas'
 faux' pas'
fa'vor·a·ble
fa'vor·a·bly
fa'vored
fa'vor·ite
fa'vor·it·ism
fawn
 (*deer; act ser-*
 vilely; see faun)

faze
  fazed faz'ing
  (*disturb;* see
  phase)
fe'al·ty
fear'ful
  fear'ful·ly
fear'less
fear'some
fea·si·bil'i·ty
fea'si·ble
fea'si·bly
feast
feat
  (*deed;* see feet)
feath'er·bed'
feath'er·
  bed'ding
feath'er·
  brain'
feath'ered
feath'er·edge'
feath'er·i·ness
feath'er·stitch'
feath'er·weight'
feath'er·y
fea'ture
  ·tured·tur·ing
fea'ture-length'
feb'ri·fuge'
fe'brile
Feb'ru·ar'y
fe'cal
fe'ces
feck'less
fe'cund
fe'cun·date'
  ·dat'ed·dat'ing
fe·cun'di·ty
fed'er·al
fed'er·al·ism
fed'er·al·i·
  za'tion
fed'er·al·ize'
  ·ized'·iz'ing
fed'er·ate'
  ·at'ed·at'ing
fed'er·a'tion
fe·do'ra
fee'ble
  ·bler·blest
fee'ble·mind'ed
feed
  fed feed'ing
feed'back'
feel
  felt feel'ing
fee'-split'ting
feet
  (*pl. of foot;*
  see feat)
feign
feint
  (*pretense;* see
  faint)
fe·lic'i·tate'
  ·tat'ed·tat'ing
fe·lic'i·ta'tion

fe·lic'i·tous
fe·lic'i·ty
  ·ties
fe'line
fel'low·ship'
fel'on
fe·lo'ni·ous
fel'o·ny
  ·nies
fe·luc'ca
fe'male
fem'i·nine
fem'i·nin'i·ty
fem'i·nism
fem'i·nize'
  ·nized'·niz'ing
femme fa·tale'
  femmes fa·tales'
fence
  fenced fenc'ing
fend'er
fen·es·tra'tion
fen'nel
fer'ment
fer'men·ta'tion
fern
fe·ro'cious
fe·roc'i·ty
fer'ret
fer'ri·age
Fer'ris wheel
fer'rule
  (*metal ring;*
  see ferule)
fer'ry
  ·ries
  ·ried·ry·ing
fer'ry·boat'
fer'tile
fer·til'i·ty
fer·til·iz'a·ble
fer'til·i·za'tion
fer'til·ize'
  ·ized'·iz'ing
fer'til·iz'er
fer'ule
  (*stick;* see
  ferrule)
fer'vent
fer'vid
fer'vor
fes'cue
fes'tal
fes'ter
fes'ti·val
fes'tive
fes·tiv'i·ty
  ·ties
fes·toon'
fe'tal
fetch'ing
fete *or* fête
  fet'ed *or* fêt'ed
  fet'ing *or* fêt'ing
fe'ti·cide'
fet'id
fet'ish
fet'ish·ism

fet'lock'
fet'ter
fet'tle
fet'tuc·ci'ne
fe'tus
  ·tus·es
feu'dal
feu'dal·ism
feu'dal·is'tic
fe'ver·ish
fez
  fez'zes
fi·an·cé' *masc.*
fi·an·cée' *fem.*
fi·as'co
  ·coes *or* ·cos
fi'at
fib
  fibbed fib'bing
fib'ber
fi'ber *or* ·bre
fi'ber·board'
Fi'ber·glas'
fi'bril·la'tion
fi'broid
fi'brous
fib'u·la
  ·lae *or* ·las
fick'le
fic'tion·al·ize'
  ·ized'·iz'ing
fic·ti'tious
  (*imaginary;* see
  factitious)
fid'dle
  ·dled·dling
fi·del'i·ty
  ·ties
fidg'et
fidg'et·i·ness
fidg'et·y
fi·du'ci·ar'y
  ·ies
field'er
field'-strip'
field'-test'
field'work'
fiend'ish
fierce
  fierc'er
  fierc'est
fierce'ly
fi'er·i·ness
fi'er·y
  ·i·er·i·est
fi·es'ta
fif'teen'
fif'ti·eth
fif'ty
  ·ties
fight
  fought
  fight'ing
fig'ment
fig'u·ra'tion
fig'u·ra·tive
fig'ure
  ·ured·ur·ing

fig'ure·head'
fig'u·rine'
fil'a·ment
fi'lar
fil'bert
file
  filed fil'ing
fi·let' mi·gnon'
fil'i·al
fil'i·a'tion
fil'i·bus'ter
fil'i·gree'
  ·greed'
  ·gree'ing
fil'ings
Fil'i·pi'no
  ·nos
fil'let
fill'-in'
fill'ing
fil'lip
fil'ly
  ·lies
film'strip'
film'y
  ·i·er·i·est
fil'ter
  (*strainer;* see
  philter)
fil'ter·a·ble
filth'i·ly
filth'i·ness
filth'y
  ·i·er·i·est
fil'trate
  ·trat·ed·trat·ing
fin'a·ble
fi·na'gle
  ·gled·gling
fi·na'le
fi'nal·ist
fi·nal'i·ty
fi'nal·ize'
  ·ized'·iz'ing
fi'nal·ly
fi·nance'
  ·nanced'
  ·nanc'ing
fi·nan'cial
fi·nan'cial·ly
fin·an·cier'
find
  found find'ing
find'er
fine
  fin'er fin'est
  fined fin'ing
fine'-cut'
fine'-drawn'
fine'-grained'
fine'ly
fine'ness
fin'er·y
  ·ies
fine'spun'
fi·nesse'
  ·nessed'
  ·ness'ing

fine'-toothed'
fin'ger·board'
fin'gered
fin'ger·nail'
fin'ger·print'
finger tip
fin'i·al
fin'i·cal
fin'ick·i·ness
fin'ick·y
fi'nis
fin'ish
fin'ished
fi'nite
fin'nan had'die
fiord
fir
  (*tree;* see fur)
fire
  fired fir'ing
fire'arm'
fire'ball'
fire'boat'
fire'bomb'
fire'box'
fire'brand'
fire'break'
fire'brick'
fire'bug'
fire'clay'
fire'crack·er
fire'-cure'
fire'damp'
fire'dog'
fire'-eat'er
fire escape
fire'fly'
  ·flies'
fire'man
fire'place'
fire'plug'
fire'pow'er
fire'proof'
fire'side'
fire'trap'
fire'wa'ter
fire'wood'
fire'works'
fir'kin
firm'ly
first'born'
first'-class'
first'-hand'
first'ly
first'-rate'
firth
fis'cal
fis'cal·ly
fish'bowl'
fish'er·man
fish'er·y
  ·ies
fish'hook'
fish'i·ness
fish'mon'ger
fish'plate'
fish'pond'

fish'tail'
fish'wife'
fish'y
  ·i·er·i·est
fis'sion
fis'sion·a·ble
fis'sure
  ·sured·sur·ing
fis'ti·cuffs'
fis'tu·lous
fit
  fit'ted fit'ting
  fit'ter fit'test
fit'ful
  fit'ful·ly
fit'ness
five'fold'
fix'ate
  ·at·ed·at·ing
fix·a'tion
fix'a·tive
fixed
fix'ed·ly
fix'ture
fiz'zle
  ·zled·zling
fjord
flab'ber·gast'
flab'bi·ness
flab'by
  ·bi·er·bi·est
flac'cid
flac·cid'i·ty
fla·con'
flag
  flagged
  flag'ging
flag'el·lant
flag'el·late'
  ·lat'ed·lat'ing
flag'el·la'tion
fla·gel'lum
  ·la *or* ·lums
flag'eo·let'
flag'on
flag'pole'
fla'gran·cy
fla'grant
flag'ship'
flag'stone'
flag'-wav'ing
flail
flair
  (*knack;* see flare)
flake
  flaked flak'ing
flak'i·ness
flak'y
  ·i·er·i·est
flam·bé'
flam'beau
  ·beaux *or* ·beaus
flam·boy'ance
flam·boy'ant
flame
  flamed flam'ing
fla·men'co
  ·cos

flame'out'
flame'proof'
fla·min'go
 ·gos or ·goes
flam'ma·bil'i·ty
flam'ma·ble
flange
flanged
flang'ing
flank
flan'nel
flan'nel·ette'
flan'nel-mouthed'
flap
flapped
flap'ping
flap'jack'
flap'per
flare
flared flar'ing
 (blaze; see flair)
flare'-up'
flash'back'
flash'bulb'
flash'card'
flash'cube'
flash'i·ly
flash'i·ness
flash'light'
flash'y
 ·i·er·i·est
flat
 flat'ter flat'test
 flat'ted flat'ting
flat'boat'
flat'car'
flat'fish'
flat'-foot'ed
flat'i·ron
flat'ten
flat'ter
flat'ter·y
flat'u·lent
flat'ware'
flat'work'
flaunt
flau'tist
fla'vor·ful
fla'vor·ing
fla'vor·less
flaw'less
flax'en
flax'seed'
flea'-bit'ten
fledg'ling
flee
 fled flee'ing
fleece
 fleeced fleec'ing
fleec'i·ness
fleec'y
 ·i·er·i·est
fleet'ing
flesh'-col'ored
flesh'i·ness
flesh'pots'
flesh'y
 ·i·er·i·est

fleur'-de-lis'
fleurs'-de-lis'
flex'i·bil'i·ty
flex'i·ble
flex'i·bly
flick'er
flied
 (only in baseball)
fli'er or fly'er
flight'i·ness
flight'less
flight'y
 ·i·er·i·est
flim'si·ly
flim'si·ness
flim'sy
 ·si·er·si·est
flinch'ing·ly
fling
 flung fling'ing
flint'lock'
flint'y
 ·i·er·i·est
flip
 flipped flip'ping
flip'pan·cy
 ·cies
flip'pant
flip'per
flir·ta'tion
flir·ta'tious
flit
 flit'ted flit'ting
float'er
float'ing
floc'cu·late'
 ·lat'ed·lat'ing
floc'cu·lent
floe
 (ice; see flow)
flog
 flogged
 flog'ging
flood'gate'
flood'light'
 ·light'ed or·lit'
 ·light'ing
floor'ing
floor'walk'er
flop
 flopped
 flop'ping
flo'ra
 ·ras or·rae
flo'ral
flo·res'cence
 (blooming; see
 fluorescence)
flo·res'cent
flo'ret
flo'ri·cul'ture
flor'id
Flor'i·da
flo·rid'i·ty
flor'in
flo'rist
floss'y
 ·i·er·i·est

flo·ta'tion
flo·til'la
flot'sam
flounce
 flounced
 flounc'ing
floun'der
flour'ish
flout
flow
 (glide; see floe)
flow'ered
flow'er·i·ness
flow'er·pot'
flow'er·y
 ·i·er·i·est
flu
 (influenza)
fluc'tu·ate'
 ·at'ed·at'ing
flue
 (pipe)
flu'en·cy
flu'ent
fluf'fi·ness
fluf'fy
 ·fi·er·fi·est
flu'id
flu·id'i·ty
flun'ky
 ·kies
flu'o·resce'
 ·resced'
 ·resc'ing
flu'o·res'cence
 (light; see
 florescence)
flu'o·res'cent
fluor'i·date'
 ·dat'ed·dat'ing
fluor'i·da'tion
fluor'i·nate'
 ·nat'ed·nat'ing
fluor'o·scope'
flu'o·ros'co·py
flur'ry
 ·ries
 ·ried·ry·ing
flus'ter
flute
 flut'ed flut'ing
flut'ist
flut'ter
flu'vi·al
fly
 flies
 flew flown
 fly'ing
fly'a·ble
fly'a·way'
fly'-by-night'
fly'catch'er
fly'leaf'
 ·leaves'
fly'pa'per
fly'speck'
fly'trap'
fly'weight'

fly'wheel'
foam'i·ness
foam'y
 ·i·er·i·est
fo'cal
fo'cal·ize'
 ·ized'·iz'ing
fo'cus
 ·cus·es or·ci
 ·cused or·cussed
 ·cus·ing or
 ·cus·sing
fod'der
fog
 fogged fog'ging
fog'bound'
fog'gi·ly
fog'gi·ness
fog'gy
 ·gi·er·gi·est
fog'horn'
fo'gy or fo'gey
 ·gies or·geys
foi'ble
foist
fold'a·way'
fold'er
fo'li·age
fo'li·ate'
 ·at'ed·at'ing
fo'li·a'tion
fo'li·o'
 ·os', ·oed'·o'ing
folk'lore'
folk'way'
fol'li·cle
fol'low·er
fol'low-through'
fol'low-up'
fol'ly
 ·lies
fo·ment'
fo·men·ta'tion
fon'dant
fon'dle
 ·dled·dling
fond'ness
fon·due'
food'stuff'
fool'har'di·ness
fool'har'dy
fool'ish·ness
fool'proof'
fools'cap'
foot
 feet
foot'age
foot'ball'
foot'bridge'
foot'-can'dle
foot'fall'
foot'hold'
foot'ing
foot'lights'
foot'lock'er
foot'loose'
foot'note'
foot'path'

foot'-pound'
foot'print'
foot'race'
foot'rest'
foot'sore'
foot'step'
foot'stool'
foot'-ton'
foot'wear'
foot'work'
fop'pish
for'age
for'ay
for·bear'
 ·bore'·borne'
 ·bear'ing
 (abstain; see
 forebear)
for·bear'ance
for·bid'
 ·bade' or·bad'
 ·bid'den
 ·bid'ding
force
 forced forc'ing
force'ful
for'ceps
 ·ceps
for'ci·ble
for'ci·bly
fore'arm'
fore·bear'
 (ancestor; see
 forbear)
fore·bode'
 ·bod'ed·bod'ing
fore'cast'
 ·cast' or·cast'ed
 ·cast'ing
fore'cas'tle
fore·close'
fore·clo'sure
fore·doom'
fore·fa'ther
fore'fin'ger
fore'foot'
fore·go'
 ·went'·gone'
 ·go'ing
 (precede; see
 forgo)
fore·go'ing
fore'ground'
fore'hand'
fore·hand'ed
fore'head
for'eign
for'eign-born'
for'eign·er
fore·knowl'edge
fore'leg'
fore'lock'
fore'man
fore'most'
fore·named'
fore·noon'
fo·ren'sic
fo·ren'si·cal·ly

fore'or·dain'
fore'paw'
fore'play'
fore'quar'ter
fore'run'ner
fore'sail'
fore·see'
 ·saw'·seen'
 ·see'ing
fore·see'a·ble
fore·se'er
fore·shad'ow
fore·short'en
fore·show'
 ·showed',
 ·shown' or
 ·showed',
 ·show'ing
fore'sight'
fore'skin'
for'est
fore·stall'
for'est·a'tion
for'est·er
for'est·ry
fore'taste'
fore·tell'
 ·told'·tell'ing
fore'thought'
for·ev'er
fore·warn'
fore'word'
 (preface; see
 forward)
for'feit
for'fei·ture
forge
 forged forg'ing
forg'er
for'ger·y
 ·ies
for·get'
 ·got'·got'ten
 or·got',
 ·get'ting
for·get'ful
for·get'-me-not'
for·get'ta·ble
for·giv'a·ble
for·give'
 ·gave'·giv'en
 ·giv'ing
for·give'ness
for·go' or fore·
 ·went'·gone'
 ·go'ing
 (do without;
 see forego)
forked
fork'lift'
for·lorn'
for'mal
form·al'de·hyde'
for·mal'i·ty
 ·ties
for'mal·i·za'tion
for'mal·ize'
 ·ized'·iz'ing

for'mal·ly
for'mat
for·ma'tion
form'a·tive
for'mer
For·mi'ca
for'mi·da·ble
for'mi·da·bly
form'less
for'mu·la
  ·las or ·lae'
for'mu·late'
  ·lat'ed ·lat'ing
for'mu·la'tion
for'ni·cate'
  ·cat'ed ·cat'ing
for'ni·ca'tion
for'ni·ca'tor
for·sake'
  ·sook' ·sak'en
  ·sak'ing
for·swear'
  ·swore' ·sworn'
  ·swear'ing
for·syth'i·a
fort
  (fortified place)
forte
  (special skill)
forth'com'ing
forth'right'
forth'with'
for'ti·eth
for·ti·fi·ca'tion
for'ti·fi'er
for'ti·fy'
  ·fied' ·fy'ing
for'ti·tude'
for'tress
for·tu'i·tous
for·tu'i·ty
  ·ties
for'tu·nate
for'tune
for'tune·tell'er
for'ty
  ·ties
fo'rum
  ·rums or ·ra
for'ward
  (to the front;
  see foreword)
fos'sil
fos'ter
foul
  (filthy; see fowl)
fou·lard'
foul'mouthed'
foun·da'tion
foun'der v.
found'er n.
found'ling
found'ry
  ·ries
foun'tain
foun'tain·head'
four'-flush'er
four'fold'

four'-foot'ed
Four'-H' club or
  4'-H' club
four'-in-hand'
four'-post'er
four'score'
four'some
four'square'
four'-star'
four'teen'
fourth
fourth'-class'
four'-way'
fowl
  (bird; see foul)
fox'hole'
fox'hound'
fox'i·ly
fox'i·ness
fox'y
  ·i·er ·i·est
foy'er
fra'cus
frac'tion
frac'tious
frac'ture
  ·tured ·tur·ing
frag'ile
fra·gil'i·ty
frag'ment
frag·men'tal·ly
frag'men·tar'y
fra'grance
fra'grant
frail'ty
  ·ties
frame
framed
fram'ing
frame'-up'
frame'work'
franc
  (coin; see frank)
fran'chise
  ·chised ·chis·ing
fran'gi·bil'i·ty
fran'gi·ble
frank
  (free; see franc)
frank'furt·er
frank'in·cense'
fran'tic
fran'ti·cal·ly
frap·pé'
fra·ter'nal
fra·ter'nal·ly
fra·ter'ni·ty
  ·ties
frat'er·ni·za'tion
frat'er·nize'
  ·nized' ·niz'ing
frat'ri·cide'
fraud'u·lence
fraud'u·lent
fraught
freak'ish
freck'le
  ·led ·ling

free
  fre'er fre'est
  freed free'ing
free'bie or ·by
  ·bies
free'born'
freed'man
free'dom
free'-for-all'
free'-form'
free'hand'
free'-lance'
free'load'er
free'man
Free'ma'son
free'-spo'ken
free'-stand'ing
free'stone'
free'think'er
free'way'
free'wheel'ing
freez'a·ble
freeze
  froze froz'en
  freez'ing
  (become ice; see
  frieze)
freeze'-dry'
  -dried' -dry'ing
freez'er
freight'age
freight'er
French cuff
French doors
French fry
  French fries
French toast
fre·net'ic
fre·net'i·cal·ly
fren'zy
  ·zies
  ·zied ·zy·ing
fre'quen·cy
  ·cies
fre'quent
fres'co
  ·coes or ·cos
fresh'en
fresh'et
fresh'man
fresh'wa'ter
fret
fret'ted
fret'ting
fret'ful
fret'ful·ly
fret'work'
Freud'i·an
fri'a·bil'i·ty
fri'a·ble
fri'ar
fric'as·see'
  ·seed' ·see'ing
fric'tion
Fri'day
friend'li·ness
friend'ly
  ·li·er ·li·est

friend'ship
frieze
  (in architecture;
  see freeze)
frig'ate
fright'ened
fright'ful
frig'id
fri·gid'i·ty
frill'y
  ·i·er ·i·est
fringe
fringed
fring'ing
frip'per·y
  ·ies
Fris'bee
fri·sé'
frisk'i·ness
frisk'y
  ·i·er ·i·est
frit'ter
fri·vol'i·ty
  ·ties
friv'o·lous
friz'zi·ness
frog'man'
frol'ic
  ·icked ·ick·ing
frol'ick·er
frol'ic·some
front'age
fron'tal
fron·tier'
fron·tiers'man
fron'tis·piece'
front'let
frost'bite'
  ·bit' ·bit'ten
  ·bit'ing
frost'i·ly
frost'i·ness
frost'ing
frost'y
  ·i·er ·i·est
froth'i·ly
froth'i·ness
froth'y
  ·i·er ·i·est
fro'ward
frown
frow'zi·ness
frow'zy
  ·zi·er ·zi·est
fro'zen
fruc'ti·fy'
  ·fied' ·fy'ing
fru'gal
fru·gal'i·ty
fru'gal·ly
fruit'cake'
fruit'ful
fruit'i·ness
fru·i'tion
fruit'less
fruit'wood'
fruit'y
  ·i·er ·i·est

frump'ish
frus'trate
  ·trat·ed ·trat·ing
frus·tra'tion
frus'tum
  ·tums or ·ta
fry
  fried fry'ing
fry'er or fri'er
f'-stop'
fuch'sia
fudge
fudged
fudg'ing
fu'el
  ·eled or ·elled
  ·el·ing or ·el·ling
fuel cell
fu'gi·tive
fugue
ful'crum
  ·crums or ·cra
ful·fill' or ·fil'
  ·filled' ·fill'ing
ful·fill'ment
  or ·fil'ment
full'back'
full'-blood'ed
full'-blown'
full'-bod'ied
full'-dress'
full'er's earth
full'-faced'
full'-fash'ioned
full'-fledged'
full'-length'
full'-scale'
full'-time'
full'y
ful'mi·nate'
  ·nat'ed ·nat'ing
ful'some
fum'ble
  ·bled ·bling
fume
  fumed fum'ing
fu'mi·gant
fu'mi·gate'
  ·gat'ed ·gat'ing
fu'mi·ga'tion
fu'mi·ga'tor
func'tion·al
func'tion·al·ly
func'tion·ar'y
  ·ar'ies
fun·da·men'tal
fun·da·men'tal·ism
fun·da·men'tal·ly
fund'-rais'er
fu'ner·al
fu·ne're·al
fun'gi·cid'al
fun'gi·cide'
fun'gous adj.
fun'gus n.
  ·gi or ·gus·es
fu·nic'u·lar

fun'nel
  ·neled or ·nelled
  ·nel·ing or
  ·nel·ling
fun'ni·ness
fun'ny
  ·ni·er ·ni·est
fur
  furred fur'ring
  (hair; see fir)
fur'be·low'
fur'bish
fu'ri·ous
fur'long
fur'lough
fur'nace
fur'nish·ings
fur'ni·ture
fu'ror
fur'ri·er
fur'ri·ness
fur'row
fur'ry
  ·ri·er ·ri·est
fur'ther
fur'ther·ance
fur'ther·more'
fur'ther·most'
fur'thest
fur'tive
fu'ry
  ·ries
fuse
  fused fus'ing
fu'se·lage'
fu·si·bil'i·ty
fu'si·ble
fu'sil·lade'
  ·lad'ed ·lad'ing
fu'sion
fuss'i·ness
fuss'y
  ·i·er ·i·est
fus'tian
fust'y
  ·i·er ·i·est
fu'tile
fu'tile·ly
fu·til'i·ty
fu'ture
fu·tu'ri·ty
  ·ties
fuzz'i·ly
fuzz'i·ness
fuzz'y
  ·i·er ·i·est

G

gab'ar·dine'
ga'ble
gad'a·bout'
gadg'et
gag
  gagged
  gag'ging

gage
(*pledge; see*
  gauge)
gag'gle
gag'man'
gai'e·ty
gai'ly
gain'er
gain'ful
gain'ful·ly
gain'li·ness
gain'ly
·li·er ·li·est
gain'say'
·said' ·say'ing
gait
(*way of walking;*
see gate)
gai'ter
ga'la
Gal'a·had'
gal'ax·y
·ies
gal'lant
gal'lant·ry
·ries
gal'le·on
gal'ler·y
·ies
·ied ·y·ing
gal'ley
·leys
gall'ing
gal'li·vant'
gal'lon
gal'lop
gal'lows
·lows·es or ·lows
gall'stone'
ga·lore'
ga·losh'
  or ·loshe'
ga·lumph'
gal·van'ic
gal'va·nism
gal'va·ni·za'tion
gal'va·nize'
·nized' ·niz'ing
gal'va·nom'e·ter
gam'bit
gam'ble
·bled ·bling
(*risk; see*
gambol)
gam'bler
gam'bol
·boled or ·bolled
·bol·ing or
·bol·ling
(*frolic; see*
gamble)
gam'brel
game'cock'
game'keep'er
games'man·ship'
gam'in
gam'i·ness
gam'ma

gam'ut
gam'y
·i·er ·i·est
gan'der
Gan'dhi·ism
ga'nef or ·nof
gang'land'
gan'gling
gan'gli·on
·gli·a or ·gli·ons
gang'plank'
gan'grene
gan'gre·nous
gang'ster
gang'way'
gant'let
gan'try
·tries
gap
gapped
gap'ping
gape
gaped gap'ing
ga·rage'
·raged' ·rag'ing
gar'bage
gar'ble
·bled ·bling
gar·çon'
·çons'
gar'den·er
gar·de'ni·a
gar'gle
·gled ·gling
gar'goyle
gar'ish
gar'land
gar'lic
gar'ment
gar'ner
gar'net
gar'nish
gar'nish·ee'
·eed' ·ee'ing
gar'nish·ment
gar'ret
gar'ri·son
gar·rote'
·rot'ed or
·rot'ted
·rot'ing or
·rot'ting
gar·ru'li·ty
gar'ru·lous
gar'ter
gas
gassed
gas'sing
gas'e·ous
gas'ket
gas'light'
gas·o·line' or
·lene'
gas'sy
·si·er ·si·est

gas'tric
gas'tro·nome'
gas'tro·nom'i·cal
gas·tron'o·my
gate
(*door; see gait*)
gate'way'
gath'er·ing
gauche
(*lacking grace;*
see gouache)
gau'che·rie'
gaud'i·ly
gaud'i·ness
gaud'y
·i·er ·i·est
gauge
gauged
gaug'ing
(*measure; see*
gage)
gauge'a·ble
gaunt
gaunt'let
gauze
gauz'y
·i·er ·i·est
gav'el
gawk'i·ness
gawk'y
·i·er ·i·est
gay'ly
gaze
gazed gaz'ing
ga·ze'bo
·bos or ·boes
ga·zelle'
ga·zette'
gaz'et·teer'
gear'box'
gear'shift'
gear'wheel'
Gei'ger
gei'sha
·sha or ·shas
gel
gelled gel'ling
gel'a·tin or ·tine
ge·lat'i·nize'
·nized' ·niz'ing
ge·lat'i·nous
geld
geld'ed or gelt
geld'ing
gel'id
ge·lid'i·ty
gem'i·nate'
·nat'ed ·nat'ing
Gem'i·ni'
gen'darme
gen'der
ge·ne·a·log'i·cal
ge·ne·al'o·gy
·gies
gen'er·al
gen'er·al'i·ty
·ties
gen'er·al·i·za'tion

gen'er·al·ize'
·ized' ·iz'ing
gen'er·al·ly
gen'er·ate'
·at'ed ·at'ing
gen'er·a'tion
gen'er·a'tor
ge·ner'ic
ge·ner'i·cal·ly
gen'er·os'i·ty
·ties
gen'er·ous
gen'e·sis
·ses'
ge·net'ic
ge·net'i·cal·ly
ge'nial
ge·ni·al'i·ty
ge'nial·ly
ge'nie
gen'i·tal
gen'ius
gen'o·cide'
gen'o·type'
gen're
gen·teel'
gen·teel'ly
gen'tile
gen·til'i·ty
gen'tle
·tler ·tlest
gen'tle·man
gen'tle·man·ly
gen'tle·wom'an
gent'ly
gen'try
gen'u·flect'
gen'u·ine
gen'u·ine·ly
ge'nus
gen'er·a
ge·o·cen'tric
ge·og'ra·pher
ge·o·graph'i·cal
ge·og'ra·phy
·phies
ge·o·log'ic
ge·o·log'i·cal·ly
ge·ol'o·gist
ge·ol'o·gy
·gies
ge·o·met'ric
ge·o·met'ri·cal·ly
ge·om'e·try
·tries
ge·o·phys'i·cal
ge·o·phys'i·cist
ge·o·phys'ics
ge·o·po·lit'i·cal
ge·o·pol'i·tics
Geor'gia
ge·o·stat'ics
ge·ot'ro·pism
ge·ra'ni·um
ger'bil or ·bille
ger·i·at'rics
ger·mane'
ger'mi·cid'al

ger'mi·cide'
ger'mi·nate'
·nat'ed ·nat'ing
ger'mi·na'tion
ger·on·tol'o·gy
ger'ry·man'der
ger'und
Ge·stalt'
ges'tate
·tat·ed ·tat·ing
ges·ta'tion
ges·tic'u·late'
·lat'ed ·lat'ing
ges·tic'u·la'tion
ges·tic'u·la'tor
ges'ture
·tured ·tur·ing
get
got, got or
got'ten,
get'ting
get'a·way'
get'-to·geth'er
gew'gaw
gey'ser
ghast'li·ness
ghast'ly
·li·er ·li·est
ghost'li·ness
ghost'ly
·li·er ·li·est
ghost'write'
ghost'writ'er
ghoul'ish
gi'ant
gib'ber·ish
gib'bet
gib'bon
gib·bos'i·ty
·ties
gib'bous
gibe
gibed gib'ing
(*taunt; see jibe*)
gib'let
gid'di·ly
gid'di·ness
gid'dy
·di·er ·di·est
gift'ed
gift'-wrap'
-wrapped'
-wrap'ping
gig
gigged gig'ging
gi·gan'tic
gi·gan'ti·cal·ly
gi·gan'tism
gig'gle
·gled ·gling
gig'o·lo'
·los'

gild
gild'ed or gilt
gild'ing
(*coat with gold;*
see guild)
gilt
(*gold; see guilt*)
gilt'-edged'
gim'bals
gim'crack'
gim'let
gim'mick
gin'ger
gin'ger·bread'
ging'ham
gi·raffe'
gird
gird'ed or girt
gird'ing
gird'er
gir'dle
·dled ·dling
girl'ish
gist
give
gave giv'en
giv'ing
give'a·way'
giz'zard
gla·cé'
·céed' ·cé'ing
gla'cial
gla'ci·ate'
·at'ed ·at'ing
gla'cier
glad
glad'der
glad'dest
glad'den
glad'i·a'tor
glad'i·o'lus or ·la
·lus·es or ·li, ·las
glad'some
glair
(*glaze; see glare*)
glam'or·ize'
·ized' ·iz'ing
glam'or·ous
glam'our or ·or
glance
glanced
glanc'ing
glan'du·lar
glare
glared glar'ing
(*strong light;*
see glair)
glar'i·ness
glar'y
·i·er ·i·est
glass'ful'
·fuls'
glass·ine'
glass'i·ness
glass'ware'
glass'y
·i·er ·i·est
glau·co'ma

glaze
　glazed glaz'ing
gla'zier
glean'ings
glee'ful
glee'ful·ly
glib
　glib'ber
　glib'best
glib'ly
glide
　glid'ed glid'ing
glid'er
glim'mer
glimpse
　glimpsed
　glimps'ing
glis·sade'
　·sad'ed ·sad'ing
glis'ten
glit'ter
glit'ter·y
gloam'ing
gloat
glob'al
globe'-trot'ter
glob'u·lar
glob'ule
glock'en·spiel'
gloom'i·ly
gloom'i·ness
gloom'y
　·i·er ·i·est
glo·ri·fi·ca'tion
glo'ri·fy'
　·fied' ·fy'ing
glo'ri·ous
glo'ry
　·ries
　·ried ·ry·ing
glos'sa·ry
　·ries
gloss'i·ness
gloss'y
　·i·er ·i·est
　·ies
glot'tal
glove
　gloved glov'ing
glow'er
glow'ing·ly
glow'worm'
glu'cose
glue
　glued glu'ing
glue'y
　glu'i·er
　glu'i·est
glum'ly
glut
　glut'ted
　glut'ting
glu'ten
glu'ten·ous
　(having gluten)
glu'ti·nous
　(gluey)
glut'ton

glut'ton·ous
　(greedy)
glut'ton·y
glyc'er·in or ·ine
gnarled
gnash
gnat
gnaw
　gnawed
　gnaw'ing
gneiss
gnoc'chi
gnome
gno'mic
gno'mon
gnos'tic
gnu
go
　went gone
go'ing
goad
go'-a·head'
goal'keep'er
goat·ee'
gob'ble
　bled ·bling
gob'ble·dy·gook'
go'-be·tween'
gob'let
gob'lin
god'child'
god'daugh·ter
god'dess
god'fa'ther
God'-giv'en
god'li·ness
god'ly
　·li·er ·li·est
god'moth'er
god'par'ent
god'send'
god'son'
God'speed'
go'-get'ter
gog'gle
　gled ·gling
go'-go'
goi'ter or ·tre
gold'en
gold'-filled'
gold'fish'
gold leaf
gold'smith'
golf'er
gon'do·la
gon'do·lier'
gon'or·rhe'a
　or ·rhoe'a
good
　bet'ter best
good'bye' or
　good'-bye'
　byes' or ·byes'
good'-for-
　noth'ing
good'-heart'ed
good'-hu'mored
good'-look'ing

good'ly
　·li·er ·li·est
good'-na'tured
good night
good'-sized'
good'-tem'pered
good'y
　·ies
goo'ey
goo'i·er goo'i·est
goo'gol
goose
　geese
goose'neck'
goose'-step'
go'pher
gore
　gored gor'ing
gorge
　gorged gorg'ing
gor'geous
go·ril'la
　(ape; see guerrilla)
gor'i·ness
gor'mand·ize'
　·ized' ·iz'ing
gor'y
　·i·er ·i·est
gos'hawk'
gos'ling
gos'pel
gos'sa·mer
gos'sip
got'ten
gouache
　(painting; see
　gauche)
gouge
　gouged
　goug'ing
gou'lash
gourd
gour'mand
gour'met
gout
gov'ern·ess
gov'ern·ment
gov'ern·men'tal
gov'er·nor
grab
　grabbed
　grab'bing
grace'ful
grace'ful·ly
grace'less
gra'cious
gra'date
　·dat·ed ·dat·ing
gra·da'tion
grade
　grad'ed grad'ing
grad'u·al
grad'u·ate'
　·at·ed ·at'ing
grad·u·a'tion
graf·fi'ti
　(sing. graf·fi'to)
graft'er

gra'ham
grain'i·ness
grain'y
　·i·er ·i·est
gram'mar
gram·mar'i·an
gram·mat'i·cal
gran'a·ry
　·ries
grand'aunt'
grand'child'
grand'daugh'ter
gran'deur
grand'fa'ther
gran·dil'o·quent
gran'di·ose'
grand'moth'er
grand'neph'ew
grand'niece'
grand'par'ent
grand'son'
grand'stand'
grand'un'cle
gran'ite
gran'ite·ware'
grant·ee'
grant'in-aid'
　grants'-in-aid'
grant'or
gran'u·lar
gran'u·late'
　·lat'ed ·lat'ing
gran'ule
grape'fruit'
grape'vine'
graph'ic
graph'i·cal·ly
graph'ite
graph·ol'o·gy
grap'nel
grap'ple
　pled ·pling
grap'pler
grasp'ing
grass'hop'per
grass'y
　·i·er ·i·est
grate
　grat'ed grat'ing
grate'ful
grate'ful·ly
grat·i·fi·ca'tion
grat'i·fy'
　·fied' ·fy'ing
gra'tis
grat'i·tude
gra·tu'i·tous
gra·tu'i·ty
　·ties
grave
　graved, grav'en
　or graved,
　grav'ing
　(carve out)
grave
　graved grav'ing
　(clean the hull)
grave'clothes'

grav'el
　·eled or ·elled
　·el·ing or ·el·ling
grav'el·ly
grave'ly
grave'side'
grave'stone'
grave'yard'
grav'i·tate'
　·tat'ed ·tat'ing
grav'i·ta'tion
grav'i·ty
　·ties
gra'vy
　·vies
gray
gray'-head'ed
graze
　grazed graz'ing
grease
　greased
　greas'ing
grease'paint'
greas'i·ness
greas'y
　·i·er ·i·est
great'-aunt'
great'coat'
great'-grand'child'
great'-grand'par'·
　ent
great'ly
great'-neph'ew
great'ness
great'-niece'
great'-un'cle
greed'i·ly
greed'i·ness
greed'y
　·i·er ·i·est
Greek'-let'ter
green'back'
green'er·y
green'-eyed'
green'gage'
green'horn'
green'house'
green'room'
green'sward'
greet'ing
gre·gar'i·ous
grem'lin
gre·nade'
gren'a·dier'
gren'a·dine'
grey'hound' or
　gray'·
grid'dle
　·dled ·dling
grid'dle·cake'
grid'i'ron
grief'-strick'en
griev'ance
grieve
　grieved
griev'ing
griev'ous
grif'fin

grill
　(broiler grid)
grille
　(open grating)
grill'room'
grim
　grim'mer
　grim'mest
gri·mace'
　·maced'
　·mac'ing
grime
　grimed grim'ing
grim'i·ly
grim'i·ness
grim'y
　·i·er ·i·est
grin
　grinned
　grin'ning
grind
　ground
　grind'ing
grind'stone'
grip
　gripped or gript
　grip'ping
　(hold)
gripe
　griped grip'ing
　(distress)
grippe
　(influenza)
gris'li·ness
gris'ly
　·li·er ·li·est
　(horrid)
gris'tle
gris'tly
　(of gristle)
grist'mill'
grit
　grit'ted
　grit'ting
grit'ti·ness
grit'ty
　·ti·er ·ti·est
griz'zly bear
groan'ing
gro'cer·y
　·ies
grog'gi·ly
grog'gi·ness
grog'gy
　·gi·er ·gi·est
groin
grom'met
groom
groove
　grooved
groov'ing
groov'y
　·i·er ·i·est
grope
　groped grop'ing
gros'grain'
gross'ly
gross'ness

gro·tesque'
gro·tesque'ly
grot'to
·toes or ·tos
grouch'i·ly
grouch'i·ness
grouch'y
·i·er ·i·est
ground'less
grounds'keep'er
ground'speed'
ground'work'
group
grout
grove
grov'el
·eled or ·elled
·el·ing or ·el·ling
grow
grew grown
grow'ing
growl'er
grown'-up'
growth
grub
grubbed
grub'bing
grub'bi·ness
grub'by
·bi·er ·bi·est
grub'stake'
grudge
grudged
grudg'ing
gru'el
gru'el·ing or
gru'el·ling
grue'some
grue'some·ly
gruff'ly
grum'ble
·bled ·bling
grum'bler
grum'bly
grump'i·ness
grump'y
·i·er ·i·est
grun'ion
grunt
Gru·yère'
G'-string'
G'-suit'
guar'an·tee'
·teed' ·tee'ing
guar'an·tor'
guar'an·ty
·ties
·tied ·ty·ing
guard'ed
guard'house'
guard'i·an
guard'rail'
guard'room'
guards'man
gua'va
gu'ber·na·to'ri·al
Guern'sey
·seys

guer·ril'la or gue·
(soldier; see
gorilla)
guess'work'
guest
guid'a·ble
guid'ance
guide
guid'ed
guid'ing
guide'book'
guide'line'
guide'post'
guild
(union; see gild)
guilds'man
guile'ful
guile'less
guil'lo·tine'
·tined' ·tin'ing
guilt
(blame; see gilt)
guilt'i·ly
guilt'i·ness
guilt'y
·i·er ·i·est
guin'ea pig
guise
gui·tar'
gui·tar'ist
gulch
gul'let
gul'li·bil'i·ty
gul'li·ble
gul'li·bly
gul'ly
·lies
gum'drop'
gum'mi·ness
gum'my
·mi·er ·mi·est
gun
gunned
gun'ning
gun'cot'ton
gun'fire'
gung'-ho'
gun'lock'
gun'man
gun'ner·y
gun'ny·sack'
gun'play'
gun'point'
gun'pow'der
gun'run'ning
gun'shot'
gun'-shy'
gun'smith'
gun'stock'
gup'py
·pies
gur'gle
·gled ·gling
gu'ru
gush'er
gush'i·ness
gush'y
·i·er ·i·est

gus'set
gus'ta·to'ry
gus'to
gust'y
·i·er ·i·est
gut
gut'ted
gut'ting
gut'ta-per'cha
gut'ter·snipe'
gut'tur·al
guy
guz'zle
·zled ·zling
guz'zler
gym·na'si·um
·si·ums or ·si·a
gym'nast
gym·nas'tics
gym'no·sperm'
gyn'e·col'o·gist
gyn'e·col'o·gy
gyp
gypped gyp'ping
gyp'sum
Gyp'sy
·sies
gy'rate
·rat·ed ·rat·ing
gy·ra'tion
gy'ro·com'pass
gy'ro·scope'
gy'ro·scop'ic
gy'ro·sta'bi·liz'er

H

ha'be·as cor'pus
hab'er·dash'er·y
·ies
ha·bil'i·tate'
·tat'ed ·tat'ing
hab'it
hab'it·a·ble
hab'i·tat'
hab'i·ta'tion
hab'it-form'ing
ha·bit'u·al
ha·bit'u·ate'
·at'ed ·at'ing
hab'i·tude'
ha·bit'u·é
ha·ci·en'da
hack'ney
·neys
hack'neyed
hack'saw'
had'dock
hag'gard
hag'gle
·gled ·gling
hai'ku
·ku
hail
(ice; see hale)
hail'stone'

hail'storm'
hair'breadth'
hair'cut'
hair'do'
hair'dress'er
hair'i·ness
hair'line'
hair'piece'
hair'-rais'ing
hair'split'ting
hair'spring'
hair'y
·i·er ·i·est
hal'cy·on
hale
haled hal'ing
(healthy; force;
see hail)
half
halves
half'back'
half'-baked'
half'-breed'
half'-caste'
half'-cocked'
half'heart'ed
half'-hour'
half'-mast'
half'-moon'
half'tone'
half'track'
half'-truth'
half'way'
half'-wit'ted
hal'i·but
hal'i·to'sis
hal'le·lu'jah
or ·iah
hall'mark'
hal'lowed
Hal'low·een'
hal·lu'ci·nate'
·nat'ed ·nat'ing
hal·lu'ci·na'tion
hal·lu'ci·na·to'ry
hal·lu'ci·no·gen
hall'way'
hal'lo
·los or ·loes
hal'ter
halt'ing·ly
ha·lutz'
ha'lutz·im'
halve
halved halv'ing
hal'yard
ham'burg'er
ham'let
ham'mer
ham'mer·head'
ham'mock
ham'per
ham'ster
ham'string'
hand'bag'
hand'ball'
hand'bill'

hand'book'
hand'breadth'
hand'clasp'
hand'cuff'
hand'ful'
·fuls'
hand'gun'
hand'i·cap'
·capped·
·cap'ping
hand'i·craft'
hand'i·ly
hand'i·ness
hand'i·work'
hand'ker·chief
·chiefs
han'dle
·dled ·dling
han'dle·bar'
hand'ler
hand'made'
hand'-me-down'
hand'out'
hand'picked'
hand'rail'
hand'saw'
hand'sel
·seled or ·selled
·sel·ing or ·sel·ling
hand'set'
hand'shake'
hands'-off'
hand'some
hand'spring'
hand'stand'
hand'-to-hand'
hand'-to-mouth'
hand'work'
hand'writ'ing
hand'y
·i·er ·i·est
han'dy·man'
hang
hung hang'ing
(suspend)
hang
hanged hang'ing
(put to death)
hang'ar
(aircraft shed)
hang'dog'
hang'er
(garment holder)
hang'er-on'
hang'ers-on'
hang'man
hang'nail'
hang'o·ver
hang'-up'
hank'er
han'ky-pan'ky
han'som (cab)
Ha'nu·ka'
hap'haz'ard
hap'less
hap'pen
hap'pen·stance'
hap'pi·ly

hap'pi·ness
hap'py
·pi·er ·pi·est
hap'py-go-luck'y
ha'ra-ki'ri
ha·rangue'
·rangued'
·rangu'ing
ha·rangu'er
har·ass'
har'bin·ger
har'bor
hard'back'
hard'-bit'ten
hard'-boiled'
hard'-bound'
hard'-core'
hard'-cov'er
hard'en
hard'fist'ed
hard'goods'
hard'head'ed
hard'heart'ed
har'di·hood'
har'di·ly
har'di·ness
hard'ly
hard'pan'
hard'-shell'
hard'ship'
hard'tack'
hard'top'
hard'ware'
hard'wood'
har'dy
·di·er ·di·est
hare'brained'
hare'lip'
ha'rem
har'le·quin
harm'ful
harm'less
har·mon'ic
har·mon'i·ca
har·mo'ni·ous
har'mo·nize'
·nized' ·niz'ing
har'mo·ny
har'ness
harp'ist
har·poon'
harp'si·chord'
har'py
·pies
har'ri·er
har'row
har'row·ing
har'ry
·ried ·ry·ing
harsh'ness
har'te·beest'
har'um-scar'um
har'vest·er
has'-been'
ha'sen·pfef'fer
hash'ish or ·eesh
has'sle
·sled ·sling

has'sock
haste
has'ten
hast'i·ly
hast'i·ness
hast'y
 ·i·er ·i·est
hat'band'
hatch'er·y
 ·ies
hatch'et
hatch'ing
hatch'way'
hate
 hat'ed hat'ing
hate'a·ble
hate'ful
hat'rack'
ha'tred
hat'ter
haugh'ti·ly
haugh'ti·ness
haugh'ty
 ·ti·er ·ti·est
haul'age
haunch
haunt'ed
haunt'ing
hau·teur'
have
 had hav'ing
have'lock
ha'ven
have'-not'
hav'er·sack'
hav'oc
Ha·wai'i
Ha·wai'ian
hawk
hawk'-eyed'
hawk'ish
haw'ser
hay fever
hay'field'
hay'loft'
hay'ride'
haz'ard
haz'ard·ous
haze
 hazed haz'ing
ha'zel·nut'
ha'zi·ly
ha'zi·ness
ha'zy
 ·zi·er ·zi·est
H'-bomb'
head'ache'
head'board'
head'cheese'
head'dress'
head'first'
head'gear'
head'hunt'er
head'i·ly
head'i·ness
head'land
head'less
head'light'

head'line'
head'long'
head'man
head'mas'ter
head'mis'tress
head'-on'
head'phone'
head'piece'
head'quar'ters
head'rest'
head'room'
head'set'
head'stand'
head start
head'stock'
head'strong'
head'wait'er
head'wa'ters
head'way'
head wind
head'y
 ·i·er ·i·est
heal
 (cure; see heel)
health'ful
health'i·ly
health'i·ness
health'y
 ·i·er ·i·est
heap
hear
 heard hear'ing
heark'en
hear'say'
hearse
heart'ache'
heart'beat'
heart'break'
heart'bro'ken
heart'burn'
heart'en
heart'felt'
hearth'stone'
heart'i·ly
heart'i·ness
heart'less
heart'-rend'ing
heart'sick'
heart'strings'
heart'-to-heart'
heart'warm'ing
heart'y
 ·i·er ·i·est
heat'ed·ly
heat'er
heath
hea'then
heath'er
heat'stroke'
heave
 heaved or hove
 heav'ing
heav'en·ly
heav'en·ward
heav'i·ly
heav'i·ness
heav'y
 ·i·er ·i·est

heav'y-du'ty
heav'y-hand'ed
heav'y-heart'ed
heav'y·set'
heav'y·weight'
He·bra'ic
He'brew
heck'le
 ·led ·ling
hec'tic
hec'ti·cal·ly
hec'to·graph'
hedge
 hedged
 hedg'ing
hedge'hop'
he'don·ism
he'do·nis'tic
heed'ful
heed'less
heel
 (foot part;
 see heal)
heft'y
 ·i·er ·i·est
heif'er
height
height'en
hei'nous
heir
 (inheritor; see
 air)
heir'ess
heir'loom'
hel'i·cal
hel'i·cop'ter
he'li·o·graph'
he'li·o·trope'
he'li·port'
he'li·um
he'lix
 ·lix·es or ·li·ces'
hell'lion
hel·lo'
 ·los'
 ·loed' ·lo'ing
hel'met
helms'man
help'ful
help'ful·ly
help'less
hel'ter-skel'ter
hem
 hemmed
 hem'ming
he'ma·tol'o·gy
hem'i·sphere'
hem'i·spher'i·cal
hem'line'
he'mo·glo'bin
he'mo·phil'i·a
hem'or·rhage
 ·rhaged
 ·rhag·ing
hem'or·rhoid'
hem'stitch'
hence'forth'
hench'man

hen'na
 ·naed ·na·ing
hen'ner·y
 ·ies
hen'pecked'
hen'ry
 ·rys or ·ries
he·pat'ic
hep'a·ti'tis
hep'ta·gon'
her'ald
he·ral'dic
her'ald·ry
her·ba'ceous
her'bi·cide'
her'bi·vore'
her·biv'o·rous
herds'man
here'a·bout'
here·af'ter
here'by'
he·red'i·tar'y
he·red'i·ty
 ·ties
here·in'
here'in·af'ter
here's
her'e·sy
 ·sies
her'e·tic
he·ret'i·cal
here'to·fore'
here·with'
her'it·a·ble
her'it·age
her·maph'ro·dite'
her·met'i·cal·ly
her'mit
her'ni·a
 ·as or ·ae'
her'ni·ate'
 ·at'ed ·at'ing
he'ro
 ·roes
he·ro'ic
he·ro'i·cal·ly
her'o·in
 (narcotic)
her'o·ine
 (female hero)
her'o·ism
her'pes
her'ring·bone'
her·self'
hes'i·tan·cy
 ·cies
hes'i·tant
hes'i·tate'
 ·tat'ed ·tat'ing
hes'i·ta'tion
het'er·o·dox'
het'er·o·dox'y
 ·ies
het'er·o·dyne'
 ·dyned' ·dyn'ing
het'er·o·ge·ne'i·ty
 ·ties
het'er·o·ge'ne·ous

het'er·o·nym'
het'er·o·sex'u·al
heu·ris'tic
heu·ris'ti·cal·ly
hew
 hewed, hewed or
 hewn, hew'ing
 (chop; see hue)
hex'a·gon'
hex·ag'o·nal
hex'a·he'dron
 ·drons or ·dra
hey'day'
H'-hour'
hi·a'tus
 ·tus·es or ·tus
hi·ba'chi
hi'ber·nate'
 ·nat'ed ·nat'ing
hi'ber·na'tion
hi'ber·na'tor
hi·bis'cus
hic'cup or ·cough
 ·cuped or ·cupped
 ·cup·ing or
 ·cup·ping
hick'o·ry
 ·ries
hide
 hid, hid'den or
 hid, hid'ing
hide'a·way'
hide'bound'
hid'e·ous
hide'-out'
hie
 hied, hie'ing
 or hy'ing
hi'er·ar'chi·cal
hi'er·ar'chy
 ·chies
hi'er·o·glyph'ic
hi'-fi'
high'ball'
high'born'
high'boy'
high'bred'
high'brow'
high'chair'
high'-class'
high'er-up'
high'fa·lu'tin
high'-flown'
high'-grade'
high'hand'ed
high'-keyed'
high'land·er
high'-lev'el
high'light'
high'ly
high'-mind'ed
high'-pitched'
high'-pow'ered
high'-pres'sure
high'-priced'
high'-rise'
high'-sound'ing
high'-spir'it·ed

high'-strung'
high'-ten'sion
high'-test'
high'-toned'
high'way'
hi'jack'
hike
 hiked hik'ing
hi·lar'i·ous
hi·lar'i·ty
hill'i·ness
hill'ock
hill'side'
hill'y
 ·i·er ·i·est
him·self'
hind
 hind'er,
 hind'most' or
 hind'er·most'
hin'der
hin'drance
hind'sight'
hinge
 hinged hing'ing
hin'ter·land'
hip'bone'
hip'pie
hip'po·drome'
hip·po·pot'a·mus
 ·mus·es or ·mi
hir'a·ble or hire'·
hire
 hired hir'ing
hire'ling
hiss'ing
his'ta·mine'
his·tol'o·gy
his·to'ri·an
his·tor'i·cal
his·tor'i·cal·ly
his'to·ry
 ·ries
his'tri·on'ic
hit
 hit hit'ting
hit'-and-run'
hitch'hike'
hith'er·to'
hit'-or-miss'
hives
hoard
 (reserve; see
 horde)
hoar'frost'
hoar'i·ness
hoarse
hoar'y
 ·i·er ·i·est
hob'ble
 ·bled ·bling
hob'by
 ·bies
hob'by·horse'
hob'gob'lin
hob'nail'
hob'nob'
 ·nobbed' ·nob'bing

ho'bo
· bos *or* · boes
hock'ey
ho'cus·po'cus
hodge'podge'
hoe
hoed hoe'ing
hoe'down'
hog'gish
hogs'head'
hog'tie'
· tied', · ty'ing
or · tie'ing
hog'wash'
hoi' pol·loi'
hoist
hold
held hold'ing
hold'out'
hold'o·ver'
hold'up'
hole
holed hol'ing
hole'y
(*with holes;* see
holy, wholly)
hol'i·day'
ho'li·ly
ho'li·ness
hol'lan·daise'
hol'low
hol'lo·ware'
hol'ly
· lies
hol'ly·hock'
hol'o·caust'
ho·log'ra·phy
Hol'stein
hol'ster
ho'ly
· li·er · li·est
· lies
(*sacred;* see
holey, wholly)
hom'age
hom'burg
home
homed hom'ing
home'bod'y
home'bred'
home'-brew'
home'com'ing
home'-grown'
home'land'
home'less
home'li·ness
home'ly
· li·er · li·est
(*plain;* see
homey)
home'made'
home'mak'er
home'own'er
home'sick'
home'spun'
home'stead'
home'stretch'
home'ward

home'work'
home'y
hom'i·er
hom'i·est
(*cozy;* see
homely)
home'y·ness
hom'i·ci'dal
hom'i·cide'
hom'i·let'ics
hom'i·ly
· lies
hom'i·ny
ho'mo·ge·ne'i·ty
ho'mo·ge'ne·ous
ho·mog'e·nize'
· nized' · niz'ing
hom'o·graph'
ho·mol'o·gous
hom'o·nym
hom'o·phone'
Ho'mo sa'pi·ens'
ho'mo·sex'u·al
ho'mo·sex'u·
al'i·ty
hone
honed hon'ing
hon'est
hon'es·ty
hon'ey
· eys, · eyed *or*
· ied, · ey·ing
hon'ey·bee'
hon'ey·comb'
hon'ey·dew'
hon'ey·moon'
hon'ey·suck'le
hon'or·a·ble
hon'o·ra'ri·um
· ri·ums *or* · ri·a
hon'or·ar'y
hon'or·if'ic
hood'ed
hood'lum
hood'wink'
hoof
hoof'beat'
hook'ah *or* · a
hook'up'
hook'y
hoo'li·gan
hoop'la
hoot'en·an'ny
· nies
hop
hopped hop'ping
hope
hoped hop'ing
hope'ful
hope'ful·ly
hope'less
hop'per
horde
hord'ed hord'ing
(*crowd;* see
hoard)
hore'hound'
ho·ri'zon

hor'i·zon'tal
hor·mo'nal
hor'mone
hor'net
horn'i·ness
horn'pipe'
horn'y
· i·er · i·est
ho·rol'o·gy
hor'o·scope'
hor·ren'dous
hor'ri·ble
hor'ri·bly
hor'rid
hor'ri·fy'
· fied' · fy'ing
hor'ror
hors' d'oeu'vre
· vres
horse'back'
horse'fly'
· flies
horse'hair'
horse'hide'
horse'laugh'
horse'man
horse'play'
horse'pow'er
horse'rad'ish
horse'shoe'
· shoed' · shoe'ing
horse'tail'
horse'whip'
horse'wom'an
hors'i·ness
hors'y
· i·er · i·est
hor'ta·to'ry
hor'ti·cul'ture
hor'ti·cul'tur·ist
ho·san'na
hose
hosed hos'ing
ho'sier·y
hos'pice
hos'pi·ta·ble
hos'pi·ta·bly
hos'pi·tal
hos'pi·tal'i·ty
· ties
hos'pi·tal·i·za'tion
hos'pi·tal·ize'
· ized' · iz'ing
hos'tage
hos'tel
(*inn;* see hostile)
hos'tel·ry
· ries
host'ess
hos'tile
(*unfriendly;* see
hostel)
hos'tile·ly
hos·til'i·ty
· ties
hos'tler
hot
hot'ter hot'test

hot'bed'
hot'-blood'ed
hot'box'
ho·tel'
ho·tel'ier'
hot'foot'
· foots'
hot'head'ed
hot'house'
hot'tem'pered
hound'ed
hour'glass'
hour'ly
house
housed hous'ing
house'boat'
house'break'
· broke' · bro'ken
· break'ing
house'clean'ing
house'dress'
house'coat'
house'fly'
· flies
house'ful'
house'hold'
house'keep'er
house'lights'
house'maid'
house'man'
house'moth'er
house organ
house party
house'-rais'ing
house'warm'ing
house'wife'
· wives'
house'work'
hous'ing
hov'el
· eled *or* · elled
· el·ing *or* · el·ling
hov'er
how'dah
how·ev'er
how'itz·er
howl'ing
how'so·ev'er
how'-to'
hoy'den
hua·ra'ches
hub'bub'
hub'cap'
huck'le·ber'ry
· ries
huck'ster
hud'dle
· dled · dling
hue
(*color;* see hew)
huff'i·ly
huff'i·ness
huff'y
· i·er · i·est
hug
hugged hug'ging
huge'ness
hulk'ing

hul'la·ba·loo'
hum
hummed
hum'ming
hu'man
hu·mane'
hu'man·ism
hu'man·is'tic
hu'man·is'ti·cal·ly
hu·man'i·tar'i·an
hu·man'i·ty
· ties
hu'man·ize'
· ized' · iz'ing
hu'man·kind'
hu'man·ly
hu'man·ness
hu'man·oid'
hum'ble
· bler · blest
· bled · bling
hum'bly
hum'bug'
hum'drum'
hu·mec'tant
hu'mer·us
· mer·i'
(*bone;* see
humorous)
hu'mid
hu·mid'i·fi·ca'tion
hu·mid'i·fi'er
hu·mid'i·fy'
· fied' · fy'ing
hu·mid'i·ty
hu'mi·dor'
hu·mil'i·ate'
· at'ed · at'ing
hu·mil'i·a'tion
hu·mil'i·ty
hum'ming·bird'
hum'mock
hu'mor
hu'mor·esque'
hu'mor·ist
hu'mor·ous
(*funny;* see
humerus)
hump'back'
hu'mus
hunch'back'
hun'dred·fold'
hun'dredth
hun'dred·weight'
hun'ger
hun'gri·ly
hun'gri·ness
hun'gry
· gri·er · gri·est
hunt'er
hunt'ress
hunts'man
hur'dle
· dled · dling
(*barrier;* see
hurtle)
hur'dy-gur'dy
hurl'er

hurl'y-burl'y
hur·rah'
hur'ri·cane'
hur'ried·ly
hur'ry
· ried · ry·ing
hurt
hurt hurt'ing
hurt'ful
hur'tle
· tled · tling
(*rush;* see hurdle)
hus'band
hus'band·ry
hush'-hush'
husk'i·ly
husk'i·ness
hus'ky
· kies
(*dog*)
husk'y
· i·er · i·est, · ies
(*hoarse; robust*)
hus'sy
· sies
hus'tle
· tled · tling
hus'tler
hy'a·cinth'
hy'brid
hy'brid·ize'
· ized' · iz'ing
hy·dran'ge·a
hy'drant
hy'drate
· drat·ed · drat·ing
hy'dra·tor
hy·drau'lic
hy'dro·chlo'ric
hy'dro·dy·nam'ics
hy'dro·e·lec'tric
hy'dro·foil'
hy'dro·gen
hy'dro·gen·ate'
· at'ed · at'ing
hy'dro·gen·a'tion
hy'dro·ki·net'ics
hy·drol'o·gy
hy·drol'y·sis
hy'dro·lyt'ic
hy'dro·me·
chan'ics
hy·drom'e·ter
hy'dro·naut'
hy'dro·pho'bi·a
hy'dro·plane'
hy'dro·pon'ics
hy'dro·ski'
hy'dro·stat'ics
hy'dro·ther'a·py
hy'drous
hy·e'na
hy'giene
hy'gi·en'ic
hy'gi·en'i·cal·ly
hy'gi·en·ist
hy·grom'e·ter
hy'gro·scope'

hy'men
hy'me·ne'al
hymn
hym'nal
hym·nol'o·gy
hy'per·a·cid'i·ty
hy'per·ac'tive
hy·per'bo·la
  (curve)
hy·per'bo·le
  (exaggeration)
hy'per·bol'ic
hy'per·crit'i·cal
  (too critical; see
  hypocritical)
hy'per·sen'si·tive
hy'per·son'ic
hy'per·ten'sion
hy'per·ven'ti·
  la'tion
hy'phen
hy'phen·ate'
  ·at'ed ·at'ing
hy'phen·a'tion
hyp·no'sis
  ·ses
hyp·not'ic
hyp·not'i·cal·ly
hyp'no·tism
hyp'no·tiz'a·ble
hyp'no·tize'
  ·tized' ·tiz'ing
hy'po·chon'dri·a
hy'po·chon'dri·ac'
hy'po·chon·
  dri'a·cal
hy'po·chon·
  dri'a·sis
hy·poc'ri·sy
  ·sies
hyp'o·crite
hyp'o·crit'i·cal
  (deceitful; see
  hypercritical)
hy'po·der'mic
hy·pot'e·nuse'
hy·poth'e·cate'
  ·cat'ed ·cat'ing
hy·poth'e·sis
  ·ses'
hy·poth'e·size'
  ·sized' ·siz'ing
hy'po·thet'i·cal
hy'po·thet'i·cal·ly
hys'ter·ec'to·my
  ·mies
hys·te'ri·a
hys·ter'ic
hys·ter'i·cal
hys·ter'i·cal·ly

I

i·am'bic
ice
  iced ic'ing

ice'berg'
ice'bound'
ice'box'
ice'break'er
ice'cap'
ice cream
ice field
ice'house'
ice'man'
ice milk
ich'thy·ol'o·gy
i'ci·cle
i'ci·ly
i'ci·ness
ic'ing
i'con
i·con'ic
i·con'o·clast'
i'cy
  i'ci·er i'ci·est
I'da·ho'
i·de'a
i·de'al
i·de'al·ism
i·de'al·ist
i'de·al·is'tic
i·de'al·i·za'tion
i·de'al·ize'
  ·ized' ·iz'ing
i·de'al·ly
i'de·ate'
  ·at'ed ·at'ing
i'de·a'tion
i·den'ti·cal
i·den'ti·cal·ly
i·den'ti·fi·ca'tion
i·den'ti·fi'a·ble
i·den'ti·fi'er
i·den'ti·fy'
  ·fied' ·fy'ing
i·den'ti·ty
  ·ties
id'e·o·gram'
id'e·o·graph'ic
i'de·o·log'i·cal
i'de·o·log'i·cal·ly
i'de·ol'o·gist
i'de·ol'o·gize'
  ·gized' ·giz'ing
i'de·ol'o·gy
  ·gies
id'i·o·cy
id'i·om
id'i·o·mat'ic
id'i·o·mat'i·cal·ly
id'i·o·syn'cra·sy
  ·sies
id'i·o·syn·crat'ic
id'i·ot
id'i·ot'ic
id'i·ot'i·cal·ly
i'dle
  i'dler i'dlest
  i'dled i'dling
  (not active; see
  idol, idyll)
i'dle·ness

i'dler
i'dly
i'dol
  (image worshiped;
  see idle, idyll)
i·dol'a·ter
i·dol'a·trous
i·dol'a·try
i'dol·ize'
  ·ized' ·iz'ing
i'dyll or i'dyl
  (pastoral poem;
  see idle, idol)
i·dyl'lic
ig'loo
  ·loos
ig'ne·ous
ig·nit'a·ble
  or ·i·ble
ig'nite'
  ·nit'ed ·nit'ing
ig·ni'tion
ig·no'ble
ig'no·min'i·ous
ig'no·min'y
  ·ies
ig'no·ra'mus
ig'no·rance
ig'no·rant
ig·nore'
  ·nored' ·nor'ing
i·gua'na
il'e·um
  (intestine)
il'i·um
  (bone)
ill
  worse worst
ill'-ad·vised'
ill'-be'ing
ill'-bod'ing
ill'-bred'
ill'-con·sid'ered
ill'-dis·posed'
i·le'gal
il'le·gal'i·ty
  ·ties
il·le'gal·ly
il'leg·i·bil'i·ty
il·leg'i·ble
il·leg'i·bly
il'le·git'i·ma·cy
  ·cies
il'le·git'i·mate
il'le·git'i·mate·ly
ill'-fat'ed
ill'-fa'vored
ill'-found'ed
ill'-got'ten
ill'-hu'mored
il·lib'er·al
il·lic'it
  (unlawful; see
  elicit)
il·lim'it·a·ble
il·lim'it·a·bly
Il'li·nois'
il·lit'er·a·cy

il·lit'er·ate
il·lit'er·ate·ly
ill'-man'nered
ill'-na'tured
ill'ness
il·log'i·cal
il·log'i·cal·ly
ill'-sort'ed
ill'-spent'
ill'-starred'
ill'-suit'ed
ill'-tem'pered
ill'-timed'
ill'-treat'
il·lu'mi·nate'
  ·nat'ed ·nat'ing
il·lu'mi·na'tion
il·lu'mi·na'tor
ill'-us'age
ill'-use'
il·lu'sion
  (false idea; see
  allusion, elusion)
il·lu'sive
  (deceptive; see
  allusive, elusive)
il·lu'so·ri·ly
il·lu'so·ri·ness
il·lu'so·ry
il'lus·trate'
  ·trat'ed ·trat'ing
il'lus·tra'tion
il·lus'tra·tive
il·lus'tra·tor
il·lus'tri·ous
im'age
  ·aged ·ag·ing
im'age·ry
  ·ries
i·mag'i·na·ble
i·mag'i·na·bly
i·mag'i·nar'i·ness
i·mag'i·nar'y
i·mag'i·na'tion
i·mag'i·na·tive
i·mag'ine
  ·ined ·in·ing
im'ag·ism
im·bal'ance
im'be·cile
im'be·cil'ic
im'be·cil'i·ty
  ·ties
im·bibe'
  ·bibed' ·bib'ing
im·bib'er
im'bri·cate'
  ·cat'ed ·cat'ing
im'bri·ca'tion
im·bro'glio
  ·glios
im·brue'
  ·brued' ·bru'ing
im·bue'
  ·bued' ·bu'ing
im'i·ta·ble
im'i·tate'
  ·tat'ed ·tat'ing

im'i·ta'tion
im'i·ta'tive
im'i·ta'tor
im·mac'u·late
im'ma·nent
  (inherent; see
  imminent)
im'ma·te'ri·al
im'ma·ture'
im'ma·tu'ri·ty
im·meas'ur·a·ble
im·me'di·a·cy
im·me'di·ate
im·me'di·ate·ly
im'me·mo'ri·al
im·mense'
im·mense'ly
im·men'si·ty
im·merge'
  ·merged'
  ·merg'ing
  (plunge; see
  emerge)
im·mer'gence
im·merse'
  ·mersed'
  ·mers'ing
im·mers'i·ble
im·mer'sion
im'mi·grant
im'mi·grate'
  ·grat'ed ·grat'ing
im'mi·gra'tion
im'mi·nence
im'mi·nent
  (impending; see
  eminent,
  immanent)
im·mis'ci·ble
im·mit'i·ga·ble
im·mo'bile
im'mo·bil'i·ty
im·mo'bi·li·
  za'tion
im·mo'bi·lize'
  ·lized' ·liz'ing
im·mod'er·ate
im·mod'er·a'tion
im·mod'est
im·mod'es·ty
im'mo·late'
  ·lat'ed ·lat'ing
im'mo·la'tion
im·mor'al
im'mo·ral'i·ty
  ·ties
im·mor'tal
im'mor·tal'i·ty
im·mor'tal·i·
  za'tion
im·mor'tal·ize'
  ·ized' ·iz'ing
im·mov'a·bil'i·ty
im·mov'a·ble
im·mune'
im·mu'ni·ty
  ·ties
im'mu·ni·za'tion

im'mu·nize'
  ·nized' ·niz'ing
im'mu·nol'o·gy
im·mure'
  ·mured' ·mur'ing
im·mu'ta·bil'i·ty
im·mu'ta·ble
im·mu'ta·bly
im·pact'ed
im·pac'tion
im·pair'
im·pale'
  ·paled' ·pal'ing
im'pal·pa·bil'i·ty
im·pal'pa·ble
im·pan'el
  ·eled or ·elled
  ·el·ing or ·el·ling
im·part'
im·part'a·ble
im·par'tial
im'par·ti·al'i·ty
im·part'i·ble
im·pas'sa·bil'i·ty
im·pass'a·ble
  (not passable;
  see impassible)
im'passe
im·pas'si·bil'i·ty
im·pas'si·ble
  (unfeeling; see
  impassable)
im·pas'sioned
im·pas'sive
im'pas·siv'i·ty
im·pa'tience
im·pa'tient
im·peach'
im·peach'a·ble
im·pec'ca·bil'i·ty
im·pec'ca·ble
im·pec'ca·bly
im·pe·cu'ni·
  os'i·ty
im·pe·cu'ni·ous
im·ped'ance
im·pede'
  ·ped'ed ·ped'ing
im·ped'i·ment
im·ped'i·men'ta
im·pel'
  ·pelled' ·pel'ling
im·pel'lent
im·pel'ler
im·pend'
im·pend'ing
im·pen'e·tra·
  bil'i·ty
im·pen'e·tra·ble
im·pen'i·tence
im·pen'i·tent
im·per'a·tive
im'per·cep'ti·ble
im'per·cep'ti·bly
im·per'fect
im'per·fec'tion
im·per'fo·rate
im·pe'ri·al

im·pe'ri·al·ism
im·pe'ri·al·is'tic
im·pe'ri·al·ly
im·per'il
im·pe'ri·ous
im·per'ish·a·ble
im·per'ma·nent
im·per'me·a·ble
im'per·mis'si·ble
im·per'son·al
im·per'son·al'i·ty
im·per'son·al·ize'
im·per'son·ate'
 ·at'ed ·at'ing
im·per'son·a'tion
im·per'son·a'tor
im·per'ti·nence
im·per'ti·nent
im'per·turb'a·
 bil'i·ty
im'per·turb'a·ble
im·per'vi·ous
im·pe·ti'go
im·pet'u·os'i·ty
im·pet'u·ous
im'pe·tus
im·pi'e·ty
 ·ties
im·pinge'
 ·pinged' ·ping'ing
im·pinge'ment
im'pi·ous
imp'ish
im·pla'ca·ble
im·plant'
im'plan·ta'tion
im·plau'si·ble
im'ple·ment
im'ple·men'tal
im'ple·men·ta'tion
im'pli·cate'
 ·cat'ed ·cat'ing
im'pli·ca'tion
im'pli·ca'tive
im·plic'it
im·plode'
 ·plod'ed ·plod'ing
im·plore'
 ·plored' ·plor'ing
im·plo'sion
im·ply'
 ·plied' ·ply'ing
im'po·lite'
im·pol'i·tic
im·pon'der·a·ble
im·port'
im·port'a·ble
im·por'tance
im·por'tant
im'por·ta'tion
im·port'er
im·por'tu·nate
im·por·tune'
 ·tuned' ·tun'ing
im'por·tu'ni·ty
 ·ties
im·pose'
 ·posed' ·pos'ing

im'po·si'tion
im·pos'si·bil'i·ty
 ·ties
im·pos'si·ble
im'post
im·pos'tor
 (deceiver)
im·pos'ture
 (deception)
im'po·tence
im'po·tent
im·pound'
im·pov'er·ish
im·prac'ti·ca·
 bil'i·ty
im·prac'ti·ca·ble
im·prac'ti·cal
im'pre·cate'
 ·cat'ed ·cat'ing
im·pre·ca'tion
im'pre·cise'
im·preg'na·bil'i·ty
im·preg'na·ble
im·preg'nate
 ·nat'ed ·nat'ing
im'preg·na'tion
im'pre·sa'ri·o
 ·ri·os
im'pre·scrip'ti·ble
im·press'
im·press'i·ble
im·pres'sion
im·pres'sion·a·ble
im·pres'sion·a·bly
im·pres'sion·ism
im·pres'sive
im·pres'sive·ly
im'pri·ma'tur
im·print'
im·pris'on
im·prob'a·ble
im·promp'tu
im·prop'er
im·pro·pri'e·ty
 ·ties
im·prov'a·ble
im·prove'
 ·proved' ·prov'ing
im·prove'ment
im·prov'i·dent
im·prov'i·sa'tion
im'pro·vise'
 ·vised' ·vis'ing
im·pru'dence
im·pru'dent
im'pu·dence
im'pu·dent
im·pugn'
im·pugn'a·ble
im'pulse
im·pul'sion
im·pul'sive
im·pul'sive·ly
im·pu'ni·ty
im·pure'
im·pu'ri·ty
 ·ties
im·put'a·bil'i·ty

im·put'a·ble
im'pu·ta'tion
im·put'a·tive
im·pute'
 ·put'ed ·put'ing
in'a·bil'i·ty
in·ac'ces·si·ble
in·ac'cu·ra·cy
 ·cies
in·ac'cu·rate
in·ac'tion
in·ac'ti·vate'
 ·vat'ed ·vat'ing
in·ac'ti·va'tion
in·ac'tive
in'ac·tiv'i·ty
in·ad'e·qua·cy
 ·cies
in·ad'e·quate
in'ad·mis'si·ble
in'ad·vert'ence
in'ad·vert'ent
in'ad·vis·a·bil'i·ty
in·al'ien·a·ble
in·al'ter·a·ble
in·ane'
in·an'i·mate
in·an'i·ty
 ·ties
in'ap·pli·ca·ble
in'ap·pre'ci·a·ble
in'ap·proach'a·ble
in'ap·pro'pri·ate
in'ar·tic'u·late
in'ar·tis'tic
in'as·much' as
in'at·ten'tion
in'at·ten'tive
in·au'di·ble
in·au'gu·ral
in·au'gu·rate'
 ·rat'ed ·rat'ing
in'aus·pi'cious
in'board'
in'born'
in'breed'
 ·bred' ·breed'ing
in·cal'cu·la·ble
in·cal'cu·la·bly
in'can·des'cence
in'can·des'cent
in'can·ta'tion
in'ca·pa·bil'i·ty
in·ca'pa·ble
in'ca·pac'i·tate'
 ·tat'ed ·tat'ing
in'ca·pac'i·ta'tion
in'ca·pac'i·ty
in·car'cer·ate'
 ·at'ed ·at'ing
in·car'cer·a'tion
in·car'nate
 ·nat·ed ·nat·ing
in'car·na'tion
in·cau'tious
in'cen·di·ar'y
 ·ies

in'cense
in·cense'
 ·censed' ·cens'ing
in·cen'tive
in·cep'tion
in·cep'tive
in·cer'ti·tude'
in·ces'sant
in'cest
in·ces'tu·ous
in·cho'ate
in·ci'dence
in'ci·dent
in'ci·den'tal
in'ci·den'tal·ly
in·cin'er·ate'
 ·at'ed ·at'ing
in·cin'er·a'tion
in·cin'er·a'tor
in·cip'i·ence
in·cip'i·ent
in·cise'
 ·cised' ·cis'ing
in·ci'sion
in·ci'sive
in·ci'sor
in·cite'
 ·cit'ed ·cit'ing
in·cit'er
in'ci·vil'i·ty
 ·ties
in·clem'en·cy
in·clem'ent
in·cli'na·ble
in'cli·na'tion
in·cline'
 ·clined' ·clin'ing
in'cli·nom'e·ter
in·clude'
 ·clud'ed
 ·clud'ing
in·clu'sion
in·clu'sive
in·co·er'ci·ble
in·cog·ni'to
 ·tos
in·cog'ni·zance
in·cog'ni·zant
in'co·her'ence
in'co·her'ent
in'com·bus'ti·ble
in'come
in'com'ing
in'com·men'su·
 ra·ble
in'com·men'su·
 rate
in'com·mode'
 ·mod'ed ·mod'ing
in'com·mo'di·ous
in'com·mu'ni·
 ca·ble
in'com·mu'ni·
 ca'do
in·com'pa·ra·ble
in'com·pat'i·
 bil'i·ty
 ·ties

in'com·pat'i·ble
in'com'pe·tence
in·com'pe·tent
in'com·plete'
in'com·pre·
 hen'si·ble
in'com·press'i·ble
in'com·put'a·ble
in'con·ceiv'a·ble
in'con·clu'sive
in·con'dite
in'con·form'i·ty
in·con'gru·ent
in·con'gru·i·ty
 ·ties
in·con'gru·ous
in·con·se·
 quen'tial
in'con·sid'er·a·ble
in'con·sid'er·ate
in'con·sid'er·
 ate·ly
in'con·sid·er·
 a'tion
in'con·sis'ten·cy
 ·cies
in'con·sis'tent
in'con·sol'a·ble
in'con·spic'u·ous
in'con·stan·cy
in·con'stant
in'con·sum'a·ble
in'con·test'a·ble
in·con'ti·nent
in'con·trol'la·ble
in'con·tro·vert'i·
 ble
in'con·ven'ience
in'con·ven'ient
in'con·vert'i·ble
in·co·or'di·nate
in·cor'po·rate'
 ·rat'ed ·rat'ing
in·cor'po·ra'tion
in·cor'po·ra'tor
in·cor·po're·al
in'cor·rect'
in·cor'ri·gi·bil'i·ty
in·cor'ri·gi·ble
in·cor'ri·gi·bly
in·cor·rupt'
in'cor·rupt'i·ble
in·creas'a·ble
in·crease'
 ·creased'
 ·creas'ing
in·creas'ing·ly
in·cred·i·bil'i·ty
in·cred'i·ble
in·cred'i·bly
in·cre·du'li·ty
in·cred'u·lous
in'cre·ment
in'cre·men'tal
in·crim'i·nate'
 ·nat'ed ·nat'ing
in·crim'i·na'tion
in·crim'i·na·to'ry

in·crust'
in'crus·ta'tion
in'cu·bate'
 ·bat'ed ·bat'ing
in'cu·ba'tion
in'cu·ba'tor
in·cul'cate
 ·cat·ed ·cat·ing
in·cul·ca'tion
in·culp'a·ble
in·cul·pa'tion
in·cum'ben·cy
 ·cies
in·cum'bent
in'cu·nab'u·la
in·cur'
 ·curred'
 ·cur'ring
in·cur·a·bil'i·ty
in·cur'a·ble
in·cur'a·bly
in·cu'ri·ous
in·cur'sion
in·debt'ed
in·de'cen·cy
 ·cies
in·de'cent
in·de·ci'pher·
 a·ble
in·de·ci'sion
in·de·ci'sive
in·de·clin'a·ble
in·dec'o·rous
in·de·co'rum
in·deed'
in·de·fat'i·ga·ble
in·de·fat'i·ga·bly
in·de·fea'si·ble
in·de·fect'i·ble
in·de·fen'si·ble
in·de·fin'a·ble
in·def'i·nite
in·del'i·ble
in·del'i·bly
in·del'i·ca·cy
 ·cies
in·del'i·cate
in·dem'ni·fi·
 ca'tion
in·dem'ni·fy'
 ·fied' ·fy'ing
in·dem'ni·ty
 ·ties
in·dent'
in·den·ta'tion
in·den'tion
in·den'ture
 ·tured ·tur·ing
in·de·pend'ence
in·de·pend'ent
in'-depth'
in·de·scrib'a·ble
in·de·scrib'a·bly
in·de·struct'i·ble
in·de·ter'mi·na·
 ble
in·de·ter'mi·na·cy
in·de·ter'mi·nate

in·de·ter'mi·
  na'tion
in'dex
  ·dex·es or ·di·ces'
In'di·an'a
in'di·cate'
  ·cat'ed ·cat'ing
in'di·ca'tion
in·dic'a·tive
in'di·ca'tor
in·dict'
  (accuse formally;
  see indite)
in·dict'a·ble
in·dict'ment
in·dif'fer·ence
in·dif'fer·ent
in'di·gence
in·dig'e·nous
in'di·gent
in'di·gest'i·ble
in'di·ges'tion
in·dig'nant
in'dig·na'tion
in·dig'ni·ty
  ·ties
in'di·go'
in'di·rect'
in'di·rec'tion
in'dis·cern'i·ble
in'dis·creet'
  (lacking prudence)
in'dis·crete'
  (not separated)
in'dis·cre'tion
  (indiscreet act)
in'dis·crim'i·nate
in'dis·pen'sa·ble
in'dis·pose'
in'dis·po·si'tion
in'dis·pu'ta·ble
in'dis·sol'u·ble
in'dis·tinct'
in'dis·tinc'tive
in'dis·tin'guish·
  a·ble
in·dite'
  ·dit'ed ·dit'ing
  (write; see indict)
in'di·vid'u·al
in'di·vid'u·al·ism
in'di·vid'u·al·
  is'tic
in'di·vid'u·al'i·ty
in'di·vid'u·al·ize'
  ·ized' ·iz'ing
in'di·vid'u·al·ly
in'di·vid'u·ate'
  ·at'ed ·at'ing
in'di·vis'i·bil'i·ty
in'di·vis'i·ble
in·doc'tri·nate'
  ·nat'ed ·nat'ing
in·doc'tri·na'tion
in·doc'tri·na'tor
in'do·lence
in'do·lent
in·dom'i·ta·ble

in·dom'i·ta·bly
in'door'
in'doors'
in·dorse'
  ·dorsed'
  ·dors'ing
in·du'bi·ta·ble
in·du'bi·ta·bly
in·duce'
  ·duced' ·duc'ing
  ·duce'ment
in·duct'
in·duct'ance
in·duct'ee'
in·duc'tile
in·duc'tion
in·duc'tive
in·duc'tor
in·dulge'
  ·dulged'
  ·dulg'ing
in·dul'gence
in·dul'gent
in'du·rate'
  ·rat'ed ·rat'ing
in'du·ra'tion
in·dus'tri·al
in·dus'tri·al·ism
in·dus'tri·al·ist
in·dus'tri·al·i·
  za'tion
in·dus'tri·al·ize'
  ·ized' ·iz'ing
in·dus'tri·ous
in'dus·try
  ·tries
in·e'bri·ate'
  ·at'ed ·at'ing
in·e'bri·a'tion
in·e·bri'e·ty
in·ed'i·ble
in·ed'u·ca·ble
in·ef'fa·ble
in·ef'fa·bly
in·ef·face'a·ble
in·ef·fec'tive
in·ef·fec'tu·al
in·ef·fi·ca'cious
in·ef'fi·ca·cy
in·ef'fi·cien·cy
in·ef'fi·cient
in·e·las'tic
in·e·las·tic'i·ty
in·el'e·gance
in·el'e·gant
in·el'i·gi·bil'i·ty
in·el'i·gi·ble
in·e·luc'ta·ble
in·e·lud'i·ble
in·ept'
in·ept'i·tude'
in·e·qual'i·ty
  ·ties
in·eq'ui·ta·ble
in·eq'ui·ty
  ·ties
  (unfairness;
  see iniquity)

in·e·rad'i·ca·ble
in·er'ra·ble
in·er'rant
in·ert'
in·er'tia
in'es·cap'a·ble
in'es·cap'a·bly
in'es·sen'tial
in·es'ti·ma·ble
in·ev'i·ta·bil'i·ty
in·ev'i·ta·ble
in·ev'i·ta·bly
in'ex·act'
in'ex·cus'a·ble
in'ex·haust'i·ble
in·ex'o·ra·ble
in'ex·pe'di·ent
in'ex·pen'sive
in'ex·pe'ri·ence
in·ex'pert
in·ex'pi·a·ble
in·ex'pli·ca·ble
in·ex'pli·ca·bly
in'ex·press'i·ble
in'ex·press'i·bly
in'ex·pres'sive
in'ex·ten'si·ble
in'ex·tin'guish·a·
  ble
in·ex'tri·ca·ble
in·ex'tri·ca·bly
in·fal'li·bil'i·ty
in·fal'li·ble
in·fal'li·bly
in'fa·mous
in'fa·my
  ·mies
in'fan·cy
  ·cies
in'fant
in·fan'ti·cide'
in'fan·tile'
in'fan·ti·lism
in'fan·try
  ·tries
in'fan·try·man
in·fat'u·ate'
  ·at'ed ·at'ing
in·fat'u·a'tion
in·fect'
in·fec'tion
in·fec'tious
in·fec'tive
in·fec'tor
in·fe·lic'i·tous
in·fe·lic'i·ty
  ·ties
in·fer'
  ·ferred'
  ·fer'ring
in·fer'a·ble
in'fer·ence
in'fer·en'tial
in·fe'ri·or
in·fe'ri·or'i·ty
in·fer'nal
in·fer'no
  ·nos

in·fer'tile
in·fest'
in·fi'del
in·fi·del'i·ty
  ·ties
in'field'
in·fil'trate
  ·trat·ed ·trat·ing
in'fil·tra'tion
in'fil·tra'tor
in'fi·nite
in'fi·nite·ly
in·fin·i·tes'i·mal
in·fin'i·tive
in·fin'i·ty
  ·ties
in·firm'
in·fir'ma·ry
  ·ries
in·fir'mi·ty
  ·ties
in·flame'
  ·flamed'
  ·flam'ing
in·flam'ma·ble
in·flam·ma'tion
in·flam'ma·to'ry
in·flate'
  ·flat'ed
  ·flat'ing
in·fla'tion
in·fla'tion·ar'y
in·flect'
in·flec'tion
in'-flight'
in'flow'
in·flu·ence
  ·enced ·enc·ing
in·flu·en'tial
in·flu·en'za
in'flux'
in·form'
in·for'mal
in·for·mal'i·ty
in·form'ant
in·for·ma'tion
in·form'a·tive
in·form'er
in·frac'tion
in·fran'gi·ble
in·fra·red'
in·fre'quent
in·fringe'
  ·fringe'ment
in·fu'ri·ate'
  ·at'ed ·at'ing
in·fuse'
  ·fused' ·fus'ing
in·fu'sion
in·gen'ious
  (clever; see
  ingenuous)
in·gé·nue'
in·ge·nu'i·ty

in·gen'u·ous
  (frank; see
  ingenious)
in·gest'
in·ges'tion
in·glo'ri·ous
in'got
in·grained'
in'grate
in·gra'ti·ate'
  ·at'ed ·at'ing
in·grat'i·tude'
in·gre'di·ent
in'gress
in'-group'
in'grown'
in·hab'it
in·hab'it·a·ble
in·hab'it·ant
in·hal'ant
in·ha·la'tion
in·hale'
  ·haled' ·hal'ing
in·hal'er
in·har·mon'ic
in·har·mo'ni·ous
in·here'
  ·hered' ·her'ing
in·her'ence
in·her'ent
in·her'it
in·her'it·a·ble
in·her'it·ance
in·her'i·tor
in·hib'it
in·hi·bi'tion
in·hib'i·tive
in·hib'i·tor
in·hos'pi·ta·ble
in·hos·pi·tal'i·ty
in'-house'
in·hu'man
in·hu·mane'
in·hu·man'i·ty
  ·ties
in·im'i·cal
in·im'i·ta·ble
in·iq'ui·tous
in·iq'ui·ty
  ·ties
  (wickedness;
  see inequity)
in·i'tial
  ·tialed or ·tialled
  ·tial·ing or ·tial·ling
in·i'tial·ly
in·i'ti·ate'
  ·at'ed ·at'ing
in·i'ti·a'tion
in·i'ti·a·tive
in·i'ti·a'tor
in·ject'
in·jec'tion
in·jec'tor
in·ju·di'cious
in·junc'tion
in'jure
  ·jured ·jur·ing

in·ju'ri·ous
in'ju·ry
  ·ries
in·jus'tice
ink'blot'
ink'ling
ink'y
  ·i·er ·i·est
in'laid'
in'land
in'-law'
in'lay'
  ·laid' ·lay'ing
  ·lays'
in'let
in'mate'
in me·mo'ri·am
in'most'
in'nards
in·nate'
in'ner·most'
in'ner·spring'
in·ner'vate
  ·vat·ed ·vat·ing
in'ning
inn'keep'er
in'no·cence
in'no·cent
in·noc'u·ous
in'no·vate'
  ·vat·ed ·vat·ing
in'no·va'tion
in'no·va'tive
in'no·va'tor
in·nu·en'do
  ·does or ·dos
in·nu'mer·a·ble
in·oc'u·late'
  ·lat'ed ·lat'ing
in·oc'u·la'tion
in·of·fen'sive
in·op'er·a·ble
in·op'er·a·tive
in·op'por·tune'
in·or'di·nate
in·or·gan'ic
in'pa'tient
in'put'
in'quest
in·qui'e·tude'
in·quire'
  ·quired'
  ·quir'ing
in'quir·y
  ·ies
in·qui·si'tion
in·quis'i·tive
in·quis'i·tor
in'road'
in·sane'
in·san'i·tar'y
in·san'i·ty
in·sa'ti·a·ble
in·scribe'
  ·scribed'
  ·scrib'ing
in·scrip'tion
in·scru'ta·bil'i·ty

in·scru'ta·ble
in'seam'
in'sect
in·sec'ti·cide'
in·se·cure'
in·se·cu'ri·ty
in·sem'i·nate'
  ·nat'ed ·nat'ing
in·sem'i·na'tion
in·sen'sate
in·sen·si·bil'i·ty
in·sen'si·ble
in·sen'si·tive
in·sen'si·tiv'i·ty
in·sep'a·ra·ble
in·sert'
in·ser'tion
in'ser'vice
in'side'
in·sid'i·ous
in'sight'
in·sig'ni·a
in·sig·nif'i·cance
in·sig·nif'i·cant
in·sin·cere'
in·sin·cere'ly
in·sin·cer'i·ty
in·sin'u·ate'
  ·at'ed ·at'ing
in·sin'u·a'tion
in·sip'id
in·si·pid'i·ty
in·sist'
in·sist'ence
in·sist'ent
in·so·bri'e·ty
in·so·far'
in'sole'
in'so·lence
in'so·lent
in·sol'u·ble
in·sol'vent
in·som'ni·a
in·sou'ci·ance
in·sou'ci·ant
in·spect'
in·spec'tion
in·spec'tor
in'spi·ra'tion
in·spire'
  ·spired' ·spir'ing
in·spir'it
in·sta·bil'i·ty
in·stall' or ·stal'
  ·stalled' ·stall'ing
in'stal·la'tion
in·stall'ment
  or ·stal'ment
in'stance
in'stant
in'stan·ta'ne·ous
in·stan'ter
in·state'
  ·stat'ed ·stat'ing
in·stead'
in'step'
in'sti·gate'
  ·gat'ed ·gat'ing

in'sti·ga'tion
in'sti·ga'tor
in·still' or ·stil'
  ·stilled' ·still'ing
in'stinct
in·stinc'tive
in'sti·tute'
  ·tut'ed ·tut'ing
in'sti·tu'tion
in'sti·tu'tion·al·
  ize'
  ·ized' ·iz'ing
in·struct'
in·struc'tion
in·struc'tive
in·struc'tor
in'stru·ment
in'stru·men'tal
in'stru·men·
  tal'i·ty
in'stru·men·
  ta'tion
in·sub·or'di·nate
in·sub·or'di·
  na'tion
in·sub·stan'tial
in·suf'fer·a·ble
in'suf·fi'cien·cy
  ·cies
in'suf·fi'cient
in'su·lar
in'su·late'
  ·lat'ed ·lat'ing
in'su·la'tion
in'su·la'tor
in'su·lin
in'sult'
in·su'per·a·ble
in'sup·port'a·ble
in'sup·press'i·ble
in·sur·a·bil'i·ty
in·sur'a·ble
in·sur'ance
in·sure'
  ·sured' ·sur'ing
in·sur'er
in·sur'gence
in·sur'gent
in·sur·mount'a·
  ble
in'sur·rec'tion
in·tact'
in·tagl'io
  ·ios
in'take'
in·tan'gi·ble
in'te·ger
in'te·gral
in'te·grate'
  ·grat'ed ·grat'ing
in'te·gra'tion
in·teg'ri·ty
in·teg'u·ment
in'tel·lect'
in'tel·lec'tu·al
in'tel·lec'tu·al·ize'
  ·ized' ·iz'ing
in'tel·lec'tu·al·ly

in·tel'li·gence
in·tel'li·gent
in·tel'li·gent'si·a
in·tel'li·gi·bil'i·ty
in·tel'li·gi·ble
in·tel'li·gi·bly
In'tel·sat'
in·tem'per·ance
in·tem'per·ate
in·tend'
in·tend'ant
in·tense'
in·tense'ly
in·ten'si·fi·ca'tion
in·ten'si·fy'
  ·fied' ·fy'ing
in·ten'si·ty
in·ten'sive
in·tent'
in·ten'tion
in·ten'tion·al
in·ten'tion·al·ly
in·ter'
  ·terred' ·ter'ring
in'ter·act'
in'ter·ac'tion
in'ter·breed'
  ·bred' ·breed'ing
in'ter·cede'
  ·ced'ed ·ced'ing
in'ter·cept'
in'ter·cep'tion
in'ter·cep'tor
in'ter·ces'sion
in'ter·change'
in'ter·change'a·
  ble
in'ter·com'
in'ter·com·mu'ni·
  cate'
in'ter·con·nect'
in'ter·course'
in'ter·de·nom'i·
  na'tion·al
in'ter·de·part'·
  men'tal
in'ter·de·pend'·
  ence
in'ter·dict'
in'ter·dis'ci·
  pli·nar'y
in'ter·est
in'ter·est·ed
in'ter·faith'
in'ter·fere'
  ·fered' ·fer'ing
in'ter·fer'ence
in'ter·fer'on
in'ter·im
in·te'ri·or
in'ter·ject'
in'ter·jec'tion
in'ter·lace'
in'ter·leaf'
  ·leaves'
in'ter·leave'
  ·leaved'
  ·leav'ing

in'ter·lin'e·ar
in'ter·lin'ing
in'ter·lock'
in'ter·lo·cu'tion
in'ter·loc'u·tor
in'ter·loc'u·to'ry
in'ter·lope'
  ·loped' ·lop'ing
in'ter·lop'er
in'ter·lude'
in'ter·mar'riage
in'ter·mar'ry
in'ter·me'di·ar'y
  ·ar'ies
in'ter·me'di·ate
in·ter'ment
in'ter·mez'zo
  ·zos or ·zi
in·ter'mi·na·ble
in'ter·min'gle
in'ter·mis'sion
in'ter·mit'tent
in'tern
  (doctor)
in·tern'
  (detain)
in·ter'nal
in·ter'nal·ize'
  ·ized' ·iz'ing
in·ter'nal·ly
in'ter·na'tion·al
in'ter·ne'cine
in'tern·ee'
in'ter·nist
in·tern'ment
in'tern·ship'
in'ter·of'fice
in'ter·pen'e·
  trate'
in'ter·per'son·al
in'ter·phone'
in'ter·plan'e·
  tar'y
in'ter·play'
in·ter'po·late'
  ·lat'ed ·lat'ing
in·ter'po·la'tion
in'ter·pose'
in·ter'pret
in·ter'pre·ta'tion
in·ter'pret·er
in'ter·ra'cial
in'ter·re·late'
in'ter·re·la'tion
in'ter·ro·gate'
  ·gat'ed ·gat'ing
in·ter'ro·ga'tion
in·ter'rog·a·tive
in·ter'ro·ga'tor
in·ter'rog·a·to'ry
in·ter·rupt'
in'ter·rup'tion
in'ter·scho·las'tic
in'ter·sect'
in'ter·sec'tion
in'ter·sperse'
  ·spersed'
  ·spers'ing

in'ter·sper'sion
in'ter·state'
in·ter·stel'lar
in·ter'stice
  ·stic·es
in'ter·twine'
in'ter·ur'ban
in'ter·val
in'ter·vene'
  ·vened' ·ven'ing
in'ter·ven'tion
in'ter·view'
in'ter·view'er
in'ter·weave'
  ·wove' ·wov'en
  ·weav'ing
in·tes'tate
in·tes'tin·al
in·tes'tine
in'ti·ma·cy
  ·cies
in'ti·mate
in'ti·ma'tion
in·tim'i·date'
  ·dat'ed ·dat'ing
in·tim'i·da'tion
in·tol'er·a·ble
in·tol'er·ance
in·tol'er·ant
in'to·na'tion
in·tone'
in·tox'i·cant
in·tox'i·cate'
  ·cat'ed ·cat'ing
in·tox'i·ca'tion
in·trac'ta·ble
in'tra·mu'ral
in'tra·mus'cu·lar
in·tran'si·gent
in·tran'si·tive
in'tra·state'
in'tra·u'ter·ine
in'tra·ve'nous
in·trep'id
in'tre·pid'i·ty
in'tri·ca·cy
  ·cies
in'tri·cate
in·trigue'
  ·trigued'
  ·trigu'ing
in·trin'sic
in'tro·duce'
  ·duced' ·duc'ing
in'tro·duc'tion
in'tro·duc'to·ry
in'tro·spec'tion
in'tro·spec'tive
in'tro·ver'sion
in'tro·vert'
in·trude'
  ·trud'ed
  ·trud'ing
in·trud'er
in·tru'sion
in·tru'sive
in'tu·i'tion
in·tu'i·tive

in'un·date'
  ·dat'ed ·dat'ing
in'un·da'tion
in·ure'
  ·ured' ·ur'ing
in·vade'
  ·vad'ed ·vad'ing
in·vad'er
in'va·lid
in·val'id
in·val'i·date'
  ·dat'ed ·dat'ing
in·val'i·da'tion
in·val'u·a·ble
in·val'u·a·bly
in·var'i·a·ble
in·var'i·a·bly
in·va'sion
in·vec'tive
in·veigh'
in·vei'gle
  ·gled ·gling
in·vent'
in·ven'tion
in·ven'tive
in·ven'tor
in'ven·to'ry
  ·ries, ·ried ·ry·ing
in·verse'
in·ver'sion
in·vert'
in·ver'te·brate
in·vert'i·ble
in·vest'
in·ves'ti·gate'
  ·gat'ed ·gat'ing
in·ves'ti·ga'tion
in·ves'ti·ga'tor
in·ves'ti·ture
in·vest'ment
in·vet'er·ate
in·vi'a·ble
in·vid'i·ous
in·vig'or·ate'
  ·at'ed ·at'ing
in·vin·ci·bil'i·ty
in·vin'ci·ble
in·vin'ci·bly
in·vi'o·la·ble
in·vi'o·late
in·vis'i·ble
in'vi·ta'tion
in·vite'
  ·vit'ed ·vit'ing
in'vo·ca'tion
in'voice
  ·voiced· ·voic·ing
in·voke'
  ·voked' ·vok'ing
in·vol'un·tar'i·ly
in·vol'un·tar'y
in'vo·lute'
in·volve'
  ·volved'
  ·volv'ing
in·vul'ner·a·ble
in'ward
i'o·dine'

i'on
i·on·i·za'tion
i'on·ize'
·ized' ·iz'ing
i·on'o·sphere'
i·o'ta
I'o·wa
ip'e·cac'
ip'so fac'to
i·ras'ci·bil'i·ty
i·ras'ci·ble
i·rate'
ire'ful·ly
ir'i·des'cence
ir'i·des'cent
irk'some
i'ron·bound'
i'ron·clad'
i·ron'i·cal
i·ron'i·cal·ly
i'ron·stone'
i'ron·work'
i'ro·ny
·nies
ir·ra'di·ate'
ir·ra'di·a'tion
ir·ra'tion·al
ir·ra'tion·al'i·ty
ir·ra'tion·al·ly
ir're·claim'a·ble
ir·rec'on·cil'a·ble
ir're·cov'er·a·ble
ir're·deem'a·ble
ir're·duc'i·ble
ir·ref'u·ta·ble
ir·reg'u·lar
ir·reg'u·lar'i·ty
·ties
ir·rel'e·vant
ir're·li'gious
ir're·me'di·a·ble
ir're·mis'si·ble
ir're·mov'a·ble
ir·rep'a·ra·ble
ir're·place'a·ble
ir're·press'i·ble
ir're·proach'a·ble
ir're·sist'i·ble
ir·res'o·lute'
ir're·spec'tive
ir're·spon'si·ble
ir're·triev'a·ble
ir·rev'er·ence
ir·rev'er·ent
ir're·vers'i·ble
ir·rev'o·ca·ble
ir'ri·ga·ble
ir'ri·gate'
·gat'ed ·gat'ing
ir'ri·ga'tion
ir'ri·ta·bil'i·ty
ir'ri·ta·ble
ir'ri·ta·bly
ir'ri·tant
ir'ri·tate'
·tat'ed ·tat'ing
ir'ri·ta'tion
ir·rupt'

ir·rup'tion
i'sin·glass'
is'land
isle
(*island;* see aisle)
is'let
(*small island;*
see eyelet)
is'n't
i'so·bar'
i'so·late'
·lat'ed ·lat'ing
i'so·la'tion
i'so·la'tion·ist
i'so·mer
i'so·met'ric
i'so·met'ri·cal·ly
i·sos'ce·les'
i'so·therm'
i'so·tope'
i'so·trop'ic
Is'ra·el
Is·rae'li
is'su·ance
is'sue
·sued ·su·ing
isth'mus
i·tal'ic
i·tal'i·cize'
·cized' ·ciz'ing
itch'i·ness
itch'y
·i·er ·i·est
i'tem·ize'
·ized' ·iz'ing
it'er·ate'
·at'ed ·at'ing
it'er·a'tion
i·tin'er·ant
i·tin'er·ar'y
·ies
i·tin'er·ate'
·at'ed ·at'ing
its
(*of it*)
it's
(*it is*)
it·self'
I've
i'vied
i'vo·ry
·ries
i'vy
i'vies

J

jab
jabbed jab'bing
jab'ber
ja·bot'
ja'cinth
jack'al
jack'a·napes'
jack'ass'

jack'boot'
jack'et
jack'ham'mer
jack'-in-the-box'
-box'es
jack'knife'
·knives'
·knifed' knif'ing
jack'-of-all'-
trades'
jacks'-
jack'-o'-lan'tern
·terns
jack'pot'
jack'screw'
jack'straw'
Jac·quard'
jade
jad'ed jad'ing
jag'ged
jag'uar
jai' a·lai'
jail'bird'
jail'er *or* ·or
jal'ou·sie'
(*door;* see
jealousy)
jam
jammed
jam'ming
jam'ba·lay'a
jam'bo·ree'
jan'gle
·gled ·gling
jan'i·tor
Jan'u·ar'y
·ar'ies
ja·pan'
·panned'
·pan'ning
jar
jarred jar'ring
jar'di·niere'
jar'gon
jas'mine
jas'per
ja'to *or* JA'TO
jaun'dice
·diced ·dic·ing
jaun'ti·ly
jaun'ti·ness
jaun'ty
·ti·er ·ti·est
jav'e·lin
jaw'bone'
jaw'break'er
Jay'cee'
jay'walk'er
jazz'i·ness
jazz'y
·i·er ·i·est
jeal'ous
jeal'ous·y
·ies
(*envy;* see
jalousie)
jeans
jeer'ing·ly

je·june'
jel'li·fy'
·fied' ·fy'ing
jel'ly
·lies, ·lied ·ly·ing
jel'ly·fish'
jel'ly·roll'
jen'ny
·nies
jeop'ard·ize'
·ized' ·iz'ing
jeop'ard·y
je·quir'i·ty
jer'e·mi'ad
jerk'i·ly
jer'kin
jerk'i·ness
jerk'wa'ter
jerk'y
·i·er ·i·est
(*moving fitfully*)
jer'ky
(*dried beef*)
Jer'sey
·seys
(*dairy cattle*)
jer'sey
·seys
(*cloth; shirt*)
jest'er
jet
jet'ted jet'ting
jet'-black'
jet'lin'er
jet'port'
jet'-pro·pelled'
jet'sam
jet stream
jet'ti·son
jet'ty
·ties, ·tied ·ty·ing
jew'el
·eled *or* ·elled
·el·ing *or* ·el·ling
jew'el·er·er *or*
·el·ler
jew'el·ry
Jew'ish
Jew'ry
·ries
jew's'-harp' *or*
jews'-harp'
Jez'e·bel
jib
jibbed jib'bing
jibe
jibed jib'ing
(*nautical; agree;*
see gibe)
jig'ger
jig'gle
·gled ·gling
jig'saw'
Jim'-Crow'
jim'my
·mies
·mied ·my·ing

jin'gle
·gled ·gling
jin'go
·goes
jin'go·ism
jin'go·is'ti·cal·ly
jin·ni'
jinn
jin·rik'i·sha
jinx
jit'ney
·neys
jit'ter·y
job
jobbed job'bing
job'ber
jock'ey
·eys
·eyed ·ey·ing
jock'strap'
jo·cose'
jo·cos'i·ty
·ties
joc'u·lar
joc'u·lar'i·ty
joc'und
jo·cun'di·ty
jodh'purs
jog
jogged jog'ging
jog'ger
jog'gle
·gled ·gling
john'ny·cake'
join'er
joint'ly
join'ture
joist
joke
joked jok'ing
jol'li·ness
jol'li·ty
jol'ly
·li·er ·li·est
jon'quil
jos'tle
·tled ·tling
jot
jot'ted jot'ting
jounce
jounced
joun'cing
jour'nal
jour'nal·ese'
jour'nal·ism
jour'nal·is'tic
jour'ney
·neys
·neyed ·ney·ing
jour'ney·man
joust
jo'vi·al
jo'vi·al'i·ty
jo'vi·al·ly
jowl
joy'ful
joy'less
joy'ous

ju'bi·lant
ju'bi·la'tion
ju'bi·lee'
Ju·da'i·ca
Ju'da·ism
judge
judged judg'ing
judg'ment *or*
judge'.
ju'di·ca·to'ry
·ries
ju·di'cial
ju·di'ci·ar'y
·ies
ju·di'cious
ju'do
jug
jugged jug'ging
jug'ger·naut'
jug'gle
·gled ·gling
jug'u·lar
juice
juiced juic'ing
juic'er
juic'i·ly
juic'i·ness
juic'y
·i·er ·i·est
ju·jit'su *or*
ju·jut'su
ju'jube
juke'box'
ju'lep
ju·li·enne'
Ju·ly'
·lies'
jum'ble
·bled ·bling
jum'bo
jump'er
jump'i·ness
jump'y
·i·er ·i·est
junc'tion
junc'ture
June
jun'gle
jun'ior
jun·ior'i·ty
ju'ni·per
junk'et
junk'man'
jun'ta
jun'to
·tos
ju·rid'i·cal
ju·rid'i·cal·ly
ju'ris·dic'tion
ju'ris·pru'dence
ju'rist
ju·ris'tic
ju'ror
ju'ry
·ries
ju'ry·man
jus'tice
jus'ti·fi'a·ble

jus'ti·fi'a·bly
jus'ti·fi·ca'tion
jus'ti·fy'
·fied' ·fy'ing
just'ly
jut
jut'ted jut'ting
jute
ju'ven·ile
jux'ta·pose'
·posed' ·pos'ing
jux'ta·po·si'tion

K

Ka·bu'ki
kaf'fee·klatsch'
kai'ser
ka·lei'do·scope'
ka·lei'do·scop'ic
kal'so·mine'
ka'mi·ka'ze
kan'ga·roo'
Kan'sas
ka'o·lin
ka'pok
ka·put'
kar'a·kul
kar'at
ka·ra'te
ka'sha
ka'ty·did'
katz'en·jam'mer
kay'ak
ka·zoo'
ke·bab'
kedge
kedged kedg'ing
keel'haul'
keel'son
keen'ness
keep
kept keep'ing
keep'sake'
keg'ler
ke'loid
kempt
ken'nel
·neled or ·nelled
·nel·ing or
·nel·ling
Ken·tuck'y
ker'a·tin
ker'chief
ker'miss or ·mess
ker'nel
(grain; see
colonel)
ker'o·sene' or
·sine'
ker'sey
·seys
ketch'up
ke'tone
ket'tle
ket'tle·drum'

key
keys
keyed key'ing
(lock; see quay)
key'board'
key club
key'hole'
key'note'
key punch
key'stone'
key'way'
kha'ki
kib'ble
kib·butz'
kib'but·zim'
kib'itz·er
kick'off'
kid'nap'
·napped' or
·naped'
·nap'ping or
·nap'ing
kid'nap'per or
kid'nap'er
kid'ney
·neys
kill'er
kill'-joy'
kiln
kil'o·gram'
kil'o·hertz'
·hertz'
kil'o·li'ter
ki·lo'me·ter
kil'o·volt'
kil'o·watt'
kil'o·watt'-hour'
kil'ter
ki·mo'no
·nos
kin'der·gar'ten
kin'der·gart'ner
kind'heart'ed
kin'dle
·dled ·dling
kind'li·ness
kind'ly
·li·er·li·est
kin'dred
kin'e·mat'ics
kin'e·scope'
ki·ne'sics
kin'es·thet'ic
ki·net'ic
kin'folk'
king'bolt'
king'dom
king'fish'
king'li·ness
king'ly
·li·er·li·est
king'pin'
king post
king'-size'
kink'i·ness
kink'y
·i·er·i·est
kin'ship'

kins'man
ki'osk
kis'met
kitch'en
kitch'en·ette'
kitch'en·ware'
kit'ten
kit'ty
·ties
kit'ty-cor'nered
klax'on
Klee'nex
klep'to·ma'ni·ac
klieg light
knack
knack'wurst'
knap'sack'
knave
(rogue; see nave)
knav'er·y
knav'ish
knead
(press; see need)
knee
kneed knee'ing
knee'cap'
knee'-deep'
knee'-high'
knee'hole'
kneel
knelt or kneeled
kneel'ing
knee'pad'
knell
knick'er·bock'ers
knick'knack'
knife
knives
knifed knif'ing
knife'-edge'
knight
(rank; see night)
knight'hood'
knit
knit'ted or knit
knit'ting
knit'ter
knob'by
·bi·er·bi·est
knock'a·bout'
knock'down'
knock'-kneed'
knock'out'
knoll
knot
knot'ted
knot'ting
knot'hole'
knot'ty
·ti·er·ti·est
know
knew known
know'ing
know'a·ble
know'-how'
know'-it-all'
knowl'edge
knowl'edge·a·ble

knowl'edge·a·bly
knuck'le
·led·ling
knurled
ko·a'la
ko'di·ak' bear
kohl'ra'bi
·bies
Ko·ran'
ko'sher
kow'tow'
ku'chen
ku'dos
küm'mel
kum'quat
kwa'shi·or'kor

L

la'bel
·beled or ·belled
·bel·ing or
·bel·ling
la'bi·al
la'bile
la'bor
lab'o·ra·to'ry
·ries
la'bor·er
la·bo'ri·ous
la'bor-saving
lab'y·rinth'
lab'y·rin'thine
lace
laced lac'ing
lac'er·ate'
·at'ed·at'ing
lac'er·a'tion
lace'work'
lach'ry·mose'
lac'i·ness
lack'a·dai'si·cal
lack'ey
·eys
lack'lus'ter
la·con'ic
la·con'i·cal·ly
lac'quer
la·crosse'
lac'tate
·tat·ed·tat·ing
lac·ta'tion
lac'te·al
lac'tic
lac'tose
la·cu'na
·nas or ·nae
lac'y
·i·er·i·est
lad'der
lad'en
lad'ing
la'dle
·dled·dling
la'dy
·dies

la'dy·bug'
la'dy·fin'ger
la'dy·like'
la'dy·ship'
lag
lagged lag'ging
la'ger
lag'gard
la·gniappe'
la·goon'
lair
(den; see layer)
lais'sez faire'
la'i·ty
la'ma
(monk; see llama)
la'ma·ser'y
·ies
lam·baste'
·bast'ed·bast'ing
lam'bent
lamb'kin
lam'bre·quin
lamb'skin'
lame
(crippled)
la·mé';
(fabric)
la·ment'
lam'en·ta·ble
lam'en·ta'tion
lam'i·nate'
·nat·ed·nat'ing
lam'i·na'tion
lamp'black'
lam·poon'
lamp'post'
lance
lanced lanc'ing
lan'dau
land'fill'
land'hold'er
land'ing
land'la'dy
land'locked'
land'lord'
land'lub'ber
land'mark'
land'own'er
land'scape'
·scaped'
·scap'ing
land'slide'
lands'man
lan'guage
lan'guid
lan'guish
lan'guor
lan'guor·ous
lank'i·ness
lank'ness
lank'y
·i·er·i·est
lan'o·lin
lan'tern
lan'yard
lap
lapped lap'ping

la·pel'
lap'i·dar'y
·ies
lap'in
lap'is laz'u·li'
lapse
lapsed laps'ing
lar'ce·nous
lar'ce·ny
lard'er
large
larg'er larg'est
large'ly
large'-scale'
lar'gess or ·gesse
lar'i·at
lar'va
·vae or ·vas
la·ryn'ge·al
lar'yn·gi'tis
lar'ynx
lar'ynx·es or
la·ryn'ges
la·sa'gna
las·civ'i·ous
lase
lased las'ing
(emit laser light;
see laze)
la'ser
lash'ing
las'si·tude'
las'so
·sos or ·soes
last'-ditch'
Las'tex
last'ing
latch'key'
latch'string'
late
lat'er or lat'ter
lat'est or last
la·teen'
late'ly
la'ten·cy
la'tent
lat'er·al
la'tex
lat'i·ces' or
la'tex·es
lath
(wood strip)
lathe
lathed lath'ing
(machine)
lath'er
lath'ing
lat'i·tude'
lat'ke
·kes
la·trine'
lat'ter-day'
lat'tice
·ticed·tic·ing
lat'tice·work'
laud'a·ble
laud'a·bly
laud'a·to'ry

laugh'a·ble
laugh'ing·stock'
laugh'ter
laun'der
laun'dress
laun'dro·mat'
laun'dry
 ·dries
laun'dry·man
lau're·ate
lau'rel
la'va
la·va'bo
 ·boes
lav'a·liere'
lav'a·to'ry
 ·ries
lav'en·der
lav'ish
law'-a·bid'ing
law'break·er
law'ful
law'ful·ly
law'giv'er
law'less
law'mak'er
lawn mower
law'suit'
law'yer
lax'a·tive
lax'i·ty
lay
 laid lay'ing
 (put; see lie)
lay'er
 (stratum; see
  lair)
lay·ette'
lay'man
lay'off'
lay'out'
lay'o'ver
laze
 lazed laz'ing
 (loaf; see lase)
la'zi·ly
la'zi·ness
la'zy
 ·zi·er ·zi·est
leach
 (filter; see leech)
lead
 led lead'ing
lead'en
lead'er·ship'
lead'-in'
lead'off'
leaf
 leaves
leaf'let
leaf'y
 ·i·er ·i·est
league
 leagued
 leagu'ing
leagu'er
leak
 (escape; see leek)

leak'age
leak'y
 ·i·er ·i·est
lean
 leaned or leant
 lean'ing
lean
 (thin; see lien)
lean'ness
lean'-to'
 -tos'
leap
 leaped or leapt
 leap'ing
leap'frog'
 ·frogged'
 ·frog'ging
learn
 learned or learnt
 learn'ing
learn'ed adj.
leas'a·ble
lease
 leased leas'ing
lease'-back'
lease'hold'er
least
leath'er
leath'er·ette'
leath'er·i·ness
leath'er·y
leave
 left leav'ing
 (let stay)
leave
 leaved leav'ing
 (bear leaves)
leav'en·ing
leave'-tak'ing
lech'er·ous
lec'i·thin
lec'tern
lec'ture
 ·tured ·tur·ing
ledge
ledg'er
leech
 (worm; see
  leach)
leek
 (vegetable; see
  leak)
leer'y
 ·i·er ·i·est
lee'ward
lee'way'
left'-hand'ed
left'ist
left'o'ver
left'-wing'er
leg
 legged leg'ging
leg'a·cy
 ·cies
le'gal·ese'
le·gal'i·ty
 ·ties
le'gal·i·za'tion

le'gal·ize'
 ·ized' ·iz'ing
le'gal·ly
leg'a·tee'
le·ga'tion
le·ga'to
leg'end
leg'end·ar'y
leg'er·de·main'
leg'gi·ness
leg'gy
 ·gi·er ·gi·est
leg'i·bil'i·ty
leg'i·ble
leg'i·bly
le'gion
le'gion·naire'
leg'is·late'
 ·lat'ed ·lat'ing
leg'is·la'tion
leg'is·la'tive
leg'is·la'tor
leg'is·la'ture
le·git'i·ma·cy
le·git'i·mate
le·git'i·mize'
 ·mized' ·miz'ing
leg'man'
leg'room'
leg'ume
lei
lei'sure
lei'sure·ly
lem'on·ade'
lend
 lent lend'ing
length'en
length'i·ness
length'wise'
length'y
 ·i·er ·i·est
le'ni·en·cy
le'ni·ent
len'i·tive
len'i·ty
lens
len'til
 (pea; see lintel)
leop'ard
le'o·tard'
lep'er
lep're·chaun'
lep'ro·sy
lep'rous
les'bi·an
le'sion
les·see'
less'en
 (make less)
less'er
 (smaller)
les'son
 (instruction)
les'sor
 (one who leases)
let
 let let'ting
let'down'

le'thal
le·thar'gic
le·thar'gi·cal·ly
leth'ar·gize'
 ·gized' ·giz'ing
leth'ar·gy
let'tered
let'ter·head'
let'ter-per'fect
let'ter·press'
let'tuce
let'up'
leu·ke'mi·a
lev'ee
 ·eed ·ee·ing
 (embankment;
  see levy)
lev'el
 ·eled or ·elled
 ·el·ing or ·el·ling
lev'el·head'ed
lev'el·ly
lev'er·age
lev'i·a·ble
lev'i·er
le'vis
lev'i·tate'
 ·tat'ed ·tat'ing
lev'i·ta'tion
lev'i·ty
lev'y
 ·ies, ·ied ·y·ing
 (tax; see levee)
lewd'ness
lex'i·cog'ra·pher
lex'i·con
li'a·bil'i·ty
 ·ties
li'a·ble
 (likely; see libel)
li'ai·son'
li'ar
 (one who tells
  lies; see lyre)
li·ba'tion
li'bel
 ·beled or ·belled
 ·bel·ing or
 ·bel·ling
 (defame; see
  liable)
li'bel·ous or
 ·bel·lous
lib'er·al
lib'er·al'i·ty
lib'er·al·ize'
 ·ized' ·iz'ing
lib'er·ate'
 ·at'ed ·at'ing
lib'er·a'tion
lib'er·a'tor
lib'er·tar'i·an
lib'er·tine'
lib'er·ty
 ·ties
li·bid'i·nous
li·bi'do
li·brar'i·an

li'brar'y
 ·ies
li·bret'tist
li·bret'to
 ·tos or ·ti
Lib'ri·um
li'cense
 ·censed ·cens·ing
li·cen'tious
li'chen
lic'it
lic'o·rice
lie
 lay lain ly'ing
 (to rest; see lay)
lie
 lied ly'ing
 (tell falsehood;
  see lye)
li'en
 (claim; see lean)
lieu
lieu·ten'an·cy
lieu·ten'ant
life
 lives
life belt
life'blood'
life'boat'
life buoy
life'-giv'ing
life'guard'
life'less
life'like'
life'line'
life'long'
life'sav'er
life'-size'
life'time'
life'work'
lift'off'
lig'a·ment
lig'a·ture
 ·tured ·tur·ing
light
 light'ed or lit
 light'ing
light'en
 ·ened ·en·ing
 (make light or less
 heavy; see lightning)
light'face'
light'-fin'gered
light'-foot'ed
light'-hand'ed
light'head'ed
light'heart'ed
light'house'
light'ly
light'-mind'ed
light'ning
 (flash of light;
 see lighten)
light'weight'
light'-year'
lig'ne·ous
lig'nite
lik'a·ble or like'-.

like
 liked lik'ing
like'li·hood'
like'ly
like'-mind'ed
lik'en
like'ness
like'wise'
li'lac
Lil'li·pu'tian
lil'y
 ·ies
lil'y-liv'ered
lil'y-white'
limb
 (branch; see limn
lim'ber
lim'bo
lime
 limed lim'ing
lime'light'
lim'er·ick
lime'stone'
lim'it·a·ble
lim'i·ta'tion
lim'it·ed
limn
 (draw; see limb)
lim'ou·sine'
lim'pid
limp'ness
lin'age or line'-.
 (number of lines
 see lineage)
linch'pin'
Lin'coln
lin'den
line
 lined lin'ing
lin'e·age
 (ancestry; see
  linage)
lin'e·al
lin'e·a·ment
 (feature; see
  liniment)
lin'e·ar
line'man
lin'en
lin'er
lines'man
line'up'
lin'ger
lin'ge·rie'
lin'go
 ·goes
lin'gual
lin'guist
lin·guis'tics
lin'i·ment
 (medication;
 see lineament)
lin'ing
link'age
links
 (golf course;
 see lynx)
li·no'le·um

lin'o·type'
lin'seed'
lin'sey-wool'sey
lin'tel
 (*beam; see* lentil)
li'on·ess
li'on-heart'ed
lip'-read'
 -read' -read'ing
lip'stick'
lip'-sync'
liq'ue·fac'tion
liq'ue·fi'a·ble
liq'ue·fi'er
liq'ue·fy'
 -fied' -fy'ing
li·ques'cent
li·queur'
liq'uid
liq'ui·date'
 ·dat'ed ·dat'ing
liq·ui·da'tion
liq'ui·da'tor
liq'uor
lisle
lisp'ing·ly
lis'some *or* ·som
lis'ten
list'less
lit'a·ny
 ·nies
li'tchi nut
li'ter
lit'er·a·cy
lit'er·al
 (*exact; see*
 littoral)
lit'er·al·ly
lit'er·ar'y
lit'er·ate
lit'er·a·ture
lithe'ly
lith'o·graph'
li·thog'ra·pher
li·thog'ra·phy
lith'o·sphere'
lit'i·ga·ble
lit'i·gant
lit'i·gate'
 ·gat'ed ·gat'ing
lit'i·ga'tion
lit'mus
li'to·tes
lit'ter
lit'ter·bug'
lit'tle
 lit'tler *or* less *or*
 less'er, lit'tlest
 or least
lit'to·ral
 (*shore; see*
 literal)
li·tur'gi·cal
lit'ur·gy
 ·gies
liv'a·ble *or* live'·
live
 lived liv'ing

live'li·hood'
live'li·ness
live'long'
live'ly
 ·li·er ·li·est
liv'en
liv'er·wurst'
liv'er·y
 ·ies
live'stock'
liv'id
liz'ard
lla'ma
 (*animal; see*
 lama
load
 (*burden; see* lode)
load'stone'
loaf
loaves
loaf'er
loam'y
 ·i·er ·i·est
loan
 (*something lent;*
 see lone)
loath
 (*unwilling*)
loathe
 loathed loath'ing
 (*detest*)
loath'some
lob
 lobbed lob'bing
lob'by
 ·bies
 ·bied ·by·ing
lob'by·ist
lobe
lob'ster
lo'cal
lo·cale'
lo'cal·ism
lo·cal'i·ty
 ·ties
lo'cal·ize'
 ·ized' ·iz'ing
lo'cal·ly
lo'cate
 ·cat·ed ·cat·ing
lo·ca'tion
lock'er
lock'et
lock'out'
lock'smith'
lo'co·mo'tion
lo'co·mo'tive
lo'co·weed'
lo'cus
 ·ci
lo'cust
lo·cu'tion
lode
 (*ore; see* load)
lode'stone'
lodge
 lodged lodg'ing
 (*house; see* loge)

lodg'er
lodg'ment
loft'i·ly
loft'i·ness
loft'y
 ·i·er ·i·est
log
 logged log'ging
log'a·rithm
loge
 (*theater box;*
 see lodge)
log'ger·head'
log'gi·a
 ·gi·as
log'ic
log'i·cal
log'i·cal·ly
lo·gi'cian
lo·gis'tics
log'o·gram'
log'o·griph'
log'or·rhe'a
lo'gy
 ·gi·er ·gi·est
loin'cloth'
loi'ter
lol'li·pop' *or* ·ly·
lone
 (*solitary;*
 see loan)
lone'li·ness
lone'ly
 ·li·er ·li·est
lone'some
long'-dis'tance
long'-drawn'
lon·gev'i·ty
long'hand'
lon'gi·tude'
lon'gi·tu'di·nal
long'-lived'
long'-play'ing
long'-range'
long'-run'
long'shore'man
long'stand'ing
long'-suf'fer·ing
long'-term'
long'-wind'ed
look'er-on'
 look'ers-on'
look'out'
loop'hole'
loose
 loosed loos'ing
 (*free;* see
 lose, loss)
loose'-joint'ed
loose'-leaf'
loose'ly
loos'en
loose'-tongued'
lop
 lopped lop'ping
lope
 loped lop'ing
lop'sid'ed

lo·qua'cious
lo·quac'i·ty
lor·do'sis
lor·gnette'
lor'ry
 ·ries
lose
 lost los'ing
 (*mislay;* see
 loose, loss)
los'er
loss
 (*thing lost; see*
 loose, lose)
Lo·thar'i·o'
lo'tion
lot'ter·y
 ·ies
loud'mouthed'
loud'speak'er
Lou·i'si·an'a
lounge
lounged
loung'ing
louse
lice
lout'ish
lou'ver
lov'a·ble *or*
 love'·
love
 loved lov'ing
love'li·ness
love'lorn'
love'ly
 ·li·er ·li·est
lov'ing-kind'ness
low'boy'
low'bred'
low'brow'
low'-cost'
low'-down'
low'er
low'er-class'man
low'-grade'
low'-key'
low'-lev'el
low'li·ness
low'ly
 ·li·er ·li·est
low'-mind'ed
low'-necked'
low'-pitched'
low'-spir'it·ed
lox
loy'al
loy'al·ly
loy'al·ty
 ·ties
loz'enge
lu·au'
lu'bri·cant
lu'bri·cate'
 ·cat'ed ·cat'ing
lu'bri·ca'tion
lu'bri·ca'tor
lu'cid
lu·cid'i·ty

luck'i·ly
luck'i·ness
luck'y
 ·i·er ·i·est
lu'cra·tive
lu'cre
lu'cu·bra'tion
lu'di·crous
lug'gage
lu·gu'bri·ous
luke'warm'
lull'a·by'
 ·bies'
lum'bar
 (*of the loins*)
lum'ber
 (*timber*)
lum'ber·jack'
lum'ber·yard'
lu'men
 ·mi·na *or* ·mens
lu'mi·nar'y
 ·ies
lu'mi·nes'cent
lu'mi·nous
lump'i·ness
lump'y
 ·i·er ·i·est
lu'na·cy
lu'nar
lu'na·tic
lunch'eon
lunge
 lunged lung'ing
lu'pine
lure
 lured lur'ing
lu'rid
lurk'ing
lus'cious
lush'ness
lus'ter
lust'i·ness
lus'trous
lust'y
 ·i·er ·i·est
lux·u'ri·ance
lux·u'ri·ant
lux·u'ri·ate'
 ·at'ed ·at'ing
lux·u'ri·ous
lux'u·ry
 ·ries
ly·ce'um
lye
 (*alkaline sub-*
 stance; see lie)
ly'ing-in'
lym·phat'ic
lynch'ing
lynx
 (*animal;* see links)
ly'on·naise'
lyre
 (*harp;* see liar)
lyr'ic
lyr'i·cal
lyr'i·cist

M

ma·ca'bre
mac·ad'am
mac·ad'am·ize'
 ·ized' ·iz'ing
mac'a·ro'ni
mac'a·roon'
mac'er·ate'
 ·at'ed ·at'ing
ma·che'te
Mach·i·a·vel'li·an
mach'i·nate'
 ·nat'ed ·nat'ing
mach'i·na'tion
ma·chine'
 ·chined'
 ·chin'ing
ma·chin'er·y
ma·chin'ist
mack'er·el
mack'i·naw'
mack'in·tosh'
 (*coat;* see
 McIntosh)
mac'ra·me'
mac'ro·bi·ot'ics
mac'ro·cosm
ma'cron
mac'u·la
 ·lae
mad
 mad'der
 mad'dest
mad'am
mad'ame
 mes·dames'
mad'cap'
mad'den·ing
Ma·dei'ra
ma'de·moi·selle'
made'-to-or'der
made'-up'
mad'house'
mad'man'
ma'dras
mad'ri·gal
mad'wo'man
mael'strom
ma'es·tro
 ·tros *or* ·tri
Ma'fi·a *or* Maf'·
mag'a·zine'
ma·gen'ta
mag'got
mag'ic
mag'i·cal·ly
ma·gi'cian
mag'is·te'ri·al
mag'is·trate'
mag·na·nim'i·ty
mag·nam'i·mous
mag'nate
 (*influential*
 person)

mag·ne'sia
mag'net
  (*iron attracter*)
mag·net'ic
mag·net'i·cal·ly
mag'net·ism
mag'net·ize'
  ·ized' ·iz'ing
mag·ne'to
  ·tos
mag·ni·fi·ca'tion
mag·nif'i·cence
mag·nif'i·cent
mag'ni·fi'er
mag'ni·fy'
  fied' ·fy'ing
mag·nil'o·quent
mag'ni·tude'
mag·no'li·a
mag'num
mag'pie
ma·ha·ra'jah *or*
  ·ra'ja
ma·ha·ra'ni *or*
  ·ra'nee
ma·hat'ma
mah'-jongg'
ma·hog'a·ny
maid'en
maid'ser'vant
mail'box'
mail'man'
maim
Maine
main'land'
main'line'
main'ly
main'spring'
main'stream'
main·tain'
main'te·nance
maî'tre d'hô·tel'
maize
  (*corn;* see maze)
ma·jes'tic
ma·jes'ti·cal·ly
maj'es·ty
  ·ties
ma·jol'i·ca
ma'jor
ma'jor-do'mo
  ·mos
ma·jor'i·ty
  ·ties
ma·jus'cule
make
  made mak'ing
make'-be·lieve'
make'shift'
make'up'
mal'a·dapt'ed
mal'ad·just'ed
mal'ad·min'is·ter
mal'a·droit'
mal'a·dy
  ·dies
ma·laise'
mal'a·prop·ism

mal'ap·ro·pos'
ma·lar'i·a
mal'con·tent'
mal de mer'
mal'e·dic'tion
mal'e·fac'tion
mal'e·fac'tor
ma·lef'i·cent
male'ness
ma·lev'o·lence
ma·lev'o·lent
mal·fea'sance
mal'for·ma'tion
mal·formed'
mal·func'tion
mal'ice
ma·li'cious
ma·lign'
ma·lig'nan·cy
ma·lig'nant
ma·lig'ni·ty
  ·ties
ma·lin'ger
ma·lin'ger·er
mall
  (*promenade;* see
  maul)
mal'lard
mal'le·a·bil'i·ty
mal'le·a·ble
mal'let
malm'sey
mal'nu·tri'tion
mal'oc·clu'sion
mal·o'dor·ous
mal·prac'tice
malt'ose
mal·treat'
mam'mal
mam·ma'li·an
mam'ma·ry
mam'mon
mam'moth
man
  men, manned
man'ning
man'a·cle
  ·cled ·cling
man'age
  ·aged ·ag·ing
man'age·a·ble
man'age·ment
man'ag·er
man'a·ge'ri·al
ma·ña'na
man'-child'
men'-chil'dren
man·da'mus
man'da·rin
man'date
  ·dat·ed ·dat·ing
man'da·to'ry
man'di·ble
man'do·lin'
man'drel *or* ·dril
  (*metal spindle*)
man'drill
  (*baboon*)

man'-eat'er
ma·nège'
  (*horsemanship;*
  see ménage)
ma·neu'ver
ma·neu'ver·a·ble
man'ful·ly
man'ga·nese'
mange
man'ger
man'gi·ness
man'gle
  ·gled ·gling
man'go
  ·goes *or* ·gos
man'grove
man'gy
  ·gi·er ·gi·est
man'han'dle
Man·hat'tan
man'hole'
man'hood'
man'-hour'
man'hunt'
ma'ni·a
ma'ni·ac'
ma·ni'a·cal
man'ic
man'i·cot'ti
man'i·cure'
  ·cured ·cur'ing
man'i·cur'ist
man'i·fest'
man'i·fes·ta'tion
man'i·fes'to
  ·toes
man'i·fold'
man'i·kin
Ma·ni'la
ma·nip'u·late'
  ·lat'ed ·lat'ing
ma·nip'u·la'tion
ma·nip'u·la'tive
ma·nip'u·la'tor
man'kind'
man'li·ness
man'ly
  ·li·er ·li·est
man'-made'
man'na
man'ne·quin
man'ner
  (*way;* see manor)
man'ner·ism
man'ner·ly
man'nish
man'-of-war'
  men'-of-war'
ma·nom'e·ter
man'or
  (*residence;*
  see manner)
man'pow'er
man'sard
man'ser'vant
  men'ser'vants
man'sion
man'-sized'

man'slaugh'ter
man'teau
  ·teaus
man'tel
  (*fireplace fac-
  ing;* see mantle)
man'tel·et
man'tel·piece'
man·til'la
man'tis
  ·tis·es *or* ·tes
man'tle
  ·tled ·tling
  (*cloak;* see
  mantel)
man'tu·a
man'u·al
man·u·fac'to·ry
  ·ries
man·u·fac'ture
  ·tured ·tur·ing
man·u·fac'tur·er
ma·nure'
  ·nured' ·nur'ing
man'u·script'
man'y
  more most
man'y-sid'ed
map
mapped
map'ping
ma'ple
mar
  marred mar'ring
mar'a·bou'
ma·ra'ca
mar·a·schi'no
ma·ras'mus
mar'a·thon'
ma·raud'
mar'ble
  ·bled ·bling
mar'ble·ize'
  ·ized' ·iz'ing
mar'ca·site'
mar·cel'
  ·celled' ·cel'ling
March
mar'chion·ess
Mar'di gras'
mare's'-nest'
mare's'-tail'
mar'ga·rine
mar'gin
mar'gin·al
mar'gin·al·ly
mar'i·gold'
ma·ri·jua'na *or*
  ·hua'na
ma·rim'ba
ma·ri'na
mar'i·nade'
  ·nad'ed ·nad'ing
mar'i·nate'
  ·nat'ed ·nat'ing
ma·rine'
mar'i·ner
mar'i·o·nette'

mar'i·tal
  (*of marriage;*
  see martial)
mar'i·time'
mar'jo·ram.
mark'down'
marked
mark'ed·ly
mar'ket·a·bil'i·ty
mar'ket·a·ble
mar'ket·place'
marks'man
mark'up'
mar'lin
  (*fish*)
mar'line
  (*cord*)
mar'line·spike'
mar'ma·lade'
mar'mo·set'
mar'mot
ma·roon'
mar·quee'
mar'quess
mar'que·try
mar·quise'
mar'qui·sette'
mar'riage
mar'riage·a·ble
mar'row
mar'row·bone'
mar'ry
  ·ried ·ry·ing
Mar·sa'la
mar'shal
  ·shaled *or*
  ·shalled
  ·shal·ing *or*
  ·shal·ling
marsh'mal'low
mar·su'pi·al
mar·su'pi·um
  ·pi·a
mar'ten
  (*animal;* see
  martin)
mar'tial
  (*military;* see
  marital)
Mar'tian
mar'tin
  (*bird;* see marten)
mar'ti·net'
mar'tin·gale'
mar·ti'ni
  ·nis
mar'tyr
mar'tyr·dom
mar'tyr·ize'
  ·ized' ·iz'ing
mar'vel
  ·veled *or* ·velled
  ·vel·ing *or*
  ·vel·ling
mar'vel·ous
Marx'ism
Mar'y·land

mar'zi·pan'
mas·ca'ra
  ·raed ·ra·ing
mas'con'
mas'cot
mas'cu·line
mas'cu·lin'i·ty
ma'ser
mash'ie
mask
  (*cover;* see
  masque)
masked
mas'och·ism
mas'och·is'tic
mas'och·is'ti·
  cal·ly
ma'son
Ma'son·ite'
ma'son·ry
masque
  (*masked ball;* see
  mask)
mas'quer·ade'
  ·ad'ed ·ad'ing
Mas'sa·chu'setts
mas'sa·cre
  ·cred ·cring
mas·sage'
  ·saged' ·sag'ing
mas·seur'
mas·seuse'
mas'sive
mas'ter·ful
mas'ter·ly
mas'ter·mind'
mas'ter·piece'
mas'ter·y
  ·ies
mast'head'
mas'tic
mas'ti·cate'
  ·cat'ed ·cat'ing
mas'ti·ca'tion
mas'tiff
mas'to·don'
mas'toid
mas'tur·bate'
  ·bat'ed ·bat'ing
mas'tur·ba'tion
mat
mat'ted
mat'ting
mat'a·dor'
match'box'
match'less
match'lock'
match'mak'er
mate
  mat'ed mat'ing
ma'te·las·sé'
ma·te'ri·al
  (*of matter;*
  see materiel)
ma·te'ri·al·ism
ma·te'ri·al·is'tic
ma·te'ri·al·ize'
  ·ized' ·iz'ing

ma·te'ri·al·ly
ma·te'ri·el'
  or ·té·ri·el'
  (equipment;
  see material)
ma·ter'nal
ma·ter'ni·ty
math'e·mat'i·cal
math'e·ma·ti'cian
math'e·mat'ics
mat'i·nee'
  or ·i·née'
ma'tri·arch'
ma'tri·ar'chal
ma'tri·ar'chy
  ·chies
ma'tri·cide'
ma·tric'u·lant
ma·tric'u·late'
  ·lat'ed ·lat'ing
ma·tric'u·la'tion
mat'ri·mo'ni·al
mat'ri·mo'ny
ma'trix
  ·tri·ces' or ·trix·es
ma'tron
ma'tron·li·ness
ma'tron·ly
mat'ter
mat'ter-of-fact'
mat'tock
mat'tress
mat'u·rate'
  ·rat'ed ·rat'ing
mat'u·ra'tion
ma·ture'
  ·tured' ·tur'ing
ma·ture'ly
ma·tu'ri·ty
mat'zo
  ·zot or ·zoth
  or ·zos
maud'lin
maul
  (mallet; injures;
  see mall)
maun'der
mau'so·le'um
  ·le'ums or ·le'a
mauve
mav'er·ick
mawk'ish
max·il'la
max'il·lar'y
max'im
max'i·mal
max'i·mize'
  ·mized' ·miz'ing
max'i·mum
  ·mums or ·ma
May
may'be
May'day'
may'hem
may'on·naise'
may'or
may'or·al·ty
  ·ties

May'pole'
maze
  (labyrinth; see
  maize)
maz'el tov'
Mc'In·tosh'
  (apple; see
  mackintosh)
mead'ow
mea'ger
meal'time'
meal'y
  ·i·er ·i·est
meal'y-mouthed'
mean v.
  meant mean'ing
mean adj., n.
  (middle; low;
  see mien)
me·an'der
mean'ing·ful
mean'ing·less
mean'ness
mean'time'
mean'while'
mea'sles
mea'sly
  ·sli·er ·sli·est
meas'ur·a·bil'i·ty
meas'ur·a·ble
meas'ur·a·bly
meas'ure
  ·ured ·ur·ing
meas'ure·less
meas'ure·ment
meas'ur·er
meat
  (flesh; see
  meet, mete)
meat'i·ness
me·a'tus
meat'y
  ·i·er ·i·est
me·chan'ic
me·chan'i·cal
mech'a·ni'cian
me·chan'ics
mech'a·nism
mech'a·ni·za'tion
mech'a·nize'
  ·nized' ·niz'ing
med'al
  (award;
  see meddle)
med'al·ist
me·dal'lion
med'dle
  ·dled ·dling
  (interfere;
  see medal)
med'dler
med'dle·some
me'di·a
  (sing. medium)
me'di·al
me'di·an
me'di·ate'
  ·at'ed ·at'ing

me'di·a'tion
me'di·a'tor
Med'i·caid'
med'i·cal
Med'i·care'
med'i·cate'
  ·cat'ed ·cat'ing
med'i·ca'tion
me·dic'i·nal
med'i·cine
me'di·e'val
  or ·ae'val
me'di·o'cre
me'di·oc'ri·ty
  ·ties
med'i·tate'
  ·tat'ed ·tat'ing
med'i·ta'tion
med'i·ta'tor
Med'i·ter·ra'ne·an
me'di·um
  ·di·ums or ·di·a
med'ley
  ·leys
meer'schaum
meet
  met meet'ing
  (come upon; see
  meat, mete)
meg'a·death'
meg'a·hertz'
meg'a·lo·ma'ni·a
meg'a·lop'o·lis
meg'a·phone'
meg'a·ton'
mel'an·cho'li·a
mel'an·chol'ic
mel'an·chol'y
me'lange'
mel'a·nin
me'lee or mê'lée
mel'io·rate'
  ·rat'ed ·rat'ing
mel'io·ra'tion
mel·lif'lu·ous
mel'low
me·lo'de·on
me·lod'ic
me·lo'di·ous
mel'o·dra'ma
mel'o·dra·mat'ic
mel'o·dy
  ·dies
mel'on
melt'a·ble
mel'ton
mem'ber·ship'
mem'brane
mem'bra·nous
me·men'to
  ·tos or ·toes
mem'oir
mem'o·ra·bil'i·a
mem'o·ra·ble
mem'o·ra·bly
mem'o·ran'dum
  ·dums or ·da
me·mo'ri·al

me·mo'ri·al·ize'
  ·ized' ·iz'ing
mem'o·ri·za'tion
mem'o·rize'
  ·rized' ·riz'ing
mem'o·ry
  ·ries
men'ace
  ·aced ·ac·ing
mé·nage' or me·
  (household; see
  manège)
me·nag'er·ie
men·da'cious
men·dac'i·ty
Men·de'li·an
men'di·cant
me'ni·al
men'in·gi'tis
me·nis'cus
  ·cus·es or ·ci
Men'non·ite'
men'o·pause'
men'ses
men'stru·al
men'stru·ate'
  ·at'ed ·at'ing
men'stru·a'tion
men'sur·a·ble
men'su·ra'tion
mens'wear'
men'tal
men·tal'i·ty
men'thol
men'tho·lat'ed
men'tion
men'tor
men'u
  ·us
me·phit'ic
me·pro'ba·mate'
mer'can·tile
mer'can·til·ism
mer'ce·nar'y
  ·nar'ies
mer'cer·ize'
  ·ized' ·iz'ing
mer'chan·dise'
  ·dized' ·diz'ing
mer'chan·dis'er
mer'chant
mer'ci·ful
mer'ci·ful·ly
mer'ci·less
mer·cu'ri·al
Mer·cu'ro·
  chrome'
mer'cu·ry
mer'cy
  ·cies
mere
mer'est
mere'ly
mer·en'gue
  (dance; see
  meringue)
mer'e·tri'cious

merge
  merged merg'ing
merg'er
me·rid'i·an
me·ringue'
  (pie topping;
  see merengue)
me·ri'no
  ·nos
mer'it
mer'i·to'ri·ous
mer'maid'
mer'ri·ly
mer'ri·ment
mer'ri·ness
mer'ry
  ·ri·er ·ri·est
mer'ry-an'drew
mer'ry-go-round'
mer'ry·mak'ing
Mer·thi'o·late'
me'sa
mé·sal'li·ance
mes·cal'
mes'ca·line'
mes'dames'
mes·de·moi·selles'
me·shu'ga
mesh'work'
mes'mer·ism
mes'mer·ize'
  ·ized' ·iz'ing
mes'on
mes'sage
mes'sen·ger
mes·si'ah
mes'sieurs'
mess'i·ly
mess'i·ness
mess'y
  ·i·er ·i·est
met'a·bol'ic
me·tab'o·lism
me·tab'o·lize'
  ·lized' ·liz'ing
met'al
  aled or ·alled
  ·al·ing or ·al·ling
  (mineral; see
  mettle)
me·tal'lic
met'al·lur'gi·cal
met'al·lur'gist
met'al·lur'gy
met'al·work'
met'a·mor'phic
met'a·mor'phism
met'a·mor'phose
  ·phosed ·phos·ing
met'a·mor'pho·sis
  ·ses
met'a·phor'
met'a·phor'i·cal
met'a·phor'i·
  cal·ly
met'a·phys'i·cal
met'a·phys'ics
met'a·tar'sal

me·tath'e·sis
  ·ses'
mete
met'ed met'ing
  (allot; see meat,
  meet)
me'te·or
me'te·or'ic
me'te·or·ite'
me'te·or·oid'
me'te·or·o·
  log'i·cal
me'te·or·ol'o·gist
me'te·or·ol'o·gy
me'ter
meth'a·done'
meth'ane
meth'a·nol'
meth'e·drine'
meth'od
me·thod'i·cal
me·thod'i·cal·ly
Meth'od·ist
meth'od·ize'
  ·ized' ·iz'ing
meth'od·ol'o·gy
me·tic'u·lous
mé·tier'
me·ton'y·my
met'ric
met'ri·cal
met'ro·nome'
me·trop'o·lis
met'ro·pol'i·tan
met'tle
  (spirit; see metal)
mez'za·nine'
mez'zo-so·pra'no
  ·nos or ·ni
mez'zo·tint'
mi·as'ma
  ·mas or ·ma·ta
mi'ca
Mich'i·gan
mi'cro·bar'
mi'crobe
mi·cro'bic
mi'cro·cop'y
mi'cro·cosm
mi'cro·dot'
mi'cro·fiche'
mi'cro·film'
mi'cro·groove'
mi·crom'e·ter
mi'cro·or'gan·
  ism
mi'cro·phone'
mi'cro·print'
mi'cro·read'er
mi'cro·scope'
mi'cro·scop'ic
mi'cro·scop'i·
  cal'ly
mi'cro·wave'
mid'air'
mid'cult'
mid'day'
mid'dle

mid·dle-aged'
mid'dle·brow'
mid'dle-class'
mid'dle·man'
mid'dle-of-the-
  road'
mid'dle-sized'
mid'dle·weight'
mid'dling
mid'dy
 ·dies
midg'et
mid'i·ron
mid'land
mid'night'
mid'point'
mid'riff
mid'ship·man
midst
mid'stream'
mid'sum'mer
mid'term'
mid'-Vic·to'ri·an
mid'way'
mid'week'
Mid'west'
Mid'west'ern·er
mid'wife'
 ·wives'
mid'win'ter
mid'year'
mien
 (manner; see
 mean)
miffed
might
 (power; see mite)
might'i·ly
might'i·ness
might'y
 ·i·er ·i·est
mi'gnon
mi'graine
mi'grant
mi'grate
 ·grat·ed ·grat·ing
mi·gra'tion
mi'gra·to'ry
mi·ka'do
 ·dos
mi·la'dy
mil'dew'
mild'ly
mile'age
mile'post'
mile'stone'
mi·lieu'
mil'i·tan·cy
mil'i·tant
mil'i·tar'i·ly
mil'i·ta·rism
mil'i·ta·ris'tic
mil'i·ta·ri·za'tion
mil'i·ta·rize'
 ·rized' ·riz'ing
mil'i·tar'y
mil'i·tate'
 ·tat'ed ·tat'ing

mi·li'tia
milk'i·ness
milk'maid'
milk'man'
milk'shake'
milk'shed'
milk'sop'
milk toast
 (food; see
 milquetoast)
milk'weed'
milk'y
 ·i·er ·i·est
mill'age
mill'dam'
milled
mil·len'ni·um
 ·ni·ums or ·ni·a
mill'er
mill'et
mil'liard
mil'li·bar'
mil'li·gram'
mil'li·li'ter
mil'li·me'ter
mill'line'
mil'li·ner
mil'li·ner'y
mill'ing
mil'lion
mil'lion·aire'
mil'lionth
mil'li·pede'
mill'pond'
mill'race'
mill'stone'
mill'stream'
 ·tries
mill wheel
mill'work'
mill'wright'
milque'toast'
 (timid person;
 see milk toast)
Mil·wau'kee
mime
 mimed mim'ing
mim'e·o·graph'
mim'er
mi·met'ic
mim'ic
 ·icked ·ick·ing
mim'ick·er
mim'ic·ry
mi·mo'sa
min·a·ret'
min'a·to'ry
mince
 minced minc'ing
mince'meat'
mind'ful
mind'less
mind reader
mine
 mined min'ing
mine'lay'er
min'er
 (mine worker;
 see minor)

min'er·al
min'er·al·i·za'tion
min'er·al·ize'
 ·ized' ·iz'ing
min'er·al'o·gist
min'er·al'o·gy
mi'ne·stro'ne
min'gle
 ·gled ·gling
min'i·a·ture
min'i·a·tur'i·
 za'tion
min'i·a·tur·ize'
 ·ized' ·iz'ing
min'i·bus'
min'i·fi·ca'tion
min'i·fy'
 ·fied' ·fy'ing
min'im
min'i·mal
min'i·mal·ly
min'i·mize'
 ·mized' ·miz'ing
min'i·mum
 ·mums or ·ma
min'ion
 (deputy; see
 minyan)
min'i·skirt'
min'is·ter
 (diplomat; clergy-
 man; see minster)
min·is·te'ri·al
min'is·trant
min'is·tra'tion
min'is·try
 ·tries
min'i·track'
min'i·ver
Min'ne·ap'o·lis
min'ne·sing'er
Min'ne·so'ta
min'now
mi'nor
 (lesser; see
 miner)
mi·nor'i·ty
 ·ties
min'ster
 (church; see
 minister)
min'strel
mint'age
min'u·end'
min'u·et'
mi'nus
mi·nus'cule
min'ute n.
mi·nute' adj.
mi·nute'ly
min'ute·man'
mi·nu'ti·ae'
 (sing. mi·nu'ti·a)
minx
min·yan'
min'ya·nim'
 (group; see
 minion)

mir'a·cle
mi·rac'u·lous
mi·rage'
mire
 mired mir'ing
mir'ror
mirth'ful
mirth'less
mir'y
 ·i·er ·i·est
mis'ad·ven'ture
mis'ad·vise'
mis·al·li'ance
mis'al·ly'
mis'an·thrope'
mis'an·throp'ic
mis·an'thro·py
mis'ap·pli·ca'tion
mis'ap·ply'
mis'ap·pre·hend'
mis'ap·pre·
 hen'sion
mis'ap·pro'pri·ate'
mis·be·got'ten
mis·be·have'
mis·be·hav'ior
mis·be·lief'
mis·be·lieve'
mis·cal'cu·late'
mis'cal·cu·la'tion
mis·car'riage
mis·car'ry
mis·cast'
mis·ce·ge·na'tion
mis'cel·la'ne·a
mis'cel·la'ne·ous
mis'cel·la'ny
 ·nies
mis·chance'
mis'chief
mis'chief-mak'er
mis'chie·vous
mis'ci·bil'i·ty
mis'ci·ble
mis'con·ceive'
mis'con·cep'tion
mis·con'duct
mis·con·
 struc'tion
mis'con·strue'
mis·count'
mis'cre·ant
mis·cue'
mis·date'
mis·deal'
 ·dealt' ·deal'ing
mis·deed'
mis'de·mean'or
mis'di·rect'
mi'ser
mis'er·a·ble
mis'er·a·bly
mi'ser·ly
mis'er·y
 ·ies
mis·es'ti·mate'
mis·fea'sance
mis·file'

mis·fire'
mis'fit'
mis·for'tune
mis·giv'ing
mis·gov'ern
mis·guid'ance
mis·guide'
mis·han'dle
mis'hap
mish'mash'
mis'in·form'
mis'in·for·ma'tion
mis'in·ter'pret
mis·judge'
mis·judg'ment
 or ·judge'ment
mis·lay'
 ·laid' ·lay'ing
mis·lead'
 ·led' ·lead'ing
mis·man'age
mis·man'age·
 ment
mis·match'
mis·mate'
mis·no'mer
mi·sog'a·mist
mi·sog'a·my
mi·sog'y·nist
mi·sog'y·ny
mis·place'
mis·print'
mis·pri'sion
mis'pro·nounce'
mis'pro·nun'ci·
 a'tion
mis'quo·ta'tion
mis·quote'
mis·read'
 ·read' ·read'ing
mis'rep·re·sent'
mis'rep·re·sen·
 ta'tion
mis·rule'
Miss
Miss'es
mis'sal
 (book; see
 missile, missive)
mis·shape'
mis·shap'en
mis'sile
 (weapon; see
 missal, missive)
mis'sion
mis'sion·ar'y
Mis'sis·sip'pi
mis'sive
 (letter; see
 missal, missive)
Mis·sour'i
mis·speak'
 ·spoke' ·spo'ken
 ·speak'ing
mis·spell'
 ·spelled' or
 ·spelt'
 ·spell'ing

mis·spend'
 ·spent'
 ·spend'ing
mis·state'
mis·state'ment
mis·step'
mis·take'
 ·took' ·tak'en
 ·tak'ing
mist'i·ly
mist'i·ness
mis'tle·toe'
mis'tral
mis·treat'ment
mis'tress
mis·tri'al
mis·trust'
mist'y
 ·i·er ·i·est
mis'un·der·stand'
 ·stood' ·stand'ing
mis·us'age
mis·use'
mis·val'ue
mis·write'
 ·wrote' ·writ'ten
 ·writ'ing
mite
 (arachnid; tiny
 thing; see might)
mi'ter
mit'i·ga·ble
mit'i·gate'
 ·gat'ed ·gat'ing
mit'i·ga'tion
mit'i·ga'tor
mi'tral
mitt
mit'ten
mix
mixed or mixt
mix'ing
mix'er
mix'ture
mix'-up'
miz'zen·mast
mne·mon'ic
moan'ing
moat
 (ditch; see mote)
mob
mobbed
mob'bing
mo'bile
mo·bil'i·ty
mo'bi·liz·a·ble
mo'bi·li·za'tion
mo'bi·lize'
 ·lized' ·liz'ing
mob·oc'ra·cy
 ·cies
moc'ca·sin
mo'cha
mock'er·y
 ·ies
mock'-he·ro'ic
mock'ing·bird'
mock'-up'

mod'a·cryl'ic

mod'al

(of a mode)

mod'el

·eled or ·elled

·el·ing or ·el·ling

(copy)

mod'er·ate'

·at'ed ·at'ing

mod'er·ate·ly

mod'er·a'tion

mod'er·a'tor

mod'ern

mod'ern·ism

mod'ern·is'tic

mo·der'ni·ty

mod'ern·i·za'tion

mod'ern·ize'

·ized' ·iz'ing

mod'ern·ness

mod'est

mod'es·ty

mod'i·cum

mod'i·fi·ca'tion

mod'i·fi'er

mod'i·fy'

·fied' ·fy'ing

mod'ish

mo·diste'

mod'u·lar

mod'u·late'

·lat'ed ·lat·ing

mod'u·la'tion

mod'u·la'tor

mod'ule

mo'gul

mo'hair

moi'e·ty

·ties

moire

moi·ré'

mois'ten

moist'ness

mois'ture

mois'tur·ize'

·ized' ·iz'ing

mo'lar

mo·las'ses

mold'board'

mold'er

mold'i·ness

mold'ing

mold'y

·i·er ·i·est

mole

mo·lec'u·lar

mol'e·cule'

mole'hill'

mole'skin'

mo·lest'

mo'les·ta'tion

mol'li·fy'

·fied' ·fy'ing

mol'lusk

mol'ly·cod'dle

·dled ·dling

molt

mol'ten

mo·lyb'de·num

mo'ment

mo'men·tar'i·ly

mo'men·tar'y

mo·men'tous

mo·men'tum

·tums or ·ta

mom'ism

mo·nan'drous

mon'arch

mo·nar'chal

mon'arch·ism

mon'arch·y

·ies

mon'as·ter'y

·ies

mo·nas'tic

mo·nas'ti·cism

mon·au'ral

Mon'day

mon'e·tar'y

mon'e·tize'

·tized' ·tiz'ing

mon'ey

·eys or ·ies

mon'ey·bag'

mon'ey-chang'er

mon'eyed

mon'ey-grub'ber

mon'ey·lend'er

mon'ey·mak'er

mon'ger

Mon'gol·ism

Mon'gol·oid'

mon'goose

·goos·es

mon'grel

mo·ni'tion

mon'i·tor

mon'i·to'ry

·ries

monk

mon'key

·keys

monk's cloth

mon'o·chro·mat'ic

mon'o·chrome'

mon'o·cle

mon'o·coque'

mo·noc'u·lar

mon'o·dra'ma

mo·nog'a·mist

mo·nog'a·mous

mo·nog'a·my

mon'o·gram'

·grammed'

·gram'ming

mon'o·graph'

mo·nog'y·ny

mon'o·lith'

mon'o·logue'

or ·log'

mo·nol'o·gu·ist or

mo·nol'o·gist

mon'o·ma'ni·a

mon'o·met'al·lism

mon'o·nu'cle·o'sis

mon'o·plane'

mo·nop'o·list

mo·nop'o·list'tic

mo·nop'o·li·

za'tion

mo·nop'o·lize'

·lized' ·liz'ing

mo·nop'o·ly

mon'o·rail'

mon'o·syl·lab'ic

mon'o·syl'la·ble

mon'o·the'ism

mon'o·the·is'tic

mon'o·tone'

mo·not'o·nous

mo·not'o·ny

mon'o·type'

mon·ox'ide

Mon'sei·gneur'

Mes'sei·gneurs'

mon·sieur'

mes'sieurs

Mon·si'gnor

mon·soon'

mon'ster

mon·stros'i·ty

·ties

mon'strous

mon·tage'

·taged' ·tag'ing

Mon·tan'a

month'ly

·lies

mon'u·ment

mon'u·men'tal

mood'i·ly

mood'i·ness

mood'y

·i·er ·i·est

moon'beam'

moon'-faced'

moon'light'

moon'light'ing

moon'lit'

moon'port'

moon'rise'

moon'set'

moon'shine'

moon'shot'

moon'stone'

moon'struck'

moor'age

moor'ing

moose

moose

(deer; see

mouse, mousse)

moot

(debatable;

see mute)

mop

mopped

mop'ping

mope

moped mop'ing

mop'pet

mop'-up'

mo·raine'

mor'al

mo·rale'

mor'al·ist

mor'al·is'tic

mor'al·is'ti·cal·ly

mo·ral'i·ty

mor'al·ize'

·ized' ·iz'ing

mor'al·ly

mo·rass'

mor'a·to'ri·um

·ri·ums or ·ri·a

mor'bid

mor·bid'i·ty

mor'dant

(corrosive)

mor'dent

(musical term)

more·o'ver

mo'res

mor·ga·nat'ic

morgue

mor'i·bund'

mor'i·bun'di·ty

Mor'mon

morn'ing

(part of day;

see mourning)

mo·roc'co

mo'ron

mo·ron'ic

mo·rose'

mor'phine

mor·phol'o·gy

mor'sel

mor'tal

mor·tal'i·ty

mor'tal·ly

mor'tar

mor'tar·board'

mort'gage

·gaged ·gag·ing

mort'ga·gee'

mort'ga·gor

mor·ti'cian

mor'ti·fi·ca'tion

mor'ti·fy'

·fied' ·fy'ing

mor'tise

·tised ·tis·ing

mor'tu·ar'y

·ies

mo·sa'ic

·icked ·ick·ing

mosque

mos·qui'to

·toes or ·tos

moss'back'

moss'i·ness

moss'y

·i·er ·i·est

most'ly

mote

(speck; see moat)

mo·tel'

moth'ball'

moth'-eat'en

moth'er·hood'

moth'er-in-law'

moth'ers-in-law'

moth'er·land'

moth'er·li·ness

moth'er·ly

moth'er-of-pearl'

moth'proof'

mo·tif'

mo'tile

mo·til'i·ty

mo'tion·less

mo'ti·vate'

·vat'ed ·vat'ing

mo'ti·va'tion

mo'ti·va'tor

mo'tive

mot'ley

mo'tor·bike'

mo'tor·boat'

mo'tor·bus'

mo'tor·cade'

mo'tor·cy'cle

mo'tor·drome'

mo'tor·ist

mo'tor·ize'

·ized' ·iz'ing

mo'tor·man

mot'tle

·tled ·tling

mot'to

·toes or ·tos

mou·lage'

mound

moun'tain

moun'tain·eer'

moun'tain·ous

moun'te·bank'

mourn'ful

mourn'ing

(grieving;

see morning)

mouse

mice

moused mous'ing

(rodent; see

moose, mousse)

mous'er

mouse'trap'

mous'i·ness

mousse

(food; see

moose, mouse)

mousse·line'

de soie'

mous'y

·i·er ·i·est

mouth'ful'

·fuls'

mouth'part'

mouth'piece'

mouth'-to-mouth'

mouth'wash'

mouth'wa'ter·ing

mou'ton'

(fur; see mutton)

mov'a·ble

or move'.

mov'a·bly

move

moved mov'ing

move'ment

mov'ie

mov'ie·go'er

mov'i·o'la

mow

mowed, mowed

or mown,

mow'ing

moz'za·rel'la

Mr.

Messrs.

Mrs.

Mmes.

mu'ci·lage

mu'ci·lag'i·nous

muck'rake'

mu'cous adj.

mu'cus n.

mud'der

mud'di·ness

mud'dle

·dled ·dling

mud'dler

mud'dy

·di·er ·di·est

mud'sling'ing

Muen'ster

mu·ez'zin

muf'fin

muf'fle

·fled ·fling

muf'fler

muf'ti

mug

mugged

mug'ging

mug'gi·ness

mug'gy

·gi·er ·gi·est

mug'wump'

muk'luk'

mu·lat'to

·toes

mul'ber'ry

·ries

mulch

mulct

mul'ish

mul'li·ga·taw'ny

mul'lion

mul'ti·col'ored

mul'ti·far'i·ous

mul'ti·form'

mul'ti·lat'er·al

mul'ti·ple

mul'ti·plex'

mul'ti·pli'a·ble

mul'ti·pli·cand'

mul'ti·pli·ca'tion

mul'ti·plic'i·ty

mul'ti·pli'er

mul'ti·ply'

·plied' ·ply'ing

mul'ti·tude'

mul'ti·tu'di·nous

mul'ti·ver'si·ty
mum'ble
·bled ·bling
mum'bler
mum'mer·y
mum'mi·fy'
·fied' ·fy'ing
mum'my
·mies
munch
mun·dane'
mu·nic'i·pal
mu·nic'i·pal'i·ty
·ties
mu·nic'i·pal·ize'
·ized' ·iz'ing
mu·nif'i·cence
mu·nif'i·cent
mu·ni'tion
mu'ral
mur'der·er
mur'der·ous
murk'i·ly
murk'i·ness
murk'y
·i·er ·i·est
mur'mur
mur'mur·er
mus'ca·dine
mus'ca·tel'
mus'cle
·cled ·cling
(*body part;*
see mussel)
mus'cle-bound'
mus'cu·lar
mus'cu·la'ture
muse
mused mus'ing
mu·sette'
mu·se'um
mush'i·ness
mush'room
mush'y
·i·er ·i·est
mu'sic
mu'si·cal *adj.*
mu'si·cale' *n.*
mu·si'cian
mu'si·col'o·gist
mu'si·col'o·gy
mus'kel·lunge'
mus'ket
musk'i·ness
musk'mel'on
musk'rat'
musk'y
·i·er ·i·est
mus'lin
mus'sel
(*shellfish;*
see muscle)
mus·tache'
or mous·
mus'tang
mus'tard
mus'ter
mus'ti·ness

mus'ty
·ti·er ·ti·est
mu'ta·bil'i·ty
mu'ta·ble
mu'tant
mu'tate
·tat·ed ·tat·ing
mu·ta'tion
mute
mut'ed mut'ing
(*silent;* see moot)
mu'ti·late'
·lat'ed ·lat'ing
mu'ti·la'tion
mu'ti·neer'
mu'ti·nous
mu'ti·ny
·nies
·nied ·ny·ing
mut'ter
mut'ton
(*food;* see
mouton)
mu'tu·al
mu'tu·al'i·ty
mu'tu·al·ly
muu'muu
Mu'zak
muz'zle
·zled ·zling
my'e·li'tis
my'e·lo·gram'
my'lar
my'na *or* ·nah
my·o'pi·a
my·op'ic
myr'i·ad
myr'i·a·pod'
myr'mi·don'
myrrh
myr'tle
my·self'
mys·te'ri·ous
mys'ter·y
·ies
mys'tic
mys'ti·cal
mys'ti·cal·ly
mys'ti·cism
mys'ti·fi·ca'tion
mys'ti·fy'
·fied' ·fy'ing
mys·tique'
myth'i·cal
myth'o·log'i·cal
my·thol'o·gize'
·gized' ·giz'ing
my·thol'o·gy
·gies
myth'os

N

nab
nabbed nab'bing
na·celle'

na'cre
na'cre·ous
na'dir
nag
nagged nag'ging
nail'head'
nain'sook
na·ive' *or* ·ïve'
na·ive·té' *or* ïve·
na'ked·ness
nam'by-pam'by
·bies
name
named nam'ing
name'a·ble
or nam'·
name'-drop'per
name'less
name'ly
name'plate'
name'sake'
nan·keen' *or* ·kin'
nap
napped nap'ping
na'palm
na'per·y
naph'tha
naph'tha·lene'
nap'kin
na·po'le·on
nap'per
nar·cis'sism
nar'cis·sist
nar'cis·sis'tic
nar·cis'sus
nar'co·lep'sy
nar·co'sis
nar·cot'ic
nar'co·tism
nar'rate
·rat·ed ·rat·ing
nar·ra'tion
nar'ra·tive
nar'ra·tor
nar'row-mind'ed
nar'whal
na'sal
na·sal'i·ty
na'sal·ize'
·ized' ·iz'ing
nas'cent
nas'ti·ly
nas'ti·ness
na·stur'tium
nas'ty
·ti·er ·ti·est
na'tal
na'tant
na·ta·to'ri·um
·ri·ums *or* ·ri·a
na'ta·to'ry
na'tion
na'tion·al
na'tion·al·ism
na'tion·al·is'ti·
cal·ly
na'tion·al'i·ty
·ties

na'tion·al·i·za'tion
na'tion·al·ize'
·ized' ·iz'ing
na'tion·al·ly
na'tion·wide'
na'tive
na'tive-born'
na·tiv'i·ty
·ties
nat'ti·ly
nat'ty
·ti·er ·ti·est
nat'u·ral
nat'u·ral·ism
nat'u·ral·ist
nat'u·ral·is'tic
nat'u·ral·i·za'tion
nat'u·ral·ize'
·ized' ·iz'ing
nat'u·ral·ly
na'ture
naug'a·hyde'
naught
naugh'ti·ly
naugh'ti·ness
naugh'ty
·ti·er ·ti·est
nau'se·a
nau'se·ate'
·at·ed ·at·ing
nau'seous
nau'ti·cal
nau'ti·lus
·lus·es *or* ·li'
na'val
(*of a navy*)
nave
(*part of a church;*
see knave)
na'vel
(*umbilicus*)
nav'i·cert
nav'i·ga·ble
nav'i·gate'
·gat·ed ·gat·ing
nav'i·ga'tion
nav'i·ga'tor
na'vy
·vies
nay
(*no;* see nee,
neigh)
Ne·an'der·thal'
near'by'
near'ly
near'sight'ed
neat'ly
neat'ness
neb'bish
Ne·bras'ka
neb'u·la
·lae' *or* ·las
neb'u·lar
neb·u·los'i·ty
neb'u·lous
nec'es·sar'i·ly
nec'es·sar'y
·ies

ne·ces'si·tate'
·tat'ed ·tat'ing
ne·ces'si·tous
ne·ces'si·ty
·ties
neck'er·chief
neck'lace
neck'line'
neck'piece'
neck'tie'
neck'wear'
ne·crol'o·gy
·gies
nec'ro·man'cy
nec'tar
nec'tar·ine'
nee *or* née
(*born;* see nay,
neigh)
need
(*require;* see
knead)
need'ful
need'i·ness
nee'dle
·dled ·dling
nee'dle·like'
nee'dle·point'
nee'dler
need'less
nee'dle·work'
need'n't
need'y
·i·er ·i·est
ne'er'-do-well'
ne·far'i·ous
ne·gate'
·gat'ed ·gat'ing
ne·ga'tion
neg'a·tive
neg'a·tiv·ism
neg·lect'
neg·lect'ful
neg'li·gee'
neg'li·gence
neg'li·gent
neg'li·gi·ble
neg'li·gi·bly
ne·go'ti·a·bil'i·ty
ne·go'ti·a·ble
ne·go'ti·ate'
·at'ed ·at'ing
ne·go'ti·a'tion
ne·go'ti·a'tor
Ne'gro
·groes
Ne'groid
neigh
(*whinny;* see
nay, nee)
neigh'bor
neigh'bor·hood'
neigh'bor·li·ness
neigh'bor·ly
nei'ther
(*not either;*
see nether)
nem'a·tode'

nem'e·sis
·ses'
ne'o·clas'sic
ne'o·lith'ic
ne·ol'o·gism
ne'o·my'cin
ne'on
ne'o·phyte'
ne'o·plasm
ne'o·prene'
ne·pen'the
neph'ew
ne·phri'tis
nep'o·tism
Nep'tune
nerve
nerved nerv'ing
nerve'-rack'ing
or -wrack'·
nerv'ous
nerv'y
·i·er ·i·est
nes'ci·ent
nes'tle
·tled ·tling
nest'ling
(*young bird*)
net
net'ted net'ting
neth'er
(*lower;* see
neither)
net'tle
·tled ·tling
net'work'
Neuf'châ·tel'
neu'ral
neu·ral'gia
neu'ras·the'ni·a
neu·ri'tis
neu'ro·log'i·cal
neu·rol'o·gist
neu·rol'o·gy
neu·ro'sis
·ses
neu·rot'ic
neu'ter
neu'tral
neu·tral'i·ty
neu'tral·i·za'tion
neu'tral·ize'
·ized' ·iz'ing
neu'tral·iz'er
neu·tri'no
neu'tron
Ne·vad'a
nev'er·more'
nev'er·the·less'
ne'vus
·vi
new'born'
new'com'er
new'el
new'fan'gled
new'-fash'ioned
New'found·land'
New Hamp'shire
New Jer'sey

new'ly·wed'
New Mex'i·co
news'boy'
news'cast'
news'deal'er
news'let'ter
news'man'
news'pa'per
new'speak'
news'print'
news'reel'
news'stand'
news'wor'thy
New York
next'-door'
nex'us
 ·us·es *or* nex'us
ni'a·cin
Ni·ag'a·ra
nib'ble
 ·bled ·bling
nib'lick
nice
 nic'er nic'est
nice'ly
ni'ce·ty
 ·ties
niche
 (*recess*)
nick
 (*notch*)
nick'el
 ·eled *or* ·elled
 ·el·ing *or* ·el·ling
nick'el·o'de·on
nick'name'
nic'o·tine'
nic'o·tin·ism
nic'ti·tate'
 ·tat'ed ·tat'ing
niece
nig'gard·ly
nig'gling
night
 (*darkness;* see
 knight)
night'cap'
night'club'
night'dress'
night'fall'
night'gown'
night'in·gale'
night'long'
night'ly
night'mare'
night'mar'ish
night'shirt'
night'time'
ni'hil·ism
ni'hil·is'tic
nim'ble
 ·bler ·blest
nim'bly
nim'bus
 ·bi *or* ·bus·es
nin'com·poop'
nine'fold'
nine'pins'

nine'teen'
nine'ti·eth
nine'ty
 ·ties
nin'ny
 ·nies
ni'non
ninth
nip
 nipped nip'ping
nip'per
nip'pi·ness
nip'ple
nip'py
 ·pi·er ·pi·est
nip'-up'
nir·va'na
ni'sei
 ·sei *or* ·seis
nit'-pick'ing
ni'tro·gen
ni'tro·glyc'er·in
 or ·er·ine
nit'ty-grit'ty
no·bil'i·ty
no'ble
 ·bler ·blest
no'ble·man
no'bly
no'bod'y
 ·ies
noc·tur'nal
noc·tur'nal·ly
noc'turne
noc'u·ous
nod
 nod'ded nod'ding
nod'al
node
nod'u·lar
nod'ule
no·el' *or* ·ël'
nog'gin
no'-hit'ter
noise
 noised nois'ing
noise'less
noise'mak'er
nois'i·ly
nois'i·ness
noi'some
nois'y
 ·i·er ·i·est
no'mad
no·mad'ic
nom' de plume'
noms' de plume'
no'men·cla'ture
nom'i·nal
nom'i·nal·ly
nom'i·nate'
 ·nat'ed ·nat'ing
nom'i·na'tion
nom'i·na·tive
nom'i·na'tor
nom'i·nee'
non'a·ge·nar'i·an
non'-book'

nonce
non'cha·lance'
non'cha·lant'
non·com'bat·ant
non'com·mit'tal
non com'pos
 men'tis
non'con·form'ist
non'co·op'er·a'·
 tion
non'de·script'
non·en'ti·ty
 ·ties
non'es·sen'tial
none'such'
none'the·less'
non'ex·ist'ent
non·fea'sance
non'he'ro
non·nu'cle·ar
no-non'sense
non'pa·reil'
non·par'ti·san
non·plus'
 ·plused' *or*
 ·plussed'
 ·plus'ing *or*
 ·plus'sing
non·prof'it
non·sched'uled
non'sec·tar'i·an
non'sense
non·sen'si·cal
non·sen'si·cal·ly
non' se'qui·tur
non'-sked'
non'skid'
non'stop'
non'sup·port'
non·un'ion
non·vi'o·lence
noo'dle
noon'day'
no one
noon'time'
noose
 noosed noos'ing
no'-par'
nor'mal
nor'mal·cy
nor·mal'i·ty
nor'mal·ize'
 ·ized' ·iz'ing
nor'mal·ly
North'bound'
North Car'o·li'na
North Da·ko'ta
north'east'
north'east'er·ly
north'east'ern
north'er·ly
north'ern
north'ward
north'west'
north'west'er·ly
north'west'ern
nose
 nosed nos'ing

nose'bleed'
nose cone
nose'-dive'
 -dived' -div'ing
nose'gay'
nose'piece'
no'-show'
nos·tal'gia
nos·tal'gic
nos'tril
nos'trum
no'ta·ble
no'ta·bly
no'ta·ri·za'tion
no'ta·rize'
 ·rized' ·riz'ing
no'ta·ry public
 no'ta·ries public
 or no'ta·ry publics
no·ta'tion
notched
note
 not'ed not'ing
note'book'
note'wor'thy
noth'ing·ness
no'tice
 ·ticed ·tic·ing
no'tice·a·ble
no'tice·a·bly
no'ti·fi'a·ble
no'ti·fi·ca'tion
no'ti·fy'
 ·fied' ·fy'ing
no'tion
no·to·ri'e·ty
no·to'ri·ous
no'-trump'
not'with·stand'ing
nou'gat
nought
nour'ish·ment
nou'veau riche'
 nou'veaux riches'
no'va
 ·vas *or* ·vae
nov'el
nov'el·ette'
nov'el·ist
no·vel'la
nov'el·ty
 ·ties
No·vem'ber
nov'ice
no·vi'ti·ate
now'a·days'
no'where'
no'wise'
nox'ious
noz'zle
nu'ance
nub'bi·ness
nub'by
 ·bi·er ·bi·est
nu'bile
nu'cle·ar
nu'cle·ate'
 ·at'ed ·at'ing

nu'cle·on'ics
nu'cle·us
 ·cle·i' *or*
 ·cle·us·es
nude
nudge
 nudged nudg'ing
nud'ist
nu'di·ty
nu'ga·to'ry
nug'get
nui'sance
nul'li·fi·ca'tion
nul'li·fy'
 ·fied' ·fy'ing
num'ber
num'ber·less
numb'ly
numb'ness
nu'mer·a·ble
nu'mer·al
nu'mer·ate'
 ·at'ed ·at'ing
nu'mer·a'tion
nu'mer·a'tor
nu·mer'i·cal
nu'mer·ol'o·gy
nu'mer·ous
nu'mis·mat'ic
nu·mis'ma·tist
num'skull'
nun'ner·y
 ·ies
nup'tial
nurse
 nursed nurs'ing
nurse'maid'
nurs'er·y
 ·ies
nur'ture
 ·tured ·tur·ing
nut'crack'er
nut'gall'
nut'meat'
nut'meg'
nut'pick'
nu'tri·a
nu'tri·ent
nu'tri·ment
nu·tri'tion
nu·tri'tious
nu'tri·tive
nut'shell'
nuz'zle
 ·zled ·zling
ny'lon
nymph
nym'pho·
 ma'ni·ac'

O

oaf'ish
oa'kum
oar
 (*pole;* see ore)

oar'lock'
oars'man
o·a'sis
 ·ses
oath
oat'meal'
ob'bli·ga'to
 ·tos *or* ·ti
ob'du·ra·cy
ob'du·rate
o·be'di·ence
o·be'di·ent
o·bei'sance
o·bei'sant
ob'e·lisk'
o·bese'
o·be'si·ty
o·bey'
ob'fus·cate'
 ·cat'ed ·cat'ing
ob'i·ter dic'tum
 ob'i·ter dic'ta
o·bit'u·ar'y
 ·ies
ob'ject
ob·jec'tion
ob·jec'tion·a·ble
ob·jec'tion·a·bly
ob·jec'tive
ob·jec'tive·ly
ob·jec·tiv'i·ty
ob·jec'tor
ob'jet d'art'
ob'jets d'art'
ob'jur·gate'
 ·gat'ed ·gat'ing
ob·jur·ga'tion
ob·la'tion
ob'li·gate'
 ·gat'ed ·gat'ing
ob'li·ga'tion
ob·lig'a·to'ry
o·blige'
 o·bliged'
 o·blig'ing
ob·lique'
ob·lique'ly
ob·liq'ui·ty
ob·lit'er·ate'
 ·at'ed ·at'ing
ob·lit'er·a'tion
ob·lit'er·a'tor
ob·liv'i·on
ob·liv'i·ous
ob'long
ob'lo·quy
 ·quies
ob·nox'ious
o'boe
o'bo·ist
ob·scene'
ob·scen'i·ty
 ·ties
ob·scure'
 ·scured' ·scur'ing
ob·scure'ly
ob·scu'ri·ty
 ·ties

ob'se·quies
ob·se'qui·ous
ob·serv'a·ble
ob·serv'ance
ob·serv'ant
ob'ser·va'tion
ob·serv'a·to'ry
·ries
ob·serve'
served' serv'ing
ob·serv'er
ob·sess'
ob·ses'sion
ob·ses'sive
ob·sid'i·an
ob'so·lesce'
lesced' lesc'ing
ob'so·les'cence
ob'so·les'cent
ob'so·lete'
ob'sta·cle
ob·stet'ric
ob·stet'ri·cal
ob'ste·tri'cian
ob'sti·na·cy
·cies
ob'sti·nate
ob'sti·nate·ly
ob·strep'er·ous
ob·struct'
ob·struc'tion
ob·struc'tion·ist
ob·struc'tive
ob·tain'
ob·trude'
trud'ed
trud'ing
ob·tru'sion
ob·tru'sive
ob·tru'sive·ly
ob·tuse'
ob·verse'
ob·vert'
ob'vi·ate'
·at'ed ·at'ing
ob'vi·ous
ob'vi·ous·ly
oc'a·ri'na
oc·ca'sion
oc·ca'sion·al
oc·ca'sion·al·ly
Oc'ci·dent
Oc'ci·den'tal
oc·cip'i·tal
oc·clude'
clud'ed
clud'ing
oc·clu'sion
oc·cult'
oc'cul·ta'tion
oc·cult'ism
oc'cu·pan·cy
·cies
oc'cu·pant
oc'cu·pa'tion
oc'cu·pa'tion·al·ly
oc'cu·py'
pied' ·py'ing

oc·cur'
·curred'
·cur'ring
oc·cur'rence
o'cean
o'cean·go'ing
o'ce·an'ic
o'ce·a·nog'ra·phy
o'ce·an·ol'o·gy
o'ce·lot'
o'cher or o'chre
o'·clock'
oc'ta·gon'
oc·tag'o·nal
oc'ta·he'dron
oc'tane
oc·tan'gu·lar
oc'tave
oc·ta'vo
·vos
oc·tet' or ·tette'
Oc·to'ber
oc'to·ge·nar'i·an
oc'to·pus
·pus·es or ·pi'
or oc·top'o·des'
oc'tu·ple
oc'tu·lar
oc'u·list
odd'i·ty
·ties
odd'ly
odds'-on'
o'di·ous
o'di·um
o·dom'e·ter
o'dor
o'dor·if'er·ous
o'dor·ous
Od'ys·sey
of'fal
off'beat'
off'-col'or
of·fend'
of·fense'
of·fen'sive
of'fer
of'fer·ing
of'fer·to'ry
·ries
off'hand'
off'hand'ed·ly
of'fice
office·hold'er
of'fi·cer
of·fi'cial·ese'
of·fi'cial
of·fi'ci·ate'
·at'ed ·at'ing
of·fi'ci·a'tion
of·fi'ci·a'tor
of·fi'cious
off'ing
off'-key'
off'-lim'its
off'-line'
off'print'
off'set'

off'shoot'
off'shore'
off'side'
off'spring'
·spring' or
·springs'
off'stage'
off'-white'
of'ten
of'ten·times'
o'gle
o'gled o'gling
o'gre
o'gre·ish or
o'grish
O·hi'o
ohm'me'ter
oil'cloth'
oil'i·ness
oil'pa'per
oil'skin'
oil'stone'
oil'y
·i·er ·i·est
oint'ment
OK or O.K.
OK's or O.K.'s
OK'd or O.K.'d
OK'ing or O.K.'ing
O'kla·ho'ma
old'-fash'ioned
old'ish
old'-line'
old'ster
old'-tim'er
old'-world'
o'le·o'
o'le·o·mar'ga·
rine or ·rin
ol·fac'tion
ol·fac'to·ry
·ries
ol'i·garch'
ol'i·garch'y
·ies
ol'i·gop'o·ly
·lies
ol'ive
O·lym'pic
o·me'ga
om'e·let or
·lette
o'men
om'i·nous
o·mis'si·ble
o·mis'sion
o·mit'
o·mit'ted
o·mit'ting
om'ni·bus'
om'ni·far'i·ous
om·nip'o·tence
om·nip'o·tent
om'ni·pres'ence
om'ni·pres'ent
om'ni·range'
om·nis'cience
om·nis'cient

om·niv'o·rous
once'-o'ver
on'com'ing
one'ness
on'er·ous
one'self'
one'-sid'ed
one'-time'
one'-track'
one'-up'
-upped'
-up'ping
one'-up'man·ship'
one'-way'
on'go'ing
on'ion·skin'
on'-line'
on'look'er
on'ly
on'o·mat'o·poe'ia
on'rush'
on'set'
on'shore'
on'side'
on'slaught'
o'nus
on'ward
on'yx
oo'long
ooze
oozed ooz'ing
oo'zi·ness
oo'zy
·zi·er ·zi·est
o·pac'i·ty
o'pal
o'pal·es'cent
o·paque'
o'pen-and-shut'
o'pen-end'
o'pen-end'ed
o'pen·er
o'pen-eyed'
o'pen·hand'ed
o'pen·heart'ed
o'pen-hearth'
o'pen·ly
o'pen-mind'ed
o'pen-mouthed'
o'pen·ness
o'pen·work'
op'er·a
op'er·a·ble
op'er·ate'
·at'ed ·at'ing
op'er·at'ic
op'er·a'tion
op'er·a'tion·al
op'er·a'tion·al·ly
op'er·a'tive
op'er·a'tor
op'er·et'ta
oph'thal·mol'o·
gist
oph'thal·mol'o·gy
oph·thal'mo·
scope'
o'pi·ate

o·pin'ion
o·pin'ion·at'ed
o·pin'ion·a'tive
o'pi·um
o·pos'sum
op·po'nent
op'por·tune'
op'por·tun'ism
op'por·tun'ist
op'por·tu'ni·ty
·ties
op·pos'a·ble
op·pose'
·posed' ·pos'ing
op·pos'er
op'po·site
op'po·si'tion
op·press'
op·pres'sion
op·pres'sive
op·pres'sive·ly
op·pres'sor
op·pro'bri·ous
op·pro'bri·um
op'tic
op'ti·cal
op·ti'cian
op'ti·mal
op'ti·mism
op'ti·mist
op'ti·mis'tic
op'ti·mis'ti·cal·ly
op'ti·mize'
·mized' ·miz'ing
op'ti·mum
·mums or ·ma
op'tion
op'tion·al
op'tion·al·ly
op·tom'e·trist
op·tom'e·try
op'u·lence
op'u·lent
o'pus
op'er·a or
o'pus·es
or'a·cle
(wise person;
see auricle)
o·rac'u·lar
o'ral
(of the mouth;
see aural)
o'ral·ly
or'ange
or'ange·ade'
or'ange·wood'
o·rang'u·tan'
o·ra'tion
or'a·tor
or'a·tor'i·cal
or'a·tor'i·o'
·os'
or'a·to'ry
·ries
or·bic'u·lar
or'bit
or'chard

or'ches·tra
or·ches'tral
or'ches·trate'
·trat'ed ·trat'ing
or'ches·tra'tion
or'chid
or·dain'
or·deal'
or'der
or'der·li·ness
or'der·ly
·lies
or'di·nal
or'di·nance
(law; see
ordnance)
or'di·nar'i·ly
or'di·nar'y
·ies
or'di·nate
or'di·na'tion
ord'nance
(artillery; see
ordinance)
or'dure
ore
(mineral; see oar)
o·reg'a·no
Or'e·gon
or'gan
or'gan·dy or ·die
or·gan'ic
or·gan'i·cal·ly
or'gan·ism
or'gan·ist
or'gan·iz'a·ble
or'gan·i·za'tion
or'gan·ize'
·ized' ·iz'ing
or'gan·iz'er
or·gan'za
or'gasm
or·gas'mic
or·gi·as'tic
or'gy
·gies
O'ri·ent n.
o'ri·ent' v.
O'ri·en'tal
o'ri·en·tate'
·tat'ed ·tat'ing
o'ri·en·ta'tion
or'i·fice
or'i·ga'mi
or'i·gin
o·rig'i·nal
o·rig'i·nal'i·ty
o·rig'i·nal·ly
o·rig'i·nate'
·nat'ed ·nat'ing
o·rig'i·na'tion
o·rig'i·na'tor
o'ri·ole'
or'lon
or'na·ment
or'na·men'tal
or'na·men·ta'tion
or·nate'

or·nate'ly
or'ni·thol'o·gy
o'ro·tund'
or'phan·age
or'thi·con'
or'tho·don'tics
or'tho·don'tist
or'tho·dox'
or'tho·dox'y
· ies
or·thog'ra·phy
or'tho·pe'dics
or'tho·pe'dist
os'cil·late'
· lat'ed · lat'ing
(*fluctuate;* see
osculate)
os'cil·la'tion
os'cil·la'tor
os·cil'lo·scope'
os'cu·late'
· lat'ed · lat'ing
(*kiss;* see
oscillate)
os·mo'sis
os'prey
· preys
os'si·fy'
· fied' · fy'ing
os·ten'si·ble
os·ten'si·bly
os·ten'sive
os·ten'sive·ly
os'ten·ta'tion
os'ten·ta'tious
os'te·o·path'
os'te·op'a·thy
os'tra·cism
os'tra·cize'
· cized' · ciz'ing
os'trich
oth'er-di·rect'ed
oth'er·wise'
o'ti·ose'
ot'ter
ot'to·man
· mans
ought
(*be obliged;* see
aught)
our·self'
our·selves'
oust'er
out'-and-out'
out'bid'
· bid' · bid'ding
out'board'
out'bound'
out'break'
out'build'ing
out'burst'
out'cast'
out'class'
out'come'
out'crop'
out'cry'
· cries'
out'dat'ed

out'dis'tance
· tanced · tanc·ing
out'do'
· did' · done'
· do'ing
out'door'
out'doors'
out'er·most'
out'er space
out'er·wear'
out'face'
out'field'er
out'fit'
out'fit'ter
out'flank'
out'flow'
out'go'
· went' · gone'
· go'ing
out'go'
· goes'
out'go'ing
· grew' · grown'
· grow'ing
out'growth'
out'guess'
out'house'
out'ing
out'land'er
out·land'ish
out·last'
out'law'
out'law·ry
· ries
out'lay'
· laid' · lay'ing
out'let'
out'li'er
out'line'
out'live'
out'look'
out'ly'ing
out'man'
out'ma·neu'ver
out'mod'ed
out'most'
out'num'ber
out'-of-date'
out'-of-doors'
out'-of-pock'et
out'-of-the-way'
out'-of-town'er
out'pa'tient
out'post'
out'pour'ing
out'put'
out'rage'
out·ra'geous
out'rank'
out'reach'
out'ride'
· rode' · rid'den
· rid'ing
out'rid'er
out'rig'ger
out'right'

out'run'
· ran' · run'
· run'ning
out'sell'
· sold' · sell'ing
out'set'
out'shine'
· shone' · shin'ing
out'side'
out'sid'er
out'sit'
· sat' · sit'ting
out'size'
out'skirts'
out'smart'
out'speak'
· spoke' · spo'ken
· speak'ing
out'spo'ken·ness
out'spread'
· spread'
· spread'ing
out'stand'ing
out'stare'
out'sta'tion
out'stay'
out'stretch'
out'strip'
out'talk'
out'think'
· thought'
· think'ing
out'vote'
out'ward
out'wear'
· wore' · worn'
· wear'ing
out'weigh'
out'wit'
· wit'ted
· wit'ting
out'work'
o'val
o'val·ly
o·var'i·an
o'va·ry
· ries
o·va'tion
ov'en
o'ver·age'
o'ver·all'
o'ver·alls'
o'ver·awe'
· awed' · aw'ing
o'ver·bal'ance
o'ver·bear'
· bore' · borne'
· bear'ing
o'ver·bid'
· bid' · bid'ding
o'ver·bite'
o'ver·blouse'
o'ver·board'
o'ver·cap'i·tal·
ize'
o'ver·cast'
o'ver·charge'
o'ver·coat'

o'ver·come'
· came' · come'
· com'ing
o'ver·com'pen·
sate'
o'ver·con'fi·dent
o'ver·crowd'ed
o'ver·do'
· did' · done'
· do'ing
o'ver·dose'
o'ver·draft'
o'ver·draw'
· drew' · drawn'
· draw'ing
o'ver·dress'
o'ver·drive'
o'ver·due'
o'ver·flight'
o'ver·flow'
o'ver·fly'
· flew' · flown'
· fly'ing
o'ver·gar'ment
o'ver·glaze'
o'ver·grow'
· grew' · grown'
· grow'ing
o'ver·hand'
o'ver·hang'
· hung'
· hang'ing
o'ver·haul'
o'ver·head'
o'ver·hear'
· heard'
· hear'ing
o'ver·heat'
o'ver·in·dul'·
gence
o'ver·is'sue
o'ver·joy'
o'ver·lad'en
o'ver·lap'
o'ver·lay'
· laid' · lay'ing
o'ver·leap'
o'ver·lie'
· lay' · lain'
· ly'ing
o'ver·load'
o'ver·look'
o'ver·ly
o'ver·nice'
o'ver·night'
o'ver·pass'
o'ver·pay'
· paid' · pay'ing
o'ver·pop'u·late'
o'ver·pow'er
o'ver·pro·duce'
o'ver·pro·tect'
o'ver·rate'
o'ver·reach'
o'ver·ride'
· rode' · rid'den
· rid'ing
o'ver·rule'

o'ver·run'
· ran' · run'
· run'ning
o'ver·seas'
o'ver·see'
· saw' · seen'
· see'ing
o'ver·se'er
o'ver·sell'
· sold' · sell'ing
o'ver·sexed'
o'ver·shad'ow
o'ver·shoe'
o'ver·shoot'
· shot' · shoot'ing
o'ver·sight'
o'ver·sim'pli·fy'
o'ver·size'
o'ver·skirt'
o'ver·slaugh'
o'ver·sleep'
· slept' · sleep'ing
o'ver·spend'
· spent' · spend'ing
o'ver·spread'
o'ver·state'
o'ver·stay'
o'ver·step'
o'ver·stock'
o'ver·strung'
o'ver·stuff'
o'ver·sub·scribe'
o'ver·sup·ply'
o·vert'
o'ver·take'
· took' · tak'en
· tak'ing
o'ver·tax'
o'ver-the-count'er
o'ver·throw'
· threw' · thrown'
· throw'ing
o'ver·time'
o'ver·tone'
o'ver·ture
o'ver·use'
o'ver·view'
o'ver·ween'ing
o'ver·weight'
o'ver·whelm'
o'ver·wind'
· wound' · wind'ing
o'ver·work'
o'ver·write'
· wrote' · writ'ten
· writ'ing
o'ver·wrought'
o·vip'a·rous
o'void
o'vu·late'
· lat'ed · lat'ing
o'vu·la'tion
o'vule
o'vum
o'va
owe
owed ow'ing
owl'ish

own'er·ship'
ox
ox'en
ox'blood'
ox'bow'
ox'ford
ox'i·da'tion
ox'i·dize'
· dized' · diz'ing
ox'tail'
ox'y·gen
ox'y·gen·ate'
· at'ed · at'ing
ox'y·gen·a'tion
ox'y·mo'ron
ox'y·tet'ra·cy'·
cline
oys'ter
o'zone

P

pab'lum
pace
paced pac'ing
pace'mak'er
pach'y·derm'
pach'y·san'dra
pac'i·fi'a·ble
pa·cif'ic
pac'i·fi·ca'tion
pac'i·fi'er
pac'i·fism
pac'i·fy'
· fied' · fy'ing
pack'age
· aged ·ag·ing
pack'et
pack'ing
pack'sad'dle
pack'thread'
pact
pad
pad'ded
pad'ding
pad'dle
· dled ·dling
pad'dock
pad'dy
· dies
(*rice;* see patty)
pad'lock'
pa'dre
· dres
pae'an
(*song;* see peon)
pa'gan
page
paged pag'ing
pag'eant
pag'eant·ry
· ries
page'boy'
pag'i·nate'
· nat'ed · nat'ing

pag'i·na'tion
pa·go'da
pail
(*bucket;* see
pale)
pail'ful'
·fuls'
pain
(*hurt;* see pane)
pain'ful
pain'less
pains'tak'ing
paint'brush'
paint'er
pair
(*two;* see pare,
pear)
pais'ley
pa·ja'mas
pal'ace
pal'an·quin'
pal'at·a·ble
pal'at·a·bly
pal'a·tal
pal'ate
(*roof of mouth;*
see palette, pallet)
pa·la'tial
pal'a·tine'
pa·lav'er
pale
paled pal'ing
(*white;* see pail)
pale'face'
pale'ly
pa'le·o·lith'ic
pa'le·on·tol'o·gy
pal'ette
(*paint board;* see
palate, pallet)
pal'in·drome'
pal'ing
pal'i·sade'
pall
palled pall'ing
pal·la'di·um
pall'bear'er
pal'let
(*tool; bed;* see
palate, palette)
pal'li·ate'
·at'ed ·at'ing
pal'li·a'tive
pal'lid
pall'-mall'
(*game;* see
pell-mell)
pal'lor
palm
pal·met'to
·tos *or* ·toes
palm'is·try
pal'o·mi'no
·nos
pal'pa·ble
pal'pa·bly
pal'pate
·pat·ed ·pat·ing

pal'pi·tate'
·tat'ed ·tat'ing
pal'pi·ta'tion
pal'sy
·sied ·sy·ing
pal'tri·ness
pal'try
·tri·er ·tri·est
(*trifling;*
see poultry)
pam'pas
pam'per
pam'phlet
pam'phlet·eer'
pan
panned pan'ning
pan'a·ce'a
pa·nache'
Pan'-A·mer'i·can
pan'a·tel'a
pan'cake'
pan'chro·mat'ic
pan'cre·as
pan'cre·at'ic
pan·dem'ic
pan'de·mo'ni·um
pan'der
pan·dow'dy
·dies
pane
(*window;* see
pain)
pan'e·gyr'ic
pan'e·gyr'i·cal
pan'el
·eled *or* ·elled
·el·ing *or* ·el·ling
pan'el·ist
pan'-fry'
·fried' ·fry'ing
pan'han'dle
pan'ic
·icked ·ick·ing
pan'ic·al·ly
pan'ick·y
pan'ic-strick'en
panne
pan'nier
pan'o·ply
·plies
pan'o·ra'ma
pan'o·ram'ic
pan'o·ram'i·cal·ly
pan'ta·loons'
pant'dress'
pan'the·ism
pan'the·is'tic
pan'the·on'
pan'ther
pant'ies
pan'to·graph
pan'to·mime'
·mimed'
·mim'ing
pan'to·mim'ic
pan'to·mim'ist
pan'try
·tries

pant'suit' *or*
pants suit
pan'ty hose
pa'pa·cy
·cies
pa'pal
pa'paw
pa·pa'ya
pa'per·back'
pa'per·bound'
pa'per·hang'er
pa'per·weight'
pa'per·y
pa'pier-mâ·ché'
pa·poose'
pa·pri'ka
pap'ule
pa·py'rus
·ri *or* ·rus·es
par
parred par'ring
par'a·ble
pa·rab'o·la
par'a·bol'ic
par'a·bol'i·cal·ly
par'a·chute'
·chut'ed
·chut'ing
pa·rade'
·rad'ed ·rad'ing
par'a·digm
par'a·dise'
par'a·dox'
par'a·dox'i·cal
par'a·dox'i·cal·ly
par'af·fin
par'a·gon'
par'a·graph'
par'a·keet'
par'al·lax'
par'al·lel'
·leled' *or* ·lelled'
·lel'ing *or*
·lel'ling
par'al·lel·ism
par'al·lel'o·gram'
pa·ral'y·sis
par'a·lyt'ic
par'a·lyze'
·lyzed' ·lyz'ing
par'a·me'ci·um
·ci·a
par'a·med'ic
par'a·med'i·cal
pa·ram'e·ter
(*math. term;* see
perimeter)
par'a·mount'
par'a·mour'
par'a·noi'a
par'a·noi'ac
par'a·noid'
par'a·pet
par'a·pher·na'li·a
par'a·phrase'
·phrased'
·phras'ing

par'a·ple'gi·a
par'a·ple'gic
par'a·prax'is
·es
par'a·psy·chol'o·
gy
par'a·res'cue
par'a-sail'
par'a·site'
par'a·sit'ic
par'a·sol'
par'a·troops'
par'boil'
par'buck·le
par'cel
·celed *or* ·celled
·cel·ing *or*
·cel·ling
parch'ment
par'don·a·ble
par'don·a·bly
pare
pared par'ing
(*trim;* see pair,
pear)
par'e·gor'ic
par'ent
par'ent·age
pa·ren'tal
pa·ren'the·sis
·ses'
pa·ren'the·size'
·sized' ·siz'ing
par'en·thet'i·cal
par'ent·hood'
pa·re'sis
par'e·ve
par ex'cel·lence'
par·fait'
par·he'li·on
·li·a
pa·ri'ah
pa·ri'e·tal
par'i·mu'tu·el
par'ish
pa·rish'ion·er
par'i·ty
·ties
par'ka
park'way'
parl'ance
par'lay
(*bet*)
par'ley
(*confer*)
par'lia·ment
par'lia·men·
tar'i·an
par'lia·men'ta·ry
par'lor
pa·ro'chi·al
par'o·dist
par'o·dy
·dies
·died ·dy·ing
pa·role'
·roled' ·rol'ing
pa·rol'ee'

pa·rot'id
par'ox·ysm
par'ox·ys'mal
par·quet'
·queted'
·quet'ing
par'quet·ry
par'ra·keet'
par'ri·cid'al
par'ri·cide'
par'rot
par'ry
·ries
·ried ·ry·ing
par'sec'
par'si·mo'ni·ous
par'si·mo'ny
pars'ley
pars'nip
par'son
par'son·age
par·take'
·took' ·tak'en
·tak'ing
par·terre'
par'the·no·gen'e·
sis
par'tial
par'ti·al'i·ty
par'tial·ly
par'ti·ble
par·tic'i·pant
par·tic'i·pate'
·pat'ed ·pat'ing
par·tic'i·pa'tion
par·tic'i·pa'tor
par'ti·cip'i·al
par'ti·ci·ple
par'ti·cle
par'ti-col'ored
par·tic'u·lar
par·tic'u·lar'i·ty
·ties
par·tic'u·lar·ize'
·ized' ·iz'ing
par·tic'u·lar·ly
par'ti·san
par·ti'tion
part'ner
part'ner·ship'
par'tridge
part'-time'
par·tu'ri·ent
par·tu·ri'tion
par'ty
·ties

pas'sen·ger
passe'-par·tout'
pass'er-by'
pass'ers-by'
pas'sion
pas'sion·ate
pas'sion·ate·ly
pas'sive
pas'sive·ly
pas·siv'i·ty
pass'key'
Pass'o'ver
pass'port'
pass'-through'
pass'word'
past
(*gone by; over;*
see passed)
paste
past'ed past'ing
paste'board'
pas·tel'
pas'teur·i·za'tion
pas'teur·ize'
·ized' ·iz'ing
pas·tille'
pas'time'
past'i·ness
pas'tor
pas'to·ral
pas'tor·ate
pas·tra'mi
pas'try
·tries
pas'ture
·tured ·tur·ing
past'y
·i·er ·i·est
pat
pat'ted pat'ting
patch'work'
patch'y
·i·er ·i·est
pâ·té' de foie'
gras'
pa·tel'la
·las *or* ·lae
pat'ent
pat'ent·ee'
pa·ter'nal
pa·ter'nal·is'tic
pa·ter'ni·ty
pa·thet'ic
pa·thet'i·cal·ly
path'find'er
path'o·gen'ic
path'o·log'i·cal
pa·thol'o·gy
·gies
pa'thos
pa'tience
pa'tient
pat'i·na
pa'ti·o'
·os'
pa·tis'se·rie
pat'ois
·ois

pa'tri·arch'
pa'tri·ar'chal
pa'tri·ar'chy
·chies
pa·tri'cian
pat'ri·cide'
pat'ri·mo'ny
·nies
pa'tri·ot
pa'tri·ot'ic
pa'tri·ot'i·cal·ly
pa'tri·ot·ism
pa·trol'
·trolled'
·trol'ling
pa·trol'man
pa'tron
pa'tron·age
pa'tron·ize'
·ized' ·iz'ing
pat'ro·nym'ic
pat'ter
pat'tern·mak·er
pat'ty
·ties
(cake; see paddy)
pau'ci·ty
paunch'i·ness
paunch'y
pau'per
pause
paused paus'ing
pave
paved pav'ing
pave'ment
pa·vil'ion
pawn'bro'ker
pawn'shop'
pay
paid pay'ing
pay'a·ble
pay'check'
pay'day'
pay·ee'
pay'load'
pay'mas·ter
pay'ment
pay'off'
pay'roll'
peace
(harmony;
see piece)
peace'a·ble
peace'a·bly
peace'ful
peace'ful·ly
peace'mak·er
peace pipe
peace'time'
peach
pea'cock'
peak
(highest point;
see peek, pique)
peaked
(pointed)
peak'ed
(thin and drawn)

peal
(sound; see peel)
pea'nut
pear
(fruit; see pair,
pare)
pearl
(gem; see purl)
pearl'y
·i·er ·i·est
pear'-shaped'
peas'ant
peas'ant·ry
peat moss
peau' de soie'
peb'ble
·bled ·bling
peb'bly
·bli·er ·bli·est
pe·can'
pec'ca·dil'lo
·loes or ·los
pec'cant
peck
pec'tin
pec'to·ral
pec'u·late'
·lat'ed ·lat'ing
pec'u·la'tion
pec'u·la'tor
pe·cul'iar
pe·cu'li·ar'i·ty
·ties
pe·cu'ni·ar'i·ly
pe·cu'ni·ar'y
ped'a·gog'ic
ped'a·gogue'
or ·gog'
ped'a·go'gy
ped'al
·aled or ·alled
·al·ing or
·al·ling
(foot lever; see
peddle)
ped'ant
pe·dan'tic
pe·dan'ti·cal·ly
ped'ant·ry
·ries
ped'dle
·dled ·dling
(sell; see pedal)
ped'dler
ped'es·tal
pe·des'tri·an
pe'di·a·tri'cian
pe'di·at'rics
ped'i·cure'
ped'i·gree'
ped'i·greed'
ped'i·ment
pe·dom'e·ter
peek
(look; see
peak, pique)
peel
(skin; see peal)

peep'hole'
peer
(equal; look;
see pier)
peer group
peer'less
peeve
peeved peev'ing
pee'vish
peg
pegged peg'ging
peg'board'
peign·oir'
pe'jo·ra'tion
pe·jo'ra·tive
Pe'king·ese'
pe'koe
pel'i·can
pel·la'gra
pel'let
pell'-mell'
(without order;
see pall-mall)
pel·lu'cid
pel'vic
pel'vis
pem'mi·can
pen
penned or pent
pen'ning
(enclose)
pen
penned pen'ning
(write with pen)
pe'nal
pe'nal·i·za'tion
pe'nal·ize'
·ized' ·iz'ing
pen'al·ty
·ties
pen'ance
pen'chant
pen'cil
·ciled or ·cilled
·cil·ing or
·cil·ling
pend'ant or
·ent n.
pend'ent or
·ant adj.
pend'ing
pen'du·lous
pen'du·lum
pen'e·tra·bil'i·ty
pen'e·tra·ble
pen'e·tra·bly
pen'e·trate'
·trat'ed ·trat'ing
pen'e·tra'tion
pen'e·trom'e·ter
pen'guin
pen'hold'er
pen'i·cil'lin
pen·in'su·la
pen·in'su·lar
pe'nis
·nis·es or ·nes
pen'i·tence

pen'i·tent
pen'i·ten'tial
pen'i·ten'tia·ry
·ries
pen'knife'
·knives'
pen'light' or ·lite'
pen'man·ship'
pen name
pen'nant
Penn'syl·va'ni·a
pen'ny
·nies
pen'ny ante
pen'ny·weight'
pen'ny-wise'
pen'ny·worth'
pe'no·log'i·cal
pe·nol'o·gist
pe·nol'o·gy
pen'sion
pen'sion·ar'y
·ies
pen'sive
pen'sive·ly
pen'stock'
pen'ta·gon'
pen·tag'o·nal
pen'ta·he'dral
pen'ta·he'dron
·drons or ·dra
pen·tam'e·ter
Pen'ta·teuch'
pen·tath'lon
Pen'te·cost'
pent'house'
pen·tom'ic
pent'-up'
pe·nu'che or ·chi
pe'nult
pe·nul'ti·mate
pe·num'bra
·brae or ·bras
pe·nu'ri·ous
pen'u·ry
pe'on
(laborer; see
paean)
pe'on·age
pe'o·ny
·nies
peo'ple
·pled ·pling
pep'lum
·lums or ·la
pep'per-and-salt'
pep'per·corn'
pep'per·i·ness
pep'per·mint'
pep'per·o'ni
·nis or ·ni
pep'per·y
·i·er ·i·est
pep'pi·ly
pep'pi·ness
pep'py
·pi·er ·pi·est

pep'sin
pep'tic
per·am'bu·late'
·lat'ed ·lat'ing
per·am'bu·la'tion
per·am'bu·la'tor
per an'num
per·cale'
per cap'i·ta
per·ceiv'a·ble
per·ceiv'a·bly
per·ceive'
·ceived' ·ceiv'ing
per·cent' or
per cent
per·cent'age
per·cen'tile
per'cept
per·cep'ti·ble
per·cep'ti·bly
per·cep'tion
per·cep'tive
per·cep'tive·ly
per·cep'tu·al
per·chance'
Per'che·ron'
per·cip'i·ent
per'co·late'
·lat'ed ·lat'ing
per'co·la'tion
per'co·la'tor
per·cus'sion
per·cus'sive
per di'em
per·di'tion
per·du' or ·due'
per·dur'a·ble
per'e·gri·nate'
·nat'ed ·nat'ing
per'e·gri·na'tion
per·emp'to·ri·ly
per·emp'to·ri·ness
per·emp'to·ry
per·en'ni·al
per'fect
per·fect'i·bil'i·ty
per·fect'i·ble
per·fec'tion
per·fec'tion·ism
per·fec'to
·tos
per·fid'i·ous
per'fi·dy
·dies
per'fo·rate'
·rat'ed ·rat'ing
per'fo·ra'tion
per'fo·ra'tor
per·force'
per·form'
per·form'ance
per·fume'
·fumed' ·fum'ing
per'fume n.
per·fum'er
per·func'to·ri·ly
per·func'to·ry
per'go·la

per·haps'
per'i·gee'
per'i·he'li·on
·li·ons or ·li·a
per'il
·iled or ·illed
·il·ing or ·il·ling
per'il·ous
per'i·lune'
pe·rim'e·ter
(boundary; see
parameter)
pe'ri·od
pe'ri·od'ic
pe'ri·od'i·cal
pe'ri·od'i·cal·ly
pe'ri·o·dic'i·ty
per'i·pa·tet'ic
pe·riph'er·al
pe·riph'er·y
·ies
pe·riph'ra·sis
per'i·phras'tic
pe·rique'
per'i·scope'
per'i·scop'ic
per'ish
per'ish·a·bil'i·ty
per'ish·a·ble
per'i·stal'sis
per'i·style'
per'i·to·ni'tis
per'jure
·jured ·jur·ing
per'jur·er
per'ju·ry
·ries
perk'i·ness
perk'y
·i·er ·i·est
per'ma·frost'
perm'al·loy
per'ma·nence
per'ma·nent
per'me·a·bil'i·ty
per'me·a·ble
per'me·ate'
·at'ed ·at'ing
per·me·a'tion
per·mis'si·bil'i·ty
per·mis'si·ble
per·mis'si·bly
per·mis'sion
per·mis'sive
per·mis'sive·ly
per·mit'
·mit'ted
·mit'ting
per·mut'a·ble
per'mu·ta'tion
per·ni'cious
per·nod'
per'o·rate'
·rat'ed ·rat'ing
per'o·ra'tion
per·ox'ide
·id·ed ·id·ing
per'pen·dic'u·lar

per'pe·trate'
 ·trat'ed ·trat'ing
per'pe·tra'tion
per'pe·tra'tor
per·pet'u·al
per·pet'u·al·ly
per·pet'u·ate'
 ·at'ed ·at'ing
per·pet'u·a'tion
per·pet'u·a'tor
per'pe·tu'i·ty
 ·ties
per·plex'
per·plexed'
per·plex'ed·ly
per·plex'i·ty
 ·ties
per'qui·site
 (privilege; see
 prerequisite)
per se
per'se·cute'
 ·cut'ed ·cut'ing
 (harass; see
 prosecute)
per'se·cu'tion
per'se·cu'tor
per'se·ver'ance
per'se·vere'
 ·vered' ·ver'ing
per'si·flage'
per·sim'mon
per·sist'
per·sist'ence
per·sist'ent
per'son
per'son·a·ble
per'son·age
per'son·al
 (private; see
 personnel)
per'son·al'i·ty
 ·ties
per'son·al·ize'
 ·ized' ·iz'ing
per'son·al·ly
per'son·ate'
 ·at'ed ·at'ing
per'son·a'tion
per'son·a'tor
per·son'i·fi·
 ca'tion
per·son'i·fy'
 ·fied' ·fy'ing
per'son·nel'
 (employees; see
 personal)
per·spec'tive
 (view; see
 prospective)
per'spi·ca'cious
per'spi·cac'i·ty
per'spi·cu'i·ty
per·spic'u·ous
per'spi·ra'tion
per·spir'a·to'ry
per·spire'
 ·spired' ·spir'ing

per·suad'a·ble
per·suade'
 ·suad'ed
 ·suad'ing
per·sua'si·bil'i·ty
per·sua'sion
per·sua'sive
per·tain'
per·ti·na'cious
per'ti·nac'i·ty
per'ti·nence
per'ti·nent
pert'ly
per·turb'
per'tur·ba'tion
pe·rus'al
pe·ruse'
 ·rused' ·rus'ing
per·vade'
 ·vad'ed ·vad'ing
per·va'sion
per·va'sive
per·verse'
per·verse'ly
per·ver'sion
per·ver'si·ty
per·vert'
per'vi·ous
Pe'sach
pe'so
 ·sos
pes'si·mism
pes'si·mist
pes'si·mis'tic
pes'si·mis'ti·
 cal·ly
pes'ter
pest'hole'
pes'ti·cide'
pes'ti·lence
pes'ti·lent
pes'ti·len'tial
pes'tle
 ·tled ·tling
pet
 pet'ted pet'ting
pet'al
pet'al·like'
pet'cock'
pe·tite'
pe'tit four'
 pe'tits fours'
 or pe'tit fours'
pe·ti'tion
pet'it jury
pe·tit' mal'
pet'it point
pe'tri dish
pet'ri·fac'tion
pet'ri·fy'
 ·fied' ·fy'ing
pet'ro·la'tum
pe·tro'le·um
pet'ti·coat'
pet'ti·fog'
 ·fogged'
 ·fog'ging
pet'ti·fog'ger

pet'ti·ly
pet'ti·ness
pet'ti·pants'
pet'tish
pet'ty
 ·ti·er ·ti·est
pet'u·lance
pet'u·lant
pew'ter
pha'e·ton
pha'lanx
 ·lanx·es or
 pha·lan'ges
phal'lic
phal'lus
 ·li or ·lus·es
phan'tasm
phan'tom
phar'i·sa'ic
phar'i·see'
phar'ma·ceu'ti·cal
phar'ma·cist
phar'ma·col'o·gy
phar'ma·co·pe'ia
phar'ma·cy
 ·cies
phar'ynx
 ·ynx·es or
 pha·ryn'ges
phase
 phased phas'ing
 (stage; see faze)
phase'-out'
pheas'ant
phe'no·bar'bi·tal'
phe·nom'e·nal
phe·nom'e·nal·ly
phe·nom'e·non'
 ·na or ·nons'
phi'al
Phil'a·del'phi·a
phi·lan'der·er
phil'an·throp'ic
phi·lan'thro·pist
phi·lan'thro·py
 ·pies
phil'a·tel'ic
phi·lat'e·list
phi·lat'e·ly
phil'har·mon'ic
Phil'ip·pine'
Phil'is·tine'
phil'o·den'dron
phil'o·log'i·cal
phi·lol'o·gist
phi·lol'o·gy
phi·los'o·pher
phil'o·soph'ic
phil'o·soph'i·
 cal·ly
phi·los'o·phize'
 ·phized' ·phiz'ing
phi·los'o·phy
 ·phies
phil'ter
 (potion; see
 filter)
phle·bi'tis

phlegm
phleg·mat'ic
phlox
pho'bi·a
pho'bic
phoe'be
Phoe'nix
phone
 phoned phon'ing
pho'neme
pho·net'ic
pho·net'i·cal·ly
pho·ne·ti'cian
phon'ics
pho'ni·ness
pho'no·graph'
pho·nol'o·gy
pho'ny
 ·ni·er ·ni·est
 ·nies
phos'phate
phos'pho·
 res'cence
phos'pho·res'cent
pho'to·chron'o·
 graph
pho'to·cop'i·er
pho'to·cop'y
 ·ies
 ·ied ·y·ing
pho'to·e·lec'tric
pho'to·en·grave'
 ·graved'
 ·grav'ing
pho'to·flash'
pho'to·flood'
pho'to·gen'ic
pho'to·graph'
pho'to·graph'ic
 cal·ly
pho·tog'ra·phy
pho'to·gra·vure'
pho'to·lith'o·
 graph
pho'to·li·thog'ra·
 phy
pho'to·map'
pho·tom'e·ter
pho'to·met'ric
pho·tom'e·try
pho'to·mon·tage'
pho'to·mu'ral
pho'to-off'set'
pho'to·sen'si·tive
pho'to·stat'
 ·stat'ed or
 ·stat'ted
 ·stat'ing or
 ·stat'ting
pho'to·stat'ic
pho'to·syn'the·sis
phras'al
phras'al·ly
phrase
phrased
phras'ing

phra'se·ol'o·gy
 ·gies
phre·net'ic
phre·nol'o·gy
phy·lac'ter·y
 ·ies
phy'lum
 ·la
phys'ic
 ·icked ·ick·ing
phys'i·cal
phys'i·cal·ly
phy·si'cian
phys'i·cist
phys'ics
phys'i·og'no·my
phys'i·og'ra·phy
phys'i·o·log'i·cal
phys'i·ol'o·gy
phys'i·o·ther'a·
 pist
phys'i·o·ther'a·py
phy·sique'
pi
pied
pie'ing or pi'ing
 (jumble; see pie)
pi
 (Greek letter;
 see pie)
pi'a·nis'si·mo'
pi·an'ist
pi·an'o
 ·os
pi·an'o·la
pi·az'za
pi'ca
pic'a·dor'
pic'a·resque'
pic'a·yune'
Pic'ca·dil'ly
pic'ca·lil'li
pic'co·lo'
 ·los'
pick'ax' or ·axe'
pick'er·el
pick'et
pick'le
 ·led ·ling
pick'pock'et
pick'up'
pic'nic
 ·nicked
 ·nick·ing
pic'nick·er
pi'cot
 ·coted ·cot·ing
pic'to·graph'
pic·to'ri·al
pic·to'ri·al·ly
pic'ture
 ·tured ·tur·ing
pic'tur·esque'
pid'dle
 ·dled ·dling
pidg'in English
pie
 (food; see pi)

pie'bald'
piece
pieced piec'ing
 (part; see peace)
pièce de ré·sis·
 tance'
piece'-dyed'
piece'meal'
piece'work'
pied'mont
pier
 (structure; see
 peer)
pierce
pierced
pierc'ing
pier glass
pi'e·tism
pi'e·ty
 ·ties
pi'geon
pi'geon·hole'
 ·holed' ·hol'ing
pi'geon-toed'
pig'gish
pig'gy·back'
pig'head'ed
pig iron
pig'let
pig'ment
pig'men·ta'tion
pig·no'li·a
pig'pen'
pig'skin'
pig'sty'
 ·sties'
pig'tail'
pi·laf' or ·laff'
pi·las'ter
pile
piled pil'ing
pi'le·ous
pile'up'
pil'fer
pil'fer·age
pil'grim
pil'grim·age
pil'lage
 ·laged ·lag·ing
pil'lar
pill'box'
pil'lion
pil'lo·ry
 ·ries
 ·ried ·ry·ing
pil'low
pil'low·case'
pi'lose
pi'lot
pi'lot·house'
Pil'sener or
 Pil'sner
pi·men'to or
 ·mien'·
 ·tos
pim'ple
pim'ply
pin'a·fore'

pi·ña'ta
pin'ball'
pince'-nez'
pin'cers
pinch'beck'
pinch'-hit'
 -hit' -hit'ting
pin'cush'ion
pine
 pined pin'ing
pine'ap'ple
pin'feath'er
ping'-pong'
pin'head'
pin'hole'
pin'ion
pink'eye'
pin'na·cle
 ·cled ·cling
 (acme)
pi'noch'le or
 ·noc'·
 (game)
pin'point'
pin stripe
pin'to
 ·tos
pint'-size'
pin'up'
pin'wale'
pin'wheel'
pin'worm'
pi'o·neer'
pi'ous
pipe
 piped pip'ing
pipe'ful'
 ·fuls'
pipe'line'
pip'er
pipe'stem'
pi·pette' or ·pet'
 pet'ted pet'ting
pip'pin
pi'quan·cy
pi'quant
pique
 piqued piqu'ing
 (offend; see
 peak, peek)
pi·qué' or ·que'
 (fabric)
pi'ra·cy
pi·ra'nha
pi'rate
 ·rat·ed ·rat·ing
pir'ou·ette'
 ·et'ted ·et'ting
pis'ca·to'ri·al
pis'ci·cul'ture
pis·ta'chi·o'
 ·os'
pis'til
 (part of plant)
pis'tol
 ·toled or ·tolled
 ·tol·ing or ·tol·ling
 (firearm)

pis'tol-whip'
pis'ton
pit
 pit'ted pit'ting
pitch'-black'
pitch'blende'
pitch'-dark'
pitch'er·ful'
 ·fuls'
pitch'fork'
pitch pipe
pit'e·ous
pit'fall'
pith'i·ness
pith'y
pit'i·a·ble
pit'i·ful
pit'i·less
pit'tance
Pitts'burgh
pi·tu'i·tar'y
pit'y
 ·ies, ·ied ·y·ing
piv'ot
piv'ot·al
pix'ie or ·y
 ·ies
piz'za
piz'ze·ri'a
piz'zi·ca'to
plac'a·bil'i·ty
plac'a·ble
plac'a·bly
plac'ard
pla'cate
 ·cat·ed ·cat·ing
place
 placed plac'ing
pla·ce'bo
 ·bos or ·boes
place'ment
pla·cen'ta
 ·tas or ·tae
plac'er
plac'id
pla·cid'i·ty
plack'et
pla'gia·rism
pla'gia·rize'
 ·rized' ·riz'ing
pla'gia·ry
 ·ries
plague
 plagued
 plagu'ing
plagu'er
plaid
plain
 (clear; simple;
 see plane)
plain'ness
plains'man
plain'song
plain'-spo'ken
plain'tiff
plain'tive
plain'tive·ly

plait
 (pleat; braid;
 see plate)
plan
 planned
 plan'ning
plane
 planed plan'ing
 (level; see plain)
plan'et
plan'e·tar'i·um
 ·i·ums or ·i·a
plan'e·tar'y
plan'e·tes'i·mal
plan'et·oid'
plank'ing
plank'ton
plan'ner
plan'tain
plan'tar
 (of the sole)
plan·ta'tion
plant'er
 (one that plants)
plan'ti·grade'
plaque
plas'ma
plas'ter
plas'ter·board'
plas'ter·er
plas'tic
plas'ti·cal·ly
plas'ti·cine
plas·tic'i·ty
plas'ti·cize'
 ·cized' ·ciz'ing
plat
 plat'ted
 plat'ting
 (map)
plate
 plat'ed plat'ing
 (dish; see plait)
pla·teau'
 ·teaus' or
 ·teaux'
plate'ful'
 ·fuls'
plat'en
plat'form'
plat'i·num
plat'i·tude'
plat'i·tu'di·nous
pla·ton'ic
pla·ton'i·cal·ly
pla·toon'
plat'ter
plau'dit
plau'si·bil'i·ty
plau'si·ble
plau'si·bly
play'back'
play'bill'
play'boy'
play'-by-play'
play'go'er
play'ful·ly
play'ground'

play'house'
play'mate'
play'-off'
play'pen'
play'room'
play'thing'
play'wright'
pla'za
plea
plead
 plead'ed or plead
 plead'ing
pleas'ant
pleas'ant·ry
 ·ries
please
 pleased
 pleas'ing
pleas'ur·a·ble
pleas'ur·a·bly
pleas'ure
pleat
ple·be'ian
pleb'i·scite'
plec'trum
 ·trums or ·tra
pledge
 pledged
 pledg'ing
pledg'ee'
ple'na·ry
plen'i·po·ten'ti·
 ar'y
 ·ies
plen'i·tude'
plen'te·ous
plen'ti·ful
plen'ti·ful·ly
plen'ty
ple'num
 ·nums or ·na
ple'o·nasm
pleth'o·ra
pleu'ral
 (of the pleura;
 see plural)
pleu'ri·sy
Plex'i·glas'
pli'a·bil'i·ty
pli'a·ble
pli'an·cy
pli'ant
pli'ers
plight
plis·sé' or ·se'
plod
 plod'ded
 plod'ding
plop
 plopped
 plop'ping
plot
 plot'ted
 plot'ting
plow'share'
pluck'i·ness
pluck'y
 ·i·er ·i·est

plug
 plugged
 plug'ging
plum
 (fruit)
plum'age
plumb
 (lead weight)
plumb'er
plumb'ing
plume
 plumed
 plum'ing
plum'met
plu'mose
plump'ness
plun'der
plunge
 plunged
 plung'ing
plung'er
plu·per'fect
plu'ral
 (more than one;
 see pleural)
plu'ral·ism
plu'ral·is'tic
plu·ral'i·ty
 ·ties
plu'ral·ize'
 ·ized' ·iz'ing
plush'i·ness
plush'y
 ·i·er ·i·est
plu·toc'ra·cy
 ·cies
plu'to·crat'
plu'to·crat'ic
plu·to'ni·um
plu'vi·al
ply
 plies
 plied ply'ing
ply'wood'
pneu·mat'ic
pneu·mo'ni·a
poached
poach'er
pock'et·book'
 (purse)
pocket book
 (small book)
pock'et·ful'
 ·fuls'
pock'et·knife'
 ·knives'
pock'et-size'
pock'mark'
po·di'a·trist
po·di'a·try
po'di·um
 ·di·a or ·di·ums
po'em
po·et'ic
po·et'i·cal·ly
po'et·ry
po·go'ni·a
po'go stick

po·grom'
poign'an·cy
poign'ant
poin·set'ti·a
point'-blank'
point'ed·ly
point'er
point'less
poise
 poised pois'ing
poi'son·ous
poke
 poked pok'ing
pok'er
pok'i·ness
pok'y
 ·i·er ·i·est
po'lar
po·lar'i·ty
po'lar·i·za'tion
po'lar·ize'
 ·ized' ·iz'ing
pole
 poled pol'ing
 (rod; see poll)
pole'ax' or ·axe'
po·lem'ic
po·lem'i·cist
pole'star'
pole'-vault' v.
po·lice'
 ·liced' ·lic'ing
po·lice'man
po·lice'wom'an
pol'i·clin'ic
 (outpatient clinic;
 see polyclinic)
pol'i·cy
 ·cies
pol'i·cy·hold'er
po'li·o·my'e·li'tis
pol'ish
po·lite'ly
po·lite'ness
pol'i·tic
 ·ticked ·tick·ing
po·lit'i·cal
po·lit'i·cal·ly
 (in a political
 manner)
pol'i·ti'cian
pol'i·tic·ly
 (shrewdly)
po·lit'i·co'
 ·cos'
pol'i·tics
pol'i·ty
 ·ties
pol'ka
pol'ka dot
poll
 (vote; see pole)
poll'ee'
pol'len
pol'li·nate'
 ·nat'ed ·nat'ing
pol'li·na'tion
pol'li·wog'

poll'ster
poll tax
pol·lu'tant
pol·lute'
·lut'ed ·lut'ing
pol·lu'tion
pol'ter·geist'
pol·troon'
pol'y·an'drous
pol'y·an'dry
pol'y·clin'ic
(hospital; see
policlinic)
pol'y·es'ter
pol'y·eth'yl·ene'
po·lyg'a·mous
po·lyg'a·my
pol'y·glot'
pol'y·gon'
pol'y·graph'
po·lyg'y·ny
pol'y·mer
pol'y·sty'rene
pol'y·syl·lab'ic
pol'y·syl'la·ble
pol'y·tech'nic
pol'y·the·ism
pol'y·un·sat'u·
rat'ed
pom'ace
(pulp; see
pumice)
po·ma'ceous
po·made'
pome'gran'ate
pom'mel
·meled or
·melled
·mel·ing or
·mel·ling
pom'pa·dour'
pom'pa·no'
Pom·pei'i
pom'pon'
pom·pos'i·ty
pom'pous
pon'cho
·chos
pon'der
pon'der·a·ble
pon'der·ous
pon·gee'
pon'iard
pon'tiff
pon·tif'i·cal
pon·tif'i·cate'
·cat'ed ·cat'ing
pon·toon'
po'ny
·nies
po'ny·tail'
poo'dle
pooh'-pooh'
pool'room'
poor'house'
pop
popped pop'ping
pop'corn'

pop'eyed'
pop'lar
(tree; see
popular)
pop'lin
pop'o'ver
pop'per
pop'pet
pop'py
·pies
pop'u·lace
(the masses;
see populous)
pop'u·lar
(liked by many;
see poplar)
pop·u·lar'i·ty
pop'u·lar·i·
za'tion
pop'u·lar·ize'
·ized' ·iz'ing
pop'u·late'
·lat'ed ·lat'ing
pop'u·la'tion
pop'u·lous
(full of people;
see populace)
por'ce·lain
por'cu·pine'
pore
pored por'ing
(ponder; tiny
opening; see
pour)
pork'er
por'no·graph'ic
por·nog'ra·phy
po·ros'i·ty
po'rous
por'phy·ry
·ries
por'poise
por'ridge
por'rin·ger
port'a·bil'i·ty
port'a·ble
por'tage
·taged ·tag·ing
por'tal
port·cul'lis
por·tend'
por'tent
por·ten'tous
por'ter
por'ter·house'
port·fo'li·o'
·os'
port'hole'
por'ti·co'
·coes' or ·cos'
por·tiere'
por'tion
port'li·ness
port'ly
·li·er ·li·est
port·man'teau
·teaus or ·teaux
por'trait

por'trai·ture
por·tray'
por·tray'al
Por'tu·guese'
por'tu·lac'a
pose
posed pos'ing
posh
po·si'tion
pos'i·tive
pos'i·tive·ly
pos'i·tiv·ism
pos'se
pos·sess'
pos·sessed'
pos·ses'sion
pos·ses'sive
pos·ses'sor
pos·si·bil'i·ty
·ties
pos'si·ble
pos'si·bly
post'age
post'al
post'box'
post card
post'date'
post'er
pos·te'ri·or
pos·ter'i·ty
post'grad'u·ate
post'haste'
post'hu·mous
post'hyp·not'ic
pos·til'ion
post'man
post'mark'
post'mas·ter
post'mis'tress
post'-mor'tem
post·na'tal
post'paid'
post·pone'
·poned' ·pon'ing
post·pone'ment
post'script'
pos'tu·late'
·lat'ed ·lat'ing
pos'tu·la'tion
pos'tu·la'tor
pos'tur·al
pos'ture
·tured ·tur·ing
post'war'
pot
pot'ted pot'ting
po'ta·ble
po·ta'tion
po·ta'to
·toes
pot'bel'lied
pot'bel'ly
·lies
pot'boil'er
po'ten·cy
po'tent
po'ten·tate'

po·ten'tial
po·ten'ti·al'i·ty
·ties
po·ten'tial·ly
po'tent·ly
poth'er
pot'hold·er
pot'hole'
pot'hook'
po'tion
pot'latch'
pot'luck'
pot'pour·ri'
pot'sherd'
pot'shot'
pot'tage
pot'ter·y
·ies
pouch'i·ness
poul'tice
poul'try
(fowls; see
paltry)
pounce
pounced
pounc'ing
pound'-fool'ish
pour
(flow; see pore)
pout
pov'er·ty
pow'der·y
·i·er ·i·est
pow'er·ful
pow'er·ful·ly
pow'er·house'
pow'er·less
pow'wow'
pox
prac'ti·ca·bil'i·ty
prac'ti·ca·ble
prac'ti·ca·bly
prac'ti·cal
prac'ti·cal'i·ty
·ties
prac'ti·cal·ly
prac'tice
·ticed ·tic·ing
prac'tic·er
prac'ti·cum
prac·ti'tion·er
prag·mat'ic
prag·mat'i·cal·ly
prag'ma·tism
prag'ma·tist
prai'rie
praise
praised
prais'ing
praise'wor'thy
pra'line
prance
pranced
pranc'ing
prank'ish
prate
prat'ed
prat'ing

prat'tle
·tled ·tling
pray
(implore; see
prey)
pray'er
(one who prays)
prayer
(an entreaty)
preach'er
pre'am·ble
pre'ar·range'
·ranged'
·rang'ing
pre'ar·range'ment
preb'end
pre·can'cel
pre·car'i·ous
pre·cau'tion
pre·cau'tion·ar'y
pre·cede'
·ced'ed ·ced'ing
(come before;
see proceed)
prec'e·dence
(priority)
prec'e·dent
(example)
pre'cen'sor
pre'cept
pre·cep'tor
pre·ces'sion
(a going before;
see procession)
pre·ces'sion·al
pre'cinct
pre·ci·os'i·ty
pre'cious
prec'i·pice
pre·cip'i·tate'
·tat'ed ·tat'ing
pre·cip'i·ta'tion
pre·cip'i·tous
pré·cis'
·cis'
(abstract)
pre·cise'
(definite)
pre·cise'ly
pre·ci'sion
pre·clude'
·clud'ed
·clud'ing
pre·clu'sion
pre·co'cious
pre'cog·ni'tion
pre·con·ceive'
pre'con·cep'tion
pre·con'scious
pre·cur'sor
pre·cur'so·ry
pre·da'cious
pre·date'
pred'a·tor
pred'a·to'ry
pre·de·cease'
pred'e·ces'sor
pre·des'ti·na'tion

pre·des'tine
·tined ·tin·ing
pre'de·ter'mine
pred'i·ca·bil'i·ty
pred'i·ca·ble
pre·dic'a·ment
pred'i·cate'
·cat'ed ·cat'ing
pred'i·ca'tion
pre·dict'
pre·dict'a·ble
pre·dic'tion
pre·dic'tive
pre·dic'tor
pre'di·gest'
pre'di·lec'tion
pre'dis·pose'
pre'dis·po·si'tion
pre·dom'i·nant
pre·dom'i·nate'
pre·em'i·nence
pre·em'i·nent
pre·empt'
pre·emp'tion
pre·emp'tive
pre·emp'tor
pre'es·tab'lish
pre'ex·ist'
pre'ex·ist'ence
pre'fab'
pre·fab'ri·cate'
pref'ace
·aced ·ac·ing
pref'a·to'ry
pre'fect
pre'fec·ture
pre·fer'
·ferred' ·fer'ring
pref'er·a·ble
pref'er·a·bly
pref'er·ence
pref'er·en'tial
pre·fer'ment
pre'fig·u·ra'tion
pre·fig'ur·a·tive
pre·fig'ure
pre'fix
pre'flight'
preg'na·ble
preg'nan·cy
·cies
preg'nant
pre·hen'sile
pre'his·tor'ic
pre·judge'
pre·judg'ment or
·judge'·
prej'u·dice
·diced ·dic·ing
prej·u·di'cial
prel'a·cy
prel'ate
pre·lim'i·nar'y
·ies
prel'ude
pre·mar'i·tal
pre·ma·ture'
pre·ma·ture'ly

pre·med'i·cal
pre·med'i·tate'
pre·mier'
　(*chief*)
pre·mière'
　·mièred'
　·mièr'ing
　(*first showing*)
prem'ise
　·ised　·is·ing
pre'mi·um
pre'mo·ni'tion
pre·mon'i·to'ry
pre·na'tal
pre·oc'cu·pan·cy
pre·oc'cu·pa'tion
pre·oc'cu·py'
　·pied'　·py'ing
pre'or·dain'
pre·pack'age
pre·paid'
prep'a·ra'tion
pre·par'a·tive
pre·par'a·to'ry
pre·pare'
　·pared'　·par'ing
pre·par'ed·ness
pre·pay'
　·paid'　·pay'ing
pre·pay'ment
pre·pon'der·ance
pre·pon'der·ant
pre·pon'der·ate'
　·at'ed　·at'ing
prep'o·si'tion
pre'pos·sess'
pre'pos·sess'ing
pre·pos'ter·ous
pre're·cord'
pre·req'ui·site
　(*requirement;* see
　perquisite)
pre·rog'a·tive
pre·sage'
　·saged'　·sag'ing
pres'by·ter
Pres'by·te'ri·an
pre'school'
pre'sci·ence
pre'sci·ent
pre·scribe'
　·scribed'
　·scrib'ing
　(*order;* see
　proscribe)
pre·scrip'tion
pre·scrip'tive
pres'ence
pres'ent
pre·sent'a·ble
pre'sen·ta'tion
pres'ent-day'
pre·sen'ti·ment
　(*premonition*)
pre·sent'ment
　(*presentation*)
pre·serv'a·ble
pres'er·va'tion

pre·serv'a·tive
pre·serve'
　·served'
　·serv'ing
pre·set'
pre'·shrunk'
pre·side'
　·sid'ed　·sid'ing
pres'i·den·cy
　·cies
pres'i·dent
pres'i·dent-e·lect'
pres'i·den'tial
pre·sid'i·um
　·i·a　*or*　·i·ums
pre·sig'ni·fy'
press box
press'ing
press'man
pres'sure
　·sured　·sur·ing
pres'sur·ize'
　·ized'　·iz'ing
press'work'
pres'ti·dig'i·ta'tor
pres·tige'
pres·ti'gious
pre'stressed'
pre·sum'a·ble
pre·sume'
　·sumed'
　·sum'ing
pre·sump'tion
pre·sump'tive
pre·sump'tu·ous
pre'sup·pose'
pre'sup·po·si'tion
pre·tend'
pre·tend'er
pre·tense'
pre·ten'sion
pre·ten'tious
pre'ter·nat'u·ral
pre'text
pre'tri'al
pret'ti·fy'
　·fied'　·fy'ing
pret'ti·ly
pret'ti·ness
pret'ty
　·ti·er　·ti·est
　·tied　·ty·ing
pret'zel
pre·vail'
pre·vail'ing
prev'a·lence
prev'a·lent
pre·var'i·cate'
　·cat'ed　·cat'ing
pre·var'i·ca'tion
pre·var'i·ca'tor
pre·ven'ient
pre·vent'
pre·vent'a·ble *or*
　·i·ble
pre·ven'tion
pre·ven'tive *or*
　·vent'a·tive

pre'view'
pre'vi·ous
pre·vi'sion
pre'war'
prey
　(*victim;* see
　pray)
pri'a·pism
price
　priced pric'ing
price'less
prick'le
　·led　·ling
prick'li·ness
prick'ly
　·li·er　·li·est
pride
　prid'ed prid'ing
pri'er
　(*one who pries;*
　see prior)
prize
　prized priz'ing
prize'fight'
prob'a·bil'i·ty
prob'a·ble
prob'a·bly
pro'bate
　·bat·ed　·bat·ing
pro·ba'tion
pro·ba'tion·ar'y
pro·ba'tion·er
pro'ba·tive
probe
　probed prob'ing
prob'i·ty
prob'lem
prob'lem·at'ic
pro·bos'cis
　·cis·es　*or*　·ci·des'
pro·ce'dur·al
pro·ce'dure
pro·ceed'
　(*go on;* see
　precede)
pro'ceeds
proc'ess
pro·ces'sion
　(*parade;* see
　precession)
pro·ces'sion·al
proc'es·sor *or*
　proc'ess·er
pro·claim'
proc'la·ma'tion
pro·cliv'i·ty
　·ties
pro·cras'ti·nate'
　·nat'ed　·nat'ing
pro·cras'ti·na'tion
pro·cras'ti·na'tor
pro'cre·ant
pro'cre·ate'
　·at'ed　·at'ing
pro'cre·a'tor
proc·tol'o·gy
proc'tor
proc'to·scope'
pro·cum'bent
pro·cur'a·ble

proc'u·ra'tor
pro·cure'
　·cured'　·cur'ing
pro·cure'ment
prod
　prod'ded
　prod'ding
prod'i·gal
prod'i·gal'i·ty
pro·di'gious
prod'i·gy
　·gies
　(*genius;* see
　protégé)
pro·duce'
　·duced'
　·duc'ing
pro·duc'er
pro·duc'i·ble
prod'uct
pro·duc'tion
pro·duc'tive
pro·duc'tive·ly
pro'duc·tiv'i·ty
prof'a·na'tion
pro·fane'
　·faned'　·fan'ing
pro·fane'ly
pro·fan'i·ty
　·ties
pro·fess'
pro·fessed'
pro·fess'ed·ly
pro·fes'sion
pro·fes'sion·al·ly
pro·fes'sor
pro·fes·so'ri·al
pro'fes·so'ri·ate
prof'fer
pro·fi'cien·cy
pro·fi'cient
pro'file
　·filed　·fil·ing
prof'it
　(*gain;* see
　prophet)
prof'it·a·ble
prof'it·a·bly
prof'i·teer'
prof'li·ga·cy
prof'li·gate
pro·found'
pro·fun'di·ty
　·ties
pro·fuse'
pro·fuse'ly
pro·fu'sion
pro·gen'i·tor
prog'e·ny
　·nies
prog'na·thous
prog·no'sis
　·ses
prog·nos'tic
prog·nos'ti·cate'
　·cat'ed　·cat'ing
prog·nos'ti·
　ca'tion

prog·nos'ti·ca'tor
pro'gram
　·grammed
　or　·gramed
　·gram·ming
　or　·gram·ing
pro'gram·mat'ic
pro'gram·mer
　or　·gram·er
prog'ress
pro·gres'sion
pro·gres'sive
pro·gres'siv·ism
pro·hib'it
pro·hi·bi'tion
pro·hib'i·tive
pro·hib'i·to'ry
proj'ect
pro·jec'tile
pro·jec'tion
pro·jec'tive
pro·jec'tor
pro·lep'sis
　·ses
pro'le·tar'i·an
pro'le·tar'i·at
pro·lif'er·ate'
　·at'ed　·at'ing
pro·lif'ic
pro·lix'
pro·lix'i·ty
pro·loc'u·tor
pro'logue
pro·long'
pro·lon'gate
　·gat·ed　·gat·ing
pro'lon·ga'tion
prom'e·nade'
　·nad'ed
　·nad'ing
prom'i·nence
prom'i·nent
prom'is·cu'i·ty
　·ties
pro·mis'cu·ous
prom'ise
　·ised　·is·ing
prom'is·so'ry
prom'on·to'ry
　·ries
pro·mot'a·ble
pro·mote'
　·mot'ed　·mot'ing
pro·mot'er
pro·mo'tion
prompt'er
prompt'i·tude'
prompt'ly
prom'ul·gate'
　·gat'ed　·gat'ing
prom'ul·ga'tion
prom'ul·ga'tor
prone
pronged
pro'noun'
pro·nounce'
　·nounced'
　·nounc'ing

pro·nounce'a·ble
pro·nounce'ment
pro·nun'ci·a'tion
proof'read'
·read' ·read'ing
prop'a·gan'da
prop'a·gan'dize
·dized ·diz·ing
prop'a·gate'
·gat'ed ·gat'ing
prop'a·ga'tion
prop'a·ga'tor
pro'pane
pro·pel'
·pelled' ·pel'ling
pro·pel'lant or
·lent
pro·pel'ler
pro·pen'si·ty
·ties
prop'er·ly
prop'er·tied
prop'er·ty
·ties
proph'e·cy n.
·cies
proph'e·sy' v.
·sied' ·sy'ing
proph'et
(predictor; see
profit)
pro·phet'ic
pro·phet'i·cal·ly
pro'phy·lac'tic
pro'phy·lax'is
·lax'es
pro·pin'qui·ty
pro·pi'ti·ate'
·at'ed ·at'ing
pro·pi'ti·a'tion
pro·pi'ti·a'tor
pro·pi'ti·a·to'ry
pro·pi'tious
pro·po'nent
pro·por'tion
pro·por'tion·al
pro·por'tion·al·ly
pro·por'tion·ate
pro·por'tion·ate·
ly
pro·pos'al
pro·pose'
·posed' ·pos'ing
prop'o·si'tion
pro·pound'
pro·pri'e·tar'y
·ies
pro·pri'e·tor
pro·pri'e·tress
pro·pri'e·ty
·ties
pro·pul'sion
pro·pul'sive
pro·ra'ta
pro·rat'a·ble
pro·rate'
·rat'ed ·rat'ing
pro·ro·ga'tion

pro·sa'ic
pro·sa'i·cal·ly
pro·sce'ni·um
·ni·ums or ·ni·a
pro·sciut'to
pro·scribe'
·scribed'
·scrib'ing
(forbid; see
prescribe)
pro·scrip'tion
prose
pros'e·cut'a·ble
pros'e·cute'
·cut'ed ·cut'ing
(legal term;
see persecute)
pros'e·cu'tion
pros'e·cu'tor
pros'e·lyte'
·lyt'ed ·lyt'ing
pros'e·lyt·ism
pros'e·lyt·ize'
·ized' ·iz'ing
pros'o·dy
·dies
pros'pect
pro·spec'tive
(expected; see
perspective)
pros'pec·tor
pro·spec'tus
pros'per
pros·per'i·ty
pros'per·ous
pros'tate
(gland; see
prostrate)
pros'the·sis
·the·ses
pros·thet'ic
pros'ti·tute'
·tut'ed ·tut'ing
pros'ti·tu'tion
pros'trate
·trat·ed ·trat·ing
(prone; see
prostate)
pros·tra'tion
pros'y
·i·er ·i·est
pro·tag'o·nist
pro·tect'
pro·tec'tion
pro·tec'tive
pro·tec'tor
pro·tec'tor·ate
pro'vo·lo'ne
pro'vost
prow'ess
prowl'er
prox'i·mal
prox'i·mate
prox·im'i·ty
prox'i·mo'
prox'y
·ies
pru'dence
pru'dent
pru·den'tial

pro·thon'o·tar'y
·ies
pro'to·col'
pro'ton
pro'to·plasm
pro'to·typ'al
pro'to·type'
pro'to·zo'an
pro·tract'
pro·tract'ed·ly
pro·tract'i·ble
pro·trac'tile
pro·trac'tion
pro·trac'tor
pro·trude'
·trud'ed
·trud'ing
pro·tru'sile
pro·tru'sion
pro·tru'sive
pro·tu'ber·ance
pro·tu'ber·ant
proud'ly
prov'a·bil'i·ty
prov'a·ble
prov'a·bly
prove
proved, proved
or prov'en,
prov'ing
prov'en·der
prov'i·dence
prov'i·dent
prov'i·den'tial
pro·vid'er
prov'ince
pro·vin'cial
pro·vin'cial·ism
pro·vin'cial·ly
pro·vi'sion
pro·vi'sion·al
pro·vi'sion·al·ly
pro·vi'so
·sos or ·soes
pro·vi'so·ry
prov'o·ca'tion
pro·voc'a·tive
pro·voc'a·tive·ly
pro·voke'
·voked' ·vok'ing
pro·té·gé'
(one helped by
another; see
prodigy)
pro'tein
pro·tem'po·re'
pro·test'
Prot'es·tant
prot'es·ta'tion
pro·test'er or
·tes'tor

pru'dent·ly
prud'er·y
prud'ish
prune
pruned prun'ing
pru'ri·ence
pru'ri·ent
pry
pries, pried pry'ing
psalm'book'
psal'mo·dy
psal'ter·y
·ies
pse·phol'o·gy
pseu'do
pseu'do·nym'
pseu'do·nym'i·ty
pseu·don'y·mous
psit'ta·co'sis
pso·ri'a·sis
psy'che
psy'che·de'li·a
psy'che·del'ic
psy'che·del'i·cal·
ly
psy·chi·at'ric
psy·chi·at'ri·cal·
ly
psy·chi'a·trist
psy·chi'a·try
psy'chic
psy'chi·cal·ly
psy'cho·a·
nal'y·sis
psy'cho·an'a·lyst
psy'cho·an'a·
lyt'ic
psy'cho·an'a·
lyt'i·cal·ly
psy'cho·an'a·lyze'
·lyzed' ·lyz'ing
psy'cho·dra'ma
psy'cho·dy·nam'·
ics
psy'cho·gen'ic
psy·cho·log'i·cal
psy·chol'o·gist
psy·chol'o·gize'
·gized' ·giz'ing
psy·chol'o·gy
psy·chom'e·try
psy'cho·neu·ro'sis
·ses
psy'cho·neu·rot'ic
psy'cho·path'ic
psy'cho·path·ol'·
o·gy
psy'cho·sex'u·al
psy·cho'sis
·ses
psy'cho·so·mat'ic
psy'cho·ther'a·py
psy·chot'ic
pter'o·dac'tyl
pto'maine
pu'ber·ty
pu·bes'cence
pu'bic

pub'lic
pub'li·ca'tion
pub'li·cist
pub·lic'i·ty
pub'li·cize'
·cized' ·ciz'ing
pub'lic·ly
pub'lish
puck'er
pud'ding
pud'dle
·dled ·dling
pudg'i·ness
pudg'y
·i·er ·i·est
pueb'lo
·los
pu'er·ile
Puer'to Ri'co
puff'i·ness
puff'y
·i·er ·i·est
pu'gil·ism
pug·na'cious
pug·nac'i·ty
pul'chri·tude'
pul'chri·tu'di·
nous
pull
pul'let
pul'ley
·leys
pull'out'
pull'o'ver
pull'mo·nar'y
pull'mo'tor
pul'pit
pulp'wood'
pulp'y
·i·er ·i·est
pul'sate
·sat·ed ·sat·ing
pul·sa'tion
pulse
pulsed puls'ing
pul'ver·iz'a·ble
pul'ver·i·za'tion
pul'ver·ize'
·ized' ·iz'ing
pum'ice
(rock; see pomace)
pum'mel
·meled or
·melled
·mel·ing or
·mel·ling
pump'er·nick'el
pump'kin
pun
punned
pun'ning
punch card
pun'cheon
punc·til'i·o'
·os'
punc·til'i·ous
punc'tu·al
punc'tu·al'i·ty

punc'tu·al·ly
punc'tu·ate'
·at'ed ·at'ing
punc'tu·a'tion
punc'tu·a'tor
punc'tur·a·ble
punc'ture
·tured ·tur'ing
pun'dit
pun'gen·cy
pun'gent
pu'ni·ness
pun'ish
pun'ish·a·ble
pun'ish·ment
pu'ni·tive
pun'ster
pu'ny
·ni·er ·ni·est
pu'pil
pup'pet
pup'pet·eer'
pup'py
·pies
pur'chas·a·ble
pur'chase
·chased
·chas·ing
pure'bred'
pu·rée'
·réed' ·rë'ing
pure'ly
pur·ga'tion
pur'ga·tive
pur'ga·to'ry
purge
purged purg'ing
pu'ri·fi·ca'tion
pu'ri·fi'er
pu'ri·fy'
·fied' ·fy'ing
pur'ism
pu'ri·tan
pu'ri·tan'i·cal
pu'ri·ty
purl
(stitch; see pearl)
pur·loin'
pu'ro·my'cin
pur'ple
pur'plish
pur·port'
pur'pose
·posed ·pos·ing
pur'pose·ful
pur'pose·ful·ly
pur'pose·less
pur'pose·ly
purr
purs'er
pur·su'ance
pur·sue'
·sued' ·su'ing
pur·suit'
pu'ru·lence
pu'ru·lent
pur·vey'
pur·vey'ance

pur·vey'or
pur'view
push'cart'
push'o·ver
push'-up'
pu·sil·lan'i·mous
pus'sy
· si·er ·si·est
(with pus)
puss'y
·ies
(cat)
pus'tu·lant
pus'tule
put
put put'ting
(place; see putt)
pu'ta·tive
pu'tre·fac'tion
pu'tre·fy'
·fied' ·fy'ing
pu·tres'cence
pu·tres'cent
pu'trid
putt
(golf term; see
put)
put·tee'
putt'er
(golf club)
put'ter
(busy oneself)
put'ty
·tied ·ty·ing
puz'zle
·zled ·zling
puz'zler
pyg'my
·mies
py'lon
py'or·rhe'a
pyr'a·mid
py·ram'i·dal
pyre
py·ret'ic
Py'rex
py·rog'ra·phy
py·ro·ma'ni·a
py·ro·ma'ni·ac'
py'ro·tech'nics
py·rox'y·lin
Py·thag'o·ras
py'thon

Q

quack'er·y
·ies
quad'ran'gle
quad·ran'gu·lar
quad'rant
quad'rate
·rat·ed ·rat·ing
quad·rat'ic
quad·ren'ni·al
quad'ri·lat'er·al

qua·drille'
quad·ril'lion
quad'ri·ple'gi·a
quad'ru·ped'
quad·ru'ple
·pled ·pling
quad·ru'plet
quad·ru'pli·cate'
·cat'ed ·cat'ing
quaff
quag'mire'
quail
quaint'ly
quake
quaked
quak'ing
qual'i·fi·ca'tion
qual'i·fi'er
qual'i·fy'
·fied' ·fy'ing
qual'i·ta'tive
qual'i·ty
·ties
qualm
quan'da·ry
·ries
quan'ti·ta'tive
quan'ti·ty
·ties
quan'tum
·ta
quar·an·tin'a·ble
quar'an·tine'
·tined' ·tin'ing
quar'rel
·reled or ·relled
·rel·ing or
·rel·ling
quar'rel·some
quar'ry
·ries
·ried ·ry·ing
quart
quar'ter
quar'ter·back'
quar'ter-deck'
quar'ter·ly
·lies
quar'ter·mas'ter
quar'ter·saw'
·sawed', ·sawed'
or ·sawn',
·saw'ing
quar·tet' or ·tette'
quar'tile
quar'to
·tos
quartz
qua'sar
quash
qua'si
qua'ter·na'ry
·ries
quat'rain
qua'ver
quay
(wharf; see key)
quea'si·ness

quea'sy
· si·er ·si·est
queen'li·ness
queen'ly
·li·er ·li·est
queen'-size'
queer
quell
quench'a·ble
quer'u·lous
que'ry
·ries
·ried ·ry·ing
quest
ques'tion
ques'tion·a·ble
ques'tion·naire'
queue
queued
queu'ing
(line; see cue)
quib'ble
·bled ·bling
quick'en
quick'-freeze'
-froze' -froz'en
-freez'ing
quick'sand'
quick'sil'ver
quick'-tem'pered
quick'-wit'ted
quid'nunc'
qui·es'cence
qui·es'cent
qui'et
(still; see quite)
qui'e·tude'
qui·e'tus
quill
quilt'ing
quince
qui·nel'la
quin·quen'ni·al
quin·tes'sence
quin·tet'
or ·tette'
quin·til'lion
quin·tu'ple
·pled ·pling
quin·tu'plet
quin·tu'pli·cate'
·cat'ed ·cat'ing
quip
quipped
quip'ping
quire
(of paper; see
choir)
quirk
quis'ling
quit
quit or quit'ted
quit'ting
quit'claim'
quite
(fully; see quiet)
quit'tance
quit'ter

quiv'er
quix·ot'ic
quiz
quiz'zes
quizzed
quiz'zing
quiz'zi·cal
quoin
(wedge; corner;
see coign, coin)
quoit
quon'dam
Quon'set hut
quo'rum
quo'ta
quot'a·ble
quo·ta'tion
quote
quot'ed quot'ing
quo'tient

R

rab'bet
(cut; see rabbit)
rab'bi
·bis or ·bies
rab·bin'i·cal
rab'bit
(hare; see rabbet)
rab'ble
·bled ·bling
rab'id
ra'bies
rac·coon'
race
raced rac'ing
race'horse'
rac'er
race track
race'way'
ra'cial
ra'cial·ly
rac'i·ly
rac'i·ness
rac'ism
rack'et
rack'et·eer'
rack'-rent'
rac'on·teur'
rac'y
·i·er ·i·est
ra'dar
ra'di·al
ra'di·ance
ra'di·ant
ra'di·ate'
·at'ed ·at'ing
ra'di·a'tion
ra'di·a'tor
rad'i·cal
rad'i·cal·ism
rad'i·cal·ly
ra'di·o'
·os', ·oed' ·o'ing
ra'di·o·ac'tive

ra'di·o·gram'
ra'di·o·graph'
ra'di·og'ra·phy
ra'di·o·i'so·tope'
ra'di·ol'o·gist
ra'di·ol'o·gy
ra'di·o·phone'
ra'di·o·pho'no·
graph'
ra'di·o·pho'to
·tos
ra'di·os'co·py
ra'di·o·sonde'
ra'di·o·tel'e·
phone'
ra'di·o·ther'a·py
ra'di·o·ther'my
rad'ish
ra'di·um
ra'di·us
·di·i' or ·di·us·es
ra'dix
ra'di·ces' or
ra'dix·es
ra'don
raf'fi·a
raf'fle
·fled ·fling
raft'er
rag'a·muffin
rage
raged rag'ing
rag'ged
rag'lan
ra·gout'
rag'pick'er
rag'time'
rag'weed'
raid'er
rail'ing
rail'ler·y
·ies
rail'road'
rail'-split'ter
rail'way'
rai'ment
rain
(water; see
reign, rein)
rain'bow'
rain check
rain'coat'
rain'drop'
rain'fall'
rain'i·ness
rain'proof'
rain'storm'
rain'y
·i·er ·i·est
raise
raised rais'ing
(lift; see raze)
rai'sin
rai'son d'être'
ra'jah or ·ja
rake
raked rak'ing
rak'ish

ral'li·er
ral'ly
·lies
·lied ·ly·ing
ram
rammed
ram'ming
ram'ble
·bled ·bling
ram'bler
ram·bunc'tious
ram'e·kin or ·quin
ram'i·fi·ca'tion
ram'i·fy'
·fied' ·fy'ing
ram'jet'
ramp
ram·page'
·paged' ·pag'ing
ram·pa'geous
ramp'ant
ram'part
ram'rod'
ram'shack'le
ranch'er
ran'cid
ran'cor
ran'cor·ous
ran'dom
ran'dom·ize'
·ized' ·iz'ing
range
ranged
rang'ing
rang'i·ness
rang'y
·i·er ·i·est
ran'kle
·kled ·kling
ran'sack
ran'som
rap
rapped rap'ping
(strike; see wrap)
ra·pa'cious
ra·pac'i·ty
rape
raped rap'ing
rap'id-fire'
ra·pid'i·ty
rap'id·ly
ra'pi·er
rap'ine
rap'ist
rap·port'
rap·proche'ment
rap·scal'lion
rap·to'ri·al
rap'ture
rap'tur·ous
rare
rar'er rar'est
rare'bit
rar'e·fy'
·fied' ·fy'ing
rare'ly
rar'i·ty
·ties

ras'cal
ras·cal'i·ty
ras'cal·ly
rash'er
rash'ness
rasp'ber'ry
·ries
rasp'i·ness
rasp'ing
rasp'y
·i·er ·i·est
rat
rat'ted rat'ting
rat'a·ble *or* rate'-
ratch'et
rate
rat'ed rat'ing
rath'er
raths'kel'ler
rat'i·fi·ca'tion
rat'i·fi'er
rat'i·fy'
·fied' ·fy'ing
ra'tio
·tios
ra'ti·o'ci·nate'
·nat'ed ·nat'ing
ra'tion·al
ra'tion·ale'
ra'tion·al·ism
ra'tion·al'i·ty
ra'tion·al·i·za'tion
ra'tion·al·ize'
·ized' ·iz'ing
ra'tion·al·ly
rat'line *or* ·lin
rat'tail'
rat·tan' *or* ra·tan'
rat'tle
·tled ·tling
rat'tle·brained'
rat'tler
rat'tle·snake'
rat'tle·trap'
rat'tly
rau'cous
rav'age
·aged ·ag·ing
rave
raved rav'ing
rav'el
·eled *or* ·elled
·el·ing *or* ·el·ling
ra'ven
rav'e·nous
ra·vine'
ra·vi·o'li
rav'ish
raw'boned'
raw'hide'
ray'on
raze
razed raz'ing
(*demolish;* see
raise)
ra'zor
ra'zor·back'
reach

re·act'
(*respond*)
re'-act'
(*act again*)
re·ac'tion
re·ac'tion·ar'y
·ies
re·ac'ti·vate'
·vat'ed ·vat'ing
re·ac'tive·ly
re·ac'tor
read
read read'ing
read'a·bil'i·ty
read'a·ble
read'i·ly
read'i·ness
re'ad·just'
read'out'
read'y
·i·er ·i·est
·ied ·y·ing
read'y-made'
re·a'gent
re'al
(*actual;* see reel)
re'al·ism
re'al·ist
re'al·is'tic
re'al·is'ti·cal·ly
re·al'i·ty
·ties
(*real thing;* see
realty)
re'al·iz'a·ble
re'al·i·za'tion
re'al·ize'
·ized' ·iz'ing
re'al-life'
re'al·ly
realm
Re'al·tor
re'al·ty
(*real estate;* see
reality)
ream'er
re·an'i·mate'
·mat'ed ·mat'ing
reap'er
re'ap·por'tion
rear guard
re·ar'ma·ment
re'ar·range'
re'ar·range'ment
rear'ward
rea'son·a·ble
rea'son·a·bly
re'as·sur'ance
re'as·sure'
·sured' ·sur'ing
re'bate
·bat·ed ·bat·ing
reb'el *n.*
re·bel' *v.*
·belled' ·bel'ling
re·bel'lion
re·bel'lious
re·birth'

re·bound'
re·buff'
(*blunt refusal*)
re'-buff'
(*buff again*)
re·buke'
·buked'
·buk'ing
re'bus
re·but'
·but'ted
·but'ting
re·but'tal
re·cal'ci·trant
re·call'
re·cant'
re·cap'
·capped'
·cap'ping
re'ca·pit'u·late'
·lat'ed ·lat'ing
re'ca·pit'u·la'tion
re·cap'pa·ble
re·cap'ture
re·cede'
·ced'ed ·ced'ing
re·ceipt'
re·ceiv'a·ble
re·ceive'
·ceived'
·ceiv'ing
re·ceiv'er·ship'
re·cen'sion
re'cent
re·cep'ta·cle
re·cep'tion
re·cep'tive
re·cep'tor
re'cess
re·ces'sion
re·ces'sive
re·charge'a·ble
re·cher'ché
re·cid'i·vism
rec'i·pe
re·cip'i·ent
re·cip'ro·cal
re·cip'ro·cal·ly
re·cip'ro·cate'
·cat'ed ·cat'ing
re·cip'ro·ca'tion
re·cip'ro·ca'tor
rec'i·proc'i·ty
re·ci'sion
re·cit'al
rec'i·ta'tion
rec'i·ta·tive'
re·cite'
·cit'ed ·cit'ing
reck'less
reck'on·ing
re·claim'
(*restore for use*)
re'-claim'
(*claim back*)
rec'la·ma'tion
re·cline'
·clined' ·clin'ing

rec'luse
re·clu'sion
rec'og·ni'tion
rec'og·niz'a·ble
re·cog'ni·zance
rec'og·nize'
·nized' ·niz'ing
re·coil'
(*draw back*)
re'-coil'
(*coil again*)
re·coil'less
rec'ol·lect'
(*remember*)
re'-col·lect'
(*collect again*)
rec'ol·lec'tion
rec'om·mend'
rec'om·men·
da'tion
re'com·mit'
rec'om·pense'
·pensed'
·pens'ing
re·con·cil'a·ble
rec'on·cile'
·ciled' ·cil'ing
rec'on·cil'i·a'tion
rec'on·dite'
re·con·di'tion
re·con'nais·sance
re'con·struct'
rec'on·noi'ter
re·con·sid'er
re'con·ver'sion
re·con·vert'
re·cord' *v.*
rec'ord *n.*
re·cord'er
re·count'
(*narrate*)
re'-count'
(*count again*)
re·coup'
re'course
re·cov'er
(*get back*)
re'-cov'er
(*cover again*)
re·cov'er·y
·ies
rec're·ant
rec're·ate'
·at'ed ·at'ing
(*refresh*)
re'-cre·ate'
·at'ed ·at'ing
(*create anew*)
rec're·a'tion
re'-cre·a'tion
re·crim'i·nate'
·nat'ed ·nat'ing
re·crim'i·na'tion
re·cruit'
rec'tal
rec'tan'gle
rec·tan'gu·lar
rec'ti·fi'a·ble

rec'ti·fi·ca'tion
rec'ti·fi'er
rec'ti·fy'
·fied' ·fy'ing
rec'ti·lin'e·ar
rec'ti·tude'
rec'tor
rec'to·ry
·ries
rec'tum
·tums *or* ·ta
re·cum'ben·cy
re·cum'bent
re·cu'per·ate'
·at'ed ·at'ing
re·cu'per·a'tion
re·cur'
·curred'
·cur'ring
re·cur'rence
re·cur'rent
rec'u·sant
re·cy'cle
re·dact'
re·dac'tion
re·dac'tor
red'bait'
red'-blood'ed
red'den
re·deem'a·ble
re·demp'tion
re'de·ploy'
re'de·vel'op·ment
red'-hand'ed
red'head'
red'-hot'
re·di·rect'
re·dis'trict
red'-let'ter
re·do'
·did' ·done'
·do'ing
red'o·lence
red'o·lent
re·dou'ble
re·doubt'
re·doubt'a·ble
re·dound'
red'out'
re·dress'
(*remedy*)
re'-dress'
(*dress again*)
re·duce'
·duced' ·duc'ing
re·duc'i·ble
re·duc'tion
re·dun'dan·cy
·cies
re·dun'dant
re·du'pli·cate'
re·du'pli·ca'tion
re·ech'o
reed'i·ness
re·ed'it
re·ed'u·cate'
reed'y
·i·er ·i·est

reek
(*emit a smell;* see
wreak)
reel
(*whirl; dance;*
spool; see real)
re'e·lect'
re'e·lec'tion
re'em·bark'
re'em·bod'y
re'em·brace'
re'e·merge'
re·em'pha·sis
re·em'pha·size'
re'em·ploy'
re'en·act'
re'en·dow'
re'en·gage'
re'en·list'
re·en'ter
re·en'try
re'e·quip'
re'es·tab'lish
re'e·val'u·ate'
re'ex·am'ine
re'ex·change'
re'ex·hib'it
re'ex·pe'ri·ence
re'ex·plain'
re'ex·port'
re·fec'tion
re·fer'
·ferred'
·fer'ring
ref'er·a·ble *or*
·i·ble
ref'er·ee'
·eed' ·ee'ing
ref'er·ence
ref'er·en'dum
·dums *or* ·da
ref'er·ent
re·fer'ral
re·fill'a·ble
re·fine'
·fined' ·fin'ing
re·fine'ment
re·fin'er·y
·ies
re·fit'
re·fla'tion
re·flect'
re·flec'tion
re·flec'tive
re·flec'tor
re'flex
re·flex'ive
re'for·est·a'tion
re·form'
(*make better*)
re'-form'
(*form again*)
ref'or·ma'tion
re·form'a·to'ry
·ries
re·fract'
re·frac'to·ry

re·frain'	reg'u·la'tion	rel'e·gate'	re·mov'a·ble	re'-pe·ti'tion	re·pub'li·can
re·fran'gi·ble	reg'u·la'tor	gat'ed gat'ing	re·mov'al	(petition again)	re·pu'di·ate'
re·fresh'	re·gur'gi·tate'	rel'e·ga'tion	re·move'	rep'e·ti'tious	at'ed at'ing
re·fresh'ment	tat'ed tat'ing	re·lent'less	moved'	re·pet'i·tive	re·pu'di·a'tion
re·frig'er·ant	re·gur'gi·ta'tion	rel'e·vance	mov'ing	re·phrase'	re·pug'nance
re·frig'er·ate'	re·ha·bil'i·tate'	rel'e·vant	re·mu'ner·ate'	re·place'	re·pug'nant
at'ed at'ing	tat'ed tat'ing	re·li'a·bil'i·ty	at'ed at'ing	re·place'a·ble	re·pulse'
re·frig'er·a'tion	re·ha·bil'i·ta'tion	re·li'a·ble	re·mu'ner·a'tion	re·place'ment	pulsed'
re·frig'er·a'tor	re·hears'al	re·li'a·bly	re·mu'ner·a'tive	re·plen'ish	puls'ing
ref'uge	re·hearse'	re·li'ance	re·mu'ner·a'tor	re·plete'	re·pul'sion
ref'u·gee'	hearsed'	re·li'ant	ren'ais·sance'	re·ple'tion	re·pul'sive
re·ful'gent	hears'ing	rel'ic	re·nas'cent	re·plev'in	rep'u·ta·bil'i·ty
re·fund'	reign	re·lief'	rend	rep'li·ca	rep'u·ta·ble
re·fur'bish	(rule; see rain, rein)	re·liev'a·ble	rent rend'ing	re·ply'	rep'u·ta·bly
re·fus'al	re·im·burs'a·ble	lieved' liev'ing	ren'der	plies'	rep'u·ta'tion
re·fuse' v.	re·im·burse'	re·liev'er	ren'dez·vous'	plied' ply'ing	re·pute'
fused' fus'ing	bursed'	re·li'gion	·vous'	re·port'ed·ly	put'ed put'ing
ref'use n.	burs'ing	re·li'gious	·vous'ing	re·port'er	re·quest'
ref'u·ta'tion	rein	re·lin'quish	ren·di'tion	re·pose'	Re'qui·em
re·fute'	(control; see	rel'i·quar'y	ren'e·gade'	posed' pos'ing	re·quire'
fut'ed fut'ing	rain, reign)	ies	re·nege'	(rest)	·quired'
re·gain'	re·in·car'nate	rel'ish	neged' neg'ing	re'-pose'	·quir'ing
re'gal adj.	nat·ed nat·ing	re·luc'tance	re·new'al	(pose again)	re·quire'ment
re·gale' v.	re·in·car·na'tion	re·luc'tant	ren'net	re·pos'i·to'ry	req'ui·site
galed' gal'ing	re·in·cur'	re·ly'	re·nounce'	ries	req'ui·si'tion
re·ga'li·a	rein'deer	lied' ly'ing	nounced'	re'pos·sess'	re·quit'al
re·gal'i·ty	re·in·force'	re·main'der	nounc'ing	re'pos·ses'sion	re·quite'
ties	forced'	re·make'	ren'o·vate'	rep're·hend'	quit'ed
re·gard'ing	forc'ing	made' mak'ing	vat'ed vat'ing	rep're·hen'si·ble	quit'ing
re·gard'less	re·in·force'ment	re·mand'	ren'o·va'tion	rep're·hen'sion	rere'dos
re·gat'ta	re·in·state'	re·mark'a·ble	re·nown'	rep're·sent'	re·route'
re'gen·cy	stat'ed	re·mark'a·bly	re·nowned'	(stand for)	re·run'
cies	stat'ing	re·me'di·a·ble	rent'al	re'-pre·sent'	·ran' ·run'
re·gen'er·ate'	re·it'er·ate'	re·me'di·al	rent'-free'	(present again)	run'ning
at'ed at'ing	at'ed at'ing	rem'e·dy	re·nun'ci·a'tion	rep're·sen·ta'tion	re·sal'a·ble
re·gen'er·a'tion	re·ject'	dies	re·or'der	rep're·sent'a·tive	re'sale'
re·gen'er·a'tive	re·jec'tion	died dy·ing	re·or'gan·i·za'tion	re·press'	re·scind'
re·gen'er·a'tor	re·joice'	re·mem'ber	re·or'gan·ize'	(restrain)	re·scind'a·ble
re'gent	joiced' joic'ing	re·mem'brance	·ized' ·iz'ing	re'-press'	re·scis'sion
reg'i·cide'	re·join'der	re·mind'er	re·pair'man	(press again)	res'cu·a·ble
re·gime' or ré·	re·ju've·nate'	rem'i·nisce'	rep'a·ra·ble	re·pressed'	res'cue
reg'i·men	nat'ed nat'ing	nisced'	rep'a·ra'tion	re·press'i·ble	·cued ·cu·ing
reg'i·ment	re·lapse'	nisc'ing	rep'ar·tee'	re·pres'sion	res'cu·er
reg'i·men'tal	lapsed'	rem'i·nis'cence	re·past'	re·prieve'	re·search'
reg'i·men·ta'tion	laps'ing	rem'i·nis'cent	re·pa'tri·ate'	prieved'	re·sem'blance
re'gion·al	re·lat'a·ble	rem'i·nis'cer	at'ed at'ing	priev'ing	re·sem'ble
reg'is·ter	re·late'	re·miss'	re·pa'tri·a'tion	rep'ri·mand'	·bled ·bling
reg'is·trant	lat'ed lat'ing	re·mis'si·ble	re·pay'	re·print'	re·sent'
reg'is·trar'	re·la'tion·ship'	re·mis'sion	paid' pay'ing	re·pris'al	(feel a hurt)
reg'is·tra'tion	rel'a·tive	re·mit'	(pay back)	re·proach'	re'-sent'
reg'is·try	rel'a·tive·ly	mit'ted	re'-pay'	re·proach'ful	(sent again)
tries	rel'a·tiv'i·ty	mit'ting	-paid' -pay'ing	rep'ro·bate'	re·sent'ful
re'gress	re·lax'	re·mit'ta·ble	(pay again)	bat'ed bat'ing	re·sent'ment
re·gres'sion	re·lax'ant	re·mit'tance	re·peal'	re·proc'essed	res'er·va'tion
re·gres'sive	re·lax·a'tion	re·mit'tent	re·peat'	re'pro·duce'	re·serve'
re·gret'	re'lay	rem'nant	re·pel'	re'pro·duc'i·ble	served'
gret'ted	layed lay·ing	re·mod'el	pelled' pel'ling	re'pro·duc'tion	serv'ing
gret'ting	(send by relay)	re·mon'strance	re·pel'lent	re'pro·duc'tive	(set aside)
re·gret'ful	re'-lay'	re·mon'strate	re·pent'	re·proof'	re'-serve'
re·gret'ful·ly	-laid' -lay'ing	strat·ed	re·pent'ance	re·prove'	(serve again)
re·gret'ta·ble	(lay again)	strat·ing	re·pent'ant	proved'	re·served'·ly
re·gret'ta·bly	re·lease'	re'mon·stra'tion	re·per·cus'sion	prov'ing	re·serv'ist
reg'u·lar	leased'	re·mon'stra·tor	rep'er·toire'	(rebuke)	res'er·voir'
reg'u·lar'i·ty	leas'ing	re·morse'ful	rep'er·to'ry	re'-prove'	re·set'
ties	(set free)	re·morse'less	ries	(prove again)	·set' ·set'ting
reg'u·late'	re'-lease'	re·mote'	rep'e·ti'tion	rep'tile	re·ship'ment
lat'ed lat'ing	(lease again)	re·mote'ly	(a repeating)	rep·til'i·an	re·side'
				re·pub'lic	·sid'ed ·sid'ing

res'i·dence
res'i·den·cy
·cies
res'i·dent
res'i·den'tial
re·sid'u·al
re·sid'u·ar'y
res'i·due'
re·sign'
(give up)
re'-sign'
(sign again)
res·ig·na'tion
re·sil'i·ence
re·sil'i·ent
res'in
res'in·ous
re·sist'
re·sist'ance
re·sist'ant
re·sist'er
(one who resists)
re·sist'i·ble
re·sis'tor
(electrical device)
re'sole'
soled' sol'ing
res'o·lute'
res'o·lu'tion
re·solv'a·ble
re·solve'
solved'
solv'ing
(break into parts)
re'-solve'
(solve again)
re·sol'vent
res'o·nance
res'o·nant
res'o·na'tor
re·sort'
(go for help)
re'-sort'
(sort again)
re·sound'
(echo)
re'-sound'
(sound again)
re'source
re·source'ful
re·spect'a·bil'i·ty
re·spect'a·ble
re·spect'ful
re·spect'ful·ly
re·spec'tive
re·spec'tive·ly
res'pi·ra'tion
res'pi·ra'tor
res'pi·ra·to'ry
re·spire'
spired'
spir'ing
res'pite
pit·ed pit·ing
re·splend'ence
re·splend'ent
re·spond'
re·spond'ent

re·sponse'
re·spon'si·bil'i·ty
·ties
re·spon'si·ble
re·spon'si·bly
re·spon'sive
re·state'
stat'ed stat'ing
res'tau·rant
res'tau·ra·teur'
rest'ful
res'ti·tu'tion
res'tive
rest'less
res'to·ra'tion
re·stor'a·tive
re·store'
stored' stor'ing
re·strain'
(hold back)
re'-strain'
(strain again)
re·straint'
re·strict'
re·stric'tion
re·stric'tive
rest'room'
re·struc'ture
re·sult'
re·sult'ant
re·sum'a·ble
re·sume' v.
·sumed'
·sum'ing
ré'su·mé' n.
re·sump'tion
re·sur'face
re·sur'gence
re·sur'gent
res'ur·rect'
res'ur·rec'tion
re·sus'ci·tate'
·tat'ed ·tat'ing
re·sus'ci·ta'tion
re·sus'ci·ta'tor
re'tail
re·tain'
re·tain'er
re·take'
·took' ·tak'en
·tak'ing
re·tal'i·ate'
·at'ed ·at'ing
re·tal'i·a'tion
re·tal'i·a·to'ry
re·tard'
re·tard'ant
re·tar'date
re·tar·da'tion
retch
(strain to vomit;
see wretch)
re·ten'tion
re·ten'tive
re'ten·tiv'i·ty
re·think'
ret'i·cence
ret'i·cent

re·tic'u·lar
re·tic'u·late'
·lat'ed ·lat'ing
ret'i·cule'
ret'i·na
·nas or ·nae'
ret'i·nue'
re·tire'
·tired' ·tir'ing
re·tir'ee'
re·tire'ment
re·tool'
re·tort'
re·touch'
re·trace'
(go back over)
re'-trace'
(trace again)
re·trace'a·ble
re·tract'
re·tract'a·ble
re·trac'tile
re·trac'tion
re·trac'tor
re'tread' v.
·tread'ed
·tread'ing
re'tread' n.
re·treat'
(go back)
re'-treat'
(treat again)
re·trench'
ret'ri·bu'tion
re·triev'a·ble
re·triev'al
re·trieve'
·trieved'
·triev'ing
re·triev'er
ret'ro·ac'tive
ret'ro·ces'sion
ret'ro·fire'
ret'ro·fit'
ret'ro·grade'
·grad'ed
·grad'ing
ret'ro·gress'
ret'ro·gres'sion
ret'ro·rock'et or
ret'ro-rock'et
ret'ro·spect'
ret'ro·spec'tion
re·turn'
re·turn'ee'
re·un'ion
re'u·nite'
re·us'a·ble
re·use'
rev
revved rev'ving
re·vamp'
re·veal'
re'veil·le
rev'el
·eled or ·elled
·el·ing or ·el·ling
rev'e·la'tion

rev'el·ry
re·venge'
·venged'
·veng'ing
re·venge'ful
re·veng'er
rev'e·nue'
re·ver'ber·ant
re·ver'ber·ate'
·at'ed ·at'ing
re·ver'ber·a'tion
re·ver'ber·a'tor
re·ver'ber·a·to'ry
re·vere'
·vered' ·ver'ing
rev'er·ence
rev'er·end
rev'er·ent
rev'er·en'tial
rev'er·ie
re·ver'sal
re·vers'
·vers'
(part of garment)
re·verse'
·versed'
·vers'ing
re·ver'sion
(turned backward)
re·vers'i·ble
re·vers'i·bly
re·ver'sion
re·ver'sion·ar'y
re·vert'
re·view'
re·view'al
re·view'er
re·vile'
·viled' ·vil'ing
re·vise'
·vised' ·vis'ing
re·vi'sion
re·vi'so·ry
re·vi'tal·ize'
re·viv'a·ble
re·viv'al
re·vive'
·vived' ·viv'ing
re·viv'i·fy'
rev'o·ca·ble
rev'o·ca·bly
rev'o·ca'tion
re·voke'
·voked' ·vok'ing
re·volt'
re·volt'ing
rev'o·lu'tion
rev'o·lu'tion·ar'y
·ies
rev'o·lu'tion·ize'
·ized' ·iz'ing
re·volv'a·ble
re·volve'
·volved'
·volv'ing
re·volv'er
re·vue' or ·view'
re·vul'sion
re·ward'

re·wind'
·wound'
·wind'ing
re·write'
·wrote' ·writ'ten
·writ'ing
rhap·sod'ic
rhap·sod'i·cal·ly
rhap'so·dize'
·dized' diz'ing
rhap'so·dy
rhe'o·stat'
rhe'sus
rhet'o·ric
rhe·tor'i·cal
rhe·tor'i·cal·ly
rhet'o·ri'cian
rheu·mat'ic
rheu'ma·tism
rheu'ma·toid'
rheum'y
·i·er ·i·est
Rh factor
rhine'stone'
rhi·ni'tis
rhi·noc'er·os
rhi'zome
Rhode Island
rho'do·den'dron
rhom'boid
rhom'bus
·bus·es or ·bi
rhu'barb
rhyme
rhymed
rhym'ing
(verse; see rime)
rhythm
rhyth'mic
rhyth'mi·cal·ly
rib
ribbed
rib'bing
rib'ald
rib'ald·ry
rib'bon
ri'bo·fla'vin
rice
riced ric'ing
rich'ness
rick'et·i·ness
rick'ets
rick·ett'si·a
·si·ae' or ·si·as
rang rung
ring'ing
(sound; see
wring)
rick'et·y
rick'ey
rick'rack'
rick'shaw or ·sha
ric'o·chet'
·cheted' or
·chet'ted
·chet'ing or
·chet'ting
ri·cot'ta
rid
rid or rid'ded
rid'ding

rid'a·ble or ride'-
rid'dance
rid'dle
·dled ·dling
ride
rode rid'den
rid'ing
rid'er·less
ridge
ridged ridg'ing
ridge'pole'
rid'i·cule'
·culed' ·cul'ing
ri·dic'u·lous
rife
rif'fle
·fled ·fling
(shoal; shuffle)
riff'raff'
ri'fle
·fled ·fling
(gun; plunder)
ri'fle·man
rig
rigged rig'ging
ri'ga·to'ni
rig'ger
(one who rigs;
see rigor)
right
(correct; see rite)
right'-an'gled
right'eous
right'ful·ly
right'-hand'ed
right'ist
rig'id
ri·gid'i·ty
rig'ma·role'
rig'or
(stiffness; see
rigger)
rig'or mor'tis
rig'or·ous
rile
riled ril'ing
rim
rimmed
rim'ming
rime
rimed rim'ing
(hoarfrost; rhyme;
see rhyme)
ring
rang rung
ring'ing
(sound; see
wring)
ring
ringed ring'ing
(circle; see
wring)
ring'er
ring'lead'er
ring'let
ring'mas'ter
ring'side'
rink

rinse
  rinsed rins'ing
ri'ot·ous
rip
  ripped rip'ping
ri·par'i·an
rip'en
ripe'ness
ri·poste' *or*
  ·post'
rip'per
rip'ple
  ·pled ·pling
rip'saw'
rip'tide'
rise
  rose ris'en
ris'ing
ris'er
ris·i·bil'i·ty
  ·ties
ris'i·ble
risk'i·ly
risk'i·ness
risk'y
  ·i·er ·i·est
ris·qué'
ris'sole
rite
  (ceremonial act;
  see right, write)
rit'u·al
rit'u·al·is'tic
rit'u·al·ly
ri'val
  ·valed *or* ·valled
  ·val·ing *or*
  ·val·ling
ri'val·ry
  ·ries
rive
  rived, rived *or*
  riv'en, riv'ing
riv'er·side'
riv'et
riv'et·er
riv'u·let
roach
road'a·bil'i·ty
road'bed'
road'block'
road'show'
road'side'
road'ster
road'way'
road'work'
roam'er
roan
roar'ing
roast'er
rob
  robbed rob'bing
rob'ber
rob'ber·y
  ·ies
robe
  robed rob'ing
rob'in

ro'bot
ro·bust'
rock'-and-roll'
rock'-bound'
rock'er
rock'et
rock'e·teer'
rock'et·ry
rock'i·ness
rock·oon'
rock'y
  ·i·er ·i·est
ro·co'co
ro'dent
ro'de·o'
  ·os'
roe
  (fish eggs; see
  row)
roent'gen
rogue
  rogued rogu'ing
ro'guer·y
  ·ies
ro'guish
roil
  (stir up; see royal)
roist'er·er
roist'er·ous
role *or* rôle
  (actor's part)
roll
  (revolve)
roll'a·way'
roll'back'
roll call
roll'er
rol'lick·ing
roll'-top'
ro·maine'
ro·mance'
  ·manced'
  ·manc'ing
ro·man'tic
ro·man'ti·cal·ly
ro·man'ti·cism
ro·man'ti·cize'
  ·cized' ·ciz'ing
ron'deau
  ·deaux
  (poem)
ron'do
  ·dos
  (music)
rood
  (cross; see rude)
roof'er
rook
rook'er·y
  ·ies
rook'ie
room'er
  (lodger; see
  rumor)
room·ette'
room'ful'
  ·fuls'
room'i·ness

room'mate'
room'y
  ·i·er ·i·est
roos'ter
root beer
root'er
root'less
root'let
rope
  roped rop'ing
rope'walk'
Roque'fort
ro'sa·ry
  ·ries
ro·sé'
ro'se·ate
rose'bud'
rose'bush'
rose'-col'ored
ro·se'o·la
ro·sette'
rose'wood'
Rosh' Ha·sha'na
ros'i·ly
ros'in
ros'i·ness
row'boat'
ros'ter
ros·trum
  ·trums *or* ·tra
ros'y
  ·i·er ·i·est
rot
rot'ted
rot'ting
ro'ta·ry
  ·ries
ro'tat·a·ble
ro'tate
  ·tat·ed ·tat·ing
ro·ta'tion
ro'ta·tor
rote
  (routine; see
  wrote)
ro·tis'ser·ie
ro'to·gra·vure'
ro'tor
rot'ten
ro·tund'
ro·tun'da
ro·tun'di·ty
rou·é'
rouge
  rouged roug'ing
rough
  (not smooth;
  see ruff)
rough'age
rough'cast'
  ·cast' ·cast'ing
rough'-dry'
  -dried' -dry'ing
rough'en
rough'-hew'
  -hewed', -hewed'
  or -hewn',
  -hew'ing
rough'ly

rough'shod'
rou·lade'
rou·leau'
  ·leaux' *or* ·leaus'
rou·lette'
round'a·bout'
roun'de·lay'
round'house'
round'up'
round'worm'
rouse
  roused rous'ing
roust'a·bout'
rout
  (noisy mob; dig
  up; defeat)
route
  rout'ed rout'ing
  (course)
rou·tine'
rove
  roved rov'ing
row *n., v.*
  (line; use oars;
  brawl; see roe)
row'di·ness
row'dy
  ·di·er ·di·est
row'dy·ism
row'el
  ·eled *or* ·elled
  ·el·ing *or* ·el·ling
roy'al
  (regal; see roil)
roy'al·ist
roy'al·ly
roy'al·ty
  ·ties
rub
  rubbed
  rub'bing
rub'ber·ize'
  ·ized' ·iz'ing
rub'ber·y
rub'bish
rub'ble
  (stone; see ruble)
rub'down'
ru·bel'la
ru'bi·cund'
ru'ble
  (money; see
  rubble)
ru'bric
ru'by
  ·bies
ruche
ruch'ing
ruck'sack'
rud'der
rud'di·ness
rud'dy
  ·di·er ·di·est
rude
  (crude; see rood)
rude'ly

ru'di·ment
ru'di·men'ta·ry
rue
  rued ru'ing
rue'ful
ruff
  (collar; see rough)
ruf'fi·an
ruf'fle
  ·fled ·fling
rug'ged
ru·in·a'tion
ru'in·ous
rule
  ruled rul'ing
rul'er
rum'ble
  ·bled ·bling
ru'mi·nant
ru'mi·nate'
  ·nat'ed ·nat'ing
ru'mi·na'tor
rum'mage
  ·maged
  ·mag·ing
ru'mor
  (hearsay; see
  roomer)
rum'ple
  ·pled ·pling
run
  ran run
run'ning
run'a·bout'
run'a·way'
run'-down'
rung
  (crossbar; pp. of
  ring; see wrung)
run'-in'
run'ner-up'
  run'ners-up'
run'ni·ness
run'ny
  ·ni·er ·ni·est
run'off'
run'-on'
run'way'
rup'ture
  ·tured ·tur·ing
ru'ral
ru'ral·ly
ruse
rush
rus'set
rus'tic
rus'ti·cal·ly
rus'ti·cate'
  ·cat'ed ·cat'ing
rus'tle
  ·tled ·tling
rus'tler
rust'proof'
rust'y
  ·i·er ·i·est
rut
rut'ted rut'ting

ru·ta·ba'ga
ruth'less
rye
  (grain; see wry)

S

Sab'bath
sab·bat'i·cal
sa'ber *or* ·bre
sa'ble
sa'bot
sab'o·tage'
  ·taged' ·tag'ing
sab'o·teur'
sac
  (pouch; see sack)
sac'cha·rin *n.*
sac'cha·rine *adj.*
sac'er·do'tal
sa·chet'
sack
  (bag; see sac)
sack'cloth'
sack'ful'
  ·fuls'
sack'ing
sac'ra·ment
sac'ra·men'tal
sa'cred
sac'ri·fice'
  ·ficed' ·fic'ing
sac'ri·fi'cial
sac'ri·lege
sac'ri·le'gious
sac'ris·tan
sac'ris·ty
  ·ties
sac'ro·il'i·ac'
sac'ro·sanct'
sa'crum
  ·cra *or* ·crums
sad
  sad'der sad'dest
sad'den
sad'dle
  ·dled ·dling
sad'dle·bag'
sad'dle·cloth'
sad'dler
sad'i'ron
sad'ism
sad'ist
sa·dis'tic
sa·dis'ti·cal·ly
sa·fa'ri
  ·ris
safe
saf'er saf'est
safe'-con'duct
safe'-de·pos'it
safe'guard'
safe'keep'ing
safe'ty
  ·ties
saf'fron

sag
 sagged sag'ging
sa'ga
sa·ga'cious
sa·gac'i·ty
sage
 sag'er sag'est
sage'brush'
sag'gy
 ·gi·er ·gi·est
sa'go
 ·gos
sail'boat'
sail'cloth'
sail'er
 (boat)
sail'fish'
sail'or
 (person; hat)
saint'li·ness
saint'ly
 ·li·er ·li·est
sa'ke
 (rice wine)
sake
 (purpose)
sa·laam'
sal'a·ble or
 sale'
sa·la'cious
sal'ad
sal'a·man'der
sa·la'mi
sal'a·ried
sal'a·ry
 ·ries
sal'e·ra'tus
sales'clerk'
sales'man
sales'man·ship'
sales'peo'ple
sales'per'son
sales'wom'an
sa'lient
sa'line
sa·lin'i·ty
sa·li'va
sal'i·var'y
sal'i·vate'
 ·vat'ed ·vat'ing
sal'low
sal'ly
 ·lies, ·lied ·ly·ing
sal'ma·gun'di
salm'on
sal'mo·nel'la
 ·lae or ·la or ·las
sa·lon'
sa·loon'
sa·loon'keep'er
sal'si·fy'
salt'box'
salt'cel'lar
salt'i·ly
salt·ine'
salt'i·ness
salt'pe'ter
salt'shak'er

salt'wa'ter
salt'works'
 ·works'
salt'y
 ·i·er ·i·est
sa·lu'bri·ous
sal'u·tar'y
sal'u·ta'tion
sa·lu'ta·to'ri·an
sa·lu'ta·to'ry
 ·ries
sa·lute'
 ·lut'ed ·lut'ing
sal'vage
 ·vaged ·vag·ing
sal'vage·a·ble
sal·va'tion
salve
 salved salv'ing
sal'ver
sal'vo
 ·vos or ·voes
Sa·mar'i·tan
same'ness
sam'i·sen'
sam'o·var'
sam'pan
sam'ple
 ·pled ·pling
sam'pler
sam'u·rai'
 ·rai'
san'a·tive
sanc'ti·fi·ca'tion
sanc'ti·fy'
 ·fied' ·fy'ing
sanc'ti·mo'ni·ous
sanc'ti·mo'ny
sanc'tion
sanc'ti·ty
sanc'tu·ar'y
 ·ies
sanc'tum
 ·tums or ·ta
san'dal
san'daled or
 ·dalled
san'dal·wood'
sand'bag'
sand bar
sand'blast'
sand'box'
san'dhi
sand'hog'
sand'i·ness
sand'lot'
sand'man'
sand'pa'per
sand'stone'
sand'storm'
sand'wich
sand'y
 ·i·er ·i·est
sane'ly
San'for·ize'
 ·ized' ·iz'ing
sang'-froid'
san'gui·nar'y

san'guine
san·i·tar'i·um
 ·i·ums or ·i·a
san'i·tar'y
san·i·ta'tion
san'i·tize'
 ·tized' ·tiz'ing
san'i·ty
San'skrit
sap
 sapped sap'ping
sa'pi·ent
sap'ling
sa·pon'i·fy'
 ·fied' ·fy'ing
sap'phire
sap'py
 ·pi·er ·pi·est
sap'suck'er
sa·ran'
sar'casm
sar·cas'tic
sar·cas'ti·cal·ly
sar·co'ma
 ·mas or ·ma·ta
sar·coph'a·gus
 ·a·gi
sar·dine'
sar·don'ic
sar·don'i·cal·ly
sar'do·nyx
sa'ri
 ·ris
sa·rong'
sar'sa·pa·ril'la
sar·to'ri·al
sas'sa·fras'
sa·tan'ic
sa·tan'i·cal·ly
satch'el
sate
 sat'ed sat'ing
sa·teen'
sat'el·lite'
sa'tia·ble
sa'ti·ate'
 ·at'ed ·at'ing
sa'ti·a'tion
sa·ti'e·ty
sat'in
sat'in·wood'
sat'in·y
sat'ire
sa·tir'i·cal
sat'i·rist
sat'i·rize'
 ·rized' ·riz'ing
sat·is·fac'tion
sat·is·fac'to·ri·ly
sat·is·fac'to·ry
sat'is·fy'
 ·fied' ·fy'ing
sa·to'ri
sa'trap
sat'su·ma
sat'u·ra·ble
sat'u·rate'
 ·rat'ed ·rat'ing

sat'u·ra'tion
Sat'ur·day
sat'ur·nine'
sat'yr
sat'y·ri'a·sis
sauce'pan'
sau'cer
sau'ci·ness
sau'cy
 ·ci·er ·ci·est
sau'er·bra'ten
sau'er·kraut'
sau'na
saun'ter
sau'sage
sau·té'
 ·téed' ·té'ing
sau·terne'
sav'a·ble or
 save'
sav'age
 ·age
sav'age·ly
sav'age·ry
sa·van'na
sa·vant'
save
 saved sav'ing
sav'ior
sa'voir-faire'
sa'vor
sa'vor·i·ness
sa'vor·y
 ·i·er ·i·est
sa·voy'
saw
 sawed saw'ing
saw'dust'
saw'horse'
saw'mill'
saw'-toothed'
saw'yer
sax'o·phone'
sax'o·phon'ist
say
 said say'ing
says
say'-so'
scab
 scabbed scab'bing
scab'bard
scab'bi·ness
scab'by
 ·bi·er ·bi·est
scab'rous
scaf'fold
scagl·io'la
scal'a·ble
scal'a·wag'
scald
scale
 scaled scal'ing
scale'less
sca·lene'
scal'i·ness
scal'lion
scal'lop
scal'op·pi'ne
scal'pel

scalp'er
scal'y
 ·i·er ·i·est
scam'per
scan
 scanned
 scan'ning
scan'dal
scan'dal·ize'
 ·ized' ·iz'ing
scan'dal·mon'ger
scan'dal·ous
scan'na·ble
scan'ner
scan'sion
scant'i·ly
scant'i·ness
scant'ling
scant'ness
scant'y
 ·i·er ·i·est
scape'goat'
scape'grace'
scap'u·la
 ·lae' or ·las
scap'u·lar
scar
 scarred
 scar'ring
scar'ab
scar'a·mouch'
scarce'ly
scar'ci·ty
 ·ties
scare
 scared scar'ing
scare'crow'
scarf
 scarfs or scarves
 (long cloth)
scarf
 scarfs
 (joint; cut)
scar'i·fi·ca'tion
scar'i·fy'
 ·fied' ·fy'ing
scar'i·ness
scar'let
scarp
scar'y
 ·i·er ·i·est
scat
 scat'ted
 scat'ting
scathe
 scathed
 scath'ing
scat'ter
scat'ter·brain'
scav'enge
 ·enged ·eng·ing
scav'eng·er
sce·nar'i·o'
 ·os'
sce·nar'ist
scene
sce'ner·y
 ·ies

sce'nic
scent
 (odor; see sent)
scep'ter
sched'ule
 ·uled ·ul·ing
sche'ma
 ·ma·ta
sche·mat'ic
sche·mat'i·cal·ly
scheme
 schemed
 schem'ing
scher'zo
 ·zos or ·zi
schism
schis·mat'ic
schiz'oid
schiz'o·phre'ni·a
schiz'o·phren'ic
schnau'zer
schol'ar·ly
schol'ar·ship'
scho·las'tic
scho·las'ti·cal·ly
scho·las'ti·cism
school'boy'
school'girl'
school'house'
school'mate'
school'room'
school'teach'er
school'work'
schoon'er
schwa
sci·at'i·ca
sci'ence
sci'en·tif'ic
sci'en·tif'i·cal·ly
sci'en·tist
scim'i·tar
scin·til'la
scin'til·late'
 ·lat'ed ·lat'ing
scin'til·la'tor
sci'on
scis'sors
scle·ro'sis
scoff
scold'ing
sconce
scone
scoop'ful'
 ·fuls'
scoot'er
scope
scorch'ing
score
 scored scor'ing
score'less
scorn'ful
scor'pi·on
scot'-free'
scoun'drel
scour
scourge
 scourged
 scourg'ing

scout'mas'ter
scowl
scrab'ble
·bled ·bling
scrag'gly
·gli·er ·gli·est
scrag'gy
·gi·er ·gi·est
scram'ble
·bled ·bling
scrap
scrapped
scrap'ping
scrap'book'
scrape
scraped
scrap'ing
scrap'er
scrap'heap'
scrap'ple
scrap'py
·pi·er ·pi·est
scratch'i·ness
scratch'y
·i·er ·i·est
scrawl
scraw'ny
·ni·er ·ni·est
scream'ing
screech'y
screen'play'
screw'driv'er
scrib'ble
·bled ·bling
scrib'bler
scribe
scribed scrib'ing
scrim'mage
·maged ·mag·ing
scrimp'i·ness
scrimp'y
·i·er ·i·est
scrip
(certificate)
script
(manuscript)
scrip'tur·al
scrof'u·la
scroll'work'
scro'tum
·ta or ·tums
scrounge
scrounged
scroung'ing
scrub
scrubbed
scrub'bing
scrub'by
·bi·er ·bi·est
scruff
scrunch
scru'ple
·pled ·pling
scru'pu·lous
scru'ta·ble
scru'ti·nize'
·nized' ·niz'ing
scru'ti·ny

scu'ba
scuff
scuf'fle
·fled ·fling
scull
(oar; boat; see skull)
scul'ler·y
·ies
sculpt
sculp'tor
sculp'tur·al
sculp'ture
·tured ·tur·ing
scum'my
·mi·er ·mi·est
scup'per·nong'
scur·ril'i·ty
·ties
scur'ril·ous
scur'ry
·ried ·ry·ing
scur'vy
·vi·er ·vi·est
scut'tle
·tled ·tling
scythe
scythed
scyth'ing
sea'board'
sea'borne'
sea'coast'
sea'far'er
sea'far'ing
sea'food'
sea'go'ing
seal'ant
sea level
seal'skin'
seam
sea'man
seam'less
seam'stress
seam'y
·i·er ·i·est
sé'ance
sea'plane'
sea'port'
sear
(burn; see seer)
search'light'
sea'scape'
sea'shell'
sea'shore'
sea'sick'ness
sea'side'
sea'son
sea'son·a·ble
sea'son·al
seat belt
sea'ward
sea'way'
sea'weed'
sea'wor'thy
se·ba'ceous
se'cant
se·cede'
·ced'ed ·ced'ing

se·ces'sion
se·clude'
·clud'ed
·clud'ing
se·clu'sion
se·clu'sive
sec'ond
sec'ond·ar'i·ly
sec'ond·ar'y
sec'ond-class'
sec'ond-guess'
sec'ond-hand'
sec'ond-rate'
se'cre·cy
se'cret
sec're·tar'i·al
sec're·tar'i·at
sec're·tar'y
·ies
se·crete'
·cret'ed ·cret'ing
se·cre'tion
se'cre·tive
se·cre'to·ry
sect
sec·tar'i·an
sec'tion·al
sec'tion·al·ize'
·ized' ·iz'ing
sec'tor
sec'u·lar
sec'u·lar·ize'
·ized' ·iz'ing
se·cur'a·ble
se·cure'
·cured' ·cur'ing
se·cure'ly
se·cu'ri·ty
·ties
se·dan'
se·date'
·dat'ed ·dat'ing
se·date'ly
se·da'tion
sed'a·tive
sed'en·tar'y
sed'i·ment
sed'i·men'ta·ry
sed'i·men·ta'tion
se·di'tion
se·di'tious
se·duce'
·duced' ·duc'ing
se·duc'i·ble
se·duc'tion
se·duc'tive
se·du'li·ty
sed'u·lous
see
saw seen see'ing
seed'bed'
seed'i·ness
seed'ling
seed'y
·i·er ·i·est
seek
sought seek'ing
seem'ing·ly

seem'li·ness
seem'ly
·li·er ·li·est
seep'age
seer
(prophet; see sear)
seer'suck'er
see'saw'
seethe
seethed
seeth'ing
seg'ment
seg·men'tal
seg'men·ta'tion
seg're·gate'
·gat'ed ·gat'ing
seg're·ga'tion
seg're·ga'tion·ist
sei'del
seis'mic
seis'mi·cal·ly
seis'mo·graph'
seis·mog'ra·pher
seis·mol'o·gist
seis·mol'o·gy
seize
seized seiz'ing
sei'zure
sel'dom
se·lect'
se·lect'ee'
se·lec'tion
se·lec'tive
se·lec'tiv'i·ty
se·lec'tor
self
selves
self'-act'ing
self'-ad·dressed'
self'-ap·point'ed
self'-as·sur'ance
self'-as·sured'
self'-cen'tered
self'-con'fi·dence
self'-con'scious
self'-con·tained'
self'-con·trol'
self'-de·fense'
self'-dis'ci·pline
self'-driv'en
self'-ed'u·cat'ed
self'-em·ployed'
self'-es·teem'
self'-ev'i·dent
self'-ex·plan'a·to'ry
self'-ex·pres'sion
self'-gov'ern·ing
self'-im'age
self'-im·por'tant
self'-im·posed'
self'-im·prove'·ment
self'-in·duced'
self'-in·dul'gence
self'-in·flict'ed
self'-in'ter·est

self'ish
self'less
self'-load'ing
self'-love'
self'-made'
self'-pit'y
self'-por'trait
self'-pos·sessed'
self'-pres·er·va'·tion
self'-reg'u·lat'ing
self'-re·li'ance
self'-re·proach'
self'-re·spect'
self'-re·straint'
self'-right'eous
self'-ris'ing
self'-sac'ri·fice'
self'same'
self'-sat'is·fied'
self'-seal'ing
self'-serv'ice
self'-start'er
self'-styled'
self'-suf·fi'cient
self'-sup·port'
self'-taught'
self'-tor'ture
self'-willed'
self'-wind'ing
sell
sold sell'ing
sell'-off'
sell'out'
sel'vage or
vedge
se·man'tic
sem'a·phore'
·phored
·phor'ing
sem'blance
se'men
sem'i·na
se·mes'ter
sem'i·an'nu·al
sem'i·au'to·mat'ic
sem'i·cir'cle
sem'i·co'lon
sem'i·con·duc'tor
sem'i·con'scious
sem'i·de·tached'
sem'i·fi'nal
sem'i·for'mal
sem'i·month'ly
sem'i·nal
sem'i·nar'
sem'i·nar'y
·ies
sem'i·of·fi'cial
sem'i·pre'cious
sem'i·pri'vate
sem'i·pro·fes'·sion·al
sem'i·rig'id
sem'i·skilled'
sem'i·sol'id
Sem'ite

Se·mit'ic
sem'i·trail'er
sem'i·trop'i·cal
sem'i·week'ly
sem'i·year'ly
sem'o·li'na
sen'ate
sen'a·tor
sen'a·to'ri·al
send
sent send'ing
send'-off'
se·nes'cent
se'nile
se·nil'i·ty
sen'ior
sen·ior'i·ty
sen·sa'tion
sen·sa'tion·al·ly
sense
sensed sens'ing
sense'less
sen·si·bil'i·ty
·ties
sen'si·ble
sen'si·bly
sen'si·tive
sen·si·tiv'i·ty
sen·si·ti·za'tion
sen'si·tize'
·tized' ·tiz'ing
sen'so·ry
sen'su·al
sen'su·al'i·ty
sen'su·ous
sent
(transmitted; see scent)
sen'tence
·tenced ·tenc·ing
sen·ten'tious
sen'tient
sen'ti·ment
sen'ti·men'tal
sen'ti·men·tal'i·ty
sen'ti·men'tal·ize'
·ized' ·iz'ing
sen'ti·nel
·neled or ·nelled
·nel·ing or
·nel·ling
sen'try
·tries
sep'a·ra·ble
sep'a·rate'
·rat'ed ·rat'ing
sep'a·ra'tion
sep'a·ra·tism
sep'a·ra'tor
se'pi·a
Sep·tem'ber
sep·tet' or
·tette'
sep'tic
sep'tu·a·ge·nar'i·an

sep·tu'ple
 ·pled ·pling
sep'ul·cher
se·pul'chral
se'quel
se'quence
se·quen'tial
se·ques'ter
se'quin
se·quoi'a
se·ra'pe
ser'e·nade'
 ·nad'ed ·nad'ing
ser'en·dip'i·ty
se·rene'
se·ren'i·ty
serf
 (slave; see surf)
serge
 (fabric; see surge)
ser'geant
se'ri·al
 (in a series; see cereal)
se'ri·al·ize'
 ·ized' ·iz'ing
se'ries
 ·ries
ser'if
se'ri·o·com'ic
se'ri·ous
se'ri·ous-mind'ed
ser'mon
se'rous
ser'pent
ser'pen·tine'
ser·rate'
 ·rat'ed ·rat'ing
se'rum
 ·rums or ·ra
ser'vant
serve
 served serv'ing
serv'ice
 ·iced ·ic·ing
serv'ice·a·bil'i·ty
serv'ice·a·ble
serv'ice·a·bly
serv'ice·man'
ser'vi·ette'
ser'vile
ser·vil'i·ty
ser'vi·tor
ser'vi·tude'
ses'a·me'
ses'qui·cen·ten'·ni·al
ses'sion
 (meeting; see cession)
set
 set set'ting
set'back'
set'-in'
set'off'
set'screw'
set·tee'
set'ter

set'tle
 ·tled ·tling
set'tle·ment
set'tler
set'-to'
 ·tos'
sev'en·teen'
sev'enth
sev'en·ti·eth
sev'en·ty
 ·ties
sev'er
sev'er·al
sev'er·al·ly
sev'er·ance
se·vere'
se·vere'ly
se·ver'i·ty
 ·ties
sew
 sewed, sewn or
 sewed, sew'ing
 (stitch; see sow)
sew'age
sew'er
sew'er·age
sex'a·ge·nar'i·an
sex'i·ly
sex'i·ness
sex'less
sex'tant
sex·tet' or
 ·tette'
sex'ton
sex·tu'ple
 ·pled ·pling
sex·tu'plet
sex'u·al
sex·u·al'i·ty
sex'u·al·ly
sex'y
 ·i·er ·i·est
shab'bi·ly
shab'bi·ness
shab'by
 ·bi·er ·bi·est
shack'le
 ·led ·ling
shade
shad'ed
shad'ing
shad'i·ness
shad'ow
shad'ow·y
shad'y
 ·i·er ·i·est
shaft
shag
shagged
shag'ging
shag'gi·ness
shag'gy
 ·gi·er ·gi·est
shak'a·ble or
shake'a·ble
shake
shook shak'en
shak'ing

Shake'speare'
Shake·spear'e·an
 or ·i·an
shake'-up'
shak'i·ly
shak'i·ness
shak'y
 ·i·er ·i·est
shal'low
sha·lom'
sham
shammed
sham'ming
sham'ble
 ·bled ·bling
shame
shamed
sham'ing
shame'faced'
shame'ful
shame'ful·ly
shame'less
sham·poo'
 ·pooed' ·poo'ing
shang'hai
 ·haied ·hai·ing
shank
shan'tung'
shan'ty
 ·ties
shape
shaped shap'ing
shape'less
shape'li·ness
shape'ly
 ·li·er ·li·est
share
shared shar'ing
share'crop'per
share'hold'er
shark'skin'
sharp'en·er
sharp'-eyed'
sharp'shoot'er
sharp'-sight'ed
sharp'-tongued'
sharp'-wit'ted
shat'ter
shat'ter·proof'
shave
shaved, shaved or shav'en,
 shav'ing
shawl
sheaf
sheaves
shear
sheared, sheared or shorn,
 shear'ing
 (cut; see sheer)
shears
sheath
 (a case; dress)
sheathe
sheathed
sheath'ing
 (put into a sheath)

sheave
sheaved
sheav'ing
shed
 shed shed'ding
sheen
sheep'ish·ly
sheep'skin'
sheep'walk'
sheer
 (thin; steep; see shear)
sheet'ing
sheik or sheikh
shelf
 shelves
shell
shel·lac' or ·lack'
 ·lacked' ·lack'ing
shell'fish'
shell'-like'
shell'proof'
shel'ter
shelve
shelved
shelv'ing
she·nan'i·gan
shep'herd
sher'bet
sher'iff
sher'ry
 ·ries
shib'bo·leth
shield
shift'i·ly
shift'i·ness
shift'less
shift'y
 ·i·er ·i·est
shil·le'lagh or
shil·la'lah
shil'ly-shal'ly
 ·lied ·ly·ing
shim
shimmed
shim'ming
shim'mer·y
shim'my
 ·mies
 ·mied ·my·ing
shin
shinned
shin'ning
shine
shone or shined
shin'ing
shin'gle
 ·gled ·gling
shin'i·ness
shin'y
 ·i·er ·i·est
ship
shipped
ship'ping
ship'board'
ship'mate'
ship'ment

ship'own'er
ship'pa·ble
ship'per
ship'shape'
ship'wreck'
ship'wright'
ship'yard'
shirk'er
shirr'ing
shirt'waist'
shiv'a·ree'
 ·reed' ·ree'ing
shiv'er
shoal
shock'ing
shock'proof'
shod'di·ly
shod'di·ness
shod'dy
 ·di·er ·di·est
shoe
shod or shoed,
shod or shoed or shod'den,
shoe'ing
shoe'horn'
shoe'lace'
shoe'mak'er
sho'er
shoe'shine'
shoe'string'
shoe tree
shoo
shooed shoo'ing
shoot
shot shoot'ing
shop
shopped
shop'ping
shop'keep'er
shop'lift'er
shop'per
shop'talk'
shop'worn'
Shor'an or
 shor'-
shore'line'
shore'ward
shor'ing
short'age
short'bread'
short'cake'
short'change'
short'-cir'cuit
short'com'ing
short'cut'
short'en
short'en·ing
short'hand'
short'-hand'ed
short'horn'
short'-lived'
short'-range'
short'sight'ed
short'stop'
short'-tem'pered
short'-term'
short'-waist'ed

short'wave'
short'-wind'ed
shot'gun'
should
shoul'der
should'n't
shov'el
 ·eled or ·elled
 ·el·ing or ·el·ling
shov'el·ful'
 ·fuls'
show
showed, shown or showed,
show'ing
show'boat'
show'case'
show'down'
show'er
show'i·ly
show'i·ness
show'man
show'off'
show'piece'
show'place'
show'room'
show'y
 ·i·er ·i·est
shrap'nel
shred
shred'ded or shred
shred'ding
shrewd
shriek
shrill'ness
shrill'ly
shrine
shrink
shrank or shrunk,
shrunk or shrunk'en,
shrink'ing
shrink'age
shriv'el
 ·eled or ·elled
 ·el·ing or ·el·ling
shroud
shrub'ber·y
shrug
shrugged
shrug'ging
shuck
shud'der
shuf'fle
 ·fled ·fling
shuf'fle·board'
shun
shunned
shun'ning
shunt
shut
shut shut'ting
shut'down'
shut'-in'
shut'-off'
shut'out'
shut'ter

shut'tle
· tled · tling
shut'tle · cock'
shy
shy'er *or* shi'er
shy'est *or* shi'est
shies
shied shy'ing
Si'a · mese'
sib'i · lance
sib'i · lant
sib'ling
sick'bed'
sick'en
sick'le
sick'li · ness
sick'ly
· li · er · li · est
sick'room'
side
sid'ed sid'ing
side'arm'
side arms
side'board'
side'burns'
side'car'
side'light'
side'line'
side'long'
si · de're · al
side'sad'dle
side'show'
side'slip'
side'split'ting
side'step' *v.*
side'stroke'
side'swipe'
side'track'
side'walk'
side'ways'
side'wise'
sid'ing
si'dle
· dled · dling
siege
si · en'na
si · er'ra
si · es'ta
sieve
sieved siev'ing
sift'er
sigh
sight
(*view;* see
cite, site)
sight'less
sight'ly
· li · er · li · est
sight'see'ing
sight'se'er
sign
(*signal;* see sine)
sig'nal
· naled *or* · nalled
· nal · ing *or*
· nal · ling
sig'nal · ize'
· ized' · iz'ing

sig'nal · ly
sig'na · to'ry
· ries
sig'na · ture
sign'board'
sig'net
sig · nif'i · cance
sig · nif'i · cant
sig'ni · fi · ca'tion
sig'ni · fy'
· fied' · fy'ing
sign'post'
si'lage
si'lence
· lenced · lenc · ing
si'lenc · er
si'lent
si'lex
sil'hou · ette'
· et'ted · et'ting
sil'i · ca
sil'i · cate
si · li'ceous
sil'i · cone'
sil'i · co'sis
silk'en
silk'i · ness
silk'-screen'
silk'worm'
silk'y
· i · er · i · est
sil'li · ness
sil'ly
· lies, · li · er · li · est
si'lo
· los, · loed · lo · ing
sil'ver
sil'ver · fish'
silver plate
sil'ver · smith'
sil'ver-tongued'
sil'ver · ware'
sil'ver · y
sim'i · an
sim'i · lar
sim'i · lar'i · ty
· ties
sim'i · le'
si · mil'i · tude'
sim'mer
si'mon-pure'
sim'per
sim'ple
· pler · plest
sim'ple-mind'ed
sim'ple · ton
sim · plic'i · ty
· ties
sim'pli · fi · ca'tion
sim'pli · fi'er
sim'pli · fy'
· fied' · fy'ing
sim'ply
sim'u · lant
sim'u · late'
· lat'ed · lat'ing
sim'u · la'tion
sim'u · la'tor

si'mul · cast'
· cast' *or* · cast'ed
· cast'ing
si'mul · ta'ne · ous
sin
sinned sin'ning
sin · cere'
· cer'er · cer'est
sin · cere'ly
sin · cer'i · ty
sine
(*ratio;* see sign)
si'ne · cure'
sin'ew · y
sin'ful
sing
sang sung
sing'ing
singe
singed
singe'ing
sin'gle
· gled · gling
sin'gle-breast'ed
sin'gle-hand'ed
sin'gle-space'
sin'gle · ton
sin'gly
sing'song'
sin'gu · lar
sin'gu · lar'i · ty
sin'gu · lar · ize'
· ized' · iz'ing
sin'is · ter
sink
sank *or* sunk,
sunk sink'ing
sin'ner
sin'u · ous
si'nus
si'nus · i'tis
sip
sipped sip'ping
si'phon
sire
sired sir'ing
si'ren
sir'loin
si · roc'co
· cos
si'sal
sis'ter · hood'
sis'ter-in-law'
sis'ters-in-law'
sis'ter · li · ness
sis'ter · ly
sit
sat sit'ting
si · tar'
sit'-down'
site
(*place;* see sight)
sit'-in'
sit'ter
sit'u · ate'
· at'ed · at'ing
sit'u · a'tion
sit'-up' *or* sit'up'

sitz bath
six'fold'
six'pen'ny
six'teenth'
sixth
six'ti · eth
six'ty
· ties
siz'a · ble *or*
size'·
size
sized siz'ing
siz'zle
· zled · zling
skate
skat'ed skat'ing
skein
skel'e · ton
skep'tic
skep'ti · cal
skep'ti · cal · ly
skep'ti · cism
sketch'book'
sketch'i · ly
sketch'i · ness
sketch'y
· i · er · i · est
skew'er
ski
skis *or* ski
skied ski'ing
skid
skid'ded
skid'ding
ski'er
skil'let
skill'ful
skim
skimmed
skim'ming
skimp'i · ly
skimp'i · ness
skimp'y
· i · er · i · est
skin
skinned
skin'ning
skin'-deep'
skin'flint'
skin'ni · ness
skin'ny
· ni · er · ni · est
skip
skipped
skip'ping
ski'plane'
skip'per
skir'mish
skit'tish
skul · dug'ger · y
or skull · ·
skulk
skull
(*head;* see scull)
skull'cap'
sky
skies
sky'cap'

sky'-dive'
· dived' · div'ing
sky'-high'
sky'lark'
sky'light'
sky'line'
sky'rock'et
sky'scrap'er
sky'ward
sky'ways'
sky'writ'ing
slack'en
slack'er
slake
slaked slak'ing
sla'lom
slam
slammed
slam'ming
slan'der
slan'der · ous
slang'y
· i · er · i · est
slant'wise'
slap
slapped
slap'ping
slap'dash'
slap'stick'
slash
slate
slat'ed slat'ing
slat'tern
slaugh'ter
slave
slaved slav'ing
slav'er
slav'er · y
slav'ish · ly
slay
slew slain
slay'ing
(*kill;* see sleigh)
slea'zi · ness
slea'zy
· zi · er · zi · est
sled
sled'ded
sled'ding
sledge
sledged
sledg'ing
sleek'ly
sleep
slept sleep'ing
sleep'i · ly
sleep'i · ness
sleep'less
sleep'walk'ing
sleep'y
· i · er · i · est
sleet
sleeve'less
sleigh
(*snow vehicle;*
see slay)
sleight
(*skill;* see slight)

slen'der
slen'der · ize'
· ized' · iz'ing
sleuth
slew *or* slue
(*a lot;* see slue)
slice
sliced slic'ing
slick'er
slide
slid slid'ing
slide rule
slight
(*frail;* see
sleight)
slim
slim'mer
slim'mest
slimmed
slim'ming
slim'i · ness
slim'ness
slim'y
· i · er · i · est
sling
slung sling'ing
sling'shot'
slink
slunk slink'ing
slip
slipped slip'ping
slip'cov'er
slip'knot'
slip'-on'
slip'page
slip'per · i · ness
slip'per · y
· i · er · i · est
slip'shod'
slip'stream'
slip'-up'
slit
slit slit'ting
slith'er
sliv'er
sli'vo · vitz'
slob'ber
sloe
(*fruit;* see slow)
sloe'-eyed'
slog
slogged
slog'ging
slo'gan
sloop
slop
slopped
slop'ping
slope
sloped slop'ing
slop'pi · ly
slop'pi · ness
slop'py
· pi · er · pi · est
slosh
slot
slot'ted slot'ting
sloth'ful

slouch'y
· i·er · i·est
slough
slov'en·li·ness
slov'en·ly
· li·er · li·est
slow
(not fast; see
sloe)
slow'-wit'ted
sludge
sludg'y
· i·er · i·est
slue or slew
slued or slewed
slu'ing or
slew'ing
(turn; see slew)
slug
slugged
slug'ging
slug'gard
slug'gish
sluice
sluiced sluic'ing
slum
slummed
slum'ming
slum'ber
slum'ber·ous
slump
slur
slurred
slur'ring
slush'y
· i·er · i·est
slut'tish
sly
sli'er or sly'er
sli'est or sly'est
sly'ly or sli'ly
smack
small'-mind'ed
small'pox'
small'-scale'
smart
smash'up'
smat'ter·ing
smear'i·ness
smear'y
· i·er · i·est
smell
smelled or smelt
smell'ing
smell'i·ness
smell'y
· i·er · i·est
smidg'en
smile
smiled smil'ing
smirch
smirk
smite
smote, smit'ten
or smote,
smit'ing
smock'ing
smog

smog'gy
· gi·er · gi·est
smok'a·ble or
smoke'a·ble
smoke
smoked
smok'ing
smok'er
smoke screen
smoke'stack'
smok'i·ness
smok'y
· i·er · i·est
smol'der
smooth
smooth'bore'
smooth'-faced'
smooth'-shav'en
smooth'-spo'ken
smor'gas·bord'
smoth'er
smudge
smudged
smudg'ing
smudg'i·ness
smudg'y
· i·er · i·est
smug
smug'ger
smug'gest
smug'gle
· gled · gling
smut'ty
· ti·er · ti·est
snack bar
snaf'fle
· fled · fling
sna·fu'
snag
snagged
snag'ging
snail'-paced'
snake
snaked snak'ing
snak'y
· i·er · i·est
snap
snapped
snap'ping
snap'drag·on
snap'pish
snap'shot'
snare
snared snar'ing
snarl'y
· i·er · i·est
snatch
sneak'i·ly
sneak'i·ness
sneak'y
· i·er · i·est
sneer'ing·ly
sneeze
sneezed
sneez'ing
snick'er
snif'fle
· fled · fling

snif'ter
snip
snipped
snip'ping
snipe
sniped snip'ing
sniv'el
·eled or ·elled
·el·ing or
·el·ling
snob'ber·y
snob'bish
snoop'er·scope'
snore
snored snor'ing
snor'kel
snout
snow'ball'
snow'-blind'
snow'bound'
snow'drift'
snow'fall'
snow'flake'
snow line
snow'mo·bile'
· biled' · bil'ing
snow'plow'
snow'shoe'
· shoed'
· shoe'ing
snow'storm'
snow'-white'
snow'y
· i·er · i·est
snub
snubbed
snub'bing
snub'-nosed'
snuff'ers
snuf'fle
· fled · fling
snug
snug'ger
snug'gest
snug'gle
· gled · gling
soak'ers
soap'box'
soap'suds'
soap'y
· i·er · i·est
soar
(fly; see sore)
sob
sobbed
sob'bing
so'ber-mind'ed
so·bri'e·ty
so'bri·quet'
so'-called'
soc'cer
so'cia·bil'i·ty
so'cia·ble
so'cia·bly
so'cial
so'cial·ism
so'cial·ite'
so'cial·i·za'tion

so'cial·ize'
· ized' iz'ing
so·ci'e·tal
so·ci'e·tal·ly
so·ci'e·ty
· ties
so'ci·o·cul'tu·ral
so'ci·o·e'co·
nom'ic
so'ci·o·gram'
so'ci·o·log'i·cal
so'ci·ol'o·gist
so'ci·ol'o·gy
so'ci·o·path'
so'ci·o·po·lit'i·cal
sock'et
sock'eye'
sod
sod'ded sod'ding
so·dal'i·ty
· ties
sod'den·ness
sod'om·y
soft'ball'
soft'-boiled'
soft'-cov'er
sof'ten·er
soft'heart'ed
soft'-shell'
soft'-spo'ken
soft'ware'
sog'gi·ness
sog'gy
· gi·er · gi·est
soil
soi·ree' or ·rée'
so'journ
sol'ace
· aced · ac·ing
so'lar
so·lar'i·um
· lar'i·a
sol'der
(metal alloy)
sol'dier
(man in an army)
sole
soled sol'ing
(bottom surface;
only; see soul)
sol'e·cism
sole'ly
sol'emn
so·lem'ni·fy'
· fied' · fy'ing
so·lem'ni·ty
· ties
sol'em·nize'
· nized' · niz'ing
so'le·noid'
sole'plate'
so·lic'it
so·lic'i·ta'tion
so·lic'i·tor
so·lic'i·tous
so·lic'i·tude'
sol'id
sol'i·dar'i·ty

so·lid'i·fi·ca'tion
so·lid'i·fy'
· fied' · fy'ing
sol'id-state'
so·lil'o·quize'
· quized'
quiz'ing
so·lil'o·quy
· quies
sol'i·taire'
sol'i·tar'y
sol'i·tude'
so'lo
· los
sol'stice
sol'u·bil'i·ty
sol'u·ble
sol'ute
so·lu'tion
solv'a·bil'i·ty
solv'a·ble
solve
solved
solv'ing
sol'ven·cy
sol'vent
som'ber
som·bre'ro
· ros
some'bod'y
some'day'
some'how'
some'one'
som'er·sault'
some'thing
some'time'
some'times'
some'what'
some'where'
som·nam'bu·late'
· lat'ed · lat'ing
som'no·lent
so'nar
so·na'ta
sonde
song'ster
son'ic
son'-in-law'
sons'-in-law'
son'net
son'net·eer'
so·nor'i·ty
so·no'rous
soon'er
soothe
soothed
sooth'ing
sooth'say'er
soot'i·ness
soot'y
· i·er · i·est
sop
sopped
sop'ping
soph'ism
soph'ist
so·phis'ti·cal

so·phis'ti·cate'
· cat'ed · cat'ing
so·phis'ti·ca'tion
soph'is·try
· tries
soph'o·more'
soph'o·mor'ic
sop'o·rif'ic
so·pra'no
· nos or · ni
sor'cer·er
sor'cer·y
· ies
sor'did
sore
(painful; see
soar)
sore'ly
sor'ghum
so·ror'i·ty
· ties
sor'rel
sor'ri·ly
sor'ri·ness
sor'row
sor'row·ful
sor'ry
· ri·er · ri·est
sor'tie
so'-so'
sou·brette'
souf·flé'
soul
(spirit; see sole)
soul'ful
soul'-search'ing
sound'proof'
soup·çon'
source'book'
sour'dough'
sour'ness
sou'sa·phone'
souse
soused sous'ing
South Caro·li'na
South Da·ko'ta
south'east'
south'east'er·ly
south'east'ern
south'east'ward
south'er·ly
south'ern
south'ern·er
south'ern·most'
south'ward
south'west'
south'west'er·ly
south'west'ern
south'west'ward
sou've·nir'
sov'er·eign
sov'er·eign·ty
· ties
so'vi·et
sow
sowed, sown or
sowed, sow'ing
(plant; see sew)

soy'bean'
space
  spaced spac'ing
space'craft'
  ·craft'
space'flight'
space'man
space'port'
space'ship'
space'suit'
space'walk'
spa'cious
spack'le
  ·led ·ling
spade
spad'ed
spad'ing
spade'work'
spa·ghet'ti
span
spanned
span'ning
span'dex
span'drel
span'gle
  ·gled ·gling
span'iel
span'sule
spar
sparred
spar'ring
spare
spared spar'ing
spare'ribs'
spar'kle
  ·kled ·kling
spar'kler
spar'row
sparse'ly
spasm
spas·mod'ic
spas·mod'i·cal·ly
spas'tic
spa'tial
spat'ter
spat'u·la
spawn
spay
speak
  spoke spo'ken
speak'ing
speak'er
spear'head'
spear'mint'
spe'cial
spe'cial·ist
spe'cial·ize'
  ·ized' iz'ing
spe'cial·ly
spe'cial·ty
  ·ties
spe'cie
  (coin money)
spe'cies
  ·cies
  (kind)
spec'i·fi'a·ble
spe·cif'ic

spe·cif'i·cal·ly
spec'i·fi·ca'tion
spec'i·fy'
  ·fied' ·fy'ing
spec'i·men
spe'cious
speck'le
  ·led ·ling
spec'ta·cle
spec'ta·cled
spec·tac'u·lar
spec'ta·tor
spec'ter
spec'tral
spec'tro·scope'
spec·tros'co·py
spec'trum
  ·tra or ·trums
spec'u·late'
  ·lat'ed ·lat'ing
spec'u·la'tion
spec'u·la'tive
spec'u·la'tor
speech'less
speed
  sped or speed'ed
speed'ing
speed'boat'
speed'i·ly
speed'i·ness
speed·om'e·ter
speed'up'
speed'y
  ·i·er ·i·est
spe·le·ol'o·gy
spell
  spelled or spelt
spell'ing
  (name the letters)
spell
  spelled spell'ing
  (work in place of)
spell'bind'
  ·bound' ·bind'ing
spell'down'
spe·lunk'er
spend
  spent spend'ing
spend'thrift'
sper'ma·ce'ti
spew
sphere
spher'i·cal
sphe'roid
sphinx
sphinx'es or
  sphin'ges
spice
spiced spic'ing
spic'i·ness
spick'-and-span'
spic'y
  ·i·er ·i·est
spi'der
spi'er
spig'ot
spike
spiked spik'ing

spill
spilled or spilt
spill'ing
spin
spun spin'ning
spin'ach
spi'nal
spin'dle
  ·dled ·dling
spin'dly
  ·dli·er dli·est
spin'drift'
spine'less
spin'et
spin'ner
spin'off'
spin'ster
spin'y
  ·i·er ·i·est
spi'ral
  ·raled or ·ralled
  ·ral·ing or
  ·ral·ling
spir'it·less
spir'it·u·al
spir'it·u·ous
spit
spit'ted
spit'ting
  (impale)
spit
spit or spat
spit'ting
  (eject saliva)
spite
spit'ed
spit'ing
spite'ful
spit'fire'
spit'tle
spit·toon'
spitz
splash'down'
splat'ter
splay'foot'
  ·feet'
spleen'ful
splen'did
splen'dor
sple·net'ic
splice
spliced
splic'ing
splin'ter
split
split split'ting
split'-lev'el
split'-up'
splotch
splurge
splurged
splurg'ing
splut'ter
spoil
spoiled or spoilt
spoil'ing
spoil'age
spoil'sport'

spoke
spoked spok'ing
spoke'shave'
spokes'man
spo'li·a'tion
sponge
sponged
spong'ing
sponge'cake'
spon'gi·ness
spon'gy
  ·gi·er ·gi·est
spon'sor
spon'ta·ne'i·ty
  ·ties
spon·ta'ne·ous
spoon'er·ism
spoon'-feed'
  -fed' -feed'ing
spoon'ful'
  ·fuls'
spo·rad'ic
sport'ing
spor'tive
sports'man
sports'wear'
spot
spot'ted
spot'ting
spot'-check'
spot'light'
spot'ti·ness
spot'ty
  ·ti·er ·ti·est
spout'less
sprain
sprawl
spray
spread
spread
spread'ing
sprig
sprigged
sprig'ging
spright'li·ness
spright'ly
  ·li·er ·li·est
spring
  sprang or
  sprung, sprung,
  spring'ing
spring'board'
spring'i·ness
spring'time'
spring'y
  ·i·er ·i·est
sprin'kle
  ·kled ·kling
sprin'kler
sprint'er
spritz
sprock'et
sprout
spruce
spruc'er
spruc'est
spruced
spruc'ing

spry
spri'er or spry'er
spri'est or
spry'est
spry'ly
spry'ness
spume
spumed
spum'ing
spu·mo'ni or ·ne
spur
spurred
spur'ring
spu'ri·ous
spurn
spurt
sput'nik
sput'ter
spu'tum
spy
spies
spied spy'ing
spy'glass'
squab'ble
  ·bled ·bling
squab'bler
squad'ron
squal'id
squall
squal'or
squan'der
square
squared
squar'ing
square'-rigged'
squar'ish
squash'i·ness
squash'y
  ·i·er ·i·est
squat
squat'ted
squat'ting
squawk
squeak'i·ly
squeak'y
  ·i·er ·i·est
squeal'er
squeam'ish
squee'gee
  ·geed ·gee·ing
squeez'a·ble
squeeze
squeezed
squeez'ing
squelch
squig'gle
  ·gled ·gling
squint'-eyed'
squire
squired
squir'ing
squirm'y
  ·i·er ·i·est
squir'rel
squirt
stab
stabbed
stab'bing

sta·bil'i·ty
sta'bi·li·za'tion
sta'bi·lize'
  ·lized' ·liz'ing
sta'bi·liz'er
sta'ble
  ·bled ·bling
sta'bly
stac·ca'to
  ·tos
stack'up'
sta'di·um
  ·di·a or di·ums
staff
  staffs or staves
  (stick; music)
  staffs
  (people)
stage
staged
stag'ing
stage'craft'
stage'hand'
stage'-struck'
stag'ger
stag'nan·cy
stag'nant
stag'nate
  ·nat·ed ·nat·ing
stag·na'tion
stag'y
  ·i·er ·i·est
staid
  (sober; see stay)
stain'less
stair'case'
stake
staked
stak'ing
  (post; share;
  see steak)
stake'hold'er
stake'out'
sta·lac'tite
sta·lag'mite
stale
stal'er stal'est
staled stal'ing
stale'mate'
  ·mat'ed ·mat'ing
stalk'ing-horse'
stall
stal'lion
stal'wart
stam'i·na
stam'mer
stam·pede'
  ·ped'ed ·ped'ing
stance
stan'chion
stand
stood stand'ing
stand'ard
stand'ard-bear'er
stand'ard·i·
  za'tion
stand'ard·ize'
  ·ized' ·iz'ing

stand'by'
 ·bys'
stand·ee'
stand'-in'
stand'off'
stand'pat'
stand'point'
stand'still'
stand'-up'
stan'za
staph'y·lo·coc'cus
 ·coc'ci
sta'ple
 ·pled ·pling
sta'pler
star
 starred
 star'ring
star'board
starch'i·ness
starch'y
 ·i·er ·i·est
star'dom
stare
 stared
 star'ing
star'gaze'
 ·gazed' ·gaz'ing
stark'-nak'ed
star'let
star'light'
star'lit'
star'ry
 ·ri·er ·ri·est
star'-span'gled
start'er
star'tle
 ·tled ·tling
star·va'tion
starve
 starved
 starv'ing
starve'ling
stat'a·ble
state
 stat'ed stat'ing
State'hood'
state'li·ness
state'ly
 ·li·er ·li·est
state'ment
state'room'
states'man
state'-wide'
stat'ic
stat'i·cal·ly
sta'tion
sta'tion·ar'y
 (not moving)
sta'tion·er
sta'tion·er'y
 (writing paper)
sta·tis'tic
sta·tis'ti·cal
sta·tis'ti·cal·ly
stat'is·ti'cian
stat'u·ar'y
 ·ies

stat'ue
stat'u·esque'
stat'u·ette'
stat'ure
sta'tus
sta'tus quo'
stat'ute
stat'u·to'ry
staunch
stave
staved or stove
stav'ing
stay
stayed stay'ing
 (stop; see staid)
stead'fast'
stead'i·ly
stead'i·ness
stead'y
 ·i·er ·i·est
 ·ied ·y·ing
steak
 (meat; see stake)
steal
 stole stol'en
 steal'ing
stealth'i·ly
stealth'y
 ·i·er ·i·est
steam'boat'
steam'er
steam'roll'er
steam'ship'
steam shovel
steam'y
 ·i·er ·i·est
steel mill
steel wool
steel'work'er
steel'yard'
stee'ple
stee'ple·chase'
stee'ple·jack'
steer'age·way'
steers'man
stein
stel'lar
stem
 stemmed
 stem'ming
stem'-wind'ing
sten'cil
 ·ciled or ·cilled
 ·cil·ing or
 ·cil·ling
ste·nog'ra·pher
sten'o·graph'ic
ste·nog'ra·phy
sten'o·type'
sten'o·typ'ist
sten'o·typ'y
sten·to'ri·an
step
 stepped
 step'ping
step'broth'er
step'child'
 ·chil'dren

step'daugh'ter
step'-down'
step'fa'ther
step'lad'der
step'moth'er
step'par'ent
steppe
 (treeless plain)
stepped'-up'
step'ping·stone'
step'sis'ter
step'son'
step'-up'
ster'e·o'
ster'e·o·phon'ic
ster'e·op'ti·con
ster'e·o·scope'
ster'e·o·scop'ic
ster'e·o·type'
 ·typed' ·typ'ing
ster'e·o·typ'ic
ster'ile
ste·ril'i·ty
ster'i·li·za'tion
ster'i·lize'
 ·lized' ·liz'ing
ster'ling
stern'ness
stern'-wheel'er
stet
stet'ted
stet'ting
steth'o·scope'
ste've·dore'
stew'ard
stew'ard·ess
stick
 stuck stick'ing
stick'i·ness
stick'le
 ·led ·ling
stick'ler
stick'pin'
stick-to'-it·ive·
 ness
stick'y
 ·i·er ·i·est
stiff'en
stiff'-necked'
sti'fle
 ·fled ·fling
stig'ma
 ·mas or ·ma·ta
stig'ma·tize'
 ·tized' ·tiz'ing
stile
 (steps; see style)
sti·let'to
 ·tos or ·toes
still'born'
still life
still'y
stilt'ed
stim'u·lant
stim'u·late'
 ·lat'ed ·lat'ing
stim'u·la'tion
stim'u·la'tive

stim'u·lus
 ·li'
sting
 stung sting'ing
stin'gi·ly
stin'gi·ness
stin'gy
 ·gi·er ·gi·est
stink
 stank or stunk,
 stunk stink'ing
stint'ing·ly
sti'pend
sti·pen'di·ar'y
 ·ar'ies
stip'ple
 ·pled ·pling
stip'u·late'
 ·lat'ed ·lat'ing
stip'u·la'tion
stip'u·la'tor
stir
 stirred stir'ring
stir'rup
stitch
stock·ade'
 ·ad'ed ·ad'ing
stock'bro'ker
stock'hold'er
stock'i·ness
stock'i·nette' or
 ·net'
stock'ing
stock'pile'
stock'room'
stock'-still'
stock'y
 ·i·er ·i·est
stock'yard'
stodg'i·ness
stodg'y
 ·i·er ·i·est
sto'gie or ·gy
 ·gies
sto'ic
sto'i·cal
sto'i·cism
stoke
 stoked stok'ing
stoke'hole'
stok'er
stole
stol'en
 (pp. of steal)
stol'id
stol'len
 (sweet bread)
stom'ach
stom'ach·ache'
stone
 stoned ston'ing
stone'-blind'
stone'cut'ter
stone'-deaf'
stone'ma'son
stone'ware'
stone'work'
ston'i·ly

ston'y
 ·i·er ·i·est
stoop
 (porch; bend;
 see stoup)
stop
 stopped
 stop'ping
stop'cock'
stop'gap'
stop'light'
stop'o'ver
stop'page
stop'per
stop'ple
 ·pled ·pling
stop'watch'
stor'a·ble
stor'age
store
 stored stor'ing
store'house'
store'keep'er
store'room'
storm'bound'
storm door
storm'i·ly
storm'i·ness
storm'y
 ·i·er ·i·est
sto'ry
 ·ries
 ·ried ·ry·ing
sto'ry·tell'er
stoup
 (basin; see
 stoop)
stout'heart'ed
stove'pipe'
stow'a·way'
stra·bis'mus
strad'dle
 ·dled ·dling
Strad'i·var'i·us
strafe
 strafed straf'ing
strag'gle
 ·gled ·gling
strag'gler
straight
 (not bent;
 see strait)
straight'a·way'
straight'edge'
straight'ened
 (made straight;
 see straitened)
straight'-faced'
straight'for'ward
strain'er
strait
 (waterway; see
 straight)
strait'ened
 (limited; see
 straightened)
strait'jack'et
strait'-laced'

strange
strang'er
strang'est
strange'ly
stran'ger
stran'gle
 gled ·gling
stran'gle·hold'
stran'gu·late'
 ·lat'ed ·lat'ing
stran·gu·la'tion
strap
 strapped
 strap'ping
strat'a·gem
stra·te'gic
stra·te'gi·cal·ly
strat'e·gist
strat'e·gy
 ·gies
strat'i·fi·ca'tion
strat'i·fy'
 ·fied' ·fy'ing
strat'o·sphere'
stra'tum
 ·ta or ·tums
stra'tus
 ·ti
straw'ber'ry
 ·ries
stray
streak'i·ness
streak'y
 ·i·er ·i·est
stream'line'
 ·lined' ·lin'ing
street'car'
strength'en
stren'u·ous
strep'to·coc'cal
strep'to·coc'cus
 ·coc'ci
strep'to·my'cin
stretch'er
stretch'i·ness
stretch'y
 ·i·er ·i·est
streu'sel
strew
 strewed, strewed
 or strewn,
 strew'ing
stri'ate
 ·at·ed ·at·ing
stri·a'tion
strict'ly
stric'ture
stride
 strode strid'den
strid'ing
stri'dent
strid'u·late'
 ·lat'ed ·lat'ing
strife
strike
 struck, struck or
 strick'en,
 strik'ing

strike'break'er
string
strung
string'ing
strin'gen·cy
·cies
strin'gent
string'halt'
string'i·ness
string'y
·i·er ·i·est
strip
stripped
strip'ping
stripe
striped
strip'ing
strip'ling
strip'tease'
strive
strove *or* strived,
striv'en *or*
strived, striv'ing
strobe
stroke
stroked
strok'ing
stroll'er
strong'-arm'
strong'box'
strong'hold'
strong'-mind'ed
strong'-willed'
stron'ti·um
strop
stropped
strop'ping
struc'tur·al
struc'ture
·tured ·tur·ing
stru'del
strug'gle
·gled ·gling
strum
strummed
strum'ming
strut
strut'ted
strut'ting
strych'nine
stub
stubbed
stub'bing
stub'ble
stub'bly
·bli·er ·bli·est
stub'born
stub'by
·bi·er ·bi·est
stuc'co
·coes *or* ·cos
·coed ·co·ing
stud
stud'ded
stud'ding
stud'book'
stu'dent
stud'horse'

stu'di·o'
·os'
stu'di·ous
stud'y
·ies, ·ied ·y·ing
stuff'i·ness
stuff'y
·i·er ·i·est
stul'ti·fy'
·fied' ·fy'ing
stum'ble
·bled ·bling
stun
stunned
stun'ning
stu'pe·fac'tion
stu'pe·fy'
·fied' ·fy'ing
stu·pen'dous
stu'pid
stu·pid'i·ty
·ties
stu'por
stur'di·ly
stur'di·ness
stur'dy
·di·er ·di·est
stur'geon
stut'ter
stut'ter·er
sty
sties
stied sty'ing
(*pig pen*)
sty *or* stye
sties
(*eyelid swelling*)
style
styled styl'ing
(*mode;* see stile)
style'book'
styl'ish
styl'ist
sty·lis'tic
styl'i·za'tion
styl'ize
·ized ·iz·ing
sty'lus
·lus·es *or* ·li
sty'mie
·mied ·mie·ing
styp'tic
sty'rene
Sty'ro·foam'
su'a·ble
sua'sion
suave
suave'ly
suav'i·ty
sub'as·sem'bly
sub'base'ment
sub'com·mit'tee
sub·con'scious
sub·con'tract
sub'cul'ture
sub'cu·ta'ne·ous
sub·di·vide'
sub·di·vi'sion

sub·due'
·dued' ·du'ing
sub'gum'
sub'ject
sub·jec'tive
sub'jec·tiv'i·ty
sub·join'der
sub'ju·gate'
·gat'ed ·gat'ing
sub'ju·ga'tion
sub'ju·ga'tor
sub·junc'tive
sub'lease'
sub·let'
·let' ·let'ting
sub'li·mate'
·mat'ed ·mat'ing
sub'li·ma'tion
sub·lime'
·limed' ·lim'ing
sub·lim'i·nal
sub·lim'i·ty
·ties
sub·mar'gin·al
sub'ma·rine'
sub·merge'
·merged'
·mer'gence
sub·mer'gi·ble
sub·merse'
·mersed'
·mers'ing
sub·mers'i·ble
sub·mer'sion
sub·mis'sion
sub·mis'sive
sub·mit'
·mit'ted
·mit'ting
sub·nor'mal
sub'nor·mal'i·ty
sub·or'di·nate'
·nat'ed ·nat'ing
sub·or'di·na'tion
sub'or·na'tion
sub'plot'
sub·poe'na
·naed ·na·ing
sub ro'sa
sub·scribe'
·scribed'
·scrib'ing
sub'script
sub·scrip'tion
sub'se·quent
sub·ser'vi·ent
sub·side'
·sid'ed ·sid'ing
sub·sid'i·ar'y
·ies
sub'si·di·za'tion
sub'si·dize'
·dized' ·diz'ing
sub'si·dy
·dies
sub·sist'ence
sub'soil'
sub'stance
sub·stand'ard
sub·stan'tial

sub·stan'tial·ly
sub·stan'ti·ate'
·at'ed ·at'ing
sub·stan'ti·a'tion
sub'stan·ti'val
sub'stan·tive
sub·sta'tion
sub'sti·tut'a·ble
sub'sti·tute'
·tut'ed ·tut'ing
sub'sti·tu'tion
sub·stra'tum
·ta *or* ·tums
sub·struc'tur·al
sub·struc'ture
sub'ter·fuge'
sub·ter·ra'ne·an
sub'ti·tle
sub'tle
·tler ·tlest
sub'tle·ty
·ties
sub'tly
sub·tract'
sub·trac'tion
sub'tra·hend'
sub·trop'i·cal
sub'urb
sub·ur'ban
sub·ur'ban·ite'
sub·ur'bi·a
sub·ver'sion
sub·ver'sive
sub·vert'
sub'way'
suc·ceed'
suc·cess'
suc·cess'ful
suc·cess'ful·ly
suc·ces'sion
suc·ces'sive
suc·ces'sor
suc·cinct'
suc'cor
(*help;* see sucker)
suc'co·tash'
suc'cu·lence
suc'cu·lent
suc·cumb'
suck'er
(*one that sucks;*
see succor)
suck'le
·led ·ling
su'crose
suc'tion
sud'den·ly
sud'den·ness
su'dor·if'ic
suds'y
·i·er ·i·est
sue
sued su'ing
suede *or* suède
su'et
suf'fer
suf'fer·ance
suf'fer·ing

suf·fice'
·ficed' ·fic'ing
suf·fi'cien·cy
suf·fi'cient
suf'fix
suf'fo·cate'
·cat'ed ·cat'ing
suf'fo·ca'tion
suf'frage
suf'fra·gette'
suf'fra·gist
suf·fuse'
·fused' ·fus'ing
suf·fu'sion
sug'ar
sug'ar·coat'
sug'ar-cured'
sug'ar·plum'
sug'ar·y
sug·gest'
sug·gest'i·ble
sug·ges'tion
sug·ges'tive
su'i·ci'dal
su'i·cide'
suit
(*set;* see suite)
suit'a·bil'i·ty
suit'a·ble
suit'a·bly
suit'case'
suite
(*rooms; furniture;*
see suit, sweet)
suit'or
su'ki·ya'ki
sul'fa
sul'fur
sulk'y
·i·er ·i·est
sul'len
sul'ly
·lied ·ly·ing
sul'tan
sul·tan'a
sul'tri·ness
sul'try
·tri·er ·tri·est
sum
summed
sum'ming
su'mac
sum·mar'i·ly
sum'ma·rize'
·rized' ·riz'ing
sum'ma·ry
·ries
(*brief account*)
sum·ma'tion
sum'mer·time'
sum'mer·y
(*like summer*)
sum'mit
sum'mon
sum'mons
·mons·es
sump'tu·ar'y
sump'tu·ous

sun
sunned sun'ning
sun bath
sun'bathe'
·bathed' ·bath'ing
sun'bath'er
sun'beam'
sun'burn'
sun'burst'
sun'-cured'
sun'dae
Sun'day
sun'di'al
sun'down'
sun'-dried'
sun'dries
sun'dry
sun'glass'es
sunk'en
sun'lamp'
sun'light'
sun'lit'
sun'ni·ness
sun'ny
·ni·er ·ni·est
sun'proof'
sun'rise'
sun'set'
sun'shade'
sun'shine'
sun'spot'
sun'stroke'
sun'tan'
sun'-tanned'
sup
supped sup'ping
su·perb'
su'per·car'go
·goes *or* ·gos
su'per·charge'
su'per·cil'i·ous
su'per·e'go
su'per·fi'cial
su'per·fi'ci·al'i·ty
·ties
su'per·fi'cial·ly
su'per·fine'
su'per·flu'i·ty
·ties
su·per'flu·ous
su'per·het'er·
o·dyne'
su'per·hu'man
su'per·im·pose'
su'per·in·duce'
su'per·in·tend'ent
su·pe'ri·or
su·pe'ri·or'i·ty
su·per'la·tive
su'per·man'
su'per·mar'ket
su'per·nat'u·ral
su'per·nu'mer·
ar'y
·ar·ies
su'per·scribe'
su'per·script'
su'per·scrip'tion

su·per·sede'
· sed'ed · sed'ing
su·per·se'dure
su·per·sen'si·tive
su·per·ses'sion
su·per·son'ic
su·per·sti'tion
su·per·sti'tious
su·per·struc'ture
su·per·vene'
· vened'
· ven'ing
su'per·ven'tion
su'per·vise'
· vised' · vis'ing
su·per·vi'sion
su·per·vi'sor
su·per·vi'so·ry
su·pine'
sup'per
sup·plant'
sup'ple
sup'ple·ly
sup'ple·ment
sup'ple·men'tal
sup'ple·men'ta·ry
sup'ple·men·
ta'tion
sup'pli·ant
sup'pli·cant
sup'pli·cate'
· cat'ed · cat'ing
sup·pli·ca'tion
sup·pli'er
sup·ply'
· plied' · ply'ing
· plies'
sup·port'
sup·port'ive
sup·pose'
· posed' · pos'ing
sup·pos'ed·ly
sup·po·si'tion
sup·pos'i·to·ry
· ries
sup·press'
sup·press'i·ble
sup·pres'sion
sup·pres'sor
sup'pu·rate'
· rat'ed · rat'ing
sup'pu·ra'tion
su·prem'a·cist
su·prem'a·cy
su·preme'ly
sur'charge
sur'cin'gle
sure
sur'er sur'est
sure'-foot'ed
sure'ly
sur'e·ty
· ties
surf
(*waves;* see serf)
sur'face
· faced · fac·ing
surf'board'

surf'boat'
surf'-cast'
surf'eit
surf'er
surge
surged surg'ing
(*sudden rush;*
see serge)
sur'geon
sur'ger·y
· ies
sur'gi·cal
sur'gi·cal·ly
sur'li·ness
sur'ly
· li·er · li·est
sur·mise'
· mised' · mis'ing
sur·mount'
sur'name'
· named'
· nam'ing
sur·pass'
sur'plice
(*cloak*)
sur'plus
(*excess*)
sur·prise'
· prised' · pris'ing
sur·pris'ing·ly
sur·re'al
sur·re'al·ism
sur·ren'der
sur·rep·ti'tious
sur'rey
· reys
sur'ro·gate'
· gat'ed · gat'ing
sur·round'
sur'tax'
sur·veil'lance
sur'vey
· veys
sur·vey'or
sur·viv'a·ble
sur·viv'al
sur·vive'
· vived' · viv'ing
sur·vi'vor
sus·cep'ti·bil'i·ty
sus·cep'ti·ble
sus·pect'
sus·pend'
sus·pense'
sus·pen'sion
sus·pen'so·ry
sus·pi'cion
sus·pi'cious
sus·tain'
sus·tain'a·ble
sus'te·nance
sut·tee'
su'ture
· tured · tur·ing
svelte
swab
swabbed
swab'bing

swad'dle
· dled · dling
swag'ger
swal'low
swal'low-tailed'
swa'mi
· mis
swamp'y
· i·er · i·est
swan's'-down'
swap
swapped
swap'ping
sward
(*turf;* see sword)
swarm
swarth'y
· i·er · i·est
swash'buck'ler
swas'ti·ka
swat
swat'ted
swat'ting
swath *n.*
(*strip*)
swathe *v., n.*
swathed
swath'ing
(*bandage*)
sway'backed'
swear
swore
sworn
swear'ing
swear'word'
sweat
sweat *or*
sweat'ed,
sweat'ing
sweat'band'
sweat'er
sweat shirt
sweat'shop'
sweat'y
· i·er · i·est
sweep
swept sweep'ing
sweep'stakes'
· stakes'
sweet
(*like sugar;*
see suite)
sweet'bread'
sweet corn
sweet'en·er
sweet'heart'
sweet'meat'
swell
swelled, swelled
or swol'len,
swell'ing
swel'ter
swept'back'
swerve
swerved
swerv'ing
swift'ness
swill

swim
swam swum
swim'ming
swim'ming·ly
swim'suit'
swin'dle
· dled · dling
swing
swung
swing'ing
swing'by'
swin'ish
swipe
swiped
swip'ing
swirl
switch'board'
switch'man
swiv'el
· eled *or* · elled
· el·ing *or* · el·ling
swol'len
sword
(*weapon;* see
sward)
sword'fish'
sword'play'
swords'man
syb'a·rite'
syc'a·more'
syc'o·phant
syc'o·phan'tic
syl·lab'ic
syl·lab'i·fi·ca'tion
syl·lab'i·fy'
· fied' · fy'ing
syl'la·ble
syl'la·bus
· bus·es *or* · bi'
syl'lo·gism
sylph
syl'van
sym·bi·ot'ic
sym'bol
(*mark;* see
cymbal)
sym·bol'ic
sym'bol·ism
sym'bol·is'tic
sym'bol·ize'
· ized' · iz'ing
sym·met'ri·cal
sym'me·try
· tries
sym'pa·thet'ic
sym'pa·thet'i·
cal·ly
sym'pa·thize'
· thized' · thiz'ing
sym'pa·thy
· thies
sym·phon'ic
sym'pho·ny
· nies
sym·po'si·um
· ums *or* · a
symp'tom
symp'to·mat'ic

syn'a·gogue'
syn'chro·mesh'
syn'chro·nism
syn'chro·ni·
za'tion
syn'chro·nize'
· nized' · niz'ing
syn'chro·nous
syn'chro·tron'
syn'co·pate'
· pat'ed · pat'ing
syn'co·pa'tion
syn'co·pe
syn'cre·tize'
· tized' · tiz'ing
syn'di·cal·ism
syn'di·cate'
· cat'ed · cat'ing
syn'drome
syn·ec'do·che
syn·e·col'o·gy
syn'er·gism
syn'od
syn·od'i·cal
syn'o·nym
syn·on'y·mous
syn·on'y·my
· mies
syn·op'sis
· ses
syn·op'size
· sized · siz·ing
syn·op'tic
syn·tac'tic
syn·tac'ti·cal·ly
syn'tax
syn'the·sis
· ses'
syn'the·size'
· sized' · siz'ing
syn·thet'ic
syn·thet'i·cal·ly
syph'i·lis
syph'i·lit'ic
sy·ringe'
· ringed' · ring'ing
syr'up
sys'tem
sys·tem·at'ic
sys'tem·at'i·
cal·ly
sys'tem·a·tize'
· tized' · tiz'ing
sys·tem'ic

T

tab'ard
tab'by
· bies
tab'er·nac'le
ta'ble
· bled · bling
tab'leau
· leaux *or* · leaus
ta'ble·cloth'

ta'ble d'hôte'
ta'ble-hop'
ta'ble·land'
ta'ble·spoon'ful
· fuls
tab'let
ta'ble·ware'
tab'loid
ta·boo' *or* · bu'
· boos' *or* · bus'
· booed' *or* · bued'
· boo'ing *or*
· bu'ing
ta'bor *or* · bour
tab'o·ret
tab'u·lar
tab'u·late'
· lat'ed · lat'ing
tab'u·la'tion
tab'u·la'tor
ta·chis'to·scope'
ta·chom'e·ter
tac'it
tac'i·turn'
tac'i·tur'ni·ty
tack'i·ness
tack'le
· led · ling
tack'y
· i·er · i·est
tact'ful
tact'ful·ly
tac'ti·cal
tac·ti'cian
tac'tics
tac'tile
tact'less
tac'tu·al
tad'pole'
taf'fe·ta
taf'fy
tag
tagged tag'ging
tail'gate'
· gat'ed · gat'ing
tail'less
tail'light'
tai'lor
tai'lor-made'
tail'piece'
tail'race'
tail'spin'
tail wind
taint'ed
tak'a·ble *or* take'·
take
took tak'en
tak'ing
take'off'
take'out'
take'o'ver
talc
tal'cum
tale'bear'er
tal'ent·ed
ta'les·man
(*juryman*)
tale'tell'er

tal'is·man
·mans
(good luck charm)
talk'a·tive
talk'y
tal'low
tal'ly
·lies, ·lied ·ly·ing
Tal'mud
tal'on
tam'a·ble or
tame'·
ta·ma'le
tam'bour
tam'bou·rine'
tame
tamed tam'ing
tam'-o'-shan'ter
tamp'er n.
tam'per v.
tam'per·er
tam'pi·on
tam'pon
tan
tan'ner tan'nest
tanned tan'ning
tan'dem
tan'ge·lo'
·los'
tan'gent
tan·gen'tial
tan'ge·rine'
tan'gi·ble
tan'gi·bly
tan'gle
·gled ·gling
tan'go
·gos
tang'y
·i·er ·i·est
tank'age
tank'ard
tank'er
tank'ful
·fuls
tan'ner·y
·ies
tan'nic
tan'nin
tan'ta·lize'
·lized' ·liz'ing
tan'ta·mount'
tan'trum
tap
tapped
tap'ping
tape
taped tap'ing
tape deck
ta'per
(candle; decrease;
see tapir)
tape'-re·cord'
tape recorder
tap'es·try
·tries
tape'worm'
tap'i·o'ca

ta'pir
(animal; see
taper)
tap'pet
tap'room'
tap'root'
tar
tarred tar'ring
tar'an·tel'la
ta·ran'tu·la
tar·boosh'
tar'di·ness
tar'dy
·di·er ·di·est
tare
tared tar'ing
(weight deduction;
see tear)
tar'get
tar'iff
tar'nish
ta'ro
·ros
(plant)
tar'ot
(playing cards)
tar·pau'lin
tar'pon
tar'ra·gon'
tar'ry
·ried ·ry·ing
tar'tan
tar'tar
tar'tar sauce
tart'ly
task force
task'mas'ter
tas'sel
·seled or ·selled
·sel·ing or
·sel·ling
taste
tast'ed tast'ing
taste'ful
taste'ful·ly
taste'less
tast'er
tast'i·ness
tast'y
·i·er ·i·est
tat'ter·de·mal'ion
tat'tered
tat'ter·sall'
tat'tle
·tled ·tling
tat'tle·tale'
tat·too'
·toos'
·tooed' ·too'ing
taught
(trained; see taut)
taunt
taupe
taut
(tight; see taught)
tau·tol'o·gy
·gies
tav'ern

taw'dry
·dri·er ·dri·est
taw'ny
·ni·er ·ni·est
tax·a·bil'i·ty
tax'a·ble
tax·a'tion
tax'-de·duct'i·ble
tax'-ex·empt'
tax'i
·is, ·ied
·i·ing or ·y·ing
tax'i·cab'
tax'i·der'mist
tax'i·der'my
tax'i·me'ter
tax'i·way'
tax·on'o·my
tax'pay'er
tea bag
teach
taught teach'ing
teach'a·ble
teach'er
teach'-in'
tea'cup'
tea'cup·ful'
·fuls'
teak
tea'ket'tle
team
(group; see teem)
team'mate'
team'ster
team'work'
tea'pot'
tear
tore torn
tear'ing
(rip; see tare)
tear
teared tear'ing
(eye fluid;
see tier)
tear'drop'
tear'ful
tear gas
tear'i·ness
tea'room'
tear'y
·i·er ·i·est
tease
teased teas'ing
tea'sel
·seled or ·selled
·sel·ing or
·sel·ling
tea'spoon·ful'
·fuls'
teat
tea'-ta·ble
tea'tast'er
tea'time'
tech'nic
tech'ni·cal
tech'ni·cal'i·ty
·ties
tech'ni·cal·ly

tech·ni'cian
tech'ni·col'or
tech·nique'
tech·noc'ra·cy
tech·nog'ra·phy
tech'no·log'i·cal
tech·nol'o·gy
te'di·ous
te'di·um
tee
teed tee'ing
teem
(abound; see
team)
teen'-age'
teen'-ag'er
tee'ter-tot'ter
teethe
teethed teeth'ing
tee·to'tal·er
tee·to'tal·ism
Tef'lon
teg'u·ment
tel·au'to·graph'
tel'e·cast'
·cast' or ·cast'ed
·cast'ing
tel'e·com·mu'
ni·ca'tion
tel'e·course'
tel'e·gen'ic
tel'e·gram'
tel'e·graph'
tel'e·graph'ic
te·leg'ra·pher
te·leg'ra·phy
tel'e·ki·ne'sis
tel'e·me'ter
te'le·o·log'i·cal
te'le·ol'o·gy
tel'e·path'ic
te·lep'a·thy
tel'e·phone'
·phoned'
·phon'ing
tel'e·phon'ic
te·leph'o·ny
tel'e·pho'to
tel'e·pho'to·graph'
tel'e·pho·tog'ra·
phy
tel'e·play'
tel'e·prompt'er
tel'e·ran'
tel'e·scope'
·scoped' scop'ing
tel'e·scop'ic
tel'e·thon'
Tel'e·type'
·typed' ·typ'ing
tel'e·type'writ'er
tel'e·view'er
tel'e·vise'
·vised' ·vis'ing
tel'e·vi'sion
tell
told tell'ing
tell'a·ble

tell'er
tell'tale'
tel'pher or ·fer
Tel'star'
te·mer'i·ty
tem'per
tem'per·a
tem'per·a·ment
tem'per·a·
men'tal
tem'per·ance
tem'per·ate
tem'per·a·ture
tem'pered
tem'pest
tem·pes'tu·ous
tem'plate or ·plet
tem'ple
tem'po
·pos or ·pi
tem'po·ral
tem'po·rar'i·ly
tem'po·rar'i·ness
tem'po·rar'y
tem'po·rize'
·rized' ·riz'ing
temp·ta'tion
tempt'er
tempt'ing
tempt'ress
tem'pus fu'git
ten'a·ble
te·na'cious
te·nac'i·ty
ten'an·cy
·cies
ten'ant
ten'ant·a·ble
ten'ant·ry
·ries
tend'en·cy
·cies
ten'der
(soft; offer)
tend'er
(one who tends)
ten'der·foot'
·foots' or ·feet'
ten'der·heart'ed
ten'der·ize'
·ized' ·iz'ing
ten'der·iz'er
ten'der·loin'
ten'don
ten'dril
ten'e·ment
ten'et
ten'fold'
Ten'nes·see'
ten'nis
ten'on
ten'or
(tendency; singer;
see tenure)
ten'pins'
tense
tens'er tens'est
tensed tens'ing

tense'ly
tense'ness
ten'sile
ten·sil'i·ty
ten'sion
ten'ta·cle
ten'ta·tive
ten'ta·tive·ly
ten'ter
ten'ter·hook'
tenth
ten·u'i·ty
ten'u·ous
ten'ure
(time held;
see tenor)
ten·u'ri·al
te'pee or tee'·
tep'id
te·pid'i·ty
te·qui'la
ter'cen·te'nar·y
·ies
ter'gi·ver·sate'
·sat'ed ·sat'ing
ter'gi·ver·sa'tor
ter'ma·gant
ter'mi·na·ble
ter'mi·na·bly
ter'mi·nal
ter'mi·nate'
·nat'ed ·nat'ing
ter'mi·na'tion
ter'mi·nol'o·gy
ter'mi·nus
·ni' or ·nus·es
ter'mite
ter'na·ry
terp'si·cho·re'an
ter'race
·raced ·rac·ing
ter'ra cot'ta
ter'ra fir'ma
ter·rain'
Ter'ra·my'cin
ter'ra·pin
ter·rar'i·um
·i·ums or ·i·a
ter·raz'zo
ter·res'tri·al
ter'ri·ble
ter'ri·bly
ter'ri·er
ter·rif'ic
ter·rif'i·cal·ly
ter'ri·fy'
·fied' ·fy'ing
ter'ri·to'ri·al
ter'ri·to'ri·al'i·ty
ter'ri·to'ry
·ries
ter'ror
ter'ror·ism
ter'ror·ist
ter'ror·is'tic
ter'ror·i·za'tion
ter'ror·ize'
·ized' ·iz'ing

ter'ry
terse
  ters'er ters'est
terse'ness
ter'ti·ar'y
tes'sel·late'
  ·lat'ed ·lat'ing
tes'sel·la'tion
test'a·ble
tes'ta·ment
tes'ta·men'ta·ry
tes'tate
tes'ta·tor
tes'ti·cle
tes'ti·fi'er
tes'ti·fy'
  ·fied' ·fy'ing
tes'ti·ly
tes'ti·mo'ni·al
tes'ti·mo'ny
  ·nies
tes'ti·ness
tes'ty
  ·ti·er ·ti·est
tet'a·nus
tête'-à-tête'
teth'er
tet'ra·cy'cline
tet'ra·he'dron
  ·drons or ·dra
te·tral'o·gy
  ·gies
Tex'as
text'book'
tex'tile
tex'tu·al
tex'tur·al
tex'ture
than *conj., prep.*
thank'ful
thank'less
thanks'giv'ing
that
  those
thatch
thaw
the'a·ter *or* ·tre
the·at'ri·cal
theft
their
  (poss. form of
  they; see there,
  they're)
theirs
  (belonging to
  them; see there's)
the'ism
the·is'tic
the·mat'ic
theme
them·selves'
then
  (at that time)
thence'forth'
the·oc'ra·cy
  ·cies
the·od'o·lite'
the·o·lo'gian

the·o·log'i·cal
the·ol'o·gy
  ·gies
the'o·rem
the·o·ret'i·cal
the·o·ret'i·cal·ly
the·o·re·ti'cian
the'o·rize'
  ·rized' ·riz'ing
the'o·ry
  ·ries
the·os'o·phy
  ·phies
ther'a·peu'tic
ther'a·pist
ther'a·py
  ·pies
there
  (at that place;
  see their, they're)
there'a·bouts'
there·af'ter
there·at'
there·by'
there·for'
  (for it)
there'fore'
  (for that reason)
there·in'
there'in·af'ter
there·in'to
there's
  (there is; see
  theirs)
there'to·fore'
there·up·on'
there·with'
ther'mal
therm'i·on'ics
ther'mo·dy·
  nam'ics
ther'mo·e·lec'·
  tric'i·ty
ther·mom'e·ter
ther'mo·nu'cle·ar
ther'mo·pile'
ther'mo·plas'tic
ther'mos
ther'mo·stat'
ther'mo·stat'i·
  cal·ly
the·sau'rus
  ·ri *or* ·rus·es
the'sis
  ·ses
they'd
they'll
they're
  (they are; see
  their, there)
they've
thi'a·mine'
thick'en·ing
thick'et
thick'ness
thick'set'
thick'-skinned'
thick'-wit'ted

thief *n.*
  thieves
thieve *v.*
  thieved thiev'ing
thiev'er·y
  ·ies
thiev'ish·ly
thigh'bone'
thim'ble·ful'
  ·fuls'
thin
  thin'ner
  thin'nest
  thinned
  thin'ning
thing
think
  thought
  think'ing
thin'-skinned'
third'-class'
third'-rate'
thirst'i·ly
thirst'i·ness
thirst'y
  ·i·er ·i·est
thir'teenth'
thir'ti·eth
thir'ty
  ·ties
this
  these
this'tle·down'
thith'er·to'
thole
thong
tho·rac'ic
tho'rax
  ·rax·es *or* ·ra·ces
tho'ri·um
thorn'y
  ·i·er ·i·est
thor'ough
thor'ough·bred'
thor'ough·fare'
thor'ough·go'ing
though
thought
thought'ful·ly
thought'ful·ness
thought'less
thou'sand·fold'
thrall'dom
thrash
thread'bare'
thread'i·ness
thread'y
  ·i·er ·i·est
threat'en
3'-D'
three'-deck'er
three'-di·men'·
  sion·al
three'fold'
three'-ply'
three'-quar'ter
three'score'
three'some

three'-way'
three'-wheel'er
thren'o·dy
  ·dies
thresh'er
thresh'old
threw
  (pt. of throw;
  see through)
thrice
thrift'i·ly
thrift'i·ness
thrift'y
  ·i·er ·i·est
thrill'er
thrive
  thrived *or* throve,
  thrived *or*
  thriv'en,
  thriv'ing
throat'y
  ·i·er ·i·est
throb
  throbbed
  throb'bing
throe
  (pang; see throw)
throm·bo'sis
throne
  throned
  thron'ing
throng
throt'tle
  ·tled ·tling
through
  (from end to end
  of; see threw)
through·out'
throw
  threw thrown
  throw'ing
  (hurl; see throe)
throw'a·way'
throw'back'
thrum
  thrummed
  thrum'ming
thrust
  thrust thrust'ing
thud
  thud'ded
  thud'ding
thumb'nail'
thumb'screw'
thumb'stall'
thumb'tack'
thump
thun'der·bolt'
thun'der·cloud'
thun'der·head'
thun'der·ous
thun'der·show'er
thun'der·squall'
thun'der·storm'
thun'der·struck'
Thurs'day
thus
thwack

thwart
thyme
  (herb; see time)
thy'mus
thy'roid
ti·ar'a
tib'i·a
tic
  (muscle spasm)
tick
  (click; insect)
tick'er tape
tick'et
tick'ing
tick'le
  ·led ·ling
tick'ler
tick'lish
tick'-tack-toe'
tick'y tack'y
tid'al
tid'bit'
tide'land'
tide'mark'
tide'wa'ter
ti'di·ly
ti'di·ness
ti'dings
ti'dy
  ·di·er ·di·est
  ·died ·dy·ing
tie
  tied ty'ing
tie'back'
tie'-dye'
  -dyed' -dye'ing
tie'-in'
tie'pin'
tier
  (row; see tear)
ti'er
  (one that ties;
  see tire)
tie tack
tie'-up'
ti'ger
ti'ger's eye
tight'en
tight'fist'ed
tight'fit'ting
tight'knit'
tight'-lipped'
tight'rope'
ti'gress
tile
  tiled til'ing
till'a·ble
tilt'-top'
tim'bale
tim'ber
  (wood)
tim'ber·line'
tim'bre
  (quality of sound)
time
  timed tim'ing
  (duration;
  see thyme)

time'card'
time clock
time'-con·sum'ing
time'-hon'ored
time'keep'er
time'less
time'li·ness
time'ly
  ·li·er ·li·est
time'out'
time'piece'
tim'er
time'sav'ing
time'ta·ble
time'-test'ed
time'worn'
time zone
ti·mid'i·ty
tim'id·ly
tim'or·ous
tim'o·thy
tim'pa·ni
tim'pa·nist
tin
  tinned tin'ning
tinc'ture
  ·tured ·tur·ing
tin'der·box'
tin'foil'
tinge
  tinged, tinge'ing
  or ting'ing
tin'gle
  ·gled ·gling
tin'gly
  ·gli·er ·gli·est
ti'ni·ness
tin'ker
tin'ker·er
tin'kle
  ·kled ·kling
tin'ni·ness
tin·ni'tus
tin'ny
  ·ni·er ·ni·est
tin'-plate'
  -plat'ed -plat'ing
tin'sel
  ·seled *or* ·selled
  ·sel·ing *or*
  ·sel·ling
tin'smith'
tin'tin·nab'u·
  la'tion
tin'type'
tin'ware'
ti'ny
  ·ni·er ·ni·est
tip
  tipped tip'ping
tip'-off'
tip'pet
tip'ple
  ·pled ·pling
tip'sy
  ·si·er ·si·est
tip'toe'
  ·toed' ·toe'ing

tip'top'
ti'rade
tire
 tired tir'ing
 (*weary; rubber*
 hoop; see tier)
tired'ly
tire'less
tire'some
tis'sue
ti'tan
tithe
 tithed tith'ing
ti'tian
tit'il·late'
 ·lat'ed ·lat'ing
tit'il·la'tion
tit'tle
 ·tled ·tling
ti'tle·hold'er
tit'mouse'
 ·mice'
tit'ter
tit'u·lar
toad'stool'
toad'y
 ·ies, ·ied ·y·ing
toad'y·ism
to'-and-fro'
toast'mas'ter
to·bac'co
 ·cos
to·bac'co·nist
to·bog'gan
toc·ca'ta
toc'sin
 (*alarm;* see toxin)
to·day'
tod'dle
 ·dled ·dling
tod'dler
tod'dy
 ·dies
to-do'
toe
 toed toe'ing
toe'-dance'
 -danced'
 -danc'ing
toe'hold'
toe'-in'
toe'less
toe'nail'
tof'fee *or* ·fy
to'ga
 ·gas *or* ·gae
to·geth'er
tog'gle
 ·gled ·gling
toi'let
toi'let·ry
 ·ries
toil'some
toil'worn'
to'ken
tole
tol'er·a·ble
tol'er·a·bly

tol'er·ance
tol'er·ant
tol'er·ate'
 ·at'ed ·at'ing
tol'er·a'tion
tol'er·a'tor
toll'booth'
toll bridge
toll call
toll'gate'
toll'keep'er
toll road
tom'a·hawk'
to·ma'to
 ·toes
tom'boy'
tomb'stone'
tom'cat'
tom'fool'er·y
to·mor'row
tom'-tom'
ton
 (*weight;* see tun)
ton'al
to·nal'i·ty
 ·ties
tone
 toned ton'ing
tone'-deaf'
tongs
tongue
 tongued
tongu'ing
tongue'-lash'ing
tongue'-tie'
 -tied' -ty'ing
ton'ic
to·night'
ton'nage
ton·neau'
 ·neaus' *or*
 ·neaux'
ton'sil
ton'sil·lec'to·my
 ·mies
ton'sil·li'tis
ton·so'ri·al
ton'sure
 ·sured ·sur·ing
ton'tine
tool'mak'er
tooth
 teeth
tooth'ache'
tooth'brush'
tooth'paste'
tooth'pick'
tooth'some
top
 topped top'ping
to'paz
top'coat'
top'-drawer'
top'-dress'ing
top'-flight'
top'-heav'y
to'pi·ar'y
top'ic

top'i·cal
top'knot'
top'less
top'-lev'el
top'most'
top'-notch'
to·pog'ra·pher
top'o·graph'i·cal
to·pog'ra·phy
 (*surface features;*
 see typography)
top'ple
 ·pled ·pling
top'sail
top'-se'cret
top'soil'
top'sy-tur'vy
toque
to'rah *or* ·ra
torch'bear'er
torch·ier' *or*
 ·iere'
torch'light'
tor'e·a·dor'
tor'ment
tor·men'tor
tor·na'do
 ·does *or* ·dos
tor·pe'do
 ·does
tor'pid
tor·pid'i·ty
tor'por
torque
tor'rent
tor·ren'tial
tor'rid
tor·rid'i·ty
tor'sion
tor'so
 ·sos *or* ·si
tort
 (*wrongful act*)
torte
 (*cake*)
tor·til'la
tor'toise
tor·to'ni
tor'tu·ous
 (*winding*)
tor'ture
 ·tured ·tur·ing
tor'tur·ous
 (*agonizing*)
toss'up'
to'tal
 ·taled *or* ·talled
 ·tal·ing *or*
 ·tal·ling
to·tal'i·tar'i·an
to·tal'i·ty
to'tal·ly
tote
 tot'ed tot'ing
to'tem
tot'ter
touch'back'

touch'down'
tou·ché'
touch'hole'
touch'i·ly
touch'i·ness
touch'stone'
touch'-type'
touch'-typ'ist
touch'y
 ·i·er ·i·est
tough'en
tough'-mind'ed
tou·pee'
tour' de force'
 tours' de force'
tour'ism
tour'ist
tour'ma·line
tour'na·ment
tour'ney
 ·neys
tour'ni·quet
tou'sle
 sled ·sling
tow'age
to·ward'
tow'boat'
tow'el
 ·eled *or* ·elled
 ·el·ing *or* ·el·ling
tow'er·ing
tow'head'
tow'line'
town'ship
towns'peo'ple
tow'path'
tow'rope'
tox·e'mi·a
tox'ic
tox'i·cant
tox'i·col'o·gy
tox'in
 (*poison;* see
 tocsin)
trace
 traced trac'ing
trace'a·ble
trac'er
trac'er·y
 ·ies
tra'che·a
 ·ae' *or* ·as
tra·cho'ma
track
 (*trace*)
tract
 (*land; leaflet*)
trac'ta·ble
trac'tile
trac'tion
trac'tor
trad'a·ble *or*
 trade'a·ble
trade
 trad'ed trad'ing
trade'-in'
trade'-last'
trade'mark'

trade name
trades'man
trades'peo'ple
trade wind
tra·di'tion
tra·di'tion·al
tra·duce'
 ·duced' ·duc'ing
traf'fic
 ·ficked ·fick·ing
traf'fick·er
tra·ge'di·an
tra·ge'di·enne'
trag'e·dy
 ·dies
trag'ic
trag'i·cal·ly
trag'i·com'e·dy
 ·dies
trag'i·com'ic
trail'blaz'er
trail'er
train·ee'
train'man
trait
trai'tor
trai'tor·ous
trai'tress
tra·jec'to·ry
 ·ries
tram'mel
 ·meled *or* ·melled
 ·mel·ing *or*
 ·mel·ling
tram'ple
 ·pled ·pling
tram'po·line'
trance
tranced
tranc'ing
tran'quil
 ·quil·er *or* ·quil·ler
 ·quil·est *or*
 ·quil·lest
tran'quil·ize'
 or ·quil·lize'
 ·ized' *or* ·lized'
 ·iz'ing *or* ·liz'ing
tran'quil·iz'er *or*
 ·quil·liz'er
tran·quil'li·ty *or*
 ·quil'i·ty
tran'quil·ly
trans·act'
trans·ac'tion
trans·ac'tor
trans'at·lan'tic
trans·ceiv'er
tran·scend'
tran·scend'ent
tran·scen·den'tal
trans'con·ti·
 nen'tal
tran·scribe'
 ·scribed' ·scrib'in
tran'script'
tran·scrip'tion
tran'sept

trans·fer'
 ·ferred'
 ·fer'ring
trans·fer'a·ble
 or ·fer'ra·ble
trans·fer'al
 or ·fer'ral
trans'fer·ee'
trans·fer'ence
trans·fer'rer
trans·fig·u·ra'tion
trans·fig'ure
trans·fix'
trans·form'
trans'for·ma'tion
trans·form'er
trans·fuse'
trans·fus'i·ble
trans·fu'sion
trans·gress'
trans·gres'sion
trans·gres'sor
tran'sient
tran·sis'tor
tran·sis'tor·ize'
 ·ized' ·iz'ing
trans'it
tran·si'tion
tran·si'tion·al·ly
tran'si·tive
tran'si·to'ry
trans·lat'a·ble
trans·late'
 ·lat'ed ·lat'ing
trans·la'tion
trans·la'tor
trans·lit'er·ate'
 ·at'ed ·at'ing
trans·lit'er·a'tion
trans·lu'cence
trans·lu'cent
trans·mi'grate
 ·grat·ed ·grat·ing
trans'mi·gra'tion
trans·mis'si·ble
trans·mis'sion
trans·mit'
 ·mit'ted
 ·mit'ting
trans·mit'tal
trans·mit'tance
trans·mit'ter
trans·mut'a·ble
trans'mu·ta'tion
trans·mute'
 ·mut'ed
 ·mut'ing
trans'o·ce·an'ic
tran'som
tran·son'ic
trans·pa·cif'ic
trans·par'en·cy
 ·cies
trans·par'ent
tran·spire'
 ·spired' ·spir'ing
trans·plant'
tran·spon'der

trans·port'
trans'por·ta'tion
trans·pos'a·ble
trans·pose'
·posed' ·pos'ing
trans'po·si'tion
trans·sex'u·al
trans·ship'
·shipped'
·ship'ping
tran'stage'
tran'sub·stan'ti·
ate'
trans·val'ue
trans·ver'sal
trans·verse'
trans·verse'ly
trans·ves'tite
trap
trapped trap'ping
trap'door'
tra·peze'
tra·pe'zi·um
trap'e·zoid'
trap'per
trap'pings
trap'shoot'ing
trash'i·ness
trash'y
·i·er ·i·est
trau'ma
·mas or ·ma·ta
trau·mat'ic
trau·mat'i·cal·ly
trav'ail
(hard work)
trav'el
·eled or ·elled
·el·ing or ·el·ling
(journey)
trav'el·er or
·el·ler
trav'e·logue' or
·log'
trav·ers'a·ble
trav·ers'al
trav·erse'
·ersed' ·ers'ing
trav'er·tine'
trav'es·ty
·ties
·tied ·ty·ing
trawl'er
tray
(holder; see
trey)
treach'er·ous
treach'er·y
·ies
trea'cle
tread
trod, trod'den or
trod, tread'ing
trea'dle
·dled ·dling
tread'mill'
trea'son
trea'son·ous

treas'ure
·ured ·ur·ing
treas'ur·er
treas'ure-trove'
treas'ur·y
·ies
treat'a·ble
trea'tise
treat'ment
trea'ty
·ties
tre'ble
·bled ·bling
tree
treed
tree'ing
tree'nail'
tree'top'
tre'foil
treil'lage
trek
trekked
trek'king
trel'lis
trem'ble
·bled ·bling
tre·men'dous
trem'o·lo'
·los'
trem'or
trem'u·lous
trench'ant
trench mouth
trend
trep'i·da'tion
tres'pass
tress'es
tres'tle
tres'tle·work'
trey
(a three; see
tray)
tri'a·ble
tri'ad
tri'al
tri'an'gle
tri·an'gu·lar
tri·an'gu·late'
·lat·ed ·lat'ing
tri·an'gu·la'tion
trib'al
trib'al·ism
tribes'man
trib'u·la'tion
tri·bu'nal
trib'une
trib'u·tar'y
·ies
trib'ute
tri'cen·ten'ni·al
tri'ceps
·cep·ses or ·ceps
tri·chi'na
·nae
trich'i·no'sis
tri·chot'o·my
tri'chro·mat'ic
trick'er·y

trick'i·ly
trick'i·ness
trick'le
·led ·ling
trick'ster
trick'y
·i·er ·i·est
tri'col'or
tri'cot
tri'cy·cle
tri'di·men'sion·al
tri·en'ni·al
tri·en'ni·um
·ums or ·a
tri'er
tri'fle
·fled ·fling
tri·fo'cal
trig'ger
trig'o·no·met'ric
trig'o·nom'e·try
tri·lat'er·al
tri·lin'gual
tril'lion
tril'li·um
tril'o·gy
·gies
trim
trimmed
trim'ming
trim'mer
trim'mest
tri·mes'ter
tri·month'ly
trin'i·ty
·ties
trin'ket
tri·no'mi·al
tri'o
·os
trip
tripped trip'ping
tri·par'tite
trip'ham'mer
tri'ple
·pled ·pling
tri'ple-space'
tri'plet
trip'li·cate'
·cat'ed ·cat'ing
tri'ply
tri'pod
trip'per
trip'tych
tri·sect'
triste
tris·tesse'
trite
trit'er trit'est
trite'ly
trit'u·rate'
·rat'ed ·rat'ing
tri'umph
tri·um'phal
tri·um'phant
tri·um'vi·rate
triv'et
triv'i·a

triv'i·al
triv'i·al'i·ty
·ties
triv'i·al·ly
tri·week'ly
·lies
tro'che
(lozenge)
tro'chee
(poetic meter)
trod'den
trof'fer
trog'lo·dyte'
troll
trol'ley
·leys
·leyed ·ley·ing
trol'lop
trom·bone'
trom·bon'ist
troop
(of soldiers;
see troupe)
troop'ship'
tro'phy
·phies
trop'ic
trop'i·cal
tro'pism
trop'o·sphere'
trot
trot'ted trot'ting
trot'ter
trou'ba·dour'
trou'ble
·bled ·bling
trou'ble·mak'er
trou'ble-shoot'er
trou'ble·some
trough
trounce
trounced
trounc'ing
troupe
trouped
troup'ing
(of actors;
see troop)
troup'er
trou'sers
trous'seau
·seaux or ·seaus
trout
trow'el
·eled or ·elled
·el·ing or ·el·ling
tru'an·cy
·cies
tru'ant
truce
truck farm
truck'le
·led ·ling
truc'u·lence
truc'u·lent
trudge
trudged
trudg'ing

true
tru'er tru'est
trued tru'ing
or true'ing
true'-blue'
true'-life'
true'love'
truf'fle
tru'ism
tru'ly
trump
trumped'-up'
trump'er·y
·ies
trum'pet
trum'pet·er
trun'cate
·cat·ed ·cat·ing
trun·ca'tion
trun'cheon
trun'dle
·dled ·dling
trunk line
trun'nion
truss
trus·tee'
·teed' ·tee'ing
(manager; see
trusty)
trus·tee'ship'
trust'ful
trust'ful·ly
trust'i·ness
trust'wor'thy
trust'y
·ies, ·i·er ·i·est
(relied upon;
see trustee)
truth'ful
truth'ful·ly
truth'ful·ness
try
tries
tried try'ing
try'out'
tryst
tset'se fly
T'-shirt'
tsim'mes
tsor'is
T square
tsu·na'mi
tub
tubbed tub'bing
tu'ba
·bas or ·bae
tub'ba·ble
tub'bi·ness
tub'by
·bi·er ·bi·est
tube
tubed tub'ing
tu'ber
tu'ber·cle
tu·ber'cu·lar
tu·ber'cu·lin
tu·ber'cu·lo'sis
tu·ber'cu·lous

tube'rose'
(plant)
tu'ber·ous
(having tubers)
tu'bu·lar
tuck'er
Tu'dor
Tues'day
tuft'ed
tug
tugged tug'ging
tug'boat'
tu·i'tion
tu'la·re'mi·a
tu'lip
tulle
tum'ble
·bled ·bling
tum'ble-down'
tum'bler
tum'ble·weed'
tum'brel
tu'me·fy'
·fied' ·fy'ing
tu·mes'cence
tu·mes'cent
tu'mid
tu'mor
tu'mor·ous
tu'mult
tu·mul'tu·ous
tun
tunned tun'ning
(cask; see ton)
tun'a·ble
or tune'·
tun'dra
tune
tuned tun'ing
tune'ful
tune'less
tun'er
tune'up' or
tune'-up'
tung'sten
tu'nic
tun'nel
·neled or ·nelled
·nel·ing or
·nel·ling
tu'pe·lo'
·los'
tur'ban
(headdress)
tur'bid
tur'bine
(engine)
tur'bo·jet'
tur'bo·prop'
tur'bu·lence
tur'bu·lent
tu·reen'
turf
tur'gid
tur'key
tur'mer·ic
tur'moil
turn'a·bout'

turn'a·round'
turn'buck·le
turn'coat'
turn'down'
tur'nip
turn'key'
·keys'
turn'off'
turn'out'
turn'o·ver
turn'pike'
turn'stile'
turn'ta·ble
tur'pen·tine'
tur'pi·tude'
tur'quoise
tur'ret
tur'tle
tur'tle·dove'
tur'tle·neck'
tus'sle
·sled ·sling
tu'te·lage
tu'te·lar'y
tu'tor
tu·to'ri·al
tut'ti-frut'ti
tu'tu
tux·e'do
·dos
TV
TVs or TV's
twang
tweak
tweed
tweed'y
·i·er ·i·est
tweeze
tweezed
tweez'ing
tweez'ers
twelfth
twelve'fold'
twen'ti·eth
twen'ty
·ties
twen'ty·fold'
twice'-told'
twid'dle
·dled ·dling
twi'light'
twi'lit
twill
twine
twined twin'ing
twin'-en'gined
twinge
twinged
twing'ing
twi'-night'
twin'kle
·kled ·kling
twirl'er
twist'er
twitch
twit'ter
two'-by-four'
two'-edged'

two'-faced'
two'-fist'ed
two'fold'
two'-hand'ed
two'-leg'ged
two'-piece'
two'-ply'
two'-sid'ed
two'some
two'-way'
ty·coon'
tym·pan'ic
typ'a·ble or type'·
typ'al
type
typed typ'ing
type'bar'
type'cast'
·cast' ·cast'ing
(in acting)
type'-cast'
-cast' -cast'ing
(in printing)
type'script'
type'set'
·set' ·set'ting
type'set'ter
type'write'
·wrote' ·writ'ten
·writ'ing
type'writ'er
ty'phoid
ty·phoon'
ty'phus
typ'i·cal
typ'i·cal·ly
typ'i·fy'
·fied' ·fy'ing
typ'ist
ty·pog'ra·pher
ty'po·graph'i·cal
ty·pog'ra·phy
(setting of type;
see topography)
ty·pol'o·gy
ty·ran'ni·cal
tyr'an·nize'
·nized' ·niz'ing
tyr'an·nous
tyr'an·ny
·nies
ty'rant
ty'ro
·ros
ty'ro·thri'cin

U

u·biq'ui·tous
u·biq'ui·ty
ud'der
(milk gland;
see utter)
u·fol'o·gist
ug'li
(fruit)

ug'li·ness
ug'ly
·li·er ·li·est
u'kase
u·ku·le'le
ul'cer
ul'cer·ate'
·at'ed ·at'ing
ul'cer·ous
ul'ster
ul·te'ri·or
ul'ti·mate
ul'ti·mate·ly
ul'ti·ma'tum
·tums or ·ta
ul'tra
ul'tra·con·serv'·
a·tive
ul'tra·ism
ul'tra·ma·rine'
ul'tra·mi'cro·
scope'
ul'tra·mod'ern
ul'tra·na'tion·al·
ism
ul'tra·son'ic
ul'tra·sound'
ul'tra·vi'o·let
ul'u·late'
·lat'ed ·lat'ing
um'ber
um·bil'i·cal
um·bil'i·cus
·ci'
um'bra
·brae or ·bras
um'brage
um·bra'geous
um·brel'la
u'mi·ak' or ·ack'
um'laut
um'pire
·pired ·pir·ing
un·a'ble
un'a·bridged'
un'ac·count'a·ble
un'ac·count'ed-
for'
un'ac·cus'tomed
un'af·fect'ed
un'-A·mer'i·can
u'na·nim'i·ty
u·nan'i·mous
un·apt'
un·armed'
un'as·sum'ing
un'at·tached'
un'a·void'a·ble
un'a·ware'
un'a·wares'
un·bal'anced
un·bear'a·ble
un·beat'a·ble
un'be·com'ing
un'be·known'
un'be·lief'
un'be·liev'a·ble
un'be·liev'er

un·bend'
·bent' or ·bend'ed,
·bend'ing
un·bi'ased or
·assed
un·bid'den
un·bolt'ed
un·bos'om
un·bound'ed
un·bri'dled
un·bro'ken
un·buck'le
un·but'ton
un·called'-for'
un·can'ni·ly
un·can'ni·ness
un·can'ny
un·cared'-for'
un'cer·e·mo'ni·
ous
un·cer'tain
un·cer'tain·ty
·ties
un·char'i·ta·ble
un·chris'tian
un'ci·al
un·civ'il
un·civ'i·lized'
un·clad'
un·class'i·fied
un'cle
un·clothe'
·clothed' or
·clad', ·cloth'ing
un·com'fort·a·ble
un·com'pro·
mis'ing
un'con·cerned'
un'con·di'tion·al
un'con·scion·a·
ble
un·con'scious
un'con·sti·
tu'tion·al
un·cou'ple
un·couth'
unc'tion
unc'tu·ous
un·daunt'ed
un'de·cid'ed
un·de·ni'a·ble
un'der·age'
un'der·age
un'der·brush'
un'der·buy'
·bought' ·buy'ing
un'der·car'riage
un'der·class'man
un'der·clothes'
un'der·coat'
un'der·cov'er
un'der·cur'rent
un'der·cut'
un'der·de·vel'·
oped
un'der·do'
·did' ·done'
·do'ing

un'der·dog'
un'der·em·ployed'
un'der·es'ti·mate'
un'der·fired'
un'der·foot'
un'der·gar'ment
un'der·glaze'
un'der·go'
·went' ·gone'
·go'ing
un'der·grad'u·ate
un'der·ground'
un'der·growth'
un'der·hand'
un'der·hand'ed
un'der·hung'
un'der·lay'
·laid' ·lay'ing
un'der·lie'
·lay' ·lain'
·ly'ing
un'der·line'
un'der·ling
un'der·lin'ing
un'der·mine'
un'der·neath'
un'der·nour'ish
un'der·pants'
un'der·part'
un'der·pass'
un'der·pay'
·paid' ·pay'ing
un'der·pin'ning
un'der·play'
un'der·priv'i·
leged
un'der·proof'
un'der·rate'
un'der·score'
un'der·sea'
un'der·sec're·
tar'y
·ies
un'der·sell'
·sold' ·sell'ing
un'der·sexed'
un'der·shirt'
un'der·shot'
un'der·side'
un'der·signed'
un'der·sized'
un'der·staffed'
un'der·stand'
·stood' ·stand'ing
un'der·stand'a·
ble
un'der·stand'a·bly
un'der·state'ment
un'der·stud'y
·ies, ·ied ·y·ing
un'der·take'
·took' ·tak'en
·tak'ing
un'der·tak'ing
un'der·tone'
un'der·tow'
un'der·val'ue
un'der·wa'ter

un'der·wear'
un'der·weight'
un'der·world'
un'der·write'
·wrote' ·writ'ten
·writ'ing
un·do'
·did' ·done'
·do'ing
un·doubt'ed·ly
un·dress'
un·due'
un'du·lant
un'du·late'
·lat'ed ·lat'ing
un·du'ly
un·dy'ing
un·earned'
un·earth'
un·eas'y
un'em·ploy'a·ble
un·e'qualed
or ·qualled
un'e·quiv'o·cal·ly
un·err'ing
un'es·sen'tial
un·e'ven·ness
un'e·vent'ful·ly
un'ex·cep'tion·
a·ble
un'ex·cep'tion·al
un'ex·pect'ed
un·faith'ful
un·fa·mil'iar
un·feel'ing
un·feigned'
un'for·get'ta·ble
un·for'tu·nate
un·found'ed
un·freeze'
·froze' ·fro'zen
·freez'ing
un·frock'
un·furl'
un·gain'ly
un·god'ly
un'guent
un'gu·late
un·hand'
un·heard'-of'
un·hoped'-for'
un·horse'
·horsed'
·hors'ing
u'ni·cam'er·al
u'ni·cel'lu·lar
u'ni·corn'
u'ni·cy'cle
u'ni·fi'a·ble
u'ni·fi·ca'tion
u'ni·fi'er
u'ni·form'
u'ni·form'i·ty
u'ni·fy'
·fied' ·fy'ing
u'ni·lat'er·al
un'im·peach'a·ble
un'in·hib'it·ed

un·in·tel'li·gi·ble
un'ion
un'ion·ize'
· ized' iz'ing
u·nique'
u'ni·son
u'nit
U'ni·tar'i·an
u·nite'
· nit'ed nit'ing
u'nit·ize'
· ized' iz'ing
u'ni·ty
· ties
u'ni·ver'sal
u'ni·ver·sal'i·ty
u'ni·ver'sal·ly
u'ni·verse'
u'ni·ver'si·ty
· ties
un·kempt'
un·known'
un·lade'
· lad'ed, lad'ed
or · lad'en,
· lad'ing
un·law'ful
un·less'
un·let'tered
un·like'li·hood'
un·like'ly
un·lim'it·ed
un·list'ed
un·looked'-for'
un·loose'
· loosed' loos'ing
un·loos'en
un·luck'y
un·make'
· made' mak'ing
un·man'
· manned'
· man'ning
un·men'tion·a·ble
un·mer'ci·ful
un'mis·tak'a·ble
un·nat'u·ral
un·nec'es·sar'y
un·nerve'
· nerved'
· nerv'ing
un·num'bered
un·oc'cu·pied'
un·or'gan·ized'
un·paid'-for'
un·par'al·leled'
un·pleas'ant
un·prec'e·dent'ed
un·prej'u·diced
un·prin'ci·pled
un·qual'i·fied
un·ques'tion·a·
bly
un'quote'
un·rav'el
· eled or · elled
· el·ing or · el·ling

un're·al·is'tic
un·rea'son·a·ble
un're·gen'er·ate
un·rest'
un·rul'i·ness
un·rul'y
· i·er · i·est
un·said'
un·sa'vor·i·ness
un·sa'vor·y
un·scathed'
un·scru'pu·lous
un·seat'
un·seem'ly
un·shod'
un·sight'li·ness
un·sight'ly
un·speak'a·ble
un·stead'y
un·strung'
un·sung'
un·tan'gle
· gled gling
un·ten'a·ble
un·think'a·ble
un·thought'-of'
un·ti'dy
un·tie'
· tied' ty'ing or
· tie'ing
un·til'
un·time'ly
un·told'
un·touch'a·ble
un·to'ward
un·truth'ful
un·tu'tored
un·u'su·al
un·veil'ing
un·want'ed
(not wanted;
see unwonted)
un·war'y
un·whole'some
un·wield'i·ness
un·wield'y
un·wit'ting·ly
un·wont'ed
(not usual;
see unwanted)
un·wor'thy
un·writ'ten
un·zip'
up'-and-com'ing
up'-and-down'
up'beat'
up·braid'
up'bring'ing
up'coun'try
up·date'
up·end'
up'grade'
up·heav'al
up'hill'
up·hold'
· held' hold'ing
up·hol'ster
up·hol'ster·er

up·hol'ster·y
· ies
up'keep'
up'land
up·lift'
up·on'
up'per-case'
-cased' -cas'ing
up'per·class'man
up'per·most'
up'right'
up'ris'ing
up'roar'
up·roar'i·ous
up·root'
up·set'
· set' set'ting
up'shot'
up'stage'
· staged'
· stag'ing
up'stairs'
up·stand'ing
up'start'
up'state'
up'stream'
up'swept'
up'swing'
up'take'
up'thrust'
up'-tight' or
up'tight'
up'-to-date'
up'town'
up·turn'
up'ward
u·ra'ni·um
ur'ban
(of the city)
ur·bane'
(socially poised)
ur'ban·ism
ur·ban'i·ty
· ties
ur'ban·i·za'tion
ur'ban·ize'
· ized' iz'ing
ur'chin
u·re'mi·a
u·re'ter
u·re'thra
· thrae or · thras
urge
urged urg'ing
ur'gen·cy
· cies
ur'gent
u'ri·nal
u'ri·nal'y·sis
· ses'
u'ri·nar'y
u'ri·nate'
· nat'ed · nat'ing
u'rine
urn
u'ro·log'i·cal
u·rol'o·gy
u·ros'co·py

us'a·ble or use'·
us'age
use
used us'ing
use'ful
use'less
us'er
ush'er
ush'er·ette'
u'su·al
u'su·al·ly
u'su·fruct'
u'su·rer
u·su'ri·ous
u·surp'
u'sur·pa'tion
u'su·ry
· ries
U'tah
u·ten'sil
u'ter·ine
u'ter·us
· ter·i'
u·til'i·tar'i·an
u·til'i·ty
· ties
u'ti·liz'a·ble
u'ti·li·za'tion
u'ti·lize'
· lized' liz'ing
ut'most'
u·to'pi·a
ut'ter
(speak; see udder)
ut'ter·ance
U'-turn'
ux·o'ri·ous

V

va'can·cy
· cies
va'cant
va'cate
· cat·ed ·cat·ing
va·ca'tion
vac'ci·nate'
· nat'ed · nat'ing
vac'ci·na'tion
vac·cine'
vac'il·late'
· lat'ed · lat'ing
vac'il·la'tion
vac'il·la'tor
va·cu'i·ty
· ties
vac'u·ous
vac'u·um
· ums or · a
vag'a·bond'
va·gar'y
· ies
va·gi'na
· nas or · nae
va'gran·cy
· cies

va'grant
vague
vague'ly
vain
(futile; conceited;
see vane, vein)
vain'glo'ri·ous
vain'glo'ry
val'ance
(drapery; see
valence)
vale
(valley; see veil)
val'e·dic'tion
val'e·dic·to'ri·an
val'e·dic'to·ry
· ries
va'lence
(term in chemis-
try; see valance)
val'en·tine'
val'et
val'iant
val'id
val'i·date'
· dat'ed dat'ing
val'i·da'tion
va·lid'i·ty
va·lise'
val'ley
· leys
val'or
val'or·i·za'tion
val'u·a·ble
val'u·a'tion
val'ue
· ued u·ing
val'ue·less
valve
val'vu·lar
vam'pire
van'dal
van'dal·ism
van'dal·ize'
· ized' iz'ing
Van·dyke'
vane
(blade; see
vain, vein)
van'guard'
va·nil'la
van'ish
van'i·ty
· ties
van'quish
van'tage
vap'id
va'por
va'por·i·za'tion
va'por·ize'
· ized' iz'ing
va'por·iz'er
va'por·ous
va·que'ro
· ros
var'i·a·ble
var'i·a·bly
var'i·ance

var'i·ant
var'i·a'tion
var'i·col'ored
var'i·cose'
var'ied
var'i·e·gate'
· gat'ed · gat'ing
var'i·e·ga'tion
va·ri'e·tal
va·ri'e·ty
· ties
var'i·o'rum
var'i·ous
var'nish
var'si·ty
· ties
var'y
· ied · y·ing
(change; see very)
vas'cu·lar
vas de'fe·rens'
vas'e·line'
vas'sal
(a subordinate;
see vessel)
vast'ness
vat
vat'ted vat'ting
vat'-dyed'
vaude'ville
vault'ing
vaunt
vec'tor
vec·to'ri·al
V'-E' Day
veer
veg'e·ta·ble
veg'e·tar'i·an
veg'e·tate'
· tat'ed · tat'ing
veg'e·ta'tion
veg'e·ta'tive
ve'he·mence
ve'he·ment
ve'hi·cle
ve·hic'u·lar
veil
(screen; see vale)
vein
(blood vessel;
streak; see
vain, vane)
Vel'cro
vel'lum
ve·loc'i·pede'
ve·loc'i·ty
· ties
ve·lour' or · lours
· lours'
ve·lure'
vel'vet
vel'vet·een'
vel'vet·y
ve'nal
(corrupt; see
venial)
ve·nal'i·ty
· ties

vend·ee'
ven·det'ta
ven'dor *or*
 vend'er
ve·neer'
ven'er·a·ble
ven'er·ate'
 ·at'ed ·at'ing
ven'er·a'tion
ve·ne're·al
Ve·ne'tian
venge'ance
venge'ful
ve'ni·al
 (*pardonable;* see
 venal)
ven'i·son
ven'om·ous
ve'nous
ven'ti·late'
 ·lat'ed ·lat'ing
ven·ti·la'tion
ven'ti·la'tor
ven'tri·cle
ven·tril'o·quist
ven'ture
 ·tured ·tur·ing
ven'ture·some
ven'tur·ous
ven'ue
ve·ra'cious
 (*truthful;* see
 voracious)
ve·rac'i·ty
ve·ran'da *or* ·dah
ver'bal
ver'bal·i·za'tion
ver'bal·ize'
 ·ized' ·iz'ing
ver'bal·ly
ver·ba'tim
ver·be'na
ver'bi·age
ver·bose'
ver·bos'i·ty
ver'dant
ver'dict
ver'di·gris'
ver'dure
verge
 verged verg'ing
ver·i·fi'a·ble
ver·i·fi·ca'tion
ver'i·fy'
 ·fied' ·fy'ing
ver'i·ly
ver·i·si·mil'i·tude'
ver'i·ta·ble
ver'i·ta·bly
ver'i·ty
 ·ties
ver'mi·cel'li
ver'mi·cide'
ver·mic'u·lar
ver·mic'u·lite'
ver'mi·form'
ver'mi·fuge'
ver·mil'lion

ver'min
Ver·mont'
ver·mouth'
ver·nac'u·lar
ver'nal
ver'ni·er
ver'sa·tile
ver'sa·tile·ly
ver·sa·til'i·ty
versed
ver'si·fi·ca'tion
ver'si·fy'
 ·fied' ·fy'ing
ver'sion
ver'sus
ver'te·bra
 ·brae' *or* ·bras
ver'te·bral
ver'te·brate
ver'tex
 ·tex·es *or* ·ti·ces'
ver'ti·cal
ver·tig'i·nous
ver'ti·go'
verve
ver'y
 ·i·er ·i·est
 (*complete; exceed-*
 ingly; see vary)
ves'i·cant
ves'i·cate'
 ·cat'ed ·cat'ing
ves'i·cle
ves'per
ves'sel
 (*container; ship;*
 see vassal)
ves'tal
ves'ti·bule
ves'tige
ves·tig'i·al
vest'ment
vest'-pock'et
ves'try
 ·tries
vet'er·an
vet'er·i·nar'i·an
vet'er·i·nar'y
 ·ies
ve'to
 ·toes
 ·toed ·to·ing
vex·a'tion
vex·a'tious
vi·a·bil'i·ty
vi'a·ble
vi'a·duct'
vi'al
 (*bottle;* see
 vile, viol)
vi'and
vi'brant
vi'bra·phone'
vi'brate
 ·brat·ed ·brat·ing
vi·bra'tion
vi·bra'to
 ·tos

vi'bra'tor
vi'bra·to'ry
vic'ar
vic'ar·age
vi·car'i·al
vi·car'i·ous
vice
 (*evil conduct;*
 flaw; see vise)
vice'-chair'man
vice'-chan'cel·lor
vice'-con'sul
vice'-pres'i·dent
vice'roy
vi'ce ver'sa
vi·cin'i·ty
 ·ties
vi'cious
vi·cis'si·tude'
vic'tim
vic'tim·ize'
 ·ized' ·iz'ing
vic'tor
vic·to'ri·a
vic·to'ri·ous
vic'to·ry
 ·ries
vi·cu'ña
vid'e·o'
vid'i·con
vie
 vied vy'ing
view'point'
vig'il
vig'i·lance
vig'i·lant
vig'i·lan'te
vi·gnette'
vig'or
vig'or·ous
vile
 (*evil; offensive;*
 see vial, viol)
vile'ly
vil'i·fi·ca'tion
vil'i·fy'
 ·fied' ·fy'ing
vil'la
vil'lage
vil'lag·er
vil'lain
 (*scoundrel;*
 see villein)
vil'lain·ous
vil'lain·y
 ·ies
vil'lein
 (*serf;* see
 villain)
vin'ai·grette'
vin'ci·ble
vin'di·cate'
 ·cat'ed ·cat'ing
vin'di·ca'tion
vin'di·ca'tive
vin'di·ca'tor
vin·dic'tive

vin'e·gar
vin'er·y
 ·ies
vine'yard
vin'i·cul'ture
vi'nous
vin'tage
vint'ner
vi'nyl
vi'ol
 (*instrument;*
 see vial, viole)
vi·o'la
vi'o·la·ble
vi'o·late'
 ·lat'ed ·lat'ing
vi'o·la'tion
vi'o·la'tor
vi'o·lence
vi'o·lent
vi'o·let
vi'o·lin'
vi·o·lin'ist
vi'o·lon·cel'lo
 ·los
VIP *or* V.I.P.
vi'per
vi·ra'go
 ·goes *or* ·gos
vi'ral
vir'gin
vir'gin·al
Vir·gin'ia
vir·gin'i·ty
vir'gule
vir'ile
vi·ril'i·ty
vi·rol'o·gy
vir·tu'
vir'tu·al
vir'tu·al·ly
vir'tue
vir·tu·os'i·ty
vir·tu·o'so
 ·sos *or* ·si
vir'tu·ous
vir'u·lence
vir'u·lent
vi'rus
vi'sa
vis'age
vis-à-vis'
vis'cer·a
vis'cid
vis·cos'i·ty
vis'count
vis'count·ess
vis'cous
vise
 vised vis'ing
 (*clamp;* see vice)
vis·i·bil'i·ty
vis'i·ble
vis'i·bly
vi'sion
vi'sion·ar'y
 ·ies
vis'it

vis'it·ant
vis·it·a'tion
vis'i·tor
vis'or
vis'ta
vis'u·al
vis'u·al·ize'
 ·ized' ·iz'ing
vi'ta
 ·tae
vi'tal
vi·tal'i·ty
 ·ties
vi'tal·ize'
 ·ized' ·iz'ing
vi'ta·min
vi'ti·a·ble
vi'ti·ate'
 ·at'ed ·at'ing
vi'ti·a'tion
vi'ti·a'tor
vit're·ous
vit'ri·fy'
 ·fied' ·fy'ing
vit'ri·ol
vit·ri·ol'ic
vi·tu'per·ate'
 ·at'ed ·at'ing
vi·tu'per·a'tion
vi·va'cious
vi·vac'i·ty
viv'id
viv'i·fy'
 ·fied' ·fy'ing
vi·vip'a·rous
viv'i·sect'
viv·i·sec'tion
vix'en
V'-J' Day
V'-neck'
vo·cab'u·lar'y
 ·ies
vo'cal cord
vo'cal·ist
vo'cal·ize'
 ·ized' ·iz'ing
vo·ca'tion
vo·cif'er·ate'
 ·at'ed ·at'ing
vo·cif'er·ous
vo'cod'er
vod'ka
vogue
voice'less
voice'print'
void'a·ble
voi·là'
voile
vol'a·tile
vol'a·til'i·ty
vol·can'ic
vol·ca'no
 ·noes *or* ·nos
vol'i·tant
vo·li'tion
vol'ley
 ·leys
 ·leyed ·ley·ing

vol'ley·ball'
volt'age
vol·ta'ic
vol·tam'e·ter
volt'me'ter
vol'u·bil'i·ty
vol'u·ble
vol'u·bly
vol'ume
vo·lu'mi·nous
vol'un·tar'i·ly
vol'un·tar'y
vol'un·teer'
vo·lup'tu·ar'y
 ·ies
vo·lup'tu·ous
vo·lute'
vo·lu'tion
vom'it
voo'doo
 ·doos
vo·ra'cious
 (*greedy;* see
 veracious)
vo·rac'i·ty
vor'tex
 ·tex·es *or* ·ti·ces'
vot'a·ble *or* vote'·
vo'ta·ry
 ·ries
vote
 vot'ed vot'ing
vo'tive
vouch'er
vouch·safe'
 ·safed' ·saf'ing
vow
vow'el
voy'age
 ·aged ·ag·ing
voy'ag·er
vo·yeur'
vroom
vul'can·i·za'tion
vul'can·ize'
 ·ized' ·iz'ing
vul'gar
vul·gar'i·an
vul'gar·ism
vul·gar'i·ty
 ·ties
vul'gar·ize'
 ·ized' ·iz'ing
vul'ner·a·bil'i·ty
vul'ner·a·ble
vul'ner·a·bly
vul'ture
vul'tur·ous
vul'va
vy'ing

W

wad
wad'ded
wad'ding

wad'dle
·dled ·dling
wade
wad'ed
wad'ing
wa'fer
waf'fle
waft
wag
wagged
wag'ging
wage
waged wag'ing
wa'ger
wag'ger·y
·ies
wag'gish
wag'gle
·gled ·gling
Wag·ne'ri·an
wag'on·load'
wa·hi'ne
waif
wail
(cry; see wale,
whale)
wain'scot
·scot·ed or
·scot·ted
·scot·ing or
·scot·ting
wain'wright'
waist'band'
waist'coat
waist'-high'
waist'line'
wait'er
wait'ress
waive
waived waiv'ing
(give up; see
wave)
waiv'er
(a relinquishing;
see waver)
wake
woke or waked,
waked or wok'·
en, wak'ing
wake'ful
wak'en
wale
waled wal'ing
(ridge; see
wail, whale)
walk
walk'a·way'
walk'ie-talk'ie
walk'-in'
walk'-on'
walk'out'
walk'-through'
walk'-up'
walk'way'
wall'board'
wal'let
wall'eyed'
wall'flow'er

wal'lop·ing
wal'low
wall'pa'per
wall'-to-wall'
wal'nut
wal'rus
waltz
wam'pum
wan
wan'ner
wan'nest
wan'der
(stray; see
wonder)
wane
waned wan'ing
wan'gle
·gled ·gling
want'ing
wan'ton
(unjustifiable;
see won ton)
war
warred war'ring
war'ble
·bled ·bling
ward
war'den
ward'robe'
ward'room'
ware'house'
·housed'
·hous'ing
war'fare'
war'head'
war'i·ly
war'i·ness
war'like'
war'lock'
warm'blood'ed
warmed'-o'ver
warm'heart'ed
war'mon'ger
warmth
warm'-up'
warn'ing
warp
war'path'
warped
war'plane'
war'rant
war'ran·ty
·ties
war'ren
war'ri·or
war'ship'
wart
war'time'
war'y
·i·er ·i·est
wash'a·ble
wash'-and-wear'
wash'board'
wash'bowl'
wash'cloth'
washed'-out'
washed'-up'

wash'er
wash'er·wom'an
Wash'ing·ton
wash'out'
wash'room'
wash'stand'
wash'tub'
was'n't
wasp'ish
was'sail
wast'age
waste
wast'ed
wast'ing
waste'bas'ket
waste'ful
waste'land'
waste'pa'per
waste pipe
wast'rel
watch'band'
watch'case'
watch'dog'
watch fire
watch'ful
watch'mak'er
watch'man
watch'tow'er
watch'word'
wa'ter·borne'
wa'ter·col'or
wa'ter-cooled'
water cooler
wa'ter·course'
wa'ter·craft'
wa'ter·cress'
wa'ter·cy'cle
wa'tered
wa'ter·fall'
wa'ter·front'
water glass
water hole
wa'ter·i·ness
wa'ter·less
wa'ter·line'
wa'ter·logged'
wa'ter·mark'
wa'ter·mel'on
water pipe
water power
wa'ter·proof'
wa'ter-re·pel'lent
wa'ter-re·sist'ant
wa'ter·scape'
wa'ter·shed'
wa'ter·side'
wa'ter-ski'
-skied' -ski'ing
wa'ter-ski'er
water skis
wa'ter-soak'
wa'ter-sol'u·ble
wa'ter·spout'
wa'ter·tight'
water tower
wa'ter·way'
water wheel
water wings

wa'ter·works'
wa'ter·worn'
wa'ter·y
watt'age
watt'-hour'
wat'tle
·tled ·tling
watt'me'ter
wave
waved wav'ing
(curving motion;
see waive)
wave'length'
wav'er
(one that waves;
see waiver)
wa'ver
(falter; see
waiver)
wav'i·ness
wav'y
·i·er ·i·est
wax
wax'en
wax'i·ness
wax'work'
wax'y
·i·er ·i·est
way
(route; manner;
see weigh, whey)
way'bill'
way'far'er
way'far'ing
way'lay'
·laid' ·lay'ing
way'side'
way'ward
weak'en
weak'-kneed'
weak'ling
weak'ly
·li·er ·li·est
weak'-mind'ed
weak'ness
weal
(ridge; welfare;
see wheal, wheel)
wealth'i·ness
wealth'y
·i·er ·i·est
wean
weap'on
wear
wore worn
wear'ing
wear'a·ble
wea'ri·ly
wea'ri·ness
wea'ri·some
wea'ry
·ri·er ·ri·est
·ried ·ry·ing
wea'sel
weath'er
(atmospheric con-
ditions; see
whether)

weath'er-beat'en
weath'er-bound'
weath'er·cock'
weath'er·man'
weath'er·proof'
weath'er·strip'
·stripped'
·strip'ping
weather vane
weave
wove, wov'en or
wove, weav'ing
(interlace)
weave
weaved
weav'ing
(move in and out
as in traffic)
weav'er
web
webbed
web'bing
web'foot'
·feet'
web'-foot'ed
wed
wed'ded,
wed'ded or
wed, wed'ding
we'd
wedge
wedged
wedg'ing
Wedg'wood'
wed'lock
Wednes'day
wee
we'er we'est
weed'i·ness
week'day'
week'end' or
week'-end'
week'ly
·lies
weep
wept weep'ing
weep'i·ness
weep'y
·i·er ·i·est
wee'vil
weigh
weighed
weigh'ing
(measure weight
of; see way, whey)
weight'i·ness
weight'less
weight'y
·i·er ·i·est
weir
(dam; see we're)
weird
wel'come
·comed ·com·ing
weld'er
wel'fare'
well'-ad·vised'
well'-ap·point'ed

well'-bal'anced
well'-be·haved'
well'-be'ing
well'-be·loved'
well'born'
well'-bred'
well'-chos'en
well'-con·tent'
well'-dis·posed'
well'do'ing
well'-done'
well'-fa'vored
well'-fed'
well'-found'ed
well'-groomed'
well'-ground'ed
well'-han'dled
well'head'
well'-in·formed'
well'-in·ten'·
tioned
well'-knit'
well'-known'
well'-made'
well'-man'nered
well'-mean'ing
well'-meant'
well'-nigh'
well'-off'
well'-or'dered
well'-pre·served'
well'-read'
well'-round'ed
well'-spo'ken
well'spring'
well'-thought'-of'
well'-timed'
well'-to-do'
well'-turned'
well'-wish'er
well'-worn'
we'll
Welsh rabbit
or rarebit
welt'er
welt'er·weight'
we're
(we are; see
weir)
weren't
were'wolf'
·wolves'
wes'kit
west'er·ly
·lies
west'ern·er
west'ern·ize'
·ized' ·iz'ing
west'-north'west'
west'-south'west'
West Vir·gin'ia
west'ward
wet
wet'ter wet'test
wet or wet'ted
wet'ting
(moistened;
see whet)

wet'back'
wet'ta·ble
whale
  whaled whal'ing
  (fishlike mammal;
  see wail, wale)
whale'boat'
whale'bone'
whal'er
  wharves *or*
  wharfs
wharf'age
wharf'in·ger
what·ev'er
what'not'
what·so·ev'er
wheal
  (pimple; see
  weal, wheel)
wheat
whee'dle
  ·dled ·dling
wheel
  (disk for turning;
  see weal, wheal)
wheel'bar'row
wheel'base'
wheel'chair'
wheel'house'
wheel'wright'
wheeze
wheezed
wheez'ing
wheez'y
  ·i·er ·i·est
whelp
when
whence
when·ev'er
where
where'a·bouts'
where·as'
where·by'
where'fore'
where·in'
where·of'
where·up·on'
wher·ev'er
where·with'
where'with·al'
wher'ry
  ·ries, ·ried ·ry·ing
whet
whet'ted
whet'ting
  (sharpen; see wet)
wheth'er
  (if; see weather)
whet'stone'
whey
  (thin part of milk;
  see way, weigh)
which·ev'er
whiff
while
  whiled whil'ing
  (time; see wile)

whim
whim'per
whim'si·cal
whim'sy
  ·sies
whine
  whined whin'ing
  (cry; see wine)
whin'i·ness
whin'ny
  ·nies
  ·nied ·ny·ing
  (neigh)
whin'y
  ·i·er ·i·est
  (complaining)
whip
whipped
whip'ping
whip'cord'
whip'lash'
whip'pet
whip'poor·will'
whip'saw'
whip'stitch'
whip'stock'
whir *or* whirr
whirred
whir'ring
whirl
whirl'pool'
whirl'wind'
whisk broom
whisk'er
whis'key
  keys *or* ·kies
whis'per
whis'tle
  ·tled ·tling
whis'tler
whit
  (bit; see wit)
white
  whit'ed whit'ing
white'cap'
white'-col'lar
white'-haired'
white'-hot'
white'-liv'ered
whit'en·er
white'ness
whit'en·ing
white room
white'wall'
white'wash'
whith'er
  (where; see
  wither)*
whit'ing
whit'tle
  ·tled ·tling
whiz *or* whizz
whizzed
whiz'zing
who·ev'er
whole'heart'ed
whole'sale'
  ·saled ·sal'ing

whole'sal'er
whole'some
whole'-wheat'
whol'ly
  (completely; see
  holey, holy)*
whom·ev'er
whom'so·ev'er
whoop'ee
whop'per
whore
whorl
who's
  (who is; who has)
whose
  (poss. of who)
who'so·ev'er
why
wick'ed
wick'er·work'
wick'et
wide'-an'gle
wide'-a·wake'
wide'-eyed'
wid'en
wide'-o'pen
wide'spread'
wid'get
wid'ow
wid'ow·er
width
wield
wield'y
  ·i·er ·i·est
wie'ner
wife
  wives
wife'ly
wig'gle
  ·gled ·gling
wig'gly
wig'let
wig'wam
wild'cat'
  ·cat'ted ·cat'ting
wil'de·beest'
wil'der·ness
wild'-eyed'
wild'fire'
wild'life'
wile
  wiled wil'ing
  (trick; see while)
wil'i·ness
will'ful *or* wil'·
  will'ing·ness
will'-o'-the-wisp'
wil'low·y
will'pow'er
wil'ly-nil'ly
wi'ly
  ·li·er ·li·est
wim'ple
  ·pled ·pling
win
  won win'ning
wince
  winced winc'ing

wind
  wound wind'ing
wind'blown'
wind'-borne'
wind'break'er
wind'burn'
wind'fall'
wind'i·ness
wind'lass
  (winch)
wind'less
  (without wind)
wind'mill'
win'dow
win'dow·pane'
win'dow·shop'
wind'row'
wind'shield'
wind'storm'
wind'-swept'
wind'up'
wind'ward
wind'y
  ·i·er ·i·est
wine
  wined win'ing
  (drink; see whine)
wine cellar
wine'-col'ored
wine'glass'
wine'grow'er
wine press
win'er·y
  ·ies
Wine'sap'
wine'skin'
wing chair
wing'span'
wing'spread'
win'ner
win'now
win'some
win'ter
win'ter·green'
win'ter·ize'
  ·ized' ·iz'ing
win'ter·time'
win'try
  ·tri·er ·tri·est
wipe
  wiped wip'ing
wire
  wired wir'ing
wire'draw'
  ·drew' ·drawn'
  ·draw'ing
wire'hair'
wire'-haired'
wire'less
Wire'pho'to
wire'pull'er
wire'tap'
wire'work'
wir'i·ness
wir'y
  ·i·er ·i·est
Wis·con'sin
wis'dom

wise
  wis'er wis'est
wise'ly
wish'bone'
wish'ful
wisp
wist'ful
wit
  (sense; see whit)
witch'craft'
witch'er·y
  ·ies
with·draw'
  ·drew' ·drawn'
  ·draw'ing
with·draw'al
with'er
  (wilt; see whither)
with·hold'
  ·held' ·hold'ing
with·in'
with·out'
with·stand'
  ·stood'
  ·stand'ing
wit'less
wit'ness
wit'ti·cism
wit'ti·ness
wit'ty
  ·ti·er ·ti·est
wiz'ard
wiz'ard·ry
wiz'ened
wob'ble
  ·bled ·bling
woe'be·gone'
woe'ful
wolf
  wolves
wolf'hound'
wom'an
  wom'en
wom'an·hood'
wom'an·kind'
wom'an·li·ness
wom'an·ly
womb
wom'en·folk'
won'der
  (marvel; see
  wander)*
won'der·ful
won'der·land'
won'der·work'
won'der·work'er
won'drous
wont
  (accustomed)
won't
  (will not)
won' ton'
  (food; see wanton)
wood'carv'ing
wood'chuck'
wood'craft'
wood'cut'
wood'ed

wood'land'
wood'peck'er
wood'pile'
wood pulp
wood'shed'
woods'man
wood'sy
  ·si·er ·si·est
wood'wind'
wood'work'
wood'y
  ·i·er ·i·est
woof'er
wool'en
wool'gath'er·ing
wool'grow'er
wool'lies *or*
  wool'ies
wool'li·ness *or*
  wool'i·ness
wool'ly *or*
  wool'y
  ·li·er *or* ·i·er
  ·li·est *or* ·i·est
Worces'ter·shire'
word'age
word'book'
word'i·ly
word'i·ness
word'less
word'-of-mouth'
word'play'
wood'y
  ·i·er ·i·est
work
  worked *or*
  wrought
work'ing
work'a·ble
work'a·day'
work'bench'
work'book'
work'day'
work'house'
work'ing·man'
work'load'
work'man·like'
work'man·ship'
work'out'
work'room'
work'shop'
work'ta·ble
work'week'
world'li·ness
world'ly
  ·li·er ·li·est
world'ly-wise'
world'-shak'ing
world'-wea'ry
world'wide'
worm'-eat'en
worm gear
worm'hole'
worm'i·ness
worm wheel
worm'wood'
worm'y
  ·i·er ·i·est

worn'-out'
wor'ri·er
wor'ri·ment
wor'ri·some
wor'ry
 ·ries
 ·ried ·ry·ing
wor'ry·wart'
worse
wors'en
wor'ship
 ·shiped or
 ·shipped
 ·ship·ing or
 ·ship·ping
wor'ship·er or
 wor'ship·per
wor'ship·ful
worst
wor'sted
wor'thi·ly
wor'thi·ness
worth'less
worth'while'
wor'thy
 ·thi·er ·thi·est
would
would'-be'
wound
wrack
wraith
wran'gle
 ·gled ·gling
wran'gler
wrap
 wrapped or
 wrapt
 wrap'ping
 (cover; see rap)
wrap'a·round'
wrap'per
wrath'ful
wreak
 (inflict; see reek)

wreath n.
wreathe v.
 wreathed
 wreath'ing
wreck'age
wreck'er
wrench
wres'tle
 ·tled ·tling
wres'tler
wretch
 (miserable
 person; see
 retch)
wretch'ed
wrig'gle
 ·gled ·gling
wring
 wrung wring'ing
 (twist; see ring)
wrin'kle
 ·kled ·kling
wrin'kly
 ·kli·er ·kli·est
wrist'band'
wrist'let
wrist pin
wrist'watch'
writ
write
 wrote writ'ten
 writ'ing
 (inscribe; see
 right, rite)
write'-in'
write'-off'
writ'er
write'-up'
writhe
 writhed
 writh'ing
wrong'do'er
wrong'do'ing
wrong'ful

wrote
 (pt. of write;
 see rote)
wrought
wrought'-up'
wrung
 (pt. and pp. of
 wring; see rung)
wry
 wried wry'ing
 wri'er wri'est
 (twisted; see rye)
wry'ly
Wy·o'ming

X

x
 x-ed or x'd
 x-ing or x'ing
xan'thous
xe'bec
xen'o·pho'bi·a
xe·rog'ra·phy
xe·roph'i·lous
Xe'rox
Xmas
X'-ray' or
 X ray
xy'lo·phone'
xy'lo·phon'ist

Y

yacht
yachts'man
Yan'kee

yard'age
yard'arm'
yard'mas'ter
yard'stick'
yarn'-dyed'
yawl
yawn
yea
year'book'
year'ling
year'long'
year'ly
yearn
year'-round'
yeast
yel'low
yelp
yen
 yenned yen'ning
yeo'man
yes
 yessed yes'sing
ye·shi'va
yes'ter·day
yes'ter·year'
yet
yew
 (tree; see ewe)
Yid'dish
yield
yip'pie
yo'del
 ·deled or ·delled
 ·del·ing or
 ·del·ling
yo'del·er or
 yo'del·ler
yo'ga
yo'gi
 ·gis
yo'gurt
yoke
 yoked yok'ing
 (harness)

yolk
 (of an egg)
Yom Kip'pur
yon'der
you'd
you'll
young'ster
your
 (poss. of you)
you're
 (you are)
yours
your·self'
 ·selves'
youth'ful
you've
yowl
yo'-yo'
yule log
yule'tide'

Z

zai'ba·tsu'
 ·tsu'
za'ni·ness
za'ny
 ·nies, ·ni·er
 ·ni·est
zeal
zeal'ot
zeal'ous
ze'bra
ze'brass'
ze'bu
Zeit'geist'
Zen
ze'nith
ze'o·lite'

ze'o·lit'ic
zeph'yr
zep'pe·lin
ze'ro
 ·ros or ·roes
 ·roed ·ro·ing
zest'ful·ly
zest'ful·ness
zig'zag'
 ·zagged'
 ·zag'ging
zinc
zincked or zinced
zinck'ing or
 zinc'ing
zin'ni·a
Zi'on·ism
zip
 zipped zip'ping
ZIP Code
zip'per
zir'con
zith'er
zo'di·ac'
zo·di'a·cal
zom'bie
zon'al
zone
 zoned zon'ing
zoo
zo'o·ge·og'ra·phy
zo'o·log'i·cal
zo·ol'o·gist
zo·ol'o·gy
zoom lens
zoy'si·a
zuc·chet'to
 ·tos
zuc·chi'ni
 ·ni or ·nis
zwie'back
zy'gote
zy·mol'o·gy
zy'mur·gy

20

Forms of Address

revised by Joyce Gold

The proper form of address is essential for creating a positive initial impression, whether in a letter, on the telephone, or in person. The chart on the following pages is arranged alphabetically by the title of the person being addressed. Where pertinent, the plural form is also given for situations in which more than one person with the same title is addressed.

A few general guidelines:

- Military officers retain their highest rank when they retire and this rank should be used when they are addressed.
- Titles such as Reverend and Honorable are used with the full name on the envelope address, but they are not used in the salutation.
- When the title Esquire is used, it is abbreviated after the full name, and no other title is used before the name—for example, John Smith, Esq.

For titles not on the chart, the common procedure to be used when addressing the person is to use the title and the surname—for example, Chief Smith.

Person Being Addressed	Envelope Address	Business Salutation	Social Salutation	In Speaking
Abbot	The Right Reverend (full name), (address of church)	Right Reverend Abbot:	Dear Father Abbot:	Abbot (surname)
Ambassador (United States)	The Honorable (full name), The Ambassador of the United States, Embassy of the United States of America (city and country)	Sir (*or* Madam):	Dear Mr. (*or* Madam) Ambassador:	Mr. Ambassador (*or* Madam Ambassador) Mr. (*or* Mrs., *or* Ms., *or* Miss) (surname) *or* Sir *or* Madam
Ambassador (Foreign)	His (*or* Her) Excellency (full name), Ambassador of (country), Washington, D.C.	Excellency:	Dear Mr. (*or* Madam) Ambassador:	Excellency *or* Mr. Ambassador (*or* Madam Ambassador) *or* Sir (*or* Madam)
Apostolic Delegate	His Excellency, The Most Reverend (full name), Archbishop of (name of church), The Apostolic Delegate, (address of church)	Your Excellency:	Dear Archbishop:	Your Excellency *or* Archbishop (surname)
Archbishop (Roman Catholic)	The Most Reverend (full name), Archbishop of (city), (city and state, etc.)	Your Excellency: *or* Most Reverend Sir:	Dear Archbishop (surname):	Your Excellency *or* Archbishop (surname)
Assemblyman (see Representative)				
Attorney General	The Honorable (full name), Attorney General, Washington, D.C. 20503	Sir (*or* Madam):	Dear Mr. (*or* Madam) Attorney General:	Mr. (*or* Madam) Attorney General *or* Mr. (*or* Mrs., Ms., *or* Miss) (surname)
Bishop (Methodist)	Bishop (full name), (city and state, etc.)	Dear Bishop (surname):	Dear Bishop (surname):	Bishop (surname)

Person Being Addressed	Envelope Address	Business Salutation	Social Salutation	In Speaking
Bishop (Protestant Episcopal)	The Right Reverend (full name), Bishop of (diocese), (city and state, etc.)	Right Reverend Sir:	Dear Bishop (surname):	Bishop (surname)
Bishop (Roman Catholic)	The Most Reverend (full name), (church), (city and state, etc.)	Most Reverend Sir:	Dear Bishop (surname):	Bishop (surname)
Brother (of a religious order)	Brother (religious name plus initials of his order), (address, city, and state)	Dear Brother:	Dear Brother (religious name):	Brother (religious name)
Cabinet Officer of the United States	The Honorable (full name), (title), Washington, D.C.	Sir (or Madam): or Dear Sir (or Dear Madam):	Dear Mr. (or Madam) Secretary: or Dear Mr. (or Mrs. or Ms. or Miss) (surname):	Mr. (or Madam) Secretary or Sir (or Madam) or Mr. (or Mrs. or Ms. or Miss) (surname)
Cardinal (Roman Catholic)	His Eminence (given name) Cardinal (surname), Archbishop of (city, etc.), (city and state, etc.)	Your Eminence:	Dear Cardinal (surname):	Your Eminence or Cardinal (surname)
Clergyman, Protestant (without degree)	The Reverend (full name), (address of his church)	Dear Sir:	Dear Mr. (surname):	Mr. (surname) or The Reverend (full name)
Clergyman, Protestant (with degree)	The Reverend (full name), D.D. (LL.D., if held), (address of his church)	Dear Sir:	Dear Dr. (surname):	Dr. (surname) or The Reverend Dr. (full name)
Clergyman, Lutheran	The Reverend (full name), (address of his church)	Dear Sir:	Dear Pastor (surname):	Pastor or Pastor (surname)

Person Being Addressed	Envelope Address	Business Salutation	Social Salutation	In Speaking
ommissioner	The Honorable (full name), Commissioner, (city, state)	Dear Mr. (or Madam) Commissioner:	Dear Mr. (or Madam) Commissioner or Mr. (or Mrs. or Miss or Ms.) (surname)	Mr. (or Mrs. or Miss or Ms.) (surname)
Common Form (Man)	Mr. (full name), (address, city, and state)	Dear Mr. (surname): or My Dear Sir: in plural, Gentlemen:	Dear Mr. (surname): in plural, Dear Messrs. (surname):	Mr. (surname)
Common Form (Woman)	Mrs. (or Miss or Ms.) (full name), (address, city, and state)	Dear Mrs. (or Miss or Ms.) (surname): or Dear Madam: in plural, Mesdames:	Dear Mrs. (or Miss or Ms.) (surname): or Dear Madam: in plural, Mesdames:	Miss (or Mrs. or Ms.) (surname)
Congressman (see Representative)				
Consul (United States or other)	(full name), Esquire, American (or other) Consul, (city and country, or state)	Sir (or Madam): or Dear Sir (or Dear Madam):	Dear Mr. (or Mrs. or Ms. or Miss) (surname):	Mr. (or Mrs. or Ms. or Miss) (surname)
Doctor (of Philosophy, Medicine, Divinity, Dentistry, etc.)	(full name), Ph.D., M.D., D.D., D.D.S., etc., or Dr. (full name), (address, city, and state)	Dear Dr. (surname): or Dear Sir (or Dear Madam):	Dear Dr. (surname):	Dr. (surname)
Former President	The Honorable (full name), (address, city, and state)	Sir:	Dear Mr. (surname):	Mr. (surname) or Sir
Governor (of a state)	The Honorable (or in some states His or Her Excellency) (full name), Governor of (state), (capital city and state)	Sir (or Madam):	Dear Governor (surname):	Governor (surname) or Sir (or Madam)

Person Being Addressed	Envelope Address	Business Salutation	Social Salutation	In Speaking
Judge (see also Supreme Court)	The Honorable (full name), Justice (name of court), (city and state)	Sir (or Madam):	Dear Judge (surname):	Judge (surname)
Lawyer	(Full name), Esq. (office address) or Mr. (or Mrs. or Miss or Ms.) (surname)	Dear Sir (or Madam):	Dear Mr. (or Mrs. or Miss or Ms.) (surname):	Mr. (or Mrs. or Miss or Ms.) (surname)
Mayor	His (or Her) Honor, The Mayor, City Hall (city and state)	Sir (or Madam):	Dear Mr. (or Madam) Mayor:	Mr. (or Madam) Mayor (surname)
Military Enlisted Personnel (American)—Army, Navy, Coast Guard, Air Force, Marine Corps	(title of rank), (full name), (address)	Sir (or Madam): or Dear Sir (or Dear Madam):	Dear Private (or Airman, or Seaman) (surname):	Private (or Airman, or Seaman) (surname)
Military Officer (American)—Army, Navy, Coast Guard, Air Force, Marine Corps	(title of rank), (full name), (address)	Sir (or Madam): or Dear Sir (or Dear Madam):	Dear General (or Admiral, Colonel, Major, Captain, etc.) (surname):	General (or Colonel, or Admiral, Major, Captain, etc.) (surname)
Minister of a Foreign Country	The Honorable (full name), The Minister of (Country), Washington, D.C.	Sir:	Dear Mr. (or Madam) Minister:	Mr. (or Madam) Minister or Mr. (or Mrs. or Miss or Ms.) (surname)
Minister Plenipotentiary of the United States	The Honorable (full name), The Minister of the United States, American Legation, (city, country)	Sir or Madam:	Dear Mr. (or Madam) Minister:	Mr. (or Madam) Minister or Mr. (or Mrs. or Miss or Ms.) (surname)

Person Being Addressed	Envelope Address	Business Salutation	Social Salutation	In Speaking
Minister (Protestant)	The Reverend (full name plus D.D. if applicable), (address, city, and state)	Dear Sir (or Dear Madam): or Sir (or Madam):	Dear Mr. (or Mrs. or Ms. or Miss or Dr.) (surname):	Mr. (or Mrs. or Ms. or Miss or Dr. or, if a Lutheran, Pastor) (surname)
Monsignor (Roman Catholic)	The Right Reverend Monsignor (surname), (church), (city and state)	Right Reverend and Monsignor (surname):	Dear Monsignor (surname):	Monsignor (surname)
Naval Enlisted Personnel (American)	(title of rank), (full name), (address)	Sir (or Madam): or Dear Sir (or Dear Madam):	Dear Seaman (or Quartermaster, etc.) (surname):	Seaman (or Quartermaster, etc.) (surname)
Naval Officer (American)	(title of rank), (full name), (address)	Sir (or Madam): or Dear Sir (or Dear Madam):	Dear Admiral (or Commodore, Captain, etc.) (surname):	Admiral (or Commodore, Captain, etc.) (surname)
Patriarch (Eastern Orthodox Church)	His Beatitude the Patriarch of (name of church), (address of his church)	Most Reverend Lord:	Your Beatitude or Most Reverend Lord:	Your Beatitude or Most Reverend Lord
Pope	His Holiness the Pope, Vatican City, Italy	Your Holiness:	Your Holiness: or Most Holy Father:	Your Holiness (or Most Holy Father)
Premier	His (or Her) Excellency (full name), Premier of (country), (city, country)	Excellency:	Dear Mr. (or Madam) Premier:	Your Excellency or Mr. (or Mrs. or Miss or Ms.) (surname)
President (of the United States)	The President, The White House, Washington, D.C. 20500	Sir: or Mr. President:	Dear Mr. President: or Dear President (surname):	Mr. President or Sir

Person Being Addressed	Envelope Address	Business Salutation	Social Salutation	In Speaking
Priest (Episcopal)	The Reverend (full name) *or* (if with degree) The Reverend Dr. (full name), (address of his church)	Dear Mr. (surname): *or* Dear Dr. (surname):	Dear Mr. (surname): *or* Dear Dr. (surname): *or* Dear Father (surname):	Mr. (surname) *or* Father (surname) *or* Dr. (surname)
Priest (Roman Catholic)	The Reverend (full name plus initials of his order), (address, city, and state)	Reverend Father:	Dear Father (surname):	Father (surname) *or* Father
Prime Minister	His (*or* Her) Excellency (full name), Prime Minister of (country), (city, country)	Excellency:	Dear Mr. (*or* Madam) Prime Minister:	Mr. (*or* Madam) Prime Minister or Mr. (*or* Mrs. *or* Miss *or* Ms.) (surname)
Professor	Professor (*or* Dr. if Ph.D.) (full name), Department of (Mathematics, History, etc.), (name of university or college), (address, city, and state)	Dear Sir (*or* Madam):	Dear Professor (surname): *or* Dear Dr.(surname):	In certain universities (*e.g.,* Harvard) all faculty members are orally addressed as Mr. (*or* Mrs. *or* Ms. *or* Miss) Professor (*or* surname) Professor (*or* Dr. *or* Mr. *or* Mrs. *or* Ms. *or* Miss) (surname)
Rabbi	Rabbi (full name plus D.D. if applicable), (address, city, and state)	Dear Sir (*or* Madam):	Dear Rabbi (*or* Dr.) (surname):	Rabbi (*or* Dr.) (surname)
Representative (of a state legislature)	The Honorable (full name), Member of Assembly (*or* other name of the legislature), (capital city and state)	Sir (*or* Madam):	Dear Mr. (*or* Mrs. *or* Ms. *or* Miss) (surname):	Mr. (*or* Mrs. *or* Ms. *or* Miss) (surname)

Person Being Addressed	Envelope Address	Business Salutation	Social Salutation	In Speaking
Representative (of the United States Congress)	The Honorable (full name), United States House of Representatives, Washington, D.C. 20515	Sir (*or* Madam):	Dear Mr. (*or* Mrs. *or* Ms. *or* Miss) (surname)	Mr. (*or* Mrs. *or* Ms. *or* Miss) (surname)
Senator (of a state legislature)	The Honorable (full name), The Senate of (state), (capital city and state)	Sir (*or* Madam):	Dear Senator (surname):	Senator (surname) *or* Mr. (*or* Madam) Senator
Senator (of the United States)	The Honorable (full name), United States Senate, Washington, D.C. 20510	Sir (*or* Madam):	Dear Senator (surname):	Senator (surname) *or* Mr. (*or* Madam) Senator
Sister (of a religious order)	Sister (religious name plus initials of her order), (address, city, and state)	Dear Sister:	Dear Sister (religious name):	Sister (religious name)
Supreme Court (of a state) (Associate Justice)	The Honorable (full name), Associate Justice of the Supreme Court of (state), (address)	Sir (*or* Madam):	Dear Justice (surname):	Mr. (*or* Madam) Justice (surname) *or* Judge (surname)
Supreme Court (of a state) (Chief Justice)	The Honorable (full name), Chief Justice of the Supreme Court of (state), (address)	Sir (*or* Madam):	Dear Mr. (*or* Madam) Chief Justice:	Mr. (*or* Madam) Chief Justice *or* Chief Justice (surname) *or* Judge (surname)
Supreme Court (of the United States) (Associate Justice)	Mr. Justice (surname), The Supreme Court, Washington, D.C. 20543	Sir (*or* Madam):	Dear Mr. (*or* Madam) Justice (surname):	Mr. (*or* Madam) Justice *or* Mr. (*or* Madam) Justice (surname) *or* Sir (*or* Madam)

Person Being Addressed	Envelope Address	Business Salutation	Social Salutation	In Speaking
Supreme Court (of the United States) (Chief Justice)	The Chief Justice, The Supreme Court, Washington, D.C. 20543	Sir:	Dear Mr. Chief Justice:	Mr. Chief Justice *or* Sir
United Nations Delegate (other than U.S.)	His (*or* Her) Excellency, (country) Representative to the United Nations, United Nations, New York 10017	Sir (*or* Madam): *or* Your Excellency:	Dear Mr. (*or* Madam) Ambassador: *or* Dear Mr. (*or* Ms. *or* Miss *or* Mrs.) (surname):	Your Excellency
United Nations Delegate (United States)	The Honorable (full name), United States Permanent Representative to the United Nations, United Nations, New York 10017	Sir (*or* Madam):	Dear Mr. (*or* Madam) Ambassador *or* Dear Mr. (*or* Ms. *or* Miss *or* Mrs.) (surname):	Mr. Ambassador (*or* Madam Ambassador)
United Nations Secretary-General	His Excellency (full name), Secretary-General of the United Nations, United Nations, New York 10017	Sir *or* Your Excellency:	Dear Mr. Secretary-General:	Your Excellency *or* Secretary-General (surname)
University Chancellor	Dr. (full name), Chancellor, (address of university)	Sir (*or* Madam):	Dear Dr. (surname):	Dr. (surname)
University or College Chaplain	The Reverend (full name), Chaplain, (address of school)	Dear Sir (*or* Madam):	Dear Chaplain (surname): *or* Dear Mr. (*or* Mrs. *or* Miss *or* Ms.) (surname): *or* Dear Father (surname):	Chaplain (surname) *or* Mr. (*or* Mrs. *or* Miss *or* Ms.) (surname) *or* Father (surname)

Person Being Addressed	Envelope Address	Business Salutation	Social Salutation	In Speaking
University or College Dean	Dean (full name) or Dr. (full name) Dean, (address of school)	Sir (or Madam):	Dear Dr. (surname): or Dear Dean (surname):	Dean (surname) or Dr. (surname)
University or College President	Dr. (full name) or President (full name) (address of school)	Sir (or Madam):	Dear President (surname): or Dear Dr. (surname):	Dr. (surname)
Vice President (of the United States)	The Vice President, United States Senate, Washington, D.C. 20510	Sir:	Dear Mr. Vice President:	Mr. Vice President (or Sir)
Warrant Officer	Warrant Officer (or Chief Warrant Officer) (full name), (address)	Sir (or Madam): or Dear Sir (or Dear Madam):	Dear Mr. (or Mrs. or Ms. or Miss) (surname):	Mr. (or Mrs. or Ms. or Miss) (surname)

Legal Information

21

General Legal Principles

by William W. Cook, J.D.
revised by Naomi Dornfeld Platt, Ed.D.

■ *Criminal Law*

> *Levels of Crime*
> *Violations*
> *Criminals and Jurisdiction*

■ *The Civil Law*

> *The Law of Torts*
> *The Law of Contracts*
> *Personal Property*
> *Real Property*
> *Estates and Trusts*

■ *The Uniform Commercial Code*

> *Sales*
> *Secured Transactions*
> *Bulk Sales or Transfers*
> *Commercial Paper*

■ *Relationships between Businesses and Employees/Agents*

> *Employer–Employee Relationships*
> *Agencies*
> *Independent Contractors*

■ *Forms of Doing Business*

> *Individual Proprietorship*
> *Partnership*
> *Limited Partnership*
> *Incorporation*

This overview of general legal principles can trace its sources and heritage to the great lawgivers: Moses, Solon, and Justinian; to the *Code of Hammurabi* and to the *Magna Carta;* and to the common law as it developed throughout English history. The common law is the basis of our legal system and, where it has not been changed by constitutional provisions or statutes, is in force and effect throughout this country. The laws of the state of Louisiana, which have their antecedents in the *Napoleonic Code,* are the exception.

The Constitution of the United States is the supreme law of the land. It creates the basic framework of our government and provides for and protects the fundamental rights of each citizen and of society as a whole. Congress is conferred with authority to pass legislation to govern in accordance with its constitutional mandate. But the Constitution reserves to the individual states: *The powers not delegated to the United States . . . nor prohibited by it to the states. . . .* Each state, therefore, has its own constitution and laws, which are markedly varied and diverse.

We have in effect 51 different "legal systems" or jurisdictions: one for the federal government and one for each of the 50 states. In addition, the states confer upon their townships and municipalities the authority to pass laws, regulations, and ordinances. Both the federal and state governments confer upon agencies the power to enact rules and regulations affecting, among other things, trade and commerce. This vastly increases the total number of legal systems that govern, regulate, and control almost every aspect of our lives.

The laws passed by the respective legislatures are codified. Federal laws can be found in the *United States Code* and state laws in the respective statutes of each state. In addition, rules and regulations passed by various agencies can be found in registers such as the *Code of Federal Regulations.* The laws passed by municipalities may be found in *Administrative Codes.* The common law is found in the published legal decisions of each court.

This overview of general legal principles is not meant to be, nor is it a substitute for, competent legal advice. Because of the marked diversity of our legal systems, legal advice must be sought from attorneys licensed in the jurisdiction where the activity, matter, or event arises and occurs.

This chapter discusses briefly criminal law, civil law, the uniform commercial code, and the forms of doing business and the service relationships involved.

CRIMINAL LAW

One of the major divisions of U.S. law is that between criminal law and civil law. The underlying purpose of criminal laws is to ensure that members of society have their constitutional rights of life, liberty, and the pursuit of happiness. To this end, criminal laws provide for the punishment of antisocial behavior. Essentially, a crime is an offense against society as a whole.

Traditionally, crimes have been punished by either a fine or imprisonment or both. Courts today are also increasingly ordering offenders to make restitution to their victims, that is, to "pay back" or compensate the victim for the loss that has been sustained. A court may, for example, punish by imprisonment one who has embezzled funds from an employer. It may also order the offender to return the embezzled funds to the rightful owner.

Generally, to be a crime, the act must be committed intentionally, although negligence, if it is sufficiently wanton and willful, may be criminal. Crimes are also classified according to their seriousness.

Levels of Crimes

There are two basic levels of crimes: felonies and misdemeanors.

Felonies

Felonies are serious crimes. They can be either violent, such as homicide, arson, rape, robbery, and assault, or nonviolent, such as embezzlement, extortion, larceny, bribery, insurance fraud, and tax fraud. Felonies are usually punishable by one or more years' imprisonment and/or a fine and, in some cases, by death.

The violent crimes (homicide, rape, robbery, arson, and assault) are committed directly against the person or his or her property by use of physical force. This endangers not only the victim's life but also the lives of others who may be injured or killed during the commission of such a crime. For example, in the case of arson (the destruction, by burning, of another person's real property), tenants in a building and not just the owner may be killed in the fire.

Nonviolent, or *white collar,* crimes are committed directly against the property of an individual, business, corporation, or government without the element of physical force. These crimes are committed by stealth, concealment, and deception.

Misdemeanors

All other crimes, less serious by their nature, are considered misdemeanors. They are usually punishable by imprisonment of less than one year and/or a fine. Examples include lesser degrees of both violent and nonviolent crimes. To determine if a crime is a misdemeanor or a felony, distinctions are made as to the amount of money involved, the extent of force used, and intent. What constitutes a crime—the definition of an act as a felony or misdemeanor—varies from state to state.

Violations

Most states and the federal government make distinctions between crimes (felonies and misdemeanors) and violations. A violation is not a crime. It is an infraction of some rule or regulation promulgated by a federal, state, or city government or regulatory agency. Such an infraction is usually punishable by a fine. Examples include traffic violations (speeding, parking, red light, and stop sign infractions); disturbing the peace; violations of Health Department no-smoking prohibitions; and Building Department construction code violations.

In our complex society, almost every phase of business is regulated, to some degree, by federal, state, and/or municipal regulatory agencies. Any breach of their regulations may constitute a violation.

Criminals and Jurisdiction

Crimes and violations may be committed by individuals and corporations. As will be subsequently discussed, the corporation is legally similar in many ways to a person. A corporation cannot, of course, do or be subject to things that are peculiar to persons. A corporation cannot, for example, commit perjury or be imprisoned. Corporate offenses can therefore be punished only by fines. A careful distinction should be made concerning a criminal offense by an individual within a corporation and an offense by the corporation itself. A corporate officer *could* commit perjury or be imprisoned for an offense committed in that officer's own right.

Other forms of doing business such as the proprietorship (one person doing business) or the partnership (two or more persons doing business jointly) cannot commit a criminal offense in the same way as a corporation.

Crimes fall under either federal or state jurisdiction. Jurisdiction is simply the power of a given type of court to hear and decide a case. A crime that crosses state lines is subject to federal jurisdiction. A federal statute—the Dyer Act, for example—prohibits transporting a vehicle known to be stolen across state lines. Crimes committed on federal property, such as a military reservation, also fall under federal jurisdiction.

THE CIVIL LAW

The civil law includes the remainder of the law after criminal law. The civil law has many branches, but the principal ones include the law of torts, contracts, real and personal property, estates and trusts, and domestic relations. Civil law exists to resolve conflicts between parties rather than between an offender and society. A civilly injured party is entitled to receive some type of compensation for the injury, and the party responsible for the injury cannot be fined or imprisoned for the act. "Injury" as used here refers not only to physical injury but to other types such as monetary damage.

The Law of Torts

A *tort* is any wrong or damage, except breach of contract, for which a civil action, usually for monetary damages, can be brought by one person against another. (As a rule, the attorney fees of the injured party cannot be recovered.)

The monetary damages that can be recovered in any tort action consist of the following:

- actual out-of-pocket expenses incurred as a direct result of the tort, such as medical bills, hospital bills, nursing bills, loss of earnings, cost of hiring replacement vehicles (in the case of loss of use of a vehicle resulting from an automobile accident)
- anticipated out-of-pocket expenses for medical, hospital, and nursing services, and anticipated loss of earnings resulting from any permanent injury or loss sustained
- compensation for pain, suffering, and mental anguish sustained as a result of the tort

Categories of Torts

Torts fall into two main categories: intentional torts and negligence.

Intentional torts. Many intentional torts may be crimes as well. Assault and battery afford an example of this. If A commits battery upon B and damages B's teeth, it will do B little good if A is criminally fined or imprisoned. But B can sue A for battery—a tort—and receive monetary damages from A not only for the dental bills and other out-of-pocket expenses B incurred as a result of the battery but also for pain, suffering, and mental anguish.

Several other intentional torts include fraud and deceit, libel and slander, the invasion of another's privacy, the maintenance of a nuisance, and antitrust violations. All of these may be committed by a business entity. Fraud and deceit, for example, involve the intentional misrepresentation of a material fact that leads another party to act upon it to his detriment and resulting damage. Such an offense could easily arise in a sales situation. But a salesperson's mere commendation of a product is not necessarily fraudulent or deceitful. A reference to a used car for sale as "a real cream puff" is a sales practice known as "puffing." Puffing is not a tort and can be best defined as *judicious exaggeration.*

Two or more persons can conspire to commit an intentional tort. In such a situation, the tortfeasors are jointly and severally liable to the injured party for the damages that party sustained. There can be *conspiracy to defraud* by false representation; to obtain delivery of goods on false credit; or to induce a breach of an existing contract, as, for example, when a merchant's competitors cause the merchant's wholesaler not to deliver the goods for the price stated in the contract between the merchant and the wholesaler.

Businesses that are involved with mass communications, such as newspapers, magazines, and the broadcast media, are apt without utmost care to commit the tort of libel or slander. The damage suffered by a victim is essentially to the person's reputation as the result of a false statement or imputation. Thus, both *libel* (written statement) and *slander* (oral statement) are included in the broad term *defamation.* The constitutional guarantee of "freedom of speech" does not protect the tortfeasor who intentionally and knowingly defames the reputation of another.

The tort of *invasion of privacy* stems from the right of the individual to be left alone and like other rights is not an absolute one. Because it is an individual right, it cannot be claimed by a corporation, institution, or business. Damages for intrusion into an individual's privacy might consist of humiliation or shame, mental distress, or outrage by a person of ordinary sensibilities.

Nuisance consists of using one's property in such an unreasonable way as to damage another. The doctrine is really a limitation on the use of property. Many businesses, as a part of a manufacturing process, could cause damage to adjacent property owners. The process could, for example, discharge noxious fumes, which the business should take every precaution to prevent. Environmental pollution may be a public nuisance, and courts could order it abated or stopped. Nuisance can be a private one as well, and the victim may be entitled to damages for the injury sustained. Public nuisance can be criminally prosecuted.

Antitrust violations involve the activities of an unlawful monopoly or combination that injure another. While state antitrust statutes provide for the recovery of actual damages by an injured party, the federal statute, the Sherman Act, provides for treble, or three times, the actual damages.

Negligence. Negligence is an unintentional tort for which a person can receive a monetary judgment for damages. In all negligence actions, the standard of care that an individual must exercise is *due care under the circumstances.* A person is negligent when he or she fails to exercise that degree of care that a reasonably prudent person would have exercised under the same circumstances. Negligence may arise from an act of omission (the failure to do an act a reasonably prudent person would have done under the same circumstances) or an act of commission (the doing of an act that a reasonably prudent person would not have done under the same circumstances). The negligent act—the wrong—must be the proximate cause of the injuries sustained.

In many instances, the law will infer negligence when injury results from inherently or abnormally dangerous activities, such as blasting with explosives. In such a situation, strict liability is imposed upon the person using the explosives. Breach of the duty to use due care need not be proved, but the injury must have been directly caused by the blast.

The law of negligence is very complex and is based upon the legal duty to use care. At the same time, the prevention of an action for negligence is largely a matter of common sense. It cannot, therefore, be overemphasized that all employees of a given business should be alert to the existence of negligent practices.

Frequently, the victim of negligence will have contributed to the cause of injury. Under the doctrine of *contributory negligence,* the victim would be barred from recovering damages. Today, most states have enacted comparative negligence statutes that allow recovery of damages from the negligent party less the proportion of the victim's contribution of negligence to the accident. The doctrine of *comparative negligence* is most commonly invoked in motor vehicle negligence cases.

The owner of property owes varying degrees of care to different classes of people who come upon the premises. Owners owe the highest degree of care to invitees on the property. Invitees are those who enter another's property and whose presence is of some interest or advantage to the owner. Customers in stores and shops and guests in hotels and restaurants would be considered invitees. To them the owner owes the care of keeping the premises reasonably safe.

The Law of Contracts

Contracts may be oral or written, express or implied. They include all agreements or promises to buy and sell personal property and real property; to perform services; to agree to do or not to do specified acts; to lease property— real or personal; to mortgage or otherwise encumber real or personal property; and to include all dealings and relationships between persons, including marriage, that are not classified as torts or crimes.

Requirements for a Contract

A contract is formed when the following three requirements are met:

1. There are at least two parties with legal capacity to enter into the agreement. Legal capacity means that the parties are adults (usually over the age of 18 years) and are not under any mental or physical disability that diminishes or impairs their capacity to enter into an agreement. If a party lacks legal capacity, the contract is voidable—that is, it can be disaffirmed and set aside by the legal representative of such person (in the case of infancy, the guardian; in the case of incompetency, the committee; in the case of physical disability, the conservator) or by the person when the disability is removed (as when an infant attains the age of 18 years). If the contract is not disaffirmed, it is fully enforceable.

2. There must be mutual assent to the terms of the agreement—that is, a *meeting of the minds* on all essential terms. This is the finality of the negotiations between the parties. It encompasses, and is the end result of, the offers, counteroffers, and acceptances of the offers made by the parties.

3. Consideration is the final requirement. It is a *quid pro quo,* an exchange of value, for the mutual promises of the parties. Consideration may consist of money, services, a product, a promise not to do something (a forbearance), a promise to do something, or simply love and affection. In some situations, where the promise is in writing and signed by

the promisor, consideration is not required in order to have a valid, enforceable contract. The New York General Obligations Law provides that a written signed promise to change or modify, or to discharge in whole or in part, any contract, obligation, lease, mortgage, or other security interest in personal or real property shall not be invalid because of lack of consideration.

Purpose of the Contract

The purpose for which the contract is entered into must be one that is not void by statute or rules of common law. Generally, any agreement entered into to commit a criminal act or any act that is against the public policy of the state is void and unenforceable. If, for example, an agreement is entered into in New York State to rent a store as a gambling casino, such agreement is void on its face (gambling in New York is a crime), and the court will not enforce the contract on behalf of either party.

Breach of Contract

When a party fails to perform what he or she has agreed to do, such party will have *breached* the contract, and an action can be maintained by the *damaged* or injured party for specific performance of the contract or for monetary damages sustained as a result of the breach. An action for *specific performance* compels the breaching party to perform his or her promises in accordance with the contract's terms and provisions. Usually, courts grant relief for specific performance because of the uniqueness of the subject matter of the contract and the fact that monetary damages would be inadequate compensation to the injured party. The equitable relief of specific performance has been traditionally granted by the courts in cases where a seller of real property (each parcel of real property is considered unique) wrongfully refuses to tender a deed to a purchaser who is ready, willing, and able to purchase the property in accordance with the terms of the contract of sale.

An action for breach of contract may be maintained when proof of the following elements exists:

1. formation of the contract between the plaintiff and the defendant
2. performance by the plaintiff
3. defendant's failure to perform
4. resulting damages to the plaintiff

Usually the monetary damage sustained is the difference between the contract price the plaintiff would have paid if the breach had not occurred and the higher cost that the plaintiff actually paid to a third party because of the defendant's breach.

Implied and Written Contracts

Every day, each of us enters into many contracts. Most of these contracts are oral and many are implied from our actions. These contracts include buying a newspaper, riding public transportation, eating in restaurants, buying items in department stores, and hiring gardeners, electricians, plumbers, painters, doctors, or dentists. The *consideration* for the products and services we buy and use is a specified sum of money. The specification of the cost of the item or service and/or its display or availability for use is the *offer.* Our taking of the item or use of the service is the acceptance of the offer, thereby giving rise to our duty to pay the consideration.

However, certain agreements are not valid or enforceable unless they are in writing; in fact, these agreements are void, as against the public policy of their terms and conditions. These contracts or agreements, which must be in writing, are specified in the *Statute of Frauds,* whose antecedents date back to seventeenth-century England. Today, all states have a Statute of Frauds in one form or another. Generally, the following contracts or agreements must be in writing or else they are void:

- all contracts concerning the sale of real property or an estate or interest in real property
- all deeds to real property
- all mortgages, liens, easements, or other encumbrances affecting real property
- all leases of real property for a term of one year or more
- a promise to answer for the debt or obligation of another
- any agreement that is not to be performed within one year of the date of the promise
- the sale of personal property of a value of $500 or more, unless there has been partial performance by the seller or purchaser

Personal Property

The law relating to the *sale* of personal property is largely contained in Article 2 of the Uniform Commercial Code, which will be discussed as a separate topic. Inherent in the ownership of property is the right to transfer or dispose of it. A sale is but one medium through which this may be done. The owner of property may transfer property by will (a bequest) or by making a gift of it. It is difficult to formulate a precise definition of personal property. Clearly the term includes objects other than real property, which consists of land and the buildings on it.

Types of Personal Property

Personal property is frequently classified as corporeal or incorporeal.

Corporeal personal property. The term *corporeal personal property* refers to personal property that is tangible and includes goods that are also referred to as *chattels*. Another distinction of corporeal personal property is that it is visible and movable.

Incorporeal personal property. Incorporeal personal property involves "rights" rather than tangible objects. Examples of such rights include patents, copyrights, and trademarks. A patent is a grant to the inventor to use, sell, or allow others to use the invention exclusively for a period of 17 years. A copyright is a grant giving an author an exclusive right to possess, publish, or sell the production of his or her intellect. Formerly a copyright was a grant for 28 years with the right to renew it for another 28 years. Today, however, for copyrights granted during and after 1978, there is a single period consisting of the lifetime of the author plus 50 years. A trademark, which is the property of a business, is a sign, mark, name, or symbol that identifies it or its product. Trademarks may be registered for a period of 20 years and may be renewed at the end of each 20-year period. Other examples of incorporeal personal property include mortgages on both real estate and chattels; leases of apartments, offices, and stores; promissory notes; stock certificates; bonds; bank accounts; and even court judgments.

Title

Title to or ownership of corporeal personal property (chattels) may be established by exclusive possession of the chattel, a bill of sale, or a certificate of title (as in the case of an automobile).

Title to or ownership of incorporeal personal property is established by the document itself: the stock certificate, the lease, the mortgage, the bond, the certificate of deposit, or the bankbook. All of these documents name the owner—the mortgagee, lessee, promisee, stockholder, payee, or judgment creditor, as the case may be, on the face of the instrument.

Single or Joint Ownership

Personal property can be owned by a single person, by two or more persons as *tenants in common* where each person owns an undivided equal interest in the property, or as *joint tenants with rights of survivorship* where two or more persons own an undivided equal interest in the property. On the death of one such tenant, the surviving tenant or tenants own the deceased tenant's share.

Ownership vs. Possession

The ownership of personal property should be distinguished from the possession of it. Frequently the owner of personal property will deliver it to another for some purpose, such as safekeeping or repair. When this happens, the possession by one other than the owner is known as a *bailment.* The one in possession (the bailee) has responsibilities for the property to the owner (the bailor). The bailee is responsible for using ordinary care as to the bailed property and returning or disposing of the property at the direction of the bailor. A bailment comes into being upon agreement of the parties and delivery of the property to the bailee.

A bailment does not exist when a party merely rents space for the safekeeping of personal property. A bank, for example, is not a bailee of goods kept in a safety-deposit box because it cannot enter the box without the owner's key. Similarly, a "park and lock" parking lot is not a bailee; but when a vehicle owner leaves the key to the vehicle with the parking lot operator, a bailment does exist. In the latter case the lot operator would be responsible if the owner's vehicle was damaged while stored.

Sometimes the law will infer what is known as a constructive bailment. A person who finds lost property is a constructive bailee who owes the owner the standard of ordinary care for it.

Real Property

Real property consists of land and all improvements (structures and buildings with appurtenant fixtures), if any, situated on the land. Fixtures are items of personal property that are affixed to the structure or building and are thereby considered part of the real property. They would include sinks, cabinets, lighting fixtures (but not lamps), spigots, etc. They do not include furniture. Each parcel of real property is unique; it is for this reason that specific performance can be obtained if a seller breaches a contract of sale.

Types of Real Property Estates

When a person owns (has title to) real property, he or she in effect owns an *estate* in real property. There are two types of real property estates: *freehold* and *leasehold.*

Freehold estate. A freehold estate is either a *fee* (sometimes referred to as a *fee simple* or *fee simple absolute*) or a *life estate.* A *fee* is the highest degree of ownership that can be had in real property, being diminished only by encumbrances (such as mortgage liens and easements for electric, gas, water, and rights-of-way). In a *life estate,* the holder of the estate owns the property during his lifetime. As an example, A, the owner of a fee, grants the fee to B for the life of B. During B's lifetime, B has all of the incidents of ownership, including absolute possession. B could sell his estate to C, who, of course, would own it only as long as B lives; B could mortgage the estate or lease it to another. In effect, B could do anything with the property that the grantor, A, could do. On B's death, however, the title to the estate would revert back to the grantor or any person the grantor designated as remainderman (the person who takes the estate on the death of the life tenant). The interest in the fee of C or any other party would terminate on the death of the life tenant.

Leasehold estate. A leasehold estate entitles the party to exclusive possession and use of the real property—the land and any and all improvements thereon—for a specified term. To have a leasehold estate, the land must be leased. If the land is not included in the lease, an estate in real property would not be created; such a lease would be incorporeal personal property. Therefore, a lease of a portion of a structure or building for a store or an apartment does not create a leasehold estate, but the lease of vacant or improved land for any specified term would create such an estate.

Tenancy

The manner in which an estate in real property, freehold or leasehold, is owned (how title is held) is called a *tenancy.* Generally there are four tenancies: in severalty; in common; joint with rights of survivorship; and by the entireties.

Tenancy in severalty. A misnomer, tenancy in severalty is individual ownership; one person owns the estate.

Tenancy in common. Tenancy in common is a form of joint ownership, whereby each individual tenant owns an equal undivided portion of the whole estate. In the case of the death of one tenant, his or her undivided equal share will be distributed in accordance with his or her last will and testament or by the laws of descent and distribution in case of intestacy. If two or more names are listed on a deed as the grantees with nothing else following their names, the law in most jurisdictions assumes that such a transfer is a tenancy in common.

Joint tenancy with rights of survivorship. This is another form of joint ownership between two or more persons. It differs from a tenancy in common in that, upon the death of one tenant, that tenant's undivided equal interest in the property will become the property of the surviving tenant or tenants. If it is the intention to create such a tenancy, the words "as joint tenants with rights of survivorship" must be placed after the names of the grantees on the deed. Otherwise, a tenancy in common will be created.

Tenancy by the entireties. Tenancy by the entireties is a joint tenancy with rights of survivorship between a husband and wife. After the names of the grantees, the words *his wife* or the Latin abbreviation *ux.* are placed to designate the creation of this tenancy.

Transfer of Real Property

The transfer of real property is called *alienation of title.* The "ownership" of the estate is evidenced by a document called a *deed.* Property is transferred by delivery of a deed from the grantor, the current owner of the estate, to the grantee, the person to whom the estate is being transferred. A grantor can transfer all or a portion of the estate owned. The most common form of transfer is by sale of property where, for example, A conveys to B a fee in a one-family house for an agreed-upon price. The delivery of the deed to B by A transfers the ownership. Property can also be transferred by deed of gift (no consideration required), by last will and testament, by the laws of descent and distribution, and by mortgage foreclosure.

Almost every jurisdiction has recording laws that require that every deed, mortgage, easement, or other encumbrance affecting real property be recorded. Usually, such document is recorded in the county clerk's office of the county in which the property is located.

Leases

When the owner of an estate in real property rents a portion of the property—for example, as an apartment or store—to a person for a period of time, a contract, called a *lease,* is created. The owner, in this situation, becomes the *lessor,* or landlord. The person to whom the premises are rented is called the *lessee,* or *tenant.* The description of the premises leased is called the *demised premises.* The length of the lease is called the *term.* The *rental* is the sum of money that the tenant will pay to the landlord, usually monthly, for the possession and use of the premises.

A lease is personal property and not an estate in real property. If the lease is for a term that is less than one year, it can be oral. If it is for a term of one year or more, most jurisdictions require it to be in writing in order to satisfy the requirements of the Statute of Frauds. Some jurisdictions will permit a lease for a term of three years or more to be recorded.

When a lease is for a fixed term, it is called a *tenancy for years.* This is true even if the term is for less than a year; the name is a misnomer. The essential characteristic is that the term is a fixed period of time, whether it be five months or five years.

When a lease is from one period to another, such as week to week or month to month, it is called a *periodic tenancy.* Such a lease may be oral or written. At the end of each period, a new lease is created, unless the landlord or tenant terminates the agreement. Usually periodic oral tenancies can be terminated by either the landlord or tenant giving proper *notice* to the other party. On a month-to-month tenancy, thirty-day notice is required. On a week-to-week tenancy, seven-day notice is required.

At the end of the term of the lease, the tenant is required to turn over possession of the premises to the landlord. When a tenant remains in possession of the premises after the term has expired without entering into a new agreement with the landlord, the tenant becomes a *holdover* and can be dispossessed.

Estates and Trusts

Distribution of an Estate by a Will

Estate law provides for the transfer of property at the time of death. Such a transfer may be by will or without a will. The maker of a will, a *testator,* provides his or her representative after death, the *executor,* with instructions for the distribution of property. In the absence of a will, distribution will be made as stipulated by law. It is certainly advisable for most people to make a will, not only so that their wishes may be effected but also because a will might be most advantageous to the relatives of the testator.

The basic requirement for a will is the *intent,* sometimes called the *donative intent,* of the maker. A will has no force until death and may be revoked or changed at any time by the testator. It creates no rights or benefits in others during the life of the maker. No special form is necessary for a will, although the maker must know and understand the contents of it. Anyone who is "sound of mind" can make a will. Through the years there has been great controversy about what a sound mind really is.

Because a will is a solemn document, the law requires with rare exceptions that it be written and signed by the testator. Signing must be attested to or witnessed in all states, although the number of witnesses required varies.

Upon the death of the testator, a probate court in the appropriate jurisdiction appoints an executor, usually the person so named in the will. The court is not bound in this respect, however, since the person named may be unavailable or unqualified at the time of probate. Following appointment, the executor distributes the property according to the will and under the supervision of the court. Finally, the executor must account to the court for the distribution.

Distribution of an Estate without a Will

When a person dies without a will, his or her property is distributed according to the various state statutes of descent and distribution. Such statutes provide for distribution to various classes of relationship.

The most preferred class of persons are the lineal descendants who are in a direct line of the decedent, such as children and grandchildren or parents and grandparents. A second relationship is that by affinity or marriage, and the third class consists of collateral relatives such as brothers and sisters and cousins. In default of the above classes, the decedent's estate goes to the "next of kin."

A person who dies without a will is said to be *intestate.* Distribution is made by an administrator rather than an executor, and the probate procedure is similar in many ways to that under a will.

Trusts

A trust is a relationship between two or more parties in which one party, a *trustee,* holds property for the enjoyment of the person creating the trust, the trustor or settler, or a third party. The reasons for the creation of trusts are endless; but a trust once created must be for an active purpose. The decision to have a second party manage one's property would be a valid reason for establishing a trust.

Any legally competent person can create a trust and must manifest an intent to do so. The trust instrument must reasonably describe the property that is entrusted, and the duties of the trustee must be clear. If a trust is to be revocable, that is, subject to cancellation by the trustor or another, this should be so stated in the instrument. Otherwise it will be irrevocable.

A trustor may also be the trustee, but in such a case he or she cannot be a beneficiary or person who is to enjoy the benefits of the trust. Trusts must, of course, have a lawful purpose. As the term implies, the trustee has a fiduciary responsibility and must act in good faith.

THE UNIFORM COMMERCIAL CODE

The basic document governing the conduct of business is the Uniform Commercial Code (UCC). It covers the sale of goods; commercial paper; bank deposits and collections; letters of credit; bulk transfers; warehouse receipts, bills of lading, and other documents of title; investment securities; and secured transactions.

The UCC is, in effect, a codification of many of the common-law rules with respect to the law of contracts, personal property, and bills and notes. It does not cover the law of real property. The UCC, in one form or another and with minor variations, has been adopted by every state.

Sales

Article 2 of the UCC contains the basic law of sales. It is sometimes referred to as "the buyer's law," because it sets out remedies for the breach of sales contracts and defines various types of warranties for goods that are sold. But it also contains remedies for abuses suffered by the seller and delineates the responsibility for goods that are in the possession of a bailee such as a trucker or railroad.

When one considers the sheer number of sales transactions that occur each day and the fact that many of them are not cash transactions, it is apparent that both buyers and sellers need the protection of the law to clearly define their respective rights and responsibilities. The article on sales should, therefore, be considered in the light of the article on secured transactions. A secured transaction is simply one in which the seller maintains a right in that which is sold until the full purchase price has been paid.

Article 2 applies specifically to the sale of "goods" that are movable and identifiable. The term excludes money that is used to pay for the goods. Even more specifically, Article 2 governs contracts for the sale of goods and recognizes different types of buyers and sellers. A "merchant," for example, is one who has special occupational skills and knowledge of the particular type of goods sold. A merchant is charged with a higher standard of care in dealing than one who is not a merchant.

Contract for the Sale of Goods

As noted, Article 2 basically governs *contracts* for the sale of goods. Most of the casual retail transactions that occur daily would thus be excluded. The Statute of Frauds in Article 2 further limits those transactions that must be covered by a written sales contract. Generally, a sales contract that provides for a price of $500 or more must be in writing. A special situation exists in Article 2 as to merchants. If a merchant receives a letter of confirmation of a transaction that is not written, he or she must, if desired, repudiate or reject the transaction within ten days just as though he or she had signed the writing. This provision cures a previous evil in which a party could repudiate a contract by simply ignoring a confirming letter. It is imperative that a buyer or seller who is in the "merchant" class closely monitor incoming mail. The secretary may therefore be instrumental in preventing an unwanted contract by default.

It should be emphasized that the requirement of the Statute of Frauds that certain contracts be in writing does not necessarily mean the existence of what most people consider a formal contract. The reason for the rule is evidentiary in the sense that as an agreement becomes more important, there is a greater need for written evidence of it. In the case of Article 2, $500 is the criterion that invokes the Statute.

A writing under the Statute must meet several requirements, however. It must be signed, although this may be done by printing, stamping, typewriting, or even initials if it is the intent of the party to authenticate the writing. The terms of the writing should give assurance that there is or was a transaction and state the quantity of goods involved. The writing may be a single one or consist of several writings such as the exchange of letters, bills of sale, or even telegrams. Lesser documents such as cash register receipts usually do not satisfy the signature requirement.

There are situations in which a transaction is taken out of the Statute of Frauds even though the price is greater than $500. If, for example, the goods are delivered by the seller and accepted by the buyer, the contract will be enforceable without a writing. Delivery and acceptance of only a part of the goods will render a contract enforceable only as to that part.

Once a valid contract, written or oral, exists, each of the parties has certain rights and responsibilities. It may seem too obvious, but the essential two acts of performance are that the seller deliver the goods and that the buyer pay for them. Such a simplistic statement raises a variety of questions. Where, for example, is delivery to be made? How is payment to be made? While goods are in transit, who bears the risk of their destruction? What if the goods are not exactly of the quantity and quality ordered? Normally it is advisable to have specific provisions in the contract that answer these questions. But in practice such specific provisions are frequently omitted, because customary practices in dealing are followed.

Delivery of Goods

The UCC, Article 2, does provide some answers. Unless otherwise stated, the place of delivery is the seller's place of business or, if there is none, the seller's residence. Or, if both parties know that the goods are at a location other than the seller's place of business, that location is the place of delivery. Such a situation might exist where the seller's goods are stored in another's warehouse.

Article 2 stipulates, unless otherwise stated, that the time for delivery is a *reasonable* time. In the event that a contract was breached on this basis, the court would decide what a reasonable time would have been. The type of goods would, of course, have a bearing upon the decision and even the hour of delivery must be reasonable. Without agreement to the contrary, a buyer is entitled to have all goods delivered at the same time.

If a contract states that the place of delivery of goods is that of the buyer, the seller must so deliver them and may do so through a carrier such as a trucking company or railroad. When the goods are turned over to the carrier, the carrier signs a bill of lading that lists goods, weight, etc. A *bill of lading* is a document by which the carrier acknowledges receipt of goods and agrees to transport them to the designated place of delivery. Generally, risk for the destruction of goods rests with the seller until time of delivery.

Acceptance or Rejection of Goods

When the goods are delivered, the buyer has the right to inspect them to ensure that they comply with the contract. The time and place for inspection are described as reasonable ones by the UCC. And sometimes because of the complexity and nature of goods, the right of inspection extends to using the goods. Such is the case of a purchaser of an automobile since a visual inspection alone might not be sufficient to discover a defect.

If upon inspection the buyer determines that goods do not conform to the terms of the contract, they may be rejected or accepted. And the buyer may also elect to accept any commercial unit or units and reject the rest. If the buyer rejects all or part of the tendered goods, he or she must promptly notify the seller and hold them with reasonable care for a period of time sufficient for the seller to remove them. The buyer cannot, of course, use the goods after rejection.

Payment for Goods

Once the buyer has accepted goods, he or she must tender payment to the seller. Any method of payment is sufficient if it is in the ordinary course of business. The seller can demand payment in legal tender (money). When this is done, the buyer must be given a reasonable extension of time to procure it. Payment by check is conditional upon its being honored on due presentment.

Warranties

The UCC sets out three kinds of warranties, the breach of which may create liability upon the seller. The most obvious warranty is an express one and need not be created by the words *warrant* or *guarantee*. Any affirmation of fact or promise by the seller may create an *express warranty* and may be determined by whether or not it is a basis for the bargain between the seller and buyer. A seller's mere "puffing" of a product—that is, an opinion or commendation of goods—does not create an express warranty. Since an express warranty is an affirmative statement, it cannot be excluded or modified as can implied warranties.

**FULL ONE YEAR WARRANTY
ON ELECTRIC HEATER**

If, within one (1) year from the date of purchase, this Electric Heater fails due to a defect in material or workmanship, we will replace it free of charge.

This warranty service is available by simply returning the Electric Heater to any Sears store throughout the United States.

This warranty gives you specific legal rights, and you may also have other rights which may vary from state to state.

SEARS, ROEBUCK & CO.   BSC 41-3   SEARS TOWER   CHICAGO, IL. 60684

Two types of *implied warranties* exist under the UCC. The first is the *warranty of merchantability.* For such a warranty to exist, the seller must be a merchant for a particular purpose as defined by the Code. Very generally, for the criteria are complex, goods are merchantable as they compare with the quality of other brands on the market and conform within variations permitted by the agreement. The reason for this warranty is that because of the merchant's special skill and knowledge, he or she is held to a higher standard for the quality of goods sold. And the UCC specifically includes the sale of food or drink for value in the warranty of merchantability.

A second implied warranty is that of *fitness* for a particular purpose. This warranty arises where the seller knows the purpose for which the goods are bought and that the buyer is relying on the seller's skill or judgment to furnish the appropriate goods.

Implied warranties may be modified or excluded. A warranty of fitness must be in writing and conspicuous. A warranty of merchantability must mention merchantability; and, if in writing, it too must be conspicuous. If a buyer examines or refuses to examine goods before entering into a contract and such examination should have revealed a defect, there can be no implied warranty.

All warranties may extend to the family or those in the household of a buyer or even guests if they could reasonably expect to use or consume the product.

Secured Transactions

In recent years credit buying has become an American way of life. The practice is not new, however, although expansion of it has largely occurred in the consumer sector. Credit buying usually consists of a person's buying something and paying for it with a commitment against future income. The real estate mortgage is a form of credit buying and has its roots in antiquity.

The problem with a credit sale is that a seller parts with property to a buyer who may default on his or her promise to pay for the goods or who subsequently sells them to a third party. Article 9 of the UCC provides an orderly system that not only allows the seller's interest in goods sold on credit to be retained but also gives notice of this interest to subsequent buyers. This system is similar in many ways to the mortgage system used in real estate.

Security Interests

Article 9 of the UCC essentially covers personal property and fixtures. Because personal property is movable and real estate is not, considerable differences also exist between Article 9 security interests and the real estate mortgage. What, then, is a security interest? It is simply an interest that, once established, secures the payment or performance of an obligation.

Security interests are not limited only to a buyer-seller sales situation. A may lend B money to buy an automobile. When B has purchased the automobile, A may have a security interest in it to secure the loan to B. In this situation A would be called a lender, B would be called a debtor, and the automobile would be called collateral.

A security interest is said by the UCC to "attach" at a certain time. In essence, this means that it becomes effective. When three requirements have been met and coexist, a security interest is said to attach. There must first be agreement between the lender and debtor that it attach; the secured party must have given value; and the debtor must have rights in the collateral. In the example in the above paragraph, attachment would not occur at the time of the loan but at the time B had an interest in the collateral, that is, the automobile.

The medium for agreement is a document called a *security agreement.* It must reasonably identify the collateral and be signed by the debtor. Although the secured party does not have to sign the security agreement, such is the usual practice.

Once a security agreement has attached, the lender (or creditor) has enforceable rights in the collateral and is thus protected against the default of the debtor. The secured party is also *usually* protected against subsequent purchasers of the collateral and other creditors.

Financing Statement

In the case of certain types of goods, the secured party must take one more step in order to have a fully protected interest. This procedure is known as "perfecting" the security interest and consists of filing a document called a financing statement with an appropriate agency. The place for filing varies from state to state, but typically it is with, say, the UCC Division in the Office of the Secretary of State. Here financing statements are filed and indexed under the name of the debtor.

The purpose behind the filing process is to give notice to another party considering extending credit to the debtor that there is a preexisting security interest in collateral. If, for example, A lends B $10,000 and takes a security interest in B's manufacturing equipment, A will file a financing statement to protect his or her interest. B might try to obtain another loan from C against the same collateral. If C checks with the place for filing, it will be apparent that there is another security interest in B's equipment and C will be well advised not to extend a loan to B. If C does so anyway or fails to check for a previously filed security interest, C's interest will be subordinate to that of A.

Financing statements may be filed on very simple forms that are supplied by the Secretary of State. They must include the names and addresses of both the creditor and debtor and be signed by the latter. The description of collateral need not be as specific as in the security agreement because, as noted, the purpose is only to give notice to one considering a subsequent loan or extension of credit that a security interest already exists. Addresses are given so that a prospective creditor may further investigate the matter.

Security interests may be filed before attachment, in which case perfection does not occur until attachment. If, for example, B borrows from A to buy equipment that will become the collateral in which A will have a security interest, A may file at the time of making the loan. The interest cannot attach until B purchases the equipment, and thus it is not perfected until that time.

A security interest is a perfected one if the creditor has the collateral in possession. The reason for this is that a prospective creditor is automatically put on notice of the security interest of a secured party.

Article 9 of the UCC generally classifies goods as consumer goods, equipment, farm products, and inventory. In the case of consumer goods, a security interest need not be perfected by filing, a rule largely based upon expediency. As a practical matter it would be nearly impossible to file the extremely large

UNIFORM COMMERCIAL CODE — FINANCING STATEMENT — FORM UCC-2

INSTRUCTIONS
1. This form is designed to avoid double typing when filing with more than one office. Place this form over UCC-1.
2. PLEASE TYPE this form. Fold only along perforation for mailing.
3. Send all 3 copies with interleaved carbon paper to the filing officer. Enclose filing fee.
4. If the space provided for any item(s) on the form is inadequate the item(s) should be continued on additional sheets, preferably 5" x 8" or 8" x 10". Only one copy of such additional sheets need be presented to the filing officer with a set of three copies of the financing statement. Long schedules of collateral, indentures, etc., may be on any size paper that is convenient for the secured party.
5. If collateral is crops or goods which are or are to become fixtures, describe generally the real estate and give name of record owner.
6. When a copy of the security agreement is used as a financing statement, it is requested that it be accompanied by a completed but unsigned set of these forms, without extra fee.
7. At the time of original filing, filing officer will return third copy as an acknowledgment. At a later date, secured party may date and sign the termination legend and use third copy as a Termination Statement.

This FINANCING STATEMENT is presented to a filing officer for filing pursuant to the Uniform Commercial Code.

1 Debtor(s) (Last Name First and address)	2 Secured Party(ies) and address	3 Maturity date (if any):
		For Filing Officer (Date, Time, Number, and Filing Office)

4 This financing statement covers the following types (or items) of property

Check ☒ if covered: ☐ Proceeds of Collateral are also covered ☐ Products of Collateral are also covered No. of additional sheets presented:

Filed with:_____

This instrument prepared by_____

By:_____ By:_____
Signature(s) of Debtor(s) Signature(s) of Secured Party(ies)

Filing Officer Copy — Alphabetical STANDARD FORM · UNIFORM COMMERCIAL CODE · FORM UCC-2
Approved by The Secretary of State

Figure 21-1. Standard financing statement of the Uniform Commercial Code

number of secured transactions in consumer goods. The burden of filing would be particularly heavy on retail merchants who typically sell their goods on installment contracts. Such a burden outweighs the interest of the possible creditor of the consumer. Consumer goods are defined by the UCC as goods ". . . used or bought primarily for personal, family, or household purposes."

It has been noted that Article 9 covers secured transactions in fixtures as well as all other kinds of personal property. The place of filing a security interest in fixtures is usually the place of filing for the real property to which an item is affixed. This would usually be in a county office such as a Registry of Deeds. Filing may therefore be either local (in a county office) or central (in the Secretary of State's Office). The UCC does not, unfortunately, define fixtures. Thus a secured party must rely on individual state interpretations. If there is any doubt, the secured party should file *both* locally and centrally.

The system for secured transactions here described results in degrees of security for the creditor. Depending on the degree of security, the UCC establishes priorities among conflicting interests in the same collateral for nonfixtures and fixtures, respectively. Under these provisions a perfected security interest has priority over an unperfected interest, and the first party to perfect has priority over a party who perfects subsequently. If A advanced credit to B on January 1 and took a security interest in B's equipment but did not file a financing statement, and if on February 1 C executed the same transaction taking a security interest in the same equipment and did file a financing statement, C's interest would have priority over that of A. Even if A filed on March 1, C's claim would be paramount. If B became insolvent on April 1, C's rights in B's equipment would allow C to take it in satisfaction of the debt and A's rights would be defeated.

The secretary will often be the person in a business responsible for the documentation of a secured transaction. It should be apparent that the secretary must be alert to the need for timeliness and correct procedure in satisfying the requirements of Article 9. Procrastination in filing a financing statement, for example, might leave the business unprotected in the event of a buyer's or borrower's default. The secretary should live by the maxim that "when in doubt, file!"

Bulk Sales or Transfers

It is not, happily, a common occurrence, but a merchant could transfer the majority of his or her materials, supplies, or inventory to another with the purpose of defeating creditors' claims. Article 6 of the Uniform Commercial Code regulates just such transactions and serves to protect the creditors in a bulk transaction. For example, A, a merchant hounded by creditors, says to his friend B, "B, I'm tired of this business. I'll sell you my stock at a good price." B accepts and pays A in cash for his stock. A leaves the area. What recourse do the creditors of A have?

Article 6 of the UCC deals with the matter between the bulk tranferee, B in the sample above, and the creditors of the transferor, A. First the transfer must be a "bulk" transfer. Article 6, Sec. 102 refers to a transfer not in the ordinary course of the transferor's business of ". . . a major part of the materials, supplies, merchandise, or other inventory." Article 6 does not proscribe bulk transfers; it merely dictates that certain procedures be followed, and the responsibility for so doing is largely on the transferee. In effect, an illegal or procedurally incorrect transfer is treated as no transfer at all with respect to the creditors.

The correct procedure is relatively simple. The transferee must require the transferor to supply him or her with a list of the transferor's property, that is, a schedule of the property transferred in bulk. The transferor is also required to furnish a list of his or her creditors. Next, the transferee must notify the creditors of the sale within ten days before either taking possession of the goods or paying for them. Finally, the transferee must maintain the list of creditors and schedule of property for six months and allow inspection or copying of them by the creditors.

Clearly, Article 6 is designed to prevent surprise or "midnight" sales that leave the creditor without protection. Since the very nature of a fraudulent bulk sale involves the absence of a transferor, the responsibility for compliance with Article 6 falls on the transferee. The creditors cannot be held responsible since they are not parties to the transaction nor do they ordinarily have knowledge of it.

Section 6-106 of the UCC requires that a bulk transferee apply the proceeds of the transferred goods to the creditors of the transferor as properly listed. Without correct procedure in the sale, creditors have a claim on the goods as though there had been no sale or transfer.

The law of bulk transactions logically follows that of secured transactions. It should again be noted that Article 6 does not invalidate a bulk transfer. It only provides protection to the creditors of the transferor and does not in any way affect the seller-buyer relationship in a bulk transfer.

Commercial Paper

The law concerning commercial paper was once known as the *law of negotiable instruments.* The latter term was possibly more descriptive than the present one because the negotiability of commercial paper is one of its main characteristics. The law concerning commercial paper is largely contained in Article 3 of the Uniform Commercial Code.

Money is, as it always has been, the principal medium for the exchange of value. But because money has value as it stands, there is always the danger of losing it or having it stolen, and the finder or thief will have little trouble in using it. Commercial paper is in a sense "substitute money," but it acquires value only when signed or endorsed.

Types of Commercial Paper

There are four types of commercial paper: promissory notes, drafts, checks, and certificates of deposit.

Promissory notes. A promissory note is basically a promise by one party to pay another party a certain sum of money either on demand or at a specific time. If the note is payable on demand, it is almost the same as money to the holder of it. If A signs a promissory note in favor of B on demand, B can use it to pay value to C because it can be immediately converted to cash. If a note is for payment on a certain future date, it serves to extend credit and is therefore not the same thing as money. Parties to a promissory note are the "maker," the one promising to pay, and the "payee," the one to whom the promise is made. Promissory notes must be in writing and signed by the maker. They may be secured by the borrower, who provides some kind of collateral to the lender. When a mortgage on property is given to the lender, the note is known as a mortgage note; in the event of nonpayment, the lender can foreclose on the property for satisfaction.

Drafts. A draft, or bill of exchange, involves three parties. One party orders a second party to pay a third party. For example, A, the drawer, orders B, the drawee, to pay a certain amount of cash to C, the payee. The system presupposes that B is in some way indebted to A. Drafts are the least common form of commercial paper.

Name of Student: _____

Student No.: _____

PROMISSORY NOTE AND DISCLOSURES

$ _____   Date: _____, 19 ____

FOR VALUE RECEIVED, the undersigned (which includes all "undersigned" jointly and severally if more than one) promises to pay to the order of _____ . (which includes any holder hereof) at its offices: (i) the Amount Financed shown in item 1 below; (ii) interest on the balance of such Amount Financed from time to time remaining unpaid, at the rate per annum shown in item 3 below, from the date hereof, in accordance with the Payment Schedule shown in item 5 below. All payments shall be applied first to interest accrued to the date upon which payment is made, and the remainder in reduction of the Amount Financed. The undersigned and any guarantor agree that _____ may from time to time grant extensions or renewals for any period. Undersigned will pay reasonable attorney's fees not in excess of 15% of the unpaid balance after default and referral to an attorney. DEFAULT shall result from any of the following events: (a) failure to make a payment as required by this Note; (b) the significant impairment of the prospect of payment or performance, which includes, but is not limited to: death, insolvency, assignment for benefit of creditors, or the commencement of any proceeding under any bankruptcy or insolvency laws by or against undersigned. In the event of default, holder may, at its option, declare the entire unpaid balance of the Amount Financed and accrued interest thereon immediately due and payable without notice or demand, subject, however, to such rights, if any, as undersigned may have to cure a default for failure to make a required payment.

Terms and Disclosures

1. Amount Financed $ _____
2. **FINANCE CHARGE:** $ _____
3. **ANNUAL PERCENTAGE RATE**   _____ %
4. Total of Payments (1+2) $ _____
5. Payment Schedule: This Note is payable in _____ consecutive monthly installments of $ _____ each and one final monthly installment of $ _____, commencing on _____ 19 ____ and on the same date of each month thereafter. If payments are not made when due, one or more additional payments may be necessary to pay in full.

NOTICE TO CONSUMER: 1. Do not sign this Note before you read it. 2. You are entitled to a copy of this Note. 3. You may prepay the unpaid balance at any time without penalty, except for minimum charges as permitted by law.

WITNESS:

_____

_____

Address

Figure 21-2. Typical form of a promissory note (including terms) agreed to by a student and the financial officer of a college. This type of note is essentially an unconditional promise to pay the stipulated sum of money (often in designated installments) by some specified future date to the party named in the document. The note may be secured or unsecured.

Checks. Checks, of course, are very common and are a part of the fabric of modern business. A check is very simply a draft drawn on a bank. Here A, who has deposited money in the bank, orders it on demand to pay an amount to another, C. The bank would be similar to B in the example of a draft above.

Checks have a utilitarian value over money. When cashed by the payee, the check is canceled by the bank and returned to the maker. It thereby serves as a receipt or at least an indication that payment has been made. One of the characteristics of commercial paper is transferability. Thus, A may write a check in favor of C, who, in turn, uses it to pay a debt to D. Transfer is done by C signing it over or "endorsing" it to D. When the check is finally returned to A, C's signature serves as evidence that C has received the face value of the check. It could also serve as evidence of the discharge of the debt of C to D.

Certificates of Deposit. A final type of commercial paper is the certificate of deposit. In recent years the certificate of deposit, or "CD," as it is commonly called, has gained in popularity. There are many forms of these certificates, but what is common to them all is redemption on demand. One popular form is the six-month CD. Usually a minimum amount of money is required, often $10,000. The purchaser is told that the money must be left in the bank for the full term of the certificate. If it is not left for the full period, a reduced interest rate will be applied. The latter situation is often referred to as a "penalty." But CDs of any kind must be redeemable on demand.

Value of Commercial Paper

The law of commercial paper is essentially protective of the rights of the various parties to it. There are problems inherent in a system that allows people to "make" money even if it is only substitute money. The maker of a check, for example, may not have sufficient funds on deposit with the bank to cover it. Another problem, especially with checks, is the possibility of forgery or an intentionally written bad check. The secretary who may receive checks on behalf of the employer should insist on identification of the party writing a check. While many checks are overdrawn through a simple mistake by the drawer and may be eventually satisfied, it may require an unreasonable amount of time to collect on such a debt.

RELATIONSHIPS BETWEEN BUSINESSES AND EMPLOYEES/AGENTS

There are various relationships common to all business entities and the people who assist them. The most common of these relationships include services, such as employment, agency, and the hiring of independent contractors.

Employer–Employee Relationships

An employer–employee, or master–servant, relationship exists when one person performs services, for a salary, under the control of and exclusively

Account No.

Date of Issuance .... , 19 ......

FIXED-RATE FIXED TERM CERTIFICATE ACCOUNT
HOME FEDERAL SAVINGS & LOAN ASSOCIATION OF LAKEWOOD
("ASSOCIATION")
LAKEWOOD, OHIO 44107

1. ACCOUNT SUMMARY SECTION

ACCOUNT
HOLDER

Opening Balance	Initial Maturity Date ....
Rate of Earnings % per annum	Extended Maturity Date ....
Frequency of Compounding	Renewal Term ....
Minimum Balance Requirement	Minimum Addition $ ....
$	

EARNINGS DISTRIBUTION DATES

Beginning .... and ....
thereafter, with the last distribution on the final maturity date.

2. GENERAL SECTION This certifies that the Accountholder holds a savings account with the Opening Balance and for the initial term expiring on the Initial Maturity Date shown hereon in Home Federal Savings & Loan Association of Lakewood, Lakewood, Ohio.

The Accountholder may, from time to time, with the consent of the Association, make additions to the balance in this account in any amount not less than the Minimum Addition provided for in Section 1. In the event of any such addition, the term of this account shall be extended so that the period from the date of such addition to the Extended Maturity Date (which shall be recorded with the entry as to such addition) shall not be less than the initial term (or Renewal Term, if the addition is made during a Renewal Term).

3. EARNINGS SECTION This account shall receive earnings at the rate and with the Frequency of Compounding as above set forth. Such earnings shall be payable on the Earnings Distribution Dates above set forth, provided the balance in the account is not reduced below the Minimum Balance Requirement. If such balance is reduced below the Minimum Balance Requirement, the Rate of Earnings on the remaining balance shall thereafter be reduced to the rate then paid on regular savings accounts. (See also Section 5).

4. AUTOMATIC RENEWAL This account shall be automatically renewed at the close of business on the Initial Maturity Date or the maturity date of any renewal or extended term unless (1) withdrawn within the 10-day period referred to in Section 5 hereof or (2) at least 15 days prior to any such date, the Association gives written notice to the Accountholder that this account will not be renewed at the Rate of Earnings and or the Renewal Term set forth above. In such event, the account will either be extended for such additional term and at such rate of earnings as set forth in said notice or the account will be converted to a regular savings account and receive earnings at the rate then paid on regular savings accounts.

Figure 21-3.   A form acknowledging that a certain person holds a certificate-of-deposit account in a particular savings and loan association. Certificates of deposit of this kind are usually time deposits; that is, they are payable on or after a stated future date at a stipulated rate of interest. They are also payable on demand or subject to withdrawal, but in either case the rate of interest is reduced. These certificates are transferable and negotiable instruments.

for the business entity. This relationship is contractual; the employment agreement may be written or oral, express, or implied.

Depending on the size of the business entity and in some instances the type of business involved, various statutes, both federal and state, may apply to and control such factors as the minimum amount of wages the employee can receive, the types of insurance coverage that must be provided by the employer (such as worker's compensation and disability insurance), and whether the employer must be an equal opportunity employer. Federal and state law provide that the employer must withhold income taxes and social security contributions from the employee's pay.

Agencies

An agency is created when one person or business entity, the *agent*, acts for and on behalf of another person or business entity; the *principal*. The principal, by an agency agreement, confers upon the agent authority to act in the principal's place and stead with a third party. This authority can be general or limited to do a specific act. Generally, any act that a business entity or individual can legally do can be delegated to the agent.

The relationship between an agent and the principal is said to be a *fiduciary relationship*. This means that the agent owes the highest degree of care and responsibility to the principal. The agent acts for the principal in dealings with a third party or parties. When the agent acts within his or her conferred authority, the principal is bound by the acts of the agent to the third party. If the agent exceeds the authority conferred, the principal is not bound to the agreement entered into by the agent with the third party unless the principal ratifies the agent's unauthorized acts. For example, if the principal retains a down payment on a contract that the agent was not specifically authorized to enter into, then ratification occurs.

The authority given to the agent can be written or oral. Some of the more common forms of agency agreements are *power of attorney* and real estate broker's *listing agreements*. Some states require that certain agency agreements concerning real property must be in writing and recorded.

The agent is not an employee of the principal, but is an independent contractor. That is, the agent solely determines how to perform and execute the limited authority given to him or her by the principal. In fact, the agent may have many principals for whom it performs services, as in the case of building managers, real estate brokers, or manufacturer's representatives. No taxes are withheld from the agent's fee or commission for services rendered. As a separate entity, the agent pays these items. The agent may have employees and may hire other independent contractors to aid him or her in performing the authorized duties or in performing any function necessary for the operation of the agent's business.

Independent Contractors

While agents are independent contractors, not all independent contractors are agents. Any business entity (a sole proprietorship, partnership, or corporation) can contract with another business entity to perform certain acts or services not involving a third party. For example, a corporation may hire a computer consultant to create a database program, or a building owner may hire a contractor to remodel an apartment. In these situations, no third party is involved, and therefore no agency situation exists.

FORMS OF DOING BUSINESS

There are several types of business entities: individual proprietorships, different types of partnerships, and corporations.

Individual Proprietorship

In a strictly legal sense a proprietor is one who has rights in something—that is, an owner. A proprietor in a business sense, then, is one who owns and operates a business alone. The proprietorship is probably the largest single form of business operation.

The term *proprietorship* gives no indication of size. A proprietor's business may be small, such as a one-chair barber shop, or large, employing thousands of people at many locations. What is common to all proprietorships is the centralization of control and authority in one person, the owner. A proprietor of a business is ultimately responsible for all decisions. For this, he or she reaps the benefits of the business out of net profits.

There are distinct advantages and disadvantages in doing business as a proprietor. With the decision-making process in but one person, there is no need to go through the lengthy process of getting agreement such as is necessary in multi-owned businesses. The greatest disadvantage of the proprietorship is that the owner has unlimited liability. The owner's personal assets, as well as business assets, are accountable and liable for the payment of business debts if the business fails.

Probably the greatest problem of the proprietorship is forming and acquiring capital for the conduct of the business. Where more than one person owns a business, each of the owners contributes or brings something of value into it. Thus by "pooling" assets, the multi-owned business is able to operate on a larger capital amount. Also, while centralized decision making may be an advantage in one sense, it may be a disadvantage in another sense. The collective skills of, say, a partnership may result in better decisions for the business. A proprietor can overcome the disadvantage of unilateral decision making by hiring those with special skills to serve in advisory roles, but he or she must also understand that those hired do not have the same proprietary interest as the owner.

No special documentation is needed to form a proprietorship, and a proprietor's earnings out of profits are taxed to the individual. This is to be compared with corporate profits, which are taxed first to the corporation and again as income to the shareholder. A double-taxation structure is therefore avoided by a proprietorship.

If the proprietor operates his or her business under an assumed name, most jurisdictions require that a certificate of doing business be filed in the county clerk's office where the business is located. This certificate shows the name under which the proprietor is doing business and the name and address of the proprietor.

Partnership

A partnership provides for ownership of a business by two or more persons, and there is no limit on the number of partners who may participate. The partners may be equal or unequal (junior partners). This is usually determined by the amount of assets each partner contributes to the partnership business.

A *partnership* is a voluntary, contractual association. Upon the formation of a partnership, each of the partners brings something of value to it, such as money, other personal or real property, or a skill. Based upon a negotiated agreement, partners usually enter a written partnership agreement that states the proportionate contribution of each partner. Partnership agreements do not necessarily have to be in writing, but they must satisfy the requirement of the Statute of Frauds, which states that contracts that cannot be performed within one year must be in writing.

Any business or profession can form a partnership. The disadvantage of the partnership form of business is that the partnership entity and each and every partner are severally and jointly liable for all partnership debts.

As in the case of a single proprietorship, many states require that a certificate of doing business as partners be filed in the county clerk's office where the partnership maintains its business office. The certificate must show the assumed business name the partnership is using, its principal business address, and the name and address of each partner. When the partnership is dissolved, a certificate of discontinuance of business as partners must also be filed in the appropriate county clerk's office.

Duties and Rights of Partners

As a practical matter, it is sensible for partners to have a written partnership agreement. The agreement should clearly specify the rights, duties, and responsibilities of all concerned.

Each partner is, in addition to being a co-owner, a principal in the conduct of the business. As such, each partner has the authority to do a variety of things on behalf of the business. The scope of a partner's authority includes making contracts that bind the partnership, selling goods (but not other assets) in the regular course of business, making purchases, obtaining loans, purchasing insurance, and hiring employees. In practice, partnerships assign the various areas of authority to individual partners.

A partnership might be formed in this way: Partner A has invented and patented a very superior mousetrap, which he brings into the business as his contribution. In the written agreement it is stated that his contribution is worth $50,000, that he will be in charge of the manufacturing process for the traps, and that he will share in the profits equally with the other partners. Partner B owns a building worth $50,000, which he will contribute and in which the mousetraps will be made. Partner B has an advertising background and it is agreed that he will be in charge of marketing. He, too, will receive a share of the profits. Partner C brings in $50,000 in cash, which will be used as start-up and as operating capital. Partner C is assigned responsibility for the general administration of the business and will also receive a proportionate share of the profits.

This example serves to show how authority might be assigned and thus limited. Partner A might have authority to purchase raw materials and manufacturing equipment and to hire plant workers. Partner B might be given authority to sell the mousetraps on the market and hire salespeople to solicit orders. Partner C would logically have authority to obtain a loan to be used for working capital, to purchase liability insurance, and to hire clerical workers. Such a division of labor is a sensible way to ensure a smoothly functioning cooperative organization. An agreement among partners as to the scope of authority of each is binding among them.

Generally, partners have certain rights in the business. These may be and should be resolved in a written partnership agreement. Without such an agreement, all partners have equal rights. One such right is to manage the business. As noted, it is not very practical for all partners to manage all areas of the business. Also, without agreement to the contrary, all partners have a right to share equally in the profits of the business. Partners do not have a right to be compensated other than by a share of profits. If two partners manage the firm while a third partner is on vacation, they are not entitled to extra compensation for their extra work.

Partners have a right to inspect the books of a firm at any time. The books should be kept at the principal place of business for this purpose.

Terminating a Partnership

Partnerships may be dissolved or terminated in several ways. First, partnerships may be formed by agreement for a specific purpose or for a specific time. Upon the accomplishment of purpose or expiration of time, dissolution occurs. Even before that time *all* partners may agree to dissolution. Where no definite term is specified, a partnership may be dissolved by the express will of one partner only. If by agreement other partners can expel a partner, such expulsion for cause will result in dissolution. Other reasons for dissolution include the death or bankruptcy of any partner or the bankruptcy of the partnership itself.

Upon application of a partner, a court will decree a dissolution in several instances. These include the insanity of a partner or a partner's incapacity to perform his or her part of the partnership contract. A court will also decree dissolution where the conduct of a partner is prejudicial to carrying on the business or where a partner willfully breaches the partnership agreement. Finally, a court will dissolve a partnership that can be continued only at a loss or dissolve it for purely equitable reasons.

Once dissolution has occurred, someone must "wind up" or finally complete the business of the partnership. This may be done by the legal representative of the last remaining partner. Winding up consists generally of satisfying partnership liabilities and distributing the partnership assets to qualifying parties.

Limited Partnership

In most jurisdictions, the creation of a limited partnership is governed by statute. It is a partnership formed by two or more persons having as members one or more general partners and one or more limited partners.

A certificate of limited partnership must be filed in the county where the limited partnership has its main office for business. In many respects, it is similar to a certificate of incorporation, showing among other things the firm name, the purpose of the business to be transacted, its principal office, the duration of the limited partnership, the name and address of each general and limited partner, and the amount of cash or property contributed by each limited partner. Many states require that the limited partnership certificate, or a notice containing the substance of the certificate, be published in newspapers in the county in which the certificate was filed. While limited partnerships can be formed to carry on any form of business activity, they are often used to form real estate syndicates and general stock brokerage businesses.

The *limited partners,* as such, are not bound by the obligations of the partnership. This is the main difference between a limited partnership and the partnership form of doing business. The limited partner's liability for the entity's debts is limited to the amount of money contributed to or invested into the limited partnership, and such a partner is not liable to creditors. The contribution of the limited partner may be cash or other property but cannot be services.

However, the *general partners,* as in the case of a partnership, are jointly and severally liable for all partnership obligations and debts. Only the general partners can act for and on behalf of the entity. They have the power and right to do anything that partners can do in the partnership form of doing business, provided that such act does not violate the certificate of limited partnership. The contribution of the general partners may be cash, property, or services to be rendered.

Incorporation

Corporations are organized, and thereby incorporated, under the laws of the state in which their principal place of business is located. In the state of incorporation, a corporation is considered to be a *domestic corporation.* If the corporation does business in any other state, it is considered to be a *foreign corporation* doing business in that state. Each foreign corporation is required to file a *certificate of doing business* in each and every state in which it operates. Many corporations, usually corporate giants with millions of stockholders, operate and conduct business not only in all fifty states but also internationally, having satisfied the legal requirements of each country in which they operate.

However, a corporation need not be large. In fact, in most states a corporation can be formed having only one person, who may simultaneously hold all of the corporate offices (president, vice president, secretary, and treasurer) and comprise the entire board of directors.

Unlike an individual, the corporation's *life* may be perpetual or for a specific term, after which it will cease to exist. In law, a corporation is considered to be an artificial person and is entitled to most of the constitutional protections afforded to a natural person, such as due process of law. In addition, a corporation, as an individual and a partnership, can avail itself of the protection of the bankruptcy laws to discharge its debts or reorganize. The corporation also has many of the same duties and obligations of a natural person, such as the payment of income taxes.

Reasons for Incorporation

The reasons for the corporate form of doing business are twofold. First, it permits a person to invest in a company and to share in the profits of it while having liability only to the degree of investment. If, for example, an individual purchases 10 shares of stock in a given company and the shares cost $100 each, he or she has a $1,000 investment. But the value of the shares may increase or decrease if they are traded on a market. If the market value rises to $120, the value of the total investment will be $1,200. If the company fails, the investor will be out of pocket $1,000.

This limitation on liability makes an investment far more attractive. In a proprietorship or partnership, the parties are responsible for all liabilities— even those above and beyond the amount invested.

The second reason for the corporate form follows from the first reason, the feature of limited liability. Because investors naturally want to keep risk at a minimum, they are more willing to invest in corporations. It is therefore easier for the corporation to acquire capital. For a corporation, the pool of investors is virtually without limit. Proprietorships and partnerships do not have such an advantage.

Types of Corporations

Corporations are classified as public, private, and quasi-public. *Public* corporations exist for some governmental purpose such as a municipality. *Private* corporations are those that are privately owned and, as will be explained, may be for profit or nonprofit. *Quasi-public* corporations are those that serve a public need but that are privately owned. Public utilities are an example of quasi-public corporations. They usually are regulated by the government and have territorial protection from competition through a licensing process. Although it may be confusing, private corporations whose stock is publicly traded are known as public corporations in the business community.

The Creation of Corporations

The creation or formation of a corporation, like other business forms, begins with an idea. Someone feels that the idea has commercial value. When a person decides to form a business and it is to be in the corporate form, he or she is known as a *promoter*. Most corporations are formed to make a profit for the owners, but they may also be designated as "not-for-profit," which results in a tax-free status. A corporation may be created for any lawful purpose such as manufacturing a product, selling goods, or providing a service. Schools, hospitals, and religious organizations are examples of nonprofit corporations, and they may not be owned as such by individuals.

Most states allow licensed professionals such as doctors, lawyers, accountants, and dentists to form *professional service corporations* in order to practice their profession for profit. When a professional service corporation is formed, all incorporators must be duly licensed to practice the same profession for which the corporation is being formed. The stock cannot be issued to or owned by any unlicensed person. When such a corporation is formed, the words *Professional Corporation* or the letters *PC* must appear after the name. However, unlike other corporations, each shareholder of a professional services corporation is personally and fully liable and accountable for any negligent or wrongful act or misconduct committed by him or her or by any person under his/her direct supervision and control while rendering professional services on behalf of such corporation.

Tasks of the promoter. Once a decision has been made to incorporate and the type of corporation has been selected, the promoter begins preparations for eventual incorporation. The promoter has three basic tasks. First, he or she must promote the original idea that gave rise to the decision to form a new business. In effect, promotion of the idea is to get financial backing for the venture. The promoter works under a considerable handicap in that all of his or her efforts are tentative and depend upon eventual incorporation. The promoter cannot sell shares in the corporation until it exists. Instead, he or she procures subscriptions or promises to buy shares when they are available.

The promoter's second task is to perform those acts that will enable the corporation to function once it has come into existence. Such acts might be to acquire a place of business, buy equipment, or hire employees. Again, the promoter is handicapped by the lack of existence of the corporation. If the promoter enters into contracts, he or she is personally bound by them unless the agreement states otherwise. While the promoter cannot bind the corporation, in practice the corporation once formed will agree to become a party in these contracts in order to relieve the promoter of personal liability. If for any reason the corporation is not formed as planned, the promoter remains liable on the contracts he or she has made.

The promoter's third and final task is to carry out the statutory procedure for incorporation. The first step is to prepare and submit a document commonly known as the Articles of Incorporation, usually to the Secretary of State.

The Articles must include certain information such as the name of the corporation, its purpose, the amount of capital stock to be authorized together with the number of shares into which it is to be divided, the place of business, the duration of existence (many states permit to be perpetual), the names of officers and directors for the first year of operation, the names and addresses of the incorporators and the number of shares for which each has subscribed, and the name and address of an agent or clerk. The latter requirement exists to give one who is suing the corporation a contact for the service of process. There are variations in these requirements from state to state.

Once submitted, the Articles of Incorporation are examined by a government official and, if approved, are returned to the new corporation. Articles may be amended at a later time if, for example, the purpose of the corporation changes. Approved Articles are in essence a contract between the state, the corporation, and the owners (shareholders). They become the document that confers authority upon the corporation.

Powers of a corporation. Once created, the corporation has powers and is required to follow certain procedures. Among the powers of a corporation are those to establish a corporate seal, make bylaws that supplement the Articles of Incorporation, issue stocks and bonds, borrow money, sell or acquire property, and even invest in other corporations.

Possibly one of the most important items of business at the first meeting of a corporation is to make bylaws for the conduct of the business. *Bylaws* are analogous to written partnership agreements. It is usually desirable to keep the Articles of Incorporation both brief and general and to provide specificity in bylaws. Articles should be effective for the life of the corporation and can be changed only upon application to the state. Bylaws can and should be changed when necessary, and this may be done within the corporation by the shareholders. Since the bylaws are a reflection of the will of the owners, they are binding on those who conduct the business of the corporation. Some states allow directors to amend bylaws. If a corporation wishes to retain this power for shareholders only, such must be done in the Articles of Incorporation.

Corporate Organization

The lines of authority in a corporation run from the shareholders who are the owners, to the board of directors, to the officers. Directors are elected by the shareholders and in turn appoint the officers of the corporation. Usually the executive officers consist of a president, one or more vice presidents, a secretary, and a treasurer. One person could be a shareholder, director, and officer; and some corporations require that directors be shareholders.

Shareholders may make policy indirectly through their power to elect directors. Frequently, too, a power is reserved to make broad policy changes such as the establishment of a pension plan. When a shareholder wishes to change policy, he or she does so by putting a resolution before the other shareholders for vote.

Frequently, because of geographical distribution or for other reasons, shareholders cannot attend meetings. In such an event, the shareholder is entitled to vote through another person, a practice known as "voting by proxy."

Although a few states forbid it, most states provide for a practice known as "cumulative voting." This process provides that each shareholder have a number of votes equal to the number of shares owned multiplied by the number of directors to be elected. Cumulative voting provides that a minority of shareholders can have representation on the board of directors.

Shareholders meet regularly, usually annually. No notice is required, although most corporations not only provide notice of regular meetings but provide forms for proxy votes as well. Special meetings do require notice and are usually called by the board of directors. In some cases special meetings are called by a fixed percentage of the shareholders. Quorum requirements for a valid meeting are based on either a specified percentage of shareholders being present or on a specified percentage of voting stock being represented. Once a quorum has been established, shareholders cannot obstruct the conduct of business by leaving and breaking a quorum.

The board of directors. The management of the corporation is the responsibility of the board of directors. Directors are considered to be fiduciaries or persons who are in a position of special trust by virtue of that position. They owe their allegiance to the corporation in general and specifically to the shareholders. As fiduciaries, directors should be careful to avoid any conflict of interest such as favoritism toward a relative or another business interest. A director should refrain from voting on a matter that might raise a conflict of interest. Similarly, a director should not use information acquired through the office for personal gain if such use is contrary to the interests of the corporation.

The bylaws of most corporations provide for regular board meetings, and directors usually cannot vote by proxy. The reason for requiring that a director be physically present is based on the idea that attendance is meeting a responsibility, whereas a shareholder's voting by proxy is the waiver of a right. As a rule, special meetings may be called by the chairperson, the president, or any two directors; bylaws frequently provide that an executive committee of the board can act on matters between meetings.

Corporate officers. As noted, officers are considered to be agents of the corporation, which, in turn, is the principal. When in this role, officers' conduct is governed by the law of agency. The scope of authority of an officer includes those actions that are consistent with the general purposes of the corporation as delineated in the articles of incorporation and the bylaws.

Officers derive their authority from the board of directors that appoints them. Rarely, officers may be appointed by the shareholders. Logically, directors should have the power of appointment because of their responsibility for management of the corporation and the fact that officers are the agents of management.

Termination of a Corporation

Corporations may be terminated by either voluntary or involuntary actions. Unfortunately, the vast majority of corporate terminations are involuntary, because of the failure of the business.

A corporation may be dissolved by written consent of shareholders, as by a vote on a resolution to dissolve. Such a resolution may be proposed by the board of directors or by shareholders possessing among them 20 percent of the outstanding shares of the corporation. After the voting procedure takes place, the corporation must file a "statement of intent to dissolve" with the Secretary of State and must notify all creditors of the filing. At this time the corporation ceases business and begins the winding-up process.

Insolvency in itself does not automatically terminate a corporation. But insolvency would probably lead to bankruptcy and that, in turn, would lead to a forced sale of the assets of the corporation. So as a practical matter, it could not continue to operate and exist without any assets.

Corporations may terminate because of a consolidation or merger of two or more corporations where it is legal under antitrust legislation. A consolidation occurs when two corporations join to form a third. If, for example, Company A and Company B consolidate to form Company C, A and B cease to exist and their combined assets are those of C. In a merger, A would acquire B and continue as A while B would terminate. There is one other multicorporate relationship, the conglomerate, which does not involve termination. A conglomerate exists when one corporation, a parent company, acquires another corporation that exists for a different purpose. If, for example, an oil company acquired a chain of motels, it would be a conglomerate. Usually corporations become conglomerates to diversify activities or to avoid the antitrust prohibition on consolidations and mergers.

Finally, corporations may be terminated for cause by the government authorizing it or by court decree. The latter method is used when a board of directors becomes so deadlocked that the company can't continue operations.

Travel Information:
Domestic and Foreign

## 22

Distances: Air and Road

AIR MILEAGE BETWEEN PRINCIPAL CITIES OF THE WORLD

	Wellington, N.Z.	Valparaiso, Chile	Tokyo, Japan	Singapore	Shanghai, China	Seattle, U.S.A.	Rome, Italy	Rio de Janeiro, Brazil	Reykjavik, Iceland	Quebec, Canada	Port Said, Egypt	Paris, France	Panama City	Oslo, Norway	New York, U.S.A.	Moscow, Russia	Mexico City	Melbourne, Aust.	Manila, Phil.	Los Angeles, U.S.A.	London, Eng.	Istanbul, Turkey	Honolulu, U.S.A.	Gibraltar	Cape Town, S. Afr.	Calcutta, India	Buenos Aires, Arg.	Bombay, India	Berlin, Germany	Beijing, China
Beijing, China	6698	11774	1307	2774	662	5396	5047	10768	4903	6423	4584	5101	8906	4360	6823	3597	7733	5667	1770	6250	5054	4379	5067	6009	8045	2024	11974	2964	4567	
Berlin, Germany	11265	7795	5538	6166	5215	5041	734	6144	1479	3583	1747	542	5849	515	3961	996	6037	9919	6128	5782	574	1078	7305	1453	5977	4376	7376	3910		4567
Bombay, India	7677	10037	4188	2429	3133	7741	3843	8257	5191	7371	2659	4359	9742	3961	7794	3131	9722	6097	3148	8701	4462	2991	8020	4814	5134	1041	9273		3910	2964
Buenos Aires, Arg.	6260	761	11400	9864	12197	6929	6918	1218	7362	5680	7613	6918	3148	7794	5297	9722	4633	7234	11042	6128	6918	7558	8020	5963	4270	10242		9273	7376	11974
Calcutta, India	7042	11400	3187	2112	1791	4496	4450	9376	3447	3506	4889	4450	10114	4590	6294	3447	10199	2189	1549	6005	5219	3646	7037	5521	6026		10242	1041	4376	2024
Cape Town, S. Afr.	7019	5556	9071	6005	5462	5249	5409	7111	7857	4590	5841	6494	6750	5000	7801	6412	8511	7525	5936	9969	6005	5219	11532	5076		6026	4270	5134	5977	8045
Gibraltar	12060	6988	6710	6646	2678	1034	2047	5000	3383	8022	964	8075	2047	8104	1874	8075		5076	5521	4270	5963	10242	6026	4814
Honolulu, U.S.A.	4708	6793	3850	4934	4959	854	8190	8738	5000	8738	7434	6750	4959	7102	1088	7033	5009	5659	5296	1551	8104		8075	8104	11532	7037	5977	8020	7305	5067
Istanbul, Turkey	10663	8172	5373	4959	6063	6646	854	6395	2558	4644	1401	6750	5009	1088	7102	5009	5659	843	1551		1874	8104	5076	5521	4270	10242	1041	1078	4379
London, Eng.	11682	7263	5938	5710	4782	887	5772	5772	1171	3101	213	714	5439	1154	3459	1549	5591	10501	6667	5439		1551	854	1094	6012	4947	6918	4462	574	5054
Los Angeles, U.S.A.	6714	5470	5470	6477	959	6326	6296	4306	5619	2579	6651	5325	3001	6016	2451	6016	1549	7931	6667		5439	6843	5278	6750	9969	8090	6128	8701	5782	6250
Manila, Phil.	5162	8423	1479	1152	1863	6457	6651	11254	8124	5619	6673	6016	8493	8493	5130	8829	9022	3941		6667	6843	5659	6667	7931	7486	2240	11042	3148	6128	1770
Melbourne, Aust.	1595	6033	5089	3761	5132	9934	8186	8186	10497	8658	10396	9926	10283	5009	8963	8422	5130		3941	5130	5591	9088	5296		6425	5515	7234	6097	9919	5667
Mexico City	6899	8088	7035	8039	2337	6759	6353	4622	4770	7671	5706	5706	1016	5009	8963	8422		5130	8829	1549	5591	5629	1549		8519	9492	4633	9722	6037	7733
Moscow, Russia	10279	7035	4650	4235	5199	5353	1474	7179	2056	4242	2454	1541	6688	4662	6688		8422	8963	8422	2451	1549	3781	7033	5629	6300	3321	5297	3131	996	3597
New York, U.S.A.	8946	5221	6735	7357	7357	1474	4273	4706	2576	1243	5706	3672	2056	4662		6688	8963	3781	5130	5009	3459	4975	4662	5009	7764	7918	5297	7794	3961	6823
Oslo, Norway	10974	7914	5094	5020	2408	4273	1243	4820	1083	3263	832	6482	6482		4662	4242	2056	5009	8829	2451	1154	1522	7179	2576	6479	4415	7921	3961	515	4360
Panama City	7433	2943	6246	5020	4591	5903	3294	3651	2659	2211	5382	5325		6482	2056	6688	5130	10283	8493	3001	5439	6595	5278	2047	7007	10499	3148	9742	5849	8906
Paris, France	11791	7251	6671	5752	4993	682	5703	5703	1380	3235	1975		5325	6482	3672	1541	5706	9926	6016	5325	213	1400	1541	1016	5786	4883	6918	4359	542	5101
Port Said, Egypt	10249	6033	5842	5088	5132	6759	1317	6244	3227	5250		1975	5382	832	5706	2454	5706	10396	6673	6651	213	884	7434	964	4633	3237	7613	2659	1747	4584
Quebec, Canada	4584	7420	6417	6981	2353	3943	5125	2189	3227		5250	3235	2211	3263	1243	4242	4622	8658	5619	2579	3101	4545	5250	5125	7599	7621	5680	7371	3583	6423
Reykjavik, Iceland	7251	6033	5504	5504	3614	2044	6118	2189		3227	5250	1380	2659	1083	2576	2056	4242	10497	8124	5619	1171	2400	5590	3383	8644	4966	7481	5191	1479	4903
Rio de Janeiro, Brazil	7349	1855	11535	11340	6891	5684	5684		2189	2189	6244	5703	2576	4820	4770	7179	4622	10544	11254	6296	5772	6389	4770	5000	3773	9377	1218	8257	6144	10768
Rome, Italy	11524	7420	6232	5677	5659	6891		5684	6118	5125	1317	5703	3294	6482	4273	1474	6353	8186	6651	6296	5772	859	8190	1034	5231	4482	6918	3843	734	5047
Seattle, U.S.A.	7242	4777	8057	5703		5659	6891	5684	3943	3943	6759	682	5903	4273	682	5353	6759	9934	6457	6326	887	5527	854	6063	10209	7040	6929	7240	5041	5396
Shanghai, China	6054	1094	2377		5703	5677	5659	6891	2353	2353	5752	4993	5132	5020	7357	5199	8039	5005	1152	6477	4782	4962	4959	2678	8061	2091	12201	3133	5215	662
Singapore	5292	10226	3304		2377	5703	5677	11340	6981	6981	5088	5088	6246	5020	7357	4235	8039	3761	1152	5470	5710	5381	4650	6710	6063	1795	9863	2429	6164	2774
Tokyo, Japan	5760	10635		3304	2377	8057	6232	11535	6232	6417	5842	6671	6246	5094	6735	4650	7035	5089	1479	5470	5938	5560	3850	6710	9156	2902	11400	4188	5538	1307
Valparaiso, Chile	5785		10635	10226	1094	4777	7420	1855	7225	7420	6033	7251	2943	7914	5221	7035	7914	6033	8423	5470	7263	8186	6793	6988	5556	11400	761	10037	7795	11774
Wellington, N.Z.		5785	5760	5292	6054	7242	11524	7349	7251	4584	10249	11791	7433	10974	8946	10279	6899	1595	5162	6714	11682	10663	4708	12060	7019	7042	6260	7677	11265	6698

567

AIR MILEAGE BETWEEN PRINCIPAL CITIES OF THE UNITED STATES

City	Atlanta, Ga.	Boston, Mass.	Buffalo, N.Y.	Charleston, S.C.	Cheyenne, Wyo.	Chicago, Ill.	Cleveland, Ohio	Dallas, Tex.	Denver, Colo.	Detroit, Mich.	Houston, Tex.	Indianapolis, Ind.	Jacksonville, Fla.	Kansas City, Mo.	Los Angeles, Cal.	Louisville, Ky.	Memphis, Tenn.	Miami, Fla.	Minneapolis, Minn.	New Orleans, La.	New York, N.Y.	Philadelphia, Pa.	Phoenix, Ariz.	Pittsburgh, Pa.	Portland, Ore.	St. Louis, Mo.	Salt Lake City, Utah	San Francisco, Cal.	Seattle, Wash.	Washington, D.C.
Atlanta, Ga.		937	697	267	1229	587	554	721	1212	596	701	426	285	676	1936	319	337	604	907	424	748	666	1592	521	2172	467	1583	2139	2182	543
Boston, Mass.	937		400	820	1735	851	551	1551	1769	613	1605	807	1017	1251	2596	826	1137	1255	1123	1359	188	271	2300	483	2540	1038	2099	2699	2493	393
Buffalo, N.Y.	697	400		699	1335	454	173	1198	1370	216	1286	435	879	861	2198	483	803	1181	731	1086	292	279	1906	178	2156	662	1699	2300	2117	292
Charleston, S.C.	267	820	699		1486	757	609	981	1474	681	936	594	197	928	2203	500	604	482	1104	641	562	528	1857	704	2405	795	1845	2428	2405	453
Cheyenne, Wyo.	1229	1735	1335	1486		891	1199	726	96	1125	956	947	1554	512	862	1096	1095	1939	757	1222	1616	1568	586	1341	1049	838	347	959	966	1477
Chicago, Ill.	587	851	454	757	891		308	803	920	238	940	165	864	414	1745	269	482	1188	355	833	713	666	1453	410	1749	262	1260	1858	1737	597
Cleveland, Ohio	554	551	173	609	1199	308		1025	1227	90	1114	263	770	700	2049	311	630	1087	630	924	405	360	1631	115	2055	492	1575	2166	2026	306
Dallas, Tex.	721	1551	1198	981	726	803	1025		663	999	225	763	879	451	1240	726	420	1111	862	443	1374	1299	887	1070	1633	547	999	1483	1681	1185
Denver, Colo.	1212	1769	1370	1474	96	920	1227	663		1156	879	999	1467	558	831	1038	879	1726	700	1082	1631	1574	586	1320	982	871	371	949	1021	1494
Detroit, Mich.	596	613	216	681	1125	238	90	999	1156		1105	240	879	645	1983	316	623	1152	543	939	482	443	1690	205	1969	455	1492	2091	1938	396
Houston, Tex.	701	1605	1286	936	956	940	1114	225	879	1105		865	816	643	1374	803	484	968	1056	305	1420	1341	1009	1137	1825	679	1200	1645	1891	1220
Indianapolis, Ind.	426	807	435	594	947	165	263	763	999	240	865		756	453	1809	107	384	1024	511	712	646	585	1499	330	1919	231	1356	1949	1872	494
Jacksonville, Fla.	285	1017	879	197	1554	864	770	879	1467	879	816	756		867	2150	649	581	326	1396	516	831	775	1831	774	2491	753	1826	2591	2585	647
Kansas City, Mo.	676	1251	861	928	512	414	700	451	558	645	643	453	867		1356	480	369	1241	413	680	1097	1038	1049	781	1506	238	1049	1506	1506	945
Los Angeles, Cal.	1936	2596	2198	2203	862	1745	2049	1240	831	1983	1374	1809	2150	1356		1829	1603	2339	1524	1673	2451	2394	357	2136	817	1589	579	347	959	2300
Louisville, Ky.	319	826	483	500	1096	269	311	726	1038	316	803	107	649	480	1829		320	919	605	623	652	582	1508	344	1919	242	1402	1949	1943	476
Memphis, Tenn.	337	1137	803	604	1095	482	630	420	879	623	484	384	581	369	1603	320		872	699	358	957	881	1263	660	1867	240	1250	1802	1867	765
Miami, Fla.	604	1255	1181	482	1939	1188	1087	1111	1726	1152	968	1024	326	1241	2339	919	872		1511	669	1092	1019	1982	1010	2708	1061	2089	2594	2734	923
Minneapolis, Minn.	907	1123	731	1104	757	355	630	862	700	543	1056	511	1396	413	1524	605	699	1511		1056	1018	985	1280	743	1426	466	987	1584	1395	934
New Orleans, La.	424	1359	1086	641	1222	833	924	443	1082	939	305	712	516	680	1673	623	358	669	1056		1171	1089	1316	919	2049	598	1434	1926	2101	966
New York, N.Y.	748	188	292	562	1616	713	405	1374	1631	482	1420	646	831	1097	2451	652	957	1092	1018	1171		83	2145	317	2445	888	1972	2571	2408	205
Philadelphia, Pa.	666	271	279	528	1568	666	360	1299	1574	443	1341	585	775	1038	2394	582	881	1019	985	1089	83		2083	259	2445	841	1972	2523	2380	123
Phoenix, Ariz.	1592	2300	1906	1857	586	1453	1631	887	586	1690	1009	1499	1831	1049	357	1508	1263	1982	1280	1316	2145	2083		1828	1009	1272	504	653	1114	1983
Pittsburgh, Pa.	521	483	178	704	1341	410	115	1070	1320	205	1137	330	774	781	2136	344	660	1010	743	919	317	259	1828		2145	559	1668	2264	2138	192
Portland, Ore.	2172	2540	2156	2405	1049	1749	2055	1633	982	1969	1825	1919	2491	1506	817	1919	1867	2708	1426	2049	2445	2445	1009	2145		1713	630	534	145	2354
St. Louis, Mo.	467	1038	662	795	838	262	492	547	871	455	679	231	753	238	1589	242	240	1061	466	598	888	841	1272	559	1713		1162	1744	1724	712
Salt Lake City, Utah	1583	2099	1699	1845	347	1260	1575	999	371	1492	1200	1356	1826	1049	579	1402	1250	2089	987	1434	1972	1972	504	1668	630	1162		599	701	1848
San Francisco, Cal.	2139	2699	2300	2428	959	1858	2166	1483	949	2091	1645	1949	2591	1506	347	1949	1802	2594	1584	1926	2571	2523	653	2264	534	1744	599		678	2442
Seattle, Wash.	2182	2493	2117	2405	966	1737	2026	1681	1021	1938	1891	1872	2585	1506	959	1943	1867	2734	1395	2101	2408	2380	1114	2138	145	1724	701	678		2329
Washington, D.C.	543	393	292	453	1477	597	306	1185	1494	396	1220	494	647	945	2300	476	765	923	934	966	205	123	1983	192	2354	712	1848	2442	2329	

ROAD MILEAGE BETWEEN PRINCIPAL CITIES OF NORTH AMERICA

	Albuquerque, N. Mex.	Atlanta, Ga.	Birmingham, Ala.	Boston, Mass.	Chicago, Ill.	Cleveland, Ohio	Dallas, Tex.	Denver, Colo.	Detroit, Mich.	Houston, Tex.	Indianapolis, Ind.	Kansas City, Mo.	Los Angeles, Cal.	Mexico City, Mex.	Miami, Fla.	Minneapolis, Minn.	Montreal, Que.	Nashville, Tenn.	New Orleans, La.	New York, N.Y.	Omaha, Neb.	Philadelphia, Pa.	Phoenix, Ariz.	Portland, Ore.	St. Louis, Mo.	Salt Lake City, Utah	San Francisco, Cal.	Seattle, Wash.	Toronto, Ont.	Washington, D.C.
Albuquerque, N. Mex.		1381	1251	2172	1281	1560	638	417	1525	834	1266	782	807	1414	1938	1190	2087	1218	1134	1979	858	1899	432	1371	1038	604	1115	1440	1847	1824
Atlanta, Ga.	1381		150	1037	674	672	795	1398	699	789	493	798	2182	1768	655	1068	1181	242	479	841	986	741	1793	2601	541	1878	2496	2618	925	608
Birmingham, Ala.	1251	150		1165	642	709	645	1286	724	639	475	697	2032	1618	751	1006	1270	196	342	969	869	898	1643	2505	465	1781	2366	2535	950	736
Boston, Mass.	2172	1037	1165		963	628	1748	1949	695	1804	906	1391	2979	2783	1504	1368	318	1088	1507	206	1412	296	2604	3046	1141	2343	3095	3095	539	429
Chicago, Ill.	1281	674	642	963		335	917	996	266	1067	181	499	2054	2367	1329	405	828	446	912	802	473	738	1713	2083	289	1390	2142	2013	492	671
Cleveland, Ohio	1560	672	709	628	335		1159	1321	170	1273	294	779	2367	2045	1352	740	561	528	1045	473	784	459	2045	2418	529	1715	2467	2366	287	346
Dallas, Tex.	638	795	645	1748	917	1159		781	1143	243	865	489	1387	1329	1352	936	1815	664	496	1552	644	1515	1058	2009	630	1242	1753	2078	1369	1319
Denver, Colo.	417	1398	1286	1949	996	1321	781		1253	1019	1058	600	1059	1746	2037	841	1815	1156	1273	1771	537	1691	865	1238	857	504	1235	1307	1479	1616
Detroit, Mich.	1525	699	724	695	266	170	1143	1253		1265	278	743	2311	2311	1387	695	561	562	1045	637	784	573	1957	2279	513	1647	2399	2399	226	506
Houston, Tex.	834	789	639	1804	1067	1273	243	1019	1265		967	710	1538	1058	1190	1157	1957	769	356	1608	865	1508	1019	2399	779	1438	1912	2274	1491	1375
Indianapolis, Ind.	1266	493	475	906	181	294	865	1058	278	967		485	2073	2311	1253	586	967	279	796	713	587	633	1698	2205	235	1504	2256	2194	504	558
Kansas City, Mo.	782	798	697	1391	499	779	489	600	743	710	485		1589	1627	1504	447	1305	556	806	1198	201	1148	1227	1835	257	1086	1835	1839	969	1043
Los Angeles, Cal.	807	2182	2032	2979	2054	2367	1387	1059	2311	1538	2073	1589		1917	2687	1889	2805	2025	1883	2786	1595	2706	389	959	1845	715	379	1131	2532	2651
Mexico City, Mex.	1414	1768	1618	2783	2367	2045	1329	1746	2311	1058	2311	1627	1917		2073	1965	2873	1747	1074	2587	1782	2487	1595	2785	1437	2016	2291	2537	2537	2354
Miami, Fla.	1938	655	751	1504	1329	1352	1352	2037	1387	1190	1253	1504	2687	2073		1748	1654	917	860	1281	1782	1198	2311	3256	1196	2532	3053	3273	1509	1075
Minneapolis, Minn.	1190	1068	1006	1368	405	740	936	841	695	1157	586	447	1889	1965	1748		1308	1041	1308	1207	357	1207	1616	1678	552	1196	1940	1608	1075	1076
Montreal, Que.	2087	1181	1270	318	828	561	1815	1815	561	1957	967	1305	2805	2873	1654	1308		1214	1591	378	1290	449	2519	2755	1143	2209	2961	2852	336	579
Nashville, Tenn.	1218	242	196	1088	446	528	664	1156	562	769	279	556	2025	1747	917	1041	1214		517	892	744	744	1650	2359	299	1636	2333	2376	754	659
New Orleans, La.	1134	479	342	1507	912	1045	496	1273	1045	356	796	806	1883	1074	860	1308	1591	517		1311	1007	1278	1494	2505	673	1738	2249	2574	1271	1078
New York, N.Y.	1979	841	969	206	802	473	1552	1771	637	1608	713	1198	2786	2587	1281	1207	378	892	1311		1251	100	2411	2885	948	2182	2934	2815	504	233
Omaha, Neb.	858	986	869	1412	473	784	644	537	784	865	587	201	1595	1782	1782	357	1290	744	1007	1251		1251	1290	1654	449	931	1683	1638	942	1116
Philadelphia, Pa.	1899	741	898	296	738	459	1515	1691	573	1508	633	1148	2706	2487	1198	1207	449	744	1278	100	1251		2331	2821	868	2114	2866	2751	453	133
Phoenix, Ariz.	432	1793	1643	2604	1713	2045	1058	865	1957	1019	1698	1227	389	1595	2311	1616	2519	1650	1494	2411	1290	2331		1266	1470	648	763	1437	2566	2256
Portland, Ore.	1371	2601	2505	3046	2083	2418	2009	1238	2279	2399	2205	1835	959	2785	3256	1678	2755	2359	2505	2885	1654	2821	1266		2060	767	636	172	2566	2754
St. Louis, Mo.	1038	541	465	1141	289	529	630	857	513	779	235	257	1845	1437	1196	552	1143	299	673	948	449	868	1470	2060		1337	2089	2081	752	793
Salt Lake City, Utah	604	1878	1781	2343	1390	1715	1242	504	1647	1438	1504	1086	715	2016	2532	1196	2209	1636	1738	2182	931	2114	648	767	1337		752	836	2089	2066
San Francisco, Cal.	1115	2496	2366	3095	2142	2467	1753	1235	2399	1912	2256	1835	379	2291	3053	1940	2961	2333	2249	2934	1683	2866	763	636	2089	752		808	2625	2799
Seattle, Wash.	1440	2618	2535	3095	2013	2366	2078	1307	2399	2274	2194	1839	1131	2537	3273	1608	2852	2376	2574	2815	1638	2751	1437	172	2081	836	808		2684	2799
Toronto, Ont.	1847	925	950	539	492	287	1369	1479	226	1491	504	969	2532	2537	1509	1075	336	754	1271	504	942	453	2566	2566	752	2089	2625	2684		456
Washington, D.C.	1824	608	736	429	671	346	1319	1616	506	1375	558	1043	2651	2354	1075	1076	579	659	1078	233	1116	133	2256	2754	793	2066	2799	2799	456	

## 23

Time

- *Time Zones*

- *Calendar Time*

- *Perpetual Calendar*

TIME ZONES

Standard Times At 12 Noon, Eastern Standard Time

Area	Time	Area	Time
Argentina	2 P.M.	Japan	2 A.M.*
Austria	6 P.M.	Korea	2 A.M.*
Australia (Sydney)	3 A.M.*	Mexico (Mexico City)	11 A.M.
Bangladesh	11 P.M.	Morocco	5 P.M.
Belgium	6 P.M.	Netherlands	6 P.M.
Brazil	2 P.M.	Netherlands Antilles	
Burma (Myanmar)	11:30 P.M.	(Aruba, Bonaire,	
Canada		Curaçao)	1 P.M.
(Newfoundland)	1:30 P.M.	New Zealand	5 A.M.*
Canada (Toronto)	12 noon	Nigeria	6 P.M.
Canada (Vancouver)	9 A.M.	Norway	6 P.M.
Chile	1 P.M.	Pakistan	10 P.M.
China (Shanghai)	1 A.M.*	Peru	12 noon
Colombia	12 noon	Philippines	1 A.M.*
Costa Rica	11 A.M.	Poland	6 P.M.
Cuba	12 noon	Portugal	6 P.M.
Czech Republic	6 P.M.	Romania	7 P.M.
Denmark	6 P.M.	Russia (Moscow,	
Dominican Republic	1 P.M.	St. Petersburg)	8 P.M.
Egypt	7 P.M.	Russia (Vladivostok)	3 A.M.*
Ethiopia	8 P.M.	Senegal	5 P.M.
Finland	7 P.M.	Singapore	12:30 A.M.*
France	6 P.M.	South Africa	7 P.M.
Germany	6 P.M.	Spain	6 P.M.
Gibraltar	6 P.M.	Sweden	6 P.M.
Greece	7 P.M.	Switzerland	6 P.M.
Haiti	12 noon	Thailand	12 midnight
Hong Kong	1 A.M.*	Tunisia	6 P.M.
Hungary	6 P.M.	Turkey	7 P.M.
India	10:30 P.M.	United Kingdom	5 P.M.
Indonesia (Java)	12 midnight	Uruguay	2 P.M.
Iran	8:30 P.M.	U.S.A. (Chicago)	11 A.M.
Iraq	8 P.M.	U.S.A. (Salt Lake	
Ireland	5 P.M.	City)	10 A.M.
Israel	7 P.M.	U.S.A. (San Francisco)	9 A.M.
Italy	6 P.M.	Venezuela	1 P.M.
Ivory Coast	5 P.M.	Vietnam	12 midnight
Jamaica	12 noon	Zaire (Kinshasa)	6 P.M.

* Morning of the following day

CALENDAR TIME

The early Roman calendar was based on the lunar month of $29^1/_2$ days and had 354 days. But the solar year (the time it takes the earth to circle the sun) is about $365^1/_4$ days. The Romans added an extra month from time to time to bring the calendar into agreement with the seasons.

A more consistent calendar was instituted by Julius Caesar in 46 B.C. Its year was 365 days with an extra day added in February every fourth year (leap year). The Julian calendar set the length of a month at 30 or 31 days, except for February.

By 1582, the calendar was again out of phase with the seasons. In October of that year, Pope Gregory XIII dropped ten days from the calendar to correct the error that had accumulated. To keep the error from recurring, the Gregorian calendar has leap year every fourth year except those centesimal years that can be divided by 400. Many countries adopted the new calendar at once, but Great Britain and its American colonies waited until 1752. Sometimes two dates are specified for an early event, "Old Style" means the Julian calendar and "New Style" means the Gregorian calendar.

A year is divided into 12 months, 52 weeks, or 365 days (except a leap year, which has 366 days):

January	31 days	July	31 days
February	28 days	August	31 days
	(leap year 29)		
March	31 days	September	30 days
April	30 days	October	31 days
May	31 days	November	30 days
June	30 days	December	31 days

1 week has 7 days
1 day has 24 hours
1 hour has 60 minutes
1 minute has 60 seconds

To compute actual days between two dates, find the number of days between months in the chart below and to that add the difference between the days (after February in a leap year, add one day).

To the Same Date in

From Any Date in	Jan.	Feb.	Mar.	Apr.	May	June	July	Aug.	Sept.	Oct.	Nov.	Dec.
January	365	31	59	90	120	151	181	212	243	273	304	334
February	334	365	28	59	89	120	150	181	212	242	273	303
March	306	337	365	31	61	92	122	153	184	214	245	275
April	275	306	334	365	30	61	91	122	153	183	214	244
May	245	276	304	335	365	31	61	92	123	153	184	214
June	214	245	273	304	334	365	30	61	92	122	153	183
July	184	215	243	274	304	335	365	31	62	92	123	153
August	153	184	212	243	273	304	334	365	31	61	92	122
September	122	153	181	212	242	273	303	334	365	30	61	91
October	92	123	151	182	212	243	273	304	335	365	31	61
November	61	92	120	151	181	212	242	273	304	334	365	30
December	31	62	90	121	151	182	212	243	274	304	335	365

PERPETUAL CALENDAR (A.D. 1–2400)

To find the calendar for any year, first find the Dominical letter for the year in the upper section of the table. Two letters are given for leap year: the first for January and February, the second for other months. In the lower section of table, find the column in which the Dominical letter for the year is in the same line as the month for which the calendar is desired; this column gives the days of the week that are to be used with the month. For example, in the table of Dominical letters we find that the letter for 1960, a leap year, is CB; in the line with July, the letter B occurs in the third column; hence July 4, 1960, is Monday.

DOMINICAL LETTERS

Century				Julian Calendar								Gregorian Calendar			
Year				0 / 700 / 1400	100 / 800 / 1500+	200 / 900	300 / 1000	400 / 1100	500 / 1200	600 / 1300	1500‡	1600 / 2000	1700 / 2100	1800 / 2200	1900 / 2300
0				DC	ED	FE	GF	AG	BA	CB		BA	C	E	G
1	29	57	85	B	C	D	E	F	G	A	F	G	B	D	F
2	30	58	86	A	B	C	D	E	F	G	E	F	A	C	E
3	31	59	87	G	A	B	C	D	E	F	D	E	G	B	D
4	32	60	88	FE	GF	AG	BA	CB	DC	ED	CB	DC	FE	AG	CB
5	33	61	89	D	E	F	G	A	B	C	A	B	D	F	A
6	34	62	90	C	D	E	F	G	A	B	G	A	C	E	G
7	35	63	91	B	C	D	E	F	G	A	F	G	B	D	F
8	36	64	92	AG	BA	CB	DC	ED	FE	GF	ED	FE	AG	CB	ED
9	37	65	93	F	G	A	B	C	D	E	C	D	F	A	C
10	38	66	94	E	F	G	A	B	C	D	B	C	E	G	B
11	39	67	95	D	E	F	G	A	B	C	A	B	D	F	A
12	40	68	96	CB	DC	ED	FE	GF	AG	BA	GF	AG	CB	ED	GF
13	41	69	97	A	B	C	D	E	F	G	E	F	A	C	E
14	42	70	98	G	A	B	C	D	E	F	D	E	G	B	D
15	43	71	99	F	G	A	B	C	D	E	C	D	F	A	C
16	44	72		ED	FE	GF	AG	BA	CB	DC	-	CB	ED	GF	BA
17	45	73		C	D	E	F	G	A	B	-	A	C	E	G
18	46	74		B	C	D	E	F	G	A	-	G	B	D	F
19	47	75		A	B	C	D	E	F	G	-	F	A	C	E
20	48	76		GF	AG	BA	CB	DC	ED	FE	-	ED	GF	BA	DC
21	49	77		E	F	G	A	B	C	D	-	C	E	G	B
22	50	78		D	E	F	G	A	B	C	-	B	D	F	A
23	51	79		C	D	E	F	G	A	B	-	A	C	E	G
24	52	80		BA	CB	DC	ED	FE	GF	AG	-	GF	BA	DC	FE
25	53	81		G	A	B	C	D	E	F	-	E	G	B	D
26	54	82		F	G	A	B	C	D	E	C	D	F	A	C
27	55	83		E	F	G	A	B	C	D	B	C	E	G	B
28	56	84		DC	ED	FE	GF	AG	BA	CB	AG	BA	DC	FE	AG

Month	Dominical letter						
Jan., Oct.	A	B	C	D	E	F	G
Feb., Mar., Nov.	D	E	F	G	A	B	C
Apr., July	G	A	B	C	D	E	F
May	B	C	D	E	F	G	A
June	E	F	G	A	B	C	D
Aug.	C	D	E	F	G	A	B
Sept., Dec.	F	G	A	B	C	D	E

Day											
1	8	15	22	29	Sun.	Sat.	Fri.	Thurs.	Wed.	Tues.	Mon.
2	9	16	23	30	Mon.	Sun.	Sat.	Fri.	Thurs.	Wed.	Tues.
3	10	17	24	31	Tues.	Mon.	Sun.	Sat.	Fri.	Thurs.	Wed.
4	11	18	25		Wed.	Tues.	Mon.	Sun.	Sat.	Fri.	Thurs.
5	12	19	26		Thurs.	Wed.	Tues.	Mon.	Sun.	Sat.	Fri.
6	13	20	27		Fri.	Thurs.	Wed.	Tues.	Mon.	Sun.	Sat.
7	14	21	28		Sat.	Fri.	Thurs.	Wed.	Tues.	Mon.	Sun.

*On and before 1582, Oct. 4 only.
‡On and after 1582, Oct. 15 only.
This calendar was prepared by G. M. Clemence, U. S. Naval Observatory, and is reprinted from the *Smithsonian Physical Tables, Ninth Edition,* by permission of the Smithsonian Institution.

24

Foreign Travel Tips

by Linda A. Bruce

- *Business and Banking Hours, and Tipping Practices in Selected Countries*

- *Business and Secretarial Services Overseas*

- *Passport, Visa, and Immunization Requirements*

- *Insurance for International Travel*

- *Money*

- *Medical Help Overseas*

- *Legal Help Overseas*

- *Jet Lag*

- *Average Temperatures by Month in Selected Cities*

- *Holidays in Selected Countries*

Increasing numbers of businesses are involved in business dealings with foreign countries. With this growth in international business has come a great increase in the amount of foreign travel by executives.

The secretary is almost always called on to help organize the executive's trip. The executive needs to know specific regulations concerning passport, visa, and immunization requirements of the country or countries to be visited. A familiarity with the rules concerning the currency of the country and plans on how to handle money—both small amounts for such items as tipping and large amounts for business deals—is very important. Information on the general business practices of the country (*e.g.*, banking hours) as well as an awareness of the culture (*e.g.*, tipping practices, holidays) will also help to make the executive's trip less stressful and possibly more profitable.

TABLE 24.1 Business and Banking Hours, and Tipping Practices in Selected Countries

Country	Business Hours	Banking Hours	Tipping*
Canada	M-F 9:00-5:00	M-F 10:00-3:00	R 15% P Meter + $1.00 T 15-20%
Denmark	M-F 9:00-5:00	M-F 9:30-4:00	R 15% P Kr5/bag T None
England	M-F 9:30-5:30	M-F 9:30-3:30	R 12-15% P 50p/bag T 20p/L fare
France	M-F 9:30-12:30; 2:30-6:00	M-F 9:00-4:00	R included in bill + chg. P F5 T 15-20%
Germany	M-F 9:00-4:00	M-F 9:00-1:00 Tu/Th 2:30-6:00	R included in bill + chg. P DM4-5/ bag T 5%
Hong Kong	M-F 9:00-4:30	M-F 9:00-4:30 Sat 9:00-12:30	R included in bill + 5% P HK$1/bag T 10%

Country	Business Hours	Banking Hours	Tipping*
Italy	M-F 8:30-1:00; 4:00-9:00	M-F 8:30-1:30	R included in bill + 5 -10% P L800/bag T 15%
Japan	M-F 9:00-6:00	M-F 9:00-3:00 Sat 9:00-12:00 closed 2nd Sat	R not custom or included P Y250/bag T none unless help w/bags
Mexico	M-F 9:00-2:30; 5:30-8:00	M-Sat 9:00-1:00 Some 2:30-8:00	R 15% P 50p/bag T 50p
Netherlands	M-F 9:00-5:30	M-F 9:00-4:00	R included in bill P fixed rate 15% T included + chg.
Norway	M-F 8:00-4:00 Summer 8:00-3:00	M-F 8:15-3:30	R included P Kr5/bag T included or round off to nearest Kr
Sweden	M-F 9:00-5:00	M-F 9:30-3:00	R included P Kr3/bag + Kr2/ add'l. T 10-15%
Switzerland	M-F 9:00-5:30	M-F 9:00-4:15	R included in bill P SF1/bag T 12-15%

* R = Restaurants; P = Porters; T = Taxi drivers

This chapter provides hints for foreign business travel. However, for any information subject to frequent or last-minute change, be sure to check with local embassies or other organizations that have up-to-the-minute information.

BUSINESS AND SECRETARIAL SERVICES OVERSEAS

If the need for business or secretarial services is occasional and/or short-term, the most convenient procedure to follow might be to investigate whether or not the hotel offers such a service. Many hotels have a completely separate office established to accommodate just such needs on a fee basis. If that is not the case, or if you expect frequent or long-term office requirements, it is possible to rent furnished offices and office/secretarial services in almost any country in the world on a daily, weekly, monthly, or annual basis.

Services that can be expected from such rental companies are:

- private office space/conference rooms/showrooms
- business mailing address
- mail collecting and forwarding service
- 24-hour telephone answering service
- multilingual secretarial services
- communication services; photocopy, dictation, telex, facsimile services
- safekeeping of documents

In addition, it is possible that assistance may be provided in making business contacts in the country in which you rent space/services or in obtaining legal and financial advice. Costs, of course, will vary depending on the space or services required.

PASSPORT, VISA, AND IMMUNIZATION REQUIREMENTS

There are a few countries that do not require a passport, but it is strongly recommended that you obtain and carry one with you at all times in any case. It is impossible to predict what circumstances might arise in your travels that would necessitate your having this important form of identification. Unexpected itinerary changes and the possibility of legal or medical problems are only a couple of the reasons you should never travel abroad without a current passport. Passport applications may be made at almost any U.S. Passport Office.

In addition to a passport, some countries require either an entry permit or a visa. Check with the country's consulate or embassy for current visa/entry permit requirements. (A travel agent or library can provide the address and telephone number of the nearest embassy or consulate.) These organizations know what, if any, immunizations are needed. A Certificate of Vaccination, as well as the "shots" themselves, can be obtained at your local board of health.

INSURANCE FOR INTERNATIONAL TRAVEL

Quite often, health and personal property insurance, whether business or personal, will cover the traveler overseas. It is very important, however, to check with either the employer or insurance agent to get all the details of coverage, including exceptions, deductibles, maximum limits, and procedures to follow in case of need.

If the traveler is not covered by an existing policy, contact International Health Service, Georgetown University Medical Center, 3800 Reservoir Road, NW, Washington, DC 20007, Tel: 202-687-1872 for information.

MONEY

Travelers checks are probably the safest and most convenient form in which to carry money while traveling abroad. Travelers checks can be cashed easily in most cities around the world. In case of loss or theft, they can also be replaced when a report is filed with the bank or agency from which the checks were purchased.

Obtaining a small amount of cash in the local currency before leaving is very helpful for paying taxis and porters on arrival at a foreign destination, particularly if the banks are closed. Banks with an international department can usually provide a limited amount of funds in the currencies of the countries you plan to visit. Currency dealers and most international airports and hotels are other sources, but the bank offers the best rate of exchange. Although the exchange rate on the "black market" may be tempting, it is extremely inadvisable, foolish, and possibly even dangerous to take this route.

When large amounts of cash will be needed in a foreign country, it is best to arrange for a line of credit with a U.S. bank before leaving. This line of credit can then be used to obtain funds at associated banks en route.

Some countries have currency restrictions to limit the amount of local currency that may be brought into or taken out of the country. Check with the appropriate consulate or embassy for the latest information in this regard.

MEDICAL HELP OVERSEAS

A few simple first aid items brought in a personal emergency kit can help ease uncomplicated illness. Such things as aspirin or an aspirin substitute, bandages, an antiseptic cream, a thermometer, sunscreen, antihistamines, nasal decongestants, antidiarrheal medication, an extra pair of prescription glasses (or at least the prescription), and sunglasses can all make life much more comfortable. For more disease-prone areas of the world, it is wise to include water purification tablets, anti-malarial medicine, and insect repellent.

Before traveling overseas, it is advisable to contact a Travelers' Clinic in the major city nearest you. These clinics offer counseling on travel health, especially in countries in which water or disease problems exist. The clinics receive weekly updates from the Centers for Disease Control in Atlanta and the World Health Organization in order to provide this information to their clients. One such clinic is the International Travel Clinic, 550 N. Broadway, Room 107, Baltimore, MD (410) 955-8931. As an alternative, the traveler can consult his or her private physician.

Another suggestion is membership in the International Association for Medical Assistance to Travelers (IAMAT), a nonprofit, donation-supported foundation located at 417 Center Street, Lewiston, NY 14092, Tel: 716-754-4883. There is no membership fee, although donations are accepted. Upon joining, the member will be sent a membership directory of doctors serving in 450 cities worldwide. The physicians have been educated in international medical practices with skills meeting Western standards. They all speak English and are available to members 24 hours a day. A fixed fee is charged for office visits and house or hotel calls, as well as holiday and Sunday visits. The traveler will also receive a Travelers Clinical Record (to be completed by a family doctor and carried with the traveler) in addition to world immunization and malaria risk charts.

Another organization providing personal and medical service for international travelers is International SOS Assistance, Inc., P.O. Box 11568, Philadelphia, PA 19116, Tel: 215-244-1500. If the local medical center is inadequate, the patient will be evacuated to the nearest adequate medical facility for treatment of the illness or injury. After stabilization, the patient will be brought to facilities near home. More details are available by contacting the organization directly.

Most major hotels around the world also have a doctor on call and arrangements with the nearest clinic or hospital to treat guests who become ill.

LEGAL HELP OVERSEAS

Legal difficulties abroad can run the gamut, including suits involving drug trafficking, personal injury, divorce, child custody, nationality, paternity, wills and estates, immigration violations, customs violations, drunk driving, etc. Because of the complicated and varied legal systems in many other parts of the world, it is advisable to consult a law firm with experience in these matters. One such firm is the International Legal Defense Counsel, which has been providing this type of assistance for many years. It is staffed by practiced American attorneys. The address is 1115 15th Street, 24th Floor, Philadelphia, PA 19102.

JET LAG

A useful item to obtain before traveling is a wallet-size card that explains the anti-jet-lag diet. To obtain one, send a stamped, self-addressed envelope to Anti-Jet Lag Diet, Argonne National Laboratory, 9700 South Cass Avenue, Argonne, IL 60439.

Essentially, what is called for is a highly structured diet for four days before embarking on a trip by air. On the first of the four days, a high-protein breakfast and lunch and a high-carbohydrate dinner are recommended. On the second day, only salads, fruits and fruit juices, and light soups are to be consumed. The same cycle followed on days one and two are followed on days three and four. Another suggestion is to eat fairly lightly when in the air. Alcohol should not be taken before or immediately after a time change, due to the lengthened period of adjustment it causes, to say nothing of decision-making and memory difficulties already brought on by jet lag.

If traveling east, it is advisable to try to retire the evening before departure one hour later than normal for each time zone that will be crossed. When traveling west, the opposite is the case: go to bed an hour earlier for every time zone to be crossed, as much as is practical.

Everyone's mood and the need for sleep are affected by exposure to sunlight. For this reason, it is wise to bring a sleeping mask to wear on long trips that will span daylight hours. If at all possible, try to eat and sleep according to the local schedule in effect at the destination. When flying east, make business appointments in the afternoon. When traveling west, early morning appointments are best.

A useful resource containing more detailed information on jet lag and other travel-related health and safety issues is the *Traveler's Health and Safety Handbook,* available for $5.00 from Agora, 824 E. Baltimore Street, Baltimore, MD 21202, Tel: (410) 234-0515.

TABLE 24.2 Average Temperatures by Month in Selected Cities

	January	February	March	April	May	June	July	August	September	October	November	December
Amsterdam	37	38	41	48	56	61	65	65	59	51	43	38
Berlin	36	32	39	49	55	66	63	61	56	48	37	32
Copenhagen	32	32	34	42	51	59	62	60	54	46	39	34
London	42	42	46	48	56	60	60	62	60	55	44	46
Melbourne	67	67	64	59	54	50	48	51	53	57	61	64
Mexico City	53	56	60	64	64	63	74	61	62	58	55	53
Milan	32	37	45	54	62	74	69	71	65	54	43	35
Montreal	12	14	25	41	55	64	74	66	58	46	33	24
Naples	44	46	48	54	66	71	74	74	68	64	53	45
Nice	46	48	51	57	58	68	71	69	69	61	52	48
Oslo	24	24	29	39	60	59	62	60	52	41	32	25
Paris	36	39	44	50	57	62	65	65	60	52	43	38
Rome	43	46	50	55	68	73	77	80	73	67	56	52
Stockholm	27	26	29	38	47	57	62	59	52	66	34	28
Sydney	73	73	69	65	57	53	53	55	59	65	67	70
Tokyo	37	38	44	54	61	68	75	77	71	60	50	41

HOLIDAYS IN SELECTED COUNTRIES*

Canada

New Year's Day, January 1; Good Friday; Easter Monday; Victoria Day; St. Jean Baptiste (Quebec); Canada Day, July 1; Fed. Gov. Holiday (Quebec), first Monday in August; Labor Day, first Monday in September; Thanksgiving Day, second Monday in October; Veteran's Day, November 11; Christmas Day, December 25; Boxing Day, December 26

Denmark

New Year's Day, January 1; Shrove Tuesday; Holy Thursday; Good Friday; Easter Sunday; Easter Monday; Prayer Day (fourth Friday after Easter); Ascension Day; Whit Monday; Constitution Day (half-day, June 5); Christmas Day, December 25; Second Day of Christmas, December 26

England

New Year's Day, January 1; Good Friday; Easter Monday; Early May Bank Holiday; Spring Holiday (last Monday in May); Queen's Birthday, June 11; Late Summer Holiday (last Monday in August); Christmas Day, December 25; Boxing Day, December 26

France

New Year's Day, January 1; Easter Monday; Labor Day, May 1; Ascension Day; Whitsuntide; Whit Monday; Bastille Day, July 14; Assumption, August 15; All Saints Day, November 1; Veterans Day, November 11; Christmas Day, December 25

Germany

New Year's Day, January 1; Epiphany, January 6; Rose Monday, February 8; Good Friday; Easter Monday; Labor Day; Ascension Day; Whit Monday; Corpus Christi; Day of German Unity, June 17; Repentance Day; Christmas Day, December 25; Boxing Day, December 26

Hong Kong

New Year's Day, January 1; Chinese New Year, February 15–17; Good Friday; day after Good Friday; Easter Monday; Ching Ming Festival, April 4; Dragon Boat Festival, June 11; Queen's Birthday, June 11; Day after Queen's Birthday, June 12; Public Holiday, August 22; Liberation Day, August 25; Mid-Autumn Festival, September 25; Chung Yeung Festival, October 19; Christmas Holiday, December 25–26

Italy

New Year's Day, January 1; Easter Monday; Liberation Day, April 25; Labor Day, May 1; Assumption, August 15; All Saints Day, November 1; Immaculate Conception, December 8; Christmas Day, December 25; St. Stephen's Day, December 26

Japan

New Year's Day, January 1; Adults' Day, January 15; National Foundation Day, February 11; Vernal Equinox Day, March 20 or 21; Emperor's Day, April 29; Constitution Day, May 3; Children's Day, May 5; Respect for the Aged Day, September 15; Autumnal Equinox, September 23 or 24; Sports Day, October 10; Cultural Day, November 3; Labor Thanksgiving Day, November 23; Government Off Season, December 29–January 3; any holiday that falls on Sunday is celebrated the following day.

Mexico

New Year's Day, January 1; Constitution Day, February 5; Benito Juarez' Birthday, March 21; Holy Thursday; Good Friday; Labor Day, May 1; Anniversary of the Puebla Battle, May 5; Independence Day, September 16; Columbus Day, October 12; All Saints Day, November 1; All Souls Day, November 2; Mexican Revolution Day, November 20; Fiesta of Our Lady of Guadelupe, December 12; Christmas Day, December 25

The Netherlands

New Year's Day, January 1; Good Friday; Easter Monday; Queen's Birthday, April 30; Liberation Day, May 5; Ascension; Whit Monday; Christmas Day, December 25; Boxing Day, December 26

Norway

New Year's Day, January 1; Holy Thursday; Good Friday; Easter Monday; Labor Day, May 1; Ascension Day; Constitution Day, May 17; Whit Monday; Christmas Day, December 25; Boxing Day, December 26

Sweden

New Year's Day, January 1; Good Friday; Easter Monday; Ascension Day; Whit Monday; Swedish Flag Day, June 6; Midsummer Day; All Saints' Day, November 1; Christmas Day, December 25; Boxing Day, December 26

Switzerland

New Year's Day, January 1; Berchtoldstag; Good Friday; Easter Sunday; Easter Monday; Labor Day, May 1; Ascension Day, Whitsuntide; Whit Monday; National Day, August 1; Federal Day of Prayers, September 21; Christmas Day, December 25; Boxing Day, December 26

* In some countries, the exact date of a holiday may vary by one or two days because holidays are based on the lunar calendar (determined by the sighting of the moon). Travelers should therefore check with the appropriate embassy before making travel plans.

General Reference

## 25

Sources of Information

Revised by Joyce Gold

- *Dictionaries*

    Desk-size
    Unabridged
    Biographical
    Foreign Language

- *Word Books*

    Books of Synonyms and Antonyms
    Books of Quotations
    Books on Usage

- *Style Books and Printing Guides*

- *Encyclopedias*

- *Atlases and Gazetteers*

- *Yearbooks and Almanacs*

- *Books on Parliamentary Procedure*

■ *Directories*
   Business, Manufacturers, Merchants
   Finance
   Education
   Who's Who
   Foreign Diplomats
   U.S. Government Offices
   Independent Government Agencies
   U.S. Government Officials

■ *Professional Associations*

■ *Indexes*

■ *Libraries*

■ *Travel Information*

   Travel Agencies
   Departments of Tourism

■ *Miscellaneous Directories, Guides, and Registers*

   Telephone Directories
   City Directories

■ *Publicity Departments*
■ *Newspaper Offices*

"The factor to be used in order to convert inches to millimeters? I think it's 25.4, but we'd better look it up."

"You are moving to Cedar Rapids, Iowa? Er . . . just how big a city is it?"

"The number of chemical elements? Well, over a hundred, certainly. The exact number escapes me."

Secretaries, business executives, students—all of us—are often faced with such questions. We "look up" the answers, and that is one form of research.

The subject for research might be the development of the computer, the hybridization of marigolds, the advertising rates for a metropolitan newspaper, the best hotel in Syracuse, New York, or the airline schedule between Nashville and London.

Resourcefulness often brings greater recognition for a researcher than does any other quality. Besides being an important part of general efficiency, it enables one to build up a reputation for knowing virtually everything.

Digging out information is first a matter of knowing *where* to dig. Following are sources of information with which all of us should be acquainted.

DICTIONARIES

A dictionary is indispensable as a quick reference for spelling, hyphenation, and syllabification of words and names. It is also valuable in finding definitions of words and phrases, synonyms, place names, biographical data, the usage of words, and the derivations of words from foreign languages.

Desk-size

The desk dictionary known as a "college edition" is of the size and scope that has proved to be most useful in a business office.

> *Webster's New World™ College Dictionary, Third Edition*

Unabridged

Some offices and families and most libraries will also have an unabridged dictionary, larger in vocabulary coverage than the "college" editions.

> *Webster's Third New International Dictionary of the English Language*
>   (Merriam-Webster)
> *Random House Dictionary of the English Language*

Biographical

Biographical dictionaries contain concise biographies of noted men and women.

> *Webster's Biographical Dictionary*

Foreign Language

Bookstores carry many foreign-language dictionaries.

Webster's New World™ French Dictionary
Webster's New World™ German Dictionary
Webster's New World™ Italian Dictionary
Webster's New World™ Spanish Dictionary

WORD BOOKS

Books of Synonyms and Antonyms

Synonyms and antonyms are groups of words with like or opposite meanings, respectively. *Sharp* and *keen* are synonyms, while *sharp* and *dull* are antonyms. Here again, your dictionary is a useful tool, but you may want a more concentrated resource. A *thesaurus* ("treasury" or "storehouse") of synonyms and antonyms is then recommended.

Webster's New World™ Thesaurus
Roget's International Thesaurus
Funk & Wagnalls *Modern Guide to Synonyms and Related Words*

Books of Quotations

John Bartlett's *Familiar Quotations*
Burton Richardson's *The Home Book of Quotations*
Bergen Evans's *Dictionary of Quotations*
H. L. Mencken's *New Dictionary of Quotations on Historical Principles*
Oxford Dictionary of Quotations

Books on Usage

Webster's New World™ Guide to Current American Usage by Bernice Randall (most up-to-date)
Elements of Style by William Strunk and E. B. White (most concise advice on usage)
Dictionary of Modern English Usage by H. W. Fowler (conservative view on usage)
Dictionary of Contemporary American Usage by Bergen and Cornelia Evans (liberal point of view)
The Careful Writer by Theodore M. Bernstein

Modern American Usage by Wilson Follett

English Grammar and Composition by John E. Warriner and Francis Griffith

STYLE BOOKS AND PRINTING GUIDES

Chicago Manual of Style, University of Chicago Press (guide for the preparation of manuscripts for printing)

United States Government Printing Office *Style Manual*

New York Times Manual of Style and Usage (newspaper and magazine style)

Words into Type by Marjorie E. Skillen, et al.

Ink on Paper by Edmund Arnold

ENCYCLOPEDIAS

A general encyclopedia is a good reference source because it summarizes what otherwise might take hours of reading to discover. Good encyclopedias also contain maps and lists of books on the subjects treated (bibliographies).

Encyclopaedia Britannica (24 volumes; generally considered the finest reference set)

Collier's Encyclopedia (24 volumes)

Encyclopedia Americana (30 volumes)

Columbia Encyclopedia (a good one-volume work)

Van Nostrand's Scientific Encyclopedia (a one-volume source of general scientific information)

McGraw-Hill Encyclopedia of Science and Technology (15 volumes, updated each year with a *Yearbook* supplement)

Encyclopedia of Associations (3 volumes)

Webster's New World™ Encyclopedia

ATLASES AND GAZETTEERS

Even the best atlases, or books of maps and geographical data, find it hard to keep up with the rapidly changing boundaries and the formation of new countries in our world today. It is important for the secretary to check the publishing dates of these works before purchase to be sure the information within is up to date. An extensive listing of geographical names is also contained in each of the atlases.

Gazetteers are dictionaries or indexes of geographic names.

Hammond's *Ambassador World Atlas*
Rand McNally *International Atlas*
Columbia Lippincott Gazetteer of the World
Webster's New World™ Atlas

YEARBOOKS AND ALMANACS

Although an almanac was originally and primarily a book of tables with astronomical information, data on tides and sunrise, etc., a number of commercial yearbooks and almanacs of a much broader scope are on the market.

The World Almanac and Book of Facts and *Information Please Almanac* are both handy, inexpensive annual guides that give information and statistical data on scores of subjects of current interest, from sports to state histories.

Facts on File is the most comprehensive of the standard hardcover yearbooks, a semimonthly periodical for which the subscriber receives at the beginning of each year a binder and updated maps along with the cumulative index of the preceding year. Additional titles are listed below.

International Yearbook and Statesman's Who's Who
Statesman's Yearbook
Political Handbook and Atlas of the World
Yearbook of American and Canadian Churches
Yearbook of International Organizations

BOOKS ON PARLIAMENTARY PROCEDURE

A secretary may be required to assist at and record executive meetings in which parliamentary procedures are followed. It is useful to have a reference for settling procedural questions.

Robert's Rules of Order
O. Garfield Jones's *Parliamentary Procedure at a Glance*

DIRECTORIES

Business, Manufacturers, Merchants

A Guide to Business Directories, United States Department of Commerce (Directories listed under type of business and subdivided by local and regional directories)

Poor's Register of Corporations, Directors and Executives (factual information about executives and directors of large American and Canadian corporations)

Directory of American Firms Operating in Foreign Countries

Thomas' Register of American Manufacturers

Kelley's Directory of Merchants, Manufacturers, and Shippers of the World

American Book Trade Directory

A Directory of Foreign Manufacturers in the United States

National Trade and Professional Associations of the United States and Canada and Labor Unions

International Business Bibliography

Finance

How to Read the Financial News by C. Norman Stabler (discussion of operation of Wall Street and stock market)

Who's Who in Finance and Industry

Dun and Bradstreet Ratings and Reports

Moody's Manuals (Reports on companies)

Ayer Directory of Publications (geographical listing of newspapers and magazines, with address, name of editor, frequency of publication, advertising rates, and circulation figures)

Education

Education Directory (published by the U.S. Office of Education; lists educational institutions, national and state educational officials and associations, county, town, and district superintendents, college presidents, etc.)

Patterson's American Education (one of several lists of schools, colleges, and other educational institutions in the U.S.)

Handbook of Private Schools

American Universities and Colleges, American Council on Education, Washington, D.C. (lists all universities and colleges in United States with information such as admission requirements, courses offered, degrees granted, number of departments, professors, students, and physical facilities)

Lovejoy's College Guide (lists information about universities, colleges, junior colleges, community colleges, and technical institutes)

Who's Who

Who's Who in American Art

Who's Who in Art

Who's Who in American Education

Who's Who in Commerce and Industry

Who's Who in Labor

Who's Who in Religion

American Men and Women of Science

American Medical Directory

Who's Who in Insurance

Leaders in Education

The World of Learning

Who's Who in Finance and Industry

Who's Who Among Black Americans

Who's Who in Computer Education and Research

Who's Who in America

Who's Who (British version)

Who's Who of American Women

International Who's Who

Who's Who in Canada

Who's Who in the World

Who's Who in Electronics

Who's Who in American Law

Dictionary of American Biography

Twentieth Century Authors, a Biographical Dictionary

Foreign Diplomats

Diplomatic List, Department of State (lists names of foreign diplomatic personnel in Washington with their addresses)

U.S. Government Offices

The United States Government is the largest publisher in the country. The Superintendent of Documents, United States Government Printing Office, Washington, D.C. 20402, has catalogs of available government publications that cover a wide range of subjects. Some of the bulletins and pamphlets are free, but for some of them and for books a charge is made. Write the Super-intendent of Documents to receive a monthly listing or to ask which government department or agency may have the specific information you are seeking. Otherwise, address the department or agency itself:

Department of Agriculture, 14th Street and Independence Avenue, SW, Washington, D.C. 20250; (202) 447-2791. For information regarding crops in general and statistics relating to agricultural production, the Forest Service, the combating of injurious insects and animal and plant pests and diseases, soil conservation, food and nutrition service, marketing, and farm prices.

Department of Commerce, 14th Street and Constitution Avenue, NW, Washington, D.C. 20230; (202) 377-4901. For information on the national census, standards of weights and measures, government fisheries, lighthouses, and coast and geodetic surveys. Within the Department of Commerce, address specific inquiries to the Patent and Trademark Office and the National Weather Service.

Department of Defense, The Pentagon, Washington, D.C. 20301; (202) 545-6700. For information regarding the armed forces, the Joint Chiefs of Staff, training academies, and military installations of the United States.

Department of Education, 400 Maryland Avenue, SW, Washington, D.C. 20202; (202) 732-4576. For information on educational programs and opportunities for learning-disabled, mentally retarded, or handicapped students, the Head Start program and vocational rehabilitation, and on special classes for gifted students.

Department of Energy, 1000 Independence Avenue, SW, Washington, D.C. 20585; (202) 586-5806. For information about energy conservation, research, development, and technology; the marketing of federal power; regulation of energy production; and the nuclear weapons program.

Department of Health and Human Services, 200 Independence Avenue, SW, Washington, D.C. 20201; (202) 245-6343. Within the department, address Public Health Services with inquiries about the Center for Disease Control or for the Food and Drug Administration, the National Health Institutes, and the Alcohol, Drug Abuse, and Mental Health Administration. Address specific inquiries about social security to the Social Security Administration.

Department of Housing and Urban Development, 451 7th Street, SW, Washington, D.C. 20401; (202) 755-6685. For information on urban renewal and public and federal housing.

Department of the Interior, 18th and C Streets, NW, Washington, D.C. 20240; (202) 343-1100. For information about government lands, national parks, national monuments, national forests, the geological survey, reclamation of wastelands, and control of mines. Within the Department of the Interior, address specific inquiries to the U.S. Fish and Wildlife Service and the Bureau of Indian Affairs.

Department of Justice, 10th Street and Constitution Avenue, NW, Washington, D.C. 20530; (202) 633-2007. For information regarding the administration of the system of federal courts, the supervision of federal prisons and the violation of federal law and for inquiries to the Immigration and Naturalization Service, the Antitrust Division, and the Federal Bureau of Investigation.

Department of Labor, 200 Constitution Avenue, NW, Washington, D.C. 20210; (202) 523-7316. For information on the welfare of wage earners' conditions in the United States, minimum wage and other wage-and-hour regulations, and statistics relating to labor and workers' compensation.

Department of State, 2201 C Street, NW, Washington, D.C. 20520; (202) 647-3686. To apply for passports for Americans traveling abroad. For information regarding ambassadors, ministers, consuls, and their staffs; the diplomatic relations of the United States with foreign countries; and activities of American citizens in foreign countries.

Department of Transportation, 400 7th Street, SW, Washington, D.C. 20590; (202) 366-5580. For information about transportation by air, road, and rail as well as programs involving urban mass transportation. Also for information about the St. Lawrence Seaway. Address the U.S. Coast Guard in the Transportation Department with inquiries about smuggling, law enforcement in coastal and other navigable waters of the United States, and assistance to vessels in distress.

Department of the Treasury, 15th Street and Pennsylvania Avenue, Washington, D.C. 20220; (202) 566-2041. For information about minting and coinage, prosecution of counterfeiters, U.S. Savings Bonds, the U.S. Secret Service, and the Bureau of Alcohol, Tobacco and Firearms. Within the Department of the Treasury, address inquiries about income taxes to the Internal Revenue Service and about duties on imported products to the U.S. Customs Service.

Department of Veterans Affairs, 810 Vermont Avenue, NW, Washington, D.C., 20420; (202) 273-5400. For information about veterans benefits including compensation payments, pensions, education and rehabilitation, and medical services.

Independent Government Agencies

In addition to the departments, there are nearly sixty independent agencies, commissions, boards, etc. of the federal government. They are listed with addresses in the *United States Government Manual.* Many of them have offices in major cities and some have offices in many smaller cities. Among these agencies are the United States Postal Service, the National Aeronautics and Space Administration, the Federal Trade Commission, the Environmental

Protection Agency, the Equal Employment Opportunity Commission, the Civil Aeronautics Board, and the Federal Reserve System.

U.S. Government Officials

Congressional Directory for the Use of the United States Congress (Gives comprehensive information regarding the legislative, judicial, and executive departments of the government, including biographical sketches of members of Congress and lists of members of diplomatic and consular services)

Office of the President of the U.S. 1600 Pennsylvania Avenue, NW, Washington, D.C. 20500; (202) 456-2343

Office of the Vice President of the U.S. Old Executive Office Building, 17th and Pennsylvania Avenue, NW, Washington, D.C. 20500; (202) 456-2326

PROFESSIONAL ASSOCIATIONS

Professional Secretaries International
301 East Armour Boulevard
Kansas City, MO 64111
(816) 531-7010
Professional organization of secretaries. Develops research and educational projects for secretaries.

American Society of Corporate Secretaries
1270 Avenue of the Americas
New York, NY 10020
(212) 765-2620
For corporate secretaries, assistant secretaries, officers and executives of corporations, and others interested in corporate practices and procedures. Maintains a central information and reference service.

Executive Women International
Spring Run Office Plaza
965 E. Van Winkle, Suite #1
Salt Lake City, UT 84117
(801) 263-3296
For women employed as executive secretaries or in administrative positions.

National Association of Legal Secretaries
2250 E. 73rd Street, Suite 550
Tulsa, OK 74136
(918) 493-3540

For legal secretaries and others employed in work of a legal nature in law offices, banks, and courts. Sponsors legal secretarial training courses.

INDEXES

Recourse to the proper indexes will uncover many important newspaper and magazine articles that may answer questions arising in your work. Such indexes list thousands of subjects and the newspapers, periodicals, etc., where articles on those matters can be found. Individual subjects in various fields are indexed in the following reference books.

> *Cumulative Book Index* (lists all currently published books)
>
> *United States Catalogue* (lists all books printed in the U.S., beginning in 1898; superseded by the *Cumulative Book Index*)
>
> *Books in Print* (lists current books by title, author, and subject)
>
> *Book Review Digest*
>
> *The New York Times Index* (possibly the most comprehensive index of news, politics, scientific progress, international development, etc.)
>
> *Reader's Guide to Periodical Literature*
>
> *Business Periodical Index*
>
> *Index to Periodical Articles By and About Negroes*
>
> *Index Medicus*
>
> *Bibliography of Medical Reviews* (part of *Index Medicus,* but also published separately)
>
> *Index to Legal Periodicals*
>
> *Education Index*
>
> *Applied Science and Technology Index*
>
> *Social Sciences and Humanities Index*
>
> *Biological and Agricultural Index*

The question will arise as to how many of the reference books listed above should be purchased for home or business use. There can be no general answer. If you find that you must visit or phone the library frequently to get information from certain books, it might be wise to buy them. But a shelf of unused books serves the dubious purpose of decoration. It is more important for you to familiarize yourself with what is available and to know where to look.

If you are asked to get the name of a paper manufacturer in Calcutta, the digest of an article on fire hoses that appeared in *The New York Times* sometime in August 1908, or the rate for sending a telegram to Belgium, just remember that there are many research avenues open and many people and books to help you.

LIBRARIES

The public-library system of the United States has a high standard of helpfulness and courtesy. It is exceptional when a reference librarian is not alert to your requests for information. In any part of the country, the great majority of librarians are not only willing but eager to help.

At libraries you will find books on special subjects, both technical and general, including the reference books listed above. You will also find information on government activities, current events, current biographies, scientific advances, industrial and commercial developments, and many other subjects.

Most libraries have photocopying devices of one kind or another for reproducing printed material. It may be helpful to have a copy of a magazine article or of a page from a reference book to take back to the office. In some library departments permission to reproduce material or assistance from the librarian may be required.

The habit of going to the library for research will uncover many hitherto unsuspected sources of information. In using reference books, always check the date of publication; if a book was published in 1934, the data it contains may have no particular value today.

In making notes for your future use, be sure to cite the year in which the book, magazine, or newspaper was published. In the case of a book, the publisher and the city in which the book was published should be included.

TRAVEL INFORMATION

Travel Agencies

In most cities and towns, full information regarding transportation schedules and rates is on file with airline, bus, railroad, or ship offices or agencies. Travel agencies give efficient service free.

The American Automobile Association (AAA) provides travel information and service to members. It will plan trips, provide maps, report on best routes and road and weather conditions, and recommend hotels and motels.

Departments of Tourism

Each of the fifty states has a Department of Tourism, and many cities also have such a department, separate from or connected with the Chamber of Commerce. Brochures about historical sites, road maps, hotel and motel listings, and calendars of coming events may be easily obtained from these sources.

MISCELLANEOUS DIRECTORIES, GUIDES, AND REGISTERS

Telephone Directories

In the larger cities, telephone directories of other large cities are usually on file at the central telephone offices and in libraries that have comprehensive reference departments. They are valuable not only for the telephone numbers listed, but for the street addresses as well. Telephone companies also publish directories in which entries are made under streets and numbers so that, given a certain address, they can tell whether there is a phone at that place. Although these directories are not available to the general public, they are rented to businesses.

If you had to secure a quantity of dry ice so that you could send a dozen brook trout in first-class condition to a friend or favored customer, the problem of finding a dealer in that unusual article might be difficult without the classified telephone directory. The Yellow Pages list the names, addresses, and telephone numbers of business houses, merchants, and professionals according to the specialties. Most big-city directories have indexes.

City Directories

These are intended to give the name, address, and occupation of each resident of the cities for which they are issued. Because Americans move frequently and businesses change names, a certain percentage of the information in each of these is out of date by the time it is published. In the cross index at the back of the book, entries are made by street and number so that by looking up a certain address, one can discover who lives there.

> *Foundations Directory*
>
> *Association Index: a Source-List of Directories and Other Publications Listing Associations*
>
> *Directory of Historical Societies in the United States and Canada*
>
> *Directory of Religious Organizations in the United States*
>
> *Lloyd's Register* (lists names and factual details of seagoing merchant ships in the world)

Another directory is the *Social Register,* which lists persons socially prominent in larger cities.

PUBLICITY DEPARTMENTS

Large corporations, groups supporting causes, and public institutions such as universities generally maintain departments of public information that handle inquiries regarding their products, services, policies, and plans. It is possible that the information they give out will seek to promote their own interests, but much valuable information may be secured from such sources. Inquiries or requests for photographs should be addressed to the director of public relations of the company or organization. Some businesses have a standard policy of enclosing a self-addressed, stamped envelope when requesting information from a charitable or other nonprofit organization.

NEWSPAPER OFFICES

Newspapers maintain libraries or "morgues" that are sometimes open to the public, or at least to businesses in the community, for reference work. Here are filed thousands of news clippings under alphabetically arranged subject headings. Editors of special departments, such as society, finance, business, sports, etc., keep their own files and are often helpful. Furthermore, most photographic departments of newspapers make prints available for a fee. *The New York Times* has developed a computerized research system available to other newspapers, public libraries, business libraries, and so on.

26

Holidays in the United States

Each state has jurisdiction over holidays that will be observed in that state. The holidays are designated either by the state legislature or by executive proclamation and therefore may be changed with each new state executive or legislature.

There are no national holidays in the United States. The President and Congress designate holidays only for the District of Columbia and for federal employees throughout the nation.

Many holidays are not observed on their actual date, but on the closest Monday to that date. The following list contains names and dates of major holidays; however, not all states observe all of these holidays.

New Year's Day—January 1

Martin Luther King, Jr.'s, Birthday—January 15

Robert E. Lee's Birthday—January 19

Inauguration Day—January 20

Mardi Gras or Shrove Tuesday—last day before Lent

Lincoln's Birthday—February 12

Washington's Birthday—February 22

Good Friday—Friday before Easter Sunday

Memorial Day—May 30

Jefferson Davis's Birthday—June 3

Independence Day—July 4

Labor Day—first Monday in September

Columbus Day—October 12

Election Day—first Tuesday after first Monday in November

Veterans Day or Armistice Day—November 11

Thanksgiving Day—fourth Thursday in November

Christmas Day—December 25

27

Signs and Symbols

BIOLOGY

○, ⊙, ①	annual plant
⊙ ⊙, ②	biennial plant
♃	perennial herb
△	evergreen plant
⊙	monocarpic plant, which bears fruit but once
♂, ♀	(1) male organism or cell (2) staminate plant or flower
♀	(1) female organism or cell (2) pistillate plant or flower
☿	perfect, or hermaphroditic, plant or flower
○	individual, especially female, organism
□	individual, especially male, organism
♂ ♀	unisexual; having male and female flowers separate
♂ — ♀	monoecious; having male and female flowers on the same plant
♂ : ♀	dioecious; having male and female flowers on different plants
♀ ♂ ♀	polygamous; having hermaphroditic and unisexual flowers on the same or different plants
∞	indefinite number, as of stamens when there are more than twenty
0	lacking or absent, as a part
)	turning or winding to the left
(	turning or winding to the right
×	crossed with: used of a hybrid
P	parental (generation)
F	filial (generation); offspring
F_1, F_2, F_3, *etc.*	offspring of the first, second, third, etc. filial generation
+	possessing a (specified) characteristic
−	lacking a (specified) characteristic
⁎̲	northern hemisphere
⁎	southern hemisphere
ǀ⁎	Old World
⁎ǀ	New World
°, ′, ″	feet, inches, lines
′, ″, ‴	feet, inches, lines (in European usage)

COMMERCE AND FINANCE

$	dollar or dollars: as, $100
¢	cent or cents: as, 13¢
£	pound or pounds sterling: as, £100
/	shilling or shillings: as, 2/6, two shillings and sixpence

@	(1) at: as, 200 @ $1 each (2) to: as, shoes per pr. $30 @ $50
₱	per
%	(1) percent: as, 5% (2) order of
‰	per thousand
a/c	account
B/L	bill of lading
B/S	bill of sale
c/d, C/D	carried down (in bookkeeping)
c/f, C/F	carried forward (in bookkeeping)
c/o	(1) care of (2) carried over (in bookkeeping)
d/a	days after acceptance
d/s	days after sight
L/C	letter of credit
O/S	out of stock
w/	with
w/o	without
#	(1) number (before a figure): as, #5 can (2) pounds (after a figure): as, 25#

COMPUTER SYSTEMS FLOWCHART

⬭	terminal: beginning, end, or interruption of a flowchart
▱	input/output: any input/output function, as processing information (input) or printout of processed information (output)
▭	process: any processing function that results in a change in form or location of information
◯	preparation: instructions to modify a program
◇	decision: choice of alternatives at this point
⬚	predefined process: a process that is specified elsewhere, as in a subroutine
○	connector: entry from or to another part of the flowchart
▽	offline storage: on perforated or magnetic tape, cards, or paper
⊂	online storage: in a storage unit, as a disk, magnetic tape, etc.
↑←	flow direction: direction of data flow: arrows not required if flow is top to bottom or left to right
⟋	communication link: transmission of data from one location to another by telephone or other telecommunications medium

⊸	annotation: addition of explanatory notes: dotted line extends to flowchart symbol
▱	manual input: data input by an online device, usually a keyboard
▽	manual operation: manual offline operation
▭	punched card
▱	punched tape
▽	document
◗	magnetic tape
◖	transmittal tape
○	display

MATHEMATICS

Numeration

Capital letters were sometimes used for the Greek numerals, and lowercase letters are often used for the Roman. In the Roman notation, the value of a character to the right of a larger numeral is added to that of the numeral: as, VI = V + 1 = 6. I, X, and sometimes C are also placed to the left of larger numerals, and when so situated their value is subtracted from that of such numerals: as, IV, that is, V – I = 4. After the sign IↃ for D, when the character Ↄ was repeated, each repetition had the effect of multiplying IↃ by ten: as, IↃↃ, 5,000; IↃↃↃ, 50,000; and the like. In writing numbers twice as great as these, C was placed as many times before the stroke I as the Ↄ was written after it. Sometimes a line was drawn over a numeral to indicate thousands: as, $\overline{\text{C}}$ = 100,000.

Arabic	Greek	Roman
0	. . .	. . .
1	α	I
2	β	II
3	γ	III
4	δ	IV *or* IIII
5	ε	V
6	ς	VI
7	ζ	VII
8	η	VIII *or* IIX
9	θ	IX *or* VIIII
10	ι	X
11	ια	XI

Arabic	Greek	Roman
12	ιβ	XII
13	ιγ	XIII or XIIV
14	ιδ	XIV or XIIII
15	ιε	XV
16	ιϛ	XVI
17	ιζ	XVII
18	ιη	XVIII or XIIX
19	ιθ	XIX or XVIIII
20	κ	XX
30	λ	XXX
40	μ	XL or XXXX
50	ν	L
60	ξ	LX
70	ο	LXX
80	π	LXXX *or* XXC
90	ϑ	XC *or* LXXXX
100	ρ	C
200	σ	CC
300	τ	CCC
400	υ	CD *or* CCCC
500	φ	D *or* IↃ
600	χ	DC *or* IↃC
700	ψ	DCC *or* IↃCC
800	ω	DCCC *or* IↃCCC
900	. . .	CM, DCCCC, *or* ICCCCC
1,000	. . .	M *or* CIↃ
2,000	. . .	MM *or* CIↃCIↃ

Calculation

+   (1) plus, the sign of addition; used also to indicate that figures are only approximately exact, some figures being omitted at the end: as, 2.1557 + (2) positive

−   (1) minus, the sign of subtraction; used also to indicate that figures have been left off from the end of a number, and that the last figure has been increased by one: as, 2.9378 = 2.94 − (2) negative

±   plus or minus: indicating that either of the signs + or − may properly be used; used also to introduce the probable error after a figure obtained by experimentation, etc.

×	multiplied by: $5 \times 4 = 20$; multiplication is also indicated by a centered dot ($5 \cdot 4 = 20$) or by placing the factors in immediate juxtaposition ($2ab = 2 \times a \times b$)
÷	divided by; division is also indicated by a colon ($x \div y = x$: y), by a straight line between the dividend and the divisor ($\frac{x}{y}$), or by an oblique line (x/y)
=	is equal to; equals
≠	is not equal to
>	is greater than: as, $x > y$; that is, x is greater than y
<	is less than: as, $x < y$; that is, x is less than y
≮, ≧, ≥	is not less than; is equal to or greater than
≯, ≦, ≤	is not greater than; is equal to or less than
⇌	is equivalent to: applied to magnitudes or quantities that are equal in area or volume but are not of the same form
≡	is identical with
≅	is congruent to
~	the difference between: used to designate the difference between two quantities without indicating which is the greater: as, $x \sim z$ = the difference between x and z
∝	varies as; is directly proportional to: as, $x \propto y$; that i, x varies as y
∺	geometric proportion: as, $\div\!\div x : y :: a : b$; that is, the geometric proportion x is to y as a is to b
:	is to; the ratio of
: :	as; equals: used between ratios
∞	indefinitely great; the symbol for infinity
!, ⌊	the factorial of, or the continued product of numbers from one upward: as, $5! = 5 \times 4 \times 3 \times 2 \times 1$
∴	therefore
	since; because
. . .	and so on
∠	angle: as, $\angle$XYZ
⊥	the perpendicular; is perpendicular to: as, EF $\perp$ MN = EF is perpendicular to MN
‖	parallel; is parallel to: as, EF ‖ DG
○	circle; circumference; 360°
⌒	arc of a circle
⊙	triangle

☐   square

▭   rectangle

▱   parallelogram

$\sqrt{\ }$, $\sqrt{\ }$ radical sign; root, indicating, when used without a figure placed above it, the square root: as, $\sqrt{9} = 3$. When any root other than the square root is meant, a figure (called the *index*) expressing the degree of the required root is placed above the sign: as, $\sqrt[3]{27} = 3$

^{1}, ^{2}, ^{3}, *etc.*   exponents, placed above and to the right of a quantity to indicate that it is raised to the first, second, third, etc. power: as, a^2, $(a+b)^3$

$'$, $''$, $'''$, *etc.*   prime, double (or second) prime, triple (or third) prime, etc., used to distinguish between different values of the same variable: as, x', x'', x''', etc.

—   vinculum: as, $x + y$

( )   parentheses: as, $2(x + y)$

[ ]   brackets: as, $a[2(x + y)]$

{ }   braces: as, $b + \{2 - a[2(x + y)]\}$

These signs indicate that the quantities connected or enclosed by them are to be taken together, as a single quantity.

f, F   function; function of: as, $f(a)$, a function of a

d   differential of: as, da

δ   variation of: as, δa

Δ   finite difference, or increment

D   differential coefficient, or derivative

∫   integral; integral of, indicating that the expression following it is to be integrated: as, $\int f(x)dx$ indicates the indefinite integral of $f(x)$ with respect to x

$\int_a^b$ definite integral, indicating the limits of integration: as, $\int_a^b f(x)dx$ indicates the integral of $f(x)$ with respect to x, between the limits a and b

Σ   sum: algebraic sum; when used to indicate the summation of finite differences, it has a sense similar to that of the symbol ∫

Π   the continued product of all terms such as (those indicated)

π   pi, the number 3.14159265 +: the ratio of the circumference of a circle to its diameter, of a semicircle to its radius, and of the area of a circle to the square of its radius

e, ∈   the number 2.7182818+: the base of the Napierian system of logarithms; also, the eccentricity of a conic section

M   the modulus of a system of logarithms, especially of the common system of logarithms, where it is equal to 0.4342944819+

°	degrees: as, 90°
'	(1) minutes of arc; (2) feet
"	(1) seconds of arc; (2) inches
h	hours
m	minutes of time
s	seconds of time

MEDICINE AND PHARMACY

ĀĀ, Ā, āā	[Gr. *ana*] of each
a.c.	[L. *ante cibum*] before meals
ad	[L.] up to; so as to make: as, *ad*3ij, so as to make three drams
add.	[L. *adde*] let there be added; add
ad lib.	[L. *ad libitum*] at pleasure; as needed or desired
aq.	[L. *aqua*] water
b. (i.) d.	[L. *bis (in) die*] twice daily
c̄.	[L. *cum*] with
coch.	[L. *cochleare*] a spoonful
D.	[L. *dosis*] a dose
dil.	[L. *dilue*] dilute or dissolve
ess.	[L. *essentia*] essence
ft. mist.	[L. *fiat mistura*] let a mixture be made
ft. pulv.	[L. *fiat pulvis*] let a powder be made
gr.	[L. *granum*] a grain
gtt.	[L. *guttae*] drops
guttatim	[L.] drop by drop
H.	[L. *hora*] hour
haust.	[L. *haustus*] a draft
hor. decub.	[L. *hora decubitus*] at bedtime
in d.	[L. *in dies*] daily
lot.	[L. *lotio*] a lotion
M.	[L. *misce*] mix
mac.	[L. *macera*] macerate
O., o.	[L. *octarius*] a pint
p.c.	[L. *post cibum*] after meals
pil.	[L. *pilula(e)*] pill(s)
p.r.n.	[L. *pro re nata*] as circumstances may require
pulv.	[L. *pulvis*] powder
q.(i.)d.	[L. *quater (in) die*] four times daily
q.l.	[L. *quantum libet*] as much as you please
q.s.	[L. *quantum suficit*] as much as will suffice

q.v.   [L. *quantum vis*] as much as you like

R͓   [L. *recipe*] take: used at the beginning of a prescription

S, Sig.   [L. *signa*] write: used in prescriptions to indicate the directions
            to be placed on the label of the medicine

t.(i.)d.   [L. *ter (in) die*] three times daily

tab.   [L. *tabella*] tablet

℥   ounce; ℥i = one ounce; ℥ij = two ounces; ℥ss = half an ounce;
            ℥iss = one ounce and a half, etc.; ƒ℥ = a fluid ounce

℈   dram; ℨi = one dram; ℨij = two drams; ℨss = half a dram; ℨiss =
            one dram and a half, etc.; ƒℨ = a fluid dram

℈   scruple; ℈i = one scruple; ℈ij = two scruples; ℈ss = half a scruple;
            ℈iss = one scruple and a half, etc.

♏, ♏   minim

WEATHER

◎   calm

○   clear

●   cloudy

◐   partly cloudy

≡   fog

∞   haze

ς   tropical storm

•   rain

❄   rain and snow

△   sleet

✳   snow

☈   thunderstorm

MISCELLANEOUS

&, (the ampersand) and: as, A. B. Smith & Co.

&c. [L. *et cetera*] and others; and so forth

© copyright; copyrighted

® registered trademark

☾ crescent: symbol of Islam

✝ cross: symbol of Christianity

✝ Celtic cross: symbol of Protestant Episcopal Church

✝ Russian cross: symbol of Russian Orthodox Church

✝ Greek cross: symbol of Greek Orthodox Church

℟, response: in religious services, used to mark the part to be uttered by the congregation in answer to the officiant

* in Roman Catholic service books, a mark used to divide each verse of a psalm into two parts, indicating where the response begins

℣,V',V versicle: in religious services, used to mark the part to be uttered by the officiant

✠ (1) a sign of the cross used by the pope, by archbishops, and by bishops, before their names; (2) in religious services, used to mark the places where the sign of the cross is to be made

✡ star of David: symbol of Judaism

🕎 menorah: symbol of Judaism

† died: used in genealogies, etc.

× (1) by: used in dimensions, as 8" × 11" paper; (2) a mark representing a signature, as on a legal document, made by someone unable to write; the name is added by someone else, *e.g.*,

> *his*
>
> *John* × *Doe*
>
> *mark*

☢ radioactive

PROOFREADER'S MARKS

⊙	Insert period
⅋	Insert comma
:/	Insert colon
;/	Insert semicolon
!	Insert exclamation point
⅋	Insert apostrophe or single quotation mark
"/⅋	Insert quotation marks
(/)	Insert parentheses
[/]	Insert brackets
=/	Insert hyphen
$\overline{t_n}$	Insert en dash
$\overline{t_m}$	Insert em dash
?/	Insert question mark
⑦	Query to author
∧	Insert marginal addition
ℓ	Delete
ℰ	Delete and close up
⌒	Close up
#	Insert space
≢	Less space
eq.#	Equalize spacing
¶	Paragraph
No ¶	Run in same paragraph
c/⊃	Move to left or to right
⊓/⊔	Raise or lower
=	Straighten type horizontally
‖	Align type vertically
tr	Transpose
stet	Let crossed-out words stand
ctr	Center
lc	Set in lowercase letters
caps	Set in capital letters
s.c.	Set in small capitals
rom	Set in roman type
ital	Set in italic type
bf	Set in boldface type
ⓧ	Replace imperfect letter
⊙	Reverse upside-down letter
⤶	Push down space that prints
wf	Wrong font (wrong size or style of type)
sp	Spell out word or figure
ld in	Insert lead, or space, between lines
cl ld	Delete lead, or space, between lines

28

Weights and Measures

U.S. CUSTOMARY AND METRIC MEASUREMENT EQUIVALENTS

Length or Distance

Linear Measure

1 inch		= 2.54	centimeters
12 inches =	1 foot	= 0.3048	meter
3 feet =	1 yard	= 0.9144	meter
5½ yards or 16½ feet =	1 rod	= 5.029	meters
40 rods =	1 furlong	= 201.17	meters
8 furlongs or 1,760 yards or 5,280 feet =	1 (statute) mile	=1,609.3	meters
3 miles =	1 (land) league	= 4.83	kilometers

Nautical Measure

6 feet = 1 fathom	= 1.829 meters
100 fathoms = 1 cable's length (ordinary) (In the U.S. Navy 120 fathoms or 720 feet = 1 cable's length; in the British Navy, 608 feet = 1 cable's length.)	
10 cables' lengths = 1 nautical mile (6,076.11549 feet, by international agreement)	= 1.852 kilometers
1 nautical mile = 1.1508 statute miles (the length of a minute of longitude at the equator)	
3 nautical miles = 1 marine league (3.45 statute miles)	= 5.56 kilometers
60 nautical miles = 1 degree of a great circle of the earth	

Area

1 square inch		=	6.452 square centimeters
144 square inches =	1 square foot	=	929 square centimeters
9 square feet =	1 square yard	=	0.8361 square meter
30¼ square yards =	1 square rod	=	25.29 square meters
160 square rods or 4,840 square yards or 43,560 square feet =	1 acre	=	0.4047 hectare
640 acres =	1 square mile	=	259 hectares or 2.59 square kilometers

Volume or Capacity

Cubic Measure

1 cubic inch			=	16.387 cubic centimeters
1,728 cubic inches	=	1 cubic foot	=	0.0283 cubic meter
27 cubic feet	=	1 cubic yard	=	0.7646 cubic meter

(in units for cordwood, etc.)

16 cubic feet	=	1 cord foot	=	0.453 cubic meter
8 cord feet	=	1 cord	=	3.625 cubic meters

Dry Measure

1 pint			=	33.60 cubic inches	=	0.5505 liter
2 pints	=	1 quart	=	67.20 cubic inches	=	1.1012 liters
8 quarts	=	1 peck	=	537.61 cubic inches	=	8.8098 liters
4 pecks	=	1 bushel	=	2,150.42 cubic inches	=	35.2383 liters

1 British dry quart = 1.032 U.S. dry quarts

According to U.S. government standards, the following are the weights avoirdupois for single bushels of the specified grains: for wheat, 60 pounds; for barley, 48 pounds; for oats, 32 pounds; for rye, 56 pounds; for corn, 56 pounds. Some states have specifications varying from these.

Liquid Measure

1 gill	=	4 fluid ounces	=	7.219 cubic inches	= 0.1183 liter
		(see next table)			
4 gills	=	1 pint	=	28.875 cubic inches	= 0.4732 liter
2 pints	=	1 quart	=	57.75 cubic inches	= 0.9464 liter
4 quarts	=	1 gallon	=	231 cubic inches	= 3.7854 liters

The British imperial gallon (4 imperial quarts) = 277.42 cubic inches = 4.546 liters. The barrel in Great Britain equals 36 imperial gallons; in the United States, usually $31\frac{1}{2}$ gallons.

Apothecaries' Fluid Measure

1 minim			=	0.0038 cubic inch	= 0.0616 milliliter
60 minims	=	1 fluid dram	=	0.2256 cubic inch	= 3.6966 milliliters
8 fluid drams	=	1 fluid ounce	=	1.8047 cubic inches	= 0.0296 liter
16 fluid ounces	=	1 pint		= 28.875 cubic inches	= 0.4732 liter

See table immediately preceding for quart and gallon equivalents. The British pint = 20 fluid ounces.

Weight

Avoirdupois Weight

(The grain, equal to 0.0648 gram, is the same in all three tables of weight.)

1 dram or 27.34 grains		= 1.772 grams
16 drams or 437.5 grains = 1 ounce		= 28.3495 grams
16 ounces or 7,000 grains = 1 pound		= 453.59 grams
100 pounds = 1 hundredweight		= 45.36 kilograms
2,000 pounds = 1 ton		= 907.18 kilograms

In Great Britain, 14 pounds (6.35 kilograms) = 1 stone, 112 pounds (50.80 kilograms) = 1 hundredweight, and 2,240 pounds (1,016.05 kilograms) = 1 long ton.

Troy Weight

(The grain, equal to 0.0648 gram, is the same in all three tables of weight.)

3.086 grains = 1 carat		= 200 milligrams
24 grains = 1 pennyweight		= 1.5552 grams
20 pennyweights or 480 grains = 1 ounce		= 31.1035 grams
12 ounces or 5,760 grains = 1 pound		= 373.24 grams

Apothecaries' Weight

(The grain, equal to 0.0648 gram, is the same in all three tables of weight.)

20 grains	= 1 scruple	=	1.296 grams
3 scruples	= 1 dram	=	3.888 grams
8 drams or 480 grains	= 1 ounce	=	31.1035 grams
12 ounces or 5,760 grains	= 1 pound	=	373.24 grams

CIRCULAR OR ANGULAR MEASUREMENT

60 seconds(")	=	1 minute(')
60 minutes	=	1 degree(°)
90 degrees	=	1 quadrant or 1 right angle
4 quadrants or 360 degrees	=	1 circle

THE METRIC SYSTEM

Length or Distance

Linear Measure

10 millimeters	=	1 centimeter	=	0.3937 inch
10 centimeters	=	1 decimeter	=	3.937 inches
10 decimeters	=	1 meter	=	39.37 inches or 3.28 feet
10 meters	=	1 decameter	=	393.7 inches
10 decameters	=	1 hectometer	=	328.08 feet
10 hectometers	=	1 kilometer	=	0.621 mile
10 kilometers	=	1 myriameter	=	6.21 miles

Area

Square Measure

100 sq. millimeters	= 1 square centimeter =	0.15499	sq. inch
100 sq. centimeters	= 1 square decimeter =	15.499	sq. inches
100 sq. decimeters	= 1 square meter =	1,549.9	sq. inches or 1.196 sq. yards
100 sq. meters	= 1 square decameter =	119.6	sq. yards
100 sq. decameters	= 1 square hectometer =	2.471	acres
100 sq. hectometers	= 1 square kilometer =	0.386	sq. mile

Land Measure

1 square meter	=	1 centiare	=	1,549.9 square inches
100 centiares	=	1 are	=	119.6 square yards
100 ares	=	1 hectare	=	2.471 acres
100 hectares	=	1 square kilometer	=	0.386 square mile

Volume or Capacity

Volume Measure

1,000 cubic millimeters	= 1 cubic centimeter =	.06102	cubic inch
1,000 cubic centimeters	= 1 cubic decimeter =	61.02	cubic inches
1,000 cubic decimeters	= 1 cubic meter =	35.314	cubic feet
	(the unit is called a *stere* in measuring firewood)		

Capacity Measure

10 milliliters	= 1 centiliter	=	.338	fluid ounce
10 centiliters	= 1 deciliter	=	3.38	fluid ounces
10 deciliters	= 1 liter	=	1.0567	liquid quarts or 0.9081 dry quart
10 liters	= 1 decaliter	=	2.64	gallons or 0.284 bushel
10 decaliters	= 1 hectoliter	=	26.418	gallons or 2.838 bushels
10 hectoliters	= 1 kiloliter	=	264.18	gallons or 35.315 cubic feet

Weight

Weights

10 milligrams	=	1 centigram	=	0.1543	grain
10 centigrams	=	1 decigram	=	1.5432	grains
10 decigrams	=	1 gram	=	15.432	grains
10 grams	=	1 decagram	=	0.3527	ounce
10 decagrams	=	1 hectogram	=	3.5274	ounces
10 hectograms	=	1 kilogram	=	2.2046	pounds
10 kilograms	=	1 myriagram	=	22.046	pounds
10 myriagrams	=	1 quintal	=	220.46	pounds
10 quintals	=	1 metric ton	=	2,204.6	pounds

Index

A

abbreviations, 265
    state, 204–205
absolute phrases, 388
abstracts, 156
    in technical reports, 64
accent marks, 424
acceptance of goods, 542
accepted spellings, 426–427
accounting, 116
acknowledgment letters, 337
addresses
    change, 226, 227
    filing rules, 270
    forms of, 513–522
    inside, 134–135
    street-address directories, 242
adjective clauses, 386
adjectives, 381–382
    nouns as, 364
adjustment letters, 338
administrative assistants. *See*
  executive secretaries
Administrative Codes, 527
adverbial clauses, 386
adverbs, 382–383
advertising secretaries, 14–15
affidavits, 51, 54
agency relationships, 552
agents, 552
agreement
    nouns, 361–363
    pronouns, 370–371
air express, domestic, 230
airmail, 217
air mileage between cities, 567–568
air travel. *See* travel
alienation of title, 537
almanacs, 598
alphabetic filing systems, 255–256,
  263–271

American Association for Medical
  Transcription (AAMT), 33–34
American Association of Medical
  Assistants (AAMA), 33–34
American Medical Association
  (AMA), 32
American National Standards Institute
  (ANSI), 113
ampersand (&), 397
answering services, 35
answers, legal, 53
antecedents, 364
antitrust violations, 531
antonyms, 596
apostrophe, 397–399
    spacing, 151
appendixes
    reports, 169, 171
    technical reports, 64
appointment books, 18–19
appointment calendars, 300
appointment letters, 339, 340
appointments, medical office, 35
appositive phrases, 388
appreciation letters, 341
appropriate behavior, 11
area measurements, 627, 630
arts secretaries, 14–15
artwork, 184–185
Association of Records Managers and
  Administrators, Inc. (ARMA), 263
    filing rules, 270
asterisks, spacing, 151
atlases, 597–598
attention lines, 134, 142–143
attorneys, dealing with, 46
authority level, 12
automobile travel, 306–307. *See also*
  travel
    expense records, 291

R

radio and television secretaries, 14–15
real property, 536–538
    leases, 538
    tenancy, 537
    transfer, 537–538
recall of mail, 226
reciprocal pronouns, 366
record keeping, 12–13
    membership, 78
records. *See also* medical records
    business, 289–290
    data management, 272
    medical, 36–37
    retention schedule, 271
    tax, 290–293
reduction/enlargement, visual aids, 195
reference initials for letters, 142
reference materials
    memos, 174–176
    telephone, 241–243
    for transcription, 123
reference pronouns, 369–370
references, reports, 169
reflexive pronouns, 366
registered mail, 219, 221
rejection letters, 348
rejection of goods, 542
relative pronouns, 365–366, 368–369
rentals, 538
reply reference notations, 143
reporters, talking to, 317
reports, 153–196
    business. *See* business reports
    membership, 80
    numbers in, 191–192
    technical, 186–188
    visual aids, 192–196
request for judicial information, 53
request for payment letters, 343
research, online services, 114
reservation letters, 349
reservations, travel, 307–308
resolutions, minutes, 181
responsibility and followup, 10

restrictive endorsement, 281
return receipt, 222
road mileage between cities, 569
rough drafts, 124–125
Rules for Alphabetical Filing, 270

S

sales, law of, 540–541
salutations, 135–136
scanners, 97–98
scheduling, 324
schools, 269
scientific manuscripts, 65
screening calls, 237–238
second class mail, 206, 210–211
secretarial services overseas, 583
secretaries
    competency, 9–13
    definition of, 5
    entering and succeeding in profession, 5–6
    future, 23
    information processing, 8–9
    language, 7–8
    professional development, 6–7
    professional reading, 8
    special employment, 16–17
    specialties, 13–16
    typical day, 17–20
secured transactions, 544–547
security interests, 544–545
semicolons, 409
    spacing, 149
seminars, 78
sentences, 388–397
    consistent construction, 395–396
    coordination, 393–394
    fragments, 391–392
    modifiers, 396–397
    parts, 388–390
    subordination, 394–395
    types, 391
sequence calls, 245–246
sequence of tenses, verbs, 379–380
sequential files, 273
serial files, 273

U